PIMLICO

86

RIOT, RISINGS AND REVOLUTION

Sir Ian Gilmour, a barrister by profession, has been an MP since 1962, first for Norfolk Central and then Chesham and Amersham. He served as Secretary of Defence under Edward Heath in 1974 and was appointed Lord Privy Seal and Deputy Foreign Secretary in Mrs Thatcher's first cabinet. His books include *The Body Politic* and *Inside Right*.

By the same author:
THE BODY POLITIC
INSIDE RIGHT
BRITAIN CAN WORK

RIOT, RISINGS AND REVOLUTION

Governance and Violence in Eighteenth-Century England

IAN GILMOUR

PIMLICO

PIMLICO

20 Vauxhall Bridge Road, London SW1V 2SA

London Melbourne Sydney Auckland Johannesburg
and agencies throughout the world

First published by Hutchinson 1992
Pimlico edition 1993

© Ian Gilmour 1992

Printed and bound in Great Britain by
Butler & Tanner Ltd, Frome and London

ISBN 0-7126-5510-7

Contents

Preface and Acknowledgements

For a politician, the problems of governance and violence in eighteenth-century England are of particular interest. In this period new difficulties were added to traditional internal and external threats. Whether or not there was an Industrial Revolution, economic developments subjected society to unusual stress. As the pace of change increased, the authorities were obliged to confront an unstable populace with resources that had not markedly improved for a hundred years: communications were poor, reliable statistics were rare and the idea of a police force was denounced as an invention of French despotism.

Whatever the difficulties of the government, those of the governed were no easier. Given the handicaps under which the state laboured, not surprisingly it often failed to act on behalf of its subjects, and when it did stir itself it sometimes made things worse. In these circumstances the response from below was frequently a violent one – thus, of course, aggravating the problems of an 'over-stretched' state.

Any attempt to write about violence in isolation would be difficult and probably unrewarding. For one thing it might seem to be little more than one damned murder or riot after another. For another, apart from much crime, violence is usually a reaction against somebody or something, and to leave out those causes would make it incomprehensible. More particularly, violence often arises from the actions or inaction of government, and popular resistance cannot be divorced from this. It is for this reason that governance must be considered together with violence – especially as the violence itself may come from the government. It follows that politics cannot be left out either, and this book tries to place eighteenth-century violence in the context of the ideas and conditions of the time.

The boundaries were difficult to set. Some reference to events after the restoration seemed necessary, so the years 1660–89 have been included as a departure platform. The terminal buffers could have been 1800, 1815 or 1832. On the whole it seemed best to choose 1800, with occasional adjustments. Considerations of space would in any case have probably dictated that date. Similarly, the need to keep within a manageable length, not an attack of 'little Englishism' – my family is Scottish – determined confining the book to England. Scotland and Ireland, therefore, have been virtually omitted except when, as in 1715, 1745 or 1798, their exclusion would have been glaringly absurd.

Part One sets the scene and describes, more or less chronologically, the chief episodes of violence up to mid-century. Part Two deals with the various patterns of recurrent violence and ranges over the century; those wishing to stick to the narrative can skip this section. Part Three reverts to a more chronological approach, giving an account of the main 'one-off' disturbances of the second half of the century and of events leading up to the revolutionary threat in the 1790's.

With trifling exceptions, eighteenth-century historians were unfailingly prompt and tolerant in answering my queries, and for various kinds of help I am grateful to Dr J.V. Beckett, Dr Jeremy Black, Professor John Cannon, Mr John Carswell, Professor Ian Christie, Professor Linda Colley, Dr Eveline Cruickshanks, Professor H.T. Dickinson, Mr H.W. Edwards, Mr John Ehrman, Professor Norman Gash, Mr Christopher Hibbert, Dr Christopher Hill, Mr Gerald Howson, Professor J.R. Jones, Mr Robert Kee, Dr Paul Langford, Dr Frank McLynn, Professor Geoffrey Pearson, Dr Roy Porter, Professor Pat Rogers, Professor George Rudé, Mr Donald Rumbelow, Dr J.A. Sharpe, and Dr John Stevenson. My debt to them and to other scholars is apparent in the references and also, I hope, in the text. I must warmly thank, too, Lord Bonham Carter, Mr Michael Hay, and Professor Ghiţa Ionescu for their wise advice and assistance.

My greatest debt is to Professor John Dunn, Dr Mark Garnett and Mr John Grigg who generously read the whole typescript and made many valuable criticisms and suggestions, which have, I hope, been incorporated in the final version. David and Andrew Gilmour kindly did the same when the text was in a more primitive form, as well as making some sensibly rigorous cuts. On good advice the references have also been drastically pruned. I am deeply obliged to Dr Garnett for undertaking the great bulk of that task with such care and skill. The errors and opinions are mine alone.

Diane Craig interpreted my handwriting with patient ingenuity and amiably typed and retyped seemingly endless drafts, as did Mrs Jane Gore Booth and Mrs Michelle Masterton at earlier stages. I owe them my profound thanks.

Finally I am, as always, greatly beholden to the staff of the House of Commons Library for their courtesy and resource in tracing innumerable books and articles. Whatever else needs reforming in the House of Commons, the Library does not.

                                                                    I.G.

Introduction: A Violent Society?

What is it which has produced, in the last hundred years, so rapid an advance, beyond what can be traced in any other period of our history? . . . Under the mild and just government of the illustrious princes of the family now on the throne, a general calm has prevailed through the country, beyond what was ever before experienced . . .

William Pitt, 1792

There are two ways of raising mobs. One by hiring, another by provoking.

Edmund Burke, 1771

Violence, being instrumental by nature, is rational to the extent that it is effective in reaching the end that must justify it. And since when we act we never know with any certainty the eventual consequences of what we are doing, violence can remain rational only if it pursues short term goals. Violence does not promote causes . . .

Hannah Arendt[1]

No western society is entirely free from violence. According to some religions, God himself has found it necessary, both in this world and the next. In the Promethean myth God cannot decide justly without violence, and in Zoroastrianism the cosmos itself is a battle. Milton pictured gunpowder and warfare in Christian heaven:

> *Millions of fierce encountring Angels fought . . .*
> > *down they fell*
> *By thousands, Angel on Archangel rolled; . . .*
> *Foul dissipation followed, and forced rout.*[2]

On earth 'men are often more squeamish than God', a Jesuit recently pointed out; they 'take exception to violence, although violence is one of the ways in which life bursts forth'. The notably unsqueamish Mussolini, a very secular figure even if Pope Pius XI called him a man sent by 'Divine Providence', was far from taking such exception. He found 'punching an exquisitely fascist means of self expression' and thought that only 'blood' made the wheels of history turn. From the opposite political pole the equally secular

Trotsky laid down that not believing in force was the same as not believing in gravity and that every state was 'based on violence'. Even if anthropologists are right in claiming that violence only began 40,000 years ago, that still leaves it pretty well entrenched. In any case a spectrum ranging from God to Mussolini and Trotsky seems conclusive.[3]

Violence, then, appears inseparable from the human condition, though its degree is subject to wild fluctuations. A society's violence depends on its history, its geography, the behaviour of its neighbours and its security from invasion, its religious and national homogeneity, the nature of its political institutions and the extent of their acceptance, the means of registering dissent and of securing change, the law and its enforcement, its prosperity, the character of its people and the traditions of its government.

The use of the word 'violence' has not here been confined to its primary meaning of the use of physical force to damage persons or property. Nor has it been so widened as to include any action running counter to stable expectations 'that deliberately or unintentionally disorients the behaviour of others'. Threatened or implied violence has been included, however; obviously people may be intimidated by a show of force or potential force even though no actual violence is employed. So has 'symbolic violence', which is intended to close the gulf between rulers and ruled by expressing the latter's equality, if not superiority. Demonstrated during the Peasants' Revolt of 1381 by Wat Tyler calling Richard II 'brother' and rinsing his mouth before the king 'in a rude and villainous manner', symbolic violence was often employed in the eighteenth century, particularly by the followers of John Wilkes.[4]

Further, the word 'violence' has been used more or less neutrally. That is to say, violence has not been considered as necessarily either bad or good, and it has been used for the actions of both rulers and ruled. Much as one man's terrorist is another man's freedom fighter, some favour the use of one word for the use of force or violence they accept and another for the kind they oppose. Sorel, the French theorist of violence, used *'violence'* for what he approved of – the violent resistance of the working class – and *'force'* for what he did not – the rule of the bourgeoisie. Most people who seek to draw a distinction use the words in the same way, while reversing Sorel's preference: 'force' for the legitimate and legally authorised coercive power of the state, and 'violence' for any unauthorised and illegal use of coercive power by the state or by anybody else.[5]*

No such distinction is made here for two main reasons. The more

---

* Similarly the word 'mob' is applied by some to a gathering whose actions or attitude are deplored, the word 'crowd' being used when its actions are considered laudable. In this book 'mob' and 'crowd' are used neutrally and interchangeably.[6]

important is that it was not drawn in the eighteenth century. In those days the word violence was used more widely and more neutrally than it is today. George III talked of using 'vigour and violence' against the Duke of Newcastle's followers; he had only their dismissal in mind. In Locke's *Two Treatises of Government*, force and violence are often almost synonymous. So were they with Burke when he told the Commons: 'Why I prefer lenity to violence is this – because force cannot be suitable to this House.'[7]

Nor did the eighteenth century use the words 'force' for government actions and 'violence' for those of private individuals. The order that was issued to soldiers on riot duty did not tell them 'not to repel violence with force'; it called upon them 'not to repel force with force unless in case of absolute necessity . . .' Conversely George Grenville told the House that 'violence must be resisted by violence'; David Hume wrote of the crown's 'violence' in the use of press gangs and of the possible 'violence' of his cousin while Scottish solicitor general; Lord Chatham spoke of the 'violence' of the House of Commons, and Lord Mansfield complained of the 'violence' of another Lord Chief Justice in giving judgements that offended George III. 'Violent' often meant only 'improper' or 'extreme'.[8]

The second reason is that the eighteenth century's use of the words seems sensible. Unless violence is defined simply as evil, or as something we are against, and force, say, is used to describe any form of violence we approve of, it is difficult to regard all violence as bad. To use the word 'force' for government violence may imply that government violence is always legitimate, and the violence of the governed always wrong, both of which are clearly untrue. Leaving aside dictatorships, even a relatively decent government may use legal but unjustifiable force or violence, making resistance inevitable, or by its reaction to resistance, a government may cause violence rather than prevent it. 'Violence,' as has been said, 'is not a solo performance, but an interaction.' In any case, whatever may be true of a democracy, in the eighteenth century some of the popular or non-governmental violence was beneficial, and eighteenth-century Englishmen did not think that all use of force by a government was legitimate. At that time, of course, not only was there no democratic government, nobody even called themselves a democrat till the century was nearly over.[9]

However the word may be used, violence is to some extent indeterminate. The varying 'dark figure' of crime – the amount of violence and crime that goes unrecorded – periodic changes in methods of recording crime, and the shifting public and governmental perceptions of different forms of violence make an exact assessment of the level of violence and crime at any particular date and place impossible. One sixteenth-century observer thought that

80 per cent of crime in England never reached the courts; similar estimates could be made in other times. It is easier, Mr Dooley once remarked, to write about a period the further you got away from it, since 'you aren't subject to interruptions by people who were there'. But even those who 'were there' often did not discern what was happening. In 1812 a few murders in Wapping created more alarm than all the Luddite disturbances put together. Dangerous riots may attract no press coverage. In 1988 an outbreak of serious violence in Gloucester in which the central police station was attacked and police reinforcements had to be summoned from neighbouring forces rated one paragraph in the national press. Further, people commonly think crime is rising, even when it is not, and they frequently look back to a golden age twenty years earlier when the country was largely free of violence, even though they had taken a much less sanguine view at that time. Because of defective reporting and occasional voluntary censorship as well as difficulties of definition, the number of riots in the eighteenth century could not be known at the time – or now.[10]

If contemporaries strongly differ about what is going on in their society, historians naturally do the same. 'Between 1780 and 1850,' wrote Professor Perkin, 'the English ceased to be one of the most aggressive, brutal, rowdy, outspoken, riotous, cruel and bloodthirsty nations in the world and became one of the most inhibited, polite, orderly, tender-minded, prudish and hypocritical.' More recently Dr Porter concluded that in the eighteenth century 'violence was as English as plum pudding'. Other historians have recalled the 'savage' rioting of the English, their 'violent' habits, and 'the old British love of violence'.[11] On the other hand, equally distinguished historians have suggested – explicitly or implicitly – that such a picture is heavily overcoloured if not downright misleading.[12]

Differing assessments are all the more likely because, as well as being indeterminate, violence and its perception are relative to both place and time. As with truth, 'one meridian' determines what is violent; 'the worst tyrant that ever had his neck wrung in modern Europe might have passed,' Macaulay said, 'for a paragon of clemency in Persia or Moscow.' Different periods of time produce similar disparities: actions, wrote Defoe,

> receive their tincture from the times,
> and as they change are virtues made or crimes.

The passing of a century, thought Sorel, had made the great revolutionary days – July 14, 1789 and August 10, 1792 – seem like 'mere scuffles'.[13]

Most people today would be disgusted by the bullbaiting and

cockfighting that Englishmen relished till almost the end of the eighteenth century, while that century would have been shocked by the twentieth's recourse to total war. Equally, violence that is humdrum in New York would be anarchy in rural Cornwall. Today's football violence would not have surprised those taking the waters in eighteenth-century Bath – a football match then was more like a battle than a game – but they would have found it weird that an international soccer match could lead to a small war in South America.[15]

Nevertheless some idea about a country's level of violence can be gained by comparing it with that of its contemporaries and of quite different societies, while the level of violence of an era can be gauged by comparing it with other ages. Thus Alan Macfarlane has demonstrated that rural life in seventeenth-century England was not in the same league of violence as that in China at the same time, in France in the eighteenth and nineteenth centuries, or in Sicily in the hundred years after 1860. And, in at least one way, undemocratic eighteenth-century Europe was less violent than today: like Periclean Athens and Republican Rome until near its end, the years 1700-89 saw few political murders.[15]

Assassination, Rebellion, Revolution

Though England reduced political killing rather later than most of Europe, assassination has never been the English vice. The only political assassins have been foreign (mainly Irish) or, evidently, mad.* Guiscard, who tried to stab Harley with a penknife in 1711, was a French spy. The would-be assassins of George III were English and probably insane; Bellingham, who assassinated Spencer Percival, the Prime Minister in 1812, was English and certainly mad. There were some Jacobite assassination plots in the 1690s and 1750s, but in the eighteenth century no politician in England died at the hands of an assassin.[16]

Similarly, though Buckingham's astrologer was lynched shortly before his master's assassination, political lynching was not an old English custom. When rioters invaded his house in 1814, Lord Eldon managed, with the help of four soldiers, to arrest two of them. One of these, the Lord Chancellor wrote, 'bid me look to myself, and told me the People were much more likely to hang me than I was to

---

* Exceptionally, Felton, the murderer of the Duke of Buckingham in 1628, was English and, mentally, a borderline case. A sufferer from morbid religious passion who thought he was God's instrument, he left instructions that he should be prayed for as a man whose mind was disordered and discontented.

procure any of them to be hanged'.* Plausible as the threat might seem, nothing was in fact less likely. Although in the Peasants' Revolt and other medieval risings, an archbishop here and there and some great officers of state were murdered, no assassinations disfigured Tudor rebellions. Likewise in the eighteenth century no English politician or ecclesiastic was lynched. Nor was any landlord lynched, even in the Swing Riots of 1830–31 when large numbers of farm labourers were judicially executed. John Horsfall, a manufacturer who was murdered by the Luddites, is just about the only victim of popular violence since the Middle Ages whose name is still remembered.[17]

Some members of unpopular groups were equally unlucky. At Tring in 1751, an old woman and her husband, allegedly a witch and a wizard, were 'beaten in a cruel and barbarous manner' by the populace. The woman died, the man survived and the ringleader was hanged. In London at least five informers who gained rewards under the Gin Act were stoned to death in the 1730s, one of them in New Palace Yard. In 1771, Clarke, who had given the principal evidence against two Spitalfields weavers which had led to their execution, was stoned by some 2000 people for three hours and eventually 'died in the greatest of agonies'. The best that can be said of the Tring witch hunt is that the Witchcraft Act prohibiting accusations of witchcraft was only sixteen years old, and many years afterwards John Wesley still had no doubts about its existence; and of the murdered informers that such people have, understandably, always been unpopular except with those they inform or misinform – they were, said Swift, 'a detestable race', though sometimes necessary.[18]

Rather than assassination or lynching, England's preferred method of getting rid of enemies was judicial murder. Some twenty-five men were executed on trumped-up charges and perjured evidence during the Popish Plot agitation. Although Charles II said he would not have hanged a dog on the evidence produced against Lord Stafford, that did not stop the House of Lords convicting him or the king agreeing to his execution. The subsequent Rye House Plot brought a smaller batch to the scaffold. The eighteenth century saw no similar orgies. The judges were no longer tools of the executive. Perjury was confined to ordinary criminal trials; and though many innocent people were hanged by due process of law, that was not deliberate. One or two unlucky Jacobite printers were executed; otherwise the

---

* In the end, surprisingly, nobody was hanged. Eldon continued on the woolsack and died in his bed. When the rioters were sent before a magistrate, 'the soldiers said they would do their duty as soldiers but would not be witnesses'. And that was that.

English had largely shed the habit of judicial murder. Legislative murder by act of attainder similarly came to an end.[19]

Religious persecution, that potent begetter of violence, also largely disappeared in the eighteenth century. There was no reversion to the opening – and still less to the closing – years of Charles II's reign. Dissenters' meeting-houses were frequently attacked by mobs and Methodist preachers assaulted, but that did not quite amount to persecution; Protestant dissent was tolerated. The penal laws against Roman Catholics were harsh, and when enforced they did amount to persecution. Fortunately, their enforcement was seldom rigorous, and the small Catholic population was usually tolerated by its neighbours if not by the law. Even during the Popish Plot and the two Jacobite risings, neighbourliness often prevailed over bigotry.[20]

Those even more potent begetters of violence, popular risings and revolutions, were almost wholly absent. Monmouth's in 1685 was the last indisputable English rebellion. Just arguably it was the savage repression of the Bloody Assizes that ensured 1685 was never repeated; more probably the enlarged standing army and improved training and military technology made it clear to everyone that a popular rising by men without arms would certainly fail. Above all, popular causes were scarce. Fear of Popery had engendered Monmouth's rebellion; a revival of that fear in the years 1774-80 led to George III, of all people, being accused of Popish leanings, and to the Gordon Riots. Otherwise, while popular hostility to Catholicism remained intense for a century after the Revolution, the threat of a British sovereign being involved in a Romanist conspiracy had palpably evaporated. The Anglicans were clearly not going to rebel against their own supremacy; the Dissenters were kept submissive by toleration despite the Test Acts; and the Roman Catholics were too few to rebel. The only issue other than the religious capable of stimulating a rising was the dynastic. For half a century the Hanoverians excited little enthusiasm – as late as 1783 Boswell agreed with Dr Johnson that they had no friends – and much hostility. Yet remarkably few Englishmen were prepared to do anything violent to get rid of them.[21]

If 1685 saw the last English rebellion, 1688 saw the last English revolution. 'In abstracted speculation,' as Johnson suggested, eighteenth-century England looked ripe for revolution. 'When many want the necessaries of nature and . . . the idle live at ease by the fatigues of the diligent . . . it seems impossible that the peace of society can long subsist.' In practice, though, until the American War the chances of social upheaval were even slenderer than those of a rebellion. The ruling rich or governing elite were a small segment of society – less than 10 per cent. Over 75 per cent of the population were working men and women and nearly half of it was dependent,

or occasionally dependent, on charity or the Poor Law for survival.
Even so, because it had more of the 'middling sort', England had a
better social balance than other countries. Disparities of wealth were
vast, but 'the space between the ploughman and the peer [was]
crammed with circle after circle', the social structure consisting of a
host of gradations rather than a few sharp cleavages, 'one ascending
slope,' as Sheridan put it, 'without a break or landing place'. The
country was getting richer and a growing number of people
possessed some property. The middling sort were on the whole
satisfied and, except in parts of London, where in 1753 John Wesley
found 'many half-starved with cold and hunger', and the bigger
cities, the vast underclass was looked after by the Poor Law. Britain
was often at war but, except against the American colonists, was
generally successful. Save possibly during 1779-80, nothing
approaching a breakdown of government ever loomed. The ruling
classes never lost their self-confidence or loosened their grip.[22]

Before 1789 a revolution was made virtually impossible by a
shortage of revolutionaries. Republicans still existed, but they were
no more operative than the English Jacobites. Nobody advocated or,
except Lord George Gordon, threatened the violent overthrow of the
regime or had the means of achieving it. Some feared a revolution in
1769, but nothing was further from the mind of John Wilkes, the
man who was supposed to be leading it. Despite widespread poverty,
there was no trigger for a revolution and, before the 1790s, no
revolutionary ideology. Far from upsetting social stability, religion
now promoted it; millenarianism had been domesticated or forgotten, and socialism not yet thought of.[23]

Whatever its defects, the citadel of the *status quo* – the Protestant
religion, a landed aristocratic hierarchical society, mixed government, the rule of law and English liberty – was not seriously
challenged. The vast legions of the poor were miserable, but few save
Tom Paine had a social policy to help them or even the conviction
that their poverty could be much alleviated. Some radicals★ had ideas
of political reform, but they seldom made much impact except in
times of economic distress. And anyway they were not revolutionaries. Both ideas and power were on the side of the rulers, as was
military and economic success. The ruled had only hardship and
numbers. 'While the gentlemen have the laws and force in their
hands,' a Northumberland lady told her husband in 1761, 'they must
exert them to the support of their authority over the commonalty.'
The gentlemen duly did so.[25]

★ Since the word radical was not used in a political sense until later, to use it of eighteenth-
century ideas or politicians is, strictly speaking, anachronistic. On the other hand, as
Lampedusa points out in *The Leopard*, tuberculosis existed before Koch discovered it.[24]

Those laws were harsh. The country's rulers continually denounced the English populace as the 'giddy multitude', the 'inferior herd of mankind', 'the dregs of the people', 'the scum of the earth', 'a lawless and furious rabble';[26]* and they acted as though a peculiarly savage criminal code was necessary to maintain law and property. Yet in most other spheres their attitude was less fierce. The mild hand of government, Burke said, made insurrections rare. And if governments seldom showed quite the 'firmness and delicacy' that Burke enjoined, and if they sometimes inflamed rather than 'concili-ated', as George Grenville recommended (when out of office), 'the heated minds of men by temper and discretion', they never treated the English as they treated Scottish Highlanders in 1746 or Irish rebels in 1798 – or as Henry VIII had treated Northern England after the Pilgrimage of Grace. They had little compunction about acting violently if it suited them to do so, but save over the criminal law they seldom in England pursued a consistent policy of violence as a means of social control. Only when they deemed their interests or their pleasures to be at serious risk did they cast off their relative forbearance in the use of force.[28]

Their restraint was well judged. A much greater degree of governmental violence in eighteenth-century England would have been fully feasible; anyone, as Cavour once remarked, can govern in a state of siege.[29] But it would have destroyed the measure of consent on which the rule of the elite rested. The extent to which government operated by law and consent rather than by force was not constant; the proportions of the mixture varied over time. But the rulers of England were adept at engineering consent; grudging and conditional though it sometimes was, it was present. 'The English believe they enjoy liberty,' said a foreign observer, 'because they have a *word* for a device; but those who find themselves invested with power, by feeding the rest with chimerical ideas find means to really enslave them.' (Disraeli took a similar view of the eighteenth century: 'a people without power or education had been induced to believe themselves the freest and most enlightened nation in the world . . .')

Yet, rightly or wrongly, Englishmen thought they were a uniquely free people. Had their belief in their liberty been destroyed, and rule by consent as well as by force been replaced by naked coercion, society would have been fundamentally changed. A proper police would have been needed and a larger standing army. By becoming

---

* But Burke's famously unfortunate phrase 'a swinish multitude' in his *Reflections on the Revolution in France* was not, strictly speaking, applied to the English masses. Burke was writing of what he feared would happen if the Revolution continued on its way: '. . . learning will be cast into the mire and trodden down under the hoofs of a swinish multitude.'[27]

more violent, the aristocracy would have cut away the branch on which they were sitting: an unintrusive central authority and largely aristocratic control of the localities. They would have handed back to the crown their captive – the central government – and undermined their own authority and prestige. They would in addition have escalated the violence of the governed. So their restraint aided their control. The narrow base and long-lasting unpopularity of the ruling house and the oligarchy also advised a policy of accommodation; so did Whig ideology which, though much changed from the original Whig ideas, still retained a belief in moderation and limited government.[30]

Of course other violence, both governmental and popular, abounded; England in the eighteenth century was far from being a Quaker haven of peace. All the same, if in that era the English eschewed judicial murder, only intermittently indulged in religious persecution, failed to massacre or assassinate each other, seldom lynched anyone, and neither supported rebellions nor attempted a revolution, how on earth, it may be wondered, did they contrive to exhibit their 'love of violence', or display their 'savage' and 'violent' habits?

Executions and the Pillory

Vast crowds watched executions at Tyburn and elsewhere; evidence, maybe, of the eighteenth century's love of violence. But before drawing conclusions we should perhaps consider what might well happen if public executions were brought back today. Politicians and others would queue up for the honour of being a hangman. Whoever was chosen, he or she (in these enlightened days the job would have to be thrown open to both sexes, and perhaps there would be both a male and a female hangperson) would immediately become a celebrity, ranking even higher in the public pantheon than pop singers or soap opera stars. The tabloid press would admiringly record every detail of their lives, their opinions would be regarded as important on all matters from religion to gardening, and at election time their endorsement would be eagerly sought by the political parties; on retirement, they would no doubt sit in the House of Lords. The last days of the condemned would be chronicled (or invented) in loving detail. And executions would be in Hyde Park near Tyburn of old, where, although they were televised, the crowd would be bigger than at a Wembley cup final; ticket touts would make a killing.[31]

For the public, eighteenth-century government provided not only the spectacle of execution, but also participation in the pillory, a punishment dubbed by the generally admiring historian of English law as 'essentially barbarous and wholly capricious'. Offenders, wrote Misson, a foreign observer, in 1698,

> are exposed in a high place, with their heads put through two pieces of notched wood; the uppermost whereof being made to slide down, shuts the neck into the notch. The criminal's hands are confined on each side of his head in this same manner; and thus he stands in this ridiculous posture for more or less time, or with more or fewer repetitions, according to his sentence.

They might then expect 'to be regaled with a hundred thousand handfuls of mud, and as many rotten eggs as can be got for money', the throwing of stones being unlawful but frequent.[32]

Part of the majesty of the law, the pillory was an invitation to violence. According to Defoe

> *The undistinguish'd fury of the street . . .*
> *No bias can the rabble draw*
> *But dirt throws dirt without respect to merit, or to law.*

In 1731 Mother Needham, a notorious procuress, died after being badly pelted in the pillory. Yet the mob did distinguish, as Defoe had happily discovered, when he himself was pilloried. The invitation to violence was not always accepted. The mob sometimes protected the offender and turned the pillory into a celebration. Only flowers were thrown at Defoe and, when the Jacobite Shebbeare was pilloried in 1758 for having satirised William III and George I, the mob gave him not dead cats but three huzzahs and allowed him to be protected from the rain by a footman holding an umbrella. Seven years later a Wilkite printer spent an hour in the pillory to cheers of 'Wilkes and Liberty', and over 200 guineas was collected for him. 'If you are sentenced to the pillory,' wrote Smollett, who hated Wilkes, 'your fortune is made – as times go, that's a sure step to honour and preferment . . .' Indeed it was to prevent the popular Admiral Cochrane having to stand in the pillory that in 1816 the government at last abolished it.[33]

Two groups at particular risk in the pillory were professional false witnesses and homosexuals. For them the pillory was 'almost as good as death', as another foreign observer suggested, and did occasionally lead to it. In 1732 John Waller, who had been put in it for perjuring himself to convict a highwayman, was severely pelted and then stripped naked and kicked to death. One of a gang which incited people to commit robberies and then gave evidence against them, and which also specialised in faking evidence against innocent men in order to get the rewards, was killed in the pillory twenty-four years later; the others just survived. Perjury's occasional usefulness to the authorities brought it lenient legal punishment even when its consequences had been lethal for innocent men. Not surprisingly, the populace took a less relaxed view of the crime.[34]

The case of homosexuals was rather different. In the eighteenth and early nineteenth centuries homosexuality was feared and hated by both rulers and ruled. Apart from anything else it was believed to be a foreign and popish importation.

> *Lust chose the torrid zone of Italy,*
> *Where blood foments in rapes and sodomy,*

wrote Defoe in *The True-Born Englishman*. And fifty years later Smollett said the same in *Roderick Random*:

> *Eternal infamy the wretch confound*
> *Who planted first, this vice on British ground!*

Though sodomy was made a capital crime in 1533, nobody had been executed for it since 1640. In the eighteenth century the Society for the Reformation of Manners started bringing prosecutions, and three men were hanged in 1726. The offence was difficult to prove and convictions were rare, but those who were convicted were, like murderers and forgers, seldom reprieved.[35]

Mere attempted sodomy was more easily proved, and it was for that offence that homosexuals faced the public's righteous indignation. In 1726 Charles Hitchin, the Under City Marshal, who was lucky to be convicted of only the minor offence, barely survived half an hour in the pillory. A homosexual was pelted to death there in 1763. Shortly before the Gordon Riots, Burke raised the case of one who had died there partly because of the attentions of the mob and partly because he had been too short to be able to stand in it; another member reported a similar case at Bury. In an attack on Burke, the *Morning Post* applauded 'the spirit of the spectators' and thought the crime deserved an 'ignominious death'.[36]

From about 1790, executions for sodomy virtually ceased on the continent. The French revolutionaries decriminalised it, with most Catholic countries following suit not long afterwards. In England, however, encouraged by Wilberforce's Society for the Suppression of Vice, horror of sodomy increased. The number of executions grew to about two a year and, in 1810, when some homosexuals who had been caught in a tavern in Vere Street were sentenced to the pillory, the crowd was said to number between 30,000 and 50,000.

Before any of them reached the place of punishment, their faces were completely disfigured by blows and mud . . . upwards of fifty women were permitted to stand in the ring, who assailed them incessantly with mud, dead cats, rotten eggs, potatoes, and buckets filled with blood, offal and dung, which were brought by a number of butchers' men from St James's market.

The newspapers called for the death penalty to be extended to attempted sodomy and rejoiced that some of the Vere Street culprits could not survive their ordeal. Surprisingly, however, they all did. A few years later when the Bishop of Clogher was caught with a guardsman, the pillory had been abolished, and he anyway fled the country on bail. But some weeks afterwards the Archbishop of Canterbury reported that it was still unsafe for a Bishop to appear on the streets.[37]

Such mob violence, particularly its more frequent outbreaks in the early nineteenth century, shocked foreign observers. The tormentors of the pilloried homosexuals were not, as they arguably were with perjurors, filling a lacuna in the law and punishing men who had intentionally harmed others. They were merely acting in accordance with what was thought to be biblical guidance, with the views of all ranks of society, and with the implicit blessing of the law against men who had harmed nobody. Jeremy Bentham likened the English attitude to sodomites, who were heretics in sexual taste, to the Spanish Inquisition's attitude to heretics in religion. He was nevertheless almost alone in that view, and he kept it carefully to himself.[38]

Visitors

Foreigners complained of insults from the English and of occasional rough treatment such as having dead dogs and cats thrown at them. Not all agreed, however; the Abbé Leblanc thought a Frenchman in London was better received than an Englishman in Paris.[39] Yet despite the brutalities of the pillory, visitors did not find the English a violent people. The Swiss, Meister, believed there were fewer affrays in London in a fortnight than there were in Paris in a morning. Visitors even accepted the common native belief that English highwaymen were more humane than those abroad. They were certainly prevalent. Horace Walpole, who had earlier been shot in the face by the highwayman McLean, wrote in 1752 'of being forced to travel, even at noon, as if one was going to battle'. Thirty years later he found his friends reluctant to travel to Twickenham for dinner. Lord North was robbed on the road when he was premier. Yet, over-glamourised though they were, 'the gentlemen of the road' (they included the occasional Old Etonian) seldom killed those they

robbed. English travellers round England, such as Celia Fiennes and
Defoe, did not go in constant fear of robbery or murder, and most
travellers were not driven to arms. In France in 1676 John Locke
noted that everybody carried pistols on the road. He clearly did not
think the same true of England.[40]

Locke was also struck by the number of murders, even in towns
like Montpellier. Visitors to England throughout the century were
struck by the rarity of murder, one even maintaining that London
was the only great city in Europe where murder did not happen. An
exaggeration of course, but visitors were right in believing that the
murder rate was low. Even during the 1752 crime wave there were
only ten murder convictions in London whose population was over
half a million.[41]

Admittedly, Smollett claimed that in 1730 England was 'infested
with robbers, assassins and incendiaries, the natural consequences of
degeneracy, corruption and the want of police . . .', but Smollett,
who was never given to understatement, was only nine years old in
1730 and living in Scotland. He was trying to make a political point
which the evidence does not support. When he described a period of
which he had personal experience, Smollett pointed to the turbulence
of the English, not their violence. The position, he discovered, was
very different on the continent. There he found the people of
Boulogne 'ferocious and much addicted to revenge'. 'Many barbarous murders are committed,' he added, 'and the peasants, from
motives of envy and resentment, frequently set their neighbours'
houses on fire.' He found the Italians little more reliable; they were
apt to use their knives on the slightest provocation, and the best he
could say of them was that their open attacks were 'not so formidable
as their premeditated schemes of revenge'.[42]

Instead of noting the violence of the English, travellers remarked
on their amiability. In 1727 de Saussure found them 'kind-hearted
and compassionate', and thought the term 'good natured' was not
found outside England. Ten years later Pollnitz wondered if any
other people were 'so good natured and happy' as the English. In
1765 Grosley deemed Londoners 'haughty and ungovernable' but
also 'good natured and humane'. During the Gordon Riots the Italian
opera singer Pacchierotti was advised to take his name off his door
and not to walk about the streets. 'Why should I fear?' he replied, 'I
am not alarmed because the English nation, it seems to me, is
composed of good-natured mild people'. In 1782 Moritz, like Misson
many years earlier, observed the kindness and indulgence of the
English to children. In the next few years Archenholz noted their
solicitude to both children and women, and Meister commented on
fathers paying great attention to their infant offspring and admired
'the humanity and mild disposition of the lower kind of people'. All

in all, Boswell had good cause to claim that nobody of sound mind could deny that the people of England possessed the quality of good nature.[43]

Riots

Partly because they despised foreigners for living under arbitrary governments, the English did not reciprocate their visitors' admiration. And for many of them arbitrary government at home remained a danger to be guarded against. If, despite the constitutional precautions, that danger materialised, if the British government acted illegitimately, they differed as to how a citizen should react. The original Tory view was that passive obedience and non-resistance were the only proper behaviour. The Nonjurors – some 400 Anglican clergy who refused to take the oath of fidelity to William and Mary – held to these doctrines and suffered for them. Such consistency was rare. Other Tories were more flexible, and by mid-century Hume could treat such ideas as a denial of common sense: even 'our high monarchical party' was forced to recognise their inadequacy in emergencies.[44]

Although 'resistance' was not closely defined – it could mean anything from full-scale rebellion to a riotous demonstration designed to bring pressure on the government – there was, in the Whig view, a right of resistance which had been properly exercised against James II. The right of resistance against Whig government was more problematic. Many Whigs thought that resistance was the prerogative of the nobility and gentry: the rabble could only join in if they were under the orders of their betters. Nevertheless the right of resistance remained part of constitutional theory, and Hume, Blackstone, Adam Smith, Burke and Archdeacon Paley all upheld it, though only, of course, in the most extreme circumstances and in the last resort. For many Englishmen, however, the right came into being rather earlier than the last resort; for them resistance was a matter of practice not theory, the right to riot being, in Halevy's words, 'an integral part of the national traditions'. A radical MP, John Sawbridge, thought resistance was justified, even to Acts of Parliament, if they were unjust and oppressive.[45]

'I have seen, within a year,' Benjamin Franklin wrote in 1769, 'riots in the country about corn; riots about elections; riots about workhouses; riots of colliers; riots of weavers; riots of coalheavers; riots of sawyers; riots of Wilkesites; riots of government [licensed?] chairmen; riots of smugglers, in which custom-house officers and excisemen have been murdered [and] the King's armed vessels and troops fired at.'[46] Franklin's list was relatively short. In the eighteenth century, Englishmen (and Englishwomen) rioted against turnpikes, enclosures and high food prices, against Roman Catholics, the Irish and the Dissenters, against the naturalisation of Jews, the impeachment of politicians, press gangs, 'crimp' houses and the Militia Act, against theatre prices, foreign actors, pimps, bawdy houses, surgeons, French footmen and alehouse keepers, against the gibbets in the Edgware Road and public whippings, against the imprisonment of London's chief magistrates, against the Excise, against the Cider Tax and the Shops Tax, against workhouses and industrial employers, against the rumoured destruction of cathedral spires, even against a change in the calendar.

There were riots at elections and after them, in prisons and outside them, in schools and colleges, at executions, at factories and workplaces, in the law courts at Westminster Hall, outside Parliament and within the Palace of Westminster, at the office of the Bow Street magistrate, in theatres, in brothels, in a cathedral close, and in Pall Mall at the gates of St James's Palace. Adam's fine screen outside the Admiralty was built to keep out sailors agitating for their pay.[47] Presumably it was cheaper than paying them.

Such an extensive catalogue seems to portray a naturally violent people and a society that resorted to riot on the slightest pretext. Yet the populace were in a considerable difficulty. Living in poverty or near it, forming the great majority of the population, excluded from politics, derided as the mob or the rabble, scorned as ill-informed and illiterate, classed as a lower order of creation, yet at the same time deemed by themselves and by the regime's rhetoric to be free-born Englishmen, living in what was generally recognised to be an unusually free country – 'the lower orders' could not win however they behaved. Condemning an 'indiscreet and mischievous' speech in which Grenville, the Foreign Secretary, took credit for the loyalty of the Irish Catholics during Hoche's expedition to Bantry Bay in 1796, Burke pointed the dilemma: '. . . if the people are turbulent and riotous, nothing is to be done for them on account of their evil dispositions. If they are obedient and loyal, nothing is to be done for them, because their being quiet and contented, is a proof that they feel no grievance.' That was of course not unique to the eighteenth century. Macaulay and Gladstone made the same point in the next century. Indeed, all subject peoples are caught on that Morton's fork.[48]

In eighteenth-century England the great majority preferred the prong of silence or had no choice – most people, said Hume, are normally acquiescent; but some, not surprisingly, were driven onto the prong of turbulence. 'The desire for freedom,' Erich Fromm maintained, 'is a biological reaction of the human organism . . . and threats to man's freedom arouse defensive aggression as do all threats to vital interests.' Whether or not that view is biologically sound, it was politically true of England. The eighteenth-century English were well endowed with 'defensive aggression'. Their rioting was normally defensive in that usually it sought to preserve what they regarded as their vital interests or undoubted rights, had a limited objective and was seldom violent against persons; the only people who got killed in riots were the rioters. It was aggressive in that it was violent against property and showed contempt for established authority. Yet the violence was rarely mindless. Riots usually had a specific and defensible objective. Even the seemingly idiotic agitation against the introduction of the Gregorian calendar in 1752 was not wholly irrational: people were not just concerned to get back their eleven days; the change of dates did bring genuine problems about wage rates, rents and annual payments.[49]

In pursuing short-term goals and ignoring long-term ones like fundamental change or revolution, the rioters were meeting one of Hannah Arendt's requirements for rational violence mentioned at the head of this chapter. Violence in pursuit of long-term objectives is usually self-defeating and hence irrational. That a crowd could ever be rational was not an idea entertained by the influential nineteenth-century theorist of crowds, Gustave Le Bon. He believed that the 'collective mind' of a crowd was necessarily stupid and irresponsible, and that by joining a crowd an individual descended 'several rungs in the ladder of civilisation'. Le Bon thus overrated the irrationality of crowds while underrating that of individuals. In fact in the eighteenth century, as we shall see below, crowds were sometimes the more rational of the two.[50]

Of course the presence of a rational, or even a good, cause for a riot does not remove its violence. But the words 'riot' and 'mob', like 'violence', were then used widely, being applied to any unlawful assembly or hostile activity whether violent or not. Sometimes, according to Henry Fielding, justices 'construed a little harmless scolding into a riot'; the navy termed strikes in the dockyards 'riots'. Similarly a 'mob' might be a few disrespectful people jeering 'the great', or a large crowd killing informers or seemingly intent on burning down London. Some of the rioting was brutal and bigotted, but often what were termed riots were in fact demonstrations. The 'rabble' were showing their betters where the shoe pinched and that it needed repair; a riot was their best, if not their only, channel of communication. Except when a mob was hired, the distinction between riots organised 'from above' and those 'spontaneously' initiated 'from below' was often more artificial than absolute. Frequently riots were a mixture of both: in 1721 a justice of the peace led a riot against two informers in Drury Lane. Yet many riots were instigated by the upper orders, who then unctuously deplored them.

In any case their violence was usually limited. Indeed, the violence was often non-violent.[51]

Though the mob was feared and despised by the propertied, its turbulence often served useful constitutional and political functions. At the beginning of the century Jonathan Swift in his *Discourse* denounced the 'rash, jealous and inconstant humour of the people'. Using the history of Rome to show that dissensions and popular tumults always led to tyranny and claiming (inaccurately) that 'the raging of the sea and the madness of the people' were put together in Holy Writ, he argued that the only way to maintain the balance of power established at the Revolution between King, Lords and Commons was for the first two 'never to give way to popular clamour'.[52]*

In his *Considérations*, published in 1734 shortly after his visit to England, Montesquieu drew a very different lesson from Roman history. Following Machiavelli, he believed that 'the dissensions' in Rome had been a necessary condition of its liberty. In a state which seemed to consist of 'nothing but commotions', there could be 'a union of harmony', just as dissonances in music cooperated 'in producing overall concord'. Abuses of power could be corrected by 'the spirit of the people'. And, writing specifically of England, Montesquieu defined a free government as one that was 'constantly subject to agitation'. No wonder Burke, who earlier described Montesquieu as 'the greatest genius which has enlightened this age', later complained that the *Considérations* was a 'manual' of the French revolutionaries![54]

Whether or not Robespierre had read the *Considérations*, Montesquieu was echoed by Thomas Jefferson. No admirer of mobs, which he likened to 'sores' on the human body, Jefferson thought that a country could only maintain its liberties if its rulers were periodically warned that their people preserved 'the spirit of resistance'. In consequence he believed that no country should be too long without a rebellion; in England, he added, they happened 'every half dozen years'.[55]

Swift would have been right and Montesquieu and Jefferson wrong if the English mob had been much more powerful, or indeed if English politicians, as in Republican Rome, had used it as a murderous route to personal power. But the English system more or less ruled out that form of politics. In a monarchy supreme power was only open to politicians through rebellion or revolution, neither of which promised hope of success. Nor could lesser power be easily

---

* Later vicissitudes led Swift to reverse his position. After the death of Queen Anne, he hoped memories of the Sacheverell Riots might curb Whig violence, and he came to regard 'the sentiments of the vulgar' as a useful constitutional safeguard.[53]

gained by using the mob. The vast social and economic gulf between England's ruling aristocracy and the populace ensured that use of the mob for personal – as opposed to party or opposition – advancement (except for generally accepted purposes such as electioneering) was usually frowned upon by the elite. The rules of the club confined politics to Parliament and the parliamentary classes; the extraparliamentary nation was there to do what it was told.[56]

At the same time the political awareness of the many and the social chasm between them and the few made the mob unamenable to all but the most exceptional politicians. The London mob was not composed of the dregs of the capital but chiefly of labourers, journeymen, small tradesmen and shopkeepers, with a sprinkling of 'well-dressed persons', and was not easily drawn to an oligarch in need of support. A hired mob, of course, could always be raised from the venal, but that was of scant political use. Finally, the mob was not a constitutional danger because it was not over-mighty. Its lack of firearms – unlike the American colonists or many people in eighteenth-century Languedoc – prevented it presenting a serious challenge to the army. Largely the consequence of post-Restoration government policy and of the Game Laws, a disarmed people was a cardinal feature of eighteenth-century England.[57]

Like other political forces and institutions, the mob was seldom wholly independent; nor was it necessarily representative. Nevertheless, unarmed though it was, the mob was still a powerful force both in its own right and as an indication of 'the inclinations of the People'. At the end of his life Burke lamented that most attention was paid to 'the cry of the people' in towns through 'fear of their multitude and combination'. The urban mob certainly inspired fear among the propertied, and ministers beat tactical retreats in the face of popular disaffection. Lord North once said that there were only two ways of changing a ministry: by the King or the mob. Yet only in 1710, 1741-42, 1756-57 and 1763 did the mob help to precipitate a change of ministry, and on the first three occasions the country was at war. As in other countries, the crowd was chiefly influential as a defensive or conservative force. What Smollett called 'the immediate danger of popular commotions' was sometimes the only check on the government. Indeed Smollett's fellow novelist, Fielding, called the mob 'the fourth estate'.* The remark was ironic, but it contained truth. From 1716 onwards the Commons and still more the Lords were more adjuncts than controllers of the executive; so often was the mob. Yet the fourth estate was probably a more effective curb on the

---

* Hazlitt later described Cobbett as 'a kind of fourth estate'. Later still, the press as a whole was given the title. The mob was probably the most capable of the three.[58]

government than either the second or the third. It was England's strongest countervailing force.[59]

The people, Burke told the Commons, would not look for illegal means of redress if they had legal ones. Perceived injustice is the root of most popular violence, and different conceptions of justice the cause of most violent social and political conflict. Governments find that difficult to accept. Marvelling at the skilful beneficence of their own rule, they are convinced that the ruled can have no cause for complaint; hence they infer that popular violence must stem from licentiousness, perversity or agitation. 'I hope,' the Bishop of Durham wrote during an industrial dispute in 1793, 'the good sense of the People will in a little time prevail and convince them of the happiness which they enjoy.' What the Bishop regarded as the people's good sense often did prevail; on other occasions the conviction that they were enjoying not happiness but injustice urged them to violence. It was often the only weapon they had.[60]

Popular and governmental violence are commonly assessed by different standards. Governments are judged by political criteria, under which consequences are at least as important as intentions or methods. Violent repression and official terrorism can thus be justified by their apparent success, and abuses of power excused by reasons of state. Popular violence is given no such latitude. Ordinary moral standards are applied, with the result that it is almost inevitably condemned. 'The wild justice of the people,' wrote James Mackintosh of the French Revolution well before the Terror, 'has a naked and undisguised horror. Its slightest exertion awakens all our indignation, while murder and rapine if arrayed in the gorgeous disguise of acts of state, may with impunity stalk abroad.' The double standards involved in denying individuals or 'the people' the indulgence that is commonly given to 'the justice' or the violence of governments probably help to cut down violence. But if, for a change, the same standards are applied to popular and governmental violence, and if the violence that was instigated from above is added to the government's own violence and that of the governing elite, then in eighteenth-century England violence came much more from the rulers than from the ruled.[61]

Part One

LEGITIMACY IN DISPUTE

We find ourselves in possession of the greatest human good, CIVIL AND RELIGIOUS LIBERTY, at a time when almost all the rest of mankind lie in slavery and error. This is no ordinary mercy . . . So that if there be any thing certain, this is not to be disputed, that we *Englishmen* (how unworthy soever) are at present most indebted to Providence of the whole race of mankind.

William Warburton, Bishop of Gloucester, 1746

ONE

Prelude: The Glorious Revolution

No man undervalues the common people of England, who are in truth the best and the honestest, aye, and the wisest common people in the world, when he says they are not fit to model the government they are to live under, or to make the laws they are to obey. . . . It is the privilege . . . of the common people of England to be represented by the greatest, and learnedest, and wealthiest, and wisest persons, that can be chose out of the nation . . .

Lord Chancellor Hyde, 1661

I am sure there was no man born marked of God above another; for none comes into the world with a saddle on his back, neither any booted or spurred to ride him.

Richard Rumbold on the scaffold, 1685

King Charles lost his life *because he did not run away*, and his son, King James, saved his life, because he *did* run away.

Daniel Defoe, 1702[1]

Earlier revolutions, wrote Tom Paine during the French one, had been little more than 'a change of persons', with the nation being then, as always, 'left out of the question'. English aristocrats were certainly anxious to keep the nation out of the Glorious Revolution. They had, after all, recently seen what happened when the nation entered into the question. In those terrible years, 1641-2, not only had the ruling elite gone to war with one another, but London mobs had intimidated the King and the Lords, prevented most of the Bishops taking their seats in Parliament, and openly threatened violence if their demands were not met. In Westminster Hall some 500 men had fought gentlemen with swords and cudgels. 'All right and property,' an MP had cautioned the Commons in 1642, 'all *meum* and *teum* must cease in a civil war and we know not what advantages the meaner sort also may take to divide the spoils of the rich and noble among them . . .,' a warning echoed by Charles I. In the event a social revolution had not occurred in what the 1662 Prayer Book called 'the late unhappy confusions'; nor had there been a Terror, either then or at the Restoration. Yet the world had almost been turned upside down. The aristocratic leaders of 1688-9 were determined to keep their world the right way up with themselves securely on top of it.[2]

Despite some further scares, the 'common people' had been relatively passive since 1660. The unconditional restoration of Charles II had ended anarchy – London apprentices had fought a street battle with soldiers – and was initially popular. Venner's tiny rising of fifty to 100 fanatics was easily suppressed by the King's Guards: twenty-six rebels were killed and another thirteen executed. The restored monarchy's popularity was soon dissipated, however, and by 1663 Londoners were described as hostile. The regime was insecure and the government remained jittery, yet there was no danger of popular insurrection.[3]

In 1668, in riots involving thousands of people and lasting five days, London apprentices pulled down bawdy houses and attacked prisons to release their arrested comrades. Before the Civil War, the apprentices, who saw themselves as moral reformers, had customarily attacked brothels on Shrove Tuesday, their traditional holiday. The revival of the custom on Easter Monday in 1668 was probably caused by a royal proclamation requiring enforcement of the laws against Dissenters. Instead of the degree of toleration Nonconformists had been expecting, they now faced renewed persecution. Bawdy houses, which like Dissenters' conventicles were illegal and symbolic of Charles's flagrantly debauched court, were a natural focus of resentment. According to Pepys, 'these idle fellows' – there were over 20,000 apprentices in London – regretted having only pulled down small bawdy houses instead of pulling down 'the great bawdy house at Whitehall'. With veterans of Cromwell's army rumoured to be involved, the government behaved as though the destruction of brothels was the prelude to civil war. Large bodies of troops were called out; their commander, said Pepys, acted like a madman and alarms were sounded, as though 'the French were coming into the town'.[4]

The reaction of the bench was equally extreme. Though the connection between attacking bawdy houses and committing high treason is not self-evident, judicial ingenuity easily coupled them. With the only distinguished judge on the bench, Hale, dissenting on the grounds that such severity was undeserved and legally mistaken, Peter Messenger and three other apprentices were adjudged guilty of high treason and were hanged, drawn and quartered. Almost anything could now be turned into treason. A few years later a Nonconformist preacher's mere likening of Charles II to that fosterer of idolatry, King Jeroboam, was found treasonable, a verdict which even Jeffreys found steep. But, despite the heavy retribution, the apprentices did not abandon their designs against London's brothels.[5]

Unlike in the United Provinces where fear of the mob elevated William of Orange to the stadholdership, in London bawdy houses were for some time about as near to politics as the populace managed to get. Apart from the Weavers' Riots seven years later, which were leniently treated because they were considered a 'rebellion begot in the belly not in the brain', there were no serious disturbances. Political rioting needed leadership – 'the people stir not without the gentry,' wrote one of Charles II's secretaries of state – and the propertied's memories of 1640–60 inhibited them from providing it.[6]

Under Charles II extraparliamentary politics were virtually confined to the Exclusion Crisis of 1678–83, when both the new Whig and Tory parties organised public opinion and encouraged demonstrations. The Whigs, some of whom were being bribed by Louis XIV, were initially the more successful, beating the Court in three general elections and narrowly controlling the City of London. Yet the Tories, basing their campaign on memories of the Civil War, also had a large public following. Indeed the parties were pretty evenly balanced until, in the reaction against the Whig attempt to exclude the Roman Catholic James from succeeding his brother, the Tories gained predominance. So long as the struggle was primarily parliamentary, the Whigs used some violent language but no direct violence – though their whipping up of the mob resulted in judicial violence against the alleged perpetrators of the Popish Plot, twenty-five of whom were executed on heavily-perjured evidence. Initially, indeed, the chief danger of civil war came from the Whigs' target, James, Duke of York, who favoured the use of force to crush them. But the King contented himself with a mere show of force when Parliament met at Oxford in 1681: 660 Horse and Foot Guards in that city, and a doubling of the garrison in London. Nevertheless the general fear of violence, greater even than that of Popery, rebounded against the Whigs, and the cry that '1641 was come again' ensured their downfall and consolidated the regime.[7]

In defeat a few Whig thoughts turned to violent resistance. The Whig leader, Lord Shaftesbury, planned armed rebellion and claimed to have a private army of 'ten thousand brisk boys from Wapping'. But they were never seen, and Shaftesbury fled to Holland. With the government seeking vengeance and with open rebellion ruled out by lack of support, conspiracy was the only alternative to exile or submission. Treason was certainly talked and armed resistance schemed, but nothing substantial emerged. The so called Rye House Plot was probably a separate affair. Yet the uncovering of an alleged plan of some fanatical republicans to murder Charles and James on their way back from Newmarket races gave the government the opportunity to get rid of the Whig leaders. This time the judicial

murders were many fewer than those instigated by the Whigs during
the Popish Plot, but according to the custom of the times Lord
Russell and Algernon Sidney among others – probably innocent as
charged though not of other activities – went to the scaffold.[8]

The Monmouth Rebellion

Popular quiescence did not imply contentment or unqualified
deference to what Hyde claimed was the most 'entirely loved'
nobility in Europe. Between 1660 and 1688 Hyde's 'common people'
were given only one brief opportunity to rebel under aristocratic
leadership and, in the South West, many took it. Charles II's
illegitimate and protestant son, the Duke of Monmouth, had shown
unexpected clemency after defeating the Scottish covenanters at
Bothwell Brig in 1679, and his looks, manners and religion gave him
popular appeal. Of his semi-royal 'progresses' round the country,
wrote Dryden,

> The admiring crowd are dazzled with surprise,
> And on his goodly person feed their eyes . . .
> The crowd, (that still believe their Kings oppress)
> With lifted hands their young Messiah bless . . .
> Fame runs before him, as the morning star;
> And shouts of joy salute him from afar.[9]

Monmouth, who had had no intention of rising while Charles was
alive, chose the wrong moment after his death, June 1685 being
strategically too soon and tactically too late. He landed at Lyme Regis
before James II had had the chance to offend his subjects – his only
Parliament was still generously voting him money and it promptly
declared the Duke a traitor – but a full four weeks after the Earl of
Argyll had set out to raise Scotland. The government was thus given
ample warning to arrest potential troublemakers before Monmouth
landed.[10]

Monmouth's rebellion was not, as used to be thought, a tragi-
farce, in which deluded and scarcely armed yokels, under a timorous,
inept leader with cart horses for cavalry and no competent officers,
embarked on an absurd enterprise that was doomed before it began.
In its results the rebellion was certainly tragic, but farcical it was not.
Monmouth, himself, was not bold enough to be an ideal leader,
being prone to morose indecisiveness, but in comparison with his
contemporary insurgent, Argyll, or with Mar in 1715, he was an
effective rebel. An experienced soldier with a good record in the Low
Countries and in Scotland, he took pains to train his force, and he

showed courage at the Norton St Philip skirmish and at Sedgemoor
– until, that is, his somewhat premature departure from the
battlefield. His friend and cavalry commander, Lord Grey, who left
with him, was fairly cowardly, wholly amateurish and ultimately
treacherous, but Monmouth had many efficient professional officers
in his army.[11]

Nor were his rank and file a rabble of star-struck rustics, incapable
of understanding the issues. Since the Restoration, Dissenters had
suffered twenty years of intermittent persecution, all the more severe
during the last four years. The local gentry and the militia had
wrecked the Dissenters' meeting-house at Bridgwater. Much the
same had happened at Lyme Regis and Bridport. In Taunton the
mayor had led the attack, pulling down the main meeting-houses of
the Dissenters and burning their contents to the accompaniment of
bell ringing and copious drinking. By 1685, with the Whigs crippled
and the towns placed under Tory control, persecution seemed
destined to be permanent. And with an avowed Catholic on the
throne, there was now the greater danger of Popery. This was no
less alarming to many churchmen than to Dissenters; hence by no
means all Monmouth's recruits were Nonconformists. Probably only
about a quarter of his army was engaged in agriculture; more than a
third were cloth workers suffering from underemployment and low
wages. They knew what they were doing. They were rebelling
against Popery and religious persecution, many of them looking back
to the Civil War and the 'good old cause.'[12]

Monmouth, who had landed with only eighty-two men, soon had
an army of some 6000 before the inevitable desertions, swelled by
James's offer of a free pardon, substantially reduced it. The militia
proved unwilling to fight him, the Somerset men deserting *en masse*,
the Dorset men being semi-mutinous and the Devonians taking
flight. Yet Argyll's Scottish rising which should have diverted
government troops to the north was snuffed out; Lord Delamere
failed to rise in Cheshire; and London remained quiet. James had not
yet alienated his people, and the opposition was divided. A leading
Dissenting minister dissuaded all he could from supporting Monmouth on the grounds that the Duke was 'ungodly'; he was content
to await deliverance from a 'holier' quarter. Monmouth, who had on
landing issued a radical declaration, offended his republican supporters in London by later proclaiming himself King. Daniel Defoe and
a few other Londoners (probably) joined the rebellion, and the
veteran republican plotter, John Wildman, sent the Duke some
horses, but apart from meagre financial support Monmouth's other
London sympathisers, as Defoe later complained, merely 'talk'd' for
him. Their caution is understandable: the King kept a strong military
presence in the capital and made hundreds of arrests.[13]

The government was in full control of London but not yet of the South West. The battle of Sedgemoor was a close-run thing. Monmouth's plan – a daring night attack – was a good one, and the gamble might well have come off. Had it done so, the government's resistance might have evaporated as it did in 1688. Monmouth probably had nearly 4000 men, enough for a surprise attack on some 2500. But surprise was lost, and the rebels were in the end routed, the slaughter on the field continuing long after the battle was over. Perhaps as many as 1400 rebels were killed; most of the rest got away, but some 1500 were soon rounded up. Of these about 100 were summarily hanged over the next four days. In some ways they were lucky; the rest awaited the attentions of His Majesty's judges.[14]

Jeffreys, the Lord Chief Justice, started slowly. At a show trial at Winchester designed to terrorise people into not harbouring rebels, Jeffreys hectored the jury into convicting the 70-year-old Dame Alice Lisle of that crime. A victim of judicial murder, she was sentenced to be burned alive but was 'graciously' permitted to be beheaded instead. Not until he reached the West Country did Jeffreys get into his stride, trying 1336 prisoners in nine sitting days; before he and his brethren arrived, many of the prisoners had been deceived into confessions by promises of the King's mercy. At Dorchester Jeffreys managed in one morning to dispatch thirty rebels, all of whom had pleaded not guilty. After trials which must have been mockeries, all but one were convicted and quickly hanged. The message was unmistakable, and most of the remaining prisoners pleaded guilty in the hope of avoiding a similar fate. Many were disappointed. As the saying went, they confessed and were hanged. The only sure way of escaping the gallows was to die in prison where conditions were so bad that many did. Some managed to buy pardons, in which there was a traffic, and 890 were transported to the West Indies, many of them dying during the voyage or on arrival. In addition to those who had been summarily hanged, about 250 more were executed by due process of law.[15]

Armed rebellion is no trifling matter to be lightly passed over in the spirit of letting bygones be bygones. Cromwell's punishment of Penruddock's royalist rebellion in 1655 was abnormally light; more typically the miniature and wholly ineffective rebellion in the North in 1663 had led to many hangings, as did the 'Fifteen' and 'Forty-five'. In 1685 severe retribution was inevitable and Monmouth himself, who had even accused James of murdering his brother and burning down London, could expect no mercy. Yet the judicial toll of what James II approvingly called Jeffreys's 'campaign' exceeded anything perpetrated by Henry VIII after the Pilgrimage of Grace or by Mary after Wyatt's rebellion; except for Elizabeth's suppression of the rising of the Northern Earls, it was the largest since the

Peasants' Revolt. Though such a massacre caused public revulsion and a royalist commander was shocked by the brutality, nobody publicly objected at the time; it would have been hazardous to do so. Some approved. The Devon magistrates issued a declaration that the sword of justice should be kept unsheathed until the 'pestilent faction' of 'impenitent and desperate rebels' had all been cut off, to which the Bishop of Exeter gave an episcopal *imprimatur* by ordering it to be read in church. (The Bishop of Winchester had commanded James's artillery at Sedgemoor.) Only after 1688 was the 'bloody Assizes' given its title. Only then, too, did James and Jeffreys start blaming each other for the carnage.[16]

The great number of executions was made worse by their manner. Save for a lucky one or two who were able to buy themselves a decent hanging, all the rebels were executed as traitors. The traditional sentence for high treason was:

> That you be carried back to the place from whence you came, and from thence be drawn upon an hurdle to the place of execution, where you shall be hanged up by the neck, but cut down again alive, your entrails and privy members cut off from your body, and burnt in your sight, your head to be severed from your body and your body divided into four parts, and disposed of at the King's pleasure. And the Lord have mercy upon your soul.

Except that they sometimes walked to the gallows or went in a cart, this sentence was executed on the rebels in 1685. Apart from its intrinsic savagery, the killing process was long drawn out. Ordinary hangings could be effected a dozen or more at a time. The refinements of burning entrails and quartering bodies required that executions for high treason be carried out individually; Jack Ketch who came to the West Country after bungling the beheading of Monmouth could manage only thirteen in a day. In consequence, a rebel's execution took considerably longer than his trial, and men often had to watch the carving up of their friends for hours before their own turn came; in consequence, too, the West Country towns and villages were long adorned with severed heads and pieces of tarred and salted corpses. Only when James visited the area in the following year and found them too vivid a reminder of his and Jeffreys's excesses were they cut down and buried.[17]

1688

Monmouth's disastrous cavalry commander, Lord Grey, was pardoned by James II for informing against his friends, and was given

an Earldom by William III, dying as Lord Privy Seal. Apart from
him, William of Orange was the only long term gainer from the
rebellion and its suppression: Monmouth was no longer a competitor
for the Protestant succession – until the birth of a son to James in
June 1688, William's wife was the heir to the English throne – and
James learned the wrong lessons. Forgetting that, militarily, morale
and loyalty are far more important than numbers, he used the
militia's unreliability during the rebellion as an excuse to retain in his
regular army the extra troops that had been raised to defeat
Monmouth. And he pressed on with his aim of 'establishing' Roman
Catholicism, by which he probably intended no more than making
his co-religionists equal with Anglicans, though his Protestant
subjects believed his sinister purpose was to make Popery the state,
if not the only, religion; probably, too, he intended to impose a
watered-down version of the absolutist monarchy of Louis XIV.
Whatever his ultimate ends, James's bullying and arbitrary means –
his engrossment of a large army with no foreign policy excuse,
browbeating of judges, wide use of the dispensing power to override
statutes, favouring of Catholics and Dissenters over Anglicans,
interference with local government and preparations to pack
Parliament – antagonised not merely the followers of 'the good old
cause' but its far more numerous Tory enemies. James had become
a danger to social order. But for a foreign invasion he would have
held onto his crown, yet in little more than three years he had
managed to transform the political nation's loyalty and active support
into sullen suspicion and resentment.

On November 5, 1688, assured in a letter of invitation from the
'Immortal Seven' of overwhelming help in England, William landed
at Torbay with some 14,000 men, a force, as he pointed out in his
Declaration giving his reasons for appearing 'in arms in England',
much too small for the 'wicked design of conquering the nation'.
Though William's army was far bigger than Monmouth's, his
gamble was no smaller: he had much more to lose than the
'Protestant Duke' and the stakes were far higher – not just the
governance of England but the defence of the Protestant cause in
Europe against French and Catholic domination. Its success depended
on James and his much larger army not giving battle; William was
careful, therefore, to observe the proprieties – insofar as that is
possible when invading somebody else's country – and ensured that
his army did the same.[18]

At first the nobility and gentry seemed little more anxious to join
the Prince of Orange than they had been to join Monmouth. The
great majority of Anglican landowners had no wish to see James
replaced by William. Yet they strongly wanted the free Parliament
that William promised as well as supremacy for their Church and

authority for themselves, none of which could be secured without William's pressure on James. Hence defections to William soon began, culminating on November 23 in that of Lord Churchill, the future Duke of Marlborough, the King's second in command. The desertions demoralised James and his army and, instead of giving battle with his much larger force, the King decided to retreat. Yet the war was not merely one of manoeuvre and morale. Blood was shed in a skirmish at Wincanton when eight of the Dutch army were killed and four of the British. Later some of James's Irish troops were killed defending Reading.[19]

Before Churchill changed sides, Lord Delamere, who had hoped to organise a diversionary rising for Monmouth, had risen in Cheshire and taken Derby, the Earl of Devonshire had seized Nottingham, where later he was joined by James's second daughter, Anne, and the Earl of Danby had captured York with a hundred mounted gentlemen, crying 'a free Parliament and the Protestant religion and no Popery'. Inflamed by these sentiments the militia refused to obey the orders of the governor of York, who, astonished that men of large estates should act contrary to the laws and their religion, was placed under house arrest. Danby also achieved the capture of Scarborough and Hull. Durham, Berwick, Northampton, Leicester, Carlisle, Newcastle, Gloucester, Norwich and King's Lynn soon joined them in William's camp. Though most of the gentry were not prepared to fight on either side – less than 10 per cent of the peerage played any part – the aristocratic risings demonstrated the absurdity of later attempts to claim that the Glorious Revolution had not involved 'resistance'.[20]

The King was urged by an aide to march to Nottingham where he could negotiate with William through Anne and, if that failed, to march on to York where Danby was 'with his broomsticks and whishtail militia' who would 'all run away' from regular troops. The advice was rejected by James who instead ran away himself. Second only to William's successful landing, the King's flight was the decisive event of the Revolution and one that nobody had anticipated.[21]

James was not frightened away by the exploits of Danby and Devonshire. Less through the efforts of the aristocratic opposition than through William's decisive moderation and James's loss of nerve, internecine strife and large-scale social upheaval were both avoided: in England armies faced each other in a virtual state of civil war but, unlike in Scotland or Ireland, major fighting did not break out. Yet the gentry did not manage to keep the nation quite out of the question. Apart of course from William's invasion, the crucial violence in 1688 came not from the aristocracy but from 'the rabble'.[22]

By the end of the Exclusion Crisis the Tories were strong in London, and the City was quiet during the years of Royalist reaction. Ominously for James, in 1686 the London mob had shown its hostility to his encouragement of Catholic worship by attacks on a priest and on Roman Catholic chapels. Two years later, too, popular feeling ran strongly against Popery and in favour of William. A week after the Prince's landing the rabble mounted a series of attacks on a Catholic chapel and monastery in Clerkenwell. As the London Trained Bands (London's militia) seemed unreliable – in Bristol, too, the Duke of Beaufort found the militia not 'to be built on' – the army had to be used. During one of the attacks a mob of 1000 fought a battle with 'several companies of soldiers'. Several of the mob were killed, but the monastery was sacked and its goods removed. At the inquest, deciding that the rioters were loyal and well-disposed persons, the jury brought in a verdict of wilful murder against the soldiers. Not only did the riots damagingly delay the King's departure to Salisbury to face William's slowly advancing army, they forced him to order the closure of all 'mass-houses' save those of his family and foreign ambassadors, and to leave behind four regiments of foot soldiers to keep 'the rabble in some awe'. That did not make James short of soldiers in the field – his troops outnumbered William's by two to one – yet his army was debilitated by desertions to the Prince, and his government was undermined by its loss of support in London.[23]

Catholic troubles were not confined to London. Priests, a 'mass-house' and the houses of 'papists' were the targets of mobs in Cambridge, Hereford, Norwich, York, Oxford and Bristol, driving many Catholics to London for safety; and at Dover a Protestant rabble seized the castle from its Catholic governor. But it was events in London that were crucial. On December 4 the so-called Third Declaration was published, allegedly by William but in fact spurious, which warned of a desperate attempt at a massacre or a burning of the city by armed papists, called on magistrates to disarm Catholics, and sentenced to death any Catholic in possession of arms or in any office contrary to the law. 'The Papists', not surprisingly, were 'frightened most wonderfully' by the Declaration, many laying down their offices and fleeing. The Lord Mayor ordered a search for Catholics and their disarming. 'It looks a Revolution,' Evelyn noted. Like his father in 1641–42 and the army and then Parliament in 1659–60, James had lost control of the capital. 'The rabble,' wrote Sir John Reresby, had reason to think 'that the counsel given the King to withdraw himself came from them.' Before dawn on December 11, James left Whitehall for France.[24]

Throwing away the Great Seal and disbanding but not disarming his troops, James hoped his absence would wreak chaos. It came on the first day. As soon as his departure was known, one journalist wrote, 'the mobile consulted to wreak their vengeance on Papists and Popery.'* On the night of the eleventh, foreign embassies, Catholic chapels and the house of the King's printer were attacked by what Macaulay termed 'human vermin'; they seem to have been in the main merely apprentices. In Lincoln's Inn Fields 'a prodigious number' of the rabble pulled down 'the large new mass-house' and burned its timber. 'The whole town seemed in a flame.' Though Spain was William's ally, the Spanish embassy was defaced and plundered; though France was William's enemy and the chief popish threat, the French embassy was merely combed for arms and priests. For the mob, diplomatic niceties were subordinate to personal considerations: the French ambassador was popular and generous; the Spaniard was unpopular because of unpaid debts. Catholics spent the day 'running into all holes to hide themselves' and carrying their goods to Protestant houses, though few dared receive them; the next day even the Queen Dowager, Catherine of Braganza, refused to give refuge to the Spanish ambassador. There was, nonetheless, no bloodshed.[26]

The London authorities at first did nothing to stop, and probably encouraged, the mob's anti-Catholic depredations. They were gratified that instead of Catholics massacring Protestants, as the Third Declaration had warned, Protestants were harrying Catholics. Their complacency was not shared by a gathering of Peers, most of whom wished to keep James on the throne and who had decided to act as a governmental body through fear of anarchy and a general threat to property; otherwise, thought the Bishop of Ely, London would certainly have been 'the spoil of the rabble'. On the twelfth the Peers sent apologies to the ambassadors 'for the insolencies' that the rabble had offered them, and directed Protestant officials to prevent any repetition. Warned that Whitehall and the Royal Chapel at St James's were threatened, the Peers ordered the Guards to disperse the rabble and 'in case of necessity to use force and to fire upon them with bullet'. The rabble were already inside St James's Palace and were defacing it when the Guards arrived. They were then 'forcibly repelled' and the Guards successfully defended Whitehall and St James's. Elsewhere, however, despite the calling out of the trained bands and the deployment of artillery and horse and foot guards throughout Westminster, violence and destruction continued, the 'detestable populace' threatening to pull down all Papists' houses in the City and crying that 'the flame should not go out till the Prince of Orange came to town'. Attacks were launched on Catholic houses

---

* The use of the word 'mobile', an abbreviation of *mobile vulgus*, to describe the rabble dates from the mid 1670s. The word 'mob' as a further abbreviation dates from 1688.[25]

and business premises, the Papal Nuncio's lodgings, the Florentine embassy and a 'mass-house' in Southwark.[27]

Also on the twelfth, Lord Chancellor Jeffreys, disguised as a sailor with shaved eyebrows, was recognised in a Wapping alehouse by a scrivener whom he had bullied in his court. The house was immediately surrounded by a hostile crowd; Jeffreys had to be rescued by the trained bands and carried before the Lord Mayor. With the mob threatening, understandably, to 'dissect' him, the terrified Chancellor was at his own request committed to the Tower.

But for Jeffreys's belief that the Tower would be safer for him than for those he had sent there, and but for an escort of two regiments of militia, he would, presumably, have been dissected. He would then have been the crowd's sole prominent victim. Even aside from the military skirmishes the Revolution was not quite bloodless. Captain Douglas of the Middlesex Trained Bands was killed in the Haymarket after ordering his force to fire on the mob, but he seems to have been shot by one of his own men, probably by accident. And some people were killed in a scuffle at Tilbury. But though much Catholic property was damaged and many Catholic deer poached, no Catholic died at the hands of the mob.[28]

In the small hours of December 13 the 'Irish Fright' hit London. The rumour was spread that great numbers of Irish had burned Uxbridge and were advancing on London. With drums and trumpets used as a tocsin, the capital was awakened to hear the alarming cry: 'Rise, arm, arm! The Irish are cutting throats.' Panics caused by the threat of imminent massacre by Irish papists were endemic in seventeenth-century England, the fact that no massacres ever materialised never providing an antidote to the next attack of paranoia. Previous alarms were local. This time the panic spread outwards from London through 'post-letters' reaching Kent, Surrey, Buckinghamshire and Norfolk the following day and then extending further afield; some credence was lent to it by the many small groups of James's disbanded Irish soldiers who were intent, however, not on massacre but on returning to Ireland. As with some previous panics, this one was deliberately disseminated. Whoever were the culprits – evidently someone in the post office was involved – James was badly damaged, and William's followers used the fright to embody the militia in the service of the Prince of Orange.[29]

'Mass-houses' and Catholic property were attacked in York, Bristol, Birmingham and throughout the country. At Bury St Edmunds a mob too large for the militia to disperse had already wrecked Catholic houses; when the Irish Fright reached the town a mob plundered both Catholics and Protestants and also demanded money; the militia refused to fire at them, laid down their arms and 'joined with the rabble'. In contrast at Hatfield, the house of the

Catholic Lord Salisbury, the militia foiled an attack. In London a peer thought that 'the rabble were the masters, if the beasts had known their own strength'. But they did not know it. Though they plundered, they had no thought of social revolution or a political coup. Their target was Popery, not power; and after the Irish panic violence gradually subsided.[30]

Discovered, like his Lord Chancellor, before he could embark for France, the King was treated with 'rudeness' at Faversham, being searched 'even to his privities'. But his return to London on the sixteenth was warmly cheered, perhaps out of sympathy, perhaps because of the violence when he was away. For James his aborted flight was frustrating; for the Prince it was potentially disastrous. With the King out of the country and the throne left empty, William could certainly fill it; with James in London almost any result was still possible. Accordingly James had to be frightened into making a second escape. Once again the means of intimidation were William's army and the enmity of the London mob. William told the City, whose Court of Aldermen had invited him to London, that the King's return was 'done without my approbation' and on the seventeenth he sent his Dutch Guards into Whitehall making the King, much to his astonishment, a prisoner in his own palace. He then ordered James to move to Ham 'for the greater safety of his person', readily consenting when the King preferred Rochester – a more convenient starting point for France.[31]

Earlier the nature of the threat to the King's person had been revealed. Opposing a Tory motion at the Court of Aldermen which congratulated James on his 'gracious return', the Whig Recorder of London pointed out that while the King had legal authority the Prince had power and, however unwarrantable, 'the mobile' was another power. He added that if the aldermen contradicted the invitation they had issued to the Prince, which had 'quieted the rabble, they might give them a provocation to commit such forcible rapes upon their houses, as they had upon others'. Even the Tory aldermen found this argument compelling, and the plan to carry congratulations to the King and to order public bonfires and the ringing of bells was abandoned. The determination of the peers to maintain James on the throne was similarly subordinated to the higher priority of maintaining law and order. James's cause had been crippled by his exodus. Deprived of the encouragement of public support, increasingly isolated, depressed by the almost 'universal running into the invader', fearful for his own safety, a king without a kingdom, James finally escaped to France two days before Christmas.[32]

William had won. Now only he could be head of the executive. Subsequent events were merely a tidying up operation, a contest over

the terms on which he was to hold power. The role of violence was
over. Though it had played an important part in destabilising James
and then provided a powerful incentive to the propertied to re-
establish strong government under William, so that 'a stop be put to
the fury of the rabble', popular violence had no influence on the
eventual constitutional settlement. When in early February crowds
assembled tumultuously at Westminster to urge the offer of the
crown to William, the Commons were outraged by the attempt to
overawe them.[33]

   Once James had gone, the differences between the parties were not
sufficiently burning for either of them to seek popular support, as
Pym had done in 1641-42. Though evidently at least one extremist
Whig peer, Lovelace, had dealings with the mob, the conservative
aristocratic wing was firmly in control of that party. The sort of
Whig who had joined Monmouth's rising was shunned, and the
struggle was confined to the Convention Parliament. The toppling
of James had also removed the chief grievance of the populace;
neither the abstruse question of whether he had 'abdicated' or
'deserted' the throne, nor the exact terms on which the crown should
be offered to William, readily lent themselves to public agitation.[34]

Effects of the Revolution

The Glorious Revolution was much more than a changing of the
guard; indeed even the mere 'change of persons' that Paine derided
was crucial. The substitution of William and Mary for James II
entailed the removal of a Catholic dynasty and the defeat of
indefeasible hereditary right in favour of a combination of hereditary
and parliamentary right. After 1688-89 the Crown was still where it
had been since the Restoration: at the centre of the stage. But it was
now joined there by Parliament, which in the previous thirty years
had played only an intermittent role and which had, from 1681-88
been almost entirely offstage. By the most important article in the
Bill of Rights a standing army in peacetime, except 'with consent of
Parliament', was declared illegal – a crucial shift in the balance of
power. William ended the practice of dismissing judges on political
grounds – Charles had removed eight and James six – and the Act of
Settlement gave them security of tenure. And the revolutionary
settlement together with the greater priority that William gave to the
war against France than to the preservation of the royal powers made
the Crown financially dependent on Parliament. Contrary to what
was happening in nearly every other European country, power was
shared by King and Parliament. In consequence, an absolute
monarchy could only have been achieved by a military coup or

complete royal control of Parliament.[35]

In that sense the Revolution of 1688 was decisive. The convenient myth of its non-violence, the fact of its virtual bloodlessness and its limited changes all served to perpetuate it. Above all, it worked; the English state was less inefficient than its rivals. At the same time 1688 blotted out its predecessor: for the next seventy-five years few expressed the radical or democratic ideas of the earlier English Revolution. England was still a monarchy, but a legal one; her government was mixed. Parliament, dominated by the landed elite, had become the monarchy's partner, though for the time being a junior one. Whether or not, as a nineteenth-century John Hampden claimed, 1688 ushered in a 'reign of aristocratic humbug', a largely aristocratic revolution had produced an aristocratic state. Like the Paris mob in the French Revolution, the populace received no reward for its help. It's role was soon forgotten or never recognised. For an aristocratic regime to have had its roots in violence was in the next century often sufficiently disturbing to need explaining away by various fictions; for those roots to have lain partly in mob violence was too abominable an idea even to explain away. It had to be suppressed.[36]

Though it was badly damaged by the Revolution the Anglican Church remained dominant. Under James, the Dissenters and the Church had been thrown together by their common fear of Popery. After the Nonconformists had defied their short-term interest by refusing the toleration offered by the King, Archbishop Sancroft urged his clergy to 'have a very tender regard to our brethren, the Protestant Dissenters . . . .' Anglican tenderness did not survive the lifting of the papist threat; still the Church clearly owed the Dissenters toleration, and that minimum debt was repaid. The so-called Toleration Act ended the Anglican monopoly of legally-recognised religion, while the continuance of the Test Acts preserved the Anglican monopoly of Parliament. Ungenerous though the Toleration Act was, it had far-reaching effects: a decline in Church congregations, an increase in the number of Dissenters' chapels, the spread of latitudinarianism, deism and even atheism, and an outbreak of severe Anglican neurosis. The loss of their monopoly led many churchmen to believe that 'impiety and infidelity' were spreading even faster than Dissent, that anti-Christ was at the gates, and that the Church was in danger not only from sin and vice but from Sancroft's 'brethren, the Protestant Dissenters', together with their secular mouthpiece, the Whigs.[37]

Despite the avoidance of civil war, at least in England, the Revolution created obvious problems for the Anglican Church's basic political doctrines of non-resistance and passive obedience, doctrines which had become, if anything, more effusively authoritarian since the Restoration, rebellion being seen 'as the sin of witchcraft'. The unstated assumption of non-resistance was that the Church would always be on the side of the King, or rather that the King would always side with the Church. Anglicans had had some uncomfortable moments with Charles II. As well as depriving the King of the sacrament because of his adultery, Archbishop Sheldon accused him of labouring to set up the 'most damnable and heretical doctrine of the Church of Rome, whore of Babylon' and of being ready 'to throw down the laws of your land at your pleasure'; yet the King's Babylonian tendencies did not inhibit the Church from giving Charles strong support in the Exclusion Crisis. Only James II, by his unequivocal embrace of the whore and his evident pleasure in throwing down the laws of his land, managed to break the Church's alliance with the monarchy. Under him non-resistance became a liability: previously it had disarmed the Church's opponents; now it disarmed the Church. In consequence its practical abandonment became temporarily unavoidable.[38]

When the Seven Bishops petitioned against the order to read James's Declaration of Indulgence in their churches, the King was understandably taken aback. They were lodged in the Tower for sedition before being acquitted amid tumultuous rejoicing. The Bishop of London signed the letter of invitation to William of Orange, and all but a small minority of Nonjurors who withdrew from the Church quickly accepted the Revolution. In so doing they laid themselves open to Defoe's charge that they were all 'apostates from the very fundamental doctrine of their Church (non-resistance), perjured in the sight of God and man'. But the fault lay with the doctrine, not with them.[39]

For all except Nonjurors and Jacobites, 1688-89 should have spelled the end of divine right, non-resistance and passive obedience. Experience, however, was easily bypassed. Tories and churchmen solved the problem of reconciling 1688-89 with their previous beliefs in a number of ways. For some William III was accepted as King *de facto*, which, said a Whig bishop, was only 'a softer word for an usurper'. For a few, the fiction of James II's abdication was the most convenient solution: by his voluntary abdication James had rendered the throne vacant, so the Glorious Revolution had not involved resistance. Yet non-resistance did not revive strongly under the Calvinist William III, whose hereditary title to the throne was slender, and whose religious outlook was displeasingly tolerant. Only under Anne, whom all except the Jacobites regarded as reigning *de jure*, did non-resistance regain its former prominence. The Queen was a devout Anglican, and provided the Pretender was forgotten or remembered only as the outcome of a warming pan (the useful Protestant legend that James's heir was not the son of Mary of

Modena but had been smuggled into her bed in a warming pan), her hereditary claim was good. Francis Atterbury, later Bishop of Rochester and, later still, a Jacobite, evolved the view that the Revolution had been an act of divine providence in favour of the Church of England. Clearly, therefore, supporters of the Revolution had not been guilty of wrongful resistance; had they opposed it, they would have been resisting a far more exalted Personage.[40]

For others, notably Archbishop Sharp, passive obedience was owed 'to the supreme authority of the place where they live', which in England was now the King in Parliament rather than just the King himself. In other words the law of the land should be obeyed even if the subject disagreed with it – which is today most people's attitude to the law. A doctrine which thus removed the distinction between a *de jure* and a *de facto* monarch struck at the root of the Jacobite belief in the indefeasible hereditary right of kings. For Jacobites the Revolution had plainly involved resistance to the Lord's anointed and was a sin. The true doctrine of non-resistance therefore demanded resistance to the usurpers, William III and the Hanoverians, in order to place on the throne the rightful sovereigns, James II and James III; to them alone were non-resistance and passive obedience properly due. As a Stuart and a devout Anglican, Anne was in a slightly different category. Wrongly believed by many Jacobites to be a secret sympathiser, she would, they thought, at the right time ensure the succession of her half-brother.[41]

If Tory difficulties stemmed from the events of 1688–89 being inconsistent with their doctrine of non-resistance, the Whig difficulty lay in limiting the right of resistance. John Locke's *Two Treatises of Government* was published in 1689. Most of it had been written during the Exclusion Crisis and in the years of Whig plotting and royal persecution that followed. Originally designed to justify armed resistance to Charles II, the *Two Treatises of Government* asserts the people's ultimate right to resist and depose an arbitrary ruler who betrays his trust. Though Locke made additions to his text to justify the Revolution of 1688, his book did not immediately receive the success it later enjoyed. It was, however, reprinted twice in the 1690s, and Locke's ideas gained wide currency through a popular plagiarism, *Political Aphorisms*, which may have been written by Defoe.[42]

Locke's philosophical defence of the people's right to rebel was meat too strong for most Whig, let alone Tory, stomachs. The popular Whig principles of the Exclusion Crisis were soon adjusted. In 1688 the Whig leaders had been concerned to prevent another people's rebellion like Monmouth's, and they certainly did not wish to foster a future one. They wanted to control the royal prerogative and to ensure the Protestant succession; they had no desire to emphasise the people's ultimate rights, and Locke's theory seemed dangerously subversive to all but the most radical.[43]

In any case, who were the people? As the Jacobite Nonjuror Charles Leslie pointed out in an attack on the *Two Treatises of Government*, 'it was never yet known, nor ever can be, what is meant by the word "people" in this scheme of government. For the whole people never chose, and a part of the people is not the whole.' And indeed, however large and influential was the electorate in comparison with both earlier and later ages, it still only included about a quarter of the adult male population. Leslie was equally withering to the conservative Whigs. 'Was your Lordship's noble family "first raised",' he asked an imaginary Whig Lord, 'to that honour by the people? Did a mob first summon your ancestor to Parliament?' Defoe confined 'the people' to freeholders.[44]

The doctrinal disarray of the two parties had unequal consequences. The Whigs did not benefit from the Revolution being seemingly more in accord with Whig than Tory principles. During the Exclusion Crisis Dryden had attributed democratic ideas to Shaftesbury, the Whig leader:

> *Maintains the Multitude can never err,*
> *And sets the people in the Papal chair.*

In fact Shaftesbury was no democrat. So far from seeking to extend the franchise, he at one point sought to reduce the electorate by three quarters. But the Whigs' anti-Popery concealed their oligarchic leanings and enabled them to

> *Drive[s] down the current with a pop'lar gale.*

That current was diverted by the Revolution, and the identity and alignment of the parties became confused. They were in flux, with a court and country antithesis cutting across that of Whig and Tory. The Whigs grew more court orientated and conservative, becoming a party of government and confining their popular appeal, while their opponents moved in the opposite direction. 'Country' Whigs under Robert Harley joined the 'country' Tories, evolving into a new Tory and Church country party, independent of the Crown and supported by the great majority of the clergy. Harley did not have a high opinion of his followers whom he regarded as 'bandits' and wrote, in 1701, that they were 'naturally selfish, peevish, narrow-spirited, ill-natured, conceited of themselves, [and] envious of any ability in others'. Not surprisingly the Whigs were much the better governmental instrument, and before 1710 the Tories as a party were only twice briefly in power. Nevertheless, the Tories, 'the gentlemen of England' as Harley later more flatteringly called his followers, were the clear majority of the political nation.[45]

Intensified by the Triennial Act of 1694 which produced ten general elections in twenty years, party strife was acute for thirty years after the revolution. Yet politics became a less violent trade – in that respect much of Europe had preceded England. Impeachments continued, but except in duels, politicians no longer tried to kill their opponents, nor did monarchs their subjects. William III was moderate and lenient. The Convention Parliament was not vindictive. The last man to be killed by an act of attainder in lieu of a judicial process was Sir John Fenwick in 1697, and although both the procedure and its motive – fear that Fenwick, unless silenced, would make embarrassing revelations of Jacobite plotting by some of the highest in the land – were dubious, Sir John had undoubtedly been engaged in at least one assassination plot. He was also a mannerless aristocratic brawler, though that in itself hardly merited the scaffold.

Anne's reign was the first for a long time to see no political killing at all. Unlike her two successors, Anne did not even execute captured Jacobite rebels. So despite Jacobite plotting and many politicians' intrigues with the Pretender, despite the schemes to resort to arms towards the end of Anne's reign, and despite, or perhaps because of, the virulent party warfare of the years 1689-1714, English politics was far healthier under William and Anne than it had been under the two previous reigns. While political language was still violent, as were elections, the rest of politics was more parliamentary and less violent and conspiratorial than before 1688. Yet all those diminutions of violence stemmed from one crucial violent act – William's invasion of England with a Dutch army – and from the ancillary violence of the London mob, which together had overthrown the legitimate King. 'Almost all' governments, said Hume, had their origin in violence. Eighteenth-century England was no exception.[46]

TWO

The Sacheverell Riots

The Church of England . . . has been rent and divided by factious and schismatical imposters; her pure doctrine has been corrupted and defiled; her primitive worship and discipline profaned and abused; her sacred orders denied and vilified; her priests and professors (like St Paul) calumniated, misrepresented and ridiculed; her altars and sacraments prostituted to hypocrites, deists, socinians and atheists; and this done . . . with impunity, not only by our professed enemies, but which is worse by our pretended friends, and FALSE BRETHREN.

Henry Sacheverell in St Paul's, November 5, 1709

Passive obedience, Non-resistance, and the Divine right of hereditary succession are *inconsistent* with the rights of the British nation . . . inconsistent with the Constitution of the British government . . . and inconsistent with the *declared*, essential foundation of the British Monarchy.

Daniel Defoe, in the Review, *January 1710*

. . . when the trumpet is sounded in Sion, when the pulpit takes up the cudgels, when the cause of the enemies of our Government is called the cause of God and of the Church, when this bitter and poisonous pill is gilded over with the specious name of loyalty . . . the Commons cannot but think it high time to put a stop to this growing evil . . .

Robert Walpole, on the second day of Sacheverell's trial[1]

For twenty years after the Revolution, the furious combat between Whig and Tory helped to keep serious political violence, though not disorder, off the streets. Comprising about 25 per cent of the male adult population, the electorate was relatively large and influential. The party chiefs, thought the Prussian representative in 1701, *'crurent devoir plutot faire leur cour au peuple, qu'au Roi'*. Almost constant electioneering excited the interest of the urban population, and widespread participation absorbed political energies in a system that was genuinely representative and widely accepted to be so. 'There is not a chambermaid, prentice or schoolboy in the whole town,' Swift claimed in 1707, 'but what is warmly engaged in one side or the other.' With both parties enjoying support all the way down the social scale, the 'common people' were divided. The party leaders not the streets set the political agenda, and Civil War memories still made the ruling elite wary of pushing their disputes to the point of popular violence. The compromise of 1688–89 anyway remained broadly acceptable to the great majority. And an additional discouragement to violence in furtherance of the party battle was the preference of both William and Anne for mixed ministries containing members of both parties.[2]

But it was not only party politics which kept the populace quiet. The English, as the French ambassador had reported even before the Revolution, were 'not easily moved to rebellion'. The English mob, like mobs in other countries, was much more royalist and conservative than revolutionary; even during the Civil War much of the popular activism had been conservative. Furthermore the expansion of the state and the professions together with an increased readiness to go into 'trade' shielded potentially discontented younger sons of the gentry from the temptation of giving upper class leadership to the mob by providing them with prosperous employment.[3]

In addition, of the three issues – dynastic, religious and economic – that might inflame the lower orders, the first two were incapable, after the Revolution, of substituting a horizontal division of the poor against the rich for the vertical division between the parties. William was always more popular with the *petit peuple* than with the upper classes; Anne was popular with both. The Jacobites had little public support and did not seek to cultivate it; they thought less of risings than of plots and invasions. Nobody suspected either William or Anne of papist inclinations, and religious persecution of Dissenters which had hit the poor harder than the rich had been ended by the Toleration Act. So while religious animosities were still intense and fears for the Protestant succession endemic, on both the religious and the dynastic issues the dividing line did not run between the populace and the elite.

For ordinary people the Revolution had done little that was tangible. Because of its ease and speed, its leaders had not needed to make concessions to gain popular support, and they were too conservative and uninterested in social matters to volunteer them. At William's suggestion, the unpopular Hearth Tax, from which the poor were exempted, was abolished, but that was all. Taxation remained heavily regressive, the Excise being particularly hated, and many people lived in miserable conditions. Though England was by 1700 already the richest nation in Europe, probably nearly half the population from time to time needed poor relief or private charity to survive. Yet, hard though life still was for the great majority, existence was less desperate than before the Civil War when the

population had been rising fast and real wages falling. In contrast
from before 1660 to about 1690 the population fell, rising again only
slowly for some time thereafter. Meanwhile the benefits of the
agricultural revolution were accruing. Harvests were occasionally
bad, especially in the 1690s, but in England unlike Scotland – where
perhaps one quarter of the population died of starvation in the 1690s
– France and many other countries, famine was unknown. Indeed
from the mid-seventies England was a net exporter of food, trade
was increasing and real wages were slowly rising.[4]

   Hence what Locke called 'some common and great distress', which
was the only thing that could make poor labourers 'forget respect'
and 'break in upon the rich,' was lacking. Rising food prices caused
occasional riots, but normal economic conditions nurtured social
stability not 'horizontal' violence against the well-off. With the most
dangerous controversies thus sterilised socially, while very much
alive politically, political violence when it came was more likley to
be orchestrated from above than to originate from below.[5]

The decision to impeach

In the wake of an abortive Jacobite invasion in 1708, the Whigs had
gained their only clear election victory between the Convention and
the Hanoverian Succession. Despite the Queen's personal dislike of
the Whig Junto – 'five tyrannising Lords' she called them – they had
been strong enough to impose their terms on Godolphin and
Marlborough, stripping the ministry of nearly all its Tories and
forcing themselves into the Cabinet. Not much else, however, had
gone right for them. After twenty years of almost continuous war,
the country had a deep longing for peace. The main financial brunt
of the war was borne by the landed interest through the Land Tax.
As a result, wrote St John in 1709, the landed interest had 'become
poor and dispirited' – poor because of the Land Tax and dispirited
because of the rise of a new 'monied' interest, spawned by the needs
of wartime finance. The financial revolution, inaugurated by the
establishment of the Bank of England in 1694, which enabled Britain
to finance much of the current war (and also later ones) by loans
rather than by taxation, and thus to win them, was profoundly
unpopular and long remained so. The money market had become a
better investment than land, and large fortunes were being made. The
largely Tory landed gentry resented the largely Whig monied men
making the profits while they were paying the taxes; they felt their
predominance threatened. Prominent among the new professional
financiers doing conspicuously well out of the war were many
foreign-born Dissenters. The passing of a general Naturalisation Act

and the arrival of 10,000 Calvinist refugees from Bavaria had fed both hostility to Dissenters and hatred of foreigners, exacerbating London's already chronic xenophobia and further identifying the Whigs with both those unpopular groups and the equally unpopular monied interest. To add to the Whigs' troubles and to those of the poorer sort, the price of wheat had more than doubled since 1707 and was higher than ever before.[6]

The Whig Junto's grip on power was plainly shaky. Safeguarding the Protestant succession was their only issue that excited popular enthusiasm, and they could not rely on a Jacobite invasion to highlight it at every election. The Tories regarded the unnatural Whig ascendancy as a threat to both the landed interest and the Church and were impatient to end it. Unlike the Whigs they were not short of popular issues: ending the war, xenophobia and 'the Church in danger' were all theirs. An Anglican backlash had been building for some years. The strongly Tory 'subalterns' of the Church did not share the moderation of their 'generals'. Not content with the Church's still vast popularity and massive influence, they wished to restore by political means the supremacy it had lost in the Revolution. High Churchmen identified the Church with the state, regarding dissent from one as like treachery to the other. Their spiritual exasperation with the growth of Dissent and the spread of infidelity was heightened by their 'scandalous' material poverty, greatly intensified by the exactions of wartime taxation. High Church fanaticism, Tory frustration and Whig anxiety to tighten their hold on power came together in the Sacheverell affair. By raising the cry of 'the Church in danger', Henry Sacheverell sought to enlist the Tory laity in the High Church crusade; the Tories united in his defence and the Whigs seized the opportunity to brand their opponents as Jacobites in disguise. The Whig Junto had picked the right issue but the wrong time. The Protestant succession eventually ruined the Tories, but not in 1710.[7]

Dr Henry Sacheverell was an overbearing, ill-natured, shallow, hard-drinking, High Church, Oxford clergyman with a fine presence and a good voice. Had his opinions not his ambition been his guide, he would have been a Nonjuror. But like many other High Tory parsons Sacheverell preferred to be, in the words of Stanhope at the trial, a 'Nonjuring Juror'. Despising moderation and hating Dissent, which he considered to be allied to Popery – together they formed a 'confederacy in iniquity' – the doctor combined violent language with extreme views. In 1702 he had launched an attack on toleration, Dissenters and occasional conformity – the practice of Dissenters qualifying themselves for office by taking the Anglican sacrament once a year – and having accused the Whigs of open enmity to 'our communion', he had called on the Church not to submit to them but to 'hang out the bloody flag and banner of defiance'. The cry of 'the Church in danger', as Sacheverell realised, was the most effective means of doing three things: inflaming congregations and 'the vulgar', uniting the Tory party and binding together the Tories and the Church.[8]

In 1709 Sacheverell was invited by Sir Samuel Garrard, the High Tory Lord Mayor of London and Member of Parliament for Amersham, to preach the annual sermon in St Paul's commemorating the Gunpowder Plot and William III's landing in England. Instead of composing a new sermon for the occasion suitable for those anniversaries, Sacheverell used, with some fermenting additions, a violent, incoherent harangue he had delivered in Oxford four years before. Taking his text from St Paul's Second Epistle to the Corinthians, Sacheverell sounded, as he said, 'a trumpet in Sion' against the false brothers in Church and State. Leaving aside such open enemies as Roman Catholics and Dissenters, these turned out to be almost everybody except High Churchmen, with Godolphin the Lord Treasurer singled out for special insult. The false brothers were bent on betraying the Church to the Dissenters and hence subverting the State. Sacheverell laid down 'an absolute and unconditional obedience to the supreme power in all things lawful' and maintained 'the utter illegality of resistance upon any pretence whatsoever'; the Revolution of 1688 had not involved resistance, the doctor contended, since William himself had disclaimed it. On that point Sacheverell won either way: if his implausible claim was accepted, the Whig glorification of the Revolution was empty; if it was rejected then the proper inference was that the Revolution had been sinful and illegal. Having attacked the Government, toleration and the Revolution, Sacheverell ended his hour-and-a-half's trumpeting with a resounding call to the Church to stand firm and excommunicate its enemies. The Whiggish Court of Aldermen having refused permission to print the sermon, the doctor, encouraged by Garrard, printed it himself and soon achieved the enormous sale of some 100,000 copies.[9]

The sermon was probably seditious, and its occasion, place of delivery and unauthorised publication were all provocative. The Whigs were duly provoked. Something, it was agreed, must be done; otherwise the ministry would have been successfully defied and its followers dispirited. Action against the doctor would bring other political benefits: Sacheverell should be prosecuted, thought the originally reluctant Marlborough, 'lest such preachers as these should preach us all out of the kingdom'; for Godolphin, action would bring revenge for having been denounced as a false brother – 'the crafty insidiousness of such wily Volpones'; for Wharton and the Whig leaders, prosecution would irrevocably cut off Godolphin from the

Tories; the isolated Lord Treasurer could then be ejected at leisure. Above all, action would enable the Whigs to dish the Tories by labelling them as Jacobites.[10]

An ordinary criminal prosecution would probably have caused no difficulties outside the courtroom; the difficulties would have been within it. Sacheverell had taken legal advice before publishing his sermon and his cloudiness of language made a conviction uncertain. The House of Commons's judicial powers were too limited to teach Sacheverell and the Tories a proper lesson. Hence it was impeachment or nothing. The doubters, who included the two great Whig lawyers, Somers and Cowper, warned that all the paraphernalia of impeachment might not lead to a heavy sentence on Sacheverell. But the something-must-be-done brigade brushed aside their objections, and the government impeached the doctor for both his 'False Brethren' sermon and an earlier one, arrestingly entitled 'The Communication of Sin'.[11]

Sacheverell was charged with suggesting that 'the necessary means used to bring about the said happy Revolution were odious and unforgiveable', for suggesting that toleration was 'unreasonable' and 'unwarrantable', for falsely suggesting that the Church of England was in great peril, and finally for defaming the Queen's administration. The last three subsidiary counts were straightforward; the first and main one was not, and the Whigs were curiously blind to its ambivalences. To deny that the Revolution had involved resistance was ridiculous: 'As if,' scoffed Defoe,

> the Prince of Orange had not brought an army with him to resist,
> but came with 14,000 men at his heels, to stand and look on while
> the English gentry and clergy, with prayers and tears, brought
> King James to run away and leave the throne vacant.

Yet, at the time and later, most people had been concerned, however implausibly, to make the Revolution look as legal as possible and to camouflage its violence. Hence the fiction of James's abdication – and even that initially went too far for the House of Lords which preferred the idea of desertion. As early as March 1689, Edward Harley had written to his brother that Toryism was 'now in the ascendant'.[12]

Ambivalence over resistance was not confined to the past. The ideological issue was from one point of view clear – for or against 1688 and by what right the monarch ruled – and made all the clearer by the Whigs' discarding of the warming-pan myth as a lie that was no longer needed, thus both basing the Queen's title solely on parliamentary sanction and branding themselves as liars. But from another it was muddled: Sacheverell preached obedience but failed to

practise it; the government did not preach obedience but tried to
enforce it. In fact, as the Whigs alleged at his trial, Sacheverell was
evidently in favour of non-resistance only to James III, while the
Whigs believed in the right of resistance but not to themselves. The
only upholder of the doctrines of absolute non-resistance and passive
obedience were Jacobites, but those doctrines would become
operative again only when the Pretender was restored. And if
resistance was always wrong and the Revolution was unjustified,
then clearly he, not the Hanoverians, should succeed the Queen.[13]

Despite the ideological pitfalls, a quick impeachment which gave
the opposition no time to organise would probably have passed off
without trouble. It was the delay, caused by the clever tactics of the
defence and the need for Wren's extensive building work in
Westminster Hall to provide seats for both Houses of Parliament and
many spectators, that was fatal to the Whigs. Their opponents put
the hiatus to good use. A popular cleric was being persecuted, they
claimed, and the Tory party was united round the cry of 'The Church
in Danger'. The Tory London clergy were as selective as Sacheverell
himself in their adherence to their sacred doctrines of passive
obedience and non-resistance. Though the toleration that he had
attacked was unquestionably the law of the land, and though the
Church taught submission to authority not the defiance of it that the
doctor had proclaimed, Tory parsons prayed four Sundays running
for God's blessing on Sacheverell and provided him with a large
clerical bodyguard for all his preliminary appearances before
Parliament. Under this incitement, public support for Sacheverell
became more and more intense. At the time of the decision to
impeach him, the Queen had told Bishop Arundel that Sacheverell's
'was a bad sermon and that he deserved well to be punished for it'.
By early February she had decided that the impeachment was a
mistake and that Sacheverell's punishment should be 'mild', lest 'the
mobb appearing on his side should occasion great commotions . . .'[14]

The trials and the riot

On the first day of the trial, February 27, the Queen's fears were
realised. The mob appeared both on and at the doctor's side. Some
400 people, many of them armed with bludgeons or swords, escorted
his procession from the Temple to Westminster Hall, and the crowd
cheered him. Later in the day the Queen was greeted on her way to
Westminster by a large crowd shouting 'God bless your Majesty and
the Church!' and 'we hope your Majesty is for High Church and
Sacheverell!'[15]

Inside Westminster Hall, which had been packed since early

morning, the Whig managers, oblivious of what had been going on outside, began the case against him. Both Montague, the Attorney-General, and Lechmere, Wharton's lawyer and a future Attorney-General, singled out Sacheverell's assertion of 'the utter illegality of resistance on any pretence whatsoever' as the essence of his sermon and hence of the trial. Using Lockean language – the popular plagiarism of Locke had just been republished in answer to Sacheverell – Lechmere claimed that when the executive broke the 'original contract' the people had not only the right but the duty to resist, an eternal truth which had been understood even when their ancestors had been 'muffled up in darkness and superstition'. Sacheverell's sermon only made sense, Lechmere suggested, if his Jacobite designs were recognised. While the Doctor was apparently affirming 'the duty of absolute non-resistance', he was in reality encouraging the taking up of 'the arms of resistance' against the Queen. Lechmere, who read a prepared speech, was not referring to what had been happening outside Westminster Hall.[16]

On the second day the crowds were bigger and more aggressive. Sacheverell had as a bodyguard 'a hired company of butchers', and those bystanders who did not salute him were roughly handled. Some lucky ones were given the doctoral hand to kiss. Inside the Hall the Whig speakers still concentrated on Sacheverell's absolute denial of the right of resistance. They again emphasised the Jacobite intent of the sermon, but they were more cautious than Lechmere on the people's right to resist. Walpole, for instance, did not mention an 'original contract'; resistance, he conceded, was nowhere 'enacted to be legal', and nobody could foresee when it should be exercised. It could only be contemplated when, as at the Revolution, the whole frame of the constitution was threatened and there was no other hope of redress.[17]

The speakers were still insulated from events outside. Part, however, of their audience was not, and after the court adjourned some peers moved that Sacheverell be taken into custody. Not surprisingly, he had already left the precincts, so they set up a select committee under the chairmanship of Lord Mohun, a Junto ally, to inquire into 'the disorder' on Sacheverell's journey to his trial.* But before it had even met, far greater disorders had occurred than those it had been set up to investigate.

On his return to the Temple Sacheverell was escorted by a crowd of thousands. The windows of Burgess's new and lavish Dissenters'

---

* Mohun was perhaps chosen because of his unrivalled knowledge of violence. He had frequently been involved in brawls and affrays, and the House of Lords had twice acquitted him of murder; shortly afterwards he and the Duke of Hamilton killed each other in a duel.

meeting-house near Lincoln's Inn were smashed, as were those of
Burgess's private house. Boyle, the Secretary of State, and other
ministers were warned by Burgess's son that ringleaders had been
overheard planning to destroy the meeting-house on the following
night. They took no action.[18]

On the third day the Doctor was accompanied to Westminster by
a 'prodigious' mob, which treated 'very rudely' all those who did not
doff their hats and say 'God bless him!' Once again 'the mob huzzaed'
the Queen on her way to the trial 'joining the Church and
Sacheverell'. The mob, perhaps 3000 strong, was not dispersed and
milled about outside Westminster Hall all day. Inside the Whig
managers concluded their case. Dolben, the son of an Archbishop of
York, denounced Sacheverell as 'a trumpeter itinerant of sedition and
rebellion' and as the devil's emissary from hell, while Sir Thomas
Parker, in the best speech of the trial, returned to the accusation of
Jacobitism, condemning the doctor for 'inciting her Majesty's
subjects to arms and violence'. Neither Parker, however, nor any of
the Whig leaders yet realised how they, just as much as Sacheverell,
had 'stirr'd up' violence or had any inkling of the form it was going
to take.[19]

The mob outside Westminster Hall had never read Locke (nor had
most people inside it) and knew little of the theoretical disputes that
occupied much of the trial, but in practice they leaned more to
Lechmere's view than to Walpole's, and if they differed from Dolben
about who had sent the doctor, they were ready to prove Parker right
about being stirred up to violence, though not to arms. Cowper, the
Lord Chancellor, and Wharton, Lord Lieutenant of Ireland, were
'insulted' on their way home from the trial. Burnet, the Whig Bishop
of Salisbury, was 'threatened', and Dolben nearly paid an expensive
price for his extremist speech: he would have been hanged had he not
successfully denied his own identity.[20]

Crowds had earlier gathered round the Temple and, when they
were joined by those returning from Westminster with Sacheverell,
the work of destruction began. The authorities were still unprepared,
but many in the crowd were not. They were equipped with crowbars
and other tools suitable for demolishing Dissenters' meeting-houses.
Burgess's, nearby in New Court, Carey Street, was the first to suffer.
In a carefully organised operation which lasted for three-and-a-half
hours, its contents were removed and piled high in Lincoln's Inn
Fields where there was no danger of the fire spreading and where
they were set alight soon after 8 o'clock. The rioters danced round
the fire and did not even 'spare the poor woman's clothes that lived
in the house, but burnt all she had but a feather bed'. Two meeting-
houses in Holborn received the same treatment, followed by one in
Drury Lane. 'High Church and Sacheverell' was the incessant cry.[21]

At about 9 o'clock the Lord Chancellor and the Duke of Newcastle, the Lord Privy Seal, who had seen the fire in Lincoln's Inn Fields, arrived at the Cockpit in Whitehall and told Lord Sunderland, the Secretary of State, that their houses were in danger. Only then did the government do anything at all. Sunderland went to St James's to see the Queen. As the militia had not been called out, the only troops available were those guarding the Queen at the Palace and their reliefs in Whitehall. Sunderland feared that an unguarded palace might be invaded by the mob, knowing that that would have spelt the end of the ministry, even if the Queen had been left unmolested. Anne, who had been 'seized with a paleness and trembling' when she first learned of the riots, was now, however, resolute, and she told Sunderland to take both her Horse and her Foot Guards. She would rely on God for her guard. The senior officer on duty, Captain Horsey, was reluctant to leave his post, only consenting when he was told that it was the Queen's command. Stanhope had no time to give the captain written orders; instead he told him to 'use his judgement and discretion' and to avoid violence 'except in the case of necessity'. Horsey was also ordered to safeguard the Bank of England, which he did by sending seven soldiers.[22]

In contrast to the later disturbances, Horsey and the soldiers were not handicapped by any misunderstanding of the Riot Act, nor were the crowd endangered by the Riot Act itself, which was still five years away. The Captain was aware, as he said, that 'he ventured his neck by going upon verbal orders' and was probably even more cautious than he would otherwise have been. He was also triumphantly successful. It took from about 11 pm until well after 2 o'clock the next morning to quell the mobs and to clear the streets round Lincoln's Inn Fields, Holborn, Hatton Garden, Blackfriars and Clerkenwell of thousands of rioters. Yet in all that time not a single shot was fired, and the military killed nobody. Mostly they used the flat of their swords. About fifty civilians were injured and a few soldiers, too, slightly hurt.[23]

So the dereliction of the authorities who had left the riots unchecked for four hours was redeemed by the discipline and efficiency of the Guards which ended them in less than another four. The care and restraint of the troops were almost matched by the rioters. Probably as many as 5000 people were involved and they gained control of much of the west end of London. Six of the most prominent dissenting meeting-houses were ravaged and a threatened attack on the Bank of England, regarded as the secular tabernacle of the Dissenters and the monied interest, was foiled by the Guards. Yet, though the houses of unpopular politicians like Wharton and Dolben and of unpopular clerics like Burnet and Hoadley would have been attacked but for the intervention of the military, not a single

private house was badly damaged and, at the most, two people lost
their lives, one from falling masonry.[24]

Causes and effects

'What,' asked Abigail, Robert Harley's sister, on the morning after,
'is mankind that a nonsensical harangue from a pragmatical
insignificant man should make such a terrible work?' Until 1780, the
Sacheverell Riots were London's worst upheaval of the century and,
predictably, many blamed them on the Whigs. Their talk of the
people being 'the original of government' and of the right of
resistance inevitably, it was held, gave the lower orders ideas above
their station and incited them to exercise that right. The Revolution,
thought a Tory Bishop, should not be boasted of or made a
precedent. But much as the Whigs saw no incongruity in appointing
an aristocratic man of violence like Lord Mohun to inquire into the
violence of the populace, they did not see that the glorification of
resistance on one occasion might lead the uninitiated to glory in it
on another.[25]

In any case, to leave Sacheverell weeks to stir up violence, and to
take no precautions to deal with it, was inviting trouble. Even when
ministers were given warning of impending violence they remained
unconcerned, and even when the violence was in full swing they did
nothing until their own houses were threatened. To many, such
inordinate nonchalance suggested governmental connivance. Indifference and negligence on top of earlier provocation can certainly be
laid at the ministry's door. Yet the Whigs did not incite the violence.
That honour belonged to the Tories and to High Church parsons,
who easily outmatched the Whigs in divorcing conduct from
doctrine. 'Methinks,' wrote Harley's sister, the mob's behaviour was
'an odd way of defending passive obedience and non-resistance.'[26]

Some of the Whigs considered the mob had prostituted itself by
acting in such a cause. One Whig pamphleteer thought they were
'slavish souls' who dishonoured the name and title of mob. Another
was angered by the sight of 'a set of illiterate, inebriated mechanics
and peasants' complimenting the Queen on her hereditary right;
others thought the mob must have been hired. By their complaints
that they had somehow been robbed of their own mob, the Whig
propagandists showed themselves both blind to the Tories' strength
in London for the last thirty years and deaf to the resonance among
'the vulgar' of the cry 'the Church in danger'.[27]

The riots were created and directed from above, and there was
undoubtedly some bribery, yet they were not the simple product of
money and free beer. The 'Sacheverell and High Church' enthusiasm

of the mob was genuine. Economic conditions had been improving since the beginning of the year and, whatever the crowd's other grievances, only one was apparent that night and on the previous two days. The cry was everywhere 'High Church and Sacheverell' and nowhere 'no war' or 'no more dear bread'. As its historian has said, this was a 'Church mob' and a 'Tory mob'.[28]

Religious passions set off and sustained the wrecking of the Dissenters' meeting-houses. Like some later disturbances, the riots were more in support of a popular individual, allegedly being persecuted by the government, than an institution or cause. At the outset they were carefully organised, though, as they ran their course, improvisation increasingly took over from planning, and as the crowd multiplied, as crowds almost invariably do, it became less single-minded. Many who were interested in destruction for its own sake and many who were drunk joined in the fun. The core of the rioters, nevertheless, had definite objectives which they pursued with care, avoiding indiscriminate destruction and killing nobody. They did not come from the dregs of society, this mob being probably the most respectable of the century. Among the seventy-six whose occupations are known, there were two lawyers, a former banker, a physician and nine 'gentlemen'. In many places gentlemen or well-dressed men were observed directing operations, and the necessary tools were always available. Like the violence, the objectives of the riots' fomentors were limited: to intimidate the Dissenters and the Whigs and to further the Tory and High Church causes. There was no thought of sedition or revolution.[29]

None of the gentlemanly planners or chief initiators was caught. Like the apprentices in 1668, two men were convicted of high treason though a change of ministry saved them from execution. One, Dammaree, was a Queen's bargeman; the other, Purchase, was a bailiff. Both had been drunk, active, and conspicuous during the riots; neither had anything to do with planning them. Out of over 100 others arrested, only a dozen or so were tried and they received light sentences.[30]

Sacheverell, too, got a light sentence. Even before the House of Lords had voted by only sixty-nine to fifty-two to convict him, Godolphin had begun to wish the trial 'had never begun', and when the House later considered the sentence the government's majority melted further. Some peers were apprehensive of 'a popular jury' if the sentence was heavy. Likewise the Queen, whose earlier wish for a light sentence for fear of 'commotions' had been strengthened by the riots, made known her view that 'the mildest punishment' would be best. Instead of the severe sentence the Whigs had intended, Sacheverell was suspended from preaching for three years. Apart from the burning of his sermons, that was all. Well might Walpole say that 'they had as good as acquitted him'! Violence had paid.[31]

London celebrated the Doctor's virtual acquittal with bonfires, illuminations, the ringing of church bells and two days' drinking. The City Trained Bands who had been mustered almost continuously since the first of March were called out and disorders continued, but the serious trouble was over. The provinces also celebrated – there were 'huge bonfires' in Derby – and Dissenters and their meeting-houses were attacked, especially in the West Country. Rival mobs fought but again without many serious casualties. There was no backlash against the violence.[32]

Before the end of the trial, Abigail Harley, probably reflecting her brother's opinion, decided that 'this business' would probably break the Whigs and raise the Tories 'to their old madness'. She was right on both counts. Prompted by Robert Harley, Anne began dismissing her Whig ministers. Godolphin lost his office in August, and Harley became the 'premier minister'. The Tories clamoured for an election, petitions to dissolve Parliament raining down upon the Queen. Harley hesitated to advise a dissolution, fearing a large Tory majority which would wreck his hopes of a mixed ministry, but the Tory pressure was irresistible.

The ensuing election was perhaps more tumultuous and violently fought than any other before or after. Riots broke out in London, Westminster and at least thirteen other towns and cities. 'The rabble came about our coach,' Swift told Stella, 'crying a Colt, a Stanhope [the Whig candidates for Westminster]. We were afraid of a dead cat, or our glasses broken, and so were always of their side.' Swift did not have a vote, and the Tory mob which 'knocked down and wounded' some Whig voters and 'obliged many of their party to return home without polling' was more effective. The Tories won easily. In the City the Tory mob broke all the windows that were not illuminated in honour of the Tory victory, including those of one of their own victorious candidates.[33]

The Whig attempt to padlock the mouths of the Tory parsons by punishing Sacheverell had fanned their political zeal in the pulpit and out of it. The clergy believed that another Whig Parliament would indeed imperil the Church; the common people thought the same. The cry of 'Sacheverell and the Church' together with that of 'Peace', ensured the return of 332 Tories and only 181 Whigs in England and Wales. To have been a Manager of the impeachment generally proved electorally disastrous. Sacheverell himself failed to profit from the Tory high tide. Anne refused to make him a bishop while he was under suspension, and though he retained his popularity outside London the Tory parliamentary leaders would have little to do with him. Harley did not relish the 'glut of Tories' he had brought in; others were jealous of his political success. In any case they did not like him, and Swift was not alone in refusing to have him as an acquaintance.[34]

Out of office and out of public favour, the Whigs in their turn aimed to use the crowd to help thwart the Tories' attempt to make peace with France. On the anniversary of Queen Elizabeth's birthday in November 1711 they designed, said Swift, 'a mighty procession by midnight'. Much money was spent, and effigies of the Pope, Dr Sacheverell, the Pretender, the Devil and other dignitaries were to be paraded and then burned. Rumours were spread that the houses of Harley, now Lord Oxford, and St John, now Lord Bolingbroke were to be attacked. The Whigs probably would have been unable to raise much of a mob, even with a large financial outlay, yet the militia was called out, the procession banned and the effigies seized.* The government had exaggerated the dangers, pretending that the Whigs planned a republican revolution; even Swift thought they had made 'too great a clutter about it'. But the Queen was pleased that the mob had been disappointed.[36]

Oxford and Bolingbroke were not the only people to learn lessons from the previous year. The riots had long-standing effects on the Whigs. Shortly after George I's accession, Swift thought that the only thing that might keep the Whigs 'from utmost violence' would be 'the fear of provoking the rabble, by remembering what passed in the business of Sacheverell'. The strength of the populace had been clearly revealed, and the Whigs did not forget it. They soon, too, came to see the wisdom of the speech of Hooper, the Tory Bishop of Wells, in the debate on the Doctor's impeachment. While allowing the necessity and legality of resistance in some extraordinary cases, the Bishop 'was of opinion that this ought to be kept from the knowledge of the people, who are naturally too apt to resist'.[37] That became Whig orthodoxy for the next seventy years.

The third lesson was no less important. The Whigs learned not to confront the enormous power of the Church. In 1719 the Stanhope ministry redeemed George I's promise to repeal the extremist Tory legislation passed at the end of Anne's reign – the Occasional Conformity Act (which the Whigs had supported) and the Schism Act – but the Whigs went no further. Walpole never forgot the Sacheverell affair. In the 1710 election he was pelted 'with dirt and stones' and came bottom of the poll in Norfolk. During his long years of power he controlled the Church, much as he controlled Parliament, by patronage, but he did not tamper with Anglican privilege. He tried to keep religion off the parliamentary agenda. In

---

* One of the Whig contributors said that the seizure of the Devil's effigy should have been followed by a sermon on the text: 'His disciples came by night and stole him away.'[35] That would have caused a riot.

consequence, apart from annual Indemnity Acts, his Dissenting supporters were continually fobbed off with cosmetic measures; the time, he explained, was not ripe for anything more substantial. The Test Act was not repealed. Thus if Sacheverell's dream – a nightmare to others – of extirpating Dissent and establishing a High Church monopoly was never within sight of being realised, equally his nightmare – and others' dream – of equality for the Dissenters also remained just that. The supremacy of the Anglican church, strongly protected by the violence of the Sacheverell Riots, survived well into the nineteenth century.[38]

THREE

The Protestant Succession and the 'Fifteen'

It was the misfortune of [George I], as well as a very great prejudice to the nation, that he had been misled into strong prepossessions against the Tories, who constituted such a considerable part of his subjects . . . the whole nation was delivered into the hands of the Whigs.

Smollett

Nothing can be more contemptible than the scum of the people, when they are instigated against a king who is supported by the two branches of the legislature. A mob may pull down a meeting house, but will never be able to overturn a government . . . The authority of the Lords and Commons of Great Britain, in conjunction with that of our sovereign, is not to be controlled by a tumultuary rabble.

Joseph Addison in The Freeholder, 1716

That party [High Church Tories] . . . do not care for venturing their carcases any further than the tavern . . . I have heard Mr Forster say he was blustered into [the 'Fifteen'] by such people as these, but that for the time to come he would never again believe a drunken Tory.

Rev Robert Patten, The History of the Late Rebellion, 1717[1]

At the Revolution, though Claverhouse had defeated William's army at Killiecrankie, few Scotsmen had been prepared to fight for James II and VII. In Scotland, however, unlike England, distance lent James enchantment, and the Stuarts soon became more popular than they had ever been on the throne. William III's off-hand treatment of the country, the government's botched and treacherous terrorism at Glencoe, the damage done to Scottish trade by William's European wars and the four years of near famine from 1695 suggested to many Scots that the dispositions of 1689-90 with their rejection of indefeasible hereditary right were frowned on by Providence. The restoration of Presbyterian government in the Church, which was forced on William by the Jacobitism of the Episcopalians, ensured

continuing pulpit support for Jacobite sentiment, since most of the
unseated Nonjuror Episcopalian ministers kept their congregations.
Above all, the Union with England in 1707 was highly unpopular,
and subsequent English behaviour did nothing to make it less so.[2]

The months just before or just after the Union came into being
would have been ideal for a Jacobite attempt, but the French delayed
until the following year and 1708 set the pattern for future forays: the
home Jacobites were not prepared to rise before the invading army
had landed; the Pretender – James II's son, James Francis Edward –
was unlucky; the French were half-hearted, and the British
government was neglectful of the country's defences. The Franco-
Jacobite plan was for James to land in Scotland with 6000 French
troops. But the Pretender had already begun to earn his nickname of
'Old Mr Misfortunate': he caught measles from his sister, delaying
the expedition; his half-brother, Berwick, an able soldier, could not
command the invading army; and the French commander, the Comte
de Forbin, regarded the expedition as madness. His pleasantry – 'As
for me, I risk nothing, I can swim,' – was scarcely heartening, even
to fellow swimmers. Eventually, under protest, he set sail. The
weather was rough, and only the Jacobites' seasickness lifted Forbin's
gloom. With most of his fleet he arrived in the Firth of Forth, but in
the wrong place. Some lairds but no magnates rose. The British
Commander-in-Chief thought that if the Jacobite army landed he
could not defend Edinburgh. Almost certainly James would then
have gained massive Scottish support; his apparent plan to take
Scotland and northern England and then negotiate was realistic. But
he did not land. Admiral Byng's fleet appeared in the Forth, and
Forbin fled north refusing to let James go ashore, even without
French troops. Thus was lost perhaps the best of the Jacobite
opportunities. All it achieved was a panic in the City and a run on
the Bank of England.[3]

Scottish Jacobites were not the only Britons ready to wage war
against their fellow countrymen. In voluntary exile from 1712, the
Duke of Marlborough plotted a foreign invasion of England to
sabotage the Tories' peace negotiations with the French and to
safeguard the Protestant succession. Hanoverian soldiers were to be
carried in Dutch ships hired by the Emperor Charles VI; the Duke's
son-in-law, Lord Sunderland, and General James Stanhope were to
be in charge at home. Hoping for a rerun of 1688, Marlborough
thought little foreign help would be needed, since most people would
support 'une révolution' to overthrow the Tories and impose on the
Queen a Whig ministry pledged not to desert its allies. Although the
Elector of Hanover, the Emperor and the Dutch all turned down the
scheme, the Duke did not abandon it. In 1714, while the Whigs in
England planned an armed rising and stockpiled arms in Scotland to

prevent a Stuart restoration, Marlborough formed another plan, accepted by the future George I, for a Hanoverian invasion of Britain to safeguard the Protestant succession.[4]

That succession was in little danger from the Pretender and none at all from the Tory ministry. Though some foreign observers thought civil war inevitable, Whig fears were largely the product of hysteria. The Pretender's half-brother, the Duke of Berwick, hoped to involve Marlborough's successor as Captain General, the Duke of Ormonde, in a *coup d'état* on Anne's death, and the French government conditionally offered to provide James with some ships. But the Jacobites had no independent military capability; they were relying on a peaceful restoration by Act of Parliament. Both the warring Tory leaders, Oxford and Bolingbroke, were in correspondence with the Jacobite Court at St Germain (as were Marlborough and the Whigs) and they made encouraging if notably vague noises about a Stuart restoration. Yet their aim was to gain the parliamentary support of the Tories' Jacobite wing, not to change the succession. In the fragmenting Tory party some fifty to sixty MP's took their orders from the Pretender, and from 1711 onwards James ordered them to support Oxford. Not until early 1714 did he realise that he had been duped and that Oxford had just been stringing him along. Unfortunately for the Tories, Oxford was also stringing along both his party and himself; he had no plan or aim except his own survival in office.[5]

The great majority of the Tory party did not favour a Stuart restoration any more than the Queen did, and neither Oxford nor Bolingbroke had any intention of restoring a non-Anglican Stuart. Bolingbroke told the Pretender that England would as soon have the Grand Turk as a Roman Catholic for king. Probably even a conversion to Anglicanism would not have made James greatly preferable to the Grand Turk; few would have thought it genuine. In any case he remained loyal to his Church, and on Anne's death fears of civil war were confounded; nobody raised a finger on his behalf. There being, Bolingbroke wrote later, 'a perfect calm and universal submission throughout the whole kingdom', the Protestant succession was achieved without trouble. But neither the calm nor the submission lasted for long. The new regime soon created first storm and then rebellion.[6]

The Tories had alienated the new King by the Peace of Utrecht, which was not, as Marlborough claimed, a 'Jacobite peace', but was as unpopular in Hanover as it was popular in Britain. And during the peace negotiations and afterwards, both Oxford and Bolingbroke had been tactless to the Elector of Hanover, who was led by his envoys and the Whigs to believe that virtually all the Tory party was Jacobite. Despite these massive handicaps the Tories expected George to employ them as well as the Whigs. They had no notion of the price they were to pay for their feckless feuding during Queen Anne's last months. After all, by using both parties William and Anne had avoided becoming what Anne called their 'slave' and avoided making the opposition party, in Harley's word, 'desperate'. Like Lord Mar, the Tories thought George I would likewise be too sensible to 'make himself but king of one party', particularly as they had recently been far more successful electorally than their opponents, having won five out of the last seven general elections.[7]

But, instead of behaving like William III and Anne, George acted as the Whigs had erroneously expected William to behave, bringing only themselves into his employment. For the first time since 1694 there was no crown 'manager' to restrain the victorious party from appropriating all the spoils of administration. Three Tories were offered posts and mistakenly refused them. Otherwise Tories were barred from ministerial offices, from the higher ranks of the Church and the army and from the judicial bench. In a much more drastic purge of the commission of the peace than was usual after a party victory, many Tories ceased to be JPs; even when Tories remained magistrates their power was diluted or nullified by the addition of Whig associates. And Tory merchants in the City of London were excluded from profitable loans, contracts and directorships. At the beginning of December 1714, Lord Carnarvon could write that hardly a Tory was left in any place, even a mean one.[8]

Even so, their parliamentary majority of over 200 seats and their previous electoral successes persuaded many Tories, including Bolingbroke, that they might win the general election. The royal onslaught, however, was not yet spent. Lord Chancellor Cowper advised George I that he could ensure 'a clear majority in all succeeding Parliaments', provided he showed his preference in time. That advice did not altogether accord with the experience of the last three reigns, but the King duly urged his 'loving subjects' to support the Whigs, and the full weight of the crown was thrown against the Tories. In consequence, what Mr Sedgwick called 'the inverse proportional representation' of the electoral system, whereby the eighty seats of the English counties had an electorate of 160,000, while the 146 seats of the smallest boroughs had an electorate of 3500, combined with the fear of Jacobitism to produce a massive Whig majority in the House of Commons. The Whigs did well, too, in the larger boroughs, yet, as Swift had pointed out four years before, the members chosen by the counties provided the truest index of opinion, and even in 1715 the Tories had an easy majority of them. So while the Whigs won the 1715 and succeeding elections, they were, and for a long time remained, a minority in the country; the Tories were the popular party and, save in 1727, won more votes than the Whigs in every election down to 1747.[9]

Popular hostility

At his accession George I was advised by his private secretary, Robethon, that if the 'very changeable . . . populace' were on the side of the court it had nothing to fear, whereas if they were against, the court was 'never safe'.[10] In London where the Tories had for the last few years become the party of 'the people', the populace soon bore him out. George I, with a largely Tory or mixed government, would have been fully acceptable; George I with an entirely Whig ministry was not. On his way back from the Lord Mayor's banquet in October, a crowd subjected the King to shouts of 'Ormonde, no Marlborough' (Ormonde was the Tory military hero); and, on the day of his coronation, riots against the celebrations occurred at Bristol, Taunton, Salisbury, Gloucester, Hereford, Shrewsbury, Canterbury, Reading, Birmingham, Norwich and many other places. The prominence of Cathedral cities indicates Tory clergy at work – the pulpit, said Defoe, had become 'a trumpet of sedition' – and much of that day's rioting was instigated from above. In Taunton, for instance, the sabotage of Hanoverian revelries was led by the mayor's son.[11]

The coronation riots were an overture to the elections. In the election itself there were riots in many places including Lancashire, Shropshire, Colchester and Brentford, where 'the rude unruly multitudes, who were encouraged . . . by several clergymen', prevented many Whig supporters from casting their votes, enabling the High Church candidates to win. A victory parade followed with the mob shouting 'High Church and Sacheverell forever'. Not, however, until the spring did the government have cause for serious concern. The disorder then and in the summer was much worse than anything that had gone before, and this time it stemmed more from below.[12]

The ministry and the dynasty lacked support among both the gentry and the populace. The Whigs' parliamentary majority was artificial. And apart from his Protestantism, nothing in George I's appearance or character made up for his rejection of the larger of the two parties. He seemed a dull, ungainly German with no regal graces but with German hangers-on and two ugly Hanoverian mistresses.* His past was no more prepossessing. He never acknowledged his illegitimate children; and if he had not been responsible, at least indirectly, for the murder of his wife's lover, he kept his wife locked up in a castle, never allowing her to see her children. Finally, his

---

* Contrary to contemporary belief, probably only one was in fact his mistress; the other was his half-sister and most likely did not play a dual role.[13]

hereditary title to the English throne was weak. Nearly sixty other people had a better one.[14]

The claim of the Jacobite Duke of Berwick that five out of six of the nation were on the side of King James was presumably exaggerated; a few years later Bristol JP's thought only two out of three of 'the vulgar in general were Jacobite inclined'. Yet the regime of King George was unquestionably unpopular, not merely with disappointed politicians and placemen but also with much of the country.★ So worried was the cabinet by the prevalent encouragement of 'Jacobite spirit' that it ordered an inquiry into the loyalty of army officers and the removal of all who were suspected of disaffection.[16]

The discontent was political not economic – food prices rose a little in 1715 and 1716, but from a low point in 1714 – and was fanned by the vindictiveness of the Whig ministers, especially Walpole, to their Tory predecessors. In 1701 the Tories had been similarly vindictive to the Whig leaders, and Walpole had been sent to the Tower for corruption in 1712. But, as with Dr Sacheverell, the Whigs provoked disorder by their impeachment of leading Tories. Such violent measures, said a peer, would make the sceptre shake in the King's hands. Violent measures were met with violence. Oxford, who was firmer in adversity than in office and who clearly had done nothing treasonable, was escorted down Piccadilly and through Holborn to the Tower by a 'great Mobb . . . crying High Church and down with the Wiggs'. The King's hostility to the Peace of Utrecht and his government's view that the ending of the last war had been criminal implied that the beginning of the next one might not be far off. Memories of the hardships of the war and resentment against those it had profited joined with fears of a new one to fuel general hostility to the Whigs. No popular measures or reforms were brought in to assuage the populace, who demonstrated and rioted against the government in Lancashire, London, Oxford, Norwich, the Midlands and the West – indeed almost everywhere except the home counties.[17]

★ George III was much more popular than his two predecessors, but Dr Johnson still thought, almost certainly wrongly, 'that if England were fairly polled, the present King would be sent away tonight, and his adherents hanged tomorrow'. Boswell was outraged. In 1715 such a remark would have been incontrovertible, though anybody making it in public would himself have been in danger of being hanged. A schoolmaster who asserted that George I had no right to the throne was sentenced to be flogged through the City and died a few days afterwards. Two clergymen were executed for adhering to what they called the 'Nonjuring church, which has kept itself free from Rebellion and Schism'. An eighteen-year-old apprentice was hanged, drawn and quartered in 1718 for writing a threatening Jacobite letter, as was a young man in the following year for printing a Jacobite pamphlet.[15]

In the West Country, George Berkeley, the philosopher and future bishop, saw riots in Gloucester which were quelled by the leading Tories of the town. An eye witness told him of mobs of up to 4000 people in Birmingham and of the killing of twenty-eight rioters. Berkeley thought that only three Dissenters' meeting-houses remained standing in Worcestershire and Staffordshire. 'It is said,' he added, 'that there are above 20,000 men at Birmingham . . . ready to take arms against the government if there was anyone to lead them.'[18]

The destruction of meeting-houses stretched far beyond the counties mentioned by Berkeley into Oxford, Shropshire and Cheshire. In Lancashire, too, mobs were active, smashing meeting-houses and parading through Warrington to cries of 'the Church in Danger!', 'Down with the Dissenters' and 'God Save King James the Third'. In Shrewsbury the 'gentlemen of the loyal mob', after destroying the Presbyterian meeting-house, issued a mock royal proclamation threatening to destroy the meeting house of any Dissenters who allowed 'that damnable faction called Presbyterian' to worship in their conventicle. Altogether more than forty Dissenting meeting-houses were pulled down. When the ringleaders of the violent Manchester mobs were sentenced to stand in the pillory, nothing was thrown at them. Disaffection was general.[19]

The Dissenters were the victims of the Tory or Jacobite mobs because they were the most vulnerable of the government's supporters and because they were believed to pose a threat to popular pleasures. Societies for the Reformation of Manners, which aimed to inculcate puritan virtues in place of drunkenness, sabbath breaking and licentiousness, were largely composed of Whigs, Low Churchmen and Dissenters. The Societies always had the pastimes of the lower orders as their target and in the thirty years after 1690 they claimed to have prompted 75,000 prosecutions for moral offences – not a passport to popularity. The Tories, on the whole more bacchanalian in their own habits, had little wish to curb plebeian roistering, and their traditional tolerance of popular culture gained them public support.[20]

In London the mob freed a prisoner who had been placed in the pillory for speaking treasonably. Some men of the First Guards staged a mini-mutiny. Instead of going on duty at the Tower, they tramped through London complaining of their clothing: 'these are Hanover shirts.' A court of inquiry set up by Marlborough, who had once again become colonel of the regiment, found the men's complaints justified. Marlborough's offer of two good shirts and a waistcoat was enough to pacify the guardsmen. Outside his regiment Marlborough was less popular. Some suspected him of profiteering at the expense of his troops, and his effigy together with those of

Cromwell and William III was displayed by mobs 'armed with great clubbs' and shouting 'No Hanoverian, No Presbyterian government'. On the King's birthday on May 28 the festivities were muted, and those who tried to celebrate were insulted or attacked by the populace and had their windows broken. In contrast, the Restoration's anniversary the next day brought great rejoicing and a forest of bonfires. Every major historical anniversary brought demonstrations of popular hostility to the Whigs.[21]

Oxford saw a similar pattern. On the King's birthday a Tory mob broke up a Whig celebration, wrecked the Presbyterian meeting-house and smashed all illuminated windows. The following day they wrecked the Quaker meeting-house, this time breaking the unilluminated windows, and attacked Oriel College from where a Whig had fired a shot at them twenty-four hours earlier.[22]

Much Jacobite rhetoric was used in the riots, and the government thought they were Jacobite inspired. The Secretary of State called them 'rebellious insurrections' fomented by Jacobites and, in a speech to Parliament, the King maintained that they had been set on foot by the disaffected who expected support from abroad. But that signified little. The Whigs always found it difficult to accept that they were disliked for themselves; hence they were prone to attribute their unpopularity to Jacobite machinations. If the disorders really had been organised by the Jacobites, they should have occurred just before or during the Jacobite rising instead of being virtually over before it began, though they may have got out of the control of Jacobite instigators – the Jacobites seem indeed to have been surprised by their apparent popular support. Yet Jacobite sentiment was rife, and whatever the exact feelings of the plebeian rioters – actually pro-Jacobite or merely anti-Whig – the Government had good cause for worry. Its unpopularity was manifest.[23]

Juries sympathised with the rioters and refused to convict; magistrates often connived at the disorders. One of the causes of public hostility – fears of a Whig campaign to curb popular liberties – now turned out to be justified. Alarmed by the unrest the Government decided that the only way to make the populace 'safe' for the court was repression. The Riot Act, which became law on July 20, 1715, was the Whigs' method of suppressing popular opposition to their rule, much as impeachment of the Tory leaders and the purge of Tory office holders was their way of suppressing the Tory opposition. Yet scarcely had the Act come into operation than the regime had to face not riot but rebellion.[24]

The 'Fifteen'

The Pretender's decision in March 1714 that London was not worth an abandonment of the mass had ruled out any chance of his gaining the throne on the death of his half-sister by parliamentary sanction or *coup d'état*. Events after her death, however, soon raised the possibility of his gaining it by a successful rebellion. Jacobitism, originally insignificant as Anne herself recognised, expanded in the second half of her reign. But in 1714 it was still not strong. The subsequent Hanoverian proscription of the Tories was less a reaction to their Jacobitism than its cause. James's suit, wrote the Prussian minister in 1715, had advanced more in eight months than in the previous four years. The King's evident intention to destroy their party inevitably weakened Tory loyalty to his regime. If the King did not want Tories to be his servants, why should they want him to be their master? Yet not only Tories trafficked with the Pretender. Marlborough, whom George I had restored to all his great offices, reinsured by sending £4000 to James.[25]

The great general presumably expected Hanoverian unpopularity to bring violent action from the Tories similar to what he himself had earlier planned, yet the great majority of them had no such inclination. 'The violence of the Whigs,' claimed Bolingbroke, who fled to France to escape impeachment, 'forced [the Tories] into the arms of the Pretender.' Whig 'violence' certainly forced Bolingbroke and Lord Mar into the Pretender's arms, and it drove many other Tories into disaffection with the House of Hanover, but it evidently forced very few of them into the Jacobite embrace. A clique of some twenty-five Tory peers and MPs conspired in the South West. A good many more Tories perhaps thought they had no reasonably safe opportunity to show their true colours. Many others presumably still preferred George I to a papist, even though for all the good he did them he might just as well have been the Grand Turk. Be that as it may, a remarkably small number of people in England were prepared to take up arms for the Stuarts or to play any part, violent or otherwise, in the rebellion.[26]

The Jacobite plan was for the main rising to take place in South West England, where the Duke of Ormonde was to lead and the Pretender was to land. Its centre was to be Bath, and Bristol and Plymouth were to be quickly seized; at the same time there were to be supporting risings in the border counties and in the Highlands. James believed that success depended on his quick entry into London, making a landing in Southern England imperative. The Whig ministers believed that in the event of rebellion the army could not be relied on, and plans were made for George I to flee to Holland. Yet rebel resolution was unsteady and Jacobite security poor.

Ormonde, under threat of impeachment, lost his nerve and fled to France instead of the West Country, leaving no instructions for a successor. The government discovered the plot, made some preventive arrests, and moved in troops. The Jacobite leaders in England had earlier told James that there was no possibility of an English rising before the arrival of a substantial foreign army: the Tories were discontented but not committed to Jacobitism and anyway lacked the power to rise because the Whigs controlled local government and the militia. The death of Louis XIV killed hopes of French help, and no other foreign army was available. When Ormonde appeared off the Devon and Cornish coasts, he was told there was no chance of a rising and returned to Brittany.[27]

George I and the Whigs could hardly have done more to make the Tories Jacobite, but it was still not enough. 'No friend can be trusted,' the French ambassador had reported three years before, 'when it is a matter of losing your head and property.' Indeed, none of the propertied raised any effective opposition to the government's precautionary measures in the South West. Those, however, who had only their heads to lose showed overt disaffection. The 'common people in Cornwall' proclaimed the Pretender King at St Columb.[28]

In Scotland that ceremony was not left to the common people; it was performed by the Earl of Mar who had been Secretary of State until dismissed by George I. London had done nothing to abate Scottish hostility to the Union. Although the British government was itself lenient in 1708, not even executing any of the 500 Jacobites who had been captured on a French ship, the reluctance of the Scottish authorities to prosecute Jacobites, the inability of Scottish witnesses to remember damaging facts, and the refusal of Scottish juries to convict, led it to impose the English law of treason on the Scots. The change was strongly resented. The Scottish treason law was clear, reasonably fair to the accused and tolerably civilised; the English law was none of those things. The Scots did not want barbarism imported from England, and all of them at Westminster opposed the Treason Act. The Scottish Privy Council was abolished to gain the support of a Scottish faction; the Scottish mint disappeared a year later. Scottish Presbyterians were offended by Anne's last Parliament setting up almost an alternative episcopal establishment in Scotland, and the Scottish nobility resented the House of Lords's blatantly inequitable ruling that Scottish peers who were given English peerages could not sit in the Upper House. These issues were not decided on their merits or in the interests of Scotland, but for reasons of factional politics or to serve English purposes, while the authorised invasion of English customs officials and discrimination against Scottish trade hit Scottish pride and Scottish pockets. The culminating blow was a Malt Tax which contravened the Act of Union and led in 1713 to a Scottish campaign at Westminster to repeal the Union. Blatant English imperialism had thus inflamed Scottish nationalism before the arrival of George I. As a German the new monarch had no claim on Scottish affections, and his accession was an affront to all believers in indefeasible hereditary right; to them the Pretender was the lawful king of Scotland.[29]

The Stuarts, with their aspirations to rule England and Ireland as well as Scotland, were not ideally fitted to be the standard bearers of Scottish nationalism. Nor was the Earl of Mar, who had been one of the architects of the Union. Yet Jacobitism was ever the residuary legatee of all kinds of discontent, ranging from nationalism to religion and from ideology to hunger, bankruptcy, smuggling and even republicanism; Mar immediately declared the end of the 'late unhappy union'.

Originally intended to be far secondary to the main rising in England, the Scottish insurrection would with only ordinary incompetence still have succeeded. Mar enjoyed widespread support in the Lowlands as well as the Highlands and in the towns as well as in the country; and this time some magnates did rise. North of the Forth, in the view of the Duke of Argyll, the British commander, there were nine Jacobites for every Whig. Only in Argyll and south of the Forth was the government in control.[30]

Had Mar fought the British commander and then advanced into England with an army some four times the size of Charles Edward's in 1745, he would have found virtually nothing to stop him. At the end of September when he expected an immediate march into England by the rebels, Berkeley feared an insurrection all over the country because of 'the general bent of the people towards Jacobitism'. (Many years later even the Whig Lord Rockingham conceded that half the nation was probably Jacobite in 1714–15.) Yet if Berkeley did not exaggerate the extent of Jacobite sentiments, he greatly overestimated the willingness of English Jacobites to risk anything for the Pretender. All the same, if Mar had ventured south, probably very few Englishmen would have helped the government. In the event, Mar's ineptitude as an insurrectionary leader prevented their being put to the test. Due to him the 'Fifteen' was an ignominious failure.[31]

In office a capable bureaucrat, Mar treated rebellion as another aspect of administration. He did not grasp that insurrection is an active not a passive business. Governments can wait because time is on their side. But rebels need movement and success to gather followers; they must strike before the government has recovered its balance and gained reinforcements. Like Charles Edward thirty years later, Mar gathered support by false claims of a French invasion and an England up in arms. 'Never,' said his nephew, 'were men so idly brought in for their lives and fortunes as we were'; others were dragooned into his army by threats of their homes being burned if they did not. Yet Mar scarcely moved from Perth, even though his army was always far larger than Argyll's. When he did at last fight at Sherriffmuir, he was as supine on the battlefield as in his preparations. After the left of each army had been routed, Mar had the opportunity to finish off Argyll whom he now outnumbered by four to one. Instead he retreated, and that was effectively the end of Jacobite hopes.[32]

The rebellion in England was no better led and fared even worse. In Northumberland some largely bankrupt and predominantly Catholic gentry, together with some Anglicans, rose in October and put themselves under Thomas Forster, the financially ruined Protestant MP for Northumberland. Forster was in the Mar class as a rebel leader, and instead of immediately striking at Newcastle he led his ill-armed band of some 200 horse – 'fox hunters armed with dress swords' – to Kelso where they joined a few hundred Jacobites who had risen in Southern Scotland under Lord Kenmure, and the larger detachment that Mar had sent under his best general, Mackintosh of Borlum. The combined force had no idea what to do next. The Scots rightly wanted to advance further into Scotland, the English to go back to England. After an abortive compromise, whereby they wandered about the borders vaguely pursuing an English army (with Kenmure commanding when in Scotland and Forster when in England) they decided to march through Cumberland and Westmoreland to raise 'loyal Lancashire'.[33]

At Penrith Fell they dispersed the scarcely formidable combination of the Cumberland Militia and the Westmoreland *posse comitatus*, yet Lancashire, like Westmoreland and Cumberland, declined to be raised; so did Cheshire. The few that did join the Jacobites were almost all Roman Catholics. The High Anglican Tories sat tight; Forster did not look like a winner. Like Mar, he did not understand that successful rebellion required aggression, and disregarding the advice of Mackintosh of Borlum he refused to attack the outnumbered English army that was shadowing him. At Preston Forster received disquieting information about the opposing forces' growing strength; he also 'received some little damage in the course of a convivial entertainment', making it necessary for him to retire to bed instead of studying military dispatches. The next day the Jacobites beat off the Hanoverian assault, inflicting heavy casualties, but they were now surrounded. The Highlanders wanted to sally out of Preston and attack the government army. Forster preferred surrender, even though the terms were abject.[34]

James landed in Scotland much too late. A month earlier Mar had asked Argyll for terms, which were not forthcoming, and 6000

Dutch troops had been landed in England. The Pretender arrived with few arms, fewer men and no ideas. A man anyway better fitted to reinforce failure than turn it into success, his only effect on the morale of his followers was to lower it. He could not even manage to get himself crowned at Scone. Mar tried to foil Argyll's advance to Perth by destroying six villages on his route. The inhabitants were driven into the snow and their houses set on fire after they had been plundered. James was mortified by the burnings which had been 'forced . . . by the violence with which my rebellious subjects acted against me'. Having destroyed the villages, Mar did not even defend Perth. The policy of 'scorched earth' was thus futile as well as barbarous.[35]

The Jacobites were guilty of no other brutality nor of any violence not inseparable from war. The government, too, was not overviolent in its reprisals, the eventual outcome being much milder than it intended. In Lancashire at the end of the rebellion, executions of thirty-four convicted rebels had proceeded without bother, but in London the first hanging, drawing and quartering created opposition to a similar sequence of slaughter. Many sympathised with the accused, probably being uneasily aware that had the rebellion flourished they would have joined it. The day after the first execution a jury acquitted two palpably guilty Jacobites, and the government, complying with public opinion, reprieved twenty-one out of the twenty-four subsequently convicted. Much the same happened in the North. By sending Scottish prisoners captured in Scotland to be tried in Carlisle, the government had violated the Act of Union and inflamed Scottish opinion. As a result, half the prisoners were released without trial and the rest were never sentenced. The only execution in Edinburgh was of the man who had tried to hand over the castle to the Jacobites. Some 700 rank and file were transported to the West Indies. Many other prisoners escaped, or were allowed to escape, from Scottish prisons.[36]

The English prisons were also leaky. With his neck at grave risk, Forster displayed qualities that would have been useful during the rising: he got the governor of Newgate drunk, locked up his servant and then escaped. Mackintosh of Borlum eschewed such subtlety. He led a rush out of the prison, scattering the turnkeys, and got away. One English and five Scottish lords were sentenced to death. The Chancellor of the Exchequer, Walpole, wanted them all beheaded and carried the Commons with a savage speech. The Lords, swayed by Nottingham, petitioned the King 'to show mercy [to] such as he judged might deserve it'. George I, preferring moderation to Walpolean revenge, reprieved three; another escaped, which pleased the King. George's decision was politic as well as merciful; even the two executions he allowed were unpopular.[37]

In the end, only forty people were hanged or beheaded; another fifty died in prison. Leaving aside the credit due to the King, the death toll was kept relatively low by the Jacobite skill in escaping, by the public backlash against the executions and by the ministry's relative lack of fright. As Berkeley recorded, hopes in London alternated with fears in the autumn of 1715, yet the government felt itself in control, and its measures were effective. It left the mistakes to the rebels. On the Jacobite side, the 'Fifteen' was a farce throughout. A far bigger rising than the 'Forty-five', it should have been a triumph. England was there for the taking. The Jacobites were much stronger than thirty years later, and the regime was correspondingly weaker. Not only Marlborough but Shrewsbury, who as Queen Anne's last Lord Treasurer had presided over the Hanoverian succession, thought it a wise precaution to send the Pretender money. Only the Jacobite ability to squander every opportunity rendered their foresight superfluous.[38]

The Duke of Newcastle's mobs

In London the Jacobite rebellion only slightly revived Whig fortunes, and the government took no chances. Troops were stationed in Hyde Park, and that show of force was supplemented by legal terror. Three soldiers of the First Foot Guards were hanged, drawn and quartered for enlisting with the Pretender, and the head of the leader was placed on Temple Bar. Still unintimidated, Londoners maintained their hostility to the government. The Riot Act, executions and the army were not enough. The Whigs felt the need to create their own mobs.[39]

Looking back more than fifty years later, the Duke of Newcastle said he loved mobs: 'I headed a mob myself once. We owe the Hanoverian succession to a mob.' The first part of his claim was true. Newcastle later became the greatest Whig boroughmonger of the age, but in 1715-16 he wielded an earlier form of aristocratic power, dealing in violence not in votes. Newcastle's mobs were organised to counter Tory militancy in London and to make the Whig government seem less unpopular than it was. Newcastle, who had become Lord Lieutenant of Middlesex at the age of 21, spent large sums of money organising the 'Loyal Societies' which would not have been necessary had the Whigs enjoyed popular support. Newcastle's 'Mugites' (from the mug-houses where they were based) did battle with the 'Jacks' (Jacobites). Between August 1715 and July of the following year, some ten major battles were fought with up to 500 people on either side taking part, resulting in a number of deaths. Newcastle himself participated without distinction in at least one of them. (He got cut off from his followers in the fighting and had to escape through the house of a cheesemonger. That worthy would have sent him back to face the mob had he realised who the fugitive was.) None of the Mugites was ever prosecuted, whereas the Tory rioters enjoyed no such immunity; five of them, the first London victims of the Riot Act, were hanged. This brought the battles to an end but increased public hostility. The second advantage enjoyed by Newcastle's mobs was the support of regular troops, and it was they and the Riot Act, not the Mugites, who suppressed the Tory mobs.[40]

The very hard winter of 1715-16, in which the Commons acknowledged that 'multitudes of poor' had been starved to death, no doubt exacerbated hatreds. The High Church clergy also played their part, though unlike in 1710 they did not go beyond incitement; this time the doctrines of passive obedience and non-resistance were flouted only in spirit. Newcastle went well beyond incitement. Mobs, however, that owed their existence purely to organisation and money rather than to popular sentiment were of limited use. Their object, wrote Ryder, a future Whig Attorney General and Chief Justice, was to 'gain over the populace'. That they never did.[41]

Nor did the ministry's relative if reluctant lenience to the Jacobite rebels bring it popular acclaim. The courage of the condemned was admired and their executions resented. Jacobite sympathies were strengthened, and in the spring of 1716 the Whigs were so unpopular that though the next election was still two years away, defeat seemed virtually certain, and with it, probably, a change of dynasty. To avert such a distressing demonstration of the nation's will, the government prolonged the life of the current Parliament for a further four years. 'The Commons, chosen by the people for three years,' Johnson later wrote, 'chose themselves for seven.' Rushed through both Houses before public opinion could be mobilised, the Septennial Act was indeed the most high-handed constitutional change of the century. The Tories and only thirty Whigs opposed it. Raymond, the future Whig law officer, pointed out that the Bill assumed that a House of Commons elected in two years time would act differently from the present one, which was 'to confess' that the House did not truly represent the people. Defending the Bill, Newcastle claimed that the Jacobites were 'as insolent as ever' and aimed to renew their 'late unnatural and monstrous rebellion . . . fomented by large contributions' from papists. He did not add that he was doing his own bit for disorder by his large contributions and his mobs. According to an opponent, Newcastle maintained that since the King had lost the affection of the people 'he must rule by the sword'. Both sides clearly believed that the electorate still could and would defeat the government. The opposition had much the better of the argument, and the court much the better of the vote.[42]

Later on some of the Whig leaders wanted yet again to extend Parliament's life by abolishing the Septennial Act. That proposal was dropped, but by the next election in 1722 the act had done its work, having enabled the Whigs to consolidate their hold on the smaller boroughs by the use of government patronage. Defending the Septennial Act some twenty years later, Walpole denied that the Jacobite danger had been its chief motive; the Triennial Act had tended too much to the form of government 'called democratical', frequent elections throwing too much power 'into the hands of the people'. Undoubtedly the Septennial Act, which completed the Whig coup d'état and the jettisoning of Whig principles, satisfactorily removed that difficulty: the influence of the electorate was reduced for more than a century. And the Septennial Act lasted until 1911.[43]

Newcastle's admission that he had organised mobs was true; his boast that his mobs had saved the Hanoverian succession was not. The Whig oligarchy and the Hanoverian dynasty were ensconced not by hired mobs but by Jacobite ineptitude, Tory divisions, manipulation of local government, the Riot and Septennial Acts, judicial terror and, above all, a standing army. Yet the Jacobite threat remained.[44]

FOUR

The Rise and Fall of Walpole

The number of troops then proposed was absolutely necessary to support his Majesty's government and would be necessary, as long as the nation enjoyed the happiness of having the present illustrious family on the throne.

Horatio Walpole, 1733

That monster, the excise! That plan of arbitrary power . . . I hope, Sir, that landed gentlemen will never consent to anything that may undo the nation, and overturn the constitution for so small a bribe . . . as that of being free from the payment of one shilling in the pound land-tax, and for one year only.

William Pulteney, 1733

The greatest men in England have fallen into the error that to be master in the cabinet is to be master of the nation . . . The general voice of the whole people were against [Sir Robert Walpole] and he fell by it.

Lord Percival circa 1747[1]

In its early years the Whig hegemony was accompanied by a crime wave lasting well into the 1720s. Highwaymen became bolder, no longer restricting their operations to the outskirts of London, which already had a population of about half a million. Not even the City itself was safe, robbers sometimes holding up three or four coaches in a night. Neither City robbers, however, nor the crime wave was confined to the lower orders. In the summer of 1720 the bursting of the South Sea Bubble revealed massive crookedness at the summit of society: in addition to the fraudulent dealings of the South Sea directors, bribes were taken from the company by the King's mistresses, ministers and MPs; so, too, very possibly, by the Prince of Wales. The King himself probably paid in full for his own stock, while knowing of the frauds of others.[2]

Unlike highwaymen, the great who had enriched themselves 'by the plunder of the nation' went largely unpunished. Walpole, who had returned to office only shortly before the crisis, himself an unsuccessful speculator in South Sea stock, shielded the court and others as far as possible from what he called 'odious inquiries', procuring lenient treatment for those he wanted to protect. One director of the South Sea Company, Sir John Blount, who offended Walpole by providing Parliament with evidence of the dishonesty of ministers and the company, was deprived of most of his money; the cashier, Robert Knight, fled to the Continent. (George I prevented his extradition; he knew too much and was not allowed to return until Walpole fell.) The worst that happened to the rest was that part of their estate was confiscated, and some were expelled from the Commons. One man, George Davis, a clerk who had absconded with a mere £4000, was hanged. His employers, who made much more, did not try to save him.[3]

Fear of revolution in London brought George I back early from an ill-timed visit to Hanover. Arthur Onslow, later Speaker of the Commons, thought that so great was the rage against the government for producing such ruin that if the Pretender could then have landed at the Tower, he 'might have rode to St James's with very few hands against him'. But James was seldom in the right place at the right time, and the Jacobites drew no benefit from the scandal. Others were not similarly passive. Some journalists thought that the directors should be hanged and that if they were saved from justice by corruption 'the abused people might do it themselves. But they did not. Though there were one or two near things, nobody was lynched.[4]

Not surprisingly, however, in view of the number of people who had been impoverished by the fraud and 'villainies' of the directors – Fielding's father lost heavily – suicide was common for some months and violence sporadic. A mob savagely attacked the especially unpopular Sir George Caswall, MP, who though not a director was heavily implicated; Lord Lonsdale, who had speculated disastrously, reputedly tried to stab the chief culprit, Sir John Blount. Before a shareholders' meeting, it was given out that some of those present would be carrying pistols, which they would use if the directors tried to impose a harsh settlement on the shareholders. As the directors merely asked for more time, the pistols stayed unused, but the next day a mob tried to murder a third director in the street; he was rescued by soldiers. The sending of one of the main political culprits, Aislabie, to the Tower caused bonfires to be made in the City. And when Walpole, with the help of the King who asked several MPs to abstain, managed by three votes to secure the acquittal of another culprit, Charles Stanhope, the Secretary of the Treasury, the result was so blatantly perverse that it provoked tumult and riots. The acquittal, wrote the Chairman of the Commons investigating committee, had 'put the town in a flame' to a scarcely imaginable degree.[5]

Walpole, as Lechmere his old associate and now enemy alleged, was virtually the counsel of the South Sea directors and other delinquents. The deluded investors who had lost their money had no such powerful defender. Several hundred of them appeared in the Commons lobby to ask for justice: they had, they pointed out, lent their money on 'Parliamentary Security'. One minister had his coat torn, and JPs and constables were summoned to deal with the riotous crowd. Meanwhile, inside the chamber, Walpole persuaded MPs that nothing could be done for the petitioners outside it. Those petitioners disregarded the JPs' order to disperse, and the Riot Act was read twice. After complaining that they had come 'as peaceable subjects and citizens to represent their grievances and did not expect to be used like a mob and scoundrels', the petitioners eventually agreed to leave. 'You first pick our pockets,' one of them told MPs, 'and then send us to gaol for complaining.'[6]

To maintain himself in office Walpole had to do five things: gain and preserve the confidence of the monarch; control Parliament; win elections; foil the Jacobites; and subdue the populace. Only the last two involved the direct use of violence by the government or its opponents, but the third, elections, nearly always produced violence, and Walpole's methods of attaining the last two were liable to provoke it.

By 'screening' the South Sea affair from public scrutiny and saving the great from punishment Walpole achieved popular execration. Yet he restored financial confidence and gained that of the King, his success as 'Skreen-Master General' being one of the main foundations of his long period of power. The other principal foundation was his handling of the Jacobite threat. Instead of profiting from the financial collapse, the Pretender's followers fell into a trap set by one of the ministers most implicated in the scandal. To gain enough Tory support to save himself from impeachment, Lord Sunderland promised the Jacobites a sudden dissolution of Parliament and no government 'buying' in the ensuing elections, which would have meant a Tory victory. Thoroughly deceived, the Jacobite leaders in a fit of madness abandoned their previous insistence on a strong invading army. Atterbury, the Bishop of Rochester, told James that he would prevail 'with very little assistance from your friends abroad,' while Lord Orrery told him they could win 'without foreign assistance'.[7]

Eventually the Jacobites realised that Sunderland was toying with them. They had given him no secrets, but they had given the Pretender an invitation, as a result of which his advisers in Paris concocted a scheme for an invasion during the forthcoming election. As usual Ormonde was to land in England with the Pretender, and as usual a diversion was to be created in Scotland; before that, an

English army to rise in support of Ormonde was to be created in secret. Orrery immediately dismissed the idea as wholly impracticable. The others went along with it until Atterbury, realising that no serious preparations had been made, dissociated himself from the scheme. Nevertheless the plotting continued. This time Lord Mar was working for both sides – his treachery to the Jacobite cause was only marginally more damaging than his previous loyalty. Though the plot had wide ramifications, it had little chance of starting, let alone succeeding. Of all the conspiracies Defoe had known, he thought this one 'the most unlikely, inconsistent and improbable attempt'. The British government knew all about it, and with Sunderland suddenly dying of pleurisy, Walpole seized his opportunity. By unveiling a vastly exaggerated Jacobite plot to the accompaniment of thousands of troops in Hyde Park, through the suspension of *habeas corpus* and a penal fine on the Roman Catholics, he was able to consolidate himself in the highest office.[8]

The Atterbury Plot showed how few Englishmen were prepared to engineer the violent overthrow of even a thoroughly unpopular regime. But, for Walpole, it also demonstrated the advantage of seeing a Jacobite under every Tory bed. From then on, wrote Speaker Onslow, he had everybody deemed a Jacobite 'who was not a professed and known Whig'. As his son said, that misrepresentation drove some men into 'Jacobite principles' but it persuaded many others, including, before long, Walpole himself. His fear of the Jacobite threat was largely genuine.[9]

There being insufficient evidence to convict Atterbury in a court of law, Walpole pushed through Parliament a bill of pains and penalties, banishing the bishop for life. (Atterbury left England as Bolingbroke returned.) Only one Jacobite was hanged, drawn and quartered: Christopher Layer. The populace suffered far higher casualties. 'Some of them must be hanged,' wrote Admiral Wager in 1734. 'That would exasperate and provoke perhaps: but we must govern the mob or they will govern us . . . they are got to a great degree of insolence.' The First Lord of the Admiralty had seamen in mind, but his words sum up the government's attitude to landsmen as well. The years 1722-41 saw the passing of thirty-one statutes which imposed the death penalty for one or more offences. Those capital statutes were in quantity no greater than that passed in other decades, but mainly because of the Waltham Black Act of 1723 the Walpole era's legislation was qualitatively more lethal than any of its successors. The Black Act, the most savage English statute of all time and, probably, the most bloodthirsty piece of legislation promulgated anywhere in eighteenth-century Europe, was directed at deer stealing and poaching, but was drafted so widely that it could be used against a variety of other activities, creating capital offences wholesale. Its ferocity was partly due to the Jacobite associations of a band of deer stealers at the time of the Atterbury Plot. Yet its use continued long after that presumed danger was past.[10]

Other legislation protecting property prescribed hanging for, *inter alia:* wilfully breaking any tools used in the manufacture of wool; bankrupts failing to present themselves for examination within forty-two days; cutting down the bank of a river; destroying turnpikes; opposing customs officers in the execution of their duty, which even Hardwicke, the Lord Chief Justice, thought went too far; and stealing one or more sheep. Hardwicke, an able self-made lawyer and a fair judge, who varnished his repressive political attitudes with a convincing legal suavity, maintained that 'the degeneracy of the present times' had necessitated these many new laws and their vigorous execution – so vigorous indeed that at Tyburn in 1741, twenty people, none of them murderers, including four women, were hanged at the same time, Tyburn's biggest haul of the century. Not content with violent legislation, attributed by others less to the depravity of the times than to the needs of the oligarchy, Sir Robert himself was on occasion not above the shady furtherance of capital prosecutions in his own interest.[11]

'Great rogues and small rogues' and 'Thieves or Prime Ministers'

The ministry's violent treatment of poor malefactors did not extend to those higher up the social scale. During the South Sea affair, the chairman of the Commons inquiry predicted that, if the Bubble were not properly probed, other scandals would soon break out 'with more virulence from the expectation of impunity'. He was right about both the scandals and the impunity. The public scorn incurred by Walpole for being the 'screen' of the South Sea racketeers did not persuade him to abandon that role. A succession of other scandals were all investigated as delicately as he could manage.

> *Who in the* Secret, *deals in Stocks secure*
> *And cheats th'unknowing widow and the poor?*
> *Who makes a* Trust, *or charity a job,*
> *And gets an Act of Parliament to rob?*

None of the MPs involved had to face the rigours of the criminal law, and most of them were able to retain much of their booty. Dennis Bond, MP for Poole, though guilty of fraud in two scandals and expelled from the Commons, was not imprisoned or even fined; instead he became church warden of St George's, Hanover Square.

Admittedly, the Lord Chancellor, Macclesfield (the Parker of the Sacheverell impeachment), was himself impeached for embezzlement and corruption, having sold masterships in Chancery for £100,000. Despite his defence that such things had 'long been practised without blame', he was fined £30,000, which George I helped to pay; yet Macclesfield had never belonged to Walpole's faction, and his impeachment headed off a wider inquiry into corruption. Walpole even opposed, unsuccessfully, the extension of an inquiry into debtors' prisons despite the appalling violence and corruption it had revealed.[12]

According to his friend, Lord Hervey, Walpole opposed all parliamentary inquiries for fear that if Parliament acquired the habit it might one day inquire into his own or his family's affairs. An inquiry into either of them would certainly have been inconvenient. Like many others, Walpole made a huge fortune from office. Having earlier acquired large sums out of being Paymaster General, he reportedly said when resuming that office in 1720 that 'he was lean and needed to get some fat on his bones'. Soon his wealth was as bulging as his carcase – George II called him 'le gros homme'.[13]

> We all of times corrupt have heard,
> When paultry minions were preferr'd;
> When all great offices, by dozens,
> Were filled by brothers, sons, and cozens.

Saint-Simon thought Cardinal Richelieu 'the best relative there ever was': he never knew Walpole. Sir Robert's eldest son was given a post worth £7000 a year and a peerage, aged twenty-two; his second son one worth £3000 a year plus other perks; his third son, Horace, was made Controller of the Pipe and Clerk of the Estreat when still at school and Usher of the Exchequer before he was twenty-one. The rest of the family similarly prospered. So did Hardwicke's. 'My Lord Chancellor,' complained George II, 'is getting every office that falls in the land for his own children.'[14]

Sinecures were part of the system of 'place' and pensions, whereby the rich became richer at the expense of everybody else, or, as Smollett put it, 'the public treasure was at their devotion'. Some later ages have looked indulgently on Walpole's corruption as being the unavoidable product of an age of political transition and lax standards; certainly, of his two chief adversaries, Bolingbroke had himself been financially dishonest when in office and Pulteney had made himself rich by robbing not the public but the Newport family. Yet even in Walpole's time not all politicians were corrupt. Henry Pelham died poor after many years in office, and many others, including his brother, the Duke of Newcastle, Townshend, Carteret,

Wyndham and Pitt were similarly honest. And it was not just the group of Tory writers round Bolingbroke who attacked Walpole for corruption. There was widespread public disapproval of him and it. As his son later wrote, 'Sir Robert never was thought [honest] till he was out.'[15]

The contrast between the impunity with which the oligarchy enriched itself and the violent punishment meted out to the poor for attempting to do the same was a happy theme for the mainly Tory satirists. In *The Beggar's Opera* John Gay, who after years at court and a meeting at Windsor with Jonathan Wild, the foremost criminal of the day, knew what he was writing about, drew a parallel between Westminster and Newgate. Politicians and prigs (thieves) were shown to operate on similar commercial principles. At the end, in case the point has not been sufficiently made, a character who represents Gay himself refers to 'such a similitude of manners in high and low life, that it is difficult to know whether (in the fashionable vices) the fine gentlemen imitate the gentlemen of the road [highwaymen], or the gentlemen of the road the fine gentlemen . . .' This was near the bone as well as being highly popular, a combination which, at Walpole's insistence, led to the banning of its successor, *Polly*, and to Gay's patrons, the Duke and Duchess of Queensberry, being banished from court.[16]

The Beggar's Opera was written at Swift's suggestion, and in his 'To Mr Gay' Swift drew the same parallel. The ends of 'the ruling rogue' (Walpole) were just the same as those of robbers:

> *A public or a private robber;*
> *A statesman or a South Sea jobber.*
> *A prelate who no God believes;*
> *A Parliament or den of thieves.*

So it was with Pope:

> *Tell me, which knave is lawful game, which not?*
> *Must great offenders, once escap'd the Crime,*
> *Like Royal Harts, be never more run down? . . .*
> *Have you less pity for the needy cheat,*
> *The poor and friendless villain than the great?*

And with Fielding too: in his *Rape upon Rape*, Justice Squeezum says '. . . if you cannot pay for your Transgressions like the Rich, you must suffer for them like the Poor'. Like Gay, Fielding had one play, *The Grub Street Opera*, banned. His attacks in his later plays on Walpole and the Government led to more drastic action. The

Government brought in a Licensing Act which effectively took political satire off the stage. Political satire in books was more difficult to suppress, and in *Jonathan Wild the Great* Walpole was once again portrayed as the famous criminal who had been hanged at Tyburn in 1725.[17]

In other countries all irreverent scribblers would have been violently suppressed. In Walpole's England, whose liberties possibly over-impressed Voltaire and Montesquieu, that would have been difficult. Whiggery, though by then very much a governmental creed, still held a residue of seventeenth-century Whig ideas. Maybe that residue prevented Walpole and the Whigs encroaching further than they did on other people's freedoms, though their treatment of the Tory leaders, the Jacobite lords, the Waltham 'Blacks' and other criminals does not suggest that they were innately moderate when it was safe not to be. Maybe they were curbed by parliamentary opposition. Or maybe their relative restraint stemmed from their fear of reprisals and the uncertainties of power; ministers were liable to be dismissed by their master, the King, and left at the mercy of their enemies. Almost certainly, however, the main deterrents to tyranny were the fear of popular agitation, which Montesquieu regarded as an essential safeguard of liberty, and the fear of Jacobitism. If there was only one governing party, there were, after all, two possible kings. The spectre of the Pretender fulfilled the function of a powerful opposition.[18]

In any case the press was far from having a free run. While subsidising pro-government papers, like his predecessors Sir Robert used existing powers to harry the opposition press and writers. The Post Office impeded the distribution of opposition journals, especially the *Craftsman*, and the law of libel was freely invoked to prosecute journalists and printers. The Attorney General even maintained that liberty of the press did not extend to attacks on the King's ministers since that was to attack the King himself. So authoritarian was the government that Dr Johnson made the ironical suggestion that schools should be closed and reading made a felony.[19]

Walpole wanted to arrest Swift at least once. Pope, too, came near arrest; and he had his windows broken when Bolingbroke was dining with him. (Pope believed that Paxton, the Treasury solicitor and Walpole's chief factotum with the press, had hired the culprits.) Whoever was the hirer, Pope was evidently silenced by the government from 1738 until Walpole's fall, and possibly in the twenties as well. All the same, not even numerous prosecutions supplemented by actual or threatened acts of violence achieved censorship of the press. To be safe, satirical allusions had to be oblique. Yet even when they were not, a conviction was far from certain, unless the jury had been picked by the government and not by the City. And under such names as Brazen-Face, Sir Robert Brass, Forage, Bob Booty, Mr Pillage and Mammon, Walpole was pilloried as a quasi-criminal.[20]

> And such was the Temper of the Times,
> He owed his preservation to his crimes.

Swift was unfair. Easily the most convincing debater of his day as well as the most effective parliamentary manager and the most accomplished courtier of the century, Walpole owed his preservation as much to his political abilities as to his 'crimes'. The violence that was effective elsewhere would clearly not do for the parliamentary classes, nor was it necessary. Walpole's enjoyment of the King's favour, his leadership of the House of Commons and his control of the secret service and the Treasury, together with one party rule and his own inclinations, enabled him to turn 'corruption' into a system that he operated with virtual impunity: parliamentary seats were bought, voters were bribed by borough patrons or the ministry, and those they elected were retained or bought by a place, a pension, an honour or a bribe – a host of places and ample secret service funds being available for government supporters. Many MPs remained independent, but Walpole's provision of 'bread and circuses' for the political nation kept enough of it in compliance.[21]

> Corruption's not of modern date;
> It hath been try'd in every state.

John Gay was largely right. Danby had attempted to control Charles II's Cavalier Parliament with methods similar to Walpole's, and those of Walpole's Whig predecessors, Stanhope and Sunderland, had been little different. Without some governmental influence over Parliament, the executive and the legislature would have fought each other, with the Commons, as Hume pointed out, probably becoming the preponderant power in the state, an outcome which would have entailed the destruction of the mixed constitution just as surely as complete control of the Commons by the court. Even Walpole's principal opponent, Bolingbroke, admitted that some corruption was necessary 'to maintain subordination and to carry on even good government'. So did Fielding. But they believed Sir Robert overdid it.[22]

Indeed, Walpole's 'corruption' undoubtedly exceeded that of his predecessors in scale, grossness and endurance. He was, said one MP, 'a tympany of corruption'. He was also the brass section, if not the whole orchestra; earlier and later ministers were more the strings or the woodwind. By 1739 about 100 peers enjoyed state employment, and over 180 placemen sat in the Commons. In an important vote on the Convention with Spain in the same year, more than two-thirds of Walpole's majority were in receipt of some *douceur* from the ministry. No wonder an MP insisted that the opposition were only 'a militia' while the government party were 'disciplined troops regularly paid'! There were still two parties, but only one party ruled and Walpole's exercise of 'corruption' was uninterrupted.[23]

Thus deprived of place and pension, the Tory and Whig oppositions saw corruption as one of the two great dangers to Britain's balanced constitution; the standing army was the other. By violently overthrowing Parliament the army might secure executive domination and put an end to liberty; by so undermining the independence of Parliament as to make it a mere satrap of government, corruption, helped by a standing army, might achieve the same result. Yet corruption went even deeper than that; the national debt and the growth of the monied interest had still not been accepted as inevitable, let alone desirable. Supposedly, the whole country was corrupt and must be recalled to virtue.

> *Hear her black trumpet thro' the land proclaim,*
> *That* NOT TO BE CORRUPTED IS THE SHAME . . .
> *See, all other nobles begging to be slaves!*
> *See, all other fools aspiring to be knaves . . .*
> *All, all look up, with reverential awe,*
> *At crimes that 'scape, or triumph o'er the law.*[24]

Denying rather than defending corruption, Walpole dismissed the whole opposition case as the mere factiousness of disappointed politicians who wanted to run the system themselves. Having himself in 1717 led probably the most factious opposition of the century, when he had reversed his position on a standing army, the repeal of the Occasional Conformity and Schism Acts and the impeachment of Lord Oxford, Walpole tended to think any opposition to him was behaving in a similar manner. After his fall, the Whig opposition's conduct largely bore him out.

All the same, the erstwhile opposition's behaviour in 1742 was not enough to dispose of the case against Walpole and the Whigs. The stage had admittedly been set by the Septennial Act and the proscription of the Tories, but neither was inevitable or need have been permanent. Corruption was the natural consequence of oligarchy. With the electorate greatly weakened and the Tories proscribed, the Whig governors, having lost their reforming impulse and largely discarded their Whig principles, had little except quarrels over the spoils to divide them. Single-party government and a one-class Parliament with a consequent paucity of issues confined politics to little more than getting office and money.

> *That statesman hat the strongest hold*
> *Whose tool of politics is gold.*

Yet English politics could have been far healthier. It was Walpole's system which removed issues from politics, not the absence of issues which created or justified the system. Even allowing for the common beliefs that since the division between rich and poor had been ordained by the Creator, man should not attempt to correct the works of God, and that the poor should remain poor and uneducated to keep them hardworking and submissive to the words of both God and the rich, there was no shortage of things for English ministries to do, had they had any inclination or electoral spur to do them. The country's conditions cried out for improvement. Even George II's government in Hanover did more than his ministers in London. As an independent MP later put it, they should have had a regard for the people's 'rights and privileges' as well as for their own 'lucrative employments'. By just looking after themselves and following what Archdeacon Coxe called 'Walpole's one great principle of government, not to rouse things which are at rest', Sir Robert's long ministry lost the opportunity to engage the affections of the nation on behalf of the Hanoverian dynasty. The penalty paid by his successors was English indifference in 1745.[25]

The Excise

Well before that, Walpole's ministry had to face worse than indifference. Early in the 'Robinocracy', the 'depravity' that Hardwicke complained of was most evident in Scotland and Ireland. In 1724 the Levellers Revolt in Galloway – a struggle against enclosure – led to one or two deaths, and in the following year an increase in the Scottish Malt Tax produced a brewers' strike and serious tumults in Glasgow. Trouble was initially avoided by the excise officers refraining from levying the tax. The arrival of Captain Bushell and two companies of Foot, who had been requested by Daniel Campbell of Shawfield, MP for Glasgow Burghs, raised the temperature. The city provost escaped with difficulty from a mob which then wrecked Campbell's house. When the mob stoned the soldiers the next day, Bushell, without complying with the Riot Act, ordered his men to fire. Nine people were killed and sixteen wounded, and the rioting only subsided when at the request of the provost the troops left the city. The Malt Tax was regressive, and the local officers of justice regarded the agitation with tolerance if not encouragement. In the end General Wade, who was already on his way north to build roads in the Highlands, had to be dispatched with some dragoons to suppress the disturbances. Bushell was tried and condemned, but then received the royal pardon and promotion.[26]

The Irish had an even more popular cause: 'Wood's halfpence', the patent sold by George I's mistress to provide a copper coinage for Ireland. Swift's polemics whipped up such a nationwide clamour and violent riots that Walpole was forced to revoke the patent. Now 'we have once more got Scotland and Ireland quiet', he told Townshend, 'if we take care to keep them so'. England needed similar care if it, too, was to be kept quiet.[27]

Following the resignations of Townshend and Carteret in 1730, Walpole was the only minister who counted. He could 'Skreen' others from investigation; he could not screen himself from public hostility. Nor could the monarchy, which was as unpopular as its chief minister. Foreign by birth and foreign by tongue, the King had no qualities except courage to compensate for those misfortunes, and a number to magnify them; he was avaricious, bad-mannered, ill-natured, and largely devoid of interest in his English subjects. Walpole and Hervey were in agreement on 'the ticklish situation' of the King and Queen, their unpopularity 'to the nation in general', and the daily increase in 'the disaffection to their persons'. Walpole was therefore the hated minister of an unloved monarchy. Indeed the hatred he engendered was more that of a royal favourite – he was likened to all of them from Piers Gaveston to Buckingham – than a mere detested politician. England was a country waiting for an explosion. It happened to come over the excise.[28]

Excise duties, paid when goods were released from warehouses, were harder to evade than customs duties, which were paid at ports when goods were landed. This Walpole well knew, having himself often imported wine and other goods without paying customs. Excise – without using the word – had effectively been extended to tea, coffee and cocoa without trouble in 1724. As Walpole pointed out, it already applied to 'ten or twelve articles of consumption' and aided the re-export trade. It did not, however, prevent smuggling: tea was one of the most smuggled commodites. In any case increased efficiency was not Walpole's primary objective. Nor was the hostile public reaction, as Adam Smith later contended, merely the result of 'factions' and 'smuggling merchants'.[29]

The excise had been introduced to pay for the New Model Army and had caused 'very foul riots' leading to its abandonment on food and clothing. Charles I also levied excise to pay for the royal army, and by James II's reign excise was the most productive branch of the revenue. After the Revolution Parliament prevented its general extension to basic commodities, but despite much opposition excise taxes grew piecemeal under both William and Anne. Apart from its distasteful origins, the excise was feared as a serious infringement of liberty, with often drunken and corrupt excisemen empowered to force their way into private premises. The need for a warrant from a magistrate was not an adequate safeguard; one MP claimed he knew of a justice who gave a warrant to search every house in five parishes.[30]

The excise was also unpopular because cases were adjudged, in Dr Johnson's words, 'not by the common judges of property, but wretches hired by those to whom Excise is paid'. To all but the government's supporters, customs and excise officers were regarded in the same light as the standing army: at best a disagreeable necessity, at worst a danger to the constitution and free elections. Customs officers had already taken the coast towns 'prisoner' and delivered them electorally to the Crown, but, unlike excise officers, they were at lest confined to the coast.[31]

In 1730 the tax – or excise – on salt had, contrary to Walpole's wishes, been abolished rather than that on candles chiefly because the House of Commons thought it was the more oppressive to the poor. The ending of the Salt Tax caused the dismissal of some 350 revenue officers. Remedying that sorry loss of patronage was not Walpole's only motive for deciding to revive it two years later. Walpole believed in taxing the poor to make them work harder. He did not just believe, as a Whig MP alleged, in grinding the poor to relieve a few of the rich. He believed in grinding the poor as a good in itself. It kept them in subjection.[32]

Walpole's third and most important reason for bringing back the Salt Tax, which he claimed to be 'no burthen upon the people of England', was to reduce the Land Tax, which in contrast was 'the most unequal, the most grievous and the most oppressive tax' that had ever been raised. He urged the House to show 'compassion' for the landed gentry burdened with mortgages, annuities and Land Tax. Though the opposition denounced the Salt Tax as unfair, neither House proved averse to showing compassion to itself. The weight of the Land Tax was a constant complaint of the gentry, and indeed the landed interest fared worse than the monied, especially as a series of good harvests had lowered corn prices and rents. Yet with indirect taxes supplying over 70 per cent of the Exchequer's revenue, the tax burden shouldered by the rich was scarcely crushing; taxes on necessaries were higher in Britain than in Holland or France, and much of the taxation paid by the poor went to paying interest to fundholders. It was, however, not the poor but the landed interest, much of it hostile to the ministry, whom Walpole was seeking to please.[33]

Walpole's object was thus more political than financial. His revival of the Salt Tax and his excise proposals the following year were part of a scheme to increase his patronage and to widen his popularity with the powerful by lowering their taxes, which entailed raising those of the poor. Had he not thought his proposals would be popular with the political nation, he would surely have followed his own advice to the Dissenters over the repeal of the Test and Corporation Acts, by bringing them forward, (if at all) in the opening, not the closing, years of a Parliament. A bad judge of public opinion, Walpole evidently thought that the reduction in the Land Tax would so ingratiate him with the landed gentry as to stifle opposition in Parliament. He soon learned better.[34]

A 'general excise' had long been feared. Walpole intended a 'general excise' only in the sense that on whichever articles it was imposed it would be paid by everybody, however poor. But 'general excise' had another more explosive meaning: a tax raised on everything used for food and clothes. Fears that Walpole intended this second form of excise were spread by his opponents, making anything to do with an excise that much more unpopular. As Swift put it in February, a general excise had not only been advised by Satan but was also 'the greatest enemy' that Satan 'could stir up against the Crown'.[35]

Walpole's intention to extend the excise to wine and tobacco was widely known. His brother had said as much and Walpole himself had dropped a heavy hint. Pope's *Epistle to Bathurst* (who had opposed the Salt Tax) published in January 1733 contained the lines:

> *Ask you why Phryne the whole Auction buys?*
> *Phryne foresees a general Excise.*

Phryne, originally a rich Athenian courtesan who exhibited herself naked at the Eleusinian games, was here Maria Skerrett, Walpole's mistress. Earlier in the same month, Walpole had assured Lord Percival that when he saw the scheme it would satisfy him. But he delayed bringing the excise before Parliament until he had completed the second stage of his plan, which was to take money out of the Sinking Fund in order to apply it 'towards the ease of the landed interest'. That also pleased the monied men, who did not want a reduction of the national debt.[36]

Walpole's delaying tactics merely provided time for the agitation to grow. *The Craftsman* had been publishing articles against the excise since the autumn and the popular papers, ballad writers an cartoonists followed it into battle. A vast number of pamphlets appeared, either sold cheaply or given away. The general slogan emphasised the excise's affinity to Popery and arbitrary government: 'Excise,

Wooden shoes, and no jury. By the end of January Percival recorded
a 'universal clamour' against the excise. The ministry, under the
delusion that the agitation was the mere product of intrigue and
incitement, was still confident that when its plans were revealed all
would be well.[37]

Outside the political system, which the oligarchy monopolised,
there remained forces which it could neither absorb nor ignore. One
of them was the crowd; another was the growing 'middle sort' and
the City of London. The richest men in the City were easily
assimilated. They bought themselves into the system by purchasing
parliamentary seats and were in turn bought by the government
which did them financial favours. But many in the City had been
increasingly hostile to Walpole since his oligarchical City Elections
Act of 1725, which restricted the franchise and temporarily crippled
the City's Common Council by giving twenty-six aldermen the right
to veto its addresses. A system under which only owners of landed
property could enter Parliament, the electorate had been cut down,
Parliaments lengthened, contested elections become rarer, corporations closed and patronage extended – in short Whig oligarchy – had
little magic for many City merchants. As well as being disenchanted
with a system that excluded them, these lesser merchants disliked a
government which pandered to the richest monied men, while doing
little for the trading interest.[38]

The City led the agitation against the excise. The crowd broke all
the windows at the Post Office, rang the church bells, built bonfires
and made every passing coach cry 'No Excise'. The clamour was not
the work of 'puppets', as Walpole claimed, nor was it confined to
London. 'The whole nation,' Hervey wrote, 'was in flames.'
Nothing like it had been seen since the Sacheverell Riots. Walpole's
scheme had provided the occasion for a national demonstration
against an unpopular government.[39]

By the time Walpole officially opened his proposals, most minds
were made up. In a powerful speech he disavowed any intention of
'a general excise', enumerated the many frauds on the customs, stated
that there were going to be only 126 extra excise officers and pointed
out that if the objections to an excise on tobacco and wine were valid
the whole system of excise laws on other commodities should be
abandoned. That was logical enough. But so, too, was Pulteney's
counterclaim that Walpole's argument pointed to a far wider
extension of the excise laws than merely to wine and tobacco. In any
case it was past the time for logic. In claiming that 'the whole nation'
had already 'declared their dislike' of the scheme, Pulteney scarcely
exaggerated. Replying to the debate Walpole remarked on the 'most
extraordinary concourse of people at our door' and, having drawn
attention to the circular letters that had brought them there, he used

the unfortunate phrase 'sturdy beggars', which laid him open to a magisterial rebuke from the City leader, Sir John Barnard. The people he had seen when he came to the House, Barnard said, 'deserved the name of sturdy beggars as little as the honourable gentleman himself . . .'[40]

The court had been warned of 'the multitude' that would come down to Parliament and was fully prepared. Magistrates and constables were in attendance and Horse and Foot Guards were on call. They were not, however, needed. Walpole left the House by the back way to avoid the threatening crowd. Some of the court party were insulted, but there was virtually no violence. Though Hervey thought fewer people attended than had been expected, the demonstration was impressive, and though it had been carefully organised, Walpole went badly astray in thinking that those taking part 'did not speak their own sentiments'. Organisation does not preclude strong feelings, and the public indignation was genuine, not bought.[41]

During the Easter recess, the clamour grew. Widespread disorder broke out, and with many authorities sympathising with its causes it was not suppressed. Indeed in many places it was the pamphlets putting Walpole's case that were officially burned. In a by-election at Chester, where in the mayoral election six months earlier Walpole had vainly drafted in a 'swarm of excise, salt and customs house officers', a Tory victory followed violence, though the excise was not the sole cause of either. So heated was the public, wrote a contemporary, that the situation was 'next to a rebellion'. Pulteney's earlier assertion – that when the disaffection became general the army was not to be depended upon – seemed to be confirmed by the soldiers' indignation at the prospect of more expensive tobacco. The King's closest friend, Lord Scarbrough, told Walpole that they were cursing the administration and 'were almost as ripe for mutiny as the nation for rebellion'; he could answer for his regiment against the Pretender, he told the Queen, but not against the opponents of the excise. James became excited by assurances that the people desired a Restoration, and individual Jacobites took part in the campaign but, despite Walpole's customary claims to the contrary the agitation owed little to Jacobite intrigue.[42]

As the result of the public clamour, Walpole's misjudgement of the public mood became a misjudgement of Parliament too. Some fifty-four constituencies instructed their members to oppose the excise. (The next election was not far off, and MPs were more than usually sensitive to public agitation.) One unreliable supporter of Walpole expressed the view of many: to force the excise on the people would be dangerous to the Royal Family. Percival recorded that 'people in public houses curse the King'. Even more alarming, some ladies going to the city 'were rudely stopped, and the cry was: "We know this coach, it comes from the St James's end of town; knock the coachman down".' Just why the coachman rather than his employers should have been singled out as the denizen of St James's suitable for punishment is not clear. Perhaps chivalry was stronger than social class antagonism. In any case the coachman was saved by one of the ladies avowing solidarity with the mob: 'We are as much against excise as you.' Even courtiers, including Scarbrough, began to desert Walpole, and, more ominous still, the bishops seemed about to defect. With his majority dwindling, Sir Robert instructed his friends to say that 'the clamour and the spirit' that had been raised made it 'necessary to give way'. In attributing his retreat to popular coercion, Walpole was telling the simple truth. Even if the erosion of his support among courtiers and MPs was the immediate cause of his surrender, it was the strength and intensity of opposition out of doors which caused that erosion, as well as undermining Walpole's own resolution. That was why Scarbrough changed sides and Percival wanted it dropped. Without the national clamour Walpole would have won by his usual majorities.[43]

On the night Walpole announced his retreat, the crowd in the lobby and in the Court of Requests just beside it was even bigger than before. Justices threatened to read the Riot Act. But the response of 'these unruly people', wrote Percival, was 'Damn your laws and proclamations'. They were, he said, inflamed by two Tory MPs asking why there were so many constables and if Walpole had sent them. This time, contrary to advice, Walpole refused to leave the House by the back way, and despite an escort of half a dozen friends and 50 constables he was duly mobbed. His son was injured, Lord Hervey was hit on the head and he himself was jostled and caught by the collar; had he fallen he might well have been trampled to death. With difficulty he escaped by getting into a coffee house and leaving by an exit unknown to the mob.[44]

That night there was tumultuous rejoicing all over London; Walpole was burned in effigy, sometimes in company with Queen Caroline and sometimes with Sarah Malcolm, a particularly atrocious murderess – Gay would have enjoyed that. While the Recorder condemned the riots to the Grand Jury of Middlesex, the Lord Mayor praised those who had taken part, drawing a distinction between public rejoicing and riotous mobbing. He was thanked by the Grand Jury. Outside London, the jubilation was similar; the rejoicings, according to one enthusiast, were more general than any since the Restoration. At Bristol the mayor declared a public holiday, the festivities including the burning of Walpole's effigy, bells were rung at Oxford and toasts drunk to the Tory leaders at Guildford. Nevertheless the celebrations were short lived. The public agitation had caused Walpole's retreat; the mobs' overt violence against him covered that retreat. Walpole decided to make the most of it. 'The incident was so well-managed,' said Hervey himself, 'that on the relation made first by Lord Hervey, then by Pelham, and then by Sir Robert Walpole, to the House, this accidental scuffle was treated as a deep-laid scheme for assassination . . .' Always adept at magnifying dangers, Walpole successfully represented the riots as a threat to parliamentary government. Even in the City, condemnation of the violence became for a time obligatory. Walpole's defeat was blurred and the damage done to him limited. His power lasted for another eight years.[45]

At first sight both Walpole and his opponents acted against their own interest over the Excise Bill: Walpole, by bringing forward an unpopular reform shortly before a general election, and the opposition, by opposing the halving of the tax that they paid on their land. In reality Walpole thought his proposals would be parliamentarily and electorally popular, and the opposition were so sure that defeating the excise would procure his fall that they put their political interest before their financial one. At the same time, though, a number of them had an evidently genuine aversion to lowering their own taxes at the expense of the poor.[46]

Dislike of Walpole and the ministry was the chief ingredient of the anti-excise agitation, both in Parliament and without doors. The City of London's campaign was Tory inspired, and the Tories supplied most of the opposition's parliamentary votes. They were implacably opposed to the 'great man', and no less so were the dissident Whigs led by Pulteny. To that extent Adam Smith was right. 'Faction' was at the bottom of the anti-excise campaign. But it was not just 'envy and malice', as Walpole claimed, that led men to oppose the excise. The agitation was a revolt against his manner of government and an expression of fear of the future consequences. It did not require envy or malice to dislike Sir Robert or to desire his removal, and the revolt might well have come sooner. The oligarchy seemed unrepresentative, over-privileged, unappealing and corrupt. Much of the country was alienated from both it and the dynasty.[47]

Walpole would have fallen had he not abandoned the Excise Bill. Even then he survived largely because of the backlash against the violence of April 11th. No such backlash had occurred against the far more serious violence of the Sacheverell Riots, but that had been against dissenting chapels, a more acceptable target than the chief minister and his friends. More important George II, whose civil list would have been augmented by the excise and who was as susceptible to bribery as any politician, fully supported his minister and dismissed Walpole's opponents. In 1710 Queen Anne's attitude to the violence had been very different. Instead of penalising her ministers' opponents, she dismissed her ministers.[48]

The 1733 backlash was confined to Westminster. Though Walpole won the following year's election, he won it because of the electoral system not because he enjoyed the electorate's support. The political nation, especially the gentry and clergy, were heavily against him. The election was particularly expensive; the recently passed Bribery and Corruption Act was generally ignored and the government spent more secret service money than on any other election between 1688 and the reform of 1782. It was more of a national contest and less a series of local struggles than any other election of the century save 1784. In the large open constituencies, where opinion counted, the government fared disastrously, losing twenty-one seats. The Whigs even lost Walpole's county, Norfolk. Only by doing even better than usual in the small constituencies, where opinion did not count and the influence of the oligarchy was decisive, did Walpole maintain his position. Even so, his losses in the larger constituencies made him dangerously dependent on the support of a few prominent borough-mongers, and when that was withdrawn in the 1741 election Walpole's majority became too small for his survival. Much as the public agitation over the excise needed the resulting defection of courtiers to defeat him on the issue, so the nation's defeat of Walpole at the 1734 election needed the subsequent defection of the Prince of Wales and other controllers of boroughs to bring about his fall.[49]

Not surprisingly, the turnout and the number of contested seats were exceptionally high, and the election was more than normally violent. A Tory mob incited by the Tory candidate beseiged Bridgenorth Town Hall; troops were needed to quell them. In Sussex an observer wrote of 'these mad riots' and thought 'the Frenzy' was as great as in Sacheverell's time. 'People of all denominations,' a Yorkshire correspondent told the Duke of Newcastle, 'are heated, some by drink, others by zeal, and the test of the latter with many is most commonly violence.' At Yarmouth the Tory mob erupted when their candidates entered the town; the arrival of the Whig candidates, one of whom was Walpole's son, produced worse violence. The Whig mayor was taken to court and ordered to pay £15 for whipping a rioter excessively. North Wales and the neighbouring English counties were even more heated. The mob attacked the government candidate in Newcastle-under-Lyme, 'vowing to wash their hands' in his blood. In Gloucestershire, Herefordshire and Worcestershire election riots were combined with riots against the new turnpikes, those built with Whig money being attacked while those built with Tory money largely escaped. No wonder the Secretary at War, called by George II 'stinking Yonge', when opposing the repeal of the Septennial Act, thought the best way of preserving 'the virtue of the people' was to have as few elections as possible. It was also the best way of keeping the Whigs in power.[50]

Turnpikes, gin and the Irish

Eight years after the excise disturbances a similar national agitation helped to bring Walpole down: between the two, violence was localised. In Gloucestershire and Herefordshire toll gates or turnpikes were destroyed. Turnpike tolls were regressive taxation which hit tradesmen or workers who frequently passed through them harder than the gentry, whose coaches did far more damage to the roads. John Wesley and other Tories thought that road repairs should be paid for by the well-off rather than by 'vile impositions of turnpikes'. In 1727 the Kingswood miners, 'a set of ungovernable men', wrote the mayor of Bristol, had attacked the new turnpikes radiating from Bristol; they complained that the magistrates had failed to enforce the laws for repairing the existing roads and the turnpike trustees had been allowed to remove furse and heath, which the colliers used for various purposes, in order to repair the roads. Despite forcing a concession that horses carrying loads did not have to pay tolls, the miners continued to destroy toll gates. When four of them were captured by a JP who was also a turnpike trustee, his house was besieged by 'a great body of colliers' and the magistrate was forced not only to release his prisoners but to provide their rescuers with ale.[51]

Most turnpikes were peacefully accepted, but a recurrence of turnpike rioting in the West brought a characteristic government response: turnpike destruction was made a capital offence, and some rioters were hanged. That did not stop the attacks. In 1735 some hundred rioters, dressed in women's clothes and armed with guns and swords, destroyed turnpikes at Ledbury in Herefordshire, others being destroyed elsewhere in that county and in Gloucestershire. Troops had to be used to suppress the riots and 'to preserve the life of a magistrate' who was under threat from the mob for diligently executing the law. Whether or not the riots were encouraged by 'gentlemen of fortune', the Kingswood colliers were Tory inclined and the Bristol turnpikes were sponsored by Whigs; in other places too, Whig turnpikes were vulnerable. Tory gentry were reluctant to prosecute the rioters. A petition for troops to be sent to Herefordshire was welcomed by the Lord Chief Justice as the first sign of country gentlemen wishing to act with spirit against the riots. Hardwicke regarded 'this sort of risings' as a dangerous symptom, fearing that if 'the People' were allowed 'to get the better of the laws' their successful 'violences' might lead them to refuse payment of 'other taxes' too. To prevent such a dangerous depletion of the national finances, the Lord Chief Justice used a stretched interpretation of the Black Act to hang one of the Hereford rioters at Tyburn.[52]

In the summer of 1736 'the people showed', Hervey wrote, 'a licentious, riotous, seditious, and almost ungovernable spirit'. The Guards in London were augmented. Two successive poor harvests in the West Country brought riots there against the export of corn. Nearer home a parcel containing papers and gunpowder exploded in Westminister Hall filling the law courts with smoke and with leaflets lampooning the administration. The lawyers treated this affront to the majesty of the law as an insult no less heinous than *lèse majesté* or sacrilege, Hardwicke considering it an impudent and audacious act of sedition coming 'very nigh high treason'. Walpole thought it merely a 'vile transaction' perpetrated by 'a set of low Jacobites'. The explosion was in fact the work of one demented clergyman, but the incident added to the sense of insecurity.[53]

Between 1727 and 1735 the consumption of gin increased by over 50 per cent. More than 7000 shops sold it in the metropolitan areas of Middlesex – up to 30,000 people were employed in London's drink trade – and in 1736 that county's magistrates informed Parliament that 'the constant and excessive use of geneva had already destroyed thousands of his Majesty's subjects'. The JPs found that the contagion had spread to the female sex: unhappy mothers became addicted, bearing weak and sickly children; others gave gin daily to their offspring. Overriding its own interests as corn producers and its allergy to social legislation, Parliament favoured immediate action, and a scheme was enacted which, by making a licence to sell gin prohibitively expensive, effectively made it impossible for the poor to buy it legally. While not opposing it, Walpole doubted if the scheme would work. Pulteney opposed its discrimination against the poor and thought it might produce 'such riots and tumults which could not be quelled without blood . . . [and without] putting an end to the liberties of the people'. Passed in May, the legislation was to come into force at Michaelmas, at which time trouble fanned by Jacobites was also expected by Walpole. In fact trouble came well before then, but was only tangentially connected with the Gin Act.[54]

In July anti-Irish rioting broke out in Shoreditch, Spitalfields and Whitechapel. The Irish were already unpopular for taking weaving jobs at lower than London rates, and when some of the English workers engaged in building a new church in Shoreditch were dismissed to be replaced by Irishmen at between one half and two-thirds of their wages, violence began. The English, complaining of being underworked and starved by the Irish, rioted three nights running. On the second night, a mob of between 2000 and 4000 attacked and gutted public houses kept by Irishmen. The Irish

defended themselves with firearms, killing one man and wounding
seven or eight others. The crowd paid no attention to a reading of
the Riot Act; only the arrival of an officer and fifty guardsmen from
the Tower brought their retreat and eventual dispersal. A similar
mob appeared on the third evening but, confronted this time by the
Tower Hamlets militia, it again offered no resistance. Irish houses
were attacked in Whitechapel. 'Other mobs arose in Southwark,
Lambeth and Tyburn Road, and took upon them to interrogate
people whether they were for the English or Irish but committed no
violence.' Elsewhere in London Horse Grenadiers dispersed mobs
preparing to demolish Irish houses. In Dartford a justice who had
imprisoned four rioters was forced to release them by a mob, which
threatened to pull his house down.[55]

The true cause of the disturbances was the ostensible one: the use
of cheap Irish labour and the resulting unemployment of English
workers. Amidst the general cry of 'Down with the Irish', the Gin
Act was denounced by some of the East London rioters. Walpole saw
a Jacobite hand behind almost every disturbance, and some Jacobites
did no doubt plan to cash in on the unpopularity of the prohibition
of gin. But anti-Irish agitation, as Walpole himself recognised, did
not provide a fertile tilling field for the Pretender's followers. The
Gin Act proved no better. The government took precautions at
Michaelmas, and the anticipated disturbances did not materialise. The
most that happened was a few shouts from mobs of 'No gin, no
King'. The Queen riposted to one such mob that if they had patience
till the next session, they should again have both. They did have
both, though not through either their patience or any action in
Parliament. For, as Walpole had feared, the Act was not enforceable.
In seven years only three of the expensive licences were taken out.
Informers had a field day: in less than two years 12,000 informations
were laid and nearly 5000 convictions secured. But the consumption
of gin went on increasing, and in the end popular violence neutered
the law. More important than minor riots was the hunting down of
informers, against whom, said Dr Johnson, the people declared war.
A number of them were murdered. Prohibition did not work. Only
when the price of malt rose and Parliament tried a very different
approach in 1751 did 'Mother Gin' begin to lose her power.[56]

Captain Porteous

That same summer saw a much more serious incident in Edinburgh
at the execution of Wilson, a popular smuggler. Wilson was popular,
because he was considered to have been badly treated by the revenue
officers, because he had generously helped a colleague to escape, and

because smuggling was an activity even more widely accepted in Scotland than in England. For fear that Wilson himself might escape his fate, the city magistrates provided guards under Captain John Porteous to escort the smuggler from the Tolbooth prison to the normal place of execution, the Grassmarket. Already disliked because of his habitual harshness, Porteous now attracted as much hatred as Wilson did sympathy through insisting on manacling his prisoner in handcuffs that were agonisingly tight and brushing aside Wilson's remonstrance with the words: 'It signifies little, your pain will soon be at an end.' No attempt to rescue was made, but after Wilson was dead the crowd began throwing stones at the Captain and his guards, wounding some of them. Instead of marching his men away, their mission completed, Porteous seized a musket from one of his soldiers, shot one man dead and ordered the others to fire. Some of them did so, and three people were killed and a dozen wounded. On their way back to the guardhouse, pursued by a mob, the guard turned and fired once killing another three people and wounding others. This time Porteous had given them no order to fire.[57]

Prosecuted by the Lord Advocate and tried by Scotland's leading judge, Porteous was convicted of murder and sentenced to death, a thoroughly congenial outcome for the large crowd which surrounded the court. Porteous was gravely at fault, and his loss of temper had had terrible consequences. Yet in view of the undoubted provocation, his delinquency scarcely amounted to murder. Accordingly, in George II's absence in Hanover, Queen Caroline reprieved him for six weeks, a decision that was vastly unpopular in Edinburgh. At Wilson's execution some of the guard, more humane than their commander, had fired over the heads of the crowd, unluckily hitting some spectators instead of rioters. As a result the victims included the innocent and the better-off as well as the guilty and the poor, and the city's hostility to Porteous was wide and deep. Instead of being removed to safety in Edinburgh Castle, the Captain was left in the Tolbooth which twice before 'within the memory of man' had not provided safe refuge from lynching mobs. This time a mob of some 4000 was carefully marshalled. The guardhouse was rushed and its weapons appropriated, their rightful users, deprived of ammunition, putting up not even token resistance. Once the gate of the prison had been burned down, Porteous was discovered halfway up a chimney. After being permitted to give his money and papers to a friend for his family, he was taken to the Grassmarket and hanged. The mob then threw away the arms they had seized and dispersed. There was no drunkenness.[58]

The 'cool resolution' of the lynchers was not matched by the forces of law and order. The army commander, General Moyle, refused to move his troops into the city to quell the disturbance without written instructions from the magistrates. Patrick Lindsay, MP for the city and a former provost, who came to seek military aid and whom Moyle reckoned to be drunk, did not carry written instructions in case the rioters found them on him. Deprived of Moyle's soldiers the other magistrates, who had been drinking together in a tavern, visited the disturbance but finding the balance of force strongly in favour of the rioters thought it prudent not to remain there. 'The behaviour of the magistrates,' Lord Islay told Walpole from Edinburgh, 'was certainly worse than can well be imagined'; some of them were 'wilfully neglectful', being in sympathy with the mob's murderous objective. Nevertheless for once it was the military, not the magistrates, who were most to blame. General Moyle's pusillanimous insistence on the protection of written orders prevented Porteous' rescue.[59]

None of the mob's 'chief agents' was ever charged. Though, as Walpole told his borther, the culprits must have been widely known, nobody was rash enough to provide evidence against them, while 'the secret patrons of the mob' were active on behalf of those minor participants who had been arrested. As a result the only alternative to the government conceding defeat was to take revenge by collective punishment. Carteret and opposition Whigs in the Lords proposed a bill to abolish Edinburgh's charter, disband its guard, knock down its gates and disqualify its provost from public office. Scotland was united against the measure but, unwilling to be outbid on law and order, Walpole unwisely supported the bill. When the opposition in the Commons denounced the proposals, Walpole was forced to compromise, the bill being whittled down to dismissal of the provost and a fine on the city of £2000 for the benefit of Porteous's widow – enough, according to Hervey, to make her 'with most unconjugal joy bless the hour in which her husband had been hanged'. A more important consequence than the widow's solace was the driving of the Duke of Argyll into opposition, and hence the government to defeat in Scotland at the next general election.[60]

Walpole's fall

Walpole had good personal reasons for stressing the dangers of frequent elections. He could not have lasted long had the Triennial Act remained in force. Even with the advantage of seven-year parliaments he paradoxically combined the longest period as first minister with the worst electoral record of the century.* Walpole

---

* Of the other long-serving first ministers, North was driven from office but not by electoral defeat; the other two – Pelham and Pitt – died, undefeated, in office. A long tenure of Downing Street was much easier before 1832 than since.

fought four elections as chief minister: the first two, in 1722 and 1727, he won comfortably, in 1734 he suffered, in Dr Langford's verdict, 'the clearest electoral rejection of any administration in the eighteenth century', and in 1741 his majority was a mere nineteen, if that. In any case, as an opposition MP wrote, if they took proper measure, 'sixteen or nothing is the same thing'. Probably not even a clear majority would have preserved Walpole for long. His position had already been fatally weakened and his unpopularity became still more intense. Since 1738 the ministry had been faced by a powerful and coordinated campaign of extra-parliamentary opposition based on hostility to corruption at home and to peace abroad – Walpole's strategy for survival.[61]

Walpole's pacific foreign policy was well judged, but as it was widely thought to stem more from a wish to keep himself in office and the Hanoverians on the throne than from the pursuit of the national interest and the furtherance of British commerce, it brought him little credit. When in 1739 belligerent mercantile and nationalist and anti-Catholic pressures eventually forced him into war with Spain, he proved no better than his successor two centuries later at waging a war he had tried to avoid. The only notable victory – Admiral Vernon's capture of Porto Bello – was of more help to the opposition than to the ministry. The Admiral who had long been Walpole's bitter critic, became a national hero and a symbol of opposition. Nominated and victorious in several constituencies, Vernon won 98.6 per cent of the vote at Ipswich on a 92 per cent turnout. [62]

The opposition belief that the election had cost Walpole his control of Parliament was soon confirmed by votes in the new House. After one narrow victory his son thought the question was: 'Downing Street or the Tower'. Out of doors the ferment was nationwide and 'prodigious'. Constituencies sent instructions to their MPs calling for Walpole's dismissal, and large demonstrations, violence, mock-funerals and effigy burnings were frequent until long after his resignation. In Exeter Sir William Courtenay MP was mobbed for not being in London to 'pull Robin down'. Lord Egmont believed, probably rightly, that 'the temper of the nation [was] so inflamed' against Walpole that his continuance in office became impossible: 'The opinion of the nation removed Walpole,' because that opinion, transmitted to ministers and MPs, convinced them that he must be toppled. Walpole himself thought his friends and fellow ministers had panicked, and only after seven defeats did he finally agree to resign.[63]

For many people that was just a beginning; they sought a violent revenge. Fifty-four English constituencies called for an inquiry into Walpole's administration, most of them adding calls for his

punishment as well as for reform. The press demanded his
impeachment, one of them reporting his execution in advance. The
lampoonists followed suit:

> Brave, independent Britons, don't
> our expectations mock,
> (No, no – such worthy members won't,)
> But bring him to the block.

Had there been a leading politician as vindictive as Walpole had
himself been to Oxford and Bolingbroke, he might have gone to the
Tower. But on his penultimate day in office, Walpolean corruption
had its final fling. Sir Robert spent £3000, almost certainly on
stultifying any probe into his conduct. The court and his former
colleagues also had their own good reasons for avoiding a penetrating
investigation into corruption, while once they had achieved office the
new ministers had quickly lost their taste for one. The parliamentary
committee of inquiry was accordingly frustrated, and the Screen-
Master General was successfully screened. But, however sleazy the
methods, the result was civilising. Political warfare became less
violent. The lenient way Walpole was treated, not the way he himself
had treated his opponents in 1714-16, became the binding precedent,
and no fallen minister was ever again put under threat of violent
punishment. Loss of office was deemed sufficient penalty.[64]

Conclusion

Whether Sir Robert was hounded out of office primarily by 'the sense
of the people' or by Parliament, he had earlier faced much popular
violence. Plebeian hostility to his ministry was undeniable. Walpole
virtually conceded it himself. Admittedly, the concession suited his
argument for the retention of a large standing army. Even so, his
admission that left to itself the militia would protect not suppress
smugglers, destroy not protect turnpikes and, over gin, side with the
public not with the authorities, was a remarkable confession of his
government's unpopularity and lack of authority. Likewise, no
minister denied the prevalence of riots. In 1737 the King's speech
complained of the general 'defiance of all authority, contempt of
magistracy and even resistance of the laws'. Earlier Hardwicke, the
Lord Chancellor, acknowledged that riots had become so frequent
and so general as in some manner to have spread over the kingdom.
'The Dunciad', a modern critic has pointed out, is a 'poem about civil
commotion.'[65]

Using an argument that became standard oposition rhetoric,

Carteret, Wyndham and Pulteney maintained that the people never became violent unless provoked. Therefore the riots should be investigated to discover their causes. The ministry did once inquire into an industrial dispute, with surprising results. But normally to inquire into riots would have been to concede the possibility of governmental provocation or oppression, which was unthinkable. Only the lowest rank of people, Hardwicke believed, had been concerned in the riots; clearly then, it was 'below the dignity of Parliament' to inquire into them. All that was necessary was to deal with their effects by punishment.[66]

Anyway the Lord Chancellor already knew their real cause: the authorities' 'want of power' to prevent or punish and the excessive liberty of others to stir up the people to disorder. The King agreed that the laws were too loose and did not allow half enough people to be hanged, vowing that they would have no mercy if they came into his hands. In fact, as Lord Bathurst pointed out in answer to Hardwicke, the authorities now had more powers against riots than ever before and the English laws against them were more severe than anybody else's.[67]

Agreeing with Hardwicke about the government's 'lenity', Walpole thought the prime cause of the tumults was Jacobite incitement. Unlike his opponents who saw many discontented but few disaffected, Walpole maintained that the people's discontent and uneasiness proceeded from disaffection. Indeed Sir Robert was sure that if the Pretender were to land with 5000 or 6000 men 'many, especially the meaner sort' would join him. Whether Walpole really believed that Jacobitism lay at the roots of popular violence or merely used it as a pretext to justify a larger army and to evade redress of well-grounded grievances matters little. If he was lying, then he knew discontent was widespread and should have taken steps to lessen it. And if he believed what he was saying, he should have wondered why after twenty years of relatively peaceful prosperity disaffection was still so deep, and again made some effort to reduce it.[68]

All the same, the oligarchy's unpopularity prompts the question not why there was so much popular disturbance but why there was not a good deal more of both plebeian and governmental violence. Almost constant electioneering had helped to keep serious violence off the streets in the twenty years after the passing of the Triennial Act in 1694. The Septennial Act removed that safety valve, but the climate provided another. Walpole was lucky. Mainly good harvests and slow growth of population ensured low food prices and a stable price level. Consequently, Walpole had to face few serious food riots – the commonest form of popular disturbance – until 1740, shortly before his fall. Low food prices were accompanied by rising prosperity. Neither had much to do with anything that the government did – except its successful protectionist policies and growth was slower than in succeeding years, but lessening economic hardship naturally dampened popular turbulence.[69]

Walpole was also fortunate in his opposition, the components of which had various inhibitions about dabbling in popular politics. Just as perpetual office had led the Whigs to abandon anti-court politics, proscription and the wilderness had driven the Tories, who were strong in the large boroughs and the counties, into espousing popular issues. The Tories had the mob on their side, a Whig candidate admitted a little later, comforting himself with the reflection that the Whigs had the army. Not only were most urban mobs Tory; most Englishmen were Tory. In 1742 the Whig Pulteney told the King that two thirds of the nation were Tories. Yet Tory populism was limited. Sweeping changes were not proposed – not even to the indefensible electoral system which ensured Tory defeat. Some Tories wanted James III, some merely wanted office under George II. But they all believed in the royal prerogative, hierarchy and authority; they were socially conservative. Tory JPs might be slow to put down riots aimed at a Whig ministry; some Tories were not above fomenting riots over, say, turnpikes, and like their opponents they fomented election riots. Some wanted to repeal the Riot Act. Yet, except over the excise and in 1742, Tories drew the line at using their popularity to incite direct political violence against the ministry. Lacking not political awareness but any political programme of its own, the populace without such incitement was as a rule politically, though not economically, quiescent. So while the Whigs were at least as good as the Tories at governing, the Tories were far less effective in opposition than the Whigs would have been.[70]

The second component of opposition, the dissident Whigs, who mostly sat for the small corrupt boroughs, had neither the capacity nor the wish to stir up popular agitation. The third component, Jacobitism, which to a varying extent and degree overlapped with the first, occasionally had both. Mobs often mouthed Jacobite slogans. There were glimmerings of a popular Jacobitism among the smugglers and deer-stealers who formed the 'Waltham Blacks'; Newcastle keelmen regularly proclaimed 'King James'; prostitutes were often considered Jacobite sympathisers. Jacobitism had become a legitimising agent for disturbance and dissent. If the Whigs became Tory, the Jacobites occasionally became Whigs. Although Jacobitism was far from being at the bottom of every disturbance, as Walpole claimed, some Jacobite gentry did incite popular violence. Yet the bad showing of the Tories in elections following Jacobite scares showed Jacobite popularity to be limited. 'The eyes of the people,' said the Attorney General after the Tory defeat in 1747, 'are much opened by rebellion.' In any case, neither the Pretender nor his leading English followers saw popular violence or a popular rising as the route to the restoration of James III. Hence, they made little effort to build up popular support. If Jacobites no longer believed with Atterbury that the voice of the people was 'the cry of hell', they still did not believe it was the voice of God.[71]

Yet it was not only Walpole's luck that cut down political rioting. His political skill and caution also deprived his opponents of popular issues. Aware that his was the minority party and mindful that the Sacheverell Riots had dislodged a Whig ministry and that those of 1715 had shaken the regime, Walpole was careful not to let the High Church parsons and the mob come together a third time. He could do nothing to stop a High Church mob rioting over the proposed destruction of Lincoln Cathedral's spires in 1726,★ but he could prevent a wider agitation by dropping his predecessor's scheme to help his party's supporters, the Dissenters. The Test Acts remained on the statute book, convocation stayed suppressed, and the clergy and the mobs were kept asunder.

More important even than luck, caution and skill, was Walpole's possession of an army. Without the army, a government speaker accepted in 1738, the Tory interest would prevail. Walpole, himself, had earlier admitted that the government needed the support of military force. Wyndham and the opposition leaders were right in their contention that unless they were provoked the people did not resort to violence; they were unarmed, and the government's use of the army was likely to make such resort painfully futile. Yet if the mob was in the last resort controlled by the army, the ministry was constrained by the mob. Though in the end it could always defeat 'popular commotion', tumults alarmed the political nation and weakened the ministry. The frequent use of soldiers to keep the peace demonstrated that the ministry lacked authority – as Carteret pointed out and Walpole implicity conceded and was governing by force. An unpopular ministry had therefore to be sparing in its employment of an unpopular army. In consequence it had to avoid adding to popular commotion and to avoid political, if not economic, provocation.[73]

In addition to its soldiers, the ministry possessed the formidable legal armoury that the Whigs had amassed since 1714. Hardwicke found the Waltham Black Act 'very useful', and he extended its utility by interpreting it broadly. The Riot Act which, provided they

---

★ The mob may have mistakenly believed that the towers as well as the spires were to be demolished. Alternatively, the mob's judgement, both aesthetically and architecturally, was superior to that of the experts – as a result of its exploits, the Cathedral authorities decided not to pull down the spires, though they were taken down as unsafe eighty years later.[72]

used the proper procedure, gave legal immunity to justices and
soldiers who used violence to quell disturbances was even more
useful. Yet 'blood', a French minister warned the British government
after the Porteous affair, instead of quietening, 'generally exasperated
riots', which then created opportunities for the disaffection to stir up
insurrection. Similarly Walpole once advised Lord Islay that 'a too
rigorous severity' could breed rancour and resentment against the
government. Although he was referring to action against Scottish
magistrates and was less inhibited about acting against the English
populace, the authorities could not wield their sweeping legal powers
regardless of popular susceptibilities. In 1735 Hardwicke regretted
having to defer to the Cornish gentry's opinion that a rioter should
be executed in the ordinary way instead of being hanged in chains,
but conceded that 'the disposition of the common people' would have
made such an example 'hazardous to attempt'. Eager as Hardwicke
and the gentry were to make examples in order to subdue the people's
'licentious spirit', they were aware that too much violence would
instead inflame its licentiousness.[74]

Not only the common people's 'disposition' limited the use of
troops and the Riot Act. The government did not always trust local
magistrates. Despite frequent Whig purges of the Commission of the
Peace, justices were not invariably supporters of the regime and the
lower social status of some JPs who were Whig supporters might
make them chary of fierce measures; even those who were both Whig
and well respected often thought their authority and prestige better
preserved by conciliation than by military force. The law moreover
was obscure. Notwithstanding the Riot Act, Hervey could write that
'the soldiers by law [could] not fire unless attacked by fire-arms; if
they do they are guilty of murder'. Similar misunderstanding of the
law, together with memories of the fate of Captains Bushell and
Porteous, predisposed army officers to avoid force when possible.[75]

By dint of the army, the law and an oppressive social policy,
Walpole managed to keep the populace down, but not wholly
intimidated. 'The insolence of the people' all over the country, said
the secretary at war, made it unsafe for magistrates to do their duty
without military aid; a mob of 5,000 in the West Country had
committed violent outrages, yet were supported by 'the country in
general'. Jekyll, the author of the Gin Act, needed a military guard,
and the Bow Street magistrate had to send for troops to save his own
house from being pulled down by a mob whose leader was tried and
acquitted. There was therefore something of a stand-off between
ministry and people, brought about not by inertia but by a balance
of power. The poorer sort were restrained by the government's
enjoyment of overwhelming force. The government was restrained
by the unpopularity of itself and of its chosen instruments as well as

by fear of the Pretender.[76]

The ministry did nothing to diminish either its own unpopularity or public discontent. A Tory clergyman suggested that the government should use its authority to relieve the needy and oppressed, affirming that if it lowered taxes on the poor by practising a little self-denial it would 'render even the disaffected loyal'. Such radicalism, however, had become unthinkable; the guiding Whig principle was now self-enrichment. For the King, Walpole and the oligarchy, lower taxation on the poor was as distasteful as self-denial for themselves. So the flaunting of 'corruption and venality' went merrily along. Such 'preying upon the public', Pulteney averred, could do nothing to mend the hearts of the people or make the disaffected loyal. The 'Forty-five' soon proved him right.[77]

FIVE

Jacobitism and the 'Forty-five'

All the good we have done has been a little bloodletting . . . and I tremble for fear that this vile spot may still be the ruin of this island and our family.

The Duke of Cumberland, writing from
Scotland three months after Culloden

'My family [said Waverley] is wealthy and powerful, inclined in principles to the Stuart race, and should a favourable opportunity –.' 'A favourable opportunity!' said Flora [MacIvor] somewhat scornfully, – 'Inclined in principles! – can such lukewarm adherence be honourable to yourselves, or gratifying to your lawful sovereign? – Think . . . what I should suffer . . . in a family where the rights which I hold most sacred are . . . only deemed worthy of support when they shall appear on the point of triumphing without it!'

Sir Walter Scott

For the two kings and their rights, I cared not a farthing which prevailed; but I was starving, and, by God, if Mahommed had set up his standard in the Highlands I had been a good Mussulman for bread, and stuck close to the party, for I must eat.

Lord Kilmarnock, executed for supporting
Charles Edward in the Forty-five[1]

No European power save the Papacy (which had opposed James II in 1688-9) actively sought a Stuart restoration except when it was fighting Britain or Hanover. The Hanoverian dynasty was therefore secure so long as Britain avoided war, a principal reason for Walpole's policy of peace at almost any price. Conversely, Jacobitism required British involvement in European war. Then the Jacobites might come in useful; in peacetime they were usually a nuisance, their claims of strong support in England being generally discounted. Unfortunately for the Pretender the twenty-five years following the Peace of Utrecht were in Western Europe the least internationally violent of any between 1494 and 1815.[2]

At war with Britain in 1719, Spain aimed to play the Jacobite card. A large scale invasion of England was planned together with a diversion in Scotland. In the event only the diversionary force of 300 Spanish soldiers and some squabbling Jacobite leaders reached North West Scotland. They were greeted with little enthusiasm, and the enterprise was doomed from the start. If even the Highlanders were reluctant to rise unless emboldened by the presence of a substantial foreign army, clearly a rising in England without outside help was unthinkable. Hence mere Jacobite plotting was useless except to the government, and many former adherents abandoned their allegiance; others became at best lukewarm. However unpopular the regime, only a rising in Scotland or a foreign invasion could make Jacobitism a plausible successor.[3]

The outbreak of war with Spain in 1739 raised Jacobite hopes, as did the war of the Austrian succession a year later. Yet geography and the strength of the British navy precluded Spain from mounting by herself an effective invasion of England, and war between France and Britain was unlikely so long as the pacific Cardinal Fleury and the pacific Robert Walpole remained the chief ministers of Louis XV and George II. Many Frenchmen were dubious of France deriving much benefit from a restoration of the Stuarts. From the French point of view the Hanoverians had the great advantage of being umbilically joined to a Hanover that was always vulnerable to French attack. A Stuart monarchy would leave the French no equivalent hostage; Britain would once more be an island. Nevertheless such long-term considerations were forgotten when use of the Jacobites promised an immediate advantage, and in 1743 it did.

Fleury had died in January, the English Jacobite leaders – the Duke of Beaufort, Lord Barrymore, Sir Watkin Williams Wynne and Sir John Hynde Cotton – had requested French assistance for a Stuart restoration and, even though Britain and France were still nominally at peace, the British, Hanoverian and other armies under the leadership of George II, clad in Hanoverian uniform, had defeated the French at Dettingen. The French sent an emissary to sound opinion in England. His estimate of Jacobite sympathisers among the gentry and in the City was wildly optimistic, but it was convenient to believe him. Louis XV decided upon an invasion of England to safeguard France, avenge Dettingen and restore the Stuarts. Backed by Spain, the invading force of 10,000 men was to be led by Marshal Saxe, a Protestant as well as one of the best generals in Europe.[4]

Because of the British navy surprise was essential. Yet, astonishingly, at the end of December 1743 the English Jacobites asked for the invasion to be postponed until February. By then the weather would be worse, and the plan might have been betrayed. The ostensible cause was that if the Jacobite leaders left Parliament before the debate on taking the Hanoverian troops into English pay, the government would suspect trouble and arrest them, a remarkably slender reason for such a momentus change of plan; or rather it would have been a momentous change, had the expedition been ready on January 9th, which it was not. Before it was, surprise had been lost. The invasion plans were sold to the English government by a French diplomat, (long in their pay), the English fleet was alerted, troops were summoned from Holland and Flanders and the weather duly deteriorated. A gale blew into Dunkirk, and twelve of Saxe's fully-loaded transports were destroyed. For the time being the danger of invasion was over.[5]

The Pretender's son, Charles Edward, had arrived in France for the expedition, and though the French government abandoned the enterprise and instead declared war on England, his appetite had been whetted. His father well knew that to attempt a rising without massive foreign aid was to invite disaster for his unfortunate adherents in Scotland. And when Charles in 1744 had floated the idea of coming 'though with a single footman', Cameron of Lochiel thought it would be 'a rash and desperate undertaking'; others replied that without French troops there would be no rising. Yet, with the help of some Franco-Irish privateering adventurers but without French troops and without telling his father, the Prince sailed for Scotland. One of his two ships was crippled by the British navy and was forced to turn back, but he himself landed in the Outer Hebrides on July 23, 1745 and on the mainland two days later, accompanied by 'the seven men of Moidart', who were in fact eight. As only half of them were Scots, there being one Englishman and three Irishmen, as well as twenty Irish officers, they were neither in quantity nor in nationality well constituted for a Scottish rising.[6]

In Scotland, as Hume said, there were no Tories; there were only Whigs and Jacobites. The Whig monopoly of Scottish politics left Jacobitism as the sole opposition. Scottish Jacobites had three further advantages over their English brethren. They were spurred on both by Scottish nationalism and by fear of Campbell hegemony, and the 'heritable jurisdictions' gave feudal authority to the Highland clan chiefs. Hence they could bring out men under arms, often by threatening to burn down their houses if they refused. English magnates had no such armed host to call upon; they could usually require their tenants to vote as they wanted, but there their powers ended.[7]

For all their feudal ascendancy, the Highland chieftains were not backward barbarians. Some of them, though, had nasty habits. In 1739 the two most powerful chieftains in Skye, Sir Alexander Macdonald and the Macleod of Macleod, planned to kidnap some of their tenants for sale in America as near slaves; the government's discovery of the plan enabled it to blackmail them into becoming its supporters – a disastrous and possibly decisive depletion of Jacobite strength. Yet many of the Highland lairds were more cultured than George II or his second son, and many of them, like Cameron of Lochiel and Lord George Murray, were improving landlords and competent businessmen. They attached greater importance than their opposite numbers in England to the idea of hereditary monarchy, but despite their hostility to the British government, they were not the sort of men to be swayed into risking their lives and estates by the mere romantic appeal of ancestral loyalties or the pull of primitive obedience. Most of them, indeed, refused to join the Young Pretender. Not one of the greatest magnates wholeheartedly supported him. Those lairds who did rise were mostly won over by his talk of French promises of support or by his own promises, as to Lochiel, of a secure income in France should the adventure miscarry.[8]

When he raised his standard at Glenfinnan, Charles Edward had only some 1300 men. To oppose him the government ordered General Cope, against his inclinations, to march north from Edinburgh with a 'raw' and ill-equipped army. Finding the country almost uniformly hostile, his baggage train sabotaged, an absence of recruits and mounting desertions, Cope decided not to risk ambush at the Corrieyairack Pass, diverting himself to Inverness and then Aberdeen. Unopposed, the Pretender* marched south and on September 17 took Edinburgh after a mere scuffle. His army grew as he went, but remained small. When the much-travelled Cope arrived from Aberdeen by ship, and Charles at Preston Pans heavily defeated him before breakfast, neither side had more than 2500 men.[10]

The march to Derby

Four things were crucial to the outcome of the 'Forty-five': the decision to invade England, the decision to retreat from Derby to Scotland, the amount of French help and the behaviour of the English Jacobites.

With most of the English army in Flanders, England, Marshal Wade believed, was for the first comer. The Prince was unable to get there first, because his own army was so small. His success depended on gaining strong support from the English Jacobites and from the

---

* Strictly speaking, of course, Charles Edward was not the Pretender. He was, Fielding maintained, only the Pretender's son, a deputy Pretender, a sort of Pretender's Pretender, a Pretender once removed. Later even staunch Whigs, according to Sir Walter Scott, thought it right to call Charles Edward not the Pretender but the Chevalier.[9]

French court, and such a small force would have impressed neither of them. Outside the North East, where the Episcopalians were strong, few adherents were gained in the Scottish Lowlands. The towns and the Presbyterian clergy were hostile. The Chevalier's support was some 70 per cent Episcopalian and 30 per cent Roman Catholic; only three Catholic clan leaders joined him. In Edinburgh the Prince could not even raise a regiment; he secured just 137 recruits. During his six weeks in the capital his army grew, but the Skye lairds whose accession to his cause would have enabled an earlier invasion, remained impervious to Preston Pans and his appeals, and the French still hesitated, sending only ammunition, guns, money and a few 'advisers'.[11]

In 1745 Jacobite support was everywhere much weaker than it had been thirty years earlier; the Prince's army was always less than half the size of that which had fought in 1715. The Chevalier had too little money to remain in the capital, where without courting unpopularity by imposing new taxes there was no more finance to be raised. The only available choices were to invade England or to gather more support in the Highlands and from France before returning to Edinburgh. The issue was debated at a council on October 31. The case against invasion, favoured by Lord George Murray and most of the clan leaders, was the reluctance of many Highlanders to fight far from home and the diminutive size of their army: 5000 men seemed far too few to defeat a Hanoverian army more than six times larger without massive help from France and from the English Jacobites, of which there had been no visible sign. The case for invasion was that it would precipitate a rising by the English Jacobites, which would in turn precipitate a French landing on the south coast of England. Charles, who strongly favoured an English expedition, insinuated that he was assured of substantial support from both English Jacobites and a French army. Even so he won by only one vote, and the price he paid was heavy. The dissimulation that enabled him to win at Edinburgh ensured he lost at Derby.[12]

The Jacobite advance from Edinburgh to Derby was marked by speed of march, scrupulous treatment of non-combatants, the brilliant generalship of Lord George Murray, apathetic resistance by the English and an ominous absence of Jacobite recruits.

Invasions not being Sunday school outings, some depredations were inevitable. But, contrary to the horror stories put out by Fielding and other subsidised propagandists, Highland behaviour on the way to Derby was almost exemplary and certainly very much better than that of James II's non-invading army on its way to the South West in 1685 or of the Dutch soldiers brought over to aid the Hanoverians against Charles Edward. The only troops that behaved similarly well were William III's invaders in 1688. The Jacobites were not violent to non combatants. Women were not raped, houses were not looted, food was paid for, not plundered; the invading army's observance of the game laws was, however, even less rigorous than that of the local inhabitants, and some deer were illegally shot. Fielding later retracted, and even the *London Gazette* admitted that 'the rebels behaved tolerably well in the march southwards'.[13]

Conducting the march with unfailing foresight and precision, while showing a concern for the welfare of his troops not shared by his opponents, save Ligonier, Lord George Murray outmanoeuvred the Duke of Cumberland and would no doubt have done the same to Marshall Wade, had that venerable and reluctant warrior ever managed to get close enough to be outwitted.

The British ministry was divided, and the King was hostile to its larger faction, the Pelhams. The Government was so ill-prepared that the militia could not be raised and legally paid. The defect could only be cured by Parliament (which with George II in Hanover could not be summoned) and when an act to remove the original defect was eventually passed, it was so badly drafted that it created a similar one. Despite the legal problems some militia were mustered, but those of Cumberland, Westmoreland and Lancashire were all stood down without firing a shot. The Lord Lieutenant of Lancashire regarded his militia as a body 'in all respects . . . very unfit for service', and stood it down in order to prevent its arms falling into the hands of the enemy – the ultimate confession of military futility.[14]

Resistance to the Highland army was minimal. Carlisle was captured with the loss of two dead, and Lancaster was initially taken by a dozen Hussars. Towns paid the public monies over to Jacobite quartermasters without demur; as a result the London government paid for the Jacobite army, and resort to unpopular methods of extorting money was rendered unnecessary. Unlike Cope in his march to the Highlands, the Jacobite army was subjected to no harrassment from soldiers or civilians. As the rebels approached Cheshire, Lord Cholmondeley could find no 'gentlemen of estate' to help defend it. So far from Wade's advice to fire on the invaders from every hedge being followed, not a single hedge was manned.[15]

Early in the rebellion Henry Pelham, the premier, complained of the 'languidness' of his supporters and the lack of zeal to defend the regime, and at the end of August Hardwicke was worried by the general 'indifference and deadness'. After Preston Pans addresses of loyalty to the throne flooded in. Associations were formed, subscriptions were opened and, with the militia militarily and politically unreliable, other local levies were raised. In a loyal address the House of Lords called on Divine Providence to give success to the King's armies, assuring George II that they would hazard their estates and their lives in defence of his 'sacred person': in the event they decided to leave it to Divine Providence. So far from hazarding their lives, the aristocracy and the gentry decamped. In Newcastle Wesley found the gentry flying southward. The Earl of Derby felt 'at liberty to save myself' by fleeing to London, 'the common asylum of the nation'. The town of Derby was no more militant. When asked to defend it, 'not one man would stir.' One rich merchant did not feel safe until he reached Holland. The new levies were little better than the militia. So discreet were the Duke of Devonshire's Derbyshire Blues that they preferred to keep at least one town between them and the Scots. Ordered by the Duke to move towards the rebels, they 'to a man refused him'; they even fled from 'a herd of horned cattle' which they mistook for the enemy.[16]

But if English resistance to the Prince was, as the Lord Chancellor admitted, remarkably 'faint', English support for him was scarcely visible. The English, indeed, were indifferent. Few were ready to fight for a German Lutheran King and the Whig oligarchy; fewer still were ready to fight for an Italian-Polish-Scottish Catholic Prince and the the Highland clans. When apparent well-wishers were invited to join the Highland army, they replied that 'they did not understand fighting'. The excuse was true. England was a disarmed country – the regime was too unpopular for it to risk arming the people – and there was little incentive to brave the treason laws by joining the Jacobites. The 'Fifteen' had not been forgotten.[17]

Nevertheless about '200 disorderly persons proclaimed the Pretender King in Ormskirk'; they were quickly suppressed by the local Protestants. Another 200 men joined the Prince's colours in Manchester, though even that recruitment did not signify enthusiastic support among a population of 30,000. O'Sullivan, the most disastrously incompetent of the Pretender's Irish sycophants, had expected at least 1500 to enlist. Thirty-nine men volunteered at Preston. Elsewhere recruits came in handfuls or not at all. One border laird tried to join, but missed the army and returned home. Three men enrolled from Northumberland; of the four from Cumberland, one was too ill to fight, another deserted and a third was a spy. Two men joined from Wales, and there were three volunteers in Derby. If the Jacobite invasion had occurred in 1740-41, after two very bad harvests and with Walpole still in power, it would probably have been far better received; by 1745 Walpole was gone, and the last four harvests had all been good.[18]

At a council in Carlisle the Prince claimed to have letters from English Jacobites promising to join him at Preston. That was enough to gain the acquiescence of those like Lord George Murray who favoured return to Scotland where the Hanoverians had retaken Edinburgh. At Preston, unabashed by his Carlisle claims proving unfounded, Charles Edward again claimed to have pledges of support from English and Welsh Jacobites, citing in particular Sir Watkin Williams Wynn. In the Manchester council he tried a variation, attributing the non-appearance of this support to the absence of a French invasion, an omission which would be repaired by a French landing on December 9th. An explanation was certainly necessary. Contrary to his assurances, not one prominent Jacobite had joined him. Whatever their enthusiasm for 'the King over the water', the English Jacobites were not prepared to help his son on dry land.[19]

Remarkably, the Prince did virtually nothing to turn his successive deceptions of his followers into truth. So far from possessing promises of support from English Jacobites, Charles Edward never succeeded in making contact with them. Even without the incentive to vindicate his promises, the persuasion of his English supporters to leave their country houses to join him should have been his most pressing task. Instead, he sent one message to sympathisers in Northumberland and wrote just two letters, to Lord Barrymore and Sir Watkin Williams Wynne, neither of which reached its intended destination.[20] The Chevalier's march through England was thus characterised by the same frivolity as his arrival in Scotland. Then he had landed without a French army; now he did not try to gain an English one.

Derby

Lord George Murray's feint to the west having sent Cumberland the wrong way, the Highland army entered Derby on December 4. It was now only 130 miles from London and nearer than the Duke. When the news reached the capital, 'Black Friday', according to Fielding, was a 'day of confusion which God will, I hope, never suffer to have its equal in this kingdom'. Philip Yorke wrote to his brother, Cumberland's ADC, that London's alarm was much increased by the news of French embarkation at Dunkirk, adding that the 'same terror but in a higher degree' had spread 'throughout the kingdom'.[21]

But already the Highland army had decided to retreat, a decision backed by Charles's entire council except himself. At Edinburgh the Prince had by one vote persuaded his followers to invade England, and at Carlisle and again at Preston to continue south, by his promises of French and English help. At Manchester, when there was again support for retreat, Lord George Murray had suggested they should continue through Derbyshire to give the French and the English Jacobites their last chance to act rather than talk. Between Manchester and Derby neither France nor the English Jacobites had done anything to suggest help was imminent. Virtually none of

Charles's council at Edinburgh would have considered embarking on the southern adventure if they had known they were going to be on their own throughout. They expected to be the initiators of an English rising and a French invasion. Instead they found themselves the only rising and the only invasion. Deep inside enemy territory, with foreign help a chimera, with no English Jacobite hand raised except to toast 'the King over the water', with three Hanoverian armies in the field against them, each of them bigger than the Jacobite army, retreat seemed the only sane course.

Lord George Murray and his supporters have been much criticised for forcing the retreat from Derby. Granted, the argument runs, that Charles's adventure was a gamble from the start, they should either have refused to leave Edinburgh in the first place or been ready at Derby to continue south; by then insisting on withdrawal they abandoned the gamble just when they were on the point of winning.[22]

This criticism ignores Charles' deceit. Ordinary gambling at roulette is one thing; that in effect was what the Chevalier was doing. In Edinburgh he told the French envoy that in two months he would either be King of England or ruined. Gambling at roulette when the wheel has been tampered with or the croupier is crooked is quite another; that was the position of his followers. Lord George Murray and the clan leaders had been induced to gamble by the Prince's bogus assurances of outside help. If at Edinburgh they had been convinced by genuine arguments that an invasion of England was the best strategy, at Derby they might well have decided differently. But their discovery that they had been tricked, that the Prince's assurances of help from the English Jacobites were worthless, that he was not even in contact with them, and that he had no firm knowledge of French plans could have led to no other decision than to return home. The council's verdict at Derby was predetermined by the Pretender's deceptions at Edinburgh, Carlisle and Preston.[23]

All the same, however wrong the Prince had been at Edinburgh, he may have been right at Derby. Some contemporaries thought (and some historians still think) that he was the best of the Jacobite strategists.[24] Yet Charles's resolve to march on London was the product not of deep strategic insight but of what Scott called his 'obstinate adherence to what he had once determined on'. A reckless adventurer,* as Lord George Murray recognised, he wanted to continue his gamble, and ignorant of England and of war he could not judge the odds. At Derby, as later at Culloden, he assumed that the British army would not fight against their lawful prince; and he

---

* The word 'adventurer' did not have the same pejorative connotation that is has today. In 'Waverley', Scott has Charles Edward referring to himself as 'a solitary adventurer'.[25]

still believed at Derby that the English Jacobites would flock to his banner. Both assumptions were naive illusions, not reasoned assessments. The Prince's wish to push on to London demonstrates not his pre-eminence as a military strategist but his eagerness always to give battle – which occasionally accorded with military realities. If he was right at Derby, he was right by chance.[26]

Whether an advance towards London would have landed Charles Edward in St James' Palace or, as Lord Elcho told him,[27] in Newgate gaol within a fortnight, would have been decided by the rival armies. But there were three other potential forces which might have affected the result by material help or violence: France, the English Jacobites and London itself.

France

The Pretender's assurances that he would be given decisive French help were nearer the truth than he knew. On October 30 Louis XV had at last decided on an invasion of England by 6000 men. Although Charles Edward's unfounded claims were thus given some retrospective justification by later French decisions, these nevertheless confirmed his irresponsibility in going to Scotland without prior promises of French help. A French invasion of England could not now be mounted in time to coincide with his own. The only significant French assistance before Derby was the sending to Scotland of 800 men of the Royal Scots under Lord George Drummond.[28]

Very probably French staff work was not capable of mounting a successful landing. Nevertheless the French seriously intended to invade England; they were not merely trying to distract English attention from the Jacobite army. Their plan, unlike that of 1744, was to land on the south coast. On December 12 the Duke of Newcastle wrongly thought a French landing was imminent, and on the following day, the second 'Black Friday', panic in London was only a little less, wrote Fielding, than 'that which had seized us the Friday before'. But by December 18, the day planned for the invasion, both the weather and the news had turned unfavourable: the wind changed and Richelieu, the French Commander, learned of the retreat from Derby. Discouraging as that undoubtedly was, it did not lead to the calling off of the invasion. Events at sea did that.[29]

Unlike the Hanoverian generals the English naval commander, Admiral Vernon, was energetic, far-sighted and resourceful, a combination as disturbing to the Admiralty as it was disheartening to the French. In consequence Vernon was replaced, but not before he had prevented the invasion. In four engagements Vernon worsted the French, and when the wind turned again to the south west from December 20-23 Richelieu was too demoralised to take advantage of it. The expedition was not formally abandoned, but once again English sea power had saved the country from invasion.[30]

But even a successful invasion on December 18, the earliest possible day, would have been too late to aid the Jacobite army on its march south from Derby. In any case the French decision to mount an invasion of England badly damaged the Chevalier. If, instead, Louis XV had sent troops and money to him in Scotland in August or September, he would have transformed the Prince's military position and probably given him victory. A little help at the right time would have done Charles Edward far more good than massive help that could only arrive too late or not at all. The only useful result of the French invasion threat was to aid his retreat from Derby. But then, as Lord Chesterfield said at the time, the Pretender was for the European powers 'only the occasional tool of their politics, not the real object of their care'.[31]

The English Jacobites

The second possible source of aid was the English sympathisers of the Stuart cause. Yet even more than in 1715 the English Jacobites lay dormant. One would have imagined, wrote Smollett, 'that all the Jacobites of England had been annihilated'. Not a single magnate or MP joined the rebels. Not one of them even sent Charles Edward either money or arms. They merely pressed for a French landing near London.[32]

Whatever their words, the actions of the English Jacobites were in support of the regime. The Jacobite leader in the Commons, Sir John Hynde Cotton, remained in the government and presented a loyal address from his constituency. Sir Watkin Williams Wynne, who refused money to Jacobite agents in 1743 and 1745, gave the Denbighshire Association £100 to defend George II. The most overtly Jacobite action of another leading supporter was to plant a clump of Scotch firs on his highest ground in Oxfordshire. When Charles Edward proclaimed attendance at the 'Elector of Hanover's' Parliament to be an overt act of treason and rebellion, the English Jacobites preferred treason to the Stuarts to suspected disloyalty to the Hanoverians and duly came to Westminster. Writing to Lord Barrymore in November, the Prince expressed the hope that his Lancashire friends would join him when he arrived in the county, for 'now', he justifiably insisted, 'is the time or never'. The English Jacobites plumped for never.[33]

Of course the English Jacobites, like the Scottish chieftains, had stressed the need for a French invasion of England before a rising, and in 1745 there had not yet been such an invasion. But whether they would have greeted an invasion by Richelieu and the French any more actively than they greeted one by their rightful Prince and the Scots is highly questionable.

Admittedly Newcastle, the Secretary of State, had claimed six years earlier that if a Spanish force of 4000 or 5000 regular troops had been landed they would have been joined by a large 'number of the disaffected', making it very difficult 'for us to support our government at home'. But the only way Newcastle could defend the Government's failure to send enough soldiers to the West Indies was to emphasise the danger of insurrection at home. The testimony from the other side is similarly suspect. A Jacobite agent wrote in 1740 that 'the English Jacobite will not fail to join such troops as the King of France shall send'. But the Jacobites, as the Bishop of Chichester observed, were perennially optimistic, and their agents particularly so.[34]

The conduct of the English Jacobites in the years 1743-5 surely provides a better indication of how they would have behaved after a French invasion than the interested estimates of their opponents and their friends. On the face of it, after all, there was no more reason for the English Jacobites to be any more enthusiastic about a French invasion by Marshal Saxe than a Scottish invasion by the Pretender's son; indeed rather less. Patriotic emotions in favour of the government were more likely to be aroused by the invasion of a French army, even if led by a Protestant, than by a Scottish one, even when led by a Catholic. The English Jacobites' apathy and fright throughout the 'Forty-five' strongly suggests that they would have done nothing if the French had landed in Kent. Sensibly, they would have waited until London had been captured before rushing to salute the victor. But however understandable was their decision not to join the Jacobite invaders, their failure even to make contact with the Prince indicates that they were only a stage army. Besides, they had already displayed their fighting qualities in 1743-4, when Cotton and others had objected to a French invasion in January 1744 on the grounds that it would be too cold to take the field. Both literally and metaphorically the English Jacobites were what Tom Paine in a later context condemned as 'summer soldiers'.[35]

Yet much of the Tory party was permeated with Jacobite sentiment. Excluded from office by the Hanoverians, it could hardly have failed to view with nostalgia the dynasty under which it had enjoyed milk and honey or to flirt with an expedient that might lead it out of the wilderness. But except for a tiny minority, such flirtation did not extend to rebellion or civil war; it was mere foreplay or fantasy. The Tory objective was a return to office, and Jacobitism was one option which was intermittently pursued. It was something like the reversionary interest, an important element of politics under the later Stuarts and the Hanoverians, whereby excluded politicians gathered round the heir to the throne to make their opposition 'loyal' and to further their careers when the reigning monarch died.

There was, however, one crucial difference between the Jacobite and the Hanoverian reversionary interest. The Hanoverian heir would in the ordinary course of events inherit; his adherents could afford to wait. A Stuart restoration on the other hand could not occur in the ordinary course of events. From the Pretender's 1714 decision not to change his Church onwards, a peaceful Stuart accession was never feasible; so just waiting would get the Jacobites nowhere. Jacobitism, in the serious sense of promoting a Stuart restoration, involved the use of violence. A rebellion, a foreign invasion, a *coup d'état* or some combination of the three was essential. Yet neither in 1715 nor in 1745 were the English Jacobites prepared to risk violence. They willed the end, but rejected the only possible means.

Hence their Jacobitism was not serious. Like Dr Johnson's in the next reign, it was more of a pose than a conviction. It merely legitimised their dissent, giving form and expression to their disaffection. The legitimising notion of the traditional 'moral economy' justified for food rioters a measure of violence in order to obtain food at a price they could afford; for most English Jacobites the legitimising notion of traditional hereditary right did not justify the far greater violence necessary to procure a Stuart restoration. Jacobitism was worth many a toast and even an intrigue here and there, but it was not worth the sacrifice of life and estates. Apart from duelling, the English aristocracy and gentry had lost the habit of using violence. When Charles Edward came to England, the Tory Member for Oxford, Thomas Rowney, who was reputed to have drunk the Pretender's health 500 times, was so frightened that for the first time in his life he ordered his chaplain to pray for King George; Gibbon's father likewise panicked. The extent to which the Tory party was Jacobite is a fascinating if not mystical question, but in the sole sense that is here relevant – readiness to use violence, the only possible way of restoring the Stuarts – it clearly was not Jacobite. No prominent Tory did anything at all.[36]

Passive or sentimental, as opposed to serious, Jacobitism solved the problem of how to react to two unappetising alternatives. Probably many Tories largely shared Hume's view of the relative merits of the Hanoverians and the Stuarts. Both had much to be said against them, Hume thought, and he came down in favour of the Hanoverians because, being in possession, they had usage on their side and because the Stuarts were Roman Catholics. Passive Jacobitism enabled the Tories to act accordingly: while theoretically favouring the Stuarts and avoiding attachment to the unattractive Hanoverians and the corrupt Whig regime, they could in practice maintain the existing order and avoid any threat to their religion or their property.[37]

English Jacobitism was thus fundamentally different from the Scottish variety. There was obviously no English counterpart to the nationalism of the Scottish Jacobites, since that was fuelled by English 'imperialism'. Again, most Scottish Jacobites were Episcopalians not Roman Catholics, but because of their dislike of the Presbyterian establishment their attachment to the Stuarts was not at odds with their religious convictions. For the great majority of English Jacobites, in contrast, their political support of the firmly Roman Catholic Stuarts was in direct opposition to their own strong Anglican prejudices. Such a fundamental contradiction between religion and politics, which did not exist in Scotland, naturally inhibited decisive action. Finally the Scottish view of hereditary right was more clear cut than the English. Lord George Murray was 'out' (i.e. rebelled) three times – in 1715, 1719 and 1745 – because he was convinced that the 'setting aside of the Royal line was an act of the highest injustice'. Insofar as the English Tories were Jacobite, that was less because the Hanoverians were the illegitimate 'Royal line' than because they were exceedingly dislikeable and only employed Whigs. As more than one Tory MP admitted, it was proscription that made them Jacobites.[38]

The English (and Welsh) Jacobites had, of course, strong practical reasons for lying low in 1745: they were not military, they had few arms, the risks were great and the French had not arrived. Yet they had long known that they had become civilianised, the shortage of arms was nothing new, the risks of treason had always been high, and the French were much more likely to arrive if they saw that the English Jacobites had risen.[39]

All in all it was less practical reasons than the intrinsic nature of their Jacobitism – what Flora MacIvor called their 'lukewarm adherence' – that kept the English Jacobites out of the field. In itself their attitude was sensible, civilised and admirably non violent, but for anyone like Forster in 1715 or the Prince thirty years later who took their words as a guide to their probable behaviour it was disastrously deceptive. Charles Edward would never have got anything from them, until he had won. The Frenchman, who warned Louis XV in 1744 that the English Jacobites were good for nothing but ruining themselves and other people, was wrong in only one respect: they were careful not to ruin themselves.*[40]

---

* They were little abashed by their inglorious role in 1745. Two years afterwards, Williams Wynn conveyed to the Prince the wish of his 'loyal subjects' to 'exert themselves more in deed than in words' in support of a foreign invasion, ascribing their earlier failure more to lack 'of concert and unanimity than of real zeal and dutiful attachment'. 'I shall do for the Welsh Jacobites,' Charles aptly remarked, 'what they did for me; I shall drink their health.'[41]

London

On Black Friday, December 6, the City was struck with an 'extraordinary panic', and in the 'great consternation' merchants started packing. Like the country gentry in the northern counties they would have speedily decamped, had the rebels continued south from Derby. In that event, the news that the lawyers had formed themselves into a regiment with the Lord Chief Justice as their colonel and had offered themselves as a royal bodyguard while the King was at Finchley, a proposal which amid much derision was rejected by George II, would neither have stayed their departure nor discouraged the Jacobite army. Even before Black Friday, London was anything but a confident and reliable bastion of the Hanoverian regime. Despite cavalcades to St James's Palace to demonstrate loyalty and pledges by bankers to support the public credit, the City had long been hostile to the ministry, and large sums of money were rumoured to have been raised for the Jacobite cause.[42]

Lord George Murray argued at Derby that, even if they reached London, 4500 men would not make a great figure 'if the mob was against the affair'. Thirty years earlier the London mob had been strongly Jacobite. By 1745 its general hostility to the government took a different form. Jacobite feeling was still widespread, and during the rebellion nearly a hundred people were arraigned for disaffection. But Jacobitism seems to have been strong chiefly among the Irish and Roman Catholic population. The government disseminated much anti-Popish propanganda, and Fielding revived his anti-Popish play *The Old Debauchers* as well as writing a pamphlet whose title gives its tone: *The Devil, the Pope and the Pretender*. It was easy to play on anti-French and anti-Catholic feeling. The Pretender, said one paper, 'comes from *Rome* to protect the *English Church*, from *France* to defeat *English Liberty*, a papist to protect protestants!' Could there be, it continued, a 'more insulting drollery'? This potent line had its effect. When some Jacobite prisoners who had been captured on a French ship were marched through the City to the Tower, they were nearly torn to pieces by a mob they found more frightening than the Battle of Dettingen. The officers of the Prince's Manchester regiment who were captured at Carlisle were pelted on their arrival in London. And on the night the news of Culloden reached the capital, Smollett and his companion were afraid to speak in case their Scottish accents provoked the 'insolence' of the mob.[43]

Even so, the authorities took elaborate precautions to deal with expected Jacobite tumults and risings, and Pitt later wondered if in the event of a Jacobite victory 'the spirit of the population would not have taken a very different turn'. London Jacobitism had markedly waned but the King was still unpopular. Probably, therefore, the best guess is that Lord George Murray's fears were unjustified and that the divided ministry could not have rallied the capital. Almost certainly the London mob would have done little to help or hinder the Jacobite cause until it was victorious. Then, like the English Jacobites and many Whigs, they would have rushed to acclaim it.[44]

So, France, the English Jacobites and London would merely have consolidated the Stuart restoration, had it been achieved. They would have done nothing to decide the outcome of a Jacobite advance on London. The issue lay entirely with the troops in the field.

Of the three Hanoverian armies, Wade's at Wetherby was too far away and too slow to have affected the issue before the Prince had reached London or been defeated by the other armies. The second, Cumberland's army, was exhausted, and the Duke of Richmond, who was on Cumberland's staff, feared that the Prince would get to London before them. Probably less than half of it could have got to Northampton before the Scots. There the Highland army, whose morale and physical condition were both superior, would surely have defeated it, but, as Lord George Murray pointed out, their own casualties would have been heavy and the remnants of Cumberland's force would have joined the third Hanoverian army outside London. Some 4000 regular troops were already waiting at Finchley, as well as the City Trained Bands. The latter would probably not have withstood a Highland charge, departing the field at least as precipitately as the regular soldiers at Preston Pans and Falkirk. And if Hogarth is to be even half-believed, the Guards were not at the peak of their disciplined efficiency. Yet they had sworn neither to give nor receive quarter, and it is anybody's guess whether the rebel army could have defeated them. To have pressed on from Derby would consequently have been a gigantic military gamble. But it might well have come off. Once the Prince reached the capital, resistance would probably have crumbled, and Tories, Whigs and the army would have sworn allegiance to the newly-proclaimed King.[45]

Prelude to Culloden

Whatever the might-have-beens, the decision to retreat looks disastrous in retrospect because it appears to have led straight to defeat of the Jacobite cause. Yet it need not have done so; it was not the Derby decision but the Chevalier's reaction to it that led to the disaster at Culloden. The Prince announced that, since he was accountable to nobody but to God and his father, he would 'no longer either ask or accept advice', words which would not have augured well for the future of limited monarchy under a Stuart restoration; in exile the last Stuarts learned less than the last Bourbons. The Prince's resentment was natural enough, but he had chiefly himself to blame. Long before Derby he should have taken serious steps to contact the English Jacobites, or at the very least made convincing efforts before the council to convert the clan leaders to the feasibility of an advance to London. He had, after all, known since Carlisle, if not since Edinburgh, how his chief officers felt.[46]

Excusable or not, the Prince's post-Derby pique ensured that the 'Forty-five' ended, as it began, as a largely Irish adventure. Charles Edward's distrust of the Scots led him to consult chiefly his Irish coterie, who told him what he wanted to hear and encouraged him to behave as his own general. This was foolish as well as fatal when he had in Lord George Murray one of the best generals in Europe; and it was all the more galling to the clan leaders who had sacrificed everything and faced the gallows if captured, whereas the Irish, who had had little to lose in the first place, were as officers in the French army in no danger of execution if taken prisoner.[47]

The Prince accepted, however, Lord George Murray's offer to conduct the retreat, and Murray commanded the rearguard throughout. Hindered by the Prince's obstructive petulance and by his insistence on leaving a garrison in Carlisle, a decision which made no strategic sense and condemned the Manchester regiment to a grisly end, and dogged by dreadful weather, but helped by old 'Grandmother Wade's' funeral tread and by Newcastle's stream of contradictory orders to Cumberland, Lord George regained Scottish soil on December 20 with his army intact. Even a fully disciplined army might have disintegrated on such a retreat. Murray had again demonstrated his superior generalship; in the march to and from Derby he lost only about two dozen men – many fewer than Wade lost in five days without ever seeing his enemy. And if the Highlanders' depredations were greater on the way back than on the way down, they were often under considerable provocation, and in general their conduct was astonishingly good, unlike the Dutch troops in Wade's army who 'plundered everywhere with a heavy hand'.[48]

The skirmish at Clifton where, by dint of ignoring an ill-judged order from the Prince to withdraw, Lord George Murray had inflicted a sharp reverse on Cumberland, should have warned the Hanoverians against over-confidence. Yet when at Falkirk on January 17 General Hawley, the new British commander in Scotland with an army of 8500 regular troops, was told that the Highlanders, now some 8000 strong, were on the march to the high ground above his camp, he was loath to interrupt his enjoyable lunch with the Jacobite Lady Kilmarnock and did not move until it was too late. Lord George Murray who commanded the Scottish right routed the English left, but the Prince had ignored Murray's requests to appoint a commander for his left wing, which was outflanked. Despite the setback on the left, Falkirk was a clear victory for the rebels. Over 300 of Hawley's army were killed and some 500 captured (including Hawley's hangmen) while the rebel losses were about fifty or sixty. Only Charles's faulty dispositions prevented the victory being decisive. With Lord George Murray, not the Prince, in command, the Hanoverian army would almost certainly have been shattered and the Chevalier the master of Scotland. Charles could have rectified his mistake had he pursued Hawley and taken Edinburgh; the argument for taking the offensive was far more clear cut than at Derby, yet, though urged to do so, the Prince refused and insisted instead on continuing the useless siege of Stirling.[49]

The Chevalier's effective assumption of control had so far led, apart from several minor blunders, to three major mistakes: the first had caused the destruction of the Manchester regiment left trapped in Carlisle; the second and third had saved the Hanoverian army from destruction at Falkirk and afterwards. The Prince may well have been right, however, in opposing his generals' wish to retire to the Highlands, even though that retreat was followed by a series of successes, which strongly suggest that Culloden was far from inevitable. In any case Charles's next two major mistakes caused the destruction of his own army and the defeat of the Jacobite cause. With Cumberland advancing on Inverness by the coast road from Culloden, the moment to gain time and inflict serious casualties was when the Hanoverian army was performing the difficult operation of fording the River Spey. The Jacobite commander had up to 2000 men lining the west bank, a strong natural position which could easily have been made even stronger. But instead of trying to disrupt the crossing, the Jacobites retreated without firing a shot.[50]

Smollett concluded that the Jacobites were 'under a total infatuation'. Certainly that seems the cause of the Prince's second major mistake. He chose to stand and fight at Drummossie Moor, Culloden, the worst possible place at the worst possible time. The battleground had been chosen by his quartermaster general, O'Sullivan, who did not bother to reconnoitre alternatives or even his chosen field. Had O'Sullivan been on Cumberland's staff, he could not have served him better. Flat and open, Culloden was ideal for a regular army with its artillery and cavalry, and exactly the terrain for a guerrilla army to avoid at all costs. The choice of O'Sullivan and the Chevalier was all the more perverse in that there was a spot nearby, just across the Nairn Water, which was well suited to the needs of the Prince's army: steep and uneven, mossy and soft, the rebels would have been sheltered from artillery, cavalry would have been of little use, and there were few places where Cumberland could have crossed the water.[51]

But Charles Edward would not listen to Lord George Murray and other officers, and refused to wait until reinforcements arrived. His determination to fight which was always his attitude – except at Clifton and after Falkirk, when he was wrong – was, as at Derby, not the result of an intelligent assessment but of delusions about his own invincibility and his enemies' unwillingness to fight him.

Having chosen a place which invited annihilation and a time when much of his army was absent, the Prince then proposed a night attack on Cumberland's camp at Nairn. Faced with disaster if a battle was fought on O'Sullivan's chosen field, Lord George Murray fell in with the plan which, if undeniably hazardous, was at least preferable to the alternative of being slaughtered on Drummossie Moor. When, however, they discovered that at least 2000 of their men had gone off in search off food and could not be fetched back in time, Lord George and the other officers wanted to call off the attack. Charles, having insisted on sticking to the plan, ensured its failure by slowing the pace of the second column so that it fell way behind the vanguard commanded by Lord George Murray. The Prince then ordered Lord George to advance with the vanguard alone. An attack by 1200 men on 8000 would have been suicidal, even at night, but the delays had prevented an attack before daylight and Murray could hear the shouts of fully alert English sentries. He therefore ordered a retreat.[52]

With the Prince's army now exhausted as well as starved, the case for moving to the favourable ground on the other side of Nairn Water was still more compelling than it had been the day before. The move would have given the Highlanders not only the advantage of ground, but also time for the 2000 absentees to return. Murray and the Scots saw that to fight where they were was sheer madness. As usual the Prince listened only to his Irish courtiers. Fatuously believing that the much larger Hanoverian army would run away from his own, which was 'half dead with hunger and fatigue', the Prince in his egotism condemned his troops to fight in O'Sullivan's chosen slaughterhouse. Lord George Murray was not alone in thinking that they were 'now putting an end to a bad affair . . .'[53]

The Prince did nothing either at or after Culloden to redeem his folly before it. He stood waiting for Cumberland to attack, while his army was being raked by the Duke's artillery. Well satisfied with the way things were going, Cumberland saw no need to move. His gunners were having a field day; their Highland targets were live but motionless. Eventually, prodded by Lochiel and Lord George, Charles ordered an attack. The Highlanders were as brave as ever. Some of them broke through Cumberland's front line, but his second was too strong for them. Cumberland's cannon 'made a frightful carnage', and soon the Highland army was in retreat, much of it in flight.

The Prince, who was supposed to be in command, played little part in the battle, and, evidently dazed by the onset of reality, played no part after it. He had not arranged a rendezvous in the event of defeat, and he showed little concern for the army he had deserted. The Highlanders could have continued the fight, as Lord George Murray wished. But three days later the Prince sent an order to the 1500 men at Ruthven under Murray: 'Let every man seek his own safety the best way he can'. He himself had already done so. Though he came much nearer success at the head of a far smaller rising than had Lord Mar in 1715, in the end Charles Edward, through his insistence on giving battle at Culloden where some 1500 to 2000 Jacobites were killed, was even more disastrous as a rebel leader. As Lord Lovat said, 'None but a mad fool would have fought that day.'*[54]

The end of the 'Forty-five'

In the eighteenth century, wars between regular armies were generally conducted in a gentlemanly manner. Armies, wrote Gibbon, were exercised by temperate and indecisive contests. The practice of murderously pursuing a routed amy had been abandoned. At the battle of Fontenoy, Lord Charles Hay of the First Guards, finding his battalion fifty paces away from the French Guards, took out his flask and drank to them; saluting with his hat, he invited them to fire first. Enemy wounded were cared for, and prisoners were treated well. The Duke of Cumberland, a brave but pompous young man – he was even younger than Charles Edward – had conformed to these rules in Flanders where his 'generosity and compassion to prisoners' was noted, and the Jacobites conformed to them in 1745. Cumberland, however, did not.[56]

Gentlemanly behaviour in war had of course strict limits. It did not often extend to the civilian population. 'War and pity,' it was held, 'did not go together', and almost any degree of violence was permissible. 'Never since the Goths,' a contemporary wrote of Frederick the Great in Moravia in 1741, 'has war been waged in such a fashion as this.' In Spain in 1702 the English were little better:

> The ravish'd nuns, the plunder'd town,
> The English honour now mispent;
> The shameful coming back, and little done.

* In the following year, after they had separately escaped to the continent, Charles asked his father to secure Lord George Murray 'in some castle' until his former general, who had sacrificed everything for the Stuart cause, justified himself for 'several demonstrative acts of disobedience, insolence and creating dissension'. The Old Pretender gently told his son that it was not a crime to differ from him. The Prince was not convinced.[55]

Raping and looting were common even when there had been no fighting, and hostages were frequently taken. In any case civilised restraint and gentlemanly behaviour did not extend to rebellion or civil war. In the American war the British government had few scruples about allowing their Red Indians to scalp the colonists, though the practice was denounced by Chatham, Burke and Wilkes.[57]

In 1745 the Jacobites were indisputably rebels, but to the Whigs they were even worse than that. A tiny army of ordinary soldiers could not possibly have reached Derby and given the government the fright of its life; only barbaric desperadoes could have managed such a feat. Determinedly ignoring the good behaviour of the Highland army, the Whigs chose to regard the Jacobites as savages who only understood the language of force and who had therefore to be taught a violent and unforgettable lesson. So in the end, as commonly happens on such occasions, the forces of 'civilisation' behaved like savages, and the 'savages' behaved like civilised human beings.

Not surprisingly the representatives of 'civilisation' and the 'savages' had very different methods of enforcing military discipline. For many years both before and after the 'Forty-five', discipline was maintained in the British army by hangings and ferocious floggings. One soldier was given 4000 lashes in 1727, having received 26,000 during the past fourteen years, and, as late as 1836, Wellington was still firmly in favour of military flogging. The years 1745-6 were no different from the others. Though popular with his own troops, the Duke of Cumberland was not much less violent to them than he was to the rebels[58]

As in the 'Fifteen', the Jacobites brought many clansmen into their ranks under duress, and the clans still had some barbarously old-fashioned habits – as when Charles could not prevent the eye for an eye execution of one clansman for the accidental shooting of another. Yet the Jacobite leaders dispensed with such aids to good order and military discipline as the noose and the cat-o'-nine-tails. Their discipline was humane but effective.[59]

Cumberland's conduct after Culloden has sometimes been excused as a natural sequel to the Highlanders' behaviour after Preston Pans. If the Duke had followed that example, however, there would have been little cause for complaint. After the rebels' lightning victory – estimates of the length of the battle vary from 4 to 10 minutes – the Highlanders for a brief period undoubtedly ran amuck and gave no quarter. But they were quickly brought under control by the Prince and Lord George Murray; Scott's account of the saving of an English officer's life by Edward Waverley was based on fact. Moreover Charles Edward gave orders for the relief of the wounded of both armies, preserving, wrote John Hume, a historian who took part in the 'Forty-five' on the Hanoverian side, 'every appearance of moderation and humanity'.* That was not an appearance that Cumberland ever gave during the 'Forty-five'. The prisoners at Preston Pans were well treated, Lord George Murray finding them quarters and providing them with food and drink of his own. Out of General Cope's army of about 2500, some 300 were killed and 1500 were taken prisoner. Some of them were badly wounded, but the high proportion of prisoners to killed testifies to Jacobite restraint. Indeed, if anybody behaved badly, it was the English prisoners, most of whom broke their parole.[61]

Cumberland's brutality thus did not have the excuse of being retaliation, and it well predated Culloden. When the rebels were in retreat from Derby, he was not able to kill prisoners, he regretfully told Newcastle, because the Jacobites held many of his army captive, but he had 'encouraged the country people to do it'. Before Carlisle surrendered, the Duke had four prisoners hanged to show the garrison what they might expect. Already he was more bloodthirsty than his father. George II was prepared to grant the rebels transportation to the West Indies; Cumberland hoped they would meet with no mercy. His allies in Scotland, the Prince of Hesse and his Hessian troops, declined to fight the Jacobite army without a cartel for prisoners. Cumberland would have nothing to do with such a civilised proposal. He preferred 'military execution'. When some of his own Highlanders 'absolutely refused' to plunder the houses of rebels, Cumberland, instead of reconsidering his attitude to Highlanders, seems to have regarded their rebuff as just another manifestation of Highland depravity.[62]

One of Cumberland's generals, Hawley, was known to his troops as 'The Hangman' and occasionally, with pardonable confusion of roles, as the 'Lord Chief Justice'. A great believer in the therapy of the gallows, Hawley liked killing both on and off the battlefield. His first act on taking up his command in Scotland was to set up gibbets in Edinburgh and Leith; he then refused to have them removed after the hanged rebels were dead. At Cumberland's dinner table the conversation turned to the honour due to the beautiful Lady

---

* At the time there was little criticism of Highland behaviour at Preston Pans. Although that very Whig prelate, the Archbishop of York, heard that brave Englishmen had been butchered in cold blood, which he hoped would fuel 'national indignation', no complaints were made in accounts of the battle published in the *Gentleman's Magazine* or in the Yorke correspondence. At Clifton, on the other hand, the Highlanders were alleged to have shouted 'No quarter, murder them'; and according to Cumberland some English officers received wounds after they had been knocked down. However, as the skirmish took place in darkness, lasted only a few minutes and resulted in few casualties, the allegation – even if true – provided no excuse or precedent for Culloden.[60]

Mackintosh – 'Colonel Anne' – who had raised her clan, though her husband supported the government. 'Damn the woman,' Hawley belched, 'I'll honour her with a mahogany gallows and a silk cord!' The Jacobites' capture of his hangmen at Falkirk did not prevent him hanging some sixty of his soldiers who ran away from that battle. Hawley himself was not above pillage and theft, plundering Callendar House near Falkirk and stealing the valuable china and household effects of an Aberdeen woman who had supported the government. On his own principles, the 'Lord Chief Justice' should have hanged himself.[63]

The urge to slaughter was not confined to psychopathic generals. That polished embodiment of civilised good manners, Lord Chester-field, then the Lord Lieutenant of Ireland, did not subject his long-suffering son to instruction in the art of 'extermination'. He nevertheless recommended it for the Highlanders, advocating the starvation of 'the loyal with the disloyal'. Other less cultured men had similar views: Henry Pelham referred to the Highlanders as 'animals'; for General Ligonier they were 'those wild beasts'; for the Duke of Richmond merely 'vermin'. The proper fate for such creatures was clearly extinction by starvation, the sword or the gallows. Richmond looked forward to the destruction of the rebels rather than to their surrender, hoping to see them put to the sword and 'a great many hanged', while Joseph Yorke, Cumberland's ADC, hoped to 'extirpate the race if we are not stopped by lenity'.[64]

The policy of slaughter was thus decided upon well before the battle of Culloden, and indeed had been followed ever since Cumberland's arrival in Scotland. His conduct after Culloden saw three phases: the pursuit and the immediate aftermath of the battle; the following few days; and the subsequent mopping–up operations.

When the rebels turned and fled at Culloden, Cumberland's cavalry gave chase, doing 'excellent execution'. An eye-witness reported that for nearly four miles the ground was 'covered with dead bodies'. Major General Bland, Cumberland recorded with satisfac-tion, 'also made great slaughter and gave quarter to none but about fifty French officers and soldiers'. That this was to some extent done in hot blood provides some excuse, yet the blood cannot have been altogether hot, or the French would have been killed too. With very few exceptions, the officers made no attempt to restrain their men or save survivors. Not only the defeated soldiers were butchered. Those who had foolishly come out from Inverness to view the battle were indiscriminately cut down, and others who had merely been imprudent enough to live nearby were similarly slain together with their children.[65]

The atrocities committed by the infantrymen were less lethal in number but without excuse. Their blood was no longer hot.

Cumberland congratulated his troops still on the battlefield and gave them whisky and biscuits, before they massacred the wounded and dying. 'The moor was covered in blood,' wrote a Hanoverian officer, 'and our men, what with killing the enemy, dabbling their feet in blood, and splashing it about one another looked like so many butchers rather than Christian soliders.' They did not merely look like butchers. Yet it was the men's chaplains and officers, by failing to order them to behave like Christian soldiers, who were to blame for this post-prandial bloodbath. Unlike Charles Edward and Lord George Murray after Preston Pans, Cumberland made no effort to stop the carnage and afterwards expressed pleasure at it, while 'Lord Chief Justice' Hawley helped it on. An officer who tried to protect a wounded clansman was cursed by that gentleman: 'Damn you, Shaw! Do you mean to preserve the life of a rebel?' The wounded man was duly slaughtered. Not only did the Hanoverians, unlike the Jacobites at Preston Pans, make no attempt to tend the enemy wounded, Cumberland in the exhilaration of victory even neglected his own injured.[66]

That was not however the end of the brutality – brutality not only by the standards of a later day but by the standards of the time. Cumberland's urge to extirpate the rebels was not slaked by the battle and the pursuit. On the following day he was still issuing orders to give no quarter and was angry with officers who had different ideas of proper conduct. The order stated: 'A captain and 50 foot to march directly and visit all the cottages in the neighbourhood of the field of battle, and to search for rebels. The officers and men will take notice that the Public orders of the rebels yesterday was to give us no quarter.' Other detachments were sent on a similar errand. Attempts were once made to explain away Cumberland's order as meaning no more than that the soldiers should be wary of treacherous Highlanders who had been told to give them no quarter. But that was not how the order was taken at the time, nor is it what the words seem to mean. For the next two days, unless a wounded Jacobite was lucky enough to be found by an officer like Lord Boyd, who did not think battlegrounds should become abbatoirs, he was butchered.[67]

Cumberland and his army have been strongly defended against charges of 'systematic butchery'.[68] But if there was no systematic butchery, there must have been systematic disregard of Cumberland's wishes, and though there were certainly some officers and men chivalrous enough to ignore them, a wholesale turning of blind eyes to their commander's order seems improbable. Certainly those officers who were merciful to the rebels incurred the Duke's displeasure.[69]

These summary executions would not have been justifiable even if, as Cumberland claimed, the Jacobite generals had on their side

ordained that no quarter should be given. But it is virtually certain
that they gave no such order. Before Culloden the Jacobites had
waged civilised warfare, and there was no reason for them suddenly
to alter their army's behaviour. The words about giving no quarter
were not in Lord George Murray's orders for the battle: the only
written evidence for the allegation is an unsigned copy of those orders
in which the vital words have clearly been inserted by another hand.
Just possibly, it has been suggested, they were part of the written or
verbal orders for the aborted Highland night attack the night before
Culloden, since that was an attempt 'to kill the royal army as it lay
asleep by stabbing the soldiers with broadswords in cold blood'. Yet
there is little evidence for such a conjecture, and in any case the idea
that a dangerous night attack on a much larger army amounts to
killing 'in cold blood' is decidedly odd. Killing in cold blood and
seeking the advantage of surprise are two quite different things. To
be able to blame the enemy for initiating the policy of 'no quarter'
was highly convenient for Cumberland and his generals, and the
strong likelihood is that the alleged order was a Hanoverian invention
or forgery.*[70]

The harrying of the guilty and the innocent continued for months.
Government supporters who favoured moderation, such as the Lord
President, had their advice rejected, because Duncan Forbes, the
leading Scottish judge who had in fact done more to hold Scotland
for the Whigs than any other man, was 'as arrant Highland mad', in
Cumberland's words, as two other Scottish Hanoverians, Lords Stair
and Crawford. The Duke sent out detachments to search for the
Prince and 'to pursue and hunt out these vermin amongst their
lurking holes'. As well as killing rebels, that meant taking their cattle
and destroying their other possessions. The wrecking was not
confined to private houses. Lord Ancrum reported destroying 'two
Roman Catholic meeting-houses and five Episcopal', as well as a
couple of libraries, thereby beating another commander who only
managed four mass-houses and a Popish academy. The officer sent
to devastate Lochiel's house and grounds was told to kill as many
rebels as he could, 'since prisoners would only embarrass him'. Some
Lowland Scottish officers were similarly murderous, ignoring the

* Dr Speck thinks Cumberland could not have been guilty of forgery, because believing
  anyway in extirpating the rebels he did not need additional justification (an argument
  which sits uneasily with the contention that there was no 'systematic butchery'), and
  because 'a diabolical conspiracy' to fabricate false rebel orders would have been out of
  character. Yet Cumberland had been warned by Scotland's chief judge about the law,
  and however besotted he was with the sacred task of wiping out the rebels, an additional
  justification would not have been unwelcome. And as he did not draw the line at
  butchery, he might well not have drawn it at the lesser crime of connivance in forgery.
  All in all, however, the most likely explanation is that Cumberland was not responsible
  for the *canard* or forgery, but eagerly took advantage of it.[71]

protection warrants which a superior officer had granted to rebels who had surrendered their arms.[72]

As Culloden receded, the urge to kill and destroy did not weaken. Cumberland's policy became even harsher. The four raiding parties that he sent out from Fort Augustus at the end of May 'in order to root out the remainder of the rebels' surpassed their predecessors in savagery. Even loyal clans were brutally treated, having their cattle stolen and their women raped. The people, wrote an offficer, had to perish either by sword or famine – 'a just reward for traitors'.[73]

Conclusion

Call fire and sword and desolation
A godly thorough reformation . . .

The ferocious coercion of the Highlands was justified by pointing to the government's relative mildness after the 'Fifteen', though that had helped to pacify them for thirty years. 'An ill-judged lenity,' Cumberland believed, was 'the greatest cruelty.' He knew more about the second than the first, but the claim that he was preventing a further rebellion gave a useful excuse for savage repression. In fact the Highlands had already begun to change well before the 'Forty-five', and a further rising in favour of the Stuarts was scarcely conceivable, especially as the Highlanders thought they had been betrayed by the French once too often. Even in 1745 relatively few Highlanders were 'out'. Maybe Cumberland never realised that a majority of the Highland clans had not supported the Young Pretender; or that Charles's army was always less than half the size of his father's; or that an army of some 5000 was a very small proportion of the male Highland population of some 250,000. Maybe he did not even know that in 1745 there were more Scotsmen fighting for the government than for Charles Edward. More likely the Duke did not care. At any rate his successor, Lord Albemarle, who hated the Scots as such as he did, discovered that the chief effect of the government's severity was to stiffen Jacobite defiance.[74]

Cumberland, who 'was beaten', Carlyle later pointed out, 'by everybody that tried, and never beat anything, except some starved Highland peasants', was probably only a little more violent than most other Hanoverian generals would have been or, indeed, than politicians like Chesterfield and Richmond. Cumberland's successor advised Newcastle not to spare those Highlanders he had in his power because 'nothing but fire and sword [could] cure their cursed, vicious ways of thinking'. The bellicose Archbishop of York, echoing the Bishop of Exeter after Sedgemoor, was not notably more charitable

or Christian. While he hoped he was not 'a sanguinary man', he did
not think mercy was called for until the rebels had 'delivered up their
arms and their mock prince'. What a sanguinary man would have
advocated, he did not disclose.[75]

The Jacobite successes put the patricians in a panic, a state in which
as Disraeli knew they lost all dignity and much else besides.[76] In
addition any fear of earning public odium by wreaking savage
vengeance on the Jacobites was allayed by the prevailing anti-Scottish
sentiment, by the Highlanders being considered especially uncivilised
and by the reign of terror taking place in a region beyond the ken of
the English public. Above all there was no danger of retaliation. The
Hanoverians possessed overwhelming force; the Highlanders were
weak and disorganised, with no devoted foreign allies to oppose the
British government. So the government had nothing to fear from
either the Pretender or the mob. The normal restraints on
government violence were in abeyance, and there was nothing to
stop it spewing out over Scotland.

The sins of Hanoverian government should not all be heaped upon
the shoulders of the young Duke of Cumberland. The Whig
oligarchy should bear their share of the blame. Yet there was some
justice in Cumberland's being made the Hanoverian scapegoat when
the general attitude to his barbarity in Scotland changed. The
responsibility was his; he was the only man who could have
controlled the carnage, had he chosen to do so. Instead he encouraged
it. Unlike his adversary, Charles Edward, who was merciful to
traitors and vetoed plots to murder Cumberland or other members
of the Royal Family, the Duke never at any stage in Scotland
displayed one atom of mercy to his defeated enemy. Even his father
later admitted that 'William had been rough with them', while adding
that he had of course not 'gone there to please them'. Cumberland
well deserved his title of 'Butcher'.[77]

That he gained it so soon demonstrated how quickly attitudes
changed. Initially Culloden was greeted with great rejoicing, and
Cumberland was soon voted a hefty pension. But as early as May 1,
Lord Bury, who had been sent to London with news of the battle,
was asked if Cumberland had ordered no quarter to be given.
Satirical pieces appeared in the press asking what had happened to
the rebel wounded since apparently none had been taken prisoner and
suggesting the sterilisation of all Jacobite women. By the end of May
it was reported that in recognition of his services the Duke was to be
made a freeman of the Butchers' company.[78]

Cumberland favoured the transportation of whole clans, and the
Crown Solicitor, P.C. Webb, advocated branding the face of all
transported prisoners to prevent them returning. Both proposals
were deemed impracticable. There being too many prisoners to be

tried individually, those in the lowest category of 'common men' drew lots and only one in twenty were tried. The rest were pardoned on condition of agreeing to be transported for life. Since nearly all those in the lowest category who were put on trial had their sentence commuted to transportation, the luck of the draw made little difference. Many were able to show that they had been forced into the Jacobite army, but few escaped on that account. 936 were transported and 222 were banished. The conditions in prisons and in the hulks for those awaiting trial were even worse than those normally suffered in eighteenth-century England. Surgeon Minshaw gave the Commissioners for Wounded an horrific report of the stench, dirt and 'malignant fever' on one of the ships. The Commissioners may have gone as far as reading it but took no other action. Officially eight-eight people died in prison, but nearly all of another 684 unaccounted for must, unofficially, have perished there.[79]

There would have been far fewer executions but for the Prince's folly in ignoring his officers' advice to send the sixty-four British officers captured at Preston Pans to France. Had they been sent, many of the Scots condemned to death could have been exchanged, not executed. The French made an appeal for clemency which, as France held few English prisoners, could be safely rejected with anger and derision. Fielding hoped for moderation; and David Hume, complaining of the violence of his cousin, the Scottish solicitor general, advised him to seek the praise of 'humanity and moderation'. That was too much to expect. Eight officers and seven sergeants of the Manchester Regiment, the only English unit to be raised for the Pretender, were hanged, drawn and quartered, and three peers were beheaded. In all, 120 men were executed. That was about half the number that were judicially killed after Sedgemoor. But the toll then exacted by James II and Jeffreys had been with one exception the worst for 300 years, and the cruelty and klllings in Somerset after Monmouth's defeat were fortunately not comparable in extent to Cumberland's barbarism after Culloden. So, if the Government after the 'Forty-five' did not add a judicial massacre to all the others, they effortlessly avoided the perils of magnanimity. While Cumberland, of course, wanted the utmost severity, George II was pleased to see the end of 'this tedious affair'.[80]

The judicial process may have been a tedious affair, though less so perhaps for the King than for many others; the rebellion itself was not. Rather it was disturbing to contemporaries and astonishing to their successors. As Gibbon concluded, it did not 'reflect much honour on the national spirit'. Certainly few emerged from it with credit – Lord George Murray, Admiral Vernon and the King being obvious exceptions.[81]

From early in the eighteenth century, Britain was one of the two
great powers of Europe, yet twice in thirty years she was not far
from being overthrown by little more than a handful of Highlanders
enjoying minimal foreign help. Between 1700 and 1760 Britain
gained glittering military successes overseas, yet if James Edward had
had a Lord George Murray instead of Lord Mar as his general in 1715,
he would surely have deposed George I; and if Charles Edward had
been able to call on the resources available to his father he would
surely have toppled George II; even as it was the Highlanders always
won except at Culloden. The contrast between Hanoverian power
abroad and Hanoverian weakness at home was stark. 'Eight millions
of people,' Hume's verdict ran, 'might have been subdued and
reduced to slavery by five thousand . . .'[82]

Writing in *The True Patriot* at the time, Fielding put his verdict into
the mouth of Parson Adams, conjured up from the pages of *Joseph
Andrews*. Doubting if history could show anything comparable to 'six
or seven men landing in a great and powerful nation, in opposition
to the inclination of the people, in defiance of a vast and mighty
army' and making 'almost unbelievable progress', Adams affirmed
that the Highlanders' success was unaccountable from human means
and demonstrated the judgement of God against 'this sinful nation';
to redress it a total amendment of life was required.[83]

Whatever the sins of the nation, the sins or omissions of
Hanoverian England were laid bare. The regime did not crumble as
had James II's in 1688, but it evoked little active loyalty. Thirty years
of Hanoverian rule had turned the political, constitutional and
religious future of England into a spectator sport, in which the great
mass of the country felt no inclination to engage. 'The people,'
Halifax the Trimmer wrote of 1688, 'can seldom agree to move
together against a government, but they can to sit still and let it be
undone.'[84] He could have said the same of the 'Forty-five'. Even
though the Protestant Hanoverians had given none of the provocations of James II, even though the English were still fiercely anti-
papist, and even though the popish danger now came from the rebels,
the people sat very still. Its verdict on thirty years of Whig rule and
the new dynasty was that it was prepared to let both of them be
undone.

Part Two

POWERS AND GRIEVANCES

A state is a human community that (successfully) claims *monopoly of the legitimate use of physical force* within a given territory.

Max Weber[1]

The English state of the eighteenth century was not over-blessed with means to help maintain that monopoly. It wholly failed to curb the upper-class custom of duelling. Or rather, it did not try to do so, because most of those running the state did not disapprove of it. Indeed they themselves were among the duellists. Equally, in the eyes of many, the powers used by the government to contain grievances, to suppress those who were articulating them, to maintain social control and to get its own way were themselves grievances and largely illegitimate.

The problem with Weber's definition, of course, is the precise meaning of the word 'legitimate'. Like duellists, many rioters felt that their own use of force, or at least the threat of it, was morally legitimate in the face of injustice. This feeling was not confined to rioters; it was sometimes shared by those who were sent to enforce the law, and even on occasion by those who sent them. This section, marking a temporary break from chronology, looks at the grievances and forms of violence which prevailed for much of the period, and at the way in which the state sustained its position.

SIX

The Army and the Riot Act

The social history of nations is largely moulded by the forms and development of their armed forces, the primary aim of national organisation being common defence.

Sir Lewis Namier

This government is founded upon resistance; it was the principle of resistance that brought about the revolution . . . Is then passive obedience and non-resistance to be established by a law [the Riot Act] the most severe and the most arbitrary in England, and that under a government which owes its very being to resistance? . . . it is a scandal it should remain in our statute books.

William Pulteney MP, 1734

The characteristic of our own government at present is imbecility. The magistrates dare not call the Guards for fear of being hanged. The Guards will not come, for fear of being given up to the blind rage of popular juries.

Dr Johnson, 1776[1]

Putting down rebellion and fighting foreign enemies were not the army's only roles. Its other tasks were diverse. Troops were the chief enforcers of public order and, in the long-running war against smugglers, the chief protectors of the customs revenue. As well as their ordinary duties at the Royal Palaces and the Tower, the Guards were required to act as auxiliary customs officers in the London area, as auxiliary gamekeepers in the royal preserves, to guard Newmarket races and to keep the peace in the Haymarket Theatre whenever a ball was held there. Such general utility made the troops popular with the government; their performance of their most important duty – the restoration of public order – made them unpopular with many of the governed. For different, partly historical reasons, the army was also suspect to many of the governing elite.[2]

The Tudors had had no standing army; they could not afford one, and Burghley thought that soldiers in peace were 'like chimneys in summer'. And for much of the seventeenth century a standing army

had been doubtfully legal and undoubtedly unpopular: James I had
no hankering for peacetime soldiers; as Hume pointed out, he
possessed not 'a single regiment of guards' to support his claims to
'divine vicegerency'. The army raised for the war with Spain, which
was as unwelcome at home as it was unsuccessful abroad, was
prominent among the grievances in the Petition of Right to Charles
I. The Interregnum brought England's first standing army and
inevitably intensified political and financial prejudices against the
military. At the Restoration, when the Cromwellian army was
disbanded, Charles II was empowered to recruit soldiers so long as
he paid them. Yet the Commons resolved in 1673 that 'the standing
army is a grievance', and during the Popish Plot Parliament forced
the disbandment of all the troops that had recently been raised. In
1685 James II prorogued his otherwise submissive Parliament because
of its hostility to his newly doubled army and his many Catholic
officers.[3]

From 1689 the Bill of Rights made the maintenance of an army in
peacetime unlawful without the consent of Parliament; and the
annual Mutiny Acts authorised courts martial to sentence soldiers to
death for a variety of offences but stressed that soldiers were not
exempted from the ordinary processes of law. This parliamentary
control of its existence and its discipline made the army legal without
making it popular. A standing army of any significant size was still
considered a threat to liberty. After the Peace of Ryswick, William
III was prepared to reduce his victorious army of nearly 90,000 men
by about two-thirds, even though he was convinced that Louis XIV
was planning to renew the war. But that was nowhere near enough
for the new 'country' coalition of Tories and Whigs, which had little
understanding of Europe and insisted on reducing the army to a
maximum of 10,000 in 1697, to 7000 in 1698, and on depriving the
King of his Dutch Guards in 1699. William considered abdication,
but he had to comply with Parliament's demands and the Bill of
Rights. In addition Parliament passed no Mutiny Acts between 1697
and 1702.[4]

During the War of the Spanish Succession the army that produced
Marlborough's triumphs was once more expanded to about 90,000
men, but with the coming of peace it was again drastically reduced.
Until 1739 the army in Britain and abroad, excluding Ireland, was
usually only some 18,000 strong. Similar expansions and contractions
continued till the defeat of Napoleon, though each war brought a
larger peacetime army.[5]

The pamphlet war over the army after the Treaty of Ryswick
reverberated into the next century. For the parliamentary opposition,
the political argument against a standing army was stronger after
1714 than in William's time. Hanoverian and Whig rule rested on

military might. Irrespective of the 'Fifteen', the first two Georges would have soon gone back to Hanover and the Whigs to opposition, had they not been buttressed by their troops. The understandable dismissal of Jacobite officers in 1715 and the arbitrary sacking of officer MPs who opposed Walpole in Parliament made the army patently political. Sir Robert freely conceded that military force was 'necessary for the support of government'. In the same debate Pulteney put it rather differently: as soon as government degenerated into faction, it had to be supported by a standing army.[6]

Not only the existence of the army was a matter of political dispute. The government's constant refrain that riots were inspired by Jacobites also made the Whig use of it to put down disputes decidedly political. Before the Civil War the army had rarely been used against the populace, not because there were no riots but because there was no army. Charles I had only 1000 soldiers; constables and the militia attempted to keep order. Charles II was better placed, militarily, than his father, but his army numbered only some 9000 and it was rarely used to quell tumults. When it was called out, as in the Bawdy House Riots of 1668, it did not fire on the rioters. During the Exclusion Crisis, order in London was kept by the militia. James II had a larger army and a strong distrust of the militia. Under him the army briefly became a much more political force, designed to suppress opposition of all kinds. But after the Revolution, as a peacekeeping body, it again faded into the background.[7]

Only in 1714 did the army become the government's regular police force. With disaffection rife the militia, which had for some time disliked its repressive role, was anything but reliable against its fellow countrymen. Walpole admitted that if used it would probably join the rioters. Hence, the army necessarily became the Whigs' engine of repression. Widespread antipathy to the regime it served ensured that in performing its peacekeeping duties the army, which by a new law was empowered to shoot rioters, was kept both busy and unpopular. Except when the rioting was serious, however, the army usually avoided using violence.[8]

With a large part of Whig power coming out of the barrel of a gun, the abolition, or at least the further reduction, of the army and reliance instead on the navy and on a citizens' militia was naturally one of the main planks of the opposition's platform under the first two Georges. In *Gulliver's Travels* Swift made that paragon of 'country' politics, the King of Brobdingnag, express amazement at the presence of 'a mercenary standing army' among a free people in the midst of peace. Swift and the opposition were echoing earlier thinkers as diverse as Sir Thomas More and Machiavelli, who identified the presence of a professional army with a corrupted people and an absolute form of government; a free state should be defended by its own citizens under arms – in other words by a militia. The natural result of standing armies, argued Fletcher of Saltoun, was slavery. By mid-century nevertheless, the army was generally accepted as a disagreeable necessity, though even in 1765 the jurist Blackstone thought a standing army regulated by the Mutiny Act introduced a 'state of servitude' into the nation.[9]

Fears of a standing army were not at all unreasonable. Till near the end of his life, such an acute observer as David Hume considered a standing army 'a mortal distemper in the British government of which it must at last inevitably perish'. The dilemma was acute. Following Louis XIV's example, other countries had large armies, and clearly a British one was needed for national defence, as well as for internal security. But equally clearly the navy was Britain's primary defensive force, and a professional army gave the executive the power to sap the mixed constitution or overthrow it by a violent coup. Oliver Cromwell and James II were homegrown warnings of the dangers involved; abroad, standing armies had frequently enabled absolutism to triumph. In the event the struggle between court and country resulted in a beneficent stand-off. The court had its way over keeping an army, but the opposition managed to keep it sufficiently small; and the election of many officers to the Commons helped to preserve parliamentary control of the army and to prevent military control of Parliament. Yet in the early eighteenth century that outcome was far from certain. Had the Hanoverians been more engaging, and had they not split the governing elite and fostered the Jacobite threat by proscribing the Tories, a standing army might have had the same consequences that it often had on the continent.[10]

In times of peace the army inspired little affection or respect. Its triumphs in war were soon forgotten; its peacetime successes in restoring order were not gratefully remembered. Nothing was so 'odious to men of all ranks and classes', Lord Hervey told George II, 'as troops'. Army pay and conditions were bad. Flogging was pervasive and brutal: at mid-century the average number of lashes ordered by courts martial for disobedience had risen to 600, and fifty years later a general order limiting sentences to 1000 lashes was not meticulously observed. 'It is poverty [that] fills armies,' said Defoe, and not surprisingly scarcely anybody who could do anything else voluntarily enlisted. Many had to be tricked into joining. Effectively they were kidnapped: after being made drunk in a tavern they woke up to find themselves soldiers. In war magistrates were empowered to conscript the unemployed, and sometimes convicts were offered the army as an alternative to prison. 'Such a set of ruffians and imbeciles,' wrote one officer, 'you may call them cannon fodder, but never soldiers.'[11]

The army, then, was scarcely 'the mirror of the people from which it is drawn', that Clausewitz later thought an army should be. Yet it was not set apart from the people, because hostility to a standing army prevented the building of barracks. The people had been taught, said General Wade in 1741, to associate the idea of barracks so closely with slavery that no ministry dared propose building them; even the Paymaster to the Forces, Henry Pelham, agreed that barracks were 'justly names of terror' to a free nation. Twenty-five years later Blackstone, echoing Montesquieu, thought the preservation of a free state required soldiers 'to live intermixed with the people', not in barracks. Only the fears of popular insurrection aroused by the French Revolution enabled the government to build barracks to keep the populace subdued.[12]

At the same time, troops could not be billeted in private houses. The Petition of Right's attempted prohibition of the practice, which had been ignored after the Restoration, was observed after 1689. In consequence the army had to be quartered in inns and alehouses, a system which was disliked both by guests and hosts. The troops were treated 'as if we had carried pestilence, robbery and pillage with us' – while according to their enemies they were 'wantoning in lewdness and luxury'. The innkeepers fared little better. They were paid late or not at all and, often, lost their regular customers. Quartering inevitably led to continual quarrels and sometimes serious riots, after which the troops were moved elsewhere and the trouble began again. All the same this depressing cycle did much to turn fears of the army into lies. The friction it caused kept the army unpopular, while the soldiers' contact with the people prevented them becoming a quasi-alien force, as ready to fight their fellow countrymen as a foreign army.[13]

An army composed of foreign mercenaries would have had no such inhibitions about subduing the English populace. Mercenaries had played an important part in building up continental absolutism. Like other states, Britain hired mercenaries to help fight her wars, and Dutch and Hessian troops were used against the Jacobite rebellions. But parliamentary opposition prevented the regular employment of mercenaries in peacetime, thus confining the constitutional threat to that from the far less dangerous English soldiers.[14]

The Law

The law under which the army was empowered to maintain order was radically changed in 1715. For riot to be an offence at common law, at least three people had to be involved in a violent act. If their use of force was for a merely private end, riot was only a misdemeanour. But if their use of force was for a public end, then rioting amounted to constructively levying war against the King, that is to say treason – as the London apprentices found to their cost. At common law, soldiers – like magistrates and everyone else – had the duty to help suppress any riot by using whatever force was necessary to restore order.[15]

In 1715 that law was not repressive enough to protect the new regime from general public hostility. In the preamble to the Riot Act the government made no attempt to conceal that the reason for that highly political measure was its fear of Jacobitism:

> Whereas of late many rebellious Riots and Tumults have been in divers Parts of this Kingdom, to the Disturbance of the publick Peace, and the endangering of His Majesty's Person and Government, and the same are yet continued and fomented by Persons disaffected to His Majesty, presuming so to do, for that the Punishments provided by the Laws now in being are not adequate to such heinous Offences . . . Therefore for the prevention and suppression of such Riots and Tumults, and for the more speedy and effectual punishing the Offenders therein; Be it enacted . . .

Rioting accordingly became a 'heinous offence'. The Act laid down that if twelve or more people, who were unlawfully or riotously assembled and had been ordered by a magistrate by a 'Proclamation to be made in the King's name' to disperse, had not done so within one hour, they were guilty of capital felony; and that those who then dispersed them were indemnified for any injury caused by the violence they had used. This drastic law achieved its immediate objective of strengthening the executive on the streets. It also tipped the balance against rioters in the courts: the scope for juries to acquit was cut down, while the scope of riot as a capital felony was greatly widened.[16]

The Riot Act merely gave the authorities additional powers; it did not touch the common law of riot. This, however, was not generally realised. Indeed the Act was so badly drafted that it puzzled ministers, magistrates, soldiers and, presumably, rioters for more than a century.* The belief which soon became widespread that it had superceded the common law in turn instilled the erroneous conviction that soldiers could not lawfully fire on rioters, unless a magistrate had requested them to do so, and that they could not

---

* The bewilderment of rioters was different from that of the authorities. When the 'proclamation' was read to the women of Bath who had boarded a food ship in 1795, they replied that they were not rioting but were merely stopping the sending of corn abroad. They then sang 'God Save the King'.[17]

forcibly disperse a mob until an hour had elapsed from the reading of the 'proclamation'.

Whatever the uncertainty about the extent of the army's legal powers and its duty to suppress riots, in exercising those powers both magistrates and troops were unquestionably subject to the law of the land. A private prosecution for murder was brought against the mayor of Carmarthen in 1757 after five colliers had been killed in a food riot. The mayor had in fact offered the colliers corn at a reasonable rate, as well as reading the Riot Act and several times asking the rioters to disperse; he was acquitted without the jury having to retire. A Southwark magistrate, Samuel Gillan, was also prosecuted for murder after the 'Massacre' of St George's Fields in 1768. William Hickey who was present thought Gillan had been stupid and overzealous and deemed the conduct of both the soldiers and the magistrate 'infamous', but Gillan, too, was easily acquitted. Yet such prosecutions were a potent deterrent to any trigger-happiness by JPs.[19]

That a soldier, too, should be subject to the common law was vital if English liberties were to be preserved and civil not to be replaced by martial law. But it made his legal position more unenviable than a magistrate's. By military law a soldier's duty was to obey orders – he was liable to sentence of death by court martial if he did not – and by common law his duty was to use only enough force to restore order, so that he was liable to civil prosecution if the force he used was deemed excessive. Writing in the 1730s, Lord Hervey conveyed something of the army's difficulties:

When . . . two or three hundred men are ordered by their officer to go against two or three thousand rioters, if they refuse to go it is mutiny, and they will be condemned by a court martial and shot; if they go and do not fire, they will probably be knocked on the head; and if they do fire and kill anybody, they will be tried by a jury and hanged. Such are the absurdities of our laws at present.

Whether they were absurdities or indispensable legal constraints, nobody removed them. 'Shall I be *shot*,' wrote General Napier 100 years later, 'for my forbearance by a court martial, or *hanged* for over zeal by a jury? . . . When a riot has taken place and all is over; when everything is known; when fear, danger, confusion, hurry, all are passed; then comes forth the wise, the heroic, the patriotic, "How undecided the officer was," exclaims the first; "he ought to have charged at once," cries the second; "that redcoated butcher must be hanged," says the third.'[20]

The legal dangers were not just theoretical. Following the prosecutions of two soldiers for firing on some smugglers in 1728, the Scottish commissioners of customs complained that if soldiers, after being attacked by a mob and 'most barbarously beat and abused' and firing in self-defence, were to be imprisoned and run the risk of execution, they would be of no further use to their officers. It was, as Hervey wrote, 'hard' on the troops that the laws and the civil power did not 'protect their own support', yet the law's uncertainties normally obliged officers to be prudent in their use of force. The commander of the troops in Bristol in 1740 explained his caution by the freshness of his memory of 'Captain Porteous's unhappy fate'.[21]

A soldier anyway gains no glory from shooting or charging his fellow citizens, but such actions are particularly distasteful when he is living 'intermixed with the people'. The army strongly disliked its policing task. Even the government admitted that riot duty was a 'most odious service'. Inevitably, the private soldiers often sympathised with the rioters. So too, sometimes, did the officers. Suppressing riots by weavers in 1756, James Wolfe called them 'poor devils' who were 'half starved' because their masters did not pay them enough to live on. Such sentiments did not predispose officers to be harsh with rioters, and soldiers often fired high whether or not they were ordered to do so. Nevertheless military intervention caused many casualties.[22]

As well as lacking martial ardour against their own countrymen, the military were aware that the army's critics in Parliament would be quick to denounce any rigorous act of suppression. Many of those who fully accepted the need for a standing army might do the same. After all, for soldiers to fire at unarmed civilians is essentially barbarous – and unlike the American colonists the English were an unarmed people. Even a tough Whig judge like Willes, LCJ, was strongly anti-militarist, while the government itself was occasionally worried by the implications of enforcing the law by troops. Frequent use of soldiers to suppress civil commotions, wrote the Secretary at War in 1765, 'has an evident tendency to introduce military government'.[23]

The good sense of the army – and often of magistrates who preferred negotiations to firearms – thus made the operation of the law less draconian than the law itself. The Riot Act was not often used. Out of forty-one riots in Devon in the 1790s, the 'proclamation' was only once read. Nevertheless the perpetual use of troops as a heavily armed police force, coupled with the knowledge that Whig power depended on the army, led the Tories under the first two Georges to advocate the Riot Act's repeal. Is this Act, Sir John Hinde Cotton asked the Commons in 1734,

> . . . no encroachment upon the rights of the people? Is it no grievance that a little dirty justice of the peace, the meanest and

vilest tool a minister can make use of . . . should have it in his
power, by reading a proclamation to put perhaps twenty or thirty
of the best subjects in England to immediate death, without any
trial or form of law?

But for the Whigs it was far too valuable a weapon for any ministry
to consider its abandonment. And the great military victories of the
Seven Years War and the ending of their proscription reconciled the
Tories to such a useful government expedient. For them, the Riot
Act and the army were no longer the despotic tools of a minority
party and an unpopular dynasty; they became the trusty, legitimate
peacekeeping instruments of the governing elite.[24]

Even after the Riot Act and the use of the army against the
populace had become generally accepted features of the political
landscape, the shooting of rioters was still liable to provoke
parliamentary criticism, and many people remained opposed to the
use of force save in the very last resort. Henry Fielding's brother,
John, who was the Bow Street magistrate for some twenty-five years
from 1754, always postponed bringing in the military as long as
possible, deeming it liable 'to provoke what it is intended to prevent'.
William Beckford, twice Lord Mayor of London, told the House of
Commons, during the Wilkite disturbances, of his unchanging view
that 'mobs might be quelled without the aid of the military'. As
Beckford had almost certainly himself raised a riot in support of Pitt
not long before, his was a fairly authoritative view. Burke did not
have Beckford's experience – he never raised a mob and deprecated
the practice – but after the St George's Fields 'massacre' in which six
people were killed he similarly maintained that 'the use of military
power, when employed in firing in places of promiscuous resort, is
attended with great danger, is contrary to the spirit of our laws, and
totally unfit for the suppression of riots and tumults in this
country.'[25]

In 1769 Burke's was very much a minority view, yet Montesquieu
and Blackstone were largely vindicated. The efforts of successive
oppositions were not in vain. Though the army was constantly used
as an instrument of coercion, military violence was employed only
against rioters. The English remained civilian through and through.
The demilitarisation resulting from virtual abstention from continental warfare in the two centuries after 1485 was not reversed.[26]

The order to the troops

Such a climate taken with the frequency of riot duty – which was
given priority over ordinary training – might have persuaded the

military authorities if not to seek some statutory protection for their soldiers at least to provide them with detailed guidance on the control of tumults. Throughout the century drill books galore were issued. Officers could compare their own military manoeuvres with those of their rivals by reading translations of the French drill book and the Prussian cavalry regulations. They could also hone their military skills by studying recently published translations of Caesar, Thucydides, Polybius, Tacitus, Xenophon, Josephus and Vegetius. Yet, aside from the constant directive to be cautious in the use of force, the War Office never issued a single page of tactical advice on how to deal with riots; and nobody else tried to fill the gap by providing for tumults the instructions that the ancient military writers furnished for battles.[27]

The omission was all the more glaring in that the matter was not one of mere theoretical speculation. There was plenty of experience to follow. Captain Horsey, after all, had quelled the extensive Sacheverell Riots without firing a shot. Luckily the good sense and moderation of the army and the caution of magistrates usually made volleys into a mob very much a last resort. Often a show of military strength was enough. If that failed, a bayonet charge by the infantry or a cavalry charge using just the flats of their swords might do the trick. Still, the often successful tactics of the troops owed nothing to the military authorities, though to be fair the War Office was not alone in its myopia. Other countries dealt with their mobs in the same way. Proper riot control lay well in the future.[28]

Nevertheless the army's unpopularity and the thankless nature of riot duties led successive Secretaries at War to seek legal instruction in order to adjust the wording of their orders to the troops. After 1715, the two immediate questions to the law officers were: was the army acting within the law in suppressing riots; and if it was, under what circumstances could it do so? In 1717 Northey, the Attorney General, answered that it was indeed legal for the army to aid the civil power. Otherwise, he made nobody much wiser: apart from one sentence about common law, his letter largely consisted of a recitation of the provisions of the Riot Act, which he had helped to draft. Four years later Raymond, the other drafter of the Riot Act, was more helpful. It was legal for everyone, whether 'a civil or a military man', to aid the magistrates in keeping the peace, but he added the caution that the army 'should not at all interpose in any of these things' except when asked to do so by the civil magistrates.[29]

That touched on the chief point of difficulty for the army which was whether the Riot Act had superceded the common law of riot or was an addition to it: in other words whether the duty of the military was simply to comply with the provisions of the Riot Act or whether, under some circumstances, the army should use force, even though no magistrate was present and the proclamation had not been read. The first interpretation which put the onus of decision exclusively on the magistrates suited the army; regrettably, though the lawyers seldom unequivocally said so, the second interpretation which left the troops with a dangerous area of discretion was, in law, the correct one.[30]

The interpretation chosen was of course crucial for the wording of the order to troops on riot duty. In 1733 the Attorney General, Yorke, produced a masterpiece of legal ambiguity. After concurring with Raymond's opinion that the army should not intervene in riots unless requested to do so by a magistrate, he recommended that the military order should read that they were 'not to repel force with force, unless it shall be found absolutely necessary'. That suggestion was unpalatable, since it removed the army from the safe protection of being able to act only under the orders of the civil magistrate. Accordingly, the Secretary at War ignored the second part of Yorke's opinion and adopted the first. The army continued to be ordered 'not to repel force with force unless thereunto required by the civil magistrates'.[31]

Unfortunately for the army, two years later the law officers preferred the second part of Yorke to the first: the words 'unless it shall be found absolutely necessary' should be substituted, they advised, for 'thereunto required by the civil magistrates'. This put the army into a difficulty; after initially following the law officers' advice, the Secretary at War once again solved it brilliantly. He included both sets of words to make the order read 'not to repel force with force, unless it shall be found absolutely necessary or being thereunto required by the civil magistrate'. This combination largely nullified the obnoxious phrase 'unless absolutely necessary' and kept the army safely under the wing of the civil magistrates. Thirty years later the Secretary at War made the protection virtually complete by altering the word 'or' to 'and'. Nevertheless his successor was still not satisfied, and in 1766 the 'absolutely necessary' phrase was dropped; commanding officers were simply told not to 'interfere' unless required by a magistrate. After mentioning that soldiers like everyone else should act to preserve the peace, Lord Mansfield, when Solicitor General, had then added the comforting qualification 'yet I suppose the soldiery from caution and for their own safety are required to obey some peace officer'.[32]

So the legal confusion was not merely the consequence of the army's natural desire to divest itself of responsibility for difficult and dangerous decisions; it was also the fault of the law officers themselves. Presumably those legal luminaries knew the law, though that is not always manifest from their advice, and presumably they knew what was worrying the army, yet none of them set out the full legal position without ambiguity. Their reticence probably stemmed from an understandable wish not to be blamed for any use of force that was deemed either excessive or inadequate, and from a creditable desire not to jeopardise soldiers on riot duty. Thus Mansfield assumed that the orders given to the troops had been 'settled with regard to prudence as well as law'. Maybe the law officers also felt that the state of the law was such that even full knowledge of it would not be of great help to the military.[33]

The army's obligations under common law to help keep the peace accordingly went into limbo. Acting in accordance with the Riot Act came to be regarded as the full extent of its obligations and powers. The army was not alone in its view; ministers and others came to believe the same thing. The common law of riot was largely forgotten. Thus while the intention of the Riot Act was to make the use of force against rioters easier and safer, which in general it unquestionably did, its effect was occasionally to make it more difficult. The Whig regime was so unpopular in 1715 that some draconian measure was necessary for its survival. But at least after 1760 the authorities, to say nothing of the rioters, would probably have been far better placed without it. The army's duties under common law to maintain the peace would not then have fallen into oblivion. And lacking the protection of the Riot Act, the army commanders would surely have been compelled to give more attention to the subject of riot control. Mowing down mobs would have been even rarer, and techniques akin to those used in the Sacheverell tumults would have been evolved or revived.

The general misunderstanding of the law – confusion even survived the trauma of the Gordon Riots, surfacing again in the 1790s and as late as the Bristol Riots in 1831 – was the next best thing to the Riot Act's repeal. By usually inducing caution in the use of force it served both the army and the country well, preventing the casualties from military action being greater than they were. Yet it only worked because the rioters, too, nearly always used limited force; and it proved disastrous in the Gordon Riots.[34]

SEVEN

Crime and the Criminal Law

It has been justly said that it is in mercy to the innocent that the guilty are punished . . . The degeneracy of the present times, fruitful in the inventions of wickedness, hath produced many new laws necessary for the present state and condition of things and to suppress mischiefs which were growing frequent amongst us.

Lord Hardwicke, Lord Chief Justice, 1735

I would . . . have the laws tuned in unison with the manners of the times; very dissonant are a gentle country and cruel laws; very dissonant that your reason is furious but your passions moderate, and that you are always equitable except in your courts of justice.

Edmund Burke in the House of Commons, 1773

The Laws are like turnpikes, only made to stop people who walk on foot, and not to interrupt those who drive through them in their coaches. – The laws are like a game at loo, where a blaze of court cards is always secure, and the knaves are the safest cards in the pack.

Henry Fielding, Rape upon Rape, *1730[1]*

The Gordon Riots caused many casualties, on the gallows as well as on the streets. Well in advance politically, economically and socially of nearly every other major state in Europe, and with a legal system easily superior to all of them, England possessed a penal code of unrivalled savagery. Most capital prosecutions continued to be brought under Tudor legislation, yet the bloody criminal code was only partly the result of 'old father antic the law'. The criminal law was so littered with acts imposing the death penalty for any offence which had caught a legislator's fancy that between the Restoration and 1820 the number of capital statutes increased by more than one a year. And a new capital statute did not necessarily create only one new capital offence. Sir Leon Radzinowicz doubted if the criminal code of any other country contained anywhere near as many capital offences as there were to be found in one English statute, the Waltham Black Act – about 200.[2]

Of course the mere counting of capital statutes or capital offences is not an adequate test of legal brutality. The hanging statute and offence of damaging Westminster bridge could have been combined with the separate hanging statute and offence of damaging Fulham bridge without making the law either more or less bloody. Or an act could have been passed making all theft, however minor, capital, and a second one passed making all violence of whatever degree capital, thereby reducing the number both of capital statutes and capital offences from over 200 to two while making the penal code even more draconian than before. All the same, the procession of capital statutes throughout the eighteenth century demonstrates at the very least that the increasing violence of the criminal law caused no revulsion among legislators. To them, Blackstone wrote, it was largely 'a matter of indifference'.[3]

Nevertheless many capital statutes were passed without debate or division; until 1772, indeed, a bill or a clause creating a new capital offence did not even have to be scrutinised by a committee of the whole House but could be agreed in a small committee consisting of as few as one member. Such legislation was the easiest to obtain and the most difficult to undo. 'When a proposal is made to emancipate or relieve,' Byron correctly told the Lords in 1812, 'you deliberate for years . . . but a death bill must be passed off hand without a thought of the consequences.' A death bill was usually passed to meet an emergency, real or imagined; hence it was both comprehensive and severe. Yet when the emergency was over, the act remained on the statute book receiving successive extensions or being made permanent. The Waltham Black Act was introduced to meet an emergency in 1723; yet as late as 1821 the Lords refused to repeal it.[4]

The more outlandish absurdities of the criminal law did not cause heavy casualties; most of those who were hanged were found guilty of some sort of theft. Yet the death penalty was applicable to an extraordinary variety of offences: not only to murder and robbery, but to such bizarre crimes as being disguised within the mint, maliciously cutting hop-binds growing on poles, being a soldier or a seaman and wandering about without a pass, pickpocketing to the amount of one shilling or over, consorting with gypsies, cutting down growing trees, stealing a fish out of any river or pond or impersonating the out-pensioners of Greenwich Hospital. In contrast, stealing a child was until 1814 virtually unpunished, and manslaughter except by stabbing was not a capital offence. Nor, except in exceptional circumstances, was attempted murder; it was only a misdemeanour.[5]

This uniquely bloody code was fettered, fortunately, to a uniquely liberal criminal procedure, which mitigated the violence of the law. Prisoners were not tortured; for most of the time *habeas corpus* was a safeguard; the judges, though cornerstones of the state and often highly political, were no longer just another arm of the executive and were not usually subject to political interference in criminal cases; trials were public; nearly all prosecutions were private, which with the government not being directly involved fostered judicial fairness and considerateness to the prisoner; above all there was the jury. Acquittals were common.

Yet, by any standards other than those on the continent at the time, English criminal procedure was highly defective. The prisoner charged with felony was not allowed to see the depositions or a list of witnesses, or to give evidence on his own behalf. Save in cases of high treason, he was not allowed counsel to defend him except on a point of law, and only then if he raised it himself without prompting. (Until the 1730s prosecuting counsel were also rare.) Gradually, however, the rules were relaxed, and defence counsel was allowed to examine and cross-examine witnesses, but never to address the jury.*

Many of those most at risk could not afford counsel anyway; as late as 1820 it was very rare for a prisoner tried in London to have a barrister. Judge Jeffries thought it 'a hard case' that a man should be allowed counsel to defend himself when he was accused of 'a twopenny trespass', but not when he was accused of a serious offence and his life was at stake. Yet this 'hard case' was not fully remedied until 150 years after even Jeffries had noticed it.[7]

The theory behind the practice of inhibiting a prisoner's full defence by counsel in felony cases was that the judge was the counsel for the prisoner. Judges did, indeed, try to protect prisoners from undue prejudice, but one stressed in 1824 that it was 'impossible' for them to go further than that. Pointing out that the judge could have no private communication with the prisoner or give him advice, Sydney Smith wondered if he ever assumed 'the appearance of believing a prisoner to be innocent whom he thinks to be guilty . . . and does he not often sum up against his own client?' Yet the legal profession persistently peddled the 'paltry and perilous fallacy' of the judge being the prisoner's counsel, and it was not until 1836, after a Royal Commission had called the fallacy 'too extravagant to require comment', that prisoners accused of felony were allowed to make their full defence by counsel.[8]

---

* At his trial before the Lords for murder in 1760, Lord Ferrers had no counsel. As his family had insisted that his defence should be insanity, this put him in an almost insuperable difficulty: the more skilfully he presented his case for his own insanity, the less likely were the Lords to accept it. (The House of Lords was not necessarily a fairer or more sophisticated tribunal than a jury: Sir James Fitzjames Stephen regarded their conviction of Lord Stafford as the most 'inexcusable' of all the bad verdicts in the Popish Plot.) By 1776, however, counsel for the Duchess of Kingston on trial for bigamy was allowed to cross-examine the prosecution's witnesses.[6]

The absence of lawyers from a process which still ressembled the unstructured 'altercation' of an Elizabethan trial necessarily made the role of the judge a more leading one than it is today. He no longer bullied the jury as he had in the previous century, but he usually got his way. In 1754 Lord Chief Justice Ryder tried a charge of infanticide against Frances Cheek. The evidence as to her sanity conflicted, the jury first saying that they doubted she was sane. Ryder, in his own words, then 'explained again to them the nature of the case rather against the prisoner', whereupon after an unusually long deliberation of an hour and a half the jury duly found her guilty. (Having pronounced himself 'very well satisfied', with the jury, Ryder sentenced Cheek to be hanged and anatomised, making a speech in which he shed so many tears that a lady provided him with 'her handkerchief dipped in lavender water'. The condemned prisoner presumably had to use her own.) Juries usually accepted the judge's view, which was often in favour of the accused, without such pressure; only when counsel were more regularly present towards the end of the century did they become more independent.[9]

The lack of a defending lawyer was not the prisoner's only handicap. Conditions in the prisons were atrocious and, despite the efforts of Oglethorpe, Howard and other reformers, remained so until well into the nineteenth century, except for those who could afford to pay; John Howard would never visit a prison before breakfast. Many more prisoners died in Newgate than left there for execution, and occasionally gaol fever (typhus) spread from the prisoners to counsel and judges, as in Dorset in 1730 and at the Old Bailey in 1750; then something was done. When prisoners had to be moved from prison for trial, conditions might well be even worse. The survivors who appeared in court were filthy, reeking and often suffering from typhus. Prisoners' chains were supposed to be struck off on their arraignment, but frequently this did not happen. Pratt, LCJ, refused to allow the chains to be removed from a Jacobite conspirator, Christopher Layer, even though he was seriously ill and was bent double under them; John Wilkes, when Sheriff of London in 1771, ordered the keeper of Newgate to end 'the present illegal and inhumane practice' of men remaining in irons during their trial. Being hungry, dirty, possibly ill and in irons, often freezing cold or oppressively hot – prisoners awaiting their case coming on at the Old Bailey were in all weathers kept in the open bail dock from 6.30 am to 8 pm – was not an encouraging prelude for a prisoner's defence of his life in court.[10]

The difficulties of the accused were magnified by the indecent speed of their trial. Based on the experience of several sessions, an observer calculated in 1833 that the average length of a criminal trial at the Old Bailey was only eight and a half minutes – the same length as a Jacobean trial. Shortly before, a French visitor noted the 'incredible rapidity' of the trials. Though eighteenth-century inefficiency made trials last a little longer, they were still quick. This did not matter much to the inveterately criminal; the scene was familiar. But many a first offender, however indulgently he was treated by the judge, scarcely had time to get his bearings before his trial was over. So short were the proceedings, there was seldom a need for a summing up; the judge had conveyed his view. When a judge did sum up, he was, according to a modern criminal court judge, seldom impartial. Juries in the first part of the century did not give a verdict after each case, but heard a dozen or so before retiring to consider them together, a procedure liable to lead to confusion. From 1738, juries at the Old Bailey returned their verdict at the end of a case. They did not retire but usually huddled in the court for a few minutes.[11]

A long trial might be more dangerous. Until 1794 criminal trials had to be completed at one session, and the jury were confined without food or drink until they had given their verdict.* Hence Pope's well known lines:

> *Meanwhile declining from the noon of day,*
> *The sun obliquely shoots his burning ray;*
> *The hungry judges soon the sentence sign,*
> *And wretches hang that jurymen may dine.*

A still greater hazard was to be in the dock after they had dined, when according to Rev Martin Madan in 1785 drunkenness was 'too frequently apparent . . . in *jurymen* and *witnesses*'. In Scotland the judges drank in court from 'black bottles of strong port' and were often 'muzzy'. In England judges did not drink wine on the bench; whether they always dined on water is conjectural.[13]

Nevertheless English criminal procedure, despite its glaring defects, produced many acquittals and was as greatly admired by foreign observers from Voltaire, Montesquieu and Beccaria downwards as the English criminal law was roundly condemned. Indeed the criticism most commonly made was that the procedure allowed too many loopholes through which the guilty could make their escape. Certainly the pedantry of the lawyers worked in favour of the accused. An indictment had to be exactly drawn. If, for example, a man's name was mispelled or his address mistaken or some technical adverb omitted, the indictment was thrown out, though

---

* In contrast, civil cases, which were profitable to the lawyers and judges, often dragged on for years or even decades. Lord Eldon, who was Lord Chancellor for twenty-five years, earned £22,730 in fees in 1810 and accumulated a vast fortune.[14]

that was rare and might merely lead to a second indictment. Not only pedantry supplied loopholes. The scope of a capital statute was generally narrowed by judicial interpretation. As a rule the judges, by sensible if artificial reasoning, contrived to exclude from the sphere of the death penalty a number of offences which according to the ordinary meaning of words were clearly within it. Juries, both grand and petty, were also much more sensible than the legislature, and they too adapted the criminal code, the first by often refusing to commit for trial, the second, frequently in cooperation with the judges, by often refusing to convict.[14]

Finally, many condemned offenders escaped execution: on average rather more than half were reprieved during the eighteenth century. Judges on assize commuted many death sentences before they moved on to the next town – Squire Allworthy told Tom Jones that he had more than once appealed to a judge on behalf of a highwayman when there were mitigating circumstances – and those who were 'left for execution' could petition the King. Death sentences passed in London and Middlesex were considered by the King in Council. In exercising the prerogative of mercy, George II usually followed the advice of the trial judge, though he occasionally, for petty reasons, refused a judge's recommendation of a reprieve. He also, notoriously, turned down the recommendation to mercy of the officers who had tried Admiral Byng.

Ideally the trial judge in making his recommendations was guided by the convict's character and previous conduct, his age, his financial circumstances – Ryder, LCJ, reprieved a highwayman because his wife was expecting her third child and he was destitute – the nature of the crime and the possibility of innocence. He could, however, be heavily prejudiced. In 1728 a judge refused a reprieve for an eighteen-year-old girl convicted of infanticide though the case for one was overwhelming; finally he gave in after strong pressure from 'people of quality'.[15]

George III, too, was nearly always guided by the advice of the judge who had tried the case. Lord Shelburne, when secretary of state, said he had never known the King to differ from the judge's opinion. As in other matters George was conscientious and unimaginative. Lord Eldon was shocked at the absence of proper machinery for the consideration of reprieves by the Council: all it had before it was a recapitulation of the trial judge's opinion. The King's almost invariable approval of that opinion would have been appropriate had there been a bureaucracy to produce all the facts – which the judge rarely had. No such bureaucracy existed; instead the King was bureaucratic, and some dreadful mistakes were made. Moreover, patronage penetrated even into the condemned cells. Prisoners who could persuade the great to intercede for them were more likely to escape the gallows than those without even the slenderest connections. The Kennedy brothers who had committed a brutal murder in 1769 had their sentences reduced to transportation after the intervention of some aristocrats who 'kept' their sister. 'The mercy of a chaste and pious prince,' wrote Junius, has been 'extended cheerfully to a wilful murderer, because that murderer is the brother of a common prostitute.' The Wilkites were incensed by the contrast between the treatment of the Kennedys and of more deserving cases; Brass Crosby, London's Lord Mayor, attempted unsuccessfully to have the case retried. That was an abnormally blatant incident. In the previous reign a request for a reprieve from the Speaker of the House of Commons and the Lord Lieutenant of Surrey was turned down. Influence was usually discreet, and the King did his best.*[16]

As a result of all these successive filters – refusal of the grand jury to commit for trial, acquittal or conviction of a minor offence by the petty jury, reprieves by the judges or the King – the hangman found the number of his clients drastically reduced. Something between 2.5 per cent and 7 per cent of those indicted, and about 10 per cent of those tried for felony, were actually executed. So while the death bills in defence of property multiplied – the process which Sheridan termed fencing gooseberry bushes around with gibbets – the numbers of those executed did not. But they did not fall. In 1725 Bernard Mandeville compared 'the droves that are carried to Tyburn for slaughter with the cattle that were sent to Smithfield for the same purpose, and the slaughter was not abated later in the century. Indeed, because of the growth of population, more people were hanged in Surrey in the 1790s than in the last decade of the previous century.[18]

Execution of the innocent and of women and children

Many of those who completed the obstacle course to Tyburn or some provincial gallows deserved to do so; others were merely unlucky.

---

* At least once, however, George III behaved rather as Czar Nicholas I behaved to Dostoyevsky, who described his experience in *The Idiot,* ordering that a highwayman should only be told of his reprieve after he had arrived at the place of execution. George II did the same. In 1758 fifteen alleged mutineers – they had merely insisted on journeying from Portsmouth to London to lay some complaint before the Admiralty – were about to be executed when they were told His Majesty had shown mercy to fourteen of them and they were to draw lots to decide the one to be hanged. On other occasions this happened through incompetence, not malice. Two seamen sentenced for mutiny in 1783 were reprieved just as they were 'ready to be hoisted up'. A marine sentenced to death in 1766 for desertion was the victim of both incompetence and malice. An officer dropped a handkerchief, which was taken by some of the firing party as the signal to fire. The officer had the reprieve in his pocket, but the marine was dead.[17]

Procedural loopholes were justified on the grounds that it was better that ten guilty people should escape than that one innocent man should be condemned. Guilty men certainly did escape. Jonathan Wild, the most notorious criminal of the age, was acquitted twice, while one of his contemporaries was twice acquitted when guilty before being condemned when innocent. No less certainly, unfortunately, many innocent people were hanged. Stephen thought that in the seventeenth century a 'frightful' amount of injustice must have been inflicted upon innocent and obscure persons. Giving evidence to a Royal Commission in 1835, Sir Frederick Pollock, a former Attorney General and later a leading judge, had no doubt that innocent people had recently been executed, while in 1866 Sir Fitzroy Kelly, another former Attorney General and later Chief Baron of the Exchequer, maintained that many innocent men had been capitally convicted and in 'formidable numbers [had] been actually executed . . .' Clearly, in the eighteenth century, many innocent people similarly met the hangman.[19]

As well as those ordinary miscarriages of justice, the practice of giving rewards for securing capital convictions led to conspiracies to frame the innocent. In the phrase used at the time, 'thief-taking' developed into 'thief-making'. Henry Fielding thought proclamations that offered rewards propagated perjuries which sometimes 'destroyed' the innocent. Just how many innocent people were hanged because of thieftakers' perjuries is not known: certainly seven in the late forties and early fifties, and evidently many more in the sixties and seventies. These 'blood-money' scandals continued into the second decade of the nineteenth century.[20]

Leaving aside the wholly innocent, the often undiscriminating violence of the criminal law undoubtedly sent to the gallows a large number of people who should not have been hanged. Some suffered because the judges, in contrast to their usual practice, extended the effect of the Waltham Black Act. Contrary to precedent and to the opinion of one of the best judges of the day, Foster, J, its capital provisions were extended to aiders and abettors, which produced a heavy toll. Again, while the Black Act seemed to suggest that more than one feature – such as shooting *and* the blacking of the face were needed to bring its ferocious provisions into operation – the judges found that only one was necessary. At Tyburn in 1736 Thomas Reynolds, a turnpike rioter who had done no more than black his face, was to his very natural surprise the first to suffer from this judicial construction.[21]

Some were sent to Tyburn for very minor offences, while others who had committed much more serious crimes either escaped the death sentence or were reprieved. One of the most notorious cases was described by Sir William Meredith MP and used by Dickens in

Barnaby Rudge. In 1770 Mary Jones, aged eighteen with two small children, was turned onto the streets after her husband had been pressganged 'on the alarm about the Falkland Islands'. She took some coarse linen off the counter of a shop and slipped it under her cloak; 'the shopman saw her, and she laid it down'. Her defence was 'that she had lived in credit, and wanted for nothing, till a press-gang came and stole her husband from her; but since then she had no bed to lie on; nothing to give her children to eat; and they were almost naked; and perhaps she might have done something wrong, for she hardly knew what she did.' The parish officers testified to the truth of her story. But, Meredith continued, there had been a good deal of shoplifting about Ludgate; an example was thought necessary; 'and this woman was hanged for the comfort and satisfaction of shopkeepers in Ludgate Street. When brought to receive sentence, she behaved in such a frantic manner, as proved her mind to be in a distracted and desponding state; and the child was sucking at her breast when she set out for Tyburn.'[22]

As the case of Mary Jones showed, neither sex nor age was a bar to execution. On at least two occasions three women were hanged for trivial offences on the same day. Even so, the hanging of women was relatively infrequent, and of the 1232 people executed at Tyburn between 1703 and 1772, only 92 were women. Moreover they were not executed if they could persuade the matrons who were sent to examine them that they were pregnant.* Murdering a husband was still petty treason and, until 1790, such offenders and female forgers were sentenced to be burned alive.† They were usually strangled before the flames reached them, but when Catherine Hayes was executed the probably drunk hangman burned his fingers, let go the rope and the woman was burned alive to the pleasure of the crowd.[24]

In 1767 an eighty-year-old man was hanged for taking from a wreck a small quantity of cotton and a piece of rope. Children, too, were hanged and burned. In 1763 a boy of fifteen was executed for shoplifting and a girl of sixteen, who was probably 'an idiot', for murder. An eleven-year-old boy was hanged for setting fire to his mother's house; a girl of seventeen was hanged with her brother in 1785. Six years later a fourteen-year-old boy was executed together with one of fifteen for a trifling crime. Indeed in the 1780s a quarter of the fifteen and sixteen-year-olds who were capitally convicted were executed. Slightly earlier, a girl of fourteen who had been ordered by her master to hide some whitewashed farthings behind her stays would have been burnt alive, had she not been reprieved just as her

---

* Evidently, however, a few women were merely reprieved until they had given birth and were then hanged.[23]

† This was because to hang, draw and quarter a woman would have offended decency.

cart was setting out as a result of 'the humane but casual interference' of the Secretary of State. As late as 1814 a fourteen-year-old boy was hanged for stealing, and two years later a sixteen-year-old drummer was executed for having been sodomised by an ensign.[25]

The criminal law was thus both harsh and unfair. Its violence did not arise from the English being especially brutal or particularly addicted to violent lawbreaking. Even in the latter part of the seventeenth century murder, which is much the best measure of crime (the well known difficulties about criminal statistics applying less strongly to that offence) was fairly rare, yet the homicide rate probably fell from about eight per 100,000 a year in 1660 to less than one per 100,000 in 1800. Eighteenth-century England probably had fewer murders in proportion to its population than any other country in Europe. Even in London and Middlesex, the most lawless part of England, only eighty-one people were convicted of murder in the twenty-three years from 1749-71. In half that period Rome, a city only a quarter of the size of London, had 4000 murders.[26]

Nor was the steady accretion of violence in the statute book directed at violent behaviour. The great majority of the new hanging statutes were concerned not with violence but with fairly trivial offences against property and money, such as shoplifting over five shillings, robbing a rabbit warren, marking the edges of any coin of the kingdom, stealing from a wharf goods worth four shillings, or stealing a sheep or a horse. This oddity was also reflected in the offenders selected for execution. Of the forty-seven prisoners executed in the Home Circuit in 1689, eighteen were murderers and two others were convicted of a serious offence against the person. But of the sixty-four executions in those same counties in 1785, only one was for murder, all the others being for offences against property. As Bernard Mandeville – who wanted to make the treatment of criminals even more rigorous – had written sixty years before, a 'multitude of unhappy wretches . . . every year are put to death for trifles in our great Metropolis . . .'[27]

Defenders and opponents of the system

However bad a man or a cause, Norman Douglas remarked of a bloodthirsty eighteenth-century cardinal, it will never lack defenders, and the 'Bloody Code' was no exception. The criminal law was, in its violence, avowedly terrorist; it had no other rationale. Its most influential apologist, Archdeacon Paley, in 1785 based his defence of it on that ground; so did the judges. For Paley, the prevention of crimes was all important; therefore the severer the punishment the better. And since capital punishment was the severest that could be devised and therefore, he believed, the most effective, Paley approved of English law sweeping 'into the net every crime which, under any possible circumstances, [might] merit the punishment of death'; he also thought it right that only a small proportion of those so sentenced should be executed. The net of capital punishment should be vast, but its mesh should be large so that many who had been caught in it should be able to escape. For the archdeacon, justice as it is normally understood did not enter into the matter. 'The crime must be prevented by some means or other,' he wrote. 'whether they be proportionable to the guilt of the criminal or not.' Or, indeed, whether the sufferer was a criminal or not. Paley was not much concerned by the hanging of the innocent; such executions still provided deterrence. 'He who falls by a mistaken sentence,' the Archdeacon believed, 'may be considered as falling for his country.' Patriotism was to be the last refuge of an innocent man.[28]

Paley's argument could have just as well led him to almost the opposite conclusion: the need to prevent crime required an adequate police force and consistent, known penalties that would not deter victims from prosecuting or frighten jurors into acquitting. Instead he extolled a system based on random retribution, not prevention. Some of Paley's legislative followers were no less frank. Introducing a bill which became law in 1788 to extend capital punishment to people who broke into a house with the intention of destroying frames, D.P. Cooke MP said that the 'present bill held out a capital punishment in terrorem, in order to deter men from committing such offences; he wished not that any person should be hanged under the authority of the Bill'. The judges had earlier adopted a similar doctrine in relation to children. In 1748 a boy of ten, William York, was sentenced to death for murdering a five-year-old girl. The Lord Chief Justice sought the advice of the other judges as to whether the execution should take place. All the judges thought that, though it might savour of cruelty, York was 'certainly a proper subject for capital punishment, and ought to suffer' in order to deter other children from similar offences.* [29]

Parliament had been acting in accordance with Paley's doctrines long before he formulated them. Indeed they were merely an eloquent rationalisation of the existing system which year after year increased the number of capital offences. Urging an end to the bloody procession, Sir William Meredith told the Commons that no 'fouler murder was ever committed against law than the murder of [Mary Jones] by law', but that it was no good blaming the judges, juries,

---

* In the end, the executive decided that to leave him under sentence of death for nine years and then pardon him on condition that he went to sea might provide sufficient deterrence to other children.

or the hangman; they were but ministerial agents; 'the true hangman', he said, was 'the member of parliament' who was answerable 'for all the blood' shed by the Bloody Code. His hearers were not concerned to blame themselves or anybody else. Only nine of them supported Meredith, which was nine more than had supported Bubb Doddington when he proposed removing the death penalty from the Mutiny Act and giving soldiers in peacetime normal civil rights. The only experience parliamentarians had of the criminal code was as property owners, where they found it satisfactory. Even after Montesquieu's *De l'Espirit des loix* and Beccaria's *Of Crimes and Punishments*, advocating certainty and moderation of punishment rather than cruelty and violence, had created considerable interest on the continent, and a number of states (though not France) had modernised their system, reform of the English Bloody Code was little more on the political agenda than the reform of Parliament. When Lord George Gordon, at his trial for a libel on the judges in 1787, attacked indiscriminate capital punishment and advocated penal reform, the jury were astonished.[30]

Others, besides Meredith, saw the iniquity of the system. Horace Walpole thought 'the monthly shambles at Tyburn' shocked humanity and should be replaced by sentences of severe labour. The poets Goldsmith and Cowper and, later, Byron, Southey, Coleridge and Shelley were, on the law as on political economy, wiser than nearly all the experts.* The exception among the experts was Blackstone who, following Montesquieu, thought it 'a kind of quackery in government . . . to apply the same universal remedy . . . to every case of difficulty'. Dr Johnson recommended 'invigorating the law by relaxation, and extirpating wickedness by

---

* In calling for more executions Henry Fielding was an important exception, although as a successful reforming magistrate he could here be classed as a lawyer rather than a writer. His *Enquiry Into the Causes of the Late Increase of Robbers* is a highly intelligent examination of the problem. Unusually, for his time, Fielding was genuinely interested in discovering causes rather than in merely punishing effects. In his novels he satirised the follies and luxury of the rich, but in the *Enquiry* he maintained that luxury among the great was more of a moral than a political evil, and he concentrated upon restraining the luxury of the poor, 'the useful part of mankind'. Also in contrast to the novels and in contrast to his own leniency as a magistrate, he complained in the *Enquiry* of 'the foolish lenity of juries' and the excessive tenderheartedness of prosecutors; Fielding advocated fewer reprieves and quicker, more private, executions. Yet such severity, he thought, would be justified only if prevention had been attempted first. Fielding believed social conditions to be so bad that he was surprised there were not far more criminals. 'With proper care and proper regulation,' he believed, the great majority of the wretches hanged at Tyburn might have been made not only happy but useful members of society. So far from Fielding's call for fewer reprieves being the result of myopic legal conservatism, it was accompanied by proposals which would have reduced the number of executions. His error lay in not seeing that the harshness of the law was not the effect but the cause of the 'foolish lenity' of juries and prosecutors.[31]

lenity'. Goldsmith thought Parliament should direct the law 'rather to reformation than severity'. Both of them believed that the indiscriminate penalty of death led people to commit greater crimes, either to prevent detection or because the distinction between murder and other crimes was blurred. Plausible and logical though that idea was, criminals, unlike Parliament, illogically preserved the distinction, as the low and declining rate of murder demonstrates. Felons might say to themselves 'hung for a sheep, hung for a lamb', but they clearly did not say 'hung for a sheep, hung for a man'. Few robbers killed their victims.[32]

Burke consistently opposed the 'multiplication' of penal laws. The whole system he deemed 'radically defective'; the criminal law was 'abominable'. The Wilkites were strongly opposed to the use of capital punishment *in terrorem*, and Wilkes himself proposed that it should be ended for 'inferior crimes'. Wilberforce thought 'the barbarous system of hanging' had been tried too long. Charles James Fox, too, favoured reform. He said of 'certain sanguinary statutes' that 'their inhumanity was manifest, their absurdity ridiculous' and that 'to leave them standing in our code was a disgrace to our statute book'. Earlier he had supported the repeal of an act passed in an emergency in the reign of Elizabeth, which dealing with the holding for ransom of people only in '*Cumberland,* Northumberland, *Westmorland* and the *Bishoprick of Duresme*', had long been as obsolete as its spelling. The crime rate in the North having scarcely differed from that in the South for at least a hundred years, Fox thought that to be a rogue or vagabond in Cumberland should be no greater an offence than to be one in Middlesex.★[33]

Defences of the code

Notwithstanding such distinguished advocates, the reformers were long in a small minority, which raises the question of why this violent and 'abominable' penal code was acceptable to the vast majority. The problem can of course be explained away by ignoring the contemporary criticisms of Burke and others, and by dismissing the modern criticisms of such scholars as Radzinowicz as the outcome

★ The Lords disagreed and threw out the bill. The Frenchman's remark about Lord Liverpool, Prime Minister from 1812 to 1827, that if he had been present at the creation he would have said '*Mon Dieu, conservons le chaos*' could more justly have been applied to the House of Lords. To be fair, the Lords did in 1808 permit the abolition of one capital statute. Passed in 1565 and dealing only with stealing 'privily' from a person – so if the victim noticed the theft the statute did not apply – it had been obsolete for many years, only one offender ever having been executed under it. The peers were prepared to risk its repeal.[34]

of mistaken Whig history unconsciously judging the Bloody Code by later ideas. The behaviour of eighteenth-century parliamentarians has been defended on four main grounds: the hanging statutes were carefully scrutinised and often defeated; they were passed in such quantity because it was only after 1689 that Parliament sat regularly every year and had the opportunity to put them on the statute book; their plethora was owing to English law lacking generality, with the consequence that offences had to be specified in minute and tedious detail which did not nevertheless greatly extend the scope of the death penalty; and finally the law may have been bad in appearance, but it was operated so selectively and sensitively that it was in practice scarcely, if at all, objectionable. Complaints against the law for valuing a man's life as worth no more than a pair of shoes or stockings were thus largely rhetorical.[35]

Taking these defences in order, unquestionably more hanging statutes were both debated and defeated than was once thought. Still, not only Meredith, who wanted fewer executions, but Madan, who wanted more, and also Blackstone, publicly testified to Parliament's casual procedures and members' lack of interest. 'Laws of this kind,' Madan wrote in 1786, 'commonly pass as of course, without observation of debate.' And if Parliament was as careful in these matters as is now claimed, why did it tolerate the continuance of the Black Act long after any possible Jacobite or other emergency had passed? Apart from one unavailing attempt in 1732 to civilise it by stripping it of its most lethal features, nothing whatever was done.[36]

Had Elizabethan and Jacobean Parliaments sat more regularly, they might have passed capital statutes as complacently as their post-Revolution successors; there is no means of knowing. But any such legislation would have been passed in response to a massive increase in violent and other crime, the years 1590-1630 seeing the crest of the long-term crime wave. In contrast, from the mid-seventeenth to the mid-eighteenth century crime of all sorts generally declined, with some short-term rises. Thereafter property crimes slowly rose absolutely, though not relative to the size of the population. Unlike their predecessors, therefore, eighteenth-century Parliaments were adding blood to the penal code not only long after crime had reached its peak but after it had been in decline for some fifty years.[37]

Another equally important difference between the situation facing eighteenth-century Parliaments and that facing their predecessors was that in Tudor and Stuart times almost no suitable alternative punishment to the gallows existed. The state of the prisons made long sentences impossible, and though sending convicts to America was authorised as early as 1597, the colonies were not in a condition to accept many prisoners; transportation was not organised and only fitfully attempted. As a result unhanged felons could only be pilloried, whipped and branded – punishments which were widely thought insufficient for many crimes. That situation was transformed by the Transportation Act of 1718 which systematised and subsidised the banishment of felons to America. Despite the ignorant fears of some, transportation was not a soft option for the criminal. As well as separation from their families and an unpleasant, sometimes fatal voyage – over a quarter of the convicts died in one ship in 1730 – transported men and women suffered virtual slavery in America. No punishment is ever ideal; transportation certainly was not. But it filled the void between the gibbet and the whip. At the same time it was for its victims, with one or two exceptions who declined it, greatly preferable to execution. It was, said Henry Fielding's brother, the magistrate Sir John Fielding, in 1773, the 'most humane and effectual punishment' they had. Between 1718 and 1769 nearly 70 per cent of the felons convicted at the Old Bailey were transported; some 36,000 convicts were sent from England before the American war brought the traffic to an end. All in all eighteenth-century legislators had much less excuse than their predecessors for extending the scope of capital punishment.[38]

The existence of that 'humane and effectual punishment' is relevant also to the third defence, which partially ascribes the multiplication of specific hanging statutes to English law's lack of generality. Yet most of those statutes concerned property offences, and at the beginning of the eighteenth century the legal position over larceny, which was always by far the commonest crime, was both clear and general. Without going into the intricacies of 'benefit of clergy', simple larceny (theft without aggravating circumstances) was not punishable by death when committed by first offenders. The grand funeral march of capital statutes across the statute book, which began after the Glorious Revolution and continued into the nineteenth century, was not caused by any lack of generality in English law, but by Parliament's constant wish to depart from the generality of the larceny laws by imposing an almost endless series of specific exceptions. After 1718 it was caused by Parliament not being content with punishment of transportation for life for such offences as theft from a ship in a navigable river of goods worth more than four shillings, and insisting on making them capital. Finally, some of the more important Hanoverian legislation such as the Riot and the Black Acts had nothing at all to do with any alleged lack of generality in English law.[39]

The fourth defence – that the flexible and highly selective operation of the system largely removed its objectionable features – is the most substantial. Ever since Elizabethan times, selectivity had characterised the criminal law. Only about half the capitally convicted felons were then executed, and that proportion remained fairly constant till the mid-eighteenth century. Thereafter the proportion fell as crimes increased with the growth of population. The estimate made by the judges and the executive of the level of hanging that would be acceptable naturally varied with the amount of crime, always rising during the postwar crime waves but remaining reasonably consistent. Selectivity was a good in itself in that it lowered the number of tumbrils journeying to Tyburn or elsewhere. But, even if it was conceded that it prevented an excessive number of executions, which it did not, the defence would only be adequate if the flexibility of the system ensured that the right people were selected for execution.[40]

Whenever capital punishment is prevalent, some quantity of convicts will inevitably be hanged for what are, effectively, other people's crimes. Their fate will depend less on all the circumstances surrounding their own case than on how many other people committed the same crime or another capital offence at the same time – in other words the judges and the executive may decide that 'an example is necessary' and that the general licentiousness of the times demand stern measures; indeed hanging some in order to frighten others from the path of crime before it was too late was the essence of the system. Within that constraint the authorities did what they could, but since they so often knew so little of the background of the cases and of the criminals whose fate they were decreeing, the system was, as Edward Gibbon Wakefield wrote, inevitably something of a lottery (though less of one in the eighteenth century than in 1827-30 when Wakefield was an inmate of Newgate and only one in eight of the capital convicts were chosen for execution). A system that allowed the hanging of Mary Jones to mollify Ludgate shopkeepers, of Thomas Reynolds because of a strained interpretation of the Black Act, of 584 people in London and Middlesex in the years 1749-71 for offences against property, and of one in four of the fifteen and sixteen year olds who were capitally convicted in the 1780s was more a brutal sweepstake than a flexible, sensitive system of justice. Sir John Fielding would not have advocated confining executions to the most incorrigible offenders if he had believed that that already happened.[41]

All four defences, then, amount to little more than somewhat despairing pleas in mitigation, and the problem of the Bloody Code's survival and expansion remains. It was not after all just the outstanding men mentioned earlier who deplored the savagery of the criminal law and its underlying idea. A sensible Tory, answering Henry Fielding in 1751 and echoing the great judge Sir Matthew Hale seventy years before, pointed out that crime would be reduced not by more stringently enforced laws but by providing jobs for those who were willing to work. Some years later John Fielding similarly attributed much criminal activity to lack of employment as well as to the weakness of the watch. In 1786 a writer pointed out that 'the legal massacres which are exhibited to a thoughtless multitude' did not deter, and pleaded for an examination into 'the manifest injustice' of the law. Others wrote in similar vein.[42]

Yet, so far from being reformed, the English criminal law grew worse, although other countries were improving theirs. Englishmen did not even have to look abroad to find a more humane and effective example. The Professor of Law at Edinburgh University reckoned in 1797 that English law contained four times as many capital crimes as the Scottish and that during the previous thirty years the average number of executions in all Scotland was not more than six a year. In London, both in 1788 and in 1786, there were fifteen on one day, none of them for murder. After one such mass sacrifice *The Gentleman's Magazine* lamented that more people were executed in England than 'in all Europe'.[43]

Attitudes to crime are seldom rational. People commonly think there is a crime wave even when there is not, and law reform, perhaps fortunately, is a minority taste. Two centuries later nobody has much idea of how to deal with crime. The English notoriously dislike tidiness and systems; hence they never thought of applying, in Burke's words, 'a remedy to the source of evil'. Also they then had a strong and, in other ways, justified respect for the law. Finally, in the eighteenth century there was little idea of evolution or reform and widespread distrust of innovation.[44] Yet after all allowances have been made, both the unleashing by Europe's most moderate ruling elite of Europe's most barbarous criminal code upon some of the best-natured and most patient poor in Europe, and the elite's failure to reform that code, remain remarkable.

Why did it survive?

One possible explanation is that the amount of organised crime and the violence of the English people required the Bloody Code or something like it. Smuggling was both highly organised and violent. With some three million pounds of tea being illegally imported into Britain every year, together with wine, brandy, lace and other goods, up to 20,000 people were regularly engaged in smuggling in Sussex and Kent alone. East Anglia and Cornwall were little different. In 1745 Pelham hit the smuggling industry, which imported more than three quarters of the tea the country consumed, by taking 80 per cent off the tea duty. Wars and consequent rises in the duty revived it, until by 1784 more than half the tea consumed in Britain was illicitly imported. All told, smuggled goods may have amounted to up to 20 per cent of total British imports. By reducing the duty on tea by 90 per cent, Pitt immediately achieved a threefold increase in legally imported tea. Smuggling continued, but it never recovered its former glories.[45]

The smuggling gangs were large and often brutal. When some smugglers killed an excise man in Dorset in 1723, they likened the murder to killing a toad. The Hawkhurst gang's torture and murder of two customs officers in 1748 was so savage that people would still have found it shocking if toads had indeed been the victims. In 1747 the same gang had fought a battle with rivals in Goudhurst, another one with the citizens of Folkestone, and raided the customs house at Poole to recover a consignment of tea which had been seized. It also threatened to burn down the town of Goudhurst and massacre its inhabitants, the attempt being foiled by the militia and the gentry. The government's unwonted zeal against these smugglers was partly due to their Jacobite associations. The guerilla war led to casualties on both sides and the hanging of thirty-five smugglers; ten more only escaped execution by dying in prison. In 1775 witnesses who were to give evidence against a smuggler at Winchester Assizes were forced back to Southampton by 'a large, regulated body of smugglers, all armed and mounted'. Four years later a pitched battle was fought in Cranbourne Chase between some dragoons and a band of fifty smugglers whom they ambushed. Despite the advantage of surprise, the dragoons were defeated, losing their arms and their horses. Other battles more satisfactory to the authorities were fought at Orford and Southwold.[46]

The difficulty was that the poorer sort did not think smuggling was wrong. Nor even did the propertied classes, when they did it themselves. Few agreed with Wesley that smuggling was 'robbing the king'. Adam Smith's view that smugglers were useful free traders was more convenient as well as being economically sound. Lady Holdernesse, wife of the Warden of the Cinque Ports who was a former Secretary of State, ran a smuggling business in French gowns and furniture from Walmer Castle. Both in and out of office Walpole smuggled linen, lace and wine, even using the Admiralty barge for his operations. More scrupulous men did much the same. The upright Parson Woodforde bought tea, brandy, gin and silk handkerchiefs from a smuggler, who worried him by whistling under his parlour window.[47]

Like smuggling, poaching both enjoyed widespread public support and required organisation. Game had to be distributed to a national market and 'production', too, was often organised with poachers operating in gangs. As with smuggling, many of the propertied classes connived at poaching by consuming the game. But whereas 'robbing the king' was eventually curbed by parliamentary action, the profits of poaching were preserved by the gentry's determination to strengthen rather than reform the Game Laws.

Other criminal activity was less highly organised. Highway robbery needed some back-up in the shape of lookouts, informants and a receiver, but highwaymen seldom operated in large groups. The partnership between Dick Turpin, a murderous horsethief very different from his glamorous legend, and his fellow highwayman, Tom King, began when Turpin tried to hold up his future partner, evidence of competition not cooperation among 'the gentlemen of the road'.[48]

Between 1721 and 1723 Jonathan Wild, one time assistant to the Under City-Marshall and self-styled 'Thief-taker General of Great Britain', destroyed four large London gangs. Nevertheless Defoe claimed in the late 1720s that in London a man was still not safe going about his business even in the daytime. A peace always produced a crime wave because of the return of many discharged soldiers and sailors without employment, and after the War of the Austrian Succession Henry Fielding likewise thought that the streets of London would shortly be impassable 'without the utmost hazard'. Asked by the ministry to suppress a large and especially dangerous gang of cutthroats, he formed a simple and successful plan. Having got money from the Treasury, he bribed one gangster to betray the others and the 'hellish society' was wiped out. Other gangs came and went, their members' readiness to double-cross each other ensuring a rapid turnover. But outside London serious crime was rare, and most lawbreaking was small in scale and opportunist. Hardened criminals apart, crime was largely the prerogative of the indigent poor. Depending on the price of bread anything from 10 to 45 per cent of the population could not, unaided, buy enough food to live. At no time in the century was there a 'criminal class' or, outside London, a 'criminal subculture'.[49]

While, therefore, crime was as always a problem, no eighteenth-century equivalent of the Mafia existed. Fornication, infidelity, idleness and other vices were generally held to be growing, but violence did not catch the eye of the vigilant overseers of other people's morality. Fielding's *Tom Jones* praised highwaymen's forbearance from cruelty, and the murder rate, as was seen above, was astonishingly low. There was nothing in English crime or national behaviour to justify 'many cartloads of our fellow creatures', as Fielding put it, being regularly carried to 'slaughter', bringing the country 'dishonour in the sight of all Christendom'.[50]

A second possible explanation for the survival of the Bloody Code is that the propertied classes thought it necessary to keep the lower orders in proper obedience, an explanation that can stand on its own or be embroidered with the notion of 'a ruling-class conspiracy'.[51] Clearly, the code was an instrument of state power and part of it, most notably the Riot Act, played a role in controlling the unpropertied, but the code as a whole does not seem to have done so; nor apparently did the ruling elite think it did. Had the elite considered their hegemony seriously at risk, they would surely have sought to shore it up by strengthening the state's fairly meagre apparatus of repression. That instead they merely lengthened the litany of punishment, while lamenting the unruly licentiousness of the populace, suggests that they regarded the penal code as the protector of their property, not of their rule. The army, not Tyburn, was the guardian of the Hanoverian regime.

On their side, the poorest sort were not conspicuously intimidated by the law. Foreign visitors did not remark on the subservience of the London crowd; they noted its turbulence and its sturdy disrespect for its superiors. And Henry Fielding thought the street was 'the absolute right of the mob'; there, because of their numbers, the poorer sort were in command. That, of course, is not conclusive. The crowd might have sought relief from habitual subservience in taunting foreigners and muddying their superiors. A better test of the criminal law as an engine of coercion is the behaviour of the populace on hanging days. With the execution of malefactors, the machinery of justice achieved its climax of terror. Then, if ever, the turbulence should have been stilled, the mob cowed, and criminals frightened into amendment of life.[52]

The theory behind the ritual of public executions was that by demonstrating in front of thousands the awful consequences of criminal activity they would deter others from continuing down the same road, drawing them back from the path of theft and violence before it was too late. To many clergymen, an execution was a religious occasion which saved souls by example. To drive the lesson home great efforts were made to persuade the condemned to confess their crimes on the scaffold, to admit the justice of their sentences and to adjure their audiences to avoid the same dreadful fate.[53]

The pressures on convicts to come in their last hours to the aid of the state were primarily religious. Unfortunately an eighteenth-century prison was not a promising venue for religious instruction. Wesley did not much exaggerate when he called them nurseries 'of all manner of wretchedness' and Newgate, specifically, 'a region of horror'; their atmosphere was more that of an overcrowded brothel or gaming house than a penitentiary or a church. While Wesley and the Methodists took great pains with the condemned and won many conversions, the Newgate 'ordinary' or prison chaplain was usually less concerned with the state of their souls than with learning (or inventing) their life stories which he could then profitably market. Jack Sheppard, whose life story (which he had already given to Defoe) was likely to have an enormous sale because of the fame he had won by his extraordinary escapes from Newgate, was eventually so exasperated by his clerical inquisitor that he told him one good file would be of more use to him than all the bibles in the world. Many other criminals similarly preferred defiance to cooperation. Undismayed, the authorities continued their efforts till the last moment, Sheppard being badgered at Tyburn by the Under Sheriff, while Monmouth was pestered on the scaffold by two bishops seeking his confession to adultery with Henrietta Wentworth.[54]

In eighteenth-century Newgate, attendance at religious services was not compulsory; the chapel was anyway too small to accommodate all the prisoners. Those who were to die, though, had, on the Sunday before their execution, to attend the 'condemned sermon', a ceremony which entailed their sitting round a coffin and being peered at by ghoulish outsiders who had paid for the privilege, as well as being preached at by the ordinary. At Newgate religious sadism did not attain its full perfection until the early nineteenth century when the condemned sermon often destroyed the composure of even the bravest criminals. Yet even in the less refined earlier days, the ordinary's pounding away at the sins of the condemned and their coming ordeal could unnerve those not already befuddled with drink who were capable of registering the preacher's eloquence above the general hubbub.[55].

The condemned often entertained the ordinary to dinner the evening before their hanging. But whether or not they had enjoyed clerical company, only a few of them spent their last night singing psalms and praying. Drink and gambling were the more normal solace. Jonathan Wild, who had avoided the condemned sermon, took laudanum; an overdose brought vomiting, not death, and he took it too late to be spared hearing the big bell of St Sepulchre's which was tolled at midnight before an execution, or the visit of that church's sexton who rang the bell outside the condemned cells before intoning a verse beginning:

> All you that in the Condemned Hold do lie;
> Prepare you for tomorrow you shall die . . .

These ministrations, thoughtfully provided by a charitable bequest, provided an additional incentive to alcoholic oblivion.[56]

On the morning of their execution the condemned were given the sacrament if they wanted it and could afford the gaoler's fee. Their irons were struck off and their arms pinioned at the elbows. Many drank heavily again. They usually wore their best clothes: 'as neat and trim', said Defoe, 'as if they were going to a wedding.' Indeed Lord Ferrers and others did wear their wedding suit. Some preferred, however, to wear their shroud, which proved for one malefactor an unfortunate choice. Managing to jump out of the cart when it reached the gallows, he might well have vanished in the crowd, had he been less pessimistically attired. However much they had drunk in Newgate, a nonstop three mile journey to Tyburn would have caused depression to succeed intoxication, particularly as they travelled in the same carts as their coffins and, usually, with the ordinary and the hangman as well. The doomed therefore required topping up on the way. Their first stop provided at best only spiritual nourishment as once again they had to listen to the tolling of St Sepulchre's bell and to the sexton urging them to repent. Their three or four other stops were more congenial, being for liquor. Many convicts were thus drunk by the time they reached Tyburn and so, frequently, was the hangman himself. He once had to be restrained from hanging the ordinary.[57]

If the principal actors were often in a condition more suitable for farce than tragedy, so was the audience. The eight hanging days a year, wrote Bernard Mandeville in the 1720s, were 'jubilees . . . All the way from Newgate to Tyburn is one continued fair for whores and rogues of the meaner sort . . . and there are none so lewd, so vile or so indigent of either sex but at the time and place aforesaid they may find a paramour'. Sex was not the only diversion. Fights were frequent and, unlike the rest of the crowd, thieves and pickpockets were not on holiday. They followed the advice of Swift's *Clever Tom Clinch* from the gallows:

> *Take courage, dear Comrades, and be not afraid,*
> *Nor slip this occasion to follow your trade.*

Executions were attended by men and women of every degree. Boswell never missed one when he was in London. Inevitably, however, because there were far more of them, most of the crowd were of the poorer sort, and they were not awed by the occasion.[58]

Despite their experiences in Newgate and *en route* to Tyburn, many convicts behaved with great decorum at the gallows. Virtually all the Jacobite victims did so, though they were seldom any use to the state. Almost invariably they defended their cause on the scaffold, proclaiming James their King. Ordinary felons were often more helpful, confessing their crimes and expressing penitence. After accompanying ten convicts from Newgate, Charles Wesley recorded that 'none showed any natural fear of death: no fear, or crying or tears . . . singing several hymns', adding that the hour he had spent under the gallows was 'the most blessed hour of my life'. *[59]

---

* Those words were not a momentary aberration. In one of his hymns he wrote: 'Oh, lovely appearance of death!/ What sight upon earth is so fair?/ Not all the gay pageants on earth/ Can with a dead body compare.' In the same spirit his brother, John, wrote to their sister Patty: 'I believe the death of your children is a great instance of the goodness of God towards you.'[60]

Even however when the condemned were becomingly penitent and did not protest their innocence, complain of the severity of the sentence or curse and kick the hangman, two things prevented the executions from serving the state's avowed purposes. The first was the bravery of nearly all the criminals in the face of an agonising death. They died by strangulation, there being no 'drop' until the second half of the century, and even then death was not instantaneous. The execution carts were driven up to the triangular gallows, and when all the preliminaries had been completed, the noose adjusted round the neck and a cap pulled down over the face, the carts were driven away and the condemned left dangling. Foreigners were impressed by their courage, which lent dignity to crime and drew admiration from both crooks and the law-abiding. 'The heroic magnanimity, the contempt of death,' said Charles Fox, 'had a most mischievous effect.'[61]

The second, as Fielding pointed out, was the frequency of executions. Having become commonplace they had largely lost the power to shock and had degenerated into entertainment. The atmosphere at 'Tyburn Fair' prevented the state conveying, or the mob receiving, the solemn warning that retribution awaited those who resorted to crime. At the gallows Charles Wesley's piety was almost as rare as the Methodist glorification of death. The novelist Richardson was shaken by what he saw at Tyburn: the clergyman was an object of ridicule; 'the psalm was sung amidst the curses and quarrelling of the most abandoned and profligate of mankind'; and 'the unhappy wretches' ' preparations for death produced barbarous mirth not humane sympathy. The noise and chaos at Jonathan Wild's execution made it almost impossible for the ordinary to say prayers, and the crowd threatened to hang the executioner for allowing Wild time to prepare himself.[62]

In France the spectators sometimes prevented executions; in London, though the mob sometimes prevented a prisoner being rehanged after the rope had broken, it only once attempted a rescue and only once, fortuitously, foiled a hanging. In the confusion caused by the serving of a writ on the hangman, William Marvell, on his way to Tyburn with three condemned men in 1717, he was attacked and knocked out. The procession continued without him to the gallows where the mob, having beaten up a bricklayer who had offered to deputise, deterred any further volunteers despite the offer of a fat fee; the criminals were eventually reprieved. But though actual rebellion against executions was avoided, the attitude of the crowd turned Tyburn into more of a festival of defiance than a ceremony of deterrence. Even so, suggestions by Fielding, Mandeville and others for altering the ritual so as to reassert its proper purpose were ignored. It was almost as though in religion the Black

Mass had superceded the real one without the Church intervening. Not until 1783 was the Tyburn parade abandoned, partly because of the objections of local residents, but mainly because of its degrading scenes and its encouragement to crime. From then on criminals were hanged outside Newgate, where the crowds were still huge and their behaviour little better. At the execution of two murderers in 1807, no fewer than thirty people were killed.[63]

Violence was frequent after Tyburn executions. Friends and relatives of the dead fought the agents of surgeons to prevent the bodies being taken for dissection. The contests, said Richardson, were 'fierce and bloody'. A false rumour that Jack Sheppard's body was being kept for dissection in Longacre caused a violent disturbance which was only quelled by the reading of the Riot Act and a company of Guards. Occasionally, too, the mob took its revenge on the prosecutors of hanged men, attacking their houses and burning their furniture. After an execution in 1769 they even attacked and destroyed the house of the Sheriff.[64]

Even, then, the most violent manifestations of the criminal law failed to intimidate the poorer sort. Indeed public executions did not even deter crime; more probably they promoted it. Mandeville thought they were 'decoys', not deterrents, and Fielding and Wakefield thought much the same. Certainly executions were regarded as promising opportunities for pickpocketing, itself a crime punishable by hanging. And many criminals who ended on the gallows had watched earlier executions. According to Dr Johnson, Dr Dodd was the first clergyman to suffer 'public execution for immorality'. The second one, Rev James Hackman, was present at the hanging of Dodd.[65]

Social control

If the violent criminal law failed as an instrument of social coercion – a rioter who had threatened to pull down the house of a Bow Street magistrate extolled after his acquittal 'the great liberty of mobbing a justice now and then' – the law as a whole was a highly effective apparatus of 'social control'. As such it did much to gain consent to the social and political system of Hanoverian England, being with the monarchy, the Church and Parliament, one of the four most important civil institutions of the state. Moreover its three companions all suffered handicaps. The divine indefeasible hereditary right of Kings, damaged by 1688–89, had been exploded by 1714; with fifty-seven people having a better hereditary claim to the throne than George I, little divinity hedged the Hanoverians.[66] Parliament enjoyed high esteem among the governing elite but was too obviously the preserve of the rich to provide by itself sufficient ideological cement for the state. With the great majority of MPs divorced from any but a tiny electorate, Parliament busied itself with its own concerns, such as whether champagne should be imported in bottles or only in casks. The machinery and activities of central government (save for the Treasury and the revenue departments) were minimal. Local government was in the hands of the country gentry. Of the nearly 3,000 acts passed between 1715 and 1754, more than two thirds were concerned with individuals or localities, usually benefiting property owners. Only some twenty a year were national, and most of those were promoted by pressure groups, usually including an extension of capital punishment. In two parts of the dominions of the Georges, Scotland and Hanover, virtually general education existed. There was no question of that or similar social provision in far richer England where the poor's ignorance was welcomed as a providential opiate. Normally the government dealt only with public finance, foreign policy and defence. As the Wilkite, John Glynn, told the Commons in 1770, 'the only point in which the present ministers seem to concern themselves about the people of this country is to get their money . . .'[67]

The Church of England inspired greater loyalty and affection than the monarchy, at least between 1714 and 1780, and religion excited passions and violence. Yet the Church's vast influence was impaired by its Bishops' prolonged residence in London during the parliamentary session and still more by its parsons' frequent non-residence in their parishes all the year round. Its doctrines, too, of non-resistance and passive obedience had been battered by 1688-89 and 1714. All the same, religion was still the director of society and opinion, and even though the Church's influence was declining in the large towns it strongly sustained the social order. But if people, as Charles I had believed, were still 'governed by the pulpit more than the sword', many did not sit under the pulpit and religion needed some auxiliary help.[68]

The social order whereby the rich were rich and the poor were poor had, of course, been ordained by God, and God's work was upheld by the Church. But the law provided an additional buttress. If the Church had lost some of its magic, the law had gained in majesty. Judges on assize in full panoply and dignity were more impressive and intimidating than bishops scurrying to the House of Lords to do the government's bidding; and, unlike the bishops, the judges did not brook dissent:[69]

Fictitious bonds, the bonds of wealth and law
Still gather strength, and force unwilling awe.

Goldsmith's well-known lines were only half right. Like those of wealth, the bonds of law forced some unwilling awe but were not fictitious. The law was not just an instrument of the rulers. It was also the protection of the ruled. Equality before the law was, of course, nowhere near complete; it seldom or never is. Wesley said that people needed money to succeed in the courts against the oppression of the rich. Guilty aristocrats were rarely punished. The great, Fielding wrote in his *Enquiry*, were 'beyond the reach of any, unless capital, laws.' But the exception is significant. The general conviction that England was ruled by law and that, whatever other inequalities existed, the law was neutral between rich and poor and was in some degree independent of government was a potent fiction, yet it was not sheer illusion. Smollett's Peregrine Pickle was arrested in France and imprisoned without trial because he had offended a prince at a masquerade. Englishmen were proud that nothing of that sort could happen in England. The law was the law, and all were subject to it. In civil cases, as in criminal, the courts often attempted to protect the weaker party. In a long-running conflict between landlords and tenants in Cumbria over forest and other rights, the courts continually upheld the rights of the tenants.[70]

Nevertheless the labouring poor, because of a £10 per year property qualification, did not serve on juries and so were not tried by their peers. They were more likely than others to be convicted, and if capitally convicted they were correspondingly much less likely to be able to procure men of standing to testify to their good character, greatly reducing their chances of a reprieve.[71] The poor were also at the mercy of often tyrannical, if usually fairly benevolent, JPs; and they fared much worse than others before Justices Frolick, Thrasher, Buzzard, Gobble and the other ignorant, biased and corrupt magistrates in the pages of Fielding and Smollett.[72]

All the same, the labouring poor were not quite outside the legal nation as they were outside the political nation. During the century many prominent people were robbed or attacked: among them were George II when Prince of Wales, George III, 'Butcher' Cumberland, the Archbishop of Canterbury, Horace Walpole, John Wesley, Lord North when premier, Charles Fox, the Duke of Devonshire, the Younger Pitt and Edmund Burke. But they were not alone. The poor, too, were frequent victims of theft, and they, like others, then resorted to law. At Essex quarter sessions between 1760 and 1800, more than 20 per cent of the prosecutions for felony were brought by labouring men; in assault cases the percentage was higher. The proportion brought by tradesmen or artisans varied between 33 and 40 per cent. Though passive obedience to the law was far from universally practised either by the rich or the poor, it was extensively and plausibly preached. When Hardwicke, on circuit exhorting grand juries to do their duty, talked of 'the best body of laws that human wisdom can frame' and adduced 'considerations which ought to make us more in love with the constitution', he expected to be, and indeed was, taken seriously.* The law enjoyed acceptance and legitimacy among all ranks of the country including, at least outside London, many of the labouring poor.[74]

Consequently the law was a powerful 'social control', buttressing 'liberty and property', the watchwords of Hanoverian England and, especially, of the ruling elite. They, after all, enjoyed much the most liberty and owned much the most property. But they had to pay a price. Both belief in the rule of law and the prestige of the courts depended on the widespread conviction that all free-born Englishmen enjoyed equality before the law. And to maintain the credibility of that fiction the rulers had to act more or less in accordance with it. Hence, with some exceptions (duelling, gambling, the frauds of Walpole's day and the plundering of India) the rulers along with the ruled consented to be governed by the law. Goldsmith's 'tyrant laws' restrained them both.[75]

Like the penal code the rule of law well suited England's rulers, but neither was the outcome of 'a ruling class conspiracy'. For one thing both of them well suited hosts of other people as well; if there was any conspiracy it was not confined to the 'ruling class'. For another, there is no evidence of any kind of conspiracy. For a third, the very notion of 'a ruling class conspiracy' is mystical, if not magical. A ruling class may accept and benefit from a given situation, but that is a very different thing from a conscious conspiracy by all its members.[76] So the explanation for the continuance of the Bloody Code must be sought elsewhere.

A different species

> Rich men . . . vilify us when there is only this difference, they rob under the cover of law, forsooth, and we plunder the rich under the protection of our own courage.
>
> *Charles Bellamy, a pirate*[77]

Maintenance of faith in the rule of law and in the law's impartiality required that a crime should be punished whoever was the criminal;

---

* Eighteenth-century politicians professed themselves to be 'in love' more freely than their successors. In 1761 Jenkinson wrote to Grenville: 'I am absolutely in love with Lord Bute . . .'. Today no politician would dare avow such a sentiment for fear of exciting the moral outrage of the tabloid press. Jenkinson was in love with Bute's patronage, not his person.[73]

it did not require that all forms of wrongdoing be visited with equal severity or even punished at all. The South Sea Bubble and Walpole's behaviour demonstrated that. Double standards were more than usually rife. The poor's pillaging of the rich and themselves brought them savage penalties; the Venetian oligarchy's pillaging of the state – Mr Pillage in Fielding's play *Eurydice Hiss'd* is Walpole – brought them money, titles and offices:

> *The manners of the great affect,*
> *Stint not your pleasure:*
> *If conscience had their genius checkt,*
> *How got they treasure?*

The rich did not regard the means they used to enrich themselves as wrong. They ignored the parallels that Gay and other satirists drew between their depredations and those of the poor, keeping the two things segregated in their minds. Burke's claim that one of Pitt's constitutional proposals was less excusable than housebreaking or highway robbery was an almost unique breach of that strict mental apartheid.[78]

The poor, too, as has been seen, had their own ideas of what constituted crime, but their views affected only the amount of crime, not the criminal law or its penalties. They were not represented in Parliament, where crime was specified and punishments decided upon. The task of a committee on criminal law reform was described by Horace Walpole as to consider 'amending the laws enacted against the vices of the lower people'. William Godwin defined crime as: 'Those offences which the wealthier part of the community has no temptation to commit.' Not only, moreover, did the rich not regard their own activities as criminal, they were seldom tempted to imitate those of the poor. 'Crime' was no longer an aristocratic or middle-class pastime.[79]

Under Elizabeth aristocratic violence was endemic. Occasionally private wars were fought, as when Sir Thomas Langton with eighty men attacked Thomas Haughton in Lancashire in 1589 and killed him. The introduction of duelling probably helped to curb such excesses, as did the growing habit of going to law. After the Restoration upper-class violence revived. In 1676 the Earl of Rochester was involved in a drunken brawl at Epsom in which one of his friends was killed. Two landowners tried to murder Robert Harley in 1693. In the later years of Queen Anne, 'Mohocks' or upper-class hooligans roamed the London streets slitting noses and beating up watchmen and passers-by. General Oglethorpe, the prison reformer and ineffectual pursuer of the Jacobite army in 1745, killed a man in a street brawl twenty years earlier. Yet, except for duelling, aristocratic violence became rare in the eighteenth century. Under Elizabeth and James I 'a poor man was hanged for stealing food for his necessities and a luxurious courtier . . . could be pardoned after killing the second or third man'; under the Georges the poor man in similar circumstances might still be hanged, but the luxurious courtier no longer killed his second or third man and probably would not have been pardoned if he had.[80]

> *Each hates his neighbour for encroaching;*
> *Squire stigmatises squire for poaching.*

Nevertheless, when laws were inconvenient they were ignored. The gentry continued to poach. Common gaming houses were illegal; the rich, though denounced by Fielding for setting a 'pernicious example', gambled openly in clubs. Faro had been illegal at least since 1738; Charles James Fox flagrantly ran the Faro bank at Brooks's in 1781-82. Electoral bribery and corruption were similarly winked at. As late as 1802 the Lord Chancellor, Eldon, thought corruption in Aylesbury was a lesser evil than extending the franchise there.[81]

Yet, with violence largely eschewed and property already in their hands, for the parliamentary classes ordinary crime had little attraction. The rich did not plunder each other; they plundered the state. So at least in conventional crime the poor, who had greatly increased in number, were on their own. The consequence was the intensification of the Bloody Code and the Game Laws. This was not just because crime was something that was committed by the poor and punished by the rich; it was also because the poor were another country, like the Scottish Highlanders and the Irish Catholics. Because of their increased numbers, the poor posed problems throughout Western Europe. England was no exception, though England had more of the middling sort than her neighbours and her poor were, on the whole, treated a good deal better than elsewhere. Fielding, like Defoe, thought they were incomparably 'more liberally provided for' than anywhere else on the globe, at the same time complaining that so little was known of their suffering, that they were often referred to with abhorrence and seldom with pity. The ruling elite regarded the poor as different beings. In *Joseph Andrews* Fielding says of 'high people' and 'low people' that 'so far from looking on each other as brethren in the Christian language, they seem scarce to regard each other as of the same species'. Later Burns wrote of

> *A creature of another kind,*
> *Some coarser substance, unrefin'd . . .*[82]

If servants in daily contact with their employers were scarcely Christian, the 'criminal' poor who were only seen in the dock or in the mass were scarcely human. Goldsmith might write that 'as their faces are like ours, their hearts are so too', but his readers were not convinced. Sympathy for criminals is scarce at any time; it vanishes when they can be regarded as a race apart. Similarly it is much easier to kill or injure somebody if the victim is considered less human than the killers. The dehumanisation of the poor was not taken half as far in England as in Ireland, where Swift took it to its satirical conclusion by suggesting that the Irish economic problem could be solved by selling most one-year-old Irish children to be eaten at the tables of the rich. But it had gone far enough for the hanging of the poor by the dozen to be perfectly acceptable to the English upper classes, who never stopped to think whether less violent methods might not serve them at least as well.[83]

Yet lack of sympathy for the labouring poor did not preclude sympathy for its individual members any more than Fielding's harsh criminal theories prevented him from being a humane justice; and the English liking for public executions was not limitless. Even during the anti-Catholic hysteria of the Popish Plot, Shaftesbury was worried that hanging so many had been a mistake. Had all those liable to the death penalty been hanged, many of the English would have felt that '*nausée de la guillotine*' that arose, rather belatedly, during the French Revolution.[84] So judges, juries and the executive acted individually to see that the system was not, as it were, given enough rope to hang itself. The criminal law became even closer to being literally draconian in that one penalty – hanging – was prescribed for nearly every offence, but the application of the law did not. Hence the system, savage as it was, did have a certain logic – so long as it applied to somebody else. And it did. Only the poor were criminals, and they were different.

The execution of Dr Dodd

Crime was not of course the complete monopoly of the poor. The mad Lord Ferrers was hanged in 1760 for murdering his valet. The nortorious Colonel Charteris was convicted of raping a maidservant in 1730, though influence won him a pardon instead of a hanging, an inglorious episode which Fielding satirised in his play *Rape upon Rape*.* Dr Dodd, the former tutor to Lord Chesterfield and one of

---

* In his Ballad 'The True English Dean to be hanged for a Rape', Swift wrote: 'Ah! dost then not envy the brave Colonel Chartres,/ Condemned for thy crime, at three score and ten./ To hang him all English would lend him their garters;/ Yet he lives, and is

the King's chaplains, was hanged for forgery in 1777. The jury had recommended mercy, and Dr Johnson and many others made prolonged efforts to win him a reprieve, but George III was almost never disposed to leniency in forgery cases and anyway felt that Dodd's social position should not procure him special favour. The two Perreau brothers (both of whose guilt was at least doubtful) had recently been executed for the same crime, and either the King or an adviser said that if Dodd did not suffer the sentence of the law, the Perreaus had been murdered.†[86]

Nothing about Dodd's crime or about the man himself was exceptionally deserving of public sympathy. Nobody doubted his guilt: he had obtained a large sum of money by false pretences and forgery. And while he wrote edifying books, he was not an edifying character. Dodd, who had once tried to bribe the Lord Chancellor, had earlier published a sermon advocating the curtailment of capital punishment. But at much the same time he had shown himself very ready to give evidence against a highwayman who had consequently been hanged. That, as Radzinowicz pointed out, was unusual. Fielding's Mrs Western refused to prosecute a highwayman who had stolen her earrings as well as her money. Not so Dr Dodd, the campaigner against excessive capital punishment who had lost nothing. And not so his fellow sufferer, Lord Ferrers, who also prosecuted a highwayman.[88]

Nevertheless, while he was lying under sentence of death, Dodd was practically canonised by public opinion. Even Newgate prison became unusually quiet in his honour. A vast public petition to save him was mounted. His execution was regarded as a calamity. It was witnessed by probably the largest crowd of the century, and more than 2000 troops were in Hyde Park for fear of trouble. Yet that enormous crowd paid little attention to the fifteen-year-old Joseph Harris, a boy executed at the same time who was accompanied to Tyburn by his father. The *Annual Register* only mentioned him as 'the other convict [who] was turned off'. His crime had been the robbing

---

ready to ravish agen . . .' Charteris, 'a man infamous for all manner of vices', had made a habit of raping girls in his service and was known as 'Rape Master General', but he died two years later, aged 57 *pace* Swift, without, as far as is known, having done so again.[85]

† Dr Johnson's famous remark – 'Depend upon it, Sir, when a man knows he is to be hanged in a fortnight it concentrates the mind wonderfully' – was made of Dodd. About him, though, it appears not to have been apposite. Dodd did not *know* he was to be hanged in a fortnight. Up to the last minute he was confident that he would be reprieved or even pardoned. Even when he knew he would be hanged, Dodd hoped to avoid death. This did sometimes happen if the hangman, as in Dodd's case, was bribed to adjust the knot in a certain way and the victim was cut down quickly and put in a hot bath. Such a plan to resuscitate Dick Sheppard was frustrated by the crowd thinking his body was being taken not to be revived but to the surgeons to be anatomised.[87]

of a stagecoach passenger of two halfguineas and seven shillings (as opposed to Dodd's £4300); neither Dr Johnson nor anybody else had made any effort to save him.[89]

> Here while the proud their long-drawn pomps display,
> There the black gibbet glooms beside the way.

The execution of the lower orders for relatively minor offences was perfectly acceptable, exciting neither interest nor concern. The hanging of a clergyman or a gentleman for such an offence was a very different matter. Dr Dodd was recognisably of the same substance as the propertied classes. He clearly had feelings to which respectable people could relate, unlike the far more deserving youth killed on the same day. For Dr Dodd tears were shed all round. The ordinary processes of the law were not meant for people like him: gentlemen were never subjected to public whipping, since that would have degraded them; and when, in 1782, a clergyman was sentenced to six months imprisonment for killing a man in a duel, the jury petitioned the King to have him excused since 'they never thought he would be subjected to so grievous a punishment'. The shock caused by Dodd's execution led many people for the first time to question the violence of the criminal law, though Parliament continued to add to it.[90]

Legal and political conservatism

The execution of Lord Ferrers had not done so. He was a murderer, and murderers whatever their social position deserved to die. Dodd's case was quite different. A string of men like him, executed for relatively trivial offences, would soon have brought an end to the Bloody Code, which owed its survival to its victims coming overwhelmingly from the poor and to the ruling elite's attitude to them or to the 'criminal' classes. Yet, as was noted above, the English poor were in other respects treated better than the poor of other countries. Visitors to France noticed the difference. Almost echoing Fielding on England, James Watt wrote from Paris to his father, the inventor, that 'one would think that the common people here were looked upon as different creatures . . .'[91] An additional reason for the persistence of the code is therefore needed, and the extreme conservatism of the lawyers and the politicians supplies it.

Between 1715 and the end of the century Parliament passed about 100 'hanging statutes', but only six notable acts reforming the criminal law. In cases of high treason, after 1747, a prisoner's counsel was allowed to speak on his behalf. The terrible punishment of *peine et forte* for refusing to plead, a torture which had not been inflicted since 1735, was abolished in two acts of 1772 and 1774. English was substituted for Latin as the language of indictments in 1730, despite the opposition of the Lord Chief Justice. Witchcraft was abolished as a crime in 1736, despite the opposition of the Scottish judge, Lord Grange. The burning of women was ended in 1790 in favour of mere drawing and hanging, despite the opposition of the Lord Chancellor. And two years later Fox's Libel Act laid down that it was for the jury not the judge to decide whether the matter published was libellous; the bill, supported by Pitt, was strongly opposed by the Lord Chancellor and all the judges. These reforms scarcely amounted to an undignified stampede to a decent criminal code.[92]

How should the responsibility be shared between the politicians and the lawyers? Sir William Meredith gave it all to the politicians, 'the true hangmen'. Clearly the ultimate power was theirs, and it was they who erected gallows all over the criminal law. How far, however, they expected the laws they passed to be carried out or how far they agreed with the judges' growing practice of recommending reprieves is not known. Probably, indeed, 'Parliament' did not have a view. Capital statutes were usually passed at the instance of a pressure group in a thin house without a division, with most MPs indifferent as to what was happening. Had they been asked, they would probably have replied that the law should be properly enforced. Equally, on the other hand, had they been asked if they approved of what the judges were doing, they would probably have expressed complete confidence in the judiciary. In any case the lawyers never showed them a path that led away from Tyburn. The law was so antique and so full of 'quibbles' that a 'quibble-loving lawyer' could, according to Bentham, only endure to hear of heavier punishments. Certainly, so far from favouring reform, the lawyers strongly opposed it.[93]

Lord Loughborough, Lord Chief Justice and later Lord Chancellor, was strongly of the opinion that if there were any defects in the criminal law, the judges were the most likely people to discover them; any proposal, therefore, to change the law should be submitted to them first. Indeed he thought such proposals should originate from the judges.* This view was not expressed, let alone acted upon, when

---

* Loughborough had only been on the bench for six years, before which he had been a remarkably untrustworthy politician. His plea for legislative deference to himself and the judges was therefore something of an impertinence. In his speech he favoured the continued burning of women because it was a better deterrent and did not make much difference as the criminal was always strangled before the flames reached her. Leaving aside Loughborough's sentiments, this was not even true, as the case of Catherine Hayes had shown. To be fair, Loughborough began by opposing the additional penalty of dissection after death being extended from murderers to burglars and robbers. His

MPs were proliferating death bills. Indeed Blackstone pointed out that even minor bills in the Lords affecting the property rights of a few were referred to the judges; yet death bills which affected the lives, liberty and property of the many were not. For the judges, only proposals to reform the Bloody Code were innovations that required judicial inspection; proposals to extend it were run of the mill and did not merit their scrutiny.[95]

While eighteenth-century judges softened the operation of the law by frequent recommendations to mercy, they never took the smallest step to ameliorate the law itself, and from 1780 until the 1820s it was they, headed by Lords Ellenborough and Eldon, who with very few exceptions took the lead in opposing any proposal to reform it. At the same time the severity of the common law had, as Holdsworth said, 'a perverting influence on the legislature'. So the lawyers were at least as culpable as the politicians.[96]

The Younger Pitt had begun by favouring reform of the criminal law, but he then came to believe that such projects should first be submitted to the judges – and that ended his career as a penal reformer. 'It would be extremely dangerous,' he claimed in 1787, 'to take any step which might have the smallest tendency to discrediting' the exiting system of criminal justice. The proposal that Pitt defeated was not a drastic measure of fundamental reform but merely an attempt to bring in a bill to set up a commission to examine 'the state of all the Penal Laws now in force'. Before that danger had been averted in England, and while Lord Loughborough was still defending the burning of women, Prussia had reduced executions to fifteen a year, Sweden had reduced them to ten a year, Austria to less than one a year, Scotland to four a year, Amsterdam, which was about one-third the size of London, to less than one a year, and Tuscany had (temporarily) abolished them. In the year of Pitt's speech, England executed ninety-two people in London and Middlesex alone.[97]

England's relatively free institutions prevented reform of the criminal law. England had no absolute monarch to override legal obscurantism and the indifference of England's governors. Well before the end of the century the Bloody Code, together with the Game Laws and the slave trade, had become part of that great wonder of the age, the British constitution, regarded by its priests as perfect,

---

argument, however, was that to do so would make the punishment for burglary the same as that for murder and would therefore increase the number of burglaries that were accompanied by murder. Since the glaring defect of the criminal code, which Loughborough so strenuously defended, was precisely that the penalty for murder was (except for dissection) exactly the same as it was for a host of trivial offences, Loughborough's speech was a triumph of tortuous judicial reasoning and demonstrated the certain consequence of leaving law reform to the judges.[94]

and untouchable by the profane hands of laymen. When Peel began
to reform the criminal law in the 1820s, he was breaking, he said,
'the sleep' of more than a century. Even then Peel and the country
were still drowsy. Only with the far more radical reforms of the
capital laws carried out in the 1830s by Lord John Russell and the
Whigs was the sleep finally broken. Indeed, granted the conservatism
of Parliament and the lawyers, the proper matter for surprise is not,
perhaps, the survival of the Bloody Code, but the abolition of the
crime of witchcraft and the introduction of the English language into
indictments.[98]

A proper police force, on the French model, would have been a
better safeguard of the rich's property than the penal code, but that
was ruled out as a threat to the liberty of the gentry who did not
want a strong and active central government. Had they been forced
to choose between property and liberty, they would no doubt have
plumped for property and settled for a police force. But no such
choice was forced upon them. They were able to enjoy both.[99]

Yet the rulers of Hanoverian England were aware that they were
few and that their power rested on a narrow base. David Hume told
them that 'force [was] always on the side of the governed' and that
the governors could only rely on opinion. Forty years later
Archdeacon Paley told them the same thing: 'The physical strength
resides in the governed . . . let civil governors learn from hence to
respect their subjects . . . civil authority is founded in opinion; that
general opinion therefore ought always to be treated with deference
and managed with delicacy and circumspection.' In theory Hume and
Paley were of course right; in practice, however, unless the
government has broken down, the strength or violence of the
governors is almost invariably much greater than that of the
governed. In any case England's rulers generally heeded the
warnings.[100]

Arguably the number of reprieves suggests delicacy and circumspection even in the treatment of crime. But the number of
executions, not reprieves, is the proper yardstick, and London was
the hanging capital of Europe. According to Mr Douglas Hay this
was inescapable: the terror of the criminal law was the foundation of
the system. And according to a historian writing from the other end
of the political spectrum, 'a sacred constitution, taking seriously the
thirty-seventh Article of Religion of the Established Church, had
defended itself with the death penalty'. Although Dr Clark does not
much elaborate, he evidently agrees that the Bloody Code was a
crucial preservative of the regime.[101]

The regime could not have survived only by means of what
Disraeli called its 'political mystification' and what Mr Thompson
calls its 'theatre', brilliant though it was.

When we with superficial view
Gaze on the rich, we're dazzled too: . . .
Thus oft the cheated crowd adore
The thriving knaves that keep them poor.

Some degree of force and violence was necessary too. And the system worked. The wealth of the country grew, and the ruled stayed in submission. The constantly-denounced 'rabble' remained 'licentious'; they did not become revolutionary. All the same, 'theatre' and violence were far from alone in securing the acquiescence of the ruled. Religion, the army, the Poor Law, the influence of landlords and the whole nexus of property relations, economic progress, success in war, and the ideology of free-born Englishmen and 'No Popery' were probably all more important in gaining the consent of the governed than was the penal code. Indeed, the criminal law's extravagant violence, whereby, as a biographer of the highwayman James Maclean asserted, hanging became close to 'a sport' and 'a pastime', almost certainly made it a less effective engine of repression than a more moderate legal system, in which executions were solemn events because of their rarity, as Fielding advocated, even one without better policing, would have been. The law was left unreformed less because the ruling elite thought it an essential weapon of control, than because a Parliament of landowners was not adversely affected by it, and the different species who were affected by it were not represented. The subject was not therefore considered important enough to merit a policy.[102]

If, however, those who believe the regime was based on terror and capital punishment are right, the ultimate controllers of 'the rabble' and the indispensable servants of England's rulers were the hangmen. 'All greatness, all power, all subordination,' de Maistre wrote, 'rests on the executioner'; and in Dahomey the executioner was so important that he normally became Prime Minister. Not so in England. But as the crimes of the vulgar, a contemporary pointed out, reflected the vices of the rulers, appropriately a number of executioners were criminals and were themselves hanged. John Price, executioner in 1714-15, was hanged for murder. Of his immediate successors, Pasha Rose was executed at Tyburn, and William Marvell only escaped the gallows and was transported to America because the jury found that the value of the goods he had stolen was less than five shillings. John Thrift, who held office from 1735 to 1752, was found guilty of murder, but then was pardoned so that he could continue to 'hang on'. His successor, Thomas Turlis, was caught stealing, but he also was too valuable a man to lose. Instead of being hanged he was made hangman of Surrey as well as of the City of London.[103]

In that respect Turlis resembled Edward Dennis, the eighteenth century's best known executioner because of his appearance in *Barnaby Rudge*. Though Dennis, who hanged both Mary Jones and Dr Dodd, did not play the prominent role in the Gordon Riots which Dickens gave him in the novel, he was sentenced to death for his part in them. So far, however, from being executed as he is in *Barnaby Rudge*, he was soon reprieved and pardoned 'so that he could hang his fellow rioters'. Dennis continued as a valued servant of the state until 1786, being presented by the Sheriffs of London with an official robe, which he promptly sold.[104] In punishing others for actions similar to those he had himself committed, Dennis symbolised part of Hanoverian England. And the criminal law which he consummated was the most violent feature of English life.

EIGHT

The Press Gang

Authority, in times of full internal peace and concord, is armed against law . . . The wild state of nature is renewed in one of the most civilised societies of mankind, and great violence and disorder are committed with impunity . . .

David Hume, on the pressing of seamen

Is it not an abominable sight in a free country like ours to have a number of sailors, with fire arms and cutlasses, frequently, in the dead of night, sometimes intoxicated with liquor, making their way into the dwellings of peaceable inhabitants, dragging a sober unoffending subject from his home and settled means of livelihood, to convey him on board an impress tender, from thence to a guardship, imprisoned among the moral and physical contagion of a miscellaneous, kidnapped crew, to be driven across the seas, no mortal can tell him where, nor for how long a time; and what is still worse, seized by surprise, not suffered to bid a kind farewell to his wife and family, nor have a thought to their future subsistence, when deprived of his care; . . . And, Sir, is it not a serious matter of reproach to this wise, this liberal nation, never yet to have provided a remedy for such dreadful and extensive sufferings?

Temple Luttrell MP, 1777[1]

Only slightly less violent than the criminal law was the press gang. In his essay, 'Of Some Remarkable Customs', David Hume cited only one English practice: the pressing of seamen, one of the oddest features of eighteenth-century England.

The English prided themselves on the rule of law, contrasting their happy state with arbitrary continental governments; yet they tolerated the press gang, which grossly offended the spirit of their constitution. Voltaire illustrated the anomaly by telling of a boatman who, having boasted that English liberty made it preferable to be a sailor in England than an archbishop in France, was then promptly press-ganged and imprisoned. In London in 1756 the inventor, James Watt, was afraid to go about the streets for fear of a similar fate.[2]

At the end of the seventeenth century, pressing was stigmatised by a merchant seaman as an 'evil custom'. Before that, it was more easily defensible. Until the 1690s pressed men were often released and paid off after only six or eight months' service. In the eighteenth century, however, they were turned over from one ship to another, and their servitude could be almost indefinite. Unquestionably the state needed seamen. Not only Britain's maritime hegemony but her national security, her prosperity and her dynasty depended upon the navy. And to man the fleet in wartime some degree of compulsion was unavoidable as the navy needed some five times as many sailors in wartime as it did in peacetime. As in twentieth century wars there would not have been enough volunteers.[3]

Yet the violence of the press gang system was not unavoidable. As was stressed in a well-informed memorandum to Walpole in about 1727, probably written by a future Admiralty secretary, pressing should have been a weapon of last resort after every effort had been made to encourage voluntary recruitment. The need for change and for putting our seamen 'into better temper', the writer concluded, was shown by 'the scarcity of them at home and the scandal we give the world in their being the ringleaders in all the piracies and robberies committed in foreign parts'. Eighteenth-century ministries and Parliaments had a choice. They could have had fleets largely staffed by volunteers, supplemented by men drafted by regulated and fair compulsion, or fleets which were, said the popular and humane Admiral Vernon, 'defrauded by injustice . . . manned by violence and maintained by cruelty'. If only by default, they always chose the latter.[4]

The capricious violence of the press gang could only have been justified by its efficiency. Yet impressment did not work well. At the beginning of wars it accentuated the shortage of seamen, drove up wages in the merchants' service and obliged slow mobilisation. Walpole conceded in 1740 that it was both 'ineffectual' and insufficient. Many of those who were picked up by press gangs were useless, while many suitable sailors escaped. Confronted with a press gang's haul, an admiral thought they were the 'scum of the earth' who might have come from 'the condemned hole at Newgate'. According to Lord Eldon, Thurlow, when Lord Chancellor, was once temporarily detailed by a press gang. But since freeholders, who were pressed, quickly found a substitute and were released, the gangs caught only the poor and voteless. On the other hand, after a press at Liverpool, a press captain said another 1500 men could have been raised there, but he did not dare land to capture his own deserters, let alone to impress merchant seamen.[5]

Little was done, however, to diminish the necessity of pressing. When Vernon advocated easing the life of seamen to increase peacetime recruitment, Admiral Wager, a Lord of the Admiralty, successfully countered him with the remarkable statement that 'it was impossible better care could be taken than was'. Yet at that time Portsmouth and Plymouth had no proper naval hospitals. In a plea for funds to build them the Admiralty admitted that sick seamen were sent ashore 'into hired places and houses' where surgeons could not see them, where the food was improper, where they were often not given 'common necessaries', and where they were placed 'two or more seamen in a bed, one recovering with one in the height of sickness, and sometimes a living man with a dead one'.[6]

On board ship things were a good deal better, otherwise the navy would not have been almost invariably victorious. Because the navy's ships were more heavily manned, seamen had to work less hard on warships than merchantmen. Naval food, too, was probably better than on merchant ships. Even so, conditions were harsh. Discipline was severe though not brutal, flogging was frequent, and the accommodation was poor. After giving an horrific description of the ship's hospital, Roderick Random 'was much less surprised to find people die on board than astonished to find anybody recover'. Having served as a surgeon's mate in the navy, Smollett knew what he was talking about.[7]

Pay was low and late, governmental meanness keeping it at its 1653 level until the mutinies of 1797. In Anne's reign seamen were said to enter the navy like men 'dragged to execution'. Not unnaturally they tried to desert. To discourage desertion, wages were withheld. When that practice was made illegal by Grenville's act passed during Pitt's ministry in 1758, sailors were paid just before their ship sailed abroad, thus lessening their opportunity to desert, while depriving their families of the money. When their ship came into harbour, the pressed men were transferred to another ship which remained beyond swimming distance from the shore. Hence Vernon's remark that pressed men were 'in effect condemned to death since they are never allowed to set foot again on shore' was a pardonable exaggeration. They certainly suffered heavy casualties. More than four-fifths of those who left on the Caribbean expedition of 1726 died in two years, and probably half of all seamen pressed between 1600 and 1800 died at sea. No wonder one in four of those who entered the navy between 1774 and 1780 deserted it![8]

Whatever their precise reasons, seamen continually voted with their feet against the navy, often also with their arms. In the second Dutch war of 1665–67, many English seamen preferred to join the Dutch navy. In later wars, too, seamen in the Mediterranean often preferred to join foreign ships and even foreign navies rather than risk impressment by joining an English merchantman. Many who were not prepared to go so far were ready to risk death to avoid impressment; affrays between warships and merchantmen were common.[9]

Inevitably the violent process of impressment provoked violent resistance. Men were rarely prepared to submit quietly to the armed gang if there was any chance of successful resistance. In 1770 a gang tried to arrest Michael Thomas during his wedding ceremony in Southwark; in the resulting 'contest' the clergyman was injured, but Thomas, a black, escaped with his white bride. Deaths and serious injuries were common. Roderick Random was not untypical in knocking out with a cudgel one of those who seized him and hurting some others, before being thrown badly wounded in the head into a hold 'among a parcel of wretches'. In 1743 Alexander Broadfoot was tried for the murder of a press gang officer while resisting impressment, but was convicted only of manslaughter as the gang had exceeded its authority. That case was far from unique. In 1779, however, a man who killed one of a party which was trying to press him was not so lucky: he was hanged at Stafford. Affrays with many casualties were common in the coast towns, and the army was frequently called on to subdue them. In one month in 1776, 800 men were seized in London and several people were killed; fatalities in Liverpool were probably higher.[10]

Rescues of impressed men were common, and informers risked their lives. In Liverpool in 1778, the mayor complained, armed seamen were freeing the press gangs' captives almost as a matter of course. The year before, a woman who had given information to a press gang against a sailor was stripped, ducked by 'some riotous people' and nearly drowned.* During the French Revolutionary Wars Pitt used additional methods of recruitment with unfortunate results: they contributed to the mutinies of 1797. But the press gang was not dispensed with, and the battles continued. In Liverpool a press gang's midshipman killed the master of a merchant ship. Though he went to goal on a charge of murder, a mob of some 500 carpenters and seamen spent seven hours destroying two recruiting houses without the authorities intervening. Between 1790 and 1800 press gangs caused twenty riots or affrays in London and many others in the North East.[12]

Pressing was more productive at sea, though resistance to it was usually greater. Those who were threatened were concentrated together and, though outgunned, they were not always outnumbered. Pressing at sea was usually directed at merchantmen when they were returning to England, not when they were on their outward voyage. After a long spell at sea, the potential victims were even more than usually averse to the involuntary service of His

---

* The woman had some cause to betray the sailor. Having married him 'in the north', she came to Liverpool only to find that he already had a wife there. Nevertheless, he refused to give her two shillings for her journey home.[11]

Majesty. In 1718 when Captain Hildesley sent a boarding party to press men on the *Philip and Mary* in the Thames, the party's commander was taken prisoner and its coxswain was killed. Hildesley brought reinforcements, struck both the master and the mate of the merchantman and committed them to prison on a charge of murder. After, however, the Solicitor General advised their release, Hildesley was himself arrested and fined £100 for assault.[13]

At the Downs in 1740 a battle over pressing was fought between the navy and some returning East India ships. Several men were wounded, one man drowned and the navy captured only 156 men when 'we should have 500'. Three years later when the warship *Dover* stopped the *Britannia*, an East India vessel, near the Scilly Isles and boarded her, five of the *Britannia*'s crew were killed in the ensuing engagement and several wounded. The *Dover*, too, had several wounded, and one man died. In later wars similar battles were fought in Liverpool, Bristol and other ports. At Shields in 1779 in the course of pressing thirty-two men out of a Greenland ship, Captain Dodds wounded three and killed two. On the advice of the Admiralty lawyer he fled to Ostend.[14]

On the tenders on which pressed men were detained before being distributed to warships, conditions were frequently deplorable and mutinies not infrequent. In 1755 pressed men took over the *Tasker* *en route* from Liverpool and many of them escaped ashore, though some preferred to remain. The following year impressed men on a tender at Hoylake took possession of the ship. The mate was killed and others were 'ill hurt in the scuffle'. Some forty of the mutineers escaped to Liverpool. Three days later two of those who had been recaptured by the navy were rescued by a mob. In 1770 over a hundred impressed seamen who were being taken down the Thames overpowered the crew and escaped across the Essex marshes. In the 1790s battles on tenders became more common; in 1797 alone three took place on the Tyne.[15]

Impressment led to corruption as well as violence. Gangs took bribes to declare sick men fit for service; alternatively they might impress, either for money or to show they had not been idle, genuinely unfit men or men who were otherwise ineligible. Government violence set an example. Masters used the press gang to rid themselves of unwanted apprentices; watermen acted similarly to their boys, whose wages legally became their property. Illicit pressing for the East India Company emulated the licit pressing for the navy.[16]

Hume was wrong, therefore, when he wrote of impressment that 'men willingly submit to it from a sense of its use and necessity'. The men who willingly submitted to it were not those who were subjected to the press gang, but the British government and

Parliament who were willing to subject others to it. Walpole, when
first minister, had doubted not only the efficacy but the legality of
the press gang. Shortly afterwards, its legality was correctly affirmed
by Foster, J, in Broadfoot's case, and put beyond doubt by Lord
Mansfield in Tubbs's case thirty years later. The grounds in both
were immemorial usage and state necessity. Despite impressment's
indubitable legality, Hume was also mistaken in suggesting that
nobody supported the sailors in their claim to possess the rights and
privileges which the law granted to all British subjects. The seamen
were not at all on their own. Pressing was widely unpopular.
Merchants needing the men for their own ships were hit in their
pockets by impressment. The Merchant Venturers of Bristol
organised a fund to support and defend people prosecuted and injured
by press gangs, and one of them, the Tory MP Sir John Phillips,
made an unsuccessful attempt to abolish the system in 1755. A similar
attempt had to be abandoned three years later.[17]

Local authorities frequently failed to cooperate with the gangs.
During the Seven Years War the Lord Mayor of London received
public thanks for defeating the press; when a gang of about 40 tried
to round up some privatiersmen in a tavern and killed one of them,
the entire gang was imprisoned and, but for the escape of one of them
who alerted the navy, might have remained there. The mayor of
Gravesend refused to sign press warrants because to do so made him
unpopular in the town; the mayor of Liverpool let drop that he would
imprison the press officers rather than allow any man in the town to
be pressed, while the Liverpool mob murdered several alleged
informers and nearly murdered the regulating captain. When
affirming the legality of pressing, Foster, J, had also emphasised that
only mariners could be pressed and that the power to do so was
confined to the officer named in the press warrant. He thus provided
loopholes for lesser legal luminaries. When a press captain in Bristol
took a man off a ship from Virginia, the recorder ruled that he was
not a mariner, and the captain and his lieutenant each had to pay
£250.[18]

Alderman John Wilkes, who later likened press gangs to 'lawless
bands of cruel bandits' and thought their use before other means of
recruitment had been tried 'totally unjustifiable', acted against them
in 1770 during a quarrel with Spain over the Falkland Islands. He
released John Shine, who had been pressed into the navy on a warrant
which had been signed by the Lords of the Admiralty and backed by
the Lord Mayor, Trecothick. Shine, a journeyman barber, may have
had nothing to do with the sea; if so, the warrant was certainly illegal.
But Wilkes ordered Shine's release without establishing the point,
erroneously declaring press warrants unlawful. Nevertheless Trecothick's successor as Lord Mayor, Brass Crosby, refused to back

press warrants, and at Wilkes's suggestion the City offered larger
bounties for volunteers, an example which was followed by Bristol,
Liverpool and other towns.[19]

Denunciations of the press gang proceeded from on high as well
as from radicals and its victims. The memorandum to Walpole called
it 'a practice equally odious to the King's officers and to the seamen'.
George II once talked of its 'force and violence'; in the forties, John
Wesley thought it contrary to Magna Carta, and Pulteney thought
anything would be better than its 'violence and compulsion'. In 1770
the Petition of His Majesty's 'dutiful and loyal, but oppressed sailors'
complained of the 'impolitic, abominable practice' under which
'thousands perish miserably, in filth and contagion, victims to its
tyranny'. Yet well before then the Admiralty's zeal for reform, such
as it was, had withered. Little was done to make the navy more
attractive to volunteers. Flogging became more pervasive after the
Seven Years War, and no move was made towards what an earlier
writer had called 'civilly impressing'. If anything, pressing became
even less civil, always remaining a weapon of first, not last, resort.[20]

The defeat of reform

The regularly recurring problem of manning the navy in wartime
other than by violence was seldom anticipated and never resolved.
Two things were required: a serious effort to recruit more volunteers
by improving the conditions of service; the introduction of a better
method of conscription.

In 1696 an act had provided for the voluntary registration of
seamen. Because many seamen did not register, while many non-
seamen did, and because the navy did not fulfil its obligations and
pressing continued side by side with the register, the experiment
failed. The French enjoyed a much better system of universal
compulsory registration, and in the first half of the century the
Admiralty favoured its introduction in Britain. With all its difficulties, a register would have brought some fairness into the procedure,
thereby reducing seamen's fears of prolonged incarceration in the
navy. Accordingly, several bills prescribing a register were brought
forward in Parliament. Grenville introduced one at the same time as
his Seamen's Wages Act. Yet none of the bills passed. The Admiralty
lost interest, and what Walpole, who tried to introduce a register in
1740, called 'the hardships of an impress' and its 'extraordinary and
violent methods' continued for the rest of the century and well
beyond.[21]

In 1777 Temple Luttrell, a Wilkite in sympathies though a brother
of Wilkes's successor as MP for Middlesex, tried to introduce a 'Bill

for the more easy Manning of the Navy'. The bill would have increased a sailor's wages, provided him with a pension and limited his time of service. During the Falklands trouble, Luttrell told the House, the Lord Mayor had warned the Admiralty that the City was so infested with press gangs that tradesmen and servants could not follow their normal business. He retailed 'some of the calamities and unconstitutional outrages affecting those manufacturers, mechanics and husbandmen' who had never had anything to do with the sea, and he pointed to the many seamen who had been drowned trying to escape, having been driven to despair by the thought that they would never be given a legal discharge. Luttrell, whose language was dramatic but not unfair – the tragedy of Mary Jones began with the pressing of her husband – thought there was not an independent gentleman who did not feel 'a strong repugnance to the iniquitous, unconstitutional mode of pressing now in use'. Nevertheless Lord Mulgrave, a naval officer, defended pressing as a good way of manning the navy, not as a disagreeable necessity. Its evils, he said, either did not exist or were very disproportionate to its advantages. Mulgrave was exceptional – Townshend said it was the first time he had ever heard pressing defended and the need for reform denied. A more typical opinion was that of Governor Johnstone, a former sea officer and a respected member, who said that impressment disgraced government, shocked the spirit of the constitution and violated the laws of humanity. Yet this 'violent', 'disgraceful', 'ineffectual' and expensive system easily survived. Luttrell was defeated by more than two to one, and his later efforts met with no result.[22]

A largely volunteer navy would have required drastically improved conditions. On a merchant ship in wartime, pay was higher and more reliable, time spent at sea shorter, discipline more moderate, and prize money fairer and more abundant. When the navy captured Havana, the admiral and the general received £244,000 betweem them. Each seaman got £3 14s 9d. Normally the distribution of prize money was less unequal, but even then the seamen's share, as Vernon said, had 'no proportion' to that of the officers.[23]

As well as better prize money and higher and more regular pay, the period of service would have had to be limited and proper pensions paid, as Vernon, Luttrell and other reformers proposed. All those things, of course, like a register of seamen, would have been expensive, and so they were left undone. Though the Admiralty, by providing more vegetables and fresh meat, did succeed in improving seamen's health in the Seven Years War, they only introduced the cure for scurvy some fifty years after Lind had discovered it; that was too hurried a reform for the press gang. When opposition MPs like Pulteney or Luttrell suggested a system based on rewards rather than punishments, the government defeated them. Equally when ministers like Walpole, Pelham, Pitt and Grenville made proposals for improvement, the shipping interests and the opposition frustrated them. Merchants did not like their seamen being stolen by the press gang, yet they were no more anxious to have them 'stolen' by higher pay. At the same time, the country gentlemen favoured economy and feared a stronger executive and any measures that could be denounced as 'French'. Late in the century the Admiralty itself took over as the saboteur of reform.[24]

Deadlock ruled, and the press gang survived – like the Bloody Code and for much the same reasons. The nature of English eighteenth-century government made reform of almost anything difficult. Few looked ahead, and anything that did not adversely affect the governing classes usually remained in place. The Parliamentary elite preferred the press gang to paying higher taxes. So both a register and higher wages for seamen were ruled out. Only the dangerous mutinies of 1797 brought some naval reform, though not, even then, to impressment. In successfully opposing Walpole's bill which would have established a general register of seamen and watermen, Sir John Barnard, the City leader, suggested that the first register should be filled 'with the despicable names of . . . placemen, sycophants, and dependants'. If that had happened, the press gang would have been abolished overnight. But as those 'despicable names' were immune – they were thought to make sufficient contribution to the state's security and prosperity by being themselves prosperous – and the press gang preyed on only the politically powerless, the ruling elite found its burdens easily endurable and its violence readily acceptable. The first war in which the navy did without the services of the press gang was the Crimean, and a naval reserve was not formed till 1859. Until then, what Hume called 'the most absurd and unaccountable' practice was persisted in, and 'a continued violence [was] permitted in the Crown'.[25]

NINE

The Game Laws and Cruelty to Animals

Many reasons have concurred for making these constitutions . . . For prevention of idleness and dissipation in husbandmen, artificers and others of lower rank . . . For prevention of popular insurrections and resistance to the government, by disarming the bulk of the people: which last is a reason oftener meant than avowed by the makers of forest or game laws.

Sir William Blackstone

The recipe to make a poacher will be found to contain a very few and simple ingredients . . . Search out (and you need not go far) a poor man with a large family, or a poor man, single, having his natural sense of right and wrong . . . give him little more than a natural disinclination to go to work, let him exist in the midst of lands where the game is preserved, keep him cool in the winter, by allowing him insufficient wages to purchase fuel; let him feel hungry upon the small pittance of parish relief; and if he be not a poacher, it will be only by the blessing of God.

Lord Suffield, in the House of Lords

Very melancholy news . . . respecting the ships wrecked and lives lost at Yarmouth . . . May those poor souls lost be O Lord better off. And send thy divine comfort to all their relatives. Mr Custance sent us a brace of partridges.

Parson Woodforde, November 7, 1789[1]

The Game Laws did not permit violence in the Crown, but they created much violence elsewhere. 'It is hard,' the *Monthly Review* lamented in 1764, 'that the first born booby of a qualified bumpkin should ride over hedge and ditch in pursuit of poor animals perhaps more sagacious than himself, while the honest farmer dares not touch the game which is sheltered and fed on the very ground he rents.' That was a passable summary of the English Game Laws, whose most remarkable feature was not that only landed gentlemen could kill game, or even that many farmers could not kill it even on their own land, but that gentlemen could pursue it onto other people's land. The privilege of hunting derived from the royal prerogative, and Game Laws dating from the fourteenth century confined it to the aristocracy.[2]

In the eighteenth and nineteenth centuries the 'preservation' of game became more widespread, being a frequent subject of legislation – between 1671 and 1831 fifty-three principal statutes concerning game, deer stealing and poaching were passed – and a copious source of violence. The basic act of 1671 laid down that only landed gentlemen could kill game, since the qualification to do so was a freehold worth £100 a year or a ninety-nine year leasehold worth £150 a year, 'there being fifty times the property required,' wrote Blackstone, 'to enable a man to kill a partridge, as to vote for a knight of the shire . . .' Virtually everybody else was prohibited from killing game, irrespective of his income, however large, from a source other than land, and irrespective of whether or not he owned the land. However, the eldest son of an esquire was also qualified, which was confusing, firstly because an eldest son was thus qualified even though his father might not be, and secondly because nobody could say for certain who exactly was 'an esquire'. Well might Blackstone comment that the game statutes were 'not a little obscure and intricate' and, after complaining of six pieces of false grammar in one act, hint that they were the work of illiterate country gentlemen![3]

As well as giving a monopoly in game and sport to country gentlemen – about 99 per cent of the population were disqualified – the 1671 act empowered lords of the manor to appoint gamekeepers with the power to search for and confiscate all guns, dogs, nets and other poaching tools in the hands of unqualified people. The Game Laws thus provided a convenient excuse for disarming the populace; indeed, as Blackstone pointed out, that was an important object of the game code. Not only did the lower orders have their guns removed under it, their dogs were frequently killed by keepers and their employers. In *Joseph Andrews*, Parsons Adams has to be restrained from pursuing the squire who had just shot the innocent spaniel belonging to his host's daughter. The squire, Adams is told, has killed all the dogs and taken away all the guns in the neighbourhood. Fielding did not exaggerate. In 1725 Lord Cardigan ordered the killing of all dogs on one of his manors in Northampton-shire, and in Yorkshire fifty years later the Duke of Devonshire did the same. The gentry themselves sometimes had their dogs killed by the gamekeepers of bigger landowners.[4]

Almost the only thing the 1671 act did not do was to increase the penalties for poaching. In the eighteenth century, only hares, partridge, pheasants and moor fowl were, strictly speaking, 'game'. Deer and rabbits were 'preserved' not by the Game Laws but by other measures. The reason for the distinction was that increasing enclosure had, by the end of the seventeenth century, led to deer and rabbits no longer being considered wild. They were therefore 'property', protected by special laws and the laws of property, and attacks on them were not poaching but theft. Game, however, was not 'property', so attacks on it were not theft or a felony, but poaching. Undeniably class legislation, as even some of their defenders conceded, the Game Laws were not till the end of the century draconian, the penalties for breaking them being less harsh than those for breaking the ordinary property laws. Yet they were often denounced as draconian as well as tyrannical, because they led to violence and because the penalties for deer and rabbit stealing were understandably but mistakenly regarded as part of the Game Laws.[5]

The increasingly artificial distinction between game and other animals was not recognised by poachers (except for the difference in penalties), or by would-be reformers like Curwen and Sheridan. Improvements in firearms made possible the large-scale massacre of pheasants and partridges, while the resulting growth in demand for birds to shoot was supplied by improved artificial methods of breeding pheasants. The rearing of pheasants and the growing enclosure of estates made pheasants less like game and more like the deer already enclosed as property in landowners' deer parks. At the same time the rising demand of landowners for game and its supply by their gamekeepers produced from other people a rising demand for game on the table and to its supply by poachers. The more game there was the less tolerable became exclusion from its enjoyment and from its fruits.[6]

Growing violence

The country gentlemen might have recognised the changes that had taken place, surrendered their unpopular monopoly, and made game, like deer and rabbits, the property of the person on whose land it was found. That would immediately have made game preservation more popular, facilitating the gentry's efforts to protect game on their own land. Yet it would have prevented them attacking it on other people's and, in abolishing their monopoly, it would have removed a prized symbol of superiority. The whole Game Laws system, as Lord Suffield observed many years later, was 'one of exclusion [whose] chief enjoyment consists in the possession of that which your neighbour has *not*, and perhaps *can not* have'.[7]

Instead, therefore, of recognising the changed facts, the country gentlemen stepped up their challenge to them. There had long been restrictions on the sale of game; in 1755 these were strengthened by an act which banned all trade in it. Now not even 'qualified' people could legally sell game; the sport of gentlemen must at no stage be sullied by money or trade. Thus while Parliament was in other fields superseding or ignoring the old Elizabethan laws which protected people and practices from the full rigours of the market, it passed a law to protect the landed gentry's monopoly in game and to abolish the market altogether. This blanket ban on the sale of game, an attempt to make a gift from the qualified the only legal source of game, was inevitably a fiasco. Unlike the Volstead Act of 1919 prohibiting alcohol in the United States, the 1755 act was not 'an experiment noble in motive': but it had similar results. Laws which carry the consent of only a few are disobeyed by the many, and like the Gin Act of 1736 and American prohibition the act of 1755 was massively flouted.[8]

> *Woods of their feather'd beauty were bereft,*
> *The beauteous victims of the silent theft;*
> *The well known shops received a large supply,*
> *That they who could not kill at least might buy.*

In the sale of game, poachers now had much less competition from landowners, and their interests were in line with those of the rest of the nation. Poaching had always been popular. Now it became a service – a black market in game flourishing wherever there was money to buy it.[9] Furthermore, poaching – previously largely an individual affair of a labourer or a collier killing for his pot, for sport or to gain a few shillings – became more like an industry, with large poaching gangs roaming the country. The conditions had been created for the violence of the poaching wars which lasted down to the end of the nineteenth century.

To combat the gangs, the penalties for poaching were made heavier. Deer poaching (or rather stealing) had, since the Black Act of 1723, been a felony punishable by death, though deer owners usually proceeded under less ferocious legislation, as juries were then more likely to convict. The Night Poaching Acts of 1770, 1773 and 1800 did not go so far as the Black Act, but they sharply increased the penalties for poaching at night – the time when game was most, and poachers least, at risk of detection. Far from diminishing poaching, however, harsher penalties merely escalated the violence as poachers fought to escape being taken prisoner.[10]

The country gentlemen were thus determined to have it both ways. They treated their own game more and more as though it were their property, while by preserving the game 'qualification' they prevented it from being other people's. They went on increasing the punishment for poaching until 1828, yet inevitably failed to put a stop either to it or to the black market. 'You will never,' Sydney

Smith correctly told them, 'separate the wealthy glutton from his pheasant.' Together with the growing exclusiveness of the privilege, the consequent alienation of farmers, and the attempted ban on the sale of game, harsher penalties did, nevertheless, fuel widespread doubts about the justification of the Game Laws. Whereas Walpole could claim in 1741 that the game code was generally accepted, none of his successors could have plausibly said the same.[11]

As with deer stealing, game preservers often did not seek the harshest available punishment for the poachers they caught. The law provided them with a wide discretion, and they could use either civil or criminal procedure. The summary trial of poachers before one or two JPs instead of a judge and jury – a development which disturbed Blackstone – was normal from 1750 onwards. Trial before a single JP ruled out a heavy punishment, which could only be imposed after a conviction by a jury. Juries, however, composed of men disqualified by the Game Laws, had a tendency to acquit in poaching cases. For the game preserver, a JP was a much more reliable tribunal, especially if the JP happened to be himself. In 1823 Richard Deller, a Hampshire farmer, who was allowed to course hares on his own farm by his own landlord was summoned by the Duke of Buckingham's gamekeeper to show that he was 'qualified' to hunt game. The Duke's gamekeeper was the informer against Deller, another of the Duke's gamekeepers was a witness, and the Duke himself was the judge. Deller's witnesses not being Buckingham's employees, the Duke prevented confusion by refusing to hear their evidence and, no doubt after earnest deliberation, found Deller guilty. How typical that notorious case was is not known. Samuel Whitbread, an opponent of the Game Laws, thought nothing of trying his own poachers, yet many landowners considered it improper to be judges in their own causes. Furthermore, it was not necessary. Their fellow justices were likely to be no less sympathetic, either because they, too, preserved game or because they were given it by the local magnate. They might even consult the prosecutor as to how they should deal with his case. So the game preserver usually secured a conviction, but the poacher suffered a relatively light punishment. Even so, the consequences for him and his family might well be grave.[12]

This legal procedure did not endear the game code to the unqualified, and as the violence increased, public sympathy remained with the poachers. In 1775 a gang of six poachers were shooting Lord Walpole's pheasants at Iteringham in Norfolk when they were interrupted by his gamekeeper and some assistants. The keeper was wounded in the thigh; four years later a shoemaker who had fired the shot was hanged at Norwich before 2000 people. In 1780 on Cranbourne Chase one keeper was killed and another had his knee smashed. The poacher's leader lost a hand in the battle; a serjeant in the dragoons, his sentence of transportation was reduced to a short term in prison.[13]

When a poaching gang was ambushed at Windsor in 1781, a sharp engagement followed. In the same year at Blickling, in Norfolk, battle was joined between the Earl of Buckinghamshire's gamekeepers and a gang of sixteen poachers. The gang, who carried guns and 'large clubs, armed with iron spikes' killed one keeper and seriously wounded another. Gamekeeping was a dangerous trade. Another Norfolk gamekeeper was beaten so badly by a gang that his skull was fractured in two places and he died a few days later; earlier one of the Duke of Richmond's assistant keepers at Goodwood was strangled. Well might that hammer of the poachers, Rev Henry Zouch, a JP and Lady Rockingham's chaplain, lament that there were 'persons assembling themselves together in the night in companies, armed with firearms, clubs and other offensive weapons . . . traversing the fields and lanes . . . impatient of rule and contemptuous of authority'.[14]

Spring guns and man traps

Zouch, a vehement opponent of Poor Law reform, favoured instead a more energetic enforcement of the criminal law and a tax on dogs to check vice and immorality. It was, he maintained, a matter 'of infinite moment that the criminal excesses of the common people should be effectively restrained, by enforcing a due degree of subordination, and a general obedience to the law of the land'. Adopting Zouch's precepts, if not his priorities, many landowners from the 1780s onwards did not seek to restrain the common people's criminal excesses merely by their gamekeepers and the law. The forces of order sought to enforce a due degree of subordination by engines of violence: spring guns and man traps. Unfortunately these engines, though economical, were no more effective than the more traditional methods in maintaining a general obedience to the law of the land.[15]

Spring guns, which were first used to defend gardens, were usually cannon that were set off by trip wires. Sir Francis Burdett exaggerated only a little when he claimed that there was scarcely a known instance of spring guns 'having taken effect' on poachers; Sir Robert Peel and Lord Suffield went nearly as far. Certainly most poachers soon learned to deal with them; otherwise they went out of business, having been maimed or killed. Poachers sometimes reset the guns against the keepers. And game preservers themselves were occasionally shot by their own guns. The usual victims, however, as both Romilly and Peel testified, were innocent passers-by. Children were often hit. The three sons of a Suffolk admiral were all seriously injured by the same shot.[16]

Man traps were instruments of torture whose names – 'The Body-squeezer', 'The Thigh-cracker' or 'The Crusher' – accurately portrayed them. Though less lethal than spring guns, they could cause fearful injuries. In 1785 a Hampshire gentleman described 'the most shocking' sight he had ever beheld: 'The hardened banditti disregarding the notice that was given of what was prepared for their destruction, ventured in the night, as had been their usual custom, into the wood, where no less than four of them were found in the morning caught in these terrible engines; three had their thighs broke by the crackers of traps, and the fourth was found dead in a body squeezer . . .' As with spring guns, however, it was not only hardened banditti who suffered. Mr Lawson, a sixty-two-year-old clergyman, was out botanising when he was caught in a man trap, and there he remained for nearly an hour and a half 'suffering under the most excruciating pain' before a gamekeeper unlocked 'this cruel instrument and extricated the worthy gentleman, whose leg was found to be much lacerated'.[17]

Even some opponents of the Game Laws defended spring guns on the grounds that they were preferable to pitched battles. Sydney Smith disagreed. He thought allowing game preservers themselves to kill trespassers would be far more humane, since a live executioner might perhaps 'spare a friend or an acquaintance, or a father of a family with ten children, or a small freeholder who voted for the Administration' – unlike the 'new rural artillery' which destroyed everything without mercy or discrimination.[18]

The ordinary principles of English law should have spiked the rural artillery after its first bombardment. Legally, homicide was justifiable only in self-defence or in order to prevent a serious crime committed by force for which the penalty was death. Killing poachers manifestly came into neither category. Yet, unlike their Scottish brethren, the English judges were equivocal. In 1827 one Scottish judge thought that if spring guns were legal, it was equally legal to dislodge a tenant with a hand grenade or by burning his house down. Another, Lord Gillies, pointed out that if a man intending to kill B killed his friend A by mistake, he committed murder, and added that whatever the law of England might be, their Scottish lordships were not bound by it.[19]

Nor, in a sense, were their English lordships, who preferred to ignore the law or adapt it so as not to declare illegal the use of spring guns in defence of game preserves. In 1818 in the civil case of *Ilot v Wilks esq*, where the defendant had put up a notice warning of spring guns, four judges gave their opinion. Abbot, LJ, considered them a

reasonable means of 'defence and protection'. Bailey, J., decided that
as the setting of spring guns was not an indictable offence its
consequences must be legal. Best, J., said that 'the links of society'
were better preserved if gentlemen resided in the country; preserving
game was the only 'diversion' they could 'partake on their estates'
and so it was 'of essential importance that this species of property
should be inviolably protected.'[20]

These judicial excuses of random violence did not impress Sydney
Smith. If gentlemen to defend their estates shot any trespasser they
saw with their own pistol, that would unquestionably be murder.
Why then, he asked the Lord Chief Justice, should doing the same
thing by a spring gun be lawful? As for Bailey, J., Smith declared
that it was not an indictable offence to go abroad with a loaded pistol
intending to shoot anybody who grinned at you; but if you shot him,
you would be hanged. To Best, J., he replied that shooting
trespassers and poachers was a strange way of preserving the links of
society in the country and that it was far better that gentlemen who
wished to do so should not reside there. Their absence would put
less strain on the links to which the judge attached importance.
Owing to the growing social attractions of London and elsewhere
many of the gentry were anyway now spending less time on their
estates, but unlike their French opposite numbers their main
residence remained in the country, not the capital.[21]

With the English judges effectively deciding that there was one law
for game preservers and another for poachers, abolition of spring
guns and man traps could come only from Parliament. Lord Suffield
led the campaign, calling the setting of spring guns 'sneaking and
assassin like', though he acquitted the noble lords listening to him of
being assassins. Charles Tennyson, Suffield's leading supporter in the
Commons, reminded the rich that it was imprudent 'to give an
example of ferocity' to the lower orders: the feudal nobility of France
and other countries had never claimed the use of such engines; the
practice was peculiar to England. Peel pointed out that if it was legal
to set a spring gun to kill one poacher, it was presumably legal to set
a land mine to kill a gang of poachers. But the Duke of Wellington
opposed the bill because it was unfair and because spring guns
prevented poaching; their violence did not disturb him or their other
defenders. Sir John Shelley thought it was an attack on gentlemen
who wished to protect their plantations and woods; he had heard
recently of two lawyers being caught in a trap, but that sort of
melancholy occurrence was too rare to be important. Lord Blandford, who used spring guns, thought objections to them stemmed
merely from 'a kind of morbid sensibility', while Lord Ellenborough
was not worried by injuries done to the innocent: the deterring object
of spring guns 'was as completely attained by hitting an innocent man

as a . . . guilty one'. Only in 1827, at the third attempt, was the bill successful, and the undiscriminating violence of spring guns made illegal.[22]

Cruelty to animals

The gentry had a monopoly only of shooting; other sports were open to all. Cockthrowing, which involved throwing missiles at a tethered cock until it was dead, was a popular pastime. So was the baiting with dogs of bulls, bears and badgers. Cockfighting and dogfighting were similarly bloody and popular, and carried the additional advantages that they could be gambled on. These were, originally, far from plebeian diversions. The courts of Charles II and James II indulged in cockthrowing, and in 1694 William III entertained Prince Lewis of Baden with bearbaiting and cockfighting.[23] In 1764 the Duke of Cumberland

> entertained a company with the following diversion; a stag was enclosed by toils in his Royal Highness's paddock at Windsor, and one of his tigers let loose at him: the tiger attempted to seize the stag by the haunch, but was beat off by his horns; a second time he appeared at his throat . . . but the stag threw him a considerable distance . . . the tiger turned tail, and ran under the foil into the forest, among a herd of deer, one of which he seized and killed him in a moment . . .[24]

If correctly reported, the 'Butcher' was a little behind the times. In the previous fifty years the gentry had tended to concentrate their sporting energies on killing pheasants and foxes, and bearbaiting and most similar activities had gone out of fashion among the elite. Only cockfighting – denounced by Wesley as the 'foul remains of Gothic barbarity' – retained its appeal among the gentry. In the 1760's Boswell attended five hours of cockfighting in the royal cockpit in St James's park. He felt 'sorry for the poor cocks [which were] mangled and torn in a most cruel manner' for as long as three-quarters of an hour, but noted that nobody else did – except foreign visitors who were usually shocked by the English taste in sports.[25]

From mid-century, nevertheless, there was a growing middle-class movement against cruelty to certain animals. Deciding which forms of violence to animals are legitimate and which are too cruel to be permitted is a notoriously difficult and subjective matter. Enthusiastic English foxhunters are shocked by the cruelty of Spanish bullfighting, and those who deplore all blood sports may still be content to digest their results. Vegetarianism and complete indifference to cruelty are the sole fully consistent positions. The eighteenth-century reformers were seldom vegetarians and they did not strive for consistency; they directed their chief criticisms against cock and dogfighting, bullbaiting and cockthrowing, all of which, save cockfighting, had, as it happened, become largely plebeian entertainments.[26]

No doubt that affected the campaign, as did the wish to cut down disorder and to inculcate industrious habits in the poor, a process which was likely to be hindered by frequent indulgence in unprofitable pleasures. Since we are ordinarily unable to exercise our 'destructive instincts on our fellow men', wrote the French theorist of crowds, Gustave Le Bon, 'we confine ourselves to exercising them on animals. The passion for the chase,' he continued, 'and the acts of ferocity of crowds proceed from one and the same source.' Whether watching and taking part in cruel sports arouses or sublimates those destructive urges Le Bon did not say. But eighteenth-century reformers had little doubt. Cruel sports, they believed, created cruel men and were productive of crime – a peril from which foxhunters and pheasant shooters were mysteriously exempt. All the same, the attempt to stamp out some popular sports had more to it than mere class prejudice. Eton College's annual Ram Hunt which culminated in the ram being bludgeoned to death by the boys was ended in 1747, and bullbaiting, cockfighting etc., have on any view little to recommend them. Cockthrowing, noted an observer in 1771, was 'a barbarous custom . . . fit only for the bloodiest savages and not for humanised men, much less for Christians'.[27]

The contrast between the attacks on the pleasures of the poor and the immunity granted to those of the rich, which was not confined to cruel sports, did not go unnoticed. In 1800 William Windham MP found it strange that the cruelty of bullbaiting should be criticised by people who had 'a most vexatious code of laws for the protection of their own animals'. Shooting, he maintained, was as cruel as 'the sport of bullbaiting' – he might have added that those who took spring guns and 'the Body-cruncher' in their stride were not well placed to jib at any sport, however brutal. 'Any cruelty may be practised to gorge the stomachs of the rich,' Sidney Smith observed a few years later, 'none to enliven the holidays of the poor.'[28]

Most such popular pastimes were already in decline, but Windham's opposition to reform was fortified by the belief that the long-established habits of the poor were a barrier to revolution. He doubted if any bullbaiter had ever flirted with Jacobinism; amusements prevented the poor from being goaded to desperation. Whether or not bullbaiting was a bulwark of the monarchy and Parliament – it was no doubt a healthier occupation than reading Tom Paine – the subject of cruelty to animals, like the reform of the

Game Laws, was left untouched by the legislature until well into the nineteenth century. When sport was not involved, Archenholz thought the English treated animals with almost as much humanity 'as if they were rational beings'.[29]

The failure to reform

The sole even remotely plausible argument for spring guns was that they restricted the violence that was endemic in the Game Laws system. The attempt to reform that system began earlier than the campaign against violent engines and ended later. In 1782, after Coke had complained of lives lost in Norfolk because of poachers, Charles Turner MP attacked the Game Laws as cruel and oppressive. He thought it a shame that the House was always enacting laws for the safety of gentlemen; he wished they would make a few for the good of the poor. Had he been a common man, he continued, he would certainly have been a poacher,* as it was the great severity of the laws that had led to the increase of poachers. Whether or not the severity of the laws increased the number of poachers, it certainly intensified the violence of poachers and gamekeepers. Those laws, Romilly later pointed out, had the effect 'of exciting a ferocious spirit not only among the lower classes but also among those in higher walks of life . . .'[31]

Yet Parliament had no time for such views, attempting as usual to deal with the effects of violence not with its causes. Indeed for many the French Revolution turned the Game Laws, like the slave trade and hanging, drawing and quartering, into pillars of the British constitution. Sweep them away, it was felt, and the constitution would come crashing down; so would social distinctions. After all, one of the earliest actions of the National Assembly in 1789 had been to abolish the French game laws, and everybody knew what had then happened. If further proof was needed, Tom Paine had attacked the game code in the *Rights of Man*. Conversely, those Whigs who supported the French Revolution denounced both Pitt's 'oppression' and the Game Laws. Supporting in 1796 J.C. Curwen's bill to permit a landowner to kill game on his own land and to allow game to be sent to market, Charles Fox described the whole Game Laws system as 'a mass of insufferable tyranny' and thought poaching no worse than purchasing seats in the House of Commons. Wilberforce, too, though no Foxite, considered the Game Laws 'extreme abomina-

---

* Lord Eldon, Lord Chancellor for twenty years, who, as the son of a prosperous coal merchant, was not quite what Turner had in mind, admitted to having been a poacher in his youth. That presumably explains why, over the Game Laws, almost uniquely for him, Eldon favoured reform.[30]

tions' which he viewed with the 'utmost abhorrence'. Nevertheless, the elite was far from being frightened into surrendering its privilege. As Cobbett complained, the 'terrible code' grew harder instead of wearing away. In 1829 as many as twenty-eight poachers were sentenced to death at Warwick Assizes, though in the end most of them were not hanged but transported.[32]

The quarrel was only partly about game and poaching; it went far wider than that. The social order was at stake, and the idea of justice played a very subsidiary role in the dispute. Opponents of the game code complained that the 'tyrannical' powers given to gamekeepers to disarm the populace dampened its martial ardour and left it in no condition to defend the country. The same criticism that the Game Laws 'disarmed' the nation was voiced during the agitation for the Militia Bill in 1756. To their upholders, of course, that was one of their greatest blessings, as Thornhill's *Shooting Directory* of 1804, quoting Blackstone, freely conceded. Lord Westmoreland later gave as the chief ground for opposing reform of the Game Laws that they made it impossible for a general arming to take place if a disposition prevailed to disturb the peace of the country; their abolition would make it possible for every man to possess arms.[33]

Furthermore, the argument ran, if the lower orders were permitted to taste the fleshpots of the country and allowed to poach with virtual impunity, they would lack the compulsion to take up more useful employment. And anyway, if they were up all night, they could not work properly in the day. Many of the country gentry did not work and had no way of killing time other than by killing game. Hence no damage was done to them or the country if they devoted their lives to game preservation and destruction. But everybody else had, or should have, better things to do; so the interests of the country and of themselves demanded that they should not fritter away their time killing hares, partridges and pheasants. Thus, in the eyes of their defenders, the Game Laws buttressed the social order both at the top and at the bottom: gentlemen were set apart by the privilege, while the lower orders were confined to useful industry.

The case for reform of the Game Laws was no more than it would end poaching than the argument for reform of the criminal law was that it would end crime. Poaching, like crime, was there to stay. There was no complete solution to either. Without some regulation, however, game laws would have become virtually extinct. When in 1818 Parliament passed an act removing, with compensation, the right of Lord Rivers to preserve deer throughout Cranborne Chase, that nobleman immediately killed vast numbers of them, and the inhabitants of the Chase shot nearly all the remainder, together with some human beings. Much the same would have happened elsewhere if all legal protection of game had been removed. Yet once game was preserved and protected, poaching, as Eldon the ex-poacher recognised, inevitably followed. Writing of deer poaching in the 1760s, White of Selborne pointed out that neither fines nor imprisonment deterred the night hunters, as it was impossible to extinguish the inherent 'spirit of sporting' in human nature. If love of 'sporting' was one motive, love of money was another. The individual labourer wanted to eat and the poaching gangster to make a profit. Lord Suffield's recipe for the making of a poacher is at the head of this chapter. His contemporary, Sir Thomas Baring, said much the same thing. As they saw, the scale of poaching depended on the social and economic conditions in the English countryside, the level of employment and agricultural distress, the relations between landlords and tenants and between large and small landowners, political attitudes, other laws such as the Poor Law, the extent of game preserves, the other diversions open to the rural poor, and the urban demand for game, rather than on the penalties for poaching or the intricacies of the game code.[34]

Poaching was as ineradicable as gaming, and the poor (and many others, too) saw as little wrong with the first as the rich saw with the second. Reform of the Game Laws would not have much cut down poaching or greatly helped the poacher. The game code's defenders rightly stressed that the distress of 'the lower agricultural classes' stemmed less from the Game Laws than from their difficulty in earning enough to live on.[35] The case for reform was simply that the Game Laws were cruel and oppressive and generated violence without even being effective. Perhaps that was what saved them. Had they stamped out poaching, and the moneyed men's dinner table become bereft of game, the code would have been swept away by a greedy torrent of aldermanic wrath. Be that as it may, the landed gentry, in defending their privilege, were prepared to tolerate a large dose of violence, of which not they but poachers and their gamekeepers were the victims. Since their ends – social stability as well as game preservation – were to them laudable, almost any means to attain them were justified, however violent. Hence spring guns, man traps and the growing savagery of the game code.[34]

With the landed gentry having a monopoly of representation in Parliament, a radical wrote in 1788, it was not to be wondered at that they granted themselves exclusive privileges including all the game in the kingdom. Certainly, over game as over other matters, English aristocrats – they were in 1800 relatively and absolutely richer than they had been in 1700 – looked after themselves at least as well as did their peers on the continent. The *folie de la chasse* was not unique to England – it kept Charles IV of Spain shooting partridges every day of the week of the Battle of Trafalgar – but the English Game Laws were as exclusive as any other country's and, after 1800, the most severe. Nowhere else were spring guns or man traps employed in the eighteenth century. In Russia game licences could be bought for a trifling consideration. Both the Scottish and the Irish laws were less restrictive than the English: the sale of game was legal in Scotland throughout the century and, for most of it, in Ireland.[36]

The ruling elite recognised, as Pitt admitted, that the law forbidding the sale of game was flouted daily. One part of the rich, the landed gentry, gave themselves a monopoly in game and imposed a legal ban on its sale; the other part of the rich, the moneyed and the merchants, consistently broke the ban by procuring poorer men to get them game. Thus 'the rich were accessary', as Charles Fox claimed, to the violation of the very laws that they insisted on maintaining. The game code was an organised hypocrisy whose violence had two sources: firstly the organised professional gangs, who supplied the wants of the commercial rich; and secondly 'the scandalous cruelty of the law' which was decreed by rich landed gentlemen.[37]

TEN

Election Skulduggery

I believe it will be granted, that the peace and quiet of the people of every city and country of the kingdom would be more uniformly preserved, if there were no such things as popular elections: such elections, we know, are often attended with great disturbance, and sometimes with dangerous tumults and riots; but this, I hope will never in this country be adopted as a good argument for depriving the people of any share in the government of their native country.

Alderman William Beckford MP, 1755

The auction of votes is become an established commerce, and his Grace [the Duke of Newcastle] did nothing but squabble for the prerogative of being sole appraiser.

Horace Walpole, circa *1755*

These visits are a mere matter of form, which a candidate makes to every elector . . . lest he should expose himself to the imputation of pride, at a time when it is expected he should appear humble. Indeed I know nothing so abject as the behaviour of a man canvassing for a seat in parliament. This mean prostration . . . has, I imagine, contributed in a great measure to raise that spirit of insolence among the vulgar, which, like the devil, will be very difficult to lay . . . The truth is, I look upon both candidates in the same light; and should think myself a traitor to the constitution of my country if I voted for either.

Smollett's Matthew Bramble in The Expedition of Humphrey Clinker[1]

Election riots were about as old as the Game Laws. They too date from the Middle Ages and did not die out until the 1870s. The franchise statute of 1430 laid down that only residents who were worth 40 shillings a year clear from free tenements should be county electors, because the presence of an excessive number of 'people of small substance and no value' had led to homicides, riots and battles. The great age of election rioting only began, however, with the enlarged seventeenth-century electorate, the heightened party feeling after the Revolution, and the unique occurrence of ten general elections in twenty years between 1695 and 1715. Westminster and

Exeter saw considerable election riots in 1695, and at Westminster three years later two of the candidates appeared to Tuthill Fields on polling day with 2000 mounted followers.[2]

In 1696 an ineffective act was passed against intimidation and bribery. The electoral system was genuinely representative, and the electorate was relatively large, influential and highly partisan. But, like all electorates, it was subjected to a variety of pressures. Under Anne the lucky voter was bribed; the unlucky one was intimidated. In the 1705 election, riots erupted at Coventry, Chester, Salisbury and elsewhere. At Coventry, where the corrupt methods of the corporation nearly always produced violence at elections until well into the nineteenth century, a mob of 600 men captured the town hall and held it for three days, controlling the voting and assaulting many of the voters. Some 150 people were prosecuted, and the election was declared void. In the 1710 election, which was particularly violent and drunken, Coventry once again figured together with at least fourteen other towns. The election three years later was less violent than the Sacheverell contest, but still far from peaceful. When the poll was level in London, the Whigs produced a horde of weavers who 'caused much fighting and quarrelling in the street'.[3]

> *Sad melancholy ev'ry visage wears;*
> *What, no election come in seven long years!*

The Septennial Act brought the era of frequent elections to an end. The growth of the electorate ceased and the increased expense of contested elections diminished the number of seats that were fought. 'The members in possession,' Philip Francis wrote of Yorkshire in 1794 where an election had not gone to the poll for half a century. 'let them behave as they might, always remain undisturbed; for who but madmen would enter into a contest for such a county, or indeed for any county?' In 1722 seventeen of the forty English counties were contested; the three elections of 1747, 1754 and 1761 averaged four such contests, the same as in 1796. One hundred and seven English boroughs went to the poll in 1722, sixty-one in 1741 and only fifty in 1747. In 1761 only forty-eight of the 315 constituencies in Great Britain went to the poll. That was the nadir, but only in 1774 were more than 30 per cent of them contested before the end of the century.[4]

As well as reducing the electorate's influence and facilitating the consolidation of Whig power, the Septennial Act obviously allowed fewer opportunities for rioting and bribery. Yet both continued as the electoral system invited them. Polling was concentrated in space and extended in time. A constituency usually had only one polling place, and polling went on for days, sometimes weeks. Excitement inevitably grew, as did the consumption of drink. In addition, to ensure the freedom of elections soldiers were removed from the towns where they were held. Their presence would probably have provoked violence; their absence did not prevent it.[5]

Large counties were represented by two members; small towns and places which scarcely existed had the same number. Some large towns had no representatives at all. Cornwall had forty-four members, one less than Scotland. The franchise was similarly varied and haphazard. The counties and some boroughs had relatively large electorates: Westminster had 8000 rising to 12,000 in mid-century, and Bristol about 4000. In contrast Truro had 24, and Malmesbury and Buckingham each had 13. By 1792 Rye had six and Helston only two. Though virtually every writer on the subject from Clarendon and Burnet to Swift, Hume and Blackstone criticised the absurdity of the system, it survived until 1832. The 'inequality', Defoe said at the beginning of the century, 'opens the door to the fraudulent practices, which have all along been made use of in elections, buying of voices, giving freedoms in corporations to people living out of corporations on purpose to make votes, debauching the electors, making whole towns drunk, and feasting to excess for a month, sometimes two or more, in order to engage their voices'. Among the freemen created by Worcester Corporation between 1731 and 1747 were 63 Tory MPs, a number of Oxford heads of houses, and the Duke of Beaufort's Gentlemen of the Horse. Cambridge University, unlike Oxford, returned government supporters from 1727 onwards, because there the crown had the power to make honorary doctors. Defoe's door remained wide open until it was closed by the enlargement of the electorate and by the Corrupt and Illegal Practices Act of 1883. Before then, few tried hard to shut it. [6]

Seats were often bought or leased to paying guests. Gatton was bought outright for £23,000 in 1751. It was sold again twenty years later and several times between 1786 and 1800. In 1801 it was sold for £90,000, and finally the Whig Lord Monson bought it for £180,000. That turned out to be an unfortunate investment. Shortly afterwards the Reform Bill abolished Gatton and made Monson a Tory. The going price for a safe seat for one parliament was £1500 in 1754, £2000 in 1761. In that year fifty-five peers could nominate or influence the election of at least 111 MPs, and fifty-six commoners that of ninety-four members – with the government immediately controlling another twenty-five, nearly half the representation of England was in very few hands and remained so for a long time. Indeed electoral patronage steadily increased. By 1798 two-thirds of the borough seats were filled by patrons. The oligarchy had partially usurped the place of the electorate – a position rationalised by Paley with the rhetorical question: 'if the properest persons be elected, what matters it by whom they are elected?'[7]

At the poll the decisions of the returning officer as to who could and who could not vote were usually partial and often venal. At Hedon in Yorkshire, a borough largely controlled by Lord Bath (the former William Pulteney,) Luke Robinson lost in 1747 to Samuel Gumley, Pulteney's brother-in-law. Robinson petitioned that the mayor,

> being gained into the interest of the said Samuel Gumley, did proceed, in taking the poll, with the utmost partiality against the petitioner, rejecting several legal voters, that were duly tendered for the petitioner and admitting several for the said Samuel Gumley who had not the least colour of right; and that by these and divers other illegal, arbitrary and corrupt methods, made use of by the said mayor, and the said Samuel Gumley and other agents, a majority of one vote only was obtained for the said Samuel Gumley.

At Marlborough in 1715 an enterprising returning officer returned as a member one Joshua Ward who had received not one solitary vote. Returning officers could go too far, however, and were occasionally committed by the House of Commons to Newgate.[8]

The final round of the electoral struggle was the hearing of election petitions to unseat members or declare their election void because of corruption, violence, or other irregularity. Until 1770, the whole House made the final decision on disputed elections, and the rights and wrongs of the case were of only marginal concern. Much more relevant was the party allegiance of the petitioners and the party complexion of the ministry. The winning opposition candidates at Bossiney in 1741 were unseated in favour of ministerialists before Walpole's fall and reseated after it.[9]

Between 1715 and 1734 the result was disputed in well over half of the 520 electoral contests that took place. Less than a third of those petitions were ever settled, opposition petitions usually languishing, even when plainly justified. In 1715 the Sheriff of Bristol returned the Whig candidates, though the Tories had clearly won; the Tory petition was never heard. Ministerial petitions had a much better chance. Between 1715 and 1747 the Tory winners at Wells were unseated and replaced by the government candidates no less than four times.[10]

Walpole aptly called this process 'weeding the House', and he sometimes shocked even his own side by his ruthless hoeing. Unusually, Walpole did not support John Scrope, the Secretary to the Treasury, when Scrope petitioned after his support of the Excise

Bill had defeated him at Bristol in 1734. Walpole 'would not espouse his cause', Lady Cowper recorded, apparently because the mob were 'resolved not to have him here and if he carried his petition were determined to rise and stone his friends'. In the end, however, Scrope did not fare too badly. Walpole found him another seat at Lyme Regis, and he remained Secretary to the Treasury and an MP until he died aged ninety.[11]

'Weeding' did not end with Walpole. Following the 1747 election, Whig petitions were determined, as Henry Pelham's secretary put it, 'as Justice requires and Whiggs desire'. Petitions were customarily treated with some levity. When Wilkes petitioned over the Berwick election of 1754 and his successful opponent talked of bribery and corruption, 'the House broke into a laughter'. It took a fierce speech from Pitt to quell the hilarity. Party feeling was weaker between 1754 and 1770, but the House seemed hostile, an MP recorded in 1768, to 'adventurers', usually 'nabobs', men who had made fortunes in India and could outbid the landed gentlemen for seats. Even though such people had been legally elected, they were liable to be unseated. Only with Grenville's Controverted Elections Act of 1770, which transferred the determination of petitions from the whole House to committees selected by lot, was a degree of fairness introduced.[12]

Clearly a House of Commons chosen in such a fashion did not very exactly represent the electorate – which, at its probable peak in 1715-22 of about 5 per cent of the country (dropping to under 4 per cent by the end of the century) or nearly one in four of all adult males, was a higher proportion of the population than the post-Reform Bill electorate. Still less did it represent the British people. Indeed, the leading Rockinghamite MP, Sir George Savile, later told it that it might as well call itself the representative of France as of the people of England. But, despite such rhetoric as Walpole's claim that the House was 'chosen by the unbiassed voice of the people in general', it was not supposed to represent them. It was, however, supposed to represent places and property, and it only did that very imperfectly. Bolingbroke computed that on the basis of the Land Tax figures, Cornwall had five times as many MPs as it deserved.[13]

Only a minority of the electorate could vote exactly as they wished. All the same a very imperfect electoral system which did not produce 'the sense of the people' was far preferable, as Beckford attested in 1755, to having no elections at all. Rousseau's well-known gibe that the English were free only during elections, even if taken at its face value, still gave the English an advantage over other nations. Although elections played a smaller part in the governmental process than they did later on, they were an indispensable demonstration that not all power and influence came from the top and therefore a warning that the oligarchy should pay some attention to the sensitivities of those below it. Conversely, by giving voters and non-voters the feeling – or illusion – of participation, elections were an important means of engineering consent to the political system and legitimising the rule of the elite.[14]

In the counties and in most boroughs an elector could normally use one of his two votes for the candidate he favoured. Only in very few of them was the borough's patron or owner in total command. The patron's control was usually conditional and rebellion against it always a possibility. Hence the patron was spurred to remember his responsibilities and to foster the economic interests of the borough. At Helston in Cornwall the Duke of Leeds, as well as erecting and maintaining the public buildings, paid the church and poor rates, which cost him £700 to £1000 a year. At St Albans the Spencers installed a water supply. Even when a patron's control was total, as was Sir William Drake's at Amersham, he did not necessarily neglect his obligations; in 1784 Drake was thanked for his 'generous and liberal benefactions to the poor'. The deference of the voters was thus matched by the paternalism of the borough's owner or patron.[15]

Public participation in elections, then, was not eliminated even in the boroughs subject to patronal influence. In any case the constituencies with the largest electorates were not amenable to patronage, and it was these largest boroughs which were most frequently contested. In such seats, as elsewhere, eighteenth-century elections were more trials of strength and demonstrations of power than opportunities to choose between candidates offering rival policies. Nevertheless in the large constituencies issues were often significant, especially from 1768 onwards, even though near-national controversies as in 1734, 1780 and 1784 were rare. Most candidates did not have policies, and one-class politics ensured that most voters were not much affected by the victory of one candidate rather than another: whoever was elected almost invariably had to pay some attention to the interests of his constituents if he wanted re-election; though Burke visited Bristol only twice between 1774 and 1780, he worked hard on his constituency's behalf; he was rejected because he had supported the Americans, free trade with Ireland and relief for Roman Catholics. A voter's self-interest pointed towards acting in accordance with the wishes of his social or economic superior, if he had one, or of accepting the highest bid if he had not. In any case voters were not under quasi-military discipline, and a substantial minority could not be relied upon to do as they were told.[16]

'Popular elections,' wrote Paley, 'procure to the common people courtesy from their superiors. That contemptuous and overbearing insolence, with which the lower orders of the community are wont to be treated by the higher, is greatly mitigated where the people have something to give.' The Archdeacon and Matthew Bramble were right; foreigners noted the same thing. Candidates did adjust their manner, or they risked defeat; the playwright Sheridan lost Stafford in 1812 through his 'tactlessness and indolence' in refusing to call upon anybody. Yet often it was the upper and not the lower orders who had something to give. In the 1780 election George III made it clear to the tradespeople of Windsor that his custom would be lost if they voted for the Whig candidate, Admiral Keppell. And when the Duke of Newcastle's candidate was beaten at Lewes in 1768, he decided to withdraw his custom from those tradesmen who had voted the wrong way, though in the end he was persuaded to relent.[17]

England was highly politicized, and political views, prejudices and allegiances remaining strong both among those who had the vote and those who did not. To Wesley's regret, 'every cobbler, tinker and hackney coachman' had political opinions. In Yarmouth, Toryism was 'the natural bent of the majority of the people', Walpole's brother was told in 1743, 'and has for many years been kept under by art, difficulty and expense'. The electoral influence of the Crown was so strong that the ministry of the day invariably won a general election. Yet it did so not because of the obedience or malleability of the voters but because of the inequity of the electoral system. In working the system almost every form of persuasion, influence and coercion was employed against the voters. If they had been prepared to do just what they were told, these efforts would have been redundant. The *Oxford Journal* gave a satirical description of campaigning in 1754: 'A Receipt to make a vote by the cook of Sir JD [Sir James Dashwood, one of the Tory candidates] – take a cottager of 30 shillings a year, tax him at 40; swear at him; bully him, take your business from him; give him your business again; make him drunk; shake him by the hand; kiss his wife; and HE IS AN HONEST FELLOW.'[18]

Election riots did not pollute an otherwise pure decision-making process. As Defoe made clear, there was no electoral purity to pollute – if indeed there ever is.

Bribery

It was 'really something very extraordinary', Sir Robert Walpole claimed in 1734, to insinuate that the government spent money on 'bribing elections'. In fact the government spent more secret service money in that year than in any other between 1688 and the civil list reform of 1782. Yet the sums spent by the government were not large; the government's electoral influence came more from patronage than corruption. Elections became ever more expensive, but most of the bribery came from other sources.[19]

If violence was usually confined to the larger electorates, bribery was obviously most appropriate to seats with small ones. The extent of electoral bribery has been exaggerated and modern experts tend to minimize it, pointing out that only in some twenty constituencies were electoral politics solely a matter of money. Yet not only radicals denounced electoral corruption. Conservative clerics as far apart as Bishop Warburton and John Wesley did the same, Warburton even complaining that 'profligate venality [had] now become universal in the choice of our representatives to Parliament'.[20]

Each of the thirteen voters at Malmesbury received in the Walpole era £100 for a general election; later they received annual payments. At Lostwithiel, with a slightly larger electorate, eight votes cost £20 each in 1727. In early nineteenth-century Wallingford voters were paid £20 by each representative, which kept them out of the workhouse and enabled them to pay taxes. At Hedon 'the prevailing custom' was twenty guineas for a plumper and ten for a split vote. Not all small boroughs were corrupt. Bath was honest, as were Salisbury and Devizes. Equally, bribery was not confined to seats with tiny electorates. At Bristol in 1727 those who 'sold their votes have received from one to five guineas for those'. At Leominster in 1796 a winning candidate paid 402 voters five guineas each; his other sixty supporters, being his debtors, men of property or Quakers, received nothing. And bribery and violence were not mutually exclusive. In the riotous mayoral election of 1732 at Chester, which had about 1500 voters, the winning candidate had to pay £20 to £30 for a vote, and bribery was as rife as violence in the Oxfordshire election of 1754. There it cost less to get the voters 'properly inspired', as the phrase went; but there were more of them.[21]

In his brash high Whig phase the young Charles Fox, MP for Midhurst, complained of the electorate's 'scandalous dishonesty'. Midhurst, which had not seen a poll since 1710, was controlled by Lord Montague who in 1768 had agreed for a consideration to let Fox and his cousin have the two seats. Speaking in favour of electoral reform in 1780, the Duke of Richmond said that in Midhurst 'he had often remarked several stones marked, 1, 2, 3, 4, etc in a park wall of a noble Lord [Montague]; having asked what were the meaning of them he had been told that they were votes and returned Members of Parliament. He immediately perceived that they were very valuable stones . . .' Fox was 19 and abroad when the stones elected him. Three years later he was blaming 'the people' for accepting bribes.[22]

Patrons and candidates complained of the venality of their own electors. At Grampound in 1747 'the villains' raised their demands extravagantly, and 'the dirty rascals despise 20 guineas as much as a king's serjeant does a half guinea fee'; sixty years later they were said 'to stick at nothing' to obtain money. Lord Harley 'met with so much open villainy and secret perfidy' in Radnorshire that he abandoned his electoral interests there. The Whig candidate at Bishop's Castle told Walpole before the 1741 election that the electors were 'very jealous of their liberty . . . which is the liberty of being as corrupt as they please'. In Wendover the electors managed to get themselves paid three guineas each even when the election was not contested.[23]

No doubt many electors similarly complained of the meanness of candidates and patrons. The relationship of corruptor and corrupted seldom engenders a mutual esteem. In any case it was scarcely the duty of the electors of Grampound or Bishop's Castle to begin the reform of the electoral system or to set an example to their betters by observing a law which was almost universally broken. In the United States at the end of the nineteenth-century when many complained of the dishonesty of politicians, an observer pointed out that he had never met a politician who had bribed himself. The voters of Grampound might have said the same. They were, after all, just pursuing their self-interest in the same way as those who bribed them. And if those who owned seats could sell them, why should not the owners of a vote do the same? Indeed Loughborough, when Lord Chief Justice in 1782, said that 'the franchise of voting was daily bought and sold, and was consequently a species of property'. Finally, Tory denunciations of electoral corruption in the early part of the century suggest that bribery, at least in the larger seats, was often less popular with the bribed than with the bribers.[24]

The bribery could be respectably collective. In an attempt to consolidate his interest at Bodmin, Lord Radnor in 1716 had that borough made an assize town in alternation with Launceston. Lord Chief Justice Willes, who had been MP for Launceston, similarly moved the summer assizes from Buckingham to Aylesbury in 1747 in a successful attempt to get his son elected there; Buckingham was a Grenville borough, and the Grenvilles, who resented its being deprived of the assizes 'merely to serve the private purposes of an ambitious judge', had them moved back again the following year. Or the bribery could also be more conventional and charitable. The hanging judge, Baron Page, paid for the paving of the streets, for the enlargement of the vicarage and for the building of a school in Banbury on the understanding that his candidate would be elected. Unfortunately, though Page was more enlightened a politician than a judge, he was less powerful in politics than in his courtroom. His candidate was defeated, and Page himself, despite the support of Walpole and the court, was cleared of corruption by only four votes.★ A hopeful candidate for Colchester bankrupted himself by building a hospital there.[26]

No clear division between influence and violence

Of the many other means of persuasion, one was religious, the parson often having great political influence. Here the Tories in the first half of the century usually had an advantage, but at Westminster the Church gave the court candidates every assistance. In the 1749 by-election a recalcitrant clergyman was marked down for conversion by the Bishop of Norwich, while the guide for the tombs in Westminster Abbey received his political guidance from the Bishop of Rochester.[27]

The threat of eviction was a more violent mode of persuasion. William Hanbury, the Whig candidate for Northamptonshire in the 1730 by-election, announced that he gave 'his tenants free liberty to vote and solicit (if they please) against him'. Hanbury could probably afford to be generous because he had few tenants, but his announcement is a rare example of the exception proving the rule. At the 1715 election the Duke of Newcastle secured compliance at Aldborough by evicting those who had defied him two years earlier. In the 1749 Westminster by-election the Duke of Bedford made himself unpopular by ordering his tenants to vote for his brother-in-law, Lord Trentham, on the pain of eviction or an increase in rent, though the threat was largely empty as most of them had long leases. Church tenants on occasion faced an additional hazard. At Lichfield in 1727 the victorious Whig candidate threatened the tenants of the Dean and Chapter not only with eviction but 'with ecclesiastical censures for incontinency'.[28]

At Stamford the tenants of Lords Exeter and Gainsborough were told in 1734 that they would be turned out not just for not supporting their landlords' nominees but for doing business with tradesmen supporting the Whigs or drinking in Whig inns. On the next occasion that the Exeter domination of Stamford was challenged – seventy-five years later – the Exeter interest again evicted disobedient tenants. An extreme form of eviction was the demolition of houses. In the early nineteenth-century Sir William Manners built a large workhouse at Ilchester for the families he had made homeless. Eviction remained an electoral

---

★ The poet Savage wrote of Page: 'But 'scapes even Innocence his harsh Harangue?/ Alas! – ev'n Innocence must hang;/ Must hang to please him, when of Spleen possest:/ Must hang to bring forth an abortive Jest.' Savage was an expert, though scarcely an impartial, witness: he had been convicted of murder before Page who, Dr Johnson said, 'treated him with his usual insolence and severity'. Both Fielding and Pope, who observed Page from a safer distance, were similarly scathing.[25]

weapon until mid-century: in 1832 the Duke of Newcastle, saying a man could do what he liked with his own, evicted some recalcitrant tenants at Newark; he was not alone in what he did.[29]

All the same, at least from about 1750, eviction was rare. The great majority of tenants did not need threats to persuade them to vote for their landlords' nominee. The eviction of tenants was proper, Dr Johnson thought, because 'the privilege of voting should [not] be independent of old family interest'; probably most tenants thought the same. Normally a tenant was allowed to use one of his votes as he wished and was only required to use the other for the landlord's candidate. Most tenants had little incentive to create unpleasantness by refusing to conform with the customs of an hierarchical society; deference often carried its own rewards. On their side, landlords usually recognised that intimidation was a sign of failure, like using force against rioters.[30]

Another weapon was the denial of access to common land to the unamenable. Similar commercial and industrial pressures existed. Licences to sell ale were useful as bribery or coercion. Justices would give them to freeholders who agreed to vote the right way and withheld them from those who did not, as they did in Bristol in 1754.[31]

For government employees, voting the way the government ordered was part of the job; non-compliance meant the end of that job. At Woolwich in 1773 the government overseer was told to order a dinner for the relevant voters with as much punch as they would drink and then get their promises 'by fair means, else by G– they shall be by foul for we have interest enough surely, to get them turned out of their places . . .' Where the government led, the universities followed. When an extreme Tory, Dr King, stood at Oxford against two moderate Tories, heads of colleges gave curates, chaplains and scholars 'this dreadful alternative', a supporter of King claimed, 'either to comply or starve'.[32]

Sometimes these methods of coercion involved violence. In 1749 a shoemaker and Chelsea Pensioner 'was taken away by three or four gentlemen and they said if he would not poll for Lord Trentham . . . he should be turned out of his pension'. At Coventry thirty years earlier several voters suffered a less mild though more official form of kidnapping: the Whig magistrates sent them to gaol until after the election for crying the names of a Tory candidate. Two voters at Gloucester in 1761 were still more unfortunate. After being made 'dead drunk' to stop them voting, they were locked up in a coach and suffocated.[33]

In any case no clear line divided the various forms of influence, coercion and violence. A hierarchy of methods of persuasion ranged from bribery at the top to violence at the bottom, and the distinctions between them were blurred. Everybody would rather be bribed than bullied. But people might be subjected to both, or might be bribed to commit violence; and it was not markedly preferable to be driven by economic or social compulsion to vote for a particular candidate than to be prevented by physical intimidation from voting at all. Nor, looking at it from the other end, was it markedly less virtuous to hire a mob by money or drink than to hire voters by direct bribery. The violence of an eighteenth-century election was just another method of electoral coercion. It did not mark a distinction between the permissible and the impermissible; broadly that distinction lay between what you did which was permissible and what your opponent did, which was not. Elections were a duel in which each participant (and occasionally the spectator) chose his weapons. The choice was wide, and participants were not confined to just one. Nor was there a distinction, as drawn by Holdsworth, between 'influence' in all its forms directed by the great from above and duress exerted by the mob from below. Mobs did sometimes riot for their own reasons, but more often mob violence was directed by the great from above and was employed as just another form of influence. Crowd participation brought two additional advantages. It gave the unenfranchised the comforting illusion that they were an important influence on the election and the successful candidates the conceit that they represented public opinion.[34]

The chief distinction between violence and the other electoral weapons in a candidate's armoury was that the latter were designed to drive supporters to the poll, whereas the usual function of violence was to keep opponents away from it or to persuade the opposition not to stand. After the Whig victory at Lichfield in 1727, the Tory petitioners claimed that they had 'a visible majority of the legal voters on the day of election' but their opponents had 'brought a great number of colliers and other riotous persons into the City who, joined with the mob, obstructed the petitioners' voters; and the sheriff . . . encouraged the said mob; so that when the petitioners had polled about 70 persons, their voters were obliged to depart, finding it impossible to obtain any justice there'. A third candidate was similarly prevented from standing at Liverpool in 1768.[35]

Sometimes the violence was openly led by the candidates or their sponsors. In the mayoral election for Chester in 1732, a Whig mob, thinking that the reigning Grosvenor interest intended to make 300 new voters during the night, expelled the aldermen and levelled the city hall. The Tory response was organised by the Jacobite Sir Watkin Williams Wynn, a friend of the Grosvenors and MP for Denbighshire. Wynn had firm views on proper electoral behaviour – he had introduced the 1729 act against electoral corruption – and decreed that the 'Whiggist rascals' should be beaten. This was achieved by the arrival of '8 or 9 hundred Welshmen . . . armed with clubs, staffs and other dangerous and offensive weapons' which were used to knock down 'every man that declared for Manley [the Whig candidate], or for King George'. Wynn and other gentlemen welcomed their Welsh followers 'with their swords drawn . . . [and] with loud huzzas and declamations'. Even so, this display of force had to be supplemented by large-scale bribery.[36]

At Stamford in 1734 violence began at the races, when supporters of the Tory Earl of Exeter stoned and drove away the supporters of the Whig, Savile Cust. The Tories' next step was to bring in some 200 outsiders, chiefly tenants of Exeter and his ally Lord Gainsborough, build them 'extempore chimneys' and lodge them 'in garrets, closets and cellars' to qualify them to vote as householders. Two days before the poll the Tory candidates 'led their riotous mob in person . . . made a formal attack on Mr Cust's house' and stoned his friends. Thirty people were hurt, and it was not Exeter's men but Cust's who were arrested and deprived of their vote. Not surprisingly, the Tories won.[37]

In the only contested county election for Staffordshire between the Restoration and the Reform Bill, the defection of Lord Gower from the Tories to the ministry in 1747 led to violence in that election and also in Lichfield and Stafford, where the house of the Whig candidate was demolished. Once again Williams Wynn was involved – one of the last occasions when the gentry were conspicuous in the violence. Later in the century they raised mobs and instigated riots but remained in the background themselves.[38]

Even in the early Hanoverian days, candidates more often hired than led mobs. In Middlesex in 1727 the Whig candidate Barker hired a mob 'of about a hundred . . . at 5/- each at an alehouse' and armed them with clubs. He seems also to have hired some JPs who imprisoned some of his opponents' voters but he still lost. Gentry and JPs customarily gave judicial help to their side's mobs and punished the leaders of their opponents'. At Westminster in 1749 Justice Fielding was openly partisan on behalf of the candidate of his patron, the Duke of Bedford. In the hard-fought Oxfordshire election of 1754 both sides hired mobs, the Tory one being known as the Regiment of Blueskins and the Whig the Regiment of Blackguards. Both were active. At the 'Battle of Chipping Norton' the Whigs armed with bludgeons stormed the White Hart and assaulted a Tory gentleman at dinner. Remarkably, a Whig grand jury found a true bill against the Whig organisers. After the scrutiny a Tory mob tried to throw into the Cherwell some Whig horsemen, one of whom shot and killed a hostile chimney sweep.[39]

Mid-century Westminster, which had one of the largest electorates in the country and where the court interest was naturally strong, displayed the two kinds of mob violence: the first organised from above by the candidates and the second springing from the mob's own resentments.

The Tories had won easily in 1722 only to be unseated on petition, and at the two subsequent elections the court candidates were returned unopposed. In 1741 the popular Admiral Vernon was suddenly nominated against the court candidates, Lord Sundon, a Lord of the Treasury, and Sir Charles Wager, the First Lord of the Admiralty. Vernon was fighting in the West Indies, but on the second day of the poll his co-candidate, Edwin, organised a mob at the hustings in Covent Garden to counteract the court interest. The mob became 'quite outrageous and threw into the Portico Dirt, Stones, Sticks, Dead Cats and Dogs' so that the candidates and officials had to take refuge in Inigo Jones's church. The violence continued for the next few days with, as Wager told Vernon, 'such mobs and riots as was never seen before'. On the sixth day, seeing a 'posse of voters' for Vernon and Edwin approaching, Sundon advised the returning officer, John Lever, to close the poll, and having sent for troops Lever did so, declaring Sundon and Wager duly elected. Both had an interest. Sundon saw he would lose if the poll continued, and the Bailiff received £1500 from secret service funds. Wager had gone to Holland with the King and his absence occasioned, an observer believed, 'all the consequent mobbings and mismanagements'.[40]

Both the Vernon voters who had been deprived of their vote and the mob who did not have a vote were 'so enraged' that Sundon once again had to take refuge in the church. After some hours he 'crept into Sir Jo Cross's coach, driving at full gallop home . . . the mob in great numbers following, hooping and hallowing, cursing and flinging stones, by which the windows were broke, plenty of dirt thrown into him, one of his footmen's skull cracked by a brick bat thrown at his head and his Lordship wounded in the hand'. Fortunately Sundon lived in Cleveland Row just beyond St James's Palace and the Guard on duty there stopped the mob, preventing his house from being pulled down. A few days later John Lever was less lucky. His 'house was much abused by the Mob . . . so that I and my family were in great danger of our lives'. The same happened to the chief Bow Street magistrate and several months later the Dean of St James's had his windows broken, because, he believed, he had favoured the court candidates for Westminster. The violence was not all one way. The other side had hired a mob led by John Broughton, 'a profest Boxer' and the English champion.[41]

After any earlier Walpole election the losers' petition would almost certainly have gone unheard. But 'the great man' was about to fall, and the petition succeeded, the House deciding that it appeared that 'a body of armed soldiers headed by officers did . . . come in a military manner and take possession of the Church Yard of St Paul,

Covent Garden . . . before the said election was ended' and that this was 'a manifest violation of the freedom of elections'.[42]

In 1747 the court candidates, Lord Trentham, the Duke of Bedford's brother-in-law, and Sir Peter Warren won easily, Bedford's 'bruising militia' removing the pollers for the Tory candidates entirely from the hustings. Two years later when his brother-in-law had to seek re-election through having taken office as a Lord of the Admiralty, Bedford did not have such an easy run. The government was unpopular because of a row over French actors and the execution of Bosavern Penlez who was alleged to have taken part in a riot against bawdy-houses, a murky episode in which Fielding was involved; Trentham was particularly unpopular because he had patronised the French players and had refused to help get a reprieve for the condemned man. He was also strongly disliked by Tories because of the defection of his Jacobite father, Lord Gower, to the Whigs. In an unusual refinement of electoral tactics, instead of voters being sent to prison to stop them voting for the opposition, prisoners and debtors were released from the prisons to vote for the court candidates. The Bedford estate again provided some 150 toughs for the hustings battle. This time, however, the Prince of Wales fielded his chairmen to take on Bedford's bruisers. The returning officer declared Trentham elected, and the opposition asked for a scrutiny which took months. Eventually Trentham's election by a small majority was confirmed and, as in 1741, the returning officer's house was threatened. The mob pelted a man, whom they took to be Trentham, from Covent Garden to the Park; unfortunately it was somebody else. Two petitions were presented, but the House of Commons had reverted to type and refused to hear them.[43]

In the Westminster election in 1784 – perhaps the most violent contest of the century – and its almost equally violent successor four years later, battle was frequently joined between the candidates' conflicting mobs, and several sailors and constables were killed. In 1788 the rival gangs, often numbering 200 or more, surrounded the hustings and intimidated opposing voters. At Coventry in 1780 the opposition candidates claimed that their voters had been kept forcibly away from the poll, 'many of them stripped naked and their clothes torn to pieces by a mob of colliers hired for that purpose; others cruelly beaten and most shamefully treated'. In the same town four years later, when the Sheriff allowed some palpably illegal votes, the supporters of the opposition candidates, Lord Sheffield and Mr Conway, destroyed the polling booths.[44]

In an industrial town like Nottingham with its large electorate, the distinction between violence from above and below was blurred; the intimidation and violence of the enfranchised framework knitters were matched by hired gangs on the other side. In 1802 the military had to be called in. A non-violent election was a rarity; a non-venal one was unthinkable.[45]

Much of the electoral violence, then, came from mobs hired by the candidates or their agents. Indeed at the vastly expensive North-ampton election of 1768, in which three peers – Lords Northampton, Halifax and Spencer – were heavily involved, this was implicitly acknowledged. The candidates, peers and representatives of corpora-tions signed an agreement 'that mobbing of all kinds shall be discontinued and discouraged by the above Lords and gentlemen and all their friends . . .'

Those who did not have the vote seldom had much to gain from the election of a Whig, a Tory or anybody else. Unless they were prompted or bribed, therefore, they rarely rioted of their own accord. For the second kind of electoral violence there usually had to be provocation: an infringement of what mobs regarded as their rights or some blatant cheating, as at Westminster in 1741. Polling was public so that the great could supervise and influence their inferiors. In 1747 the Duke of Newcastle was so anxious to secure Pitt's election at Seaford that he sat beside the returning officer. And when the great manifestly broke the rules, the voteless crowd attempted to punish or influence their superiors. Enraged by official skullduggery, their social resentments and antagonism came to the surface. The great had many electoral weapons. The little only had one: the riot. And on occasion the threat of it provided an effective incentive to improved behaviour by the authorities.[46]

The most frequent cause of the second kind of electoral violence was a 'dry' election. Treating was regarded as one of the rules to be observed. The Duke of Newcastle was especially lavish in Sussex. In 1749 the Duke of Bedford opened 222 taverns and coffeehouses for his brother-in-law at Westminster. The court spent £1800 in 1754 entertaining their supporters there, even though the election was not contested. At Carlisle in 1768 Sir James Lowther spent £400 on drink alone. In 1784 anybody in Buckinghamshire who promised Thomas Grenville his vote received a card entitling him to be 'properly accommodated' at any of seventeen houses. On a less munificent scale, treating was a customary feature of eighteenth-century elections, and candidates who broke the custom risked trouble. At Pontefract in 1768 an East India nabob decided to end the treating of electors. The crowd reacted by surrounding the polling booths, prevented some voters from polling and defeated the nabob. At the following election mobs rioted in both Northampton and York against candidates who refused to treat. Presumably, they felt that they had as much right to a drink as to a vote and that one without the other was scarcely worth having.[47]

An agreement between opposing candidates to share the representatives and avoid a poll could also be explosive. An uncontested poll was liable to be even more of a desert for voters than a dry election. When the four candidates at Leicester in 1790 agreed to return one from each party, 'the mob was so exasperated at being bilked of further extortion on the several candidates' that they gutted the Town Hall and burnt a public library. A similar agreement at Liverpool provoked a much lower degree of violence in the same year but enough to produce another candidate and ensure a contest. Any unilateral decision not to provide liquor meant finishing at the bottom of the poll.[48]

Despite a claim that the Leicester mob would have 'murdered the coalitionists, could they have got at them', electoral violence of all kinds was usually fairly mild: two people were killed at a by-election in Taunton in 1754 and another two in Nottingham in the same year, but there were few serious injuries. And it was seldom decisive. Much of it, like electoral activity in the twentieth century, was ritualistic and did not affect the outcome. Often it merely confirmed electoral superiority, or it provoked counter-violence and was cancelled out. Similarly the knowledge that the other side would respond in kind was the prime deterrent. 'Great expenses were made, great threats ushered in the day,' Walpole wrote to Norwich in 1734, 'but a due provision to repel force, by force, made it a quiet election.'[49]

The attitude of the great to electoral violence was similar to their attitude to bribery. They denounced and practised both. 'The freedom of this House is the freedom of this country, which can continue no longer than while the votes of the electors are influenced by any base or venal motive,' the Speaker, in all apparent seriousness, told the Commons in 1768.* Over electoral violence, hypocrisy similarly reigned. No words were too hard for the mobs, which many MPs and their defeated opponents had diligently hired. Legislators did not object to violence as such any more than they objected to corruption as such. 'The Cavendish family who supported the mob at Brentford will nevertheless,' wrote *The Times*, 'be very much displeased with the mob' in their own borough of Knaresborough. MPs' horror of the mob was fear it might act on its own. 'Miserable are the times,' Percival wrote of the Westminster Riot in 1741, 'when liberty is grown into licentiousness.'[51] Licentiousness was when the crowd rioted of its own accord; that might lead to damaging social change. When, however, the crowd rioted under direction from above, it created no such fears; that was liberty.

---

* Twenty years earlier Sir William Stanhope was more candid. 'For Aylesbury . . . I have no particular partiality,' he told the House, 'I never got a vote there I did not pay for.' Pitt commented that as Stanhope was a man of honour no one would doubt the truth of what he had said.[50]

ELEVEN

Food Riots

A riotous spirit in a people is generally owing to one or more of the following causes: carelessness in those at the helm of the true interest of the subjects; – negligence in the magistrates in executing the laws; – oppression of the poor by the rich or those in power; – or lastly to a spirit of licentiousness and immorality, diffused among the common people.

Thomas Andrews, 'Essay on Riots', 1739

We may calmly discuss matters over a bottle of claret after a plentiful dinner, and say that the poor in Ireland live on potatoes, and in France and other countries upon turnips or cabbage. We must take these things as we find them, our poor are not accustomed to live in that manner, nor will they easily give up bread etc . . . especially if they know they are deprived of them by the oppression of taxes.

Gentleman's Magazine, 1766

I think myself bound in justice to bear attestation to the good conduct of the labouring poor in this neighbourhood . . . But I very much fear this patience will soon be exhausted if some beneficial alteration in the price of provisions does not immediately take place. They will be unwilling to starve in the midst of plenty, and quietly to behold their oppressors growing rich out of their bowels and fattening upon their afflictions.

Rev James Hartley to the Home Office, November 1800[1]

Like election riots, food riots began well before the eighteenth century and continued beyond it. They were the staple of eighteenth-century agitation and probably accounted for well over half of all disturbances. If grain was insufficient or its price so high that they could not afford to buy it, the poor could either go hungry or riot. Unless the scarcity was purely the consequence of famine and had no human causes, the sensible course was a mild riot to bring their plight to the attention of the authorities. An even more rational course would have been to get other people to riot.[2]

Up to the Civil War the interests of the eaters of food were theoretically paramount, though the authorities occasionally had to be reminded of that priority. In 1629 100 or so women, having boarded one of several foreign ships that were exporting grain from Maldon, Essex, forced its crew to fill the bonnets and aprons of women and children with rye. This both jolted the central government into stopping the export of corn and prodded the corporation of Maldon into buying corn at a 'convenient price' for the poor. The rioters were leniently treated, but when 200 or 300 cloth workers took part in a larger repeat performance shortly afterwards, four of the leaders were hanged, the only food rioters to be executed in the early seventeenth century. Relief was again ordered, however, and in the similar economic crisis of the following year the export of corn was forbidden, and extra grain was imported and sold to the poor at below the market price. The market did not yet rule.[3]

After the Restoration, the corn producer came into his own. Imports were taxed and exports were permitted, whatever the corn price at home; bounties on exports were soon added. Trouble was initially averted by an extraordinary sequence of good harvests. A disastrous run followed in the 1690s, which in 1693 brought food riots at Worcester, when some factors arrived 'to buy up corn, bacon and cheese to export them', and also in Shrewsbury, Herefordshire and Oxfordshire. Though the years from 1692 saw seven out of eight bad harvests and much social distress, the government did not impose an embargo upon the export of corn until 1699. In the subsequent century, failure of the government to stop the export of corn in time was a common cause of food riots.[4]

Meanwhile the long agricultural revolution, the main achievements of which were before 1720, so increased the output of English agriculture that till mid-century, despite the rise in population, the country nearly always had a surplus of food; only when the harvest failed in 1709, 1726-8 and 1740, were there major disturbances. Britain, Defoe wrote in the 1720s, might 'truly be called a corn country', and from then until about mid-century food prices fell to the obvious benefit of the poorer classes. Food exports rose, and in 1750 grain accounted for one-fifth of British exports. In the second half of the century a faster growth of population and a much smaller growth in agricultural production ended the agricultural depression, raised food prices and turned Britain into a net importer of grain.[5]

Regions and occupations did not of course fare the same, but broadly, from mid-century on, except in the North, real wages stagnated or fell. Bad harvests and high food prices became more frequent, and in 1756-7, 1766-7, 1772-3, 1795-6 and 1800-1, food riots were widespread. With working families forming about three-quarters of the population and spending at least half and sometimes up to four-fifths of their incomes on food, chiefly on bread, its price was vital to most of the country.

Of course by no means all labouring families were poor. Many were skilled workers, and French and German visitors noted that the English standard of living was higher than elsewhere; French wage earners ate an even higher proportion of their income. Yet clearly many were vulnerable to high food prices or low wages and, above all, to both. And that was a combination which frequently confronted them. Agriculture's predominance in the economy and the dependence of most other industries upon it for their materials usually ensured that high food prices entailed a trade depression.[6]

Unlike most other European countries, however, England experienced no famine in the sense of mass deaths from starvation. Yet 'famine', in the sense used in 1795 by a member of the Board of Trade to Pitt of 'the want of wheat sufficient to furnish the lower and labouring classes', causing deaths due to hunger-related disease, did occur. Few starved outside London and the provincial cities, but the death rate rose appreciably in periods of dearth and immediately after them.[7]

The Poor Law cushioned hardship and, except in London and the large towns, usually prevented destitution. Local taxation only amounted to between 10 and 15 per cent of central government levies, but for the poor it provided a welcome contrast: the poor paid central government taxation but derived little benefit; they did not pay local taxes but at least three-quarters of that money was spent on poor relief. The English Poor Law had its deep stains – chiefly its often violent treatment of vagrants, the sometimes brutal removal from the parish of those who did not possess 'settlement' there and the consequent tying of labourers to their own village and their lowly status – and, like everything else, it was not proof against meanness, corruption and inefficiency. Furthermore conditions in workhouses were often squalid. Visiting a 'House of Industry' near Dereham in Norfolk in March 1780, Parson Woodforde found that the 380 poor in it did not 'look either healthy or cheerful, a great number die there, 27 have died since Christmas last'. Yet till towards the end of the century 'outdoor' relief was as a rule generously administered, providing a system of public assistance that was almost unique. Whether regarded as charity or as ransom paid to keep the poor quiet, it was money well spent.

Unemployment relief and pensions were paid by the parish, and payments were made for food, shoes, rent, lying-in expenses, burial, nursing and many other needs. In the nature of things the Poor Law worked best in the rural areas where everybody was known to the parish authorities and where between a quarter and a half of village populations needed assistance. In London and the cities conditions

were often appalling, with widows and their children being the worst
sufferers. In perhaps the worst year of all, 1740, 'many people who
wanted heat and victuals' died, and one woman 'perished with cold
after she had been delivered'. In the 1760s a magistrate told Dr
Johnson that in London more than twenty people a week died of
starvation. Fielding had thought the same ten years before.[8]

The nature of food riots

The starving and the freezing seldom riot. Too weak to combine,
their refuge is despair not violence. Food rioting was therefore not
the prerogative of only the indigent poor – rioters were often
respectable artisans. Yet food rioters were commonly hungry. The
looting Wiltshire mob at Bradley in 1766 may have exaggerated
when they told the local MP that 'they had not eat a morsel of bread
for three days but had subsisted on grains etc, and that their wives
and families were in the same miserable condition', but probably only
a little. Efficient food production and a usually effective system of
distribution should have enabled the government to avert the resort
to force by those who were strong enough to combine and protest,
yet time and again it acted too late.[9]

The three broad types of food riot – simple looting, either the
result of criminality or of desperate want; riots against the movement
of corn to somewhere else in Britain or to another country; and riots
to lower the price of corn either by forcing JPs to set a maximum
price or by requisitioning corn from farmers or millers and selling it
at a price fixed by the mob – often shaded into each other. Simple
looting, indeed, was relatively rare. Early in 1741 some colliers at
Blyth broke into two sets of granaries carrying away £500 of fine
wheat and doing 'considerable damage'. Destruction and plunder
rather than discipline and bargaining were the features, too, of food
riots in Manchester in 1757, 1762 and 1795, five people being killed
in the middle year. Looting, however, was more often combined
with one of the other types of riot. In 1740 a crowd marched out of
Norwich to extort money and strong ale from gentlemen and
farmers, and when the response was less generous than expected
'they showed their resentment by treading down corn in the fields';
but before leaving Norwich they had forced down prices in the city.
Again, looting was often the consequence of farmers or traders
rejecting the prices proposed by the crowd; an anti-export riot
sometimes developed into price-fixing or *taxation populaire*, and
looting often followed more orderly proceedings. At Cambridge in
1757 'a mob (chiefly of women) . . . broke open a storehouse in
which were lodging about fifteen quarters of wheat, the property of

a farmer who had that day refused 9s 6d for it, and carry'd it all off'.[10]

In the price-fixing riots the crowd's behaviour, though illegal, was usually disciplined and correct. If they seized corn which was about to be exported, they paid what they believed to be a fair price for it. If they decreed the price of grain which should reign in the market, they saw that that price was duly paid to the owners. In 1766 workers at Honiton, who had taken corn from farmers and sold it at what they considered to be a proper price, brought back to the farmers the sacks as well as the proceeds.[11]

At Brixham and Plymouth in 1801 those who stole food were made to return it by the crowd. In 1753 at Shepton Mallet about '700 coal miners assembled in a riotous manner on account of the great quantity of corn exported abroad [and] went to all the inns where the corn was lodged, and obliged the owners to sell at such prices as they thought proper'. In Devon in 1795 crowds fixed the price of wheat and potatoes about 25 per cent lower than the farmers' price and then bought it; or they pushed the magistrates into fixing a compromise price. Six years later they were more sophisticated: they marched out from the towns and forced farmers to sign 'contracts' to sell their produce at lower prices. In Oldham at the same period the mob not only controlled the price and handed over the proceeds of sale to the owner, it also rationed buyers.[12]

The often disciplined and rational behaviour of food and other rioters led Mr E.P. Thompson to write in a fine phrase of 'the moral economy' of the English crowd. In almost every eighteenth-century crowd action, he maintained, there was 'some legitimising notion': the crowd believed that 'they were defending traditional rights or customs' and were generally supported 'by the wider consensus of the community'. According to this moral economy of the poor, the authorities were under an obligation, by checking speculation and controlling food markets, to ensure that sufficient food was available at reasonable prices.[13]

Certainly there was nothing outlandish in food rioters considering their behaviour justified. Locke, like St Thomas Aquinas, believed that everybody had a right to enough food, 'having a title to so much out of another's plenty' as 'would save him from extreme want'. Even today, 'excessive' profits are seldom considered wholly legitimate, and the idea of fairness has not been entirely banished from the consideration of economic issues. In the eighteenth century the crowd was not alone in declining to accept the right of corn traders and farmers to make what profits they chose. Lord Kenyon, Lord Chief Justice at the end of the century, thought the country suffered 'most grievously' from food profiteers. Again, though corn exports were valuable to the country, the continued export of food when prices were high was provocative to those in difficulties. The growth of a national and international market in corn was, after all, small consolation to the poor if the market failed locally. To believe that the authorities should occasionally subsidise consumers rather than rich traders who might indeed be selling abroad to 'our enemies' was not unreasonable.[14]

For three-quarters of the century, furthermore, the crowd's aim accorded not only with decent common sense but with the laws of the land. Containing legislation based on the ideas that corn should be sold openly in the local market and that the poor should have the chance to buy it before the big dealers stepped in, the statute book supported the crowd's 'legitimising notion', that it was acting in defence of immemorial rights and customs. 'Engrossing', the buying up of growing crops, 'forestalling', the buying of food before it came to the market; and 'regrating', the resale of food after a market were all prohibited. These customs, however, while damaging to the poor and the small consumer, were of course indispensable, if London and the large towns were to be fed; they were almost as indispensable for the export of corn. Yet they were illegal.[15]

Prosecutions under these ancient laws were infrequent. But in the worst years of hunger and food rioting before the 1790s, in 1698, 1709, 1740, 1756 and 1766, royal proclamations stressed the illegality of these practices and instructed JPs to enforce the law. If Adam Smith was right in thinking popular fears of engrossing and forestalling were comparable to 'suspicion of witchcraft', the government led the witch-hunt. Even when in 1772 all the statutes that restricted dealers were repealed, local regulations often continued in force. John Wilkes, when Lord Mayor of London in 1774–5, was active against forestallers and did what he could to keep prices down. In the 1790s Kenyon, LCJ, deciding that these wholesaling practices were still illegal at common law, denounced them in addresses to the Grand Jury and presided over the conviction of a notorious speculator. In Devon several prosecutions were brought in both 1795 and 1800 for forestalling etc., and market regulations were tightened. Finally, the Assize of Bread, which controlled the profits of bakers, endured in London and many market towns. It was not repealed until the 1820s, though its enforcement was patchy.[16]

The price-fixing crowds, then, had plenty of cause to think that if the magistrates failed to enforce the law, direct action on their part to bring down food prices was justified and was in support of the law, even if itself unlawful. Hunger, the fear of starvation, the belief that people had a right to eat and the authorities the duty to see that they were able to do so were quite enough to engender genuine intimations of legitimacy. That those intimations were derived from ancient or anti-capitalist ideas is much more doubtful. The ideas were conservative. But food rioters did not hark back to some 'fair' price in the distant past. The price that they themselves fixed was more often than not the price that had recently prevailed. In Lancashire where the price of grain more than doubled between 1799 and 1801, the rioters sold their commandeered grain at 1798 prices. The Devon rioters did much the same. Further, just as the structure of a national food market already existed, food rioters were themselves often engaged in economic activities in which medieval notions had long since been abandoned. Indeed industrial workers were the normal food rioters. Finally, had there been a very general belief in a moral economy, food riots instead of being sporadic would in bad years have been ubiquitous. In 1756-57 they affected thirty counties, but in no year did they spread over the whole country, and some areas seem never to have had a food riot at all. Most disturbances had highly specific causes. Food riots were caused less by the assertion of the poor's moral economy than by the breakdown of the government's political economy.[17]

The poor traditionally look back to a golden age when the King and the rich did their duty and the poor were properly cared for, much as the propertied classes look back to a lost utopia when crime was almost unknown and both the poor and the young knew their place. Yet the crowd's deeply felt convictions about its rights and about the duties both of the authorities and of food producers and traders were not the sole cause of food riots. Nor, even, was hunger or the fear of it. Unless the crowd were all saints on the march, which is improbable, envy and social resentment were also present, and belief in the moral economy was laced with collective defiance. 'The rude and unpolished multitude,' Bernard Mandeville plausibly claimed, 'rail at their betters . . . murmur at Providence and loudly complain that the good things of this world are chiefly enjoyed by those who do not deserve them.' In 1740 a four-day riot at Dewsbury and Wakefield began with an attempt to stop a load of meal and flour being sent to Manchester. When that failed, the mob damaged some mills and attacked the High Sheriff and another man. Joseph Pollard successfully defended his mill with gunfire, wounding several rioters. The mob then went to Wakefield, declaring that they would release the prisoners taken earlier, 'pull down Pollard's house, hang him up, and skin him like a rat'.* They were blocked, however, by a magistrate and the army, who took several prisoners. Pollard's house and skin were both saved. After a Bristol riot had been quelled in 1795 by the threat of gunfire, some women vowed that they would have fresh butter and would 'live as well as ye gentry'.[19]

---

* 'Pulling down' a house in the eighteenth century rarely meant its total destruction. Usually, it merely involved the pulling out of windows and the smashing of shutters, bannisters, doors, moveable furniture and other accessible woodwork.[18]

All the same the violence of the food rioters was usually controlled, even when it was not ritualistic. The property of millers and traders and occasionally of local dignitaries was at risk, but seldom their persons. Unusually, in Yarmouth in 1793, because of 'the dearness of provisions', the mayor was attacked, an East Indiaman captain warding off the blow. With one or two exceptions the only people who lost their lives in food riots were the rioters themselves. Probably about fifty of them were killed. In addition a substantial number were executed, at least seven in 1766 and ten in 1795-96.[20]

Food riots were at the time often called 'risings of the people' or 'insurrections'. Yet they were very far from being risings or insurrections in the modern sense; they were often acts of defiance, but they had strictly limited objectives. Except in the 1790s, when it was sometimes tinged with radicalism, food rioting was essentially conservative. The food rioters were seeking to preserve their rights and often to secure the enforcement of ancient laws. They wanted cheaper food. They were not attempting to overthrow the social order.[21]

1795 was called 'the revolt of the housewives' by the Hammonds. In Carlisle women seized grain from houses and shops and then formed a committee to regulate its selling price. Women rioted also in Aylesbury, Ipswich, Tewkesbury and Blandford. In Liverpool they bit the local constable and pulled his hair, and in Ashton they seized the vicar who was trying to stop the riot. All this was not a new departure. Women had been prominent in food rioting for some 200 years. They tended to go to market and they were thought to be less vulnerable to the sanctions of the law, though in fact some were hanged. In 1740, for example, a crowd of women in Dover who objected to the export of corn when prices were high, 'rose in a tumultuous manner, cut the sacks, and took away the grain that some farmers were bringing to the ports for shipping'. They followed this up by 'pelting the teams and their drivers with stones for three miles out of town'.[22]

More important in setting off a food riot than the determination of the local women were two other features of the disturbance at Dover: its geographical position and the export of corn. The sight or the knowledge of grain being moved out of the area when prices were high naturally excited opposition. There was a general feeling, an observer not surprisingly noted, that 'charity should begin at home'. Hence many food riots took place at ports, either coastal or canal, or in small market towns from which grain was sent to London or other cities.[23]

Apart from the conduct of the authorities, the other prime determinant of the incidence of food riots was the presence of industrial workers. One of the differences between English and

French food riots – price-fixing riots or *taxation populaire* in France
were not as common as in England but often involved much bigger
crowds – was that except in Norfolk English agricultural labourers
were seldom involved. Their readiness to riot against the Militia Act
in 1756-57 and, sometimes, against enclosures suggests that this
quiescence was not due to mere deference or doltishness; they could
usually get grain from farmers, they could not anyway afford to
antagonise their employers, and they were mostly scattered. With
few factories and much industrial work done in the home and with
many manufacturing workers partially engaged in agriculture, the
distinction between industrial and agricultural work was far from
clear cut. Yet industrial workers did not have the same inhibitions or
difficulties as the agricultural labourers. Their work bred militancy,
they were a ready-made crowd with feelings of communal solidarity,
they were vulnerable to a sudden rise in prices especially when it
coincided with unemployment, and they were better placed than
more scattered labourers to resist it. Hence the prominent part in
eighteenth-century food riots played by colliers, tin miners, dockyard workers, keelmen, potters and cloth workers.[24]

In 1709, when the price of wheat had doubled since the previous
year, some 400 colliers from Kingswood marched on Bristol and
successfully demanded cheap bread. Cornish tin miners prevented the
export of corn from Falmouth in 1727, objecting that the King had
not given merchants permission to send it to 'their enemies'. In 1740
the Kingswood colliers again protested in Bristol against the high
price of corn. The presence of the army kept the protest peaceful, but
in 1753, a bad food year in the South West, over 1000 Kingswood
colliers entered Bristol, broke into the goal and released a prisoner at
the cost of four killed and many wounded. In 1756 the 'half-starved'
manufacturing people of Kidderminster 'did great damage to the
farmers and dealers in grain', while 300 colliers invaded Coventry but
left after a promise of redress of grievances from the mayor. Ten
years later the clothworkers dominated the West Country riots, some
of them against their inclinations. 'The rioters come into our
workshops,' wrote the Sheriff of Gloucestershire, 'and force out all
the men willing or unwilling to join them.' Earlier the Kingswood
colliers had been similarly conscripted. 'Satan,' said Charles Wesley,
had made a 'general assault', and Methodist colliers who had been
taught not to resist evil were 'forced' into joining their militant
colleagues; others joined because they were threatened with burial
alive if they refused.[25]

The reaction of the authorities

A conspicuous provocation – the removal of grain from an area where there was a shortage – and the presence of people united enough to respond to it were the commonest antecedents of a food riot. But a third factor was no less material: the likely behaviour of the authorities. Unless food rioters were famished and desperate, they knew rioting to be futile if it did not lead the authorities to take some remedial action, and worse than futile if it merely led to fierce judicial retribution. Food rioting often contained an element of ritual or game, and if the authorities did not play along then rioting was pointless. The object was to persuade the authorities to provide more food or to lower its price. So, unless the crowd was starving, incapable of forethought or just got out of hand, it had to judge, initially at least, what amount of violence, if any, would secure its objective. Often its first move was peaceful if menacing. In Blackburn in 1800 the crowd only demonstrated. It used no violence, but it was armed with sticks and its message was plain. The gentry, the magistrates (when they were not gentry), the army, the War Office, and even the government often had reasons for preferring negotiations and concessions to suppressing the violence by mere force and firepower, but whether those reasons would apply in any particular case was highly problematic.[26]

Apart from sending troops which might arrive too late, the government in London was too far away to affect the local outcome. It was the reaction of the local authorities that was important to the rioters and was, to some extent, predictable. The reasons that often inclined the authorities to accommodation rather than suppression were political, economic, local, legal and military in varying combinations.

In general, of course, the ruling elite was against riots and violence and in favour of order. But only in general. The Duke of Newcastle, as we have seen, organised riots after 1715 to make the Whigs seem less unpopular in London. Wesley, speaking from personal experience, thought many religious disturbances should be imputed more to the justices than to 'the rabble'. In 1743 his JPs at Wednesbury in Staffordshire helped to stir a mob against 'several disorderly persons styling themselves Methodist preachers'. Wesley himself was at the mercy of the mob for five hours. Much the same happened to him in Cornwall. Election riots were usually promoted by the candidates. The crowd was a useful ally, though the politicians who used it then dutifully denounced its excesses.[27]

In food riots, too, politics often took a hand. Under the first two Georges, the Tories' virtual exclusion from the bench and from central government, if it did not breed solidarity with the excluded crowd, sometimes bred an inclination to popular politics and inhibited their wholehearted attachment to those responsible for their proscription. So, Tory justices might be little dismayed by the difficulties suffered by Whig authorities in dealing with rioters and plead inability to help them. Either might feel the interests of their own areas more important than the presumed interests of the nation as represented by central government. Thus they sometimes forbade the transport of food outside their locality notwithstanding contrary orders from Whitehall. They left central government to get on with its business, while they got on with theirs.[28]

With the ending of Tory proscription in 1760, the fissure in the political elite was largely closed, and the propertied presented a more united front to the lower orders. Even towards the end of the century, however, when the 'haves' coalesced still more against the 'have-nots', the country gentry had no great affection for corn traders and middlemen, whom they regarded as jumped-up profiteers. Often they were Dissenters as well; in 1756 the mob destroyed three Quaker meeting houses in the Midlands because corn dealers worshipped in them. Hence gentlemen magistrates could have considerable sympathy with the attempts of the crowd to curb their depredations. In 1766 some rioters in Gloucester claimed that they had all the gentry on their side and that the Earl of Berkeley had given them three guineas.[29]

Not everybody feels protective to profits they do not share, and the gentry were aware that often excessive food profits were gained by methods that were harmful in their social effects as well as technically illegal. In 1756, a government inquiry into the price of corn in various market towns, a gratified Lord Rockingham told the Secretary of State, had made the hoarders disgorge their corn 'very expeditiously'. Two years later Wesley approved of a food riot because forestallers were near to starving the poor. A parliamentary committee even favoured tightening the laws against forestalling and engrossing, and a middleman complained of justices failing to act when 'your law-giving mob' had prevented the export of corn from the Severn and Wye Valleys. Even if it was farmers not dealers who were making the large profits, the landowners could feel above the quarrel between them and townspeople, and not necessarily side with the former. Not only the poor believed that food shortages were not always natural and that prices were sometimes kept artificially high. A report to the Board of Agriculture in 1795 maintained that rich farmers rigged the market by fixing prices and coercing their smaller colleagues into compliance. The president of the Board of Trade reached a similar conclusion five years later.[30]

Industrialists, too, were not necessarily dismayed by food riots. For the poor's resentment to be directed at high food prices rather than low wages or unemployment was a bonus which they gratefully accepted, often discovering pressing business needs that demanded their presence elsewhere until the trouble was over.

Reasons more admirable than factionalism, economic jealousy or political advantage brought food rioters some understanding from the well off, who often recognised their grievances. With Pitt as minister, the King's speech in 1756 expressed sympathy for 'the sufferings of the poorer sort' caused by the high price of grain, and recommended Parliament take measures to prevent troubles in future. Even George III, who disliked London because of its mob, sometimes had ambivalent feelings. In September 1766 he lamented 'the present risings' as further proof of the general 'licentiousness', but four days later he conceded that the distress was 'real'. Earlier the Secretary at War, Lord Barrington, took a similar attitude. He wrote of an 'ignorant and miserable multitude' with sometimes real grievances, who were to be pitied, though their efforts to redress those grievances had to be repressed.[31]

The pity was likely to be greater on the spot. Both the soldiers sent to deal with the rioters and the gentry living in the affected areas could see for themselves that the distress was genuine. Three years before Quebec, the future General Wolfe on riot duty in Gloucestershire was worried that he might have to use weapons against 'hungry weavers' who had a good case. Among the gentry paternalism was still alive, though often sullied by other motives. In any case even those who were fully convinced that poverty was the poor's own fault or the will of God or the result of inexorable economic laws found it difficult to be unaffected by the sight of hunger and hardship. Merely reproving them for breaking the law was futile. To a gentleman who asked why they had not appealed to the government and the laws instead of taking the law into their own hands, the crowd at Brixham, Devon, replied that the government had been applied to without result and therefore they had 'to do something to keep their families from starving'. All too often that was clearly true.[32]

Attempts were accordingly made to persuade dealers and farmers to moderate their prices: at Bridgenorth in 1756 two landowners 'obliged their tenants to sell wheat at 5/- a bushel or under', and promised to compensate them by lowering their rents. A friend of the local MP prevented a riot at Ashburton by subsidising potatoes out of his own pocket. In 1800 a Somerset vicar sold his own wheat cheap to his parishioners but could not persuade his farmers to do the same. The authorities sometimes assuaged the populace by making charitable collections, as did Reading Corporation in 1757 and the magistrates at Chelmsford in 1772, or they tried to persuade Whitehall to prohibit the export of food, or they bought food to sell cheaply. At the end of the century Manchester organised a soup charity, and Devon ensured that there were substitute foods to be sold at subsidised prices.[33]

Paternalism, which depended on face-to-face relationships and on rejection or, at most, limited acceptance of *laissez-faire* dogma, tended to decline as the century wore on. In 1767 Burke was scathing about the Chatham ministry's failure to produce a 'plan for speedy relief of the people' from high food prices. Later, under the impact of the French Revolution, poor health and family misfortune, he became contemptuously dismissive of any project for 'the further relief of the poor', declaring any such actions to be beyond the competence of the government, since the laws of commerce were the laws of God. Yet the new, harsher political ideas were in practice partially offset by a growth in humanitarian feelings and by greater sympathy for the distress caused by unemployment. 'The true test of civilisation,' Johnson said in 1770, was 'a decent provision for the poor.'[34]

Besides, paternalism remained strong in many rural areas. When the Home Secretary, the Duke of Portland, told Lords Lieutenant and JPs in 1800 that scarcity was a natural disaster and markets must proceed unhindered in order to allow rationing of supplies by high prices to prevent famine, many of his correspondents knew that Portland's dogma was at variance with reality: because the poor could not afford the high prices they could not participate in Portland's system. 'His Grace,' wrote the Home Office, required 'effectual suppression' of 'such dangerous proceedings' as food riots. Lord Clifford, a Devon landowner, thought, however, that only 'the greatest energy' by the government in meeting the people's grievances could make us a 'united people'; and while he conceded that his tenants and neighbours had the right to dispose of their grain as they wished, he reminded them of the importance of preserving public peace and undertook to repay them if they lowered their prices. They agreed to do so, and a riot was prevented.[35]

Magistrates' attitudes to the use of troops obviously depended on their own characters and their opinion of the rioters' grievance, as well as on the behaviour of the crowd and on the relationship in the area between authority and the lower orders. JPs were customarily restrained and lenient. They had to go on living in their town and were mindful of their social prestige. The use of force was liable to bring on them contempt from their peers and hatred from the crowd. Clerical magistrates faced an additional hazard. After the vicar of Rochdale, Dr Drake, ordered the Volunteers to fire on the crowd in 1795 and two bystanders were killed, his congregation took the obvious reprisal: they stayed away.[36]

In Devon, one of the most turbulent counties at the end of the century, riots usually occurred in small market towns where consumers still dealt with farmers face to face. The magistrates were mainly middle-class tradesmen and merchants who knew and were known by many of the rioters. In such a situation accommodation was almost a necessity. In South Lancashire, too, magistrates at the end of the century always attempted to negotiate with the crowd and sometimes persuaded dealers to sell their corn cheaply, making negotiations unnecessary. Even when all peaceful methods had been tried and failed, the Riot Act had been read and volunteers were at the ready, JPs were reluctant to give orders to fire. Perhaps they remembered the impetuosity and resulting unpopularity of Dr Drake.[37]

In the larger towns, many JPs had little social prestige to endanger and no relationships with the crowd to be damaged. Their authority, such as it was, lay merely in their office: they did not know personally those over whom they were set. Even if troops were present, however, JPs might not want to use them because they sympathised with the rioters, rejoiced in the discomfiture of the middlemen or because they were frightened. In Plymouth, by the end of the century a large town of 23,000 people where the dockyard workers were powerful, face-to-face relationships between magistrates and populace were rare; hence food riots were not orderly disturbances but destructive outbreaks of looting. After one such outbreak in 1801, the Riot Act was read, Dragoons charged, wounding several, and arrests were made. The dockyard men marched to the guardhouse and, unintimidated by the artillery, the cavalry, the militia and the volunteers assembled by the authorities, demanded the release of the prisoners. The magistrates gave way, explaining that had they used force 'many hundreds must have fallen'.[38]

Magistrates could often be exasperating to the army. Wolfe found them unhelpful in the West Country because they had, 'perhaps, different interests to pursue'. Those interests or their sympathy with the crowd, combined with fear of future reprisals, might lead to their making themselves scarce and leaving the soldiers without authority to act. Or they might just surrender. In 1756 the Nottingham magistrates having read the Riot Act seized three ringleaders of rioting colliers armed with hatchets and pick axes, but then grew fearful of the mob and released them. Others were bold and firm. In 1756, the mayor of Coventry, a town noted for its election riots sponsored by the parties, allowed a roomful of food rioters into his house and 'desired their patience whilst I ate my dinner'. Though perhaps feeling this request lacking in tact, the rioters agreed to postpone discussion of their food needs until the mayor had enjoyed his repast. Suitably fortified, he then told them that he would always listen to complaints, but breakers of the law would be punished. To complete his evenhandedness, he sent statements to the press against forestalling and asked the government to send troops.[39]

The War Office was always ready to send troops if they were really needed, but the army was overstretched when rioting was wide-spread, and it preferred the local authorities to settle the trouble themselves if at all possible. Indeed the procedure for sending troops might have been designed to curtail their use. A JP reported a riot to the Secretary of State and asked for troops to be sent. If the Secretary of State approved the request, he sent it to the War Office. The Secretary at War then sent an order to the nearest body of troops to march to the trouble spot. With communications still bad, this cumbersome procedure necessitated delay unless the riot area was near London. It was occasionally short-circuited by a magistrate applying directly to the nearest troops, but that seldom made any difference, since a commanding officer would probably not move his force, let alone take drastic action, until he had received authorisation from London. The resulting delay in the army's arrival was an additional incentive to those on the spot to restore calm without outside intervention.[40]

Inevitably, then, the authorities' reaction to food riots was mixed. It varied from place to place and from time to time. JPs were often not sure what the law was, let alone whether they wished or were able to enforce it. The traditional economy was in its death throes; the free market had taken its place or was in the process of doing so. Magistrates were bound to recognise that London and the large towns could not feed themselves; food had therefore to be moved from areas where it was grown, and middlemen were necessary. Nevertheless, many of the propertied nation retained a residual attachment to the moral economy. Furthermore, the gentry could not easily rely solely on repression when they saw hardship all around them. The crowd was not alone in its confusion. The moral economy of the poor was not confronted by a settled political economy of the rich.

Uncertainty about the law, natural confusion of ideas, local relationships, frequent sympathy with food rioters' grievances and agreement on middlemen as scapegoats inclined many authorities to accommodation with the rioters. In addition they were apprehensive of what a frustrated or inflamed crowd might do. A serious riot, the use of force and its judicial aftermath could poison local relations for many years to come. Compromise was far preferable. For all these reasons the usual restraint of food rioters was mirrored by the usual restraint of the authorities. The blunderbuss was laid aside and the political arts taken up. Often, of course, accommodation did not work. The traders were obdurate or the magistrates were not able to keep their promises. The crowd was provoked and set off on the rampage. Or accommodation was not tried. The crowd was too big, or the presence of troops or well-armed supporters made the magistrates feel secure. Accommodation in looting riots was anyway impossible.

Sometimes the riot was nearer a battle. In a five-day riot in Shropshire in November 1756 colliers forced sellers to reduce their prices but also broke into the houses of grocers, farmers and bakers, handled the householders roughly and even 'stript' the poor 'of everything'. An army of some 2500 tenants, townspeople and servants was needed to disperse them. The riot at Kidderminster ten years later was shorter but far bloodier. A mob of 300 or 400, protesting, they claimed, at farmers sending their corn to Bristol for exportation, invaded the town and were met by soldiers who 'killed eight persons upon the spot'. In the 'Shudehill fight' in Manchester the following year colliers marched to Manchester to demand a maximum price for oatmeal, potatoes and flour 'for 12 months to come' and fought a pitched battle with a small band of troops. Four of them were killed. Before the troops opened fire, one soldier had been killed, probably the only person to be killed by food rioters during the century.[41]

In Newcastle-on-Tyne in 1740, after traders had broken their promise to lower their grain prices, some 'gentlemen' fired at the crowd, killing one man and wounding others. As a contemporary wrote of a similar incident, a blunderbuss 'does not appease a mob much' and, enraged, the mob marched to the Guildhall. 'Stones flew in upon us,' wrote an observer, 'through the windows like cannon shot . . . at length the mob broke in upon us in the most terrible outrage. They spared our lives indeed but obliged us to quit the place, then fell to plundering and destroying all about them.' Much the same thing happened in Norwich in the same year. Before there had been violence, 'an unthinking gentleman' took a 'musket out of the hands of a Dragoon and shot a man through the head'. The crowd was provoked, the troops opened fire and at least five people were killed.[42]

The export of corn

Apart from sending troops to pacify troubled areas and setting up special commissions to try arrested rioters, there was not at that stage much that the government could usefully do. But what little it could do, it usually did too late. Adam Smith thought that their subsistence was so important to the people that the government must yield to their prejudices over laws concerning corn and 'establish a system they approved of'. Such a system, Smith believed, was unlikely to be reasonable.[43]

In fact 'the people' were often rather more reasonable than the ministry. What in times of shortage and high prices most inflamed the hungry was the sending abroad of corn. Clearly exports, on which moreover the government paid a bounty, did aggravate the shortage, and they could largely be stopped by government action. Yet from the early seventeenth century onwards government time and again was much slower than 'the people' in seeing that an embargo on exports had to be imposed.* The claim of Devon food rioters in July 1766 that all the calamities suffered by the poor were caused by the 'vast quantity of corn exported' was an exaggeration, yet it was nearer the mark than the ministry proved to be. Governments never learned. On virtually every occasion that there were shortages the ministry prohibited the export of corn, but never soon enough. In other words it embargoed the export of grain to subdue food riots, but not to forestall them.[45]

The classic case of government provoking rather than preventing food riots was in the years of economic slump, 1765–66. The bounty on corn exports stopped on April 1, 1765 when wheat reached 48/- a quarter. As a result of disturbances in several places including Braintree where 'a large mob . . . did considerable mischief', Parliament authorised the import of corn duty free from May 10 until August 10. With the new Rockingham ministry taking no action, the ending of duty-free imports on that date made a bounty on exports of 5/- a quarter automatically payable. Merchants who had been importing corn duty free could therefore immediately export the same corn and be paid for doing so. Naturally there was a flood of exports. In December a Yorkshire correspondent in the *Gentleman's Magazine* assumed that the government was unaware of the real state of affairs in the North; otherwise they would not permit exportation. 'Hunger,' he added, 'will break through stone walls.'[46]

For the moment, however, hunger did not do so. Some serious disturbances in East Anglia were caused by the building of new large workhouses, one of which was destroyed, rather than by food prices. In the new year the only purely food riots were in Hampshire and Dorset. Parliament then re-enacted an embargo on the export of corn until August 24, and that kept the populace quiet until the summer. The weather in 1766 was peculiar, producing an excellent harvest in the North and a disastrous one in the South, which endured one of the wettest summers of the century. The bad weather and the buying

---

* The 'people' of course infringed free trade principles by opposing the export of corn, but then so did the government by subsidising that export. In mid-century Lord Townshend attacked the export bounty, pointing to the folly of subsidising foreigners by enabling them to feed their workers more cheaply than could their British competitors. He converted Dean Tucker, the forerunner of Adam Smith.[44]

of corn by millers, anticipating the end of the corn embargo, sent up food prices. Riots followed in the West Country and the Thames Valley, both of them areas through which grain passed even when not sent abroad.[47]

The weather in August was dry, reviving hopes of a decent harvest. In consequence speculators unloaded stocks of corn, which brought food prices down sharply; in turn the wave of riots which lasted for a fortnight was over by August 10. A renewal of the export embargo would have maintained tranquillity, but the new Chatham administration did not know what was happening and was anyway engaged in 'high politics': trying to split the Bedford faction by enticing Lord Gower into the government. 'While the attention of the great world,' wrote Horace Walpole, 'was fixed on the political revolution, the people laboured under the dearness of corn and the apprehension of famine.' The ministry having no time for 'low' politics, the events of the past sixteen months were ignored, the export embargo was allowed to end on August 26 and the bounty on exports was paid once more. Heavy orders from Southern Europe where, too, the harvest was bad, sent grain pouring out of the country; prices soared, and food riots duly recommenced in Berkshire and the South West. The poor, said the *Annual Register*, had 'been driven to desperation and madness by the exorbitant prices of all manner of provisions'.[48]

The ministry's first response intensified the trouble. On September 10 it issued a proclamation against forestalling, regrating and engrossing, urging the laws against them to be 'put in speedy and effective execution'; the price of corn, said the proclamation, had already greatly risen and was likely 'to grow much dearer to the great oppression of the poor' partly because those laws were not being enforced. At the same time Parliament, which was to have met on September 16, was prorogued until November 11. These two announcements were almost an invitation to violence. The government was saying firstly that the shortage of corn was to some extent artificial, its being the fault of middlemen, and secondly, since export embargoes were always imposed by Act of Parliament, that at least until November those same middlemen were to go on being paid to send corn abroad, while the poor suffered.[49]

The ministry soon realised that its position was untenable. Not only were the poor rioting, but the propertied classes were clamouring for action too. The cities of London, Bristol, Norwich and many other corporations sent addresses, and on September 28, with doubtful legality, the government by proclamation prohibited the export of corn. This came too late to head off some of the worst food riots of the century. Not until the middle of November was the country largely pacified.[50]

Import and export matters were not the Chatham ministry's forte; its later imposition of the 'Townshend' duties did as much as anything else to lose the American colonies. Both Barrington, the Secretary at War, and Conway, a Secretary of State, were critical of local magistrates' initially easy-going treatment of the riots. Barrington complained that they had not used troops sent to help them and had shown less spirit or prudence than usual. Conway went further and thought the magistrates' inactivity was one of the chief causes of these continual outrages. That charge had weight, but JPs were taking their cue from the published opinions of the ministry, and they could with better ground have made a similar charge against Whitehall. On the face of it, indeed, the government's performance in 1766 was so maladroit as to raise the suspicion that it intended to direct violence away from the landed interest towards the middlemen.[51]

There is nothing intrinsically implausible in such a conspiracy theory. The new ministry was weak, and scapegoats are always useful. Yet, almost certainly, negligent ignorance, not malice, governed its conduct. Uninformed of what was going on outside London, its primary concern was its own survival not that of the governed. That the government was acting from inadvertence not design is strongly suggested by its handling of the export embargo. Chatham afterwards defended it as a measure of necessity to save a starving people from famine. That was fair enough, but it did not explain why the ministry had not earlier asked for powers from Parliament or later obtained them by allowing it to meet instead of proroguing it until November. The effect, though not the intention, of its proclamation against regrating, of its prorogation of Parliament, and of its failure until too late to stop the export of corn was to set off widespread violence, in which a number of rioters and bystanders lost their lives. The ministry was guilty in everything but design.[52]

'The great work' that a government had to do, Thomas Andrews wrote in 1739, was to discover the causes of discontent and then to use its 'authority to relieve the needy and oppressed . . .' No eighteenth-century government did that great work. The Chatham ministry, like others, did nothing or merely adopted traditional and temporary palliatives, such as its proclamation against forestalling. An automatic ban on distilling and on export when corn reached a certain price would have been a better curb on hoarding and speculation than belated temporary bans. Parliament might have been difficult, but the export trade in corn was declining in importance, and something of the sort was enacted in 1773.[53]

The ministry was aware of the problem. The King's Speech in 1766 requested 'the wisdom of Parliament' to be directed to the high price of wheat that particularly affected 'the poorer sort'. An amendment to the speech proposing either that corn should be bought for the poor or that bounties should be paid on corn that farmers brought to market was defeated. In the following year the King's Speech admitted that nothing yet had been done to give sufficient relief to the poor but again it contained no recommendation or policy. The ministry's sole contribution to a solution was once again to ask Parliament to give the dearness of corn earnest deliberation and to judge whether further promises could be made. The government could cause food riots by allowing too much corn to leave the country and by stirring up resentments against middlemen, but evidently it could do nothing to avert them.[54]

Punishment

It could, however, see that punishment was doled out. We might 'as well be hanged as starved to death' was a frequent cry of food rioters, and some judges were ready to take them at their word.* The culprits' sorry want of civic virtue attracted much judicial eloquence. At Norwich in 1766, Gould, J., was astonished that 'a licentious rabble, in open defiance of those laws, under which they enjoyed all the privileges of free born Englishmen' should have destroyed 'the property of their fellow subjects'. Even more surprisingly, they had not even been grateful for the King's 'parental tenderness' in removing the export bounty. Accordingly Gould sentenced eight of them to death. At York some twenty years later another judge descanted on the duty of 'us all' to submit to the food shortage with patient 'resignation as the act of providence'.[56] Unfortunately the 'rabble', on whom lay the duty of submission, remained unconvinced that their troubles were the fault of providence rather than profiteers or politicians. Nor did they value the freeborn Englishman's liberty to starve to death as highly as did their freedom-loving brethren on the bench.

During the riots at Nuneaton, 1756, Sir John Willes, LCJ, announced that he would immediately execute all rioters who were convicted. Four were arrested on Friday, condemned on the Saturday, and their execution was ordered for the Monday. In the event Willes hanged two of them and told the other two that if the rioters dispersed immediately they would be reprieved. He also kept

---

* In Brussels in 1768 rioters who looted the food market declared that they would rather be hanged than starved. When the authorities immediately erected a gallows, the crowd having saved themselves from starvation saw no need to exercise their preference and dispersed.[55]

four other people as hostages for the good behaviour of the crowd. While legal purists might question the propriety of a judge, in effect, taking hostages and making men's lives dependent upon the behaviour of others – conduct more appropriate perhaps to a soldier acting under martial law than to a judge administering the ordinary law of the land – Willes's methods were undeniably effective, and he received the congratulations of the Secretary of State for his successful blackmail of those 'insolent rioters'. (Willes's methods were only successful locally; in Derby and Nottingham rioting increased.) A highly political judge and a libertine intolerant of the sins of others, Willes regarded the crime of food rioting as 'heinous', yet he did not favour wholesale hangings for it. Ten of the prisoners taken during the long Shropshire riot in the same year were sentenced to death, but Willes thought the execution of so many would cause 'a general uneasiness in the county' and recommended transportation instead.[57]

For similar reasons those on the spot were often inclined to let matters rest after a food riot. Following one in Taunton in 1753, the Lord Lieutenant reported that he could get the ringleaders convicted if the Government told him to do so, but 'the disposition of the town and neighbouring gentlemen was against it'. Sometimes witnesses were intimidated. Sometimes the victims refused to prosecute. Sometimes the grand jury imposed leniency. Sometimes, though the authorities sought some exemplary punishments, they did not want them in their own immediate area. Sometimes the laws' delays allowed tempers to cool and prosecutions were abandoned in order not 'to rekindle the flames'.[58]

No such considerations applied in 1766, when there was a rash of death sentences: eight at Norwich, four at Salisbury, three at Reading, nine at Gloucester. Though most of the condemned were reprieved and the Secretary at War grumbled at what he considered excessive leniency to rioters near his Berkshire home, the English repression of the 1766 disturbances was probably more severe than that after the comparable riots in France nine years later. Burke's warning that legal punishments lost all appearance of justice 'when too strictly inflicted on men compelled by the last extremity of distress to incur them' went unheeded.[59]

After other outbreaks the repression was usually lighter. There was always an execution or two but, save in 1795-96, fewer than in 1756 or 1766. The authorities tried to punish only the leaders; large numbers of convictions even without executions would have created resentment without corresponding benefit. Once the law had been vindicated by a few heavy sentences, the remaining rioters could be treated leniently. As with other operations of the law, many of the guilty escaped and a number of the innocent suffered.[60]

Conclusion

Food riots were one type of disturbance which came, unambiguously, from below. But frequent as they were, they did not demonstrate a peculiar eighteenth-century English propensity to violence. Whether food rioters were driven by hunger or by a sense of injustice, they were exhibiting 'defensive aggression', with more defence than aggression in price-fixing riots, and more aggression than defence in the looting expeditions. But whatever the mixture, the reaction of the crowds, as Whitehaven JPs told the government in 1800, was not to be wondered at. And France, Italy and Germany, which achieved a national market in food later than England, all saw food disturbances in the 1850s that bore a close resemblance to the typical English food riot of the previous century.* In Piedmont free trade in cereals was called by Cavour 'the happy application of a great idea', yet that happy application produced violent food riots and an attack on Cavour's house – though that may have been caused as much by allegations that he had cornered the wheat market as by his free trade principles. Unless governments took adequate steps to cushion its impact on the poor, which they almost never did, the advent of free trade in corn was invariably accompanied by food riots.[62]

Notwithstanding political outrage at 'daring insurrections', royal insistence on 'strict observance of order' being necessary to the people's 'real welfare', and judicial indignation at their 'heinous' criminality, food riots were frequently successful. Sometimes, of course, they only moved the shortage from one place to another. Sometimes they made scarcity worse because farmers, fearful of suffering a loss, did not bring their food to market. Yet fear worked in both directions. In addition to scaring farmers and dealers, food riots reminded the authorities that they had responsibilities to the small consumer as well as to the more politically influential exporters and dealers, and showed them where intervention was necessary to prevent disaffection and destitution. In a thoroughly imperfect market, which was still partly regulated, both in theory and practice, food riots played the part which relative prices should play in a free market that is working properly. They were useful indicators of scarcity and trouble.[63]

If, in the eighteenth century, government never looked carefully at a riot's real causes, as the 'Essay on Riots' adjured, or used all possible means 'to redress all true grievances of the people', it reacted to food riots by embargoing the export of corn in twenty-three of

---

* There were food riots in Cumberland over the high price of potatoes in 1917.[61]

the years between 1698 and 1800; in addition the export bounty was withheld in three other years. Thus in the century as a whole, the government altered its preferred pattern of trade in corn in one year in four and, from 1750 onwards, in one year in two. Late as these interventions were, without food riots they would have been later still and might not have happened at all. Imports, too, would probably have been smaller and later.[64]

Like the central government, magistrates and many private individuals often responded to food riots other than by coercion. And the poor more often got their food at a lower price – either directly as the result of their own actions or indirectly as the result of government measures – than they would if they had remained quiescent. Or they were given relief. Even when the riot was a disaster for those taking part, as was the 1753 Bristol one for the Kingswood colliers who much overdid the violence, the authorities were likely to take conciliatory steps to avert a repetition.[65]

Food riots were, of course, advantageous only so long as the food market was not working properly and the dearth was not genuine and general. As the market became freer and more national, food riots instead of indicating shortages were likely to exacerbate them. Hence Hannah More, Arthur Young and others tried to explain to the poor that, while they were entitled to complain, rioting merely aggravated the evil. Those who were 'so deluded as to riot', Kenyon, LCJ, told the Worcestershire Grand Jury in 1795, dried up the markets. Four years later craftsmen in Manchester agreed: they thought food rioting 'would aggravate the evil'. All the same, the poor had few other ways of complaining, and until the end of the eighteenth century food riots were the best way both of registering a complaint against scarcity and of procuring action to remedy it.[65]

TWELVE

Industrial Disputes

Find work for idle men, do anything to employ them, go to any expense, no exertions can be too great. If ten or twenty thousand men are out of employment, yet willing and able to work, make some great roads, cut some convenient canals, erect some useful edifice, build some necessary bridges, establish some new manufacturers, at all events set them to work. If the statesman omits this, he deserves riots, and all their consequences.

Lloyd's Evening Post, *1774*

. . . you do not labour as cheap, and are not content to live and fare as hard as the manufacturers in other countries . . . Too many will not accept of work one part of the week but upon such terms only, as may enable them to live in vice and idleness the rest . . . you are worse, much worse, than the common people of any other nation.

Dr Josiah Tucker, 1745

There is such a face of industry in all ages and degrees of people, and so much civility and obliging behaviour, as they look upon all that come among them as customers, that it makes one of the most agreeable scenes I ever saw.

Dr Pocock on the Potteries, 1750[1]

Other than food riots, the most common eighteenth-century disturbances were industrial. Labour disputes bore many resemblances to food riots and were complementary to them; the same sort of people took part in both. Money to buy food was as necessary as the food itself, and employment was necessary to get the money. Much as England was better supplied with food than any other country in Europe, so English workers were better off than all but their Dutch contemporaries abroad. Yet that relative prosperity was precarious. Even tradesmen, a French visitor noted, often lived from hand to mouth. The life of artisans and labourers was far more hazardous: disaster in the shape of underemployment or unemployment was seldom far away.[2]

In the first half of the century when the idea that workers should be protected by legislation had not been abandoned, the ruling view was that they should be subject to a double squeeze: wages should be kept low to make exports cheap and competitive, and the price of necessities should be kept high to prevent workers aping the idleness of their betters; hence, as Defoe pointed out, 'almost all the necessaries of life' were taxed. Walpole's reintroduction of the Salt Tax was a practical application of this principle which an American historian christened the 'utility of poverty'. A corollary of the need to keep the poor poor was that they should be denied education, a view shared by Secker, the Bishop of London, Bernard Mandeville and other thinkers, on the ground that once the poor lost their ignorance they would also lose their willingness to do menial labour and to remain poor.[3]

A minority which included Bishop Berkeley, Defoe and, to some extent, David Hume rejected the utility of poverty theory as savage and erroneous. They believed on the contrary that an improved standard of living for labourers would not only help them but, by increasing effective demand, would also strengthen the national economy. After mid-century when the idea of legislative protection for workers became increasingly unfashionable, the minority gradually became a majority. Dr Josiah Tucker, a notable economist who became Dean of Gloucester and who was said by his Bishop (Warburton) to have made religion his trade and trade his religion, converted Hume to the view that a rich country need not be worsted by the apparent greater competitiveness of a poor one; so wages did not have to be kept low. 'That policy is violent,' Hume subsequently wrote, 'which aggrandises the public by the poverty of individuals.' Like Tucker, Dr Johnson pointed to the cruelty of entailing 'irreversible poverty upon generation after generation' and to the need for a commercial nation to give every individual the chance of improving 'his condition by his diligence'. By 1776 the intellectual battle had almost been won; *The Wealth of Nations* put the victory beyond doubt, though pockets of resistance held out. 'The liberal reward of labour,' Adam Smith laid down, was 'the necessary effect and cause of the greatest national prosperity.'[4]

So 'mercantilist' ideas of protecting the poor by legislation went hand in hand with the theory that their poverty was both necessary and desirable, while *laissez-faire* ideas of stripping workers of their legislative protection went hand in hand with the theory that their poverty should be diminished. In practice, of course, they lost their protection while retaining their poverty. Indeed, as facts are much stronger than ideas, their standard of living advanced when the prevailing orthodoxy advocated their poverty, and it remained static or retreated when the orthodoxy favoured their relative enrichment. Up to about mid-century real wages increased because of a fast growth in agricultural production and a slow growth of population.

After 1750 the population grew faster and agricultural productivity more slowly. In consequence, except in the North, real wages stagnated or declined.[5]

In any case, whatever the statute book might say, workmen in both periods were largely on their own. Though the 1563 Statute of Artificers was not finally repealed until 1813, the Tudor and Stuart legislation empowering the justices to fix wages at Quarter Session was, like that on food marketing, falling into disuse. Unreconciled to this decay of the old laws, workers did not see themselves as merely a commodity whose price should go up and down in accordance with supply and demand. To them the economy was not purely a mechanism; it had not been shorn of all elements of law and morality. Accordingly they continually sought for their wages to be regulated so as to ward off their destitution. Only seldom were their pleas answered; and nothing was put in the place of regulation of wages. As over food prices, the authorities' failure to act seemed to the workers to justify action by themselves to fill the vacuum.[6]

Workmen's 'combinations' were prohibited by many Acts of Parliament and were illegal at common law. Inevitably, however, they were widespread, becoming more so as employers and workmen grew more polarised during the century. 'Box clubs', which were primitive friendly societies usually meeting in public houses and which facilitated 'trade union' organisation, were tolerated. An observer wrote in 1797 that during the century friendly societies had extended to most parts of Britain. Indeed combinations themselves were tolerated so long as they did nothing; only when they acted to raise wages or regulate their trade were the laws wheeled into action. And in some incorporated trades, journeymen's clubs were recognised.[7]

Industrial workers who did not like the wages or the conditions of work on offer had three choices: submission, a strike, or a strike reinforced by violence. The choices were not clear cut. Submission might be joined with muted protest, or a strike might begin peacefully before degenerating into violence – as did the Northumberland miners' strike of 1765 – and a strike that was violent from the start always had some elements of order at its core.[8] Further, in the absence of authorised negotiating procedures, some element of coercion was virtually inseparable from strike action, and the distinction between that and violence was often fine.

With most work being done in small workshops often by the side of the master, the first choice was generally automatic. The master was not an adversary but an ally. The conflict of interest was not within the shop but between the shop and parts of the outside world. Not only was there much paternalist legislation still, at least nominally, in place, there was an acceptance of paternalist attitudes by both men and masters. On several occasions in the 1760s and 1770s, master weavers and their journeymen together marched to Parliament.[9]

A nonviolent strike needed both a well-organised union and abnormally favourable circumstances to succeed. Even if the masters did not attempt to break it they could, as Adam Smith pointed out, combine more easily and hold out for longer than their employees, many of whom could not exist a week and few a month without work. Occasionally time was on the side of the employees, as when the masters had quantities of perishable raw materials on their hands or had the chance to make large profits or when war made it too costly and dangerous to risk a long stoppage in naval dockyards. Sometimes, too, the men had built up an adequate strike fund, as did Kent papermakers in the 1780s, or themselves found alternative work, as when Newbury weavers left their looms in 1724 and went harvesting until the employers met their terms. More often the odds were stacked the other way.[10]

The most powerful union in London, the tailors', even had a 'house of representatives' and a 'grand committee for management of the town'. The Bow Street magistrate, Sir John Fielding, complained in 1764 that they had formed themselves into a kind of a republic and held illegal meetings at forty-two different public houses. Much earlier, in 1720-21, they had been strong enough to bring 7000 men together and to frighten the masters into persuading Parliament to fix a maximum wage; even then the masters had to concede a shorter working day, as they had to again in 1768. But powerful as they were the tailors did not eschew violence: they denounced one man who had aided the bringing in of strikebreakers from the country as an 'enemy of the trade' and tried to demolish his public house. In their strike in 1751 they were accused of having committed 'many riots, tumults and outrages', of having sent letters to masters threatening to murder them and of having assaulted and beaten some of them. Henry Fielding sentenced a number of them to a month's imprisonment. The almost equally well-organised hatters were similarly not above violence. In 1742 they so badly beat up a man for working without having served his apprenticeship that he died from his injuries.[11]

Peaceful strikes were not unknown. In 1761 journeymen cabinet-makers in London all attended their respective masters to demand more money and shorter hours. When both were refused, 'they immediately quitted their services'. Norwich woolcombers struck against the employment of an unauthorised man in 1752, moved three miles out of the city and lived there peacefully until the employers gave in. In the 1790s peaceful strikes were common. Still, if even the powerful tailors and hatters occasionally resorted to violence, less well-organised workers naturally did so. Indeed for most unions, a peaceful strike was a luxury they could not afford; it was merely the prelude to submission.[12]

Most combinations, therefore, either adopted or were driven to the third choice. They tried to outweigh the masters' natural advantages by coercion. In the absence of legal trade unions, violence either against property and machines or against men was often the only means of making a strike effective. Otherwise alternative workers were usually available to take the strikers' place; in 1764 London master tailors managed to recruit more than 1,000 strikebreakers from the provinces and from abroad. Mere withdrawal of labour was liable to be futile.[13]

In the first half of the century, West Country woolcombers and weavers were especially militant. When Tiverton clothiers started importing Irish wool in 1720, the woolcombers broke into the clothiers' shops and burned much of the wool before fighting a pitched battle with constables. In 1738 the woolcombers announced that, because the merchants were paying their masters such low prices that the masters could not pay them a wage on which they could live, they were going to enter Tiverton and pull down the merchants' houses. They fought a battle with 100 special constables in which one man was killed, then entered the town, whereupon the merchants conceded higher prices before their houses suffered, but not before one merchant had had his serges cut and had himself been 'horsed on a staff' through the town and dropped at the door of the mayor. Very possibly, the masters were behind the woolcombers' invasion. The dispute was replayed in 1749. It began peacefully, but when strike funds were exhausted fighting broke out. This time, however, the main battle was between the woolcombers and the weavers, who much preferred weaving Irish wool to not weaving at all. After the military and the Riot Act had restored order, the clothiers offered to limit their imports of wool, a concession which was refused by the woolcombers, many of whom left Tiverton for good.[14]

The weavers did not confine their fights to the woolcombers. In November 1717 nearly 1000 of them marched through various towns in Devon cutting looms and damaging the masters' stores. Nine years later the weavers began a protest march from Bradford-on-Avon to London against a new act prohibiting any combination to raise wages or regulate the trade and imposing heavy penalties for strike offences. They got as far as Frome before being forced to retreat to Melksham by two troops of Dragoons; at Melksham the Riot Act and the prospect of more dragoons was enough to disperse them. Nevertheless the march and the rioting concentrated the mind of the government, which for once investigated their causes. Discovering that the employers were mainly responsible, it passed another act which embodied an agreement between the two sides on payment and measurement of work, while reaffirming the Elizabethan principle of adjustment of wages by quarter sessions. In addition 'truck' (ie paying wages in goods not money) was prohibited. The clothiers largely evaded that act and broke their agreement, while supporting the earlier legislation. Conversely the weavers sought enforcement of the wage-fixing provisions, while ignoring the prohibition of combinations. So the struggle continued.[15]

A year later weavers at Bristol burned thirty looms and went on to do the same at three other places. In 1729 a leading Bristol clothier, Stephen Fitcham, managed to foil two attempts to pull down his house, and after making some concessions he was regarded as 'the weavers' friend'. When a competitor lowered wages Fitcham refused to copy him, and most clothiers followed his lead. A few days later, however, when the weavers asked for a rise, Fitcham refused that too. Hundreds of weavers marched upon his house, disregarding some soldiers who had been ordered to fire with powder only. Fitcham and his family were under no such inhibition; opening fire from his house they killed seven weavers and the sergeant in charge of the soldiers. Fitcham came to no legal harm.[16]

A revival of trade brought peace until, in the recession of 1738, the masters again lowered their rates of payment. Looms were severed in Trowbridge and other places to persuade them to restore the pay cut. Henry Coulthurst, a rich Melksham merchant, incurred the weavers' particular resentment. After at first refusing a pay rise, Coulthurst conceded it on the entry into the town of a large band of weavers who were clearly not bent on amicable discussion. The men then substantially raised their demands. After one of their leaders was arrested for entering a workshop through a broken window, a crowd of some 1500 weavers marched to Melksham to demand his release. Coulthurst agreed to try to secure it, but that was not sufficient to save his property. The weavers cut 'all the chains in [his] looms . . . on account of his lowering of the prices' and demolished nine of his houses as well as his mills. The rioters 'extorted money from many' before departing to try their luck of Trowbridge. Many clothiers made a more permanent departure to the more peaceful North Country, and three of the weavers were hanged at Salisbury.[17]

William Temple, a West Country clothier, JP and, later, Wilkite, wrote in 1739 of the 'insolence, idleness, debauchery, frauds and dishonesty', of the workforce, suggesting that the cause of the poor was popular only with those who did not really know them. His friend, Dr Josiah Tucker, also maintained that journeymen were intent on getting as much money for as little work as possible; they were prepared to lie and cheat and do anything, only provided it was

against their master whom they looked upon as their common
enemy. Unlike Temple, however, Tucker added that the master
considered his people as 'the scum of the earth' whom he had the
right to squeeze and to keep low so that they could not compete with
their superiors. Indeed so high was the master placed above the
condition of the journeymen that both their conditions approached
'much nearer to that of a planter and slave in our American colonies
than might be expected in such a country as England'. The remarks
of Tucker, who had no bias in favour of 'the common people',
regarding them as 'the most depraved and licentious creatures on
earth', explain the combative behaviour of the West Country
weavers.[18]

Tucker contrasted the conditions in the West Country with those
in Yorkshire, where the journeymen were so little 'removed from
the degree and condition of their masters' and, before long, so likely
to become masters themselves that they did not see their interest as
being opposed to the masters'. In consequence they did not enter into
clubs or combinations, they were industrious and sober, and mobs
and riots were almost unknown. Yorkshire was not as harmonious
as Tucker suggested, but it was much less discordant than the West
Country.[19]

The West Country tumults were far from the only industrial riots
in the first half of the century. They were merely the most
spectacular. The London silk weavers, concentrated in Spitalfields,
were in recurrent difficulties from the last quarter of the seventeenth-
century when they broke machines and, on two occasions, marched
on Parliament, being only with difficulty prevented from entering.
(The trained bands killed two of them and wounded others.) As well
as being too large, the silk industry was subject to disastrous
fluctuations from many causes, including frequent periods of court
mourning. In consequence the silk workers constantly found
themselves underemployed or unemployed and, in response to
destitution or in an attempt to avoid it, they reacted. In 1719
thousands of them – about 40,000 people were employed in silk
manufacture and allied trades – marched through London, molesting
women wearing Indian calico instead of British wool and throwing
ink at them; as a result an act was passed prohibiting the wearing of
calicoes, but not before weavers had the following year resumed their
attacks on women calico wearers. The act also made the weavers'
violence a capital offence, and one weaver was hanged in the
summer. In 1736 the weavers attacked Irish workers who, they
maintained, were working too cheaply. Thirty years later they
attacked first the Duke of Bedford and then his house, when that
nobleman temporarily defeated a bill prohibiting the import of
all foreign silks. Shortly afterwards the bill went through.[20]

In 1768 they were prominent in what became London's worst industrial violence of the century, the result of unemployment and a sharp fall in real wages brought on by the postwar depression of trade and the quarrel with the American colonists. A dispute with the masters over the reduction of their pay rates turned into a violent dispute between 'engine loom' weavers and 'single-handed' weavers; a battalion of Guards was stationed in Spitalfields to maintain order. A more imaginative step was the King's halving of future periods of court mourning; a grand procession, of both masters and weavers, marched from Spitalfields to St James's to thank him.

Later the violence and the cutting of silk began again. A soldier was shot, troops were again quartered in Spitalfields and two weavers were hanged. The chief violence came, however, from other workmen. Coalheavers besieged the house of their employer's agents; three of them were killed before the Guards arrived. In revenge the agents's sister was later torn to death. The coalheavers tried to cut off London from its supply of coal. And when the sailors helped to break the coalheavers' strike, war broke out between them. At least three pitched battles were fought. Many were killed, and seven coalheavers were hanged for murder. A sailors' strike then blockaded London.[21]

In the North East industrial disputes were frequent. Northumberland miners burned machinery in frequent riots in the 1740s and again in 1765. On both occasions they eventually won their point. The keelmen of Tyneside – the keels were small boats which took coal down the river from the collieries to be loaded at Newcastle – enforced several lengthy strikes. In 1750 they effectively blockaded Newcastle and the Tyne and beat up blackleg crews. Some of them even proclaimed the Pretender 'King of England, France and Ireland'. But prosecutions, the army and hunger drove them back to work after seven weeks with little to show from the stoppage. In 1785 the magistrates and principal inhabitants of Sunderland asked for a permanent military force to protect them against the pitmen, seamen and keelmen. The most dramatic violence, however, occurred in the North West.[22]

The Liverpool seamen's strike

In August 1775 the whaling season had ended and the American war had closed the American market for slaves, leading to the collapse of the African trade. In consequence many Liverpool ships were laid up, and some 3000 sailors were out of work. This pool of unemployment induced the owner of the *Derby*, a slave ship, to offer the sailors who had finished fitting her twenty shillings a month instead of the thirty shillings that had been agreed. The men's response on Friday August 25 was to wreck the work they had done and demolish the whole of the ship's rigging. Nine of the ringleaders were seized and imprisoned, whereupon more than 2000 sailors 'armed with handspikes, clubs etc' swarmed to the prison to release their comrades, a common enough custom in Liverpool and other towns. They ignored the reading of the Riot Act, but after breaking some windows further action was rendered unnecessary by the authorities freeing the prisoners.[23]

In the next few days sailors boarded all the ships in the docks, 'taking out all the people they found on board' and unrigging all the ships that were ready for sail. Gangs also visited the houses of leading merchants to levy contributions. On both the Monday and Tuesday the seamen marched to the Exchange (the Town Hall) to ask the mayor, Alderman Rigby, to intervene. Having for a second time gained no satisfaction, they threatened to return and pull down the building. The magistrates' reaction was to hire 120 men to defend the Exchange and another 300, it was rumoured, to arrest the strike leaders. When the seamen surrounded the Exchange that evening, the Riot Act was probably read; accounts differ as to whether the seamen offered some minimal violence. There is no dispute, however, that they had no firearms. In any event the defenders opened fire, killing several seamen and wounding up to forty.[24]

So far from quelling the seamen, that imprudent fusillade merely convinced them that they too needed firearms. On the morning of Wednesday the thirtieth about 1800 sailors, all with red ribbons in their hats, 'broke open warehouses for powder and musquets' and also gunsmiths's shops. But infantry weapons were not enough. Deciding that artillery was required they removed two cannon from a whaler. Suitably equipped 'they then hoisted the bloody flag' and began to bombard the Exchange. Either on purpose or through drunkenness they aimed high and did not level the building, though the reverberations of their cannonfire broke its windows and those of all neighbouring houses and shops. Four of the sailors were killed in the attacks and others wounded.[25]

Switching the attack to the houses of leading merchants, the seamen destroyed the home of the merchant who was said to have been the first man to fire on them and drank his cellar. 'Inflamed by liquor', they then destroyed the houses of other 'obnoxious persons'. Money was levied both from merchant houses and from those unwise enough to venture onto the streets. 'I could not help thinking we had Boston here,' wrote one eye witness, 'and I fear this is only the beginning of our sorrows.' It was in fact near the end of them. Military help had been summoned from Manchester and Chester on Wednesday afternoon, though it was not until Thursday afternoon

that a detachment of six officers and 100 men of Lord Pembroke's
Royal Regiment of Horse arrived from Manchester – Chester did not
answer the summons. The Manchester men were, however,
sufficient. They made about fifty arrests and quickly restored order.[26]

A week or so later when the Liverpool Common Council
presented a loyal address to the King expressing their 'abhorrence of
all traitorous and rebellious disturbers of his Majesty's peace', the
councillors were not condemning the sailors or their employers.
They were reproving the rebellious Americans, who were doubtless
a greater threat to Liverpool's slave trade. In seeking to forget or
obliterate its large local difficulty, the Common Council was not
alone. The fear of further disorders caused a virtual news embargo
to be imposed locally until the following April. Though the London
papers were not similarly inhibited, the *Gentleman's Magazine*
dismissed the whole affair in two sentences.[27]

The embargo was probably needless. No further disorders
occurred. A large insurrection – a 'Boston' – had never been
intended. 'The affair was accidental', the men having been inflamed
by the lowering of wages, by the original arrests, by the threat of
many more, by the first volley from the Exchange and, of course,
by drink. 'Accidental' though it was, however, the Liverpool tumult
was in one respect the most violent disturbance of the century. In
almost no other commotion were even small arms used by the
rioters, let alone the cannon employed by the Liverpool seamen. Yet
the judicial retribution was practically nil. The authorities turned the
other cheek. Maybe they thought that the seamen had had a genuine
grievance. Maybe they were wise enough to see that the episode was
effectively over and that loyal sailors were needed for the American
war. Whatever the reason, only twelve of the sixty arrested were
indicted, and even those instead of being tried were allowed to join
the navy; most of their followers did the same. The local elite was
similarly magnanimous. The sailors who had been 'so long confined
in the country gaol' published in Liverpool 'their most grateful
thanks to Alderman Rigby of this town, and to the ladies and
gentlemen of Lancaster, for their charitable contributions during their
distressed situation.'[28]

Machine breaking

Cannon not being available to most workers, the breaking of
machinery was their most effective way of coercing employers and
controlling the labour market without violence to persons; destruction of expensive material such as cloth had much the same effect.
This machine-breaking was thus not the result of blanket hostility to

machines or of an attempt to prevent technological advance. It was part of wider violence against employers and their property, a bargaining weapon against them. Before the arrival of machines, tools had been destroyed for similar reasons. Mere withdrawal of labour left the way open for the employment of other workers, who could be deterred only by threatened or actual violence. Moreover, until Parliament made the destruction of cloth or machinery a capital offence in the 1760s, machine breaking was often only a little more illegal than any other collective action by workmen to improve their lot.[29]

Yet machine-breaking was often not just a technique of collective bargaining, but the direct result of hostility to new machinery. A workman's only capital being his technical skill, not surprisingly he often saw the introduction of something which made that skill dispensable as a dangerous threat to his and his family's livelihood; and as the pace of technical innovations quickened in the latter half of the century, so this second sort of machine-breaking also increased. In 1768 500 sawyers attacked a new mechanical sawmill in London because, they explained, they objected to its being at work when thousands of them were starving for want of bread. In the following year the inventor of the spinning jenny, James Hargreaves, had his house and jennies in Blackburn destroyed by cotton workers – the probable cause of his moving to Nottingham. In 1776 the spinners and other woollen workers at Shepton Mallett petitioned the Commons against the introduction of the spinning jenny because it tended 'to the damage and ruin of many thousands of the industrious poor employed in that manufacture'. When the Commons refused to hear the petition, serious riots broke out.[30]

Three years later, during the depression caused by the American War, large mobs attacked buildings and cotton machinery at Chorley, Blackburn, Bolton, Wigan and Preston. Some 2000 people assaulted a mill at Chorley, losing two killed and eight wounded. Strongly reinforced they returned the next day and destroyed the machinery built by Arkwright. The factory of Robert Peel (Sir Robert's grandfather) at Altham was captured and destroyed. Arkwright had artillery and 'all the gentlemen in this neighbourhood' to defend his own factory at Cromford, but the arrival of the Yorkshire Militia saved factories in Manchester and prevented further violence elsewhere. The sole cause of the riots, the quarter sessions decided, was 'the erection of certain engines' for manufacturing cotton. Arkwright moved to the Midlands, and Peel to Burton-on-Trent.[31]

Gig-mills – they were machines, not buildings – had been declared illegal in the reign of Edward VI, but there was some doubt whether those in current use came within the statute. Illegal or not, they excited violent animosity. When destroying one at Warminster in 1767, shearmen claimed that two people with it could do as much in two hours as thirty men could do in a day without it; that was an exaggeration, but gig-mills were certainly very economical of manpower. In the 1790s some mills in Yorkshire had to be garrisoned, while the introduction of the gig-mill into Wiltshire and Somerset provoked serious violence in 1802. In cotton spinning, though not in weaving, things had changed by the 1790s. A writer thought that it might then be a prohibition of machinery that would cause riots.[32]

Both sorts of machine-breakers – those who broke machines as a means to a bargaining end and those who broke them as an end in itself – were often selective in their violence. When Northumberland miners struck in 1765 against the coalowners' attempt to prevent them moving from one pit to another without their master's permission, they allowed one especially humane employer to continue working his mine while destroying the machine of another particularly unpopular one. In the Lancashire machine-breaking riots of 1779-80, only the large spinning jennies which were used in factories were wrecked; the smaller ones which could be used in homes were considered 'just' machines and were spared.[33]

Economists naturally favoured the introduction of machinery. Dr Tucker had no doubt of the benefits conferred on workers by its introduction and increased efficiency. Since the price of goods would be 'prodigiously lowered', many more people could buy them and many more people would be employed. Adam Smith had little to say about machinery but favoured it. Ricardo, too, initially agreed with Tucker, but then decided that it was 'often injurious to the interests of the class of labourers' since some of them would be thrown out of employment. Eighteenth-century strikers would have been gratified to learn that their opposition to machinery, far from being 'founded on prejudice and error', was in accordance with 'the correct principles of political economy'. At the time, however, their being sound political economists did them little good. While their destruction of machinery was usually an understandable reaction to the threat of unemployment and not mere mindless violence – even Tucker conceded that more people would be employed only 'in the end . . . not immediately' – it was often destructive to themselves as well as to the machines: they were likely to be hanged or transported, and employers moved elsewhere.[34]

Nevertheless the strikers often gained a good deal of popular support. That men should not be put out of work by machines was a feeling not confined to the workers. Economic efficiency at all costs was not yet the prevailing idea; indeed efficiency of any sort in the eighteenth-century was rarely given high priority. Employers often sympathised with the men either because they were humane, or because they were inefficient and did not want to use machines themselves. Few however took their sympathy as far as Robert Oastler, a Methodist merchant in Leeds. Oastler, the father of Richard Oastler the Tory radical, gave up his cloth business because he disapproved of the growing use of gig-mills. Inventors sometimes had similar worries. But, fortunately for the country's future prosperity, Lawrence Earnshaw was unusual in destroying a cotton spinning machine he had invented because of the damage it would do to the poor.[35]

The reaction of the authorities

The attitude of Parliament and government hardened during the century, an evolution illustrated by the experience of the West Country weavers. As was seen above, Parliament passed an act against weavers' combinations in 1726, but then, after investigation, followed it with another act which favoured the weavers, empowering the justices to fix wages. The depression at the beginning of the Seven Years War brought a reprise of that dispute. The Gloucester weavers petitioned Parliament for the 1727 wage-fixing act to be observed. Parliament responded by passing another Act empowering quarter sessions to fix wages. At the instance of the masters, however, the Gloucester justices refused to do so. In consequence weavers 'committed great outrages' over a period of six weeks. The masters then asked Parliament to repeal the new act and, despite a petition from the gentry of the district requesting it to preserve the powers of the justices, Parliament duly did so.[36]

Yet Parliament's actions never followed a consistent pattern. Riots sometimes helped to procure legislation, as did petitions. In 1701 the import of cheap Indian and Chinese textiles was prohibited by 'an Act for the more effective employing of the poor by encouraging the manufactures of this kingdom'. Smuggling stopped the act satisfying the weavers and, after the Spitalfields riots of 1719, another one was passed. Action against Indian textiles was not out of line with British trade policy. British manufacturing industry in the eighteenth-century grew up behind a high tariff wall. To pay for the wars against France, import duties were roughly quadrupled between 1690 and 1704 and were then raised again in each successive war. The purpose of the duties was to gain revenue. No conscious policy of protecting industry existed, as it did in the United States after Alexander Hamilton's 'Report of Manufactures', yet that was the result. Still less was there a policy, conscious or otherwise, of protecting the workers. Increasing protection from abroad and increasing *laissez-faire* at home became the largely accidental formula for trade and

industry. Only in the next century when British industry was strong
enough to beat all comers was 'laissez faire abroad', that is to say the
policy of free trade, adopted.[37]

The last act regulating wages passed as a result of violence was as
late as 1773, the year after the ancient laws regulating the corn trade
had been swept away. The Spitalfields weavers had, after massive
riots, only recently secured an act prohibiting the import of all
foreign silks, even though Indian silks were already heavily curtailed
and French silks were subject to a duty of about 66 per cent. Yet
unrest continued, and after the Lord Mayor, who had supported the
weavers in an earlier dispute, had ordered an inquiry into their
grievances, an act was passed providing for their wages to be fixed
by the magistrates. The act did not make the weavers prosperous.
The industry's disease was incurable, and parts of the trade continued
to leave London. Yet the act brought to an end the violence which
had been endemic for most of the century, and for the next fifty years
the weavers enjoyed rates of pay which were on the whole fair.[38]

Whatever the law might say, the attitude of the authorities to
violent strikes was, as with food riots, inevitably mixed. Landed
gentry on the bench were not natural admirers of the industrial
interest; often they thought it to be causing unnecessary trouble as
well as treating its employees with insufficient consideration. In 1726
a Tory landowner in Wiltshire was said to have sided with the
weavers against their employers because he had been removed from
the Commission of the Peace. In the following decade the West
Country employers complained of the bias of JPs against them.
Certainly the Tory author of the 'Essay on Riots', writing in 1739,
put the main blame for the riots on the oppression of the clothiers,
suggesting that they paid their workers in 'truck', conspired together
to lower their wages, made them buy food in certain shops where
both the weight and the prices were suspect, and charged exorbitant
rents. He also thought they made excessive profits without having
great abilities. Nearly twenty years later Colonel Wolfe on anti-riot
duty was also inclined to blame the clothiers for oppressing their
weavers.[39]

The mid-century writer who considered workers' 'clubs' to be 'the
grand obstacle to oppression and tyranny' was, however, almost
unique. More typically Lord Hardwicke, CJ, thought in 1737 that
the 'oppression' came from the journeymen who formed 'unlawful
combinations' to maintain their wages. Twenty years later Lord
Mansfield, CJ, inveighed against the 'dangerous and illegal regulations' made by Lancashire trade unionists. In the very same year a
better-informed Oldham magistrate described the population as
being composed of 'a few rich traders amongst the numerous, half-
starved, half-clothed poor weavers'. Combinations to raise wages

were at common law an illegal conspiracy in restraint of trade, and numerous statutes were passed against them to add to the legal armoury. Judges were therefore bound to condemn combinations when cases were brought against trade unionists, especially as a strike was almost invariably accompanied by intimidation. Even Lord Kenyon, who took a firm line against regrating and forestalling, regarding a strike *cum* demonstration by some Essex farmworkers in 1800 as 'little short of raising troops and levying war against the King'. Yet industrial relations, unlike the criminal law, was not a subject on which the judges could conceivably be thought experts, and the unreality of the law, if not the judicial hyperbole on the subject, was the fault of Parliament.[40]

Notwithstanding the arrival of *laissez-faire*, Parliament's harsher laws and judicial thunderbolts against striking workmen, paternalism was a long time dying. At the instance of Yorkshire worsted manufacturers, Parliament in 1777 passed the so-called Worsted Acts toughening the law against the embezzlement of yarn by their employees. Yet the employers were frustrated by the local magistrates, who sympathised with the spinners and weavers and enforced the acts half-heartedly if at all. The Richmond justices described them as 'arbitrary and not fit to be put into execution'.[41]

Whenever Parliament attempted to regulate industry, wrote Adam Smith, its counsellors were always the masters. The greater unity of the ruling elite after mid-century and the new ideas of *laissez-faire* led government and Parliament to abandon any semblance of neutrality between masters and men and to take an increasingly stern view of industrial unrest. *Laissez-faire* was becoming the dominant dogma, and the duty to protect the weak was neglected. There was, as Carlyle later put it, an 'abdication on the part of the governors'. Following Adam Smith when it suited, and ignoring him when it did not, Parliament embraced the fiction that 'free contract' existed between a powerful employer and a poverty-stricken workman, and nothing else was needed.[42]

The French Revolutionary wars brought marked economic fluctuations and disruption. The 1790s saw disastrous harvests, trade depressions, hardship and distress, as well as booms, industrial advance, a tightening of the labour market because of massive recruitment into the armed forces, and severe inflation. Inevitably all this led to a mass of strikes for higher wages – the decade saw perhaps one third of all the century's strikes – and a growth of trade unionism. The government's Combination Act of 1799, which coincided with suppression of the radical political societies and derived as much from fear of political subversion as of industrial trouble, did not introduce heavy penalties but it prescribed objectionable procedures: the law of evidence was rigged and the right to trial by jury was removed; the accused could be tried by a single magistrate, even if that magistrate was an employer in the industry concerned.[43]

Lancaster textile workers protested that they 'must either have positive laws to protect them from imposition' or be allowed to associate to defend their interests; otherwise in a state of slavery they would be 'subject to the capricious disposition of those who employ them'. The government paid little attention, though the Combination Act of 1800 was a slight improvement on its predecessor. The acts were repressive but seldom invoked. Most combinations were already illegal – as they were in France – and trade unionism proceeded irrespective of the new legislation. The government itself disregarded its own law and negotiated with the Devonport dock workers.[44]

Before and after the Combination Acts, the authorities often preferred conciliation to violence. In 1792, during a seamen's strike in Newcastle, the magistrates refused to side with the employers, though both military and naval support had been sent to the area. The naval commander who discovered that the employers had often cheated their men in the past also favoured mediation. The strikers similarly preferred moderation. When one of the navy's ships ran aground and her crew could not free her, she was rescued by the strikers. The strike was settled on favourable terms. In a dispute at Newcastle after the 1799 Combination Act the mayor remained determinedly neutral, despite the threat to London's food supplies. Not all strikes ended happily, but at the end of the century, whatever Parliament might say, paternalistic attitudes had not been quite killed off.[45]

THIRTEEN

Duelling

Those insolent persons take upon them to frame a law and commonwealth to themselves, as if they had power to cast off the yoke of obedience to peace and justice. And therefore they enact among themselves as an undoubted position, that a man wronged may with his sword in his hand require satisfaction of any man . . . which arrogancy and rebellion must be subdued by this court, censuring the best.

Hobart, C.J., in the Star Chamber, 1616

My religious and moral principles are strongly opposed to the practice of duelling; and it would give me pain to shed the blood of a fellow creature in a private combat forbidden by the laws. Secondly my wife and children are extremely dear to me and my life is of the utmost importance to them . . . Thirdly I feel a sense of obligation towards my creditors . . . lastly I shall hazard much, and can possibly gain nothing, by the issue of the interview.

Alexander Hamilton, 1804

'For mere fighting', answered Flora, 'I believe all men . . . are pretty much alike; there is generally more courage to run away. They have besides, when confronted with each other, a certain instinct for strife, as we see in other male animals, such as dogs, bulls, and so forth.'

Sir Walter Scott, Waverley[1]

Paternalism was part of the aristocratic ethic or ideal which embraced a hierarchical society; the belief that protection and support were the right of all; and a sense of community, together with honesty, courtesy, courage and good taste. As with all such ethics, observance was at best patchy, the ideal often being a thin disguise for callous selfishness, though even the aristocracy's vices, according to Burke's famous dithyramb, lost half their evil by losing all their grossness. The ideal also had its aggressive side. By definition the gentleman was superior to everybody else and deservedly enjoyed great privileges which he ruthlessly defended. And though by the eighteenth century the English aristocracy and gentry were civilian in outlook, behaviour and descent, in one respect they looked back to the military origins of aristocracy, if not to their own. The gentleman's 'honour' was sacred, and he had the right, or rather the duty, to avenge an insult by a duel if the offender was a gentleman or by common assault if he was not.★ [2]

Duels of honour began in Italy and at the beginning of the sixteenth century spread to France, which soon became a slave, wrote the Duc de Sully, to a mistaken notion of honour, some 4000 noble men allegedly dying in duels between 1589 and 1607. Even for those like Henry IV who favoured duelling, this was rather too drastic a culling of the French nobility, and draconian edicts against it were issued but rarely enforced. Cardinal Richelieu, whose elder brother had been killed in a duel, did once invoke the full rigour of the law, and the Comte de Bouteville, a veteran of twenty-two duels and the possessor, he claimed, of the finest moustachios in France, was beheaded together with his second. Louis XIV issued eleven edicts against duelling, culminating in one of 1679 which prescribed the death penalty for all principals, seconds and thirds, in addition to confiscation of property and deprivation of Christian burial. Voltaire regarded Louis XIV's 'abolition of duels' as one of his greatest achievements. Yet while French duelling was past its peak except in the army and declined again under Louis XVI, it was far from being abolished. Indeed only in Scandinavia, the Netherlands, Portugal and, to some extent, Spain was the duel dealt with early and effectively. Duelling was a purely Christian European pastime. The Turks thought it ridiculous. So did the Persians and the Abyssinians. [4]

Duels of honour arrived in England in the later sixteenth-century, relatively late, and were rare until the beginning of the seventeenth. When gentlemen carried swords and the consequence of a quarrel was likely to be, if not a duel fought with seconds under prescribed rules, an immediate sword fight, duelling was defensible. To begin with, it probably cut down violence, being a partial substitute for affrays, ambushes, gang warfare, blood feuds and assassination. Unfortunately its advent coincided with the supersession of the relatively innocuous broadsword by the lethal rapier as the personal weapon of the aristocracy. The rising death toll among courtiers as well as the

---

★ When the young Voltaire had the presumption to challenge de Rohan to a duel in 1725, the Chevalier's servants beat him up and a *lettre de cachet* drove him to England. When the skilled swordsman, Arthur Thistlewood, (later hanged for the Cato Street conspiracy) presumptuously challenged Addington in 1818, the more bourgeois Addington merely had him arrested. In 1634 a gentleman was punished for his 'high insolence' in challenging a peer; in the eighteenth century that distinction had narrowed. Lord Oxington's initial reaction to Matthew Bramble's challenge was: 'What! A commoner send a challenge to a peer of the realm! Privilege! Privilege!' But he ended up apologising. [3]

frequently absurd pretexts for challenges induced James I to try to end it. The King, who believed like many Frenchman that Heaven had permitted the murder of Henry IV because he had tolerated the practice, issued a proclamation condemning duelling, and Bacon, his Attorney General, said he would prosecute anybody who issued or accepted a challenge. In telling the Star Chamber that the great would abandon the custom of duelling when they found it had been 'accepted by barbers, surgeons and butchers', Bacon's logic was right. Had the practice spread down to tradesmen, the great would indeed have forsaken it, much of its attraction being that, like the Game Laws, it set gentlemen apart. But Bacon's premise was wrong. Butchers and barbers were too sagacious or too timid to ape the folly of their betters; and the practice continued despite another proclamation by Charles I. All the same, the actions of the first two Stuarts were enough to keep the custom within bounds.[5]

Cromwell issued an ordinance that anybody sending, accepting or not reporting a challenge should go to prison for six months; and Lord Chesterfield was sent to the Tower. With the Restoration came a revival of the duel and an immediate proclamation against it. To Pepys, the prevalence of duelling illustrated the general complexion of the country;* the Duke of Buckingham, he lamented, was 'a fellow of no more sobriety than to fight about a whore'. In 1668 a bill which would have given the Earl Marshal power to determine questions of 'place and precedency' and to penalise the issuance and acceptance of challenges was supported by Charles II and his brother, but was soon dropped. Ten years later yet another proclamation appeared without effect. James II similarly discouraged duelling with little noticeable result. So while Louis XIV was acting ferociously against the admittedly more widespread evil in France, little was done in England.[7]

A basic rule of law, laid down by Coke in the seventeenth-century, is that 'revenge belongeth to the magistrate'. Duelling was a violent assertion of the right to private vengeance and a direct repudiation of that rule. Yet the common lawyers introduced no innovation into English law to deal with the new custom, nor did the legislators; they just went on duelling – and adding to the Bloody Code. The law on duels was both clear and ineffective. Anybody fighting a duel was guilty of an affray; a duel which ended in death was manslaughter if fought immediately in hot blood and murder if fought in cold blood. Thus the law was both too lenient towards the practice of duelling and too severe towards a surviving dueller. As Sully had recognised,

---

* Even doctors fought. When Dr Mead fought Dr Woodward and the latter fell, Dr Mead said: 'Take your life.' 'Anything but your physic,' replied Dr Woodward.[6]

the death penalty for 'this pernicious and savage abuse' only made
the law difficult to enforce.[8]

Except when there was strong suspicion of foul play, juries
invariably acquitted duellists or found them guilty of manslaughter,
which led only to a small fine, a short imprisonment, or both. This
was partly because, as duellists thought, juries accepted the
aristocratic code of their social superiors. But juries also commonly
avoided a murder verdict on those who had killed with their fists in
the plebeian version of the duel. Evidently, therefore, more sensible
as usual than the law, juries were unable to regard as murder a killing
which had occurred by consent after a fair fight. Death in a duel was
indeed more nearly suicide than murder, a duel being in the nature
of a mutual, if contingent, suicide pact.[9]

Foul play

'Duels of honour' were not always honourable affairs. The
Sacheverell trial led to several fatal duels, and the most notorious duel
of the century, between Lord Mohun and the Duke of Hamilton in
1712, was probably caused in part by the continuing party animosity
– the Duke's recent appointment as Ambassador Extraordinary in
Paris to speed up the peace negotiations was anathema to the Whigs
because of his suspected Jacobite inclinations. Had Mohun not been
a peer he would have been hanged long before. Twenty years earlier,
a Captain Hill, after failing to abduct a popular actress with whom
he was furiously in love, had killed William Mountford, the leading
actor of the day, who was wrongly assumed to be the actress's lover.
Mohun had been with Hill at both the attempted abduction and the
killing, but by 69 votes to 14 the House of Lords acquitted him of
murder, one peer remarking of the dead man that the fellow was only
an actor, and all actors were rogues. Mohun would not have been so
lucky before a judge and jury. Seven years later the Lords again
acquitted him of murder, this time probably rightly. As well as being
involved in other murderous affrays, Mohun, whose father had been
killed in a duel, had himself fought at least three before taking to
politics as a Whig.[10]

One of Mohun's more peaceful activities was a lengthy lawsuit
with the Duke of Hamilton. When the Duke remarked before a
master in Chancery that a witness had no truth in him, Mohun issued
a challenge to Hamilton who was some seventeen years his senior
Mohun's second, General MacCartney, who in 1709 had been
convicted of raping his housekeeper and the following year forced to
sell his regiment for 'licentious insolence' in damning the Harley
ministry, also fought the Duke's second, Colonel Hamilton of the

Foot Guards. Having run Mohun through, the Duke dropped his sword and bent down to help the wounded man, whereupon Mohun stabbed him. Had Mohun lived, even the Lords might have convicted him of murder, but like Hamilton he died. The Duke had four wounds, Mohun a mere three. Both the seconds were unhurt, then and later. MacCartney, who wisely fled to France, was accused by Colonel Hamilton of having also stabbed the Duke. On his return after the Whigs were in office, the colonel did not persist with the allegation; MacCartney was acquitted of murder and, like the colonel earlier, only found guilty of manslaughter. The duel further heightened party hatreds – Tories believing that it was a Whig plot to prevent Hamilton help negotiate a peace – but led to no changes in the law. A bill to suppress duelling did not get through the Commons, let alone the Lords.[11]

The second most famous duel of the century, between Lord Byron and Mr Chaworth in 1765, arose out of the momentous question as to which of them had more game on his estate. It, too, was a poor advertisement for the practice. In one of the last duels to be fought with swords, Byron, with no seconds present, killed Chaworth in a small dark room.[12]

The coroner's verdict of murder entailed, Byron being a peer, a trial before the House of Lords. Dismissive of the 'solemn puppet show', Horace Walpole was not interested in 'an obscure lord, whose birth alone procures his being treated like an overgrown criminal'; as the quarrel was about game it should have been dealt with at quarter sessions. The rest of London was enthralled. The trial was presided over by the Lord Chancellor, Northington, whose son-in-law was later killed in a duel; Lord Pomfret, who had killed a man in a duel, had the decency to stay away. The Lords found Byron guilty only of manslaughter, which meant that as a peer he went free. Byron was apparently within the rules of honour in taking advantage of Chaworth's mistaken belief that he, Byron, was mortally wounded to stab Chaworth to death. Yet duelling purists were shocked by the impropriety of fighting without seconds because it allowed the possibility of 'the foulest treachery', and general opinion was against Byron. He lost his mastership of the royal staghounds, his wife left him, and he consoled himself with his servant 'Lady Betty'; he became the 'wicked Lord', and a recluse at Newstead which he proceeded to denude of its deer, timber and pictures, leaving a dilapidated inheritance to his great nephew, the poet.[13]

Those were not the only duels in which honour was scarce. In 1703 the fifty-five-year-old Lord Wharton, who had gone to Bath to recover his health, was challenged by a young Tory, Dashwood, for no other reason than political differences. Weak as he was, Wharton accepted and survived unscathed without wounding his opponent.

Dashwood died shortly afterwards, allegedly of chagrin.*

In 1726 Major Oneby was the aggressor in a gambling quarrel and, though given time to cool down, insisted on a duel, fought without seconds. He was sentenced to death and committed suicide. In 1789 Robert Keon shot Mr Reynolds in the head before he was ready. When Reynold's second objected, Keon's brother tried to shoot him too. Keon was hanged. Twenty years later, after a quarrel over the correct word of command, Major Campbell, who like Oneby had had time to cool down, forced a pistol into Captain Boyd's hand and killed him after a fight without seconds. He, too, was executed. But unless there were strong indications of villainy, duellists suffered little or no legal penalty. In Hogarth's *Marriage à la Mode* the lover caught in bed by the lady's husband whom he then killed in a duel was hanged for murder; in real life he would have gone free.[15]

Political duels

Duels arising out of something said in Parliament were rare but became less so from about 1770. The Speaker or members not involved sometimes prevented a duel, as in 1717 when a fight between Walpole and Stanhope, the head of the ministry, who had made some wounding criticisms of Walpole's use of office to enrich his relations, his friends and himself, was avoided, and in 1732 after the head of the South Sea Company took personally Admiral Vernon's strictures on the directors' behaviour. The Speaker also prevented a duel between William Pulteney and Henry Pelham. Pulteney did, however, fight a bloodless duel with Lord Hervey after having accused him of, amongst other things, homosexuality.[16]

In 1743 William Chetwynd, in answer to a private pleasantry behind the Speaker's chair, told old Horace Walpole that he deserved to be hanged, a view which, because of the money Horace had amassed from office during his brother's reign, was widely shared. But that did not make it any more palatable to Horace, and after he had seized Chetwynd by the nose they fought at the bottom of the stairs leading out of the lobby of the House. Walpole had the better of the conflict and was about to run his adversary through, when a clerk intervened and knocked down both swords. Chetwynd was slightly wounded.[17]

That seems to have been the only duel fought within the precincts of Parliament. During the American War Fox ridiculed William

---

* Like his father, Wharton was a skilled swordsman and a practised duellist. If duelling had an attractive side, his claim at the end of his life embodied it; he said he had never refused a challenge, never offered one and never killed a man.[14]

Adam for excusing his change of sides by the argument that bad as the ministry was the nation would not definitely be better off with their opponents. After failing to persuade Fox to publish a disclaimer in the newspapers, Adam issued a challenge and they met in Hyde Park. Fox declined Adam's invitation to fire first, saying: 'Sir, I have no quarrel with you, do you fire.' After both had fired, seemingly without effect, and Fox still refused to apologise, Adam missed, and Fox fired in the air, declaring he could not say that he had intended no more personal affront to Adam than to the two seconds. He then mentioned he had been hit by the first shot, fortunately very mildly, attributing his escape to Adam's use of government powder.[18]

Fox's exemplary conduct illustrated one of the crucial defects of the duelling code. The threat of a duel inhibited a gentleman from giving an explanation or apology, even if one was deserved, for fear of seeming a coward. An apology could therefore be made only after the duel had taken place, by which time of course it was often too late.

A few months later, in March 1780, William Fullarton MP, who had lent Adam his pistols, complained in the Commons of Lord Shelburne's 'aristocratical insolence' in having said in the Lords that he and his regiment would be as ready to act against the liberties of their country as against its foes. Fullarton then published some insults in a newspaper and sent them to Shelburne, who desired Fullerton to meet him in Hyde Park the next morning. Shelburne behaved much as Fox had done but was hit by the second shot and was more seriously wounded. The City of London enquired after his lordship's safety, which had been 'highly endangered in consequence of his upright and spirited conduct in Parliament'.[19]

These political duels were a threat to the freedom of parliamentary debate, as Fox, who was in a good position to know, had pointed out when Fullarton first raised the matter, and as Sir James Lowther complained in the Commons afterwards. Lowther did not of course wish 'to put men of spirit into a dishonourable situation' – he himself fought a non-political duel against a barrister four years later – but if free debate was to be treated as personal attack and public questions were to be decided by the sword, Parliament would resemble a Polish diet. Burke supported him but Rigby, the quintessential placeman, thought the matter should be dropped since every gentleman had his own particular feelings and would preserve his honour in his own way. The very attempt, he thought, to prevent one man fighting with another was absurd; duels would continue so long as the world should endure.[20] Rigby expressed the conventional feeling, and nothing more happened.

Possibly because of that discussion, however, the duel became a less common form of parliamentary debate. Nevertheless Fox was second to a colleague in 1792 and Tierney challenged Pitt six years later. Pitt hoped that a bill to improve the manning of the navy would pass through all its stages in one day. When Tierney opposed this 'precipitous course', Pitt asked how Tierney's opposition to the measure could be accounted for but from a desire to obstruct the defence of the country. Though clearly in the wrong, Pitt refused to explain or retract. The Speaker, Addington, failed to order him to withdraw, and Tierney issued a challenge. On Putney Common Tierney missed twice and Pitt once, firing his second pistol in the air.[21]

This was perhaps the strangest duel of all. Like his father Pitt had no great admiration for the aristocracy and was Prime Minister in time of war. But rather than say that under such circumstances he could not fight a duel, or that he had used stronger language than he had intended and what he had really meant to say was . . . etc, etc, he insisted on going through with it. Pitt, whose obstinacy may be partly explained by his illness and the stress of unsuccessful war, said he was 'perfectly satisfied' with himself and his antagonist. Others were not. Wilberforce was shocked and tabled notice of a motion to stop duelling. In rare agreement with Wilberforce, the King trusted that there would be no repetition: public characters, he wrote, should not just think of themselves but what was due to their country. And Hannah More exclaimed that it was a dreadful thing that 'a life of such importance should be risked . . . on the miserable notion of false honour!' To complete the horror, she lamented, 'they chose a Sunday!'[22]

Political duels continued in both war and peace. In 1809 Castlereagh, incensed to learn of the plotting that had preceded his resignation from the War Office, challenged Canning, the Foreign Secretary. Though Portland, the Prime Minister, not Canning was primarily to blame for the concealment, they fought on Putney Heath and, with Castlereagh insisting on a second shot, Canning was wounded in the thigh. The King conceded to Canning that he could not have avoided the challenge but was shocked by his and Castlereagh's conduct.[23]

Shortly after Waterloo, O'Connell reacted to some mild criticism from Peel in Parliament by saying that Peel would not dare to criticise him in his presence, and Peel issued a challenge. They were to meet in Ostend, but O'Connell, who had recently killed a man in a duel, was arrested in London and forced to return to Dublin. Peel was left wandering about the Netherlands incognito, and the seconds fought instead of the principals. Peel then wanted to challenge O'Connell's second, and followed him to Calais. Fortunately, some negotiations and an apology brought an unsatisfactory settlement.[24]

Wellington's only duel was when he was fifty-seven and Prime

Minister. Lord Winchilsea accused him of 'insidious designs for the infringement of our liberties, and the introduction of popery into every department of state', and refused to apologise. The Duke issued a challenge. On Battersea Fields Wellington, ignoring some sage advice from labourers to settle the matter with his fists, displayed his usual battleground *sang froid*. He intended to hit Winchilsea in the thigh, but when Winchilsea did not fire, he fired wide. Winchilsea then felt that 'honour' permitted him to apologise.[25]

Thus of the fourteen Prime Ministers between 1779 and the repeal of the Corn Laws, six – Shelburne, Fox, Pitt, Canning, Wellington and Peel – fought or tried to fight a duel. For choleric, dyspeptic majors of small abilities, flushed with wine from a heavy evening in the mess, to give or take offence and then shoot one another was little more than the small change of military life; for mature and highly intelligent politicians, sober and with plenty of time to cool down, to risk their own lives and those of their opponents by giving an advance imitation of *The Three Musketeers* or the heroes of Stanley Weyman was at the very least, as the King complained, a total dereliction of duty and a violation of 'the laws which they were bound to maintain by the authority vested in them.'[26]

As a soldier Wellington was of course in a different category from the others. Battle was natural to him. All the same, great generals did not have to countenance duelling. Napoleon's maxim was '*Bon duelliste, mauvais soldat*', and when the King of Sweden challenged him, he replied that he would order a fencing master to wait on the King; Marshal Ney, 'the bravest of the brave', also discouraged duelling, while Wellington himself never duelled when he was in the army and frowned on it during the Peninsular War.[27] None of the other five prime ministerial duellists was ever a soldier or was in any way martial. Yet their propensity to duel did not stem from aristocratic frivolity or disdain for hard work. Some of them were barely aristocratic, and they were a rather more distinguished bunch than their non-duelling fellow premiers.

Presumably prominent politicians had become more touchy of their 'honours'; perhaps some were not confident of their social position. But a weightier reason for the increase in their duelling was purely technical: the introduction of duelling pistols, the use of which could be learned much more easily than sword play – indeed, as the pistols did not shoot straight, pistol duels might be survived without any training at all – and in which disparities of skill were less glaring. Both for the elderly and for politicians, therefore, pistols were convenient; Charles Fox and the others could scarcely have pranced about with swords. And with the country's leaders setting such an example, there was no danger of duelling becoming unfashionable.[28]

No attempt at suppression

Archdeacon Paley was probably right in thinking that it was impossible to suppress the code of honour which, wrote a Frenchman, 'is a law that no power may oppose'. In France it survived the Revolution. In Britain no serious attempt was made even to diminish duelling, though much could have been done. No great ingenuity was required to close the legal loopholes.* The common law did nothing to prevent duels, only seeking to punish duellists. None of the arrangements for a duel was illegal, only the duel itself. Apart therefore from forbidding duelling in the army and navy (as was achieved in Haiti) and strengthening the legal remedies for slander (as Bentham suggested) what was needed, as the Star Chamber and Cromwell had realised, was to treat as an offence both a challenge to fight and its acceptance. At the same time the penalty for a fatal duel should have been made a long term in prison. Juries would then have had no compunction in convicting the survivor, and duellists could have seen no glory in undergoing the punishment. Yet no remedies were produced because the absurdity of the law was convenient to those who made it: duelling could 'safely' continue, while it remained technically capital.[30]

The arguments against duelling have probably never been better put or their futility better illustrated than by Alexander Hamilton, who wrote the words at the head of this chapter just two days before Aaron Burr killed him in the most famous of American duels. Earlier Hamilton had claimed that as they did 'not now live in the days of chivalry' he would not fight a traducer, adding that the good sense of the times had found out that the worst way of proving innocence was to run an accuser through the body or shoot him through the head. Yet when Burr issued his 'invitation', Hamilton decided that what men of the world called 'honour' made it impossible to 'decide the call'.[31]

The third of Hamilton's arguments against duels, his obligation to his creditors, had no cogency in Britain. The problems of tradesmen wrung no aristocratic hearts; the living were little better than the dead at paying their tailors' bills. The code of honour applied only to equals. Hamilton's first argument, religion, stood little more chance of acceptance. In a conflict between the religious and the secular codes Christianity almost invariably loses; 'I love my religion very well,' says the worthy lieutenant in *Tom Jones*, 'but I love my honour

---

* Or to create practical difficulties, as did the Prince of Melfi, a sixteenth-century viceroy of Piedmont. Finding his loss of officers from duelling excessive, he decreed that all duels should be fought on the parapet of the Ponte Vecchio at Turin and that if one of the fighters fell in he was not to be pulled out. Since the strong likelihood was that both would fall in, duelling effectively ended.[29]

more.' Hamilton's two other considerations, however, family feeling and the law, should have been more powerful. Many duellists left distraught wives and families; Major Campbell had four infant children. Finally, the law was one of the main buttresses of the system, at the top of which the duelling class happily perched.[32]

But whatever the strengths of the various arguments, they were seldom put. Though duelling was plainly contrary to Christian teaching, churchmen, as Wilberforce complained, were lukewarm in their criticisms; indeed they themselves occasionally duelled.* The clergy tended to be gentlemen first and Christians second. The Council of Trent stigmatised the duel as a 'detestable invention of the devil to compass the destruction of souls together with the bloody death of the body'. Two hundred years later the Anglican Church, though opposed to duelling, could manage no such forthright a condemnation. In assize sermons to the county elite, when preachers encouraged the wielding of 'the sword of justice' and warned against 'an excessive tenderness' to offenders, they never touched on duelling. For prelates or parsons to admonish gentlemen to avoid violence and obey the law would have introduced into the proceedings a distinctly jarring note; the point of having bishops, said Paley, was 'to provide friends' for the superior orders of the community, and the assize sermon was devoted to denouncing the lawlessness of the ruled, not the rulers. Hence, apart from some obscure scribblers, and the Nonjuror Jeremy Collier (who thought duellists were worse than highwaymen as they were 'murderers by *principle*') and John Wesley, the clerical denunciation of duelling was largely left to Paley himself, who found the custom absurd as well as unchristian.[34]

Lord Hardwicke privately thought duelling an 'ill-grounded and unhappy custom', but neither his nor any other judge's stirring addresses to grand juries on the need to curb the spirit of licentious insubordination among the lower orders ever included an appeal to the gentry to set a law-abiding example by eschewing the violence of duelling. Such homilies would not have fostered the festive camaraderie of assize dinners. In court, judges sometimes sided with duellists against the law in their summings up as well as by their light sentences. Trying a bad case in 1783 Baron Eyre told the jury that the strict rule of law on duelling was 'in direct opposition to the feelings of mankind and the prevailing manners of the time'. He urged the jury to do their duty, which for once meant not convicting, and they duly acquitted. Abbot, LCJ, at the trial of a duellist and his

---

* The *Gentleman's Magazine* said of one clerical duellist, ''tis supposed that the parson never fights a man but that he buries him'. In 1783 a married Derbyshire curate killed a schoolmaster after a violent altercation 'concerning a brisk gay widow'. Probably, as was said of yet another parsonical duellist, he was 'of rather too volatile a turn for his profession'.[33]

second for the murder of the editor of the *London Magazine* in 1821, left it to the jury to decide whether there was sufficient proof to identify the prisoners as those who had been involved, remarked that they had no proof of how 'the fatal occurrence' had 'originated', and said that they had to consider what sort of deliberations there had been; so little doubt was there on the first two points that even the defence had not disputed them, while the deliberation was no less than in other duelling cases. Not surprisingly the jury's verdict was 'not guilty'.[35]

The monarchy, too, condoned duelling. Unlike the Stuarts, unlike Peter the Great who made the sending of a challenge a capital offence, unlike Frederick the Great who discouraged duelling and set up courts of honour, and unlike the Emperor Joseph who forbade it in his army, the Hanoverians did nothing to suppress it. Because duelling was most prevalent in the armed services where the monarchy's influence was highest, this royal toleration was more decisive than the passivity of the clergy and the judges.[36]

The Articles of War, which supposedly governed the conduct of the army, were specific:

> Nor shall any officer or soldier presume to send a challenge to any other officer or soldier to fight a duel upon pain of being cashiered . . . nor shall any officer or soldier upbraid another for refusing a challenge . . .

That prohibition had little more practical effect than the common law. Duels 'always will be honourable, though unlawful,' Hobbes had written in 1650, 'until such time as there shall be honour ordained for them that refuse, and ignominy for them that make the challenge'. Moreover, under the code of honour, seeking 'satisfaction' after an insult was as obligatory as the acceptance of a challenge, and nearly all officers put protecting their 'honour' well above obeying the law. An officer who duelled thus broke the law, but an officer who did not duel was liable to be ostracised by his fellow officers and even court martialled 'for conduct unbecoming an officer and a gentleman'. George II shared the preference of his officers. In direct contravention of his own Articles of War and of the decision of a court martial, he let it be known that an officer who had been knocked down by a junior must either fight a duel or forfeit his commission, and he himself once challenged the King of Prussia.[37]

The moral crusade of George III extended to adultery but not duelling. Had an anti-duelling clause been included in his coronation oath, as it was in that of Louis XVI, he would no doubt have acted upon it. George III 'mortally' disapproved of duels, especially when his ministers were involved, but he never attempted their suppression. His favourite son, the Duke of York, fought a duel with Colonel Lennox of the Coldstream Guards, who later as Duke of Richmond and Lord Lieutenant of Ireland tried to cut down duelling. The Duke behaved well on the field, coolly receiving Lennox's fire though it 'grazed His Royal Highness's curl' and himself firing into the air, but he was almost entirely to blame for the quarrel. By the end of the century, the Admiralty tended to deprecate duels, and in 1812 an officer was cashiered for trying to compel offficers to settle their quarrels by duelling. The army, however, positively encouraged them. An officer who failed to issue a challenge when he had been insulted was still dubbed a coward, and his military career was ruined. In 1814 an ensign was dismissed the service for not duelling. Though the War Office denied it, similar incidents occurred as late as the 1840s. The King and the government could have ended such behaviour many years before.[38]

Duelling was so strongly entrenched a fashion that men who preached against it in print found themselves practising it on the ground. Steele attacked the barbarism of duelling in the *Tatler*, calling it a 'custom which all men wish exploded, though no man has courage to resist it'. Shortly afterwards he proved the truth of his words. When challenged he accepted, and though he tried to avoid wounding his opponent, he ran him through and nearly killed him. Sixty years later Sheridan reversed the process. He successfully defended the reputation of his future wife against Captain Matthews in a duel in Covent Garden. Matthews, annoyed by the publicity given to his defeat, demanded another meeting and Sheridan, though the code of honour decreed that he was entitled to refuse a return match, accepted the challenge. After pistols had been discharged, they fought with swords and wounded each other; having fallen, they continued to struggle on the ground, with Matthews stabbing the now unarmed Sheridan five times. In addition to his wounds, Sheridan's face was 'nearly beaten to a jelly with the hilt of Matthews's sword' and he had part of that sword sticking through his ear. Three years later he satirised duelling in *The Rivals*.[39]

Religion, law and the family counted for nothing against the code of honour. With few exceptions, nobody in the duelling classes, however radical they were, thought of refusing a challenge. John Wilkes accepted two; he had to prove himself a gentleman. Sir Francis Burdett, too, was injured in a duel. Though the strongly Christian Dr Johnson never fought a duel, he believed a man had as much right to shoot a man who 'invaded his character' as one who broke into his house. Wilberforce on the other hand loathed the 'system of Honour (what *honour*!)', and when challenged by a slave trader, Captain Rolleston, he declined on religious grounds. Lord Shaftesbury did the same sixty years later, as did Cobden. But in the eighteenth century Wilberforce, the Duke of Grafton in 1779, and Lord Leicester, who in 1758 refused a challenge on the grounds that he was too old and ill, could not shoot and had not touched a sword for years, were almost the only men of note to prove Richard Steele wrong.[40]

With the satirists masking their own fire and the moralists muffled, duelling in the eighteenth-century did not attract sufficient disapproval or ridicule to kill it. Nevertheless, it abounded in absurdity. In 1792 after a quarrel about her age, Lady Almeria Braddock fought Mrs Elphinstone in Hyde Park. Beginning with pistols, Mrs Elphinstone hit Lady Almeria's hat; continuing with swords Lady Almeria slightly wounded Mrs Elphinstone in the arm. Honour was then satisified. There was also at least one nude duel. As a former military surgeon, Humphrey Howarth MP knew that wounds were often aggravated by clothing being driven into the body by the bullet. He therefore stripped for his encounter with Lord Barrymore in 1806. His lordship felt, however, that to fight naked was to treat the proceedings with unbecoming levity, and that ended the matter.[41]

Naked or female duellists were no more absurd than the cause of many hostile meetings. One duel was caused by deafness, another by whether a window should be open or shut, a third because a man refused to dismiss his servant, the last two both being fatal. A man died because he said at 1 am that he could drink no more. An infantry officer fought a French officer who claimed that 'the English army had more phlegm than spirit'. While Mr Cochrane, a retired naval officer, Major Lockyer and others were drinking in a tavern prior to going to South America, Cochrane said 'they were all in debt and were seeking their fortunes'; the major challenged and killed him. Lord Lonsdale fought Captain Cuthbert after Lonsdale, finding his carriage obstructed, said: 'you rascal, do you know that I am a peer of the realm?' Cuthbert replied: 'I don't know that you are a peer, but I know you are a scoundrel for applying such a term to an officer on duty.' A fatal duel occurred solely because a man had successfully prevented another one from taking place. An MP fought an Irish peer because he had ben asked to pay a long-overdue debt. Lord Falkland was killed because when drunk he said to Mr Powell, who was also drunk, 'What drunk again tonight, Pogey?' A man died in 1818, even though he and his opponent had not quarrelled; only their mutual friends had. Sixteen years after the battle of Trafalgar a naval officer wounded his opponent for having reflected on Lord Nelson. Hence Lord Fellamar's challenge to Squire Western in *Tom Jones* because the squire refused him Sophia Western's hand on the grounds that she was 'bespoke already' was relatively reasonable.[42]

In 1803 Captain Macnamara killed Colonel Montgomery for having insulted his dog. Macnamara, who was given a good character by Admirals Nelson, Hood and others, told the jury that while it was impossible to define the feelings of a gentleman, their existence had 'supported this country for many ages and she might perish if they were lost'. The judge directed the jury that on his own admission Macnamara was guilty of manslaughter. Yet either because the jury were impressed by the character references of the admirals or because they accepted the view that England's future would be jeopardised if gentlemen were not allowed to kill each other for insulting their dogs, the jury acquitted him.[43]

These pretexts were not ludicrous only in twentieth-century eyes. Smollett wrote of 'the trade of assassination', the idiocy of friends murdering each other and the hardship of a worthy man having to die because he was unlucky enough to be 'insulted by a brute, a bully, a drunkard, or a madman'. The poet Byron disliked 'seeing men play the fool for nothing' and thought a second could make up the quarrel nine times out of ten if he was not 'a bully or a butcher'. And an Edinburgh sheriff found the cause of one duel so unsatisfactory and the behaviour of the parties so strange that he ordered the fines he imposed to be paid to the local lunatic asylum.[44]

Occasionally, of course, a duel did have a substantial cause. When in 1668 Lord Shrewsbury fought the Duke of Buckingham for living with his wife, his honour was clearly involved, even if his wife, as Pepys maintained, was 'a whore'.[45] Such cases were rare. Most duels had nothing whatever to do with anything that could properly be called 'honour'. They were merely the outcome of boredom, pique or tipsy ill temper. Indeed many, if not most, duels were a form of drunken brawling, only distinguishable from an ordinary tavern squabble through being more dangerous and in the actual fight taking place in the period of hangover not intoxication.

The spread of duelling and its end

The frequency of duels is difficult to gauge. In 1844 shortly after Queen Victoria's abhorrence of the 'barbarous custom' of duelling had been conveyed to the Commons, Mr Turner estimated the number of duels fought during the reign of George III as 172. That is the figure given by James Gilchrist in his history of duelling from 1760 to 1821. Gilchrist's book is useful, but he claimed only to deal with the principal duels; he even omitted the ones between Warren Hastings and Philip Francis in 1780 – had Hastings been killed, the whole British position in Asia, Macaulay thought, might have collapsed as it had in America – and between Henry Grattan and Isaac Cory; and he omitted four in 1769 while including several French and American combats as well as fifteen in 1821. The figure of 172 for

1760-1820 therefore has no validity; the real figure must have been very much higher.[46]

In the early seventies Walpole thought duelling was in fashion. In 1778 Lord Kames believed 'the frequency of duels' to be a symptom of degeneracy. Complaining seven years later that a duellist had been buried in Westminster Abbey with military pomp, the *Gentleman's Magazine* referred to 'the gothic practice' seeming to grow every day. And in 1791 *The Times* stated that there had been thirty-three duels in the previous year. Shortly after Waterloo England was estimated to be the country most addicted to duelling and at least fourteen duels were fought in the last three months of 1835 alone.[47]

Britain was usually at war between 1790 and 1815, but that was nothing new. For many Englishmen war was merely the pursuit of trade by other means; in eighty-seven of the years between 1689 and 1815 the country was involved in major military operations. Yet at no stage was either the aristocracy or society as a whole in any sense militarist. Very few peers or gentlemen were prepared to risk life or limb in King William's wars. Generally speaking, wrote Bolingbroke, 'men of estates' had not served in the War of the Spanish Succession. The aristocracy and the gentry showed a marked reluctance to fight on either side in 1715 and 1745. The purchase of commissions, which was opposed by both William III and George I, certainly gave the aristocracy a privileged place in military affairs. Out of 102 colonels of regiments in 1769, fifty-four were peers or the sons or grandsons of peers, or married to peers' daughters; in 1780 nearly a third of the generals had titles. As the army grew bigger, it contained more aristocrats and gentlemen, and its prestige was enhanced. There was a military and an aristocratic resurgence. Yet if the younger Pitt in his mass creation of peers did not, as Disraeli claimed, clutch them 'from the counting houses of Cornhill', relatively few generals or admirals were among those ennobled. The aristocracy was even further from being a warrior caste in 1790 than a hundred years earlier. It was still much more at home in the drawing room than on the battlefield. Only over duelling did the paramilitary ethic take strong root. Admittedly duelling, unlike rebellion, carried no threat of forfeiture of estates; had it done so, 'honour' would have been less impetuously asserted and defended. All the same, duelling did carry considerable threat to life and demanded great physical courage. Of the 344 duellists mentioned in a book published in 1822 nearly half were wounded and at least sixty-nine were killed. Duelling was far from a formality. Yet, instead of declining in line with a softening of manners, a revival of religion and a growth of the prosperity of the upper classes, duelling increased in the last third of the eighteenth-century and flourished until well after the Reform Bill.[48]

Peel told the Commons in 1844 that 'the influence of civilisation' was bringing a fall in duelling. 'Civilisation' had had no such influence in the eighteenth-century or, indeed, on Peel himself when he was challenging O'Connel thirty years earlier. Yet the monarchy at last exerted itself. After a notorious duel between two military brothers-in-law in which one was killed, civilisation, in the shape of Prince Albert and Queen Victoria, managed to get the Articles of War amended so as to encourage apologies and to make the sending or acceptance of a challenge an offence punishable by cashierment for both principals and seconds. Only after the long-overdue reform did the British duel begin to die.[49]

Elsewhere Prince Albert's writ did not run. In America the Irish Code duello was brought up to date and in 1859 a former chief justice of California killed a United States senator. In Italy, despite the law, Cavour fought a duel on a wholly unimportant issue. In France Clémenceau fought twenty-two duels, nearly all bloodless. In Germany duelling lasted until after World War I. Both Hitler and Mussolini encouraged it, but continental duelling was not the prerogative of the Right. Socialist luminaries like Proudhon, Marx and Engels also fought them, and Lassalle was killed in a contest over a girl.[50]

The appeal of violence

A thug like Lord Mohun was a natural duellist as well as a tavern brawler, and he fought bravely in France in 1694.[51] The civilians who fired at each other at the end of the next century and encouraged soldiers to do the same were neither natural duellists nor brawlers, and they did not fight the French. The displacement of the sword by the pistol had made duelling easy, but that only partly accounts for the growth of the custom. As arms races seldom cause wars, so the availability of a convenient weapon was not the sole cause of duels.

Duelling was the natural outcome of the ruling elite's attitude to violence, to the law and to those they ruled. So long as it came from the top, violence was tolerated or encouraged. And duelling did not just come from the top; it was confined to the top. Then at the end of the eighteenth-century it began to seep down the social scale. In 1798 an attorney's clerk and a scavenger's clerk's attempt to duel was regarded as 'thoroughly contemptible', and a few years later Lord Ellenborough, LCJ, spoke with disdain of the 'spurious chivalry of the compting house and the clinker'. Earlier only the gentry were licenced to kill one another when they fell out, just as only the gentry were licenced to kill game. The ability to do those two things were the conspicuous badges of a gentleman.[52]

The ruling elite obeyed the laws for most of the time. They did not find that too difficult: after all, as Goldsmith pointed out, they made them. But from passing legislation giving themselves privileges, like the Game Laws, to thinking themselves above the law and selectively breaking it was only a short step, It was a further gesture of supremacy. Otherwise the matter for surprise would be not that no effective measures were taken against duelling – after all the rest of the criminal law was far more in need of improvement, yet was merely made worse – but that duelling for gentlemen was not legalised. That would have put it on a par with the Game Laws; indeed, because of the often preposterous pretexts for making a challenge, duelling was little less random in its effects than spring guns or man traps.* But to have legalised duelling would have robbed it of its attraction. While it was illegal, or rather while to kill a man in a duel was a criminal offence, the giving and acceptance of challenges showed that gentlemen were effectively above the law. 'Men can not enjoy,' wrote Burke, 'the rights of an uncivil and of a civil state together.' Yet the elite did just that. And to have brought duelling within the law would only have cheapened the privilege; Bacon would have been belatedly vindicated.[54]

The appeal to a 'higher' law than the law of the land had its dangers. If the rulers permitted themselves to carry out acts of private vengeance unimpeded by the law, the ruled might claim the same privilege of nonlegal vengeance. The French Revolutionaries instituted a popular justice which took a far heavier toll of life than duelling. In their talk of the need for revenge and violence, Saint-Just and Robespierre, who denounced 'honour' as a 'spirit at once tyrannical and servile, base and arrogant', were probably not consciously following the example of the French aristocracy, yet an example had been set. England avoided both revolution and popular justice. But fears were sometimes expressed that the violence of the governors would undermine respect for the law and inspire emulation by the governed. If the duelling class could pick and choose which laws to obey, why should the lower orders not do the same? The fears proved unfounded; stability was never threatened. Duelling demonstrated the justified confidence of the rulers in the continued deference of the ruled.[55]

Originally duelling was, like Bacon's revenge, 'a kind of wild justice'. Probably because many in Southern Europe preferred the even wilder justice of assassination and the blood feud, the duel did not become firmly established there: in a duel, after all, the offended party might be killed and the offender escape; assassination was,

---

* The grandson of the Mr Chaworth killed in the Byron duel was badly wounded by one of his father's spring guns.[53]

therefore, a more judicious procedure. At first, in England, duelling probably canalised aggression into more acceptable channels than casual assassination and, in doing so, weakened it. But that phase soon ended. Instead of cutting down violence and settling disputes, duelling exacerbated quarrels and became an excuse for violence, while enhancing self-esteem, asserting superiority and attracting the admiration of ladies.[56]

James I talked of 'the bewitching duel'. Its violence did indeed appeal and bewitch. For duellists, obligations to wives and children, to religion or to the law were powerless against the demands of 'honour', the pressures of society and the urge to violence. Indeed underneath the polish and good manners and the talk of gentlemen's feelings and honour, duelling was largely violence for its own sake. Sometimes the violence sought for was suicide. Whenever a war broke out, Nietzsche wrote of Germans, there also broke out, especially among the nobility, 'a secret desire: they throw themselves with delight against the new danger of death, because in the sacrifice for the fatherland they believe they have found at last the permission they have been seeking, the permission to evade their human purpose. War is for them a short-cut to suicide, it enables them to commit suicide with a good conscience.' The glum fatalism with which many challenges were made and accepted suggests that similar feelings were often present among duellists. When Lord Windsor refused to fight because his would-be opponent was too old, his challenger committed suicide. Yet the violence that was predominantly sought was murderous. In France Montaigne complained of duellists' invariable desire to kill. Assassination, thought Byron, none of whose challenges ended in a duel, was little worse than duelling and also its origin. 'The trash about honour,' he believed, was only 'stuff'. The urge to kill was the important thing; that was 'amiable and natural'. Many challengers, of course, did not want to kill: Wellington for one, and Byron's own loathing of Brougham and Southey was not sufficient to bring him back to England to fight them. Nevertheless Byron was basically correct: killing was the heart of the matter.[57]

With prize-fighting it was not. Largely because of 'Gentleman' John Jackson, whom Byron admired and used to spar with, and his two predecessors as champions, Johnson and Mendoza, prize-fighting, like duelling, enjoyed a resurgence in the 1780s. Boxing had been made temporarily fashionable by two earlier champions, Figg and Broughton. Figg was admired by Walpole, Hogarth and Pope; Broughton's chief patron was the Duke of Cumberland. In eleven years Figg never lost a fight. Unfortunately for boxing, Broughton was defeated in 1750. In consequence 'the Butcher', who had bet Lord Chesterfield £10,000 to £400 on Broughton, withdrew his

patronage and encouraged legislation against prize-fighting, which
was put into partial eclipse for thirty years.[58]

Duelling and prize-fighting obviously had much in common,
above all their violence. But prize-fighters were at least fighting for
money – their violence was not for its own sake. In addition
prize-fighting provided a public spectacle popular among all classes,
while duelling was a hole-in-the-corner affair. Indeed because the
large attendances at prize-fights easily led to public disorder, the
authorities devoted much greater efforts to stopping boxing matches
than to stopping duels that were far more lethal. A long time before,
John Locke had thought boys should be taught wrestling rather than
fencing. The Prussian, Archenholz, thought in 1785 that duelling had
become more fashionable as boxing had declined. In the nineteenth
century that process was reversed. The growing popularity of boxing
in the nineteenth century helped to bring duelling into disrepute.*[59]

Both the rich and the poor appealed on occasion to a 'higher'
justice. The poor appealed to the moral economy to obtain cheap
food; the rich appealed to the code of honour to obtain satisfaction.
In doing so, both only endangered themselves. Neither duellists nor
food rioters killed outsiders. But there the similarity ended. Duellists
killed each other; food rioters were killed by the state. Food rioting
was usually a last resort and was often an attempt to persuade the
authorities to enforce the law. Duelling was often a first resort and
its essence was not an appeal to the law but a defiance of it.

Much has been written of the violence and irrationality of mobs,
which except in stock exchanges and legislatures are usually
composed of the poor. In 1896 the crowd theorist Gustave Le Bon
wrote of the 'collective mind' of a crowd, which formed 'a single
being' and lacked 'all sense of responsibility'. In that stupid mind
which lacked all critical spirit, 'unconcious qualities obtained the
upper hand'. 'An individual forming part of a crowd,' Le Bon
contended, 'is no longer himself but has become an automaton' who
has 'ceased to be guided by his will'. Le Bon exaggerated in both
directions the difference between the irrationality of the crowd and
the alleged rationality of the individual. He wanted, after all, to
contrast the stupid primitive mob with the intelligent civilised elite
which he thought it threatened. Yet in one respect, at least, in
eighteenth-century England it was the elite which behaved most like
Le Bon's idea of a crowd. Over duelling the elite had a stupid
collective mind, wholly lacking in critical spirit. In France duelling

---

* Similarly at the end of the nineteenth-century Theodore Roosevelt thought the best cure
  for violence in New York city would be the formation of boxing clubs. A little later
  H.L. Menchken advocated a brass band in every Southern town as a cure for lynching.
  Music in British army messes would have alleviated the pervading boredom there and
  probably prevented many military duels.[60]

was seen as a 'plague', a 'continual frenzy' and collective madness. In England, similarly, men offered and accepted challenges like automatons without any sense of responsibility, fighting duels though they knew them to be wrong. Colonel Thomas of the First Guards, who was killed in a duel in 1784, left a will expressing his horror at the barbarous custom of duelling but saying the customs of society had compelled him to accept the challenge. Letters of duellists, written shortly before they fought, likewise show that they had ceased to be guided by their will. Instead, the laws of honour imposed upon them that 'mental unity' of a crowd which is 'often criminal but also . . . often heroic'. Bewitched, they stumbled into killing or death.[61]

The mob, too, was occasionally mindless as well as violent. Yet the violence of the plebeian crowd in pursuit of the moral economy was often rational and usually minimal; the violence of the individual gentleman duellist in defence of his honour was usually irrational and often fatal. The collective madness of the crowd was comfortably outstripped by the individual madness of the gentleman.

Part Three

AVOIDANCE OF REVOLUTION

I am sorry to say that if no instructions had ever been addressed in political crises to the people of this country except to remember to hate violence and love order and exercise patience, the liberties of this country would never have been attained.

W.E. Gladstone, 1884[1]

FOURTEEN

The 'Jew Bill', Pitt and the Militia

I . . . am not a little hurt at the spirit and disturbances showed in many parts of England against a law passed after many considerations and debates by the legislature. What is our prospect if [the people] are to set themselves up for judges whether we do right or wrong?
General Sir Charles Howard MP on the Jewish Naturalisation Act, 1753

The establishment of the militia . . . would be in time the ruin of the constitution and the immediate destruction of the Whig party.
The Duke of Newcastle, 1760

The lower rank of people . . . hold an odd language indeed, and talk, when they have arms in their hands, of fighting for those who will give them most, so thoroughly debauched is this unfortunate country, but when they are more disciplined they will have other sentiments . . .
Lord Poulett to Pitt, 1758[1]

By the early 1750s parliamentary opposition had been reduced, Smollett thought, to a state of 'imbecility'. As a result of the suppression of the Jacobite rising, the emollient policies of the Pelham ministry, the end of the War of the Austrian Succession and the death of the Prince of Wales, the party battle disintegrated into factional skirmishing. In 1750 Jacobite rioting in Walsall, Birmingham and Wednesbury lasted intermittently for nearly two months and almost amounted to a mini-insurrection. Later in the year Charles Edward visited London and was belatedly converted to Anglicanism. The Elibank Plot of 1752-53, concocted by Alexander Murray, planned the abduction of the King and the Royal Family – the Prince vetoed their projected assassination – and a diversionary rising in the Highlands. But as normal the government knew all about it and the plot fizzled out. Jacobitism was fast ebbing away and the Prince was increasingly sozzled.[2]

The House of Commons, wrote Horace Walpole, had become 'a mere quarter sessions', concerned only with turnpikes and poor rates. Parliament was so far from being 'mutinous' that at one moment during the Seven Years War the most engrossing political topic was whether a main road out of London should bring more profit to the Duke of Grafton or the Duke of Bedford. Out of doors, however, opposition was not similarly infected by the 'servility of the times'. Before retiring to join the Pretender in France, Alexander Murray was called before the Commons charged with inciting violence at the violent (on both sides) Westminster by-election in 1750. Found guilty he refused to go on his knees to the Speaker, saying he only knelt to God, and became a popular hero. More than once public clamour decisively altered events and the passing of one measure which was intended to be popular caused some of the worst violence of the century.[3]

During the 'Forty-five' and afterwards, English Jewry had been helpful to the government, and the 'Jew Bill' – an appellation which did not have the offensive connotations that it would have today – was supposed to be their reward. This simple innocuous measure, enabling Jews to be naturalised by Act of Parliament without taking the sacrament, passed through the Lords virtually unnoticed in 1753. Two years earlier a similar bill to naturalise foreign Protestants had been abandoned after opposition from the Tories and the City; yet this time, despite a similar combination, the bill got through the Commons too. Only while it was waiting for the Royal Assent did intense public clamour break out.[4]

The agitation against the bill was more religious, economic and anti-immigrant than directly anti-semitic – the anti-semitism was religious not racial. It was a rerun of the Sacheverell case, engaging Church-Dissent passions and giving the Tories a potent cry for the elections; it was not a precursor of the twentieth-century persecution of the Jews. One unpleasant minor demonstration took place against some Jews in a theatre, but English theatre audiences were notoriously rowdy (a few years later Boswell was enraged by a similar shower of apples against two Scots officers at the opera). The target in 1753 was not English Jewry but English court politicians. So far from the Archbishop of Canterbury's fears of a massacre being realised, the agitation over the Bill led to no violence against Jewish individuals or property. In contrast the Bishop of Norwich was attacked by mobs in his diocese and Dr Josiah Tucker, who had remarked that the real cause of the clamour was merchants' fears of Jews breaking their monopoly, was attacked in the streets of Bristol, burned in effigy and dubbed Josiah ben Tucker ben Judas Iscariot.[5]

Nevertheless much of the propaganda against the bill was grotesque. 'The impure conjunction with Jewish blood' was held to be 'worse than the leprosy'. As a private Act of Parliament was expensive, only rich foreign Jews would have been able to take advantage of the bill; yet it would lead, said Sir John Barnard the

City leader, to 'a general naturalisation of Jews'. It would also, its opponents claimed, produce 'a swarm of foreigners', thereby endangering the Anglican Church. Some people even affirmed that Judaism would become the fashionable religion of England. Hence it was not only the Church but the livelihood of butchers which was in danger.[6]

The agitation evoked frequent comparisons with the Sacheverell commotions, with the subsequent fate of the then Whig ministers providing a worrying precedent. According to Lord Chesterfield, the public clamour 'frightened' Newcastle 'out of his wits'. Preferring ignominy in Parliament to humiliation at the polls, the Duke moved in November the repeal of the bill which had only become law in June. The bench of bishops approved both the bill and its repeal 'with the same passive discretion'. Hardwicke, the Lord Chancellor, who thought that there would already have been violence had the people not expected immediate repeal, compared the situation to the Public Quarantine Bill of 1721 when public protests had driven the government to abandon some draconian measures against the last major outbreak of plague in Western Europe. The Excise Bill would have been a better parallel. Even Hardwicke's language echoed Walpole's on that occasion. It was not, Walpole had told the Commons, 'prudent to press a thing which the nation expressed so general a dislike to, however they were deceived'. 'However much the people may be misled,' Hardwicke now told the Lords, 'yet, in a free country, I do not think an unpopular measure ought to be obstinately persisted in' – or at least, both might have added, not shortly before an election. In the Commons William Pitt reluctantly supported the government's retreat 'out of complaisance to the people', and the repeal passed easily enough, enabling the ministry to enter the election unencumbered by a vastly unpopular bill.[7]

As usual, the election saw some violence. At Worcester Horace Walpole witnessed a Tory mob attack its opponents' headquarters 'shouting "No Tracy! [the sitting whig MP] No Jews!" It almost murdered the ostler and then carried him off to prison for being murdered.' At Bristol, Bury, Leicester, and other places, the mob 'rose very high'. In Nottingham a Dissenting Chapel was destroyed; in revenge the windows of all the Churches were broken and two men were killed. In the hard-fought Oxfordshire contest 'a drunken rabble' of Tories attacked a Whig dinner in Banbury taking two prisoners, and Whig and Tory mobs skirmished at Chipping Norton. Yet the 1754 election was one of the quietest of the century with only sixty-two constituencies being contested. The prominent part the Lord Mayor of London, Sir Crisp Gascoigne, had played against the bill was not enough to get him elected. In a sensational criminal case he had taken the right but unpopular side and saved the life of a

wrongly convicted gypsy. That outweighed his having taken the
popular but wrong side over the Jews. Reviled as 'King of the
Gypsies' he was pelted and threatened with murder, and he came
bottom of the poll in Southwark.[8]

Gascoigne's experience confirmed what the absence of violence
against Jews had already suggested: the Jewish question, as such, did
not run deep. In the same year, two other legislative provisions
benefitting Jews provoked no opposition campaign. A satirical
account of the election gives a flavour of the controversy:

> I am at present in — where the election is coming on . . . The
> Town . . . is divided into two parties, who are distinguished by
> the appellation of *Christians* and *Jews*. The Jews, it seems, are those,
> who are in the interest of a nobleman who gave his vote for passing
> the Jew Bill, and are held in abomination by the Christians. The
> zeal of the latter is still further inflamed by the vicar, who every
> Sunday . . . preaches up the pious doctrine of persecution . . . Sir
> Rowland swears that his lordship is actually circumcised, and that
> the chapel in this nobleman's house is turned into a synagogue. The
> knight had never been seen in a church, till the later clamour about
> the Jew Bill; but he now attends it regularly every Sunday, when
> he devoutly takes his nap all the service . . . Every Saturday he has
> a hunt, because it is the Jewish Sabbath; and in the evening he is
> sure to get drunk with the vicar in defence of religion . . .[9]

The agitation and the quick repeal of the bill revealed three things:
the continuing strength of English xenophobia, the latent power of
public opinion, and the caution and insecurity of the ministry. As in
the Quarantine Act and the Excise Bill, so in the Jewish Naturalisation Act the voice of the people was the voice of God – in the sixth
year of a Parliament.

Pitt's rise to office

Shortly before the elections Pelham died, and 'our tranquillity',
wrote a court Whig, Lord Waldegrave, 'expired with him'. The
Duke of Newcastle succeeded his brother, inaugurating a period of
ministerial instability which, save for the years of the Pitt-Newcastle
coalition, lasted until the advent of Lord North. Like Walpole,
Newcastle pursued a defensible but unpopular foreign policy, and
like Walpole he was incapable of waging war. His leadership or
anti-leadership – Pitt said he could not call it an administration, it was
so unsteady – made his ministry at least as calamitous as North's.
And when in the summer of 1756 Admiral Byng failed to relieve

Minorca and the island fell to the French, 'popular discontent and clamour . . . overturned his administration,' or rather, Lord Waldegrave continued, 'occasioned the panic which obliged ministers to abdicate'.[10]

Of course much intrigue and high political manoeuvring intervened before Newcastle resigned and the Devonshire-Pitt administration came into office. Yet it was what Newcastle himself called the 'almost universal uneasiness and discontent throughout the whole kingdom,' and 'the violence without doors' – which he expected soon to come within – that undermined him; at the same time it was the 'prodigious popularity' of Pitt which enabled him to tell the Lord Chancellor that 'the sense of the nation' prevented him siding with Newcastle. In September the Duke was himself mobbed. His carriage was pelted in Greenwich and, while he retreated to the Observatory, the mob enjoined his coachman to deliver him to the Tower.[11]

Nevertheless most of 'the violence without doors' had little to do with Newcastle, Minorca or Pitt. An appalling harvest had caused sky-high food prices and widespread food riots. Central England was the worst affected. Mobs destroyed mills in Warwickshire, Derbyshire, Staffordshire and Northampton. Hundreds of colliers invaded Nottingham and Coventry. In Nottingham they released some prisoners and burned down a mill. In Sheffield a riot lasting three days needed 'stout men, all armed with bludgeons', to suppress it. On top of the clamour over military defeats, this violence did nothing to calm political nerves. 'The nation is in a ferment . . .,' wrote Horace Walpole, 'instructions from counties, boroughs . . . in the style of 1641, and really in the spirit of 1715 and 1745, have raised a great flame, and lastly the countenance of Leicester House [the home of the 'reversionary' court of the Princess of Wales and her son, the future George III] . . . all these tell Pitt he may command such numbers without doors as may make the majorities within the House tremble.' In the City Sir John Barnard similarly thought the national ferment, much stimulated by the opposition, was too high for Newcastle to withstand. The Duke agreed. Despite the King's unwavering backing and a large parliamentary majority, Newcastle found 'the flame' too fierce and resigned his office.[12]

Not controlling either House and resented by George II, who regarded Pitt and his colleagues as 'scoundrels', the Devonshire-Pitt minority government was not built to last. 'The mob,' Waldegrave wrote, could 'sometimes raise a minister', but the support of the higher ranks was needed as well. The great bulk of Whigs still adhered, however, to Newcastle, and there were only a hundred Tories; Pitt did not even have enough adherents to staff the ministry. Not only could he not force 'patriot' measures through either House, the compulsions of office entailed the abandonment of such popular rallying cries as his opposition to subsidies for a continental war. 'Patriot' rhetoric was doused by the realities of power.[13]

For Pitt the most damaging issue of all was the fate of Admiral Byng. Despite the unanimous recommendation to mercy by the officers who had convicted Byng (while acquitting him of cowardice and treachery), George II, Newcastle, Fox and other ex-ministers were still out for his blood, if not mainly to save their own skins – 'Hang Byng or take care of your king' was one cry – at least to proclaim that he, not they, was to blame for losing Minorca. Partly to demonstrate the contrary but mainly for more creditable reasons, Pitt and his supporters tried to save the disgraced admiral. But when Pitt told George II that the Commons seemed inclined to mercy, the monarch riposted that Pitt had taught him to look for 'the sense of my people in other places than the House of Commons'. On Byng the feelings of the people were not in doubt; hence Pitt's concern for justice temporarily cost him his popularity with the mob. Only in supporting the militia and in sending back the German mercenaries brought over by Newcastle were Pitt's actions consistent with his popular rhetoric in opposition.[14]

Oppositions were perennially short of issues. A workable Gin Act was finally passed in 1751, but social questions were not normally a Westminster concern. Sir Francis Dashwood introduced a bill to relieve the poor and unemployed by providing for voluntary public works; it got nowhere. A landowners' parliament had its own priorities: the first day proposed for the inquiry into the loss of Minorca raised objections in the Commons because it clashed with Newmarket races. 'A line of class supremacy,' as Sir Keith Feiling put it, 'a social apathy, was drawn over the statute book.' With parliamentary interest thus confined largely to finance, defence and foreign affairs, military matters were a central political issue. From 1688 onwards, as we have seen, a standard prop of 'country' and 'patriot' oratory was suspicion of the standing army because of its threat to liberty and, as a substitute, the championing of an armed citizenry. Indeed even a court Whig like Pelham thought that under Cumberland's command the army was dangerous. Nevertheless, well before the 1750s the need for it had been generally accepted. Its size, however, remained controversial, and one way of keeping it small while avoiding the use of foreign troops was to revive the militia. This force had proved ineffective in both Jacobite risings and was almost defunct, yet unlike the army, which in its critics' eyes contained mercenaries, criminals and the dregs of society, a militia composed of freedom-loving Englishmen could not be a harbinger of arbitrary or absolute government.[15]

The idea did not appeal to the court. The monarchy's suspicion of parliamentary meddling with the militia long predated the

Hanoverians. Asked to grant Parliament control of it for a short time, Charles I replied: 'By God, not for an hour.' Though in a far stronger position because of possessing a regular army, early Hanoverian governments were almost as touchy. They had no fears of their standing army; instead they feared Jacobitism and they feared the people, and wanted them kept unarmed. In 1738 Walpole had maintained that so far from putting down riots the militia would join them. Then and later many believed that it might also join a Jacobite rising. Notwithstanding rumours of disaffection during the Excise Crisis, the army was unlikely to do the same.[16]

To the political argument for a reborn militia, the invasion scares of the forties and fifties added a convincing military case. So did experience abroad. France and Prussia had demonstrated the usefulness of part-time soldiers. Britain probably had less local defence than any other country; she certainly had too few troops. For George II and the court Whigs, however, the political dangers of a militia still far outweighed its military benefits. For all Pitt's philippics against foreign soldiers as 'an eyesore' and against the sending of 'money abroad to buy courage and defence', the court felt much safer with foreign regiments. When George Townshend MP, a brave and experienced soldier, brought forward a plan for a militia in 1756, strongly supported by Pitt, the bill was too popular for the Newcastle ministry to oppose in the Commons; it had to be killed in the Lords. Hardwicke maintained that it strengthened the 'democratical' tendencies of the age and was a threat to limited government. Even worse, the bill might militarise 'the very lowest rank of our people', who should confine themselves to industry or labour. Clearly, therefore, it was far better for the country (and especially for its rulers) to be defended by reliable professional soldiers, even if they were too few and foreign, than by a citizen army.[17]

The installation of the Devonshire-Pitt ministry banished such sentiments to opposition. As one of Pitt's conditions for accepting office a second Militia Bill was shortly afterwards introduced by Townshend. The early disasters of the war were attributed by some to the decline of Sunday observance, and the bill's opponents were able to prevent the militia drilling on Sundays. Otherwise it passed through the Commons without damage. Before its debate in the Lords, the King, pushed by 'Butcher' Cumberland and ignoring the lesson Pitt had taught him about the sense of his people, dismissed his Secretary of State. As as a result, in the middle of an apparently disastrous war, Britain was left without an administration for nearly three months. While France invaded Germany, English politicians struggled for office and George II fought for the exclusion of Pitt.[18]

Pitt's unpopularity was immediately cancelled. His dismissal

demonstrated that however much his administration had truckled to
the views of the court he himself had not become part of the court
circle. He thus 'came back to the mob' barely sullied by office. His
opponents alleged that his followers had by 'clamours' falsely
adopted 'the name of the *people* of *Great Britain*' and were attempting
to transfer 'the royal power into the hands of the mob'. Yet, genuine
or not, Pitt's popular support was accepted by George II, Newcastle
and Hardwicke. 'The popular cry without doors,' Waldegrave told
the King, 'was violent in favour of Pitt,' adding the even more
disturbing intelligence that 'there was a mutinous spirit, in the lower
class of people, which might in a moment break out in acts of the
greatest violence.'[19]

Pitt's public support was not, of course, the sole foundation of the
new Pitt-Newcastle administration, any more than it had been in the
formation of the Devonshire-Pitt ministry. Pitt still enjoyed the
backing of Leicester House – the rising sun – and was preeminent in
the Commons; the only parliamentarian capable of standing up to
him was Henry Fox, whose slippery behaviour and close association
with Cumberland made him even less acceptable to many orthodox
Whigs than his alarming rival. Nevertheless, Pitt had added a new
dimension to politics: he stood single, he said, and dared 'to appeal
to his country at large'. In 1757 as in 1756 and as never before, the
popularity of a politician was crucial in shaping the ministry. When
Newcastle talked of 'the violence and virulence' against him, he was
using the former word in the wider eighteenth-century sense: overt
violence in support of Pitt was even less in 1757 than in the previous
year. All the same the threat of violence, as Waldegrave indicated to
the King, was always there; hence George should 'give way to the
necessity of the times.' Twenty years earlier, Carteret had remarked
of the Porteous mob that its discipline had made it all the more
dreaded and dangerous. Now the mere threat of violence was more
effective still; and Pitt was called, in his own words, 'to invigorate
government and to overrule the influences of feeble and shortsighted
men'.[20]

Well before Britain once more had a government, the Militia Bill
had become law. With Pitt out of office, Newcastle and Hardwicke
could tailor it to their political wishes, passing amendments in the
Lords which the bill's promoters in the Commons, more anxious to
create a militia than to play politics, largely accepted. In consequence
executive control of the militia was strengthened, its size was halved
to 30,000 men and its existence was limited to five years. Before long
its life semed likely to be a great deal shorter.[21]

The Militia Riots

Food shortages and compulsory military service stir similar feelings, the risk of death in a war whose objectives are irrelevant or offensive being as chilling a prospect as starvation. In 1793 the imposition of conscription set off the mass rising in the Vendée against the revolutionary government in Paris; five years later conscription provoked a rising of Belgian peasants; in 1863 some 50,000 people in New York took part in riots against the draft far more violent than those 100 years later against the war in Vietnam. In eighteenth-century England, wartime acts authorising impressment for the regular army – the royal prerogative only covered pressing for the navy – were unpopular and periodically produced rioting, as in London and Newbury in 1706. Mistakes were occasionally made – sometimes intentionally to conscript Methodist preachers or political opponents – but only the unemployed or vagabonds were properly liable to impressment. In contrast the militia affected practically everyone and caused far larger disturbances.[22]

The public reaction to the 1757 Militia Act revealed the chasm between the political nation's notion of popularity and the real thing. The setting up of a citizen army, which in the eyes of its 'country' advocates would safeguard not only England against her enemies abroad but also English liberties against an unpopular government at home, proved no more congenial to the citizens than to the court. Few of them had any desire to join in. The act laid down that a census should be taken of able-bodied men aged between eighteen and fifty and that a proportion chosen by ballot should be enlisted in the militia for three years. Anybody so chosen could escape, however, by finding a substitute or paying a fine of £10. The main burden, therefore, fell on those who could not afford a substitute or £10. In addition MPs, looking after their own interests, had decided that the new militia was to be paid for by the taxpayer out of general taxation and not, like the old militia, by landowners out of the Land Tax. In consequence both the poor, who were going to staff the militia and help pay for it by their taxes, and the middling sort, who were merely going to pay for it, understandably regarded it less as a protection against arbitrary government than as yet another arbitrary emanation of that government. Like impressment for the navy and the army, recruitment of the militia was indeed unfair, but unlike the earlier impressment on land it was not just individuals who were involved but whole communities.[23]

Popular hostility to enlistment in the militia was aggravated firstly by the *canard* spread by its opponents that it would be sent overseas. In violation of a promise to the contrary, some regular army recruits had in the previous year been forcibly sent abroad; the Militia Act expressly ruled out service overseas, yet a similar fate was feared for its recruits. Secondly, because the subject of pay had misguidely been left for another act, the belief was general that militiamen would not be paid for the days they spent on exercise. Finally the disastrous harvest of 1756 was followed by a bad one in 1757, exacerbating the militia controversy and once again causing food riots.[24]

By July the army had been used to suppress food riots in twenty-five places. Trouble over the militia began in Bedfordshire at the end of August. The object of the rioters there and elsewhere was to destroy the ballot lists; a mob of several hundreds achieved this in Biggleswade, also extorting payment for their trouble in money and drink. The sending of troops produced a complaint from the Duke of Bedford that fifty-nine men were not sufficient to defend the whole country 'from the influence of a riotous rabble'. Earlier the Duke had warned of the dangers for the rest of the kingdom of allowing 'a giddy and riotous populace' to defy an Act of Parliament. The rest of the kingdom, however, needed no example from Bedfordshire. Across the country, wrote Horace Walpole, 'the peasants became refractory beyond measure'.[25]

Yorkshire, where one mob was said to be over 3000 strong, was the county worst affected, the gentry having delayed the arrival of troops by sending their requests to Lord Holderness, a Yorkshire magnate as well as a Secretary of State, instead of to the Secretary at War, Lord Barrington. At Beverley in the East Riding, the mob forced the chief constable to give up his list and then threatened to burn down the town; after damaging one house, some guineas for drink induced them to leave. The High Sheriff of Yorkshire was forced by another crowd to promise not to help execute the act. The mob, 'arm'd with guns, scythes, and clubs', claimed that the Militia Act 'was a great hardship upon the country, by compelling the poorer sort of people to contribute equally with the rich . . .' They seized any lists they could find and threatened violence against persons and houses if new lists were compiled. The Lord Lieutenant ordered no lists to be returned until instructions had been received from the King. In the North Riding, mobs visited the houses of several magistrates to find the lists and, probably, to stop the JPs from attending a meeting in York where the lists were to be received. If so, they were successful. Yet some still went to York to destroy the house where the meeting was to have taken place. The Sheriff and the Lord Mayor of York pacified them by promising to try to prevent further meetings, and the next one was indeed abandoned. In the West Riding the Lord Lieutenant, Lord Rockingham, was less pliant. Refusing requests from his deputies to be allowed to surrender the lists and arming his tenants and servants, he deterred an invasion by a Sheffield mob. Normally, a JP told Newcastle, a gentleman did not have enough servants 'to put a stop to a mobb of 200 or 300 people'.[26]

Around Lincoln there was a general rising. The mob levied contributions from the gentry, threatening to go to Lincoln races to attack the nobility, and to 'lay . . . in ashes', the Duke of Ancaster told Newcastle, 'a town (which principally belongs to me)'. In the event it contented itself with breaking Lord Vere Bertie's windows. The Dean of Lincoln, profoundly shocked by his flock's contempt for authority and the public welfare, complained that they refused to fight for what only belonged to their landlords and did not concern them. In Nottinghamshire, where fifty lists were destroyed, Sir George Savile and Lord Robert Sutton were manhandled. The cry went up that it was better to be hanged in England than scalped in America. In Kent Lord George Sackville was besieged at Knole till he was relieved by his servants under the command to his ADC, a brush that perhaps affected his nerve two years later at the Battle of Minden. Lord Hardwicke was spared the attentions of the mob, initially because they knew he had opposed the militia and later because the Horse Guards warded them off, but there were disturbances elsewhere in Cambridgeshire, as well as in six other counties.[27]

Hardwicke, who believed several of his tenants to be among the mob, thought that the Cambridgeshire disorders were encouraged by the farmers and that 'most of our own servants are on their side, for they none of them like to be *lotted*'. Certainly middle-class disaffection provided some middle-class leadership. Constables headed a mob in the East Riding, and in Lincolnshire 'our disturbances', wrote the Dean, 'were made by farmers'. The middling sort complained of high parish rates and the failure to lower rents after the previous year's bad harvest.

The militia was thought to be an upperclass plot. Gentlemen, it was said, kept poor people alive only so that they could fight for them. According to George Townshend's brother, Charles, the militia riots were caused by 'the temper of the times', there being an indifference to public affairs, 'the natural effect of habitual disappointment and constant oppression'. Certainly the gentry were little keener to serve than the populace. The war against France was still going badly: so was the economy. Riots against the militia mingled with food riots, enclosure riots and attacks on mills and millers. More than fifty towns in thirty-one different counties were affected, and some of the riots lasted for weeks.[28]

'If the legislature don't speedily use some method to suppress the present spirit of rioting,' a correspondent told the *Gentleman's Magazine*, there would be 'no protection from the plundering mob. The mob must be conquered!!' Doubting the possibility of imprison-

ing or prosecuting '1000 or 500 men in a county at once,' Hardwicke
believed the ministry would have to give way to 'popular dissent and
violence'. He, of course, wanted the Militia Act amended or
repealed.★ The supporters of the act minimised the dangers, ascribing
the troubles to mob incitement by the act's opponents. Certainly false
rumours had been circulated. Pitt complained to Newcastle that 'the
people had been inflamed by art and management', and according to
Horace Walpole, Lord Townshend, who was on bad terms with his
son, the author of the bill, 'began a mob' in Norfolk 'attended by a
parson and a few low people'. Nevertheless Hardwicke's fears turned
out to be exaggerated. A cavalry charge which caused many
casualties was deemed necessary in Northampton, but otherwise
there were few battles outside Yorkshire. Martial oratory was
sufficient to disperse a mob in Cambridgeshire, and though resources
were stretched – about half of the cavalry in England, some 1200 men
and about 4000 infantry were employed – the army put down all the
disturbances without much difficulty. The attempt to set up a
popular force as a partial substitute for the army had resulted in
popular uprisings and the use of that army to suppress them.[30]

Rather than rely solely on military force, the militia's supporters
favoured an amending, explanatory bill as a protection from the
plundering mob. Their bill's fate was bound up with that of another
bill similarly backed by Pitt, which sought to extend the Habeas
Corpus Act. A gentleman who had been wrongly impressed into the
army was refused a writ of *habeas corpus* on the grounds that he was
not being detained on a criminal charge. Convenient though that
legal decision undoubtedly was for a government fighting a war,
Pratt, the Attorney General, sought to amend the law. Pitt told
Newcastle that 'the nation insisted' upon the bill, which easily passed
the Commons, and that if it was defeated 'the spirits of men would
not subside'; he also told Lady Yarmouth that the nation would be
in a flame if the bill was rejected. Alarmed by Pitt's use of his
popularity, Newcastle feared that letting 'the mob loose in this
manner' would lead to them threatening the Lords if it presumed to
differ from the Commons. Yet the Duke was not on this occasion
intimidated by what he called Pitt's 'rhapsody of violence and
virulence', and the Lords threw out the bill, leaving 'the nation' to
wait until 1816 for the reform of *habeas corpus*. But Pitt being, in
Waldegrave's words, 'the sole conductor of the war', and enjoying a
prestige and popularity that no other politician came in sight of,

---

★ Hardwicke was wiser than the wartime coalition in 1943. When it prosecuted 1000 Kent
  miners for striking illegally, three leaders were sent to prison, the remainder being fined
  £1, with the alternative of 14 days in prison. Only nine men paid the fine, and all refused
  to work while their leaders were imprisoned. In consequence, they had to be released,
  the strike was settled in the miners' favour, and the fines were left unpaid.[29]

Newcastle and Hardwicke did not dare defy him over the Militia Bill as well as over *habeas corpus*; they feared 'convulsions' if they did.[31]

In addition to explaining the militia, the new Militia Act made concessions to popular grievances, the most important of which was the payment of allowances to the families of militiamen on active service. These were not, however, sufficient to prevent further violence in Kent, Warwickshire, Buckinghamshire and Huntingdon-shire. Indeed the worst episode of the whole militia saga was yet to come. In 1761 some Durham men marched into Gateshead 'armed with clubs' and told the magistrates that 'they who have lands should hire men to maintain them'. The magistrates obediently promised that 'the gentlemen in the country would find men to fill up the vacancies'. Further successes at Morpeth and Whittingham embolde-ned another mob of 8000 or 9000 miners to march to Hexham in the expectation of meeting similar compliance. Instead they met the Yorkshire Militia. 'No words would pacify them,' wrote the militia commander the next day. 'The Riot Act was read several times, all to no purpose. The mob came to the very point of the bayonets endeavouring to break in upon our men, who bore the greatest insults for over two hours. At last they were commanded to fire. The mob took to their heels, leaving about twenty dead upon the spot, and several wounded.' An officer and two privates in the militia were also killed. Two other contemporary reports put the death toll at twenty-four and forty-four, while eight years later the Secretary at War stated that 'sixty persons were killed'. Even if about twenty-four is accepted as the most probable and authoritative estimate, the dead and wounded at the Hexham affray numbered about a hundred, making it still the bloodiest provincial riot of the century and the only one where the fatal casualties exceeded the largest single day's toll at Tyburn.[32]

The supporters of the militia had seen it as a genuine popular force; its opponents were apprehensive that it would subvert the regime. The successful use of the militia to put down a rising against the Militia Act at least showed the political fears of the act's opponents to be no better founded than the hopes of its supporters.

Even Hexham was a mere dust-up compared with the riots against conscription during the American Civil War. In four days of rioting in New York, twelve hundred rioters were killed, about fifty negroes were lynched or otherwise murdered by the rioters, and three policemen and some fifty soldiers and militia lost their lives.[33]

The anti-draft riots in New York were of a different sort of magnitude and savagery from the English militia riots, yet the two episodes had resemblances as well as contrasts. Just as Englishmen could escape the militia by raising £10 or finding a substitute, so Americans could avoid the draft if they could produce a substitute or

subscribe $300. Class feelings were similar. Gentlemen in England
were said to keep the poor alive only to fight for them; in America
it was said to be 'a rich man's war and a poor man's fight'. (The
unfairness of the operation of the draft during the Vietnam War
aroused similar grievances.) The last thing the Irish poor of New
York wished to fight for was negroes' emancipation in the South;
they would have been readier to fight for their enslavement in the
North. Many of the English gentry encouraged plebeian hostility to
a militia by their own opposition and their unwillingness to serve in
it; the split over the draft among America's rulers was even wider.
A week before the riots, the Democratic Governor of New York had
denounced conscription as unconstitutional, adjuring his listeners to
remember 'that the bloody, treasonable and revolutionary doctrine
of public necessity can be proclaimed by a mob as well as a
government.' And when the Irish Roman Catholic Bishop of New
York was asked to urge his flock to lay aside violence and obey the
law, he declined, postponing his plea for peace until the riots were
over.[34]

The aftermath of the two tumults diverged. Despite the scale of
the New York violence and criminality, only twenty people were
tried, of whom nineteen were convicted and sent to prison for up to
five years. There were no death sentences. The lesser English
violence was met with at least four death sentences and at least two
executions; appropriately, the law was the only sphere in which
English violence exceeded American. The American violence
achieved nothing. The lesser English violence achieved better terms
of service for those called up and greater fairness in the rules for the
ballot, but it only postponed – it did not prevent – the setting up of
a new militia.[35].

By the time the militia's future was finally assured in 1762, Pitt
was out of office. Yet well before the 'battle at Hexham', both the
militia and the regime had won acceptance. The militia was saved by
the invasion scare of 1759, which made it suddenly popular. Amid
scenes of enthusiasm the King even reviewed the Norfolk contingent
at Kensington; he had not, however, undergone a conversion.
Newcastle, too, though alarmed by France's invasion plans, continued to think that the militia would destroy liberty and the
constitution. Lord Leicester told him that the Suffolk militia had
Jacobite tendencies and the Norfolk one was little better. In fact
neither Newcastle nor George II had cause to worry. The great
victories of the war organised by Pitt had ended the Jacobite threat
and made the Hanoverian regime unassailable.[36]

FIFTEEN

Wilkes and Liberty

'That rascal . . .' 'This audacious criminal . . .'

George III on Wilkes

Dear Lady, do not ask me [to play cards]. I am so ignorant that I cannot tell a king from a knave.

John Wilkes

Does not there seem to be a fatality attending the Court whenever they meddle with that man? What instance is there of such a demagogue maintaining a war against a King, Ministries, Courts of Law, a whole Legislature and all Scotland for nine years together? Wilkes in prison is chosen Member of Parliament and then Alderman of London. His colleagues betray him, desert him, expose him, and he becomes Sheriff of London. I believe, if he was to be hanged, he would be made King of England.

Horace Walpole[1]

John Wilkes entered politics in 1754 when he stood for Berwick, backed by the Grenvilles and the Duke of Newcastle. His actions at that election prefigured the rest of his career. 'Gentlemen,' he told the Berwick electors, 'I have come here *uncorrupted* and I promise you I shall ever be *uncorrupted*.' He immediately spent some £3000 buying votes. In his later political life, too, he was often ready to say things which were palpably at variance with what he was doing. But this was abnormal candour, not normal hypocrisy. Most people try to conceal the discrepancies between their words and their behaviour; Wilkes delighted in revealing them.[2]

A number of Berwick voters lived in London; and Wilkes's first original political stroke, it is said, was to ship some of those who supported his opponent not to Berwick but 'by accident' to Norway,[3] which was more effective and probably cheaper than bribery. Wilkes's defeat was the one part of the Berwick election which was notably different from the rest of his political career. Though he never attained office except in the City of London, the causes he supported ultimately prevailed.

Wilkes had no liking for religious dogma. And his marriage to a dull, lazy, plain but rich Buckinghamshire heiress, a sacrifice, as he later said, 'to Plutus, not to Venus', ensured that he did not live a life of conventional respectability, becoming one of the Monks of Medmenham, together with Sir Francis Dashwood and Lord Sandwich among others. This entailed rather more than conventional dissipation, though the diabolism and debauchery of what was called the Hell Fire Club have been exaggerated and, possibly, invented. In any case Wilkes was not only a rake. He was an assiduous magistrate at Aylesbury; he cultivated the friendship of the local magnate, Lord Temple, through whom he became on friendly terms with Temple's brother and brother-in-law, George Grenville and William Pitt, and was appointed a captain in the Buckinghamshire militia.[4]

Benjamin Franklin thought that if the King had had a bad character and Wilkes a good one, George III would have lost his throne. Wilkes himself reckoned that dissipation and profligacy renewed his mind, and he claimed that he wrote his best *North Briton* in bed with Betsy Green. His style was almost as important to his popularity as his skill in choosing issues. His wit, courage, irreverence, geniality and flamboyance caught the popular imagination. A thoroughly domesticated and pious Wilkes, a sort of radical George III, would never have become a popular hero. On the other hand such a puritanical 'Robespierrian' Wilkes might have been a dangerous though unpopular revolutionary. Wilkes, the rake, was anything but that.[5]

George III's private life was impeccable, as both he and Wilkes testified. This stood him in good stead in the political crisis of 1784; unfortunately, among the admirers of the monarch's rectitude was the King himself. He knew the 'uprightness of [his own] intentions' and while others might look on public measures as 'a game', he always acted from 'conviction'. Had that damaging certainty of being right been dented by an occasional indiscretion, George III might have been a better King and his throne even safer. Still, even if doubly wrong, Franklin's *bon mot* vividly illustrated the popularity of Wilkes.[6]

Denunciation of Wilkes's morals entailed much hypocrisy. One MP, Henry Cavendish, wanted to put Wilkes among the cabinet 'to see which of those revered, grave, and pious sages would throw the first stone at him'. Such honesty was rare; in the hail of stones there was little danger of being the first thrower. Of the three Secretaries of State who prosecuted Wilkes in 1763, the first, Halifax, was a rake who had two children by his daughter's governess. The second, Sandwich, a prominent stone thrower, had at least five illegitimate children and made Wilkes seem almost celibate. Only the third, Egremont, was perhaps entitled to toss a pebble or two; he was merely gluttonous, ill-natured, untruthful and avaricious. In the world outside, Wilkes's morals were not held against him, and he was easily the most popular politician of his day. But in the closed political circle, while the morals of Halifax, Sandwich and others were accepted or ignored, those of Wilkes were condemned because he was considered to be a threat to that circle as well as being insufficiently well bred to merit the privilege of profligacy.[7]

Much the same is true of Wilkes's chronic indebtedness. Many other politicians, from Chatham and Fox to Sandwich and Weymouth, were plagued by debts without, unlike Wilkes, incurring censure. As an old acquaintance of Wilkes told Burke, people were inclined to think much worse of his character than it really deserved. He was certainly a libertine but, unlike most eighteenth-century politicians, whom Lecky thought to be 'deeply tainted with treachery and duplicity', he never turned his coat.[8]

Three years after his defeat at Berwick, Wilkes entered Parliament, after what his friend and biographer called 'a good deal of manoeuvre and trick'. A supporter of Pitt, Wilkes did not attempt to make a mark in the Commons. He was outside the charmed circle and his chief ambition was to escape from his creditors by being given a post abroad. His applications in 1761 for the Constantinople embassy and the Governorship of Canada failed, but the dismissal of Pitt and Temple shortly afterwards and the advance of Lord Bute enabled Wilkes to show his talent for opposition: with Temple's money he founded the *North Briton* – the name was inspired by Smollett's heavily ministerial weekly the *Briton* – to defend Pitt against the attacks of Bute's hirelings in the press, to harry the ministry and to return Pitt to office.[9]

Though the dynasty was now secure, the 1760s were both politically and economically unstable. George III, who despised Newcastle's 'old corps' of Whigs and hated Pitt, began with 'independent' or 'country-party' views. He ended Tory proscription and he wanted to cut down corruption and 'to put an end to those unhappy distinctions of party called Whigs and Tories'. Predictably, however, that ambition led not to non-party rule but to the unhappy distinctions of factions. The disintegration of both the old parties which had begun in the 1750s brought not stability but volatility; and the old oligarchy's disarray was intensified by a stirring of popular forces and a widening of politics, by George III's treatment of the politicians, by the vagaries of Pitt and by the general suspicion of Bute and his Scottish retinue.[10]

The economic dislocation that in the eighteenth century always came with peace was particularly severe after the Seven Years War. A depression reigned for most of the 1760s, trade was in decline after 1764 accentuated by the quarrel with the Americans, and harvests were usually bad. The population was increasing, and unemployment and prices rose while wages lagged behind. In consequence food and industrial disturbances were frequent – most of them independent of Wilkes, others affected by him.[11]

The ministry had been unpopular since Pitt's resignation. Later in his reign George III was venerated, but not in his early years. His raising of Lord Bute, his favourite and former tutor, to be Secretary of State and then First Lord of the Treasury was execrated and only just constitutional.[12] To the obloquy commonly attached to favourites Bute had the added disadvantage of being a Scotsman. By the later standards of the reign he was not, perhaps, uniquely unfitted for his post, but he was distrusted by those who knew him and disliked by those who did not. On Lord Mayor's day in 1761, while Pitt and Temple were received with great enthusiasm, Bute was pelted by the crowd who shouted 'Damn all Scotch rogues!' and 'No Bute'. He had hired a body of 'butchers and bruisers' for protection, but these further inflamed the mob and Bute was saved by a party of constables. Beckford, the City leader and a Pittite, had probably organised the demonstration, though he claimed innocence and later said that those who raised mobs raised the devil.[13]

At the opening of Parliament, a year later, Bute fared still worse. On his way to Westminster he was again hissed and pelted; he was saved by the arrival of the Guards. To avoid the same treatment on the way back, he abandoned his coach and took an ordinary hackney chair. But the mob spotted him, smashed the glasses of his chair and put him, it was reported, 'very reasonably in great fear' of being 'demolished'. 'The wicked designs of the mob' drove the King, who had also been insulted, to conclude that this was 'the wickedest age that ever was seen.' Though the ministry failed to trace the organiser of the riots, Henry Fox apparently believed that Newcastle had hired the mob. Bute and the King went further: they believed that there was a plot to assassinate the favourite. That his unpopularity had natural causes and that the crowd needed little or no stimulus from disaffected noblemen did not occur to Bute or his royal master.[14]

The attentions of the crowd and of Wilkes were the main causes of Bute's loss of nerve,

> *When, with a sudden panic struck, he fled,*
> *Sneak'd out of pow'r, and hid his recreant head.*

Despite Walpole's experience, one of the last acts of the Bute ministry was to impose an Excise Tax on cider. Reputedly the Cider Tax was chosen because the Chancellor of the Exchequer, Wilkes's old friend Dashwood, was unable to understand a far more suitable tax on linen, a story that was credible to Wilkes who told his readers that Dashwood had all his life found even his 'tavern bills' puzzling.[15]

The Cider Tax, strongly attacked in the *North Briton*, created uproar and riots in many cider counties as well as in London, and three years later it had to be withdrawn.[16] Bute's successor, Grenville, evidently decided that the opposition of his relations, Pitt and Temple, and their followers must be cut down to size, and the man singled out for punishment was John Wilkes.

Wilkes and general warrants

The political style of both Wilkes and the ministry was well demonstrated in their first confrontation. Previous numbers of the *North Briton* had given much pleasure to many people including Boswell who read it 'with vast relish'. Yet by likening the relationship of Bute and the Princess Dowager – almost certainly unfairly – to that of Mortimer and the mother of Edward III, Wilkes had incurred the particular enmity of the King. *N° 45*, which came out in April 1763, was less scurrilous than many of its predecessors, but it called the King's speech extolling the Treaty of Paris, 'the most abandoned instance of ministerial effrontery ever attempted' and lamented that 'a prince of so many great and amiable qualities' could 'be brought to give the sanction of his sacred name to the most odious measures, and to the most unjustifiable, public declarations, from a throne ever renowned for truth, honour and unsullied virtue'. Though Britain made large gains, she had by deserting Frederick the Great alienated her allies without conciliating her enemies. Hence Wilkes's remark that it was 'certainly the peace of God, for it passeth all understanding'.[17]

In *N° 45* Wilkes claimed that the King's speech had long been recognised to be that 'of the Minister'; criticism of it was therefore permissible. Though that was correct constitutional doctrine, it did not make *N° 45* any more palatable to George III or his ministers. The King was still head of the executive, and *N° 45* implied that if he was not a liar he was the puppet of lying ministers. Probably even more wounding was Wilkes's claim that Bute was still the power behind the administration. The ministry, which had considered prosecuting earlier issues of the paper, decided to prosecute Wilkes for seditious libel and to proceed under a general warrant. Such a warrant ordered the arrest of unnamed persons or the seizure of unspecified papers or both. General warrants were therefore a powerful weapon against the press – they could close a paper by imprisoning all its staff even if no prosecution followed – and the unlimited power of search that they authorised was, potentially at least, a formidable engine of arbitrary government.[18]

Wilkes had been prepared for a battle since the previous November when the writers of another opposition paper, the *Monitor*, had been arrested under a general warrant, and he had concerted plans with Temple. In the first stages he made all the right moves with stylish courage; the government made all the wrong ones with ponderous arrogance. Legality lay with him; the violence came from the ministry who seemed, thought Charles Townshend, to have been brought together by 'some general party jail delivery'. They began by arresting the wrong printer, Leach, who had had nothing to do with *N° 45*, and by the time they tried to arrest Wilkes, they had apprehended forty-eight people. Although the Secretary of State's officers had been ordered to enter his home even at midnight, they did not arrest Wilkes when he came home, explaining later that he was 'in liquor'; nor did they arrest him when he left his house the next morning, thus enabling him to destroy incriminating papers and type at his printers in the City. When the officers finally did approach Wilkes on his return, he asked to see their warrant and said it was illegal. Since it did not name him, he asked why the officer had served it on him rather than on the Lord Chancellor, the Secretaries of State, Lord Bute or his next-door neighbour.[19]

The Secretary of State who had signed the warrant, Lord Halifax, asked Wilkes to visit him. Wilkes refused on the grounds that he did not know him and that 'this application was rather rude and ungentlemanlike'. Eventually the messengers, who now numbered thirteen and had naturally lost the argument, persuaded Wilkes 'by violence' to go to Halifax's house, though he was able to insist on travelling the few yards between the two houses by sedan chair. Halifax and Lord Egremont, the other Secretary of State and Grenville's brother-in-law, fared little better with Wilkes than their messengers.[20]

Meanwhile, through the agency of Temple, a writ of *habeas corpus* had been obtained from Pratt, the Chief Justice in the Court of Common Pleas. The Secretaries of State evaded it on the technicality that it was made out to the man who had arrested Wilkes, whereas he was now in their custody, and Wilkes was sent to the Tower under a warrant which named him. When Wilkes left his house, the messengers were joined by Wood, an Under-Secretary, and the Treasury solicitor P.C. Webb – last heard of advocating branding all transported Jacobites on the face – who broke open every drawer and ransacked his papers. Temple and some MPs who arrived while this was going on were invited to see them sealed up but declined to witness such a 'barbarous' proceeding. A number of Whig nobles, including Temple and the Dukes of Grafton and Bolton, signified their disapproval of the ministry's behaviour by visiting the Tower; they were not allowed to see the prisoner. Colonel Wilkes was dismissed from the Buckinghamshire Militia and Lord Temple from the Lord Lieutenancy of the County.[21]

A new writ of *habeas corpus* having been procured, Wilkes appeared before an overflowing Court of Common Pleas and made a popular, defiant but muddled speech. The court reserved judgement, having noted the messengers' trickery in evading the first writ. *Habeas corpus* was normally obtained from the Court of King's Bench, but the Chief Justice of that court was Lord Mansfield, whose political principles and 'partiality in the seat of justice' had been attacked by Wilkes in earlier numbers of the *North Briton* and who, in addition, was a Scot and a member of the cabinet. Wilkes would therefore have received short shrift in the King's Bench, as indeed he later did, and most unusually application was made instead to the Court of Common Pleas whose Chief Justice, Pratt, was a friend and supporter of Pitt.[22]

At his second appearance before the court three days later Wilkes made a brilliant speech well designed to gain popular support. 'The liberty,' Wilkes told the court, 'of all peers and gentlemen and what touches me more sensibly, that of all the middling and inferior set of people who stand most in need of protection – is in my case this day to be finally decided upon; a question of such importance as to determine at once whether English liberty shall be a reality or a shadow.' That may have been the political issue; it was not the legal issue. Since Wilkes had been sent to the Tower not on a general warrant but on a warrant that named him, the issue of general warrants was not before the court. The case turned solely on the extent of the privileges of MPs, which was no doubt important in its way but scarcely touched the liberty of the middling or the inferior sets of people. Giving the unanimous judgement of the court, Pratt said that since a libel was not a breach of the peace Wilkes was entitled to the privilege of Parliament and must be discharged.[23]

Wilkes was escorted home by many thousands of people 'of a far higher rank than the common Mob', and for the first time the cry 'Wilkes and Liberty' was heard. Before long the words had become almost synonymous. 'This morning,' Boswell recorded on May 6, 'the famous Wilkes was discharged from confinement and followed to his house in Great George Street by an immense mob who saluted him with loud huzzas while he stood bowing from his window.' In July Wilkes could write that the City was firmly his friend and that the County of Surrey, too, was almost unanimous in the cause of liberty. The Duke of Devonshire described him as 'the life and soul of the Opposition'.[24]

The next step was for all forty-nine people who had been arrested on the general warrant to sue the King's messengers and the Secretaries and Under-Secretary of State. The juries could be relied upon, and the printers recovered damages. Yet the law on general warrants was far from clear. Precedent was on the Secretaries' side. But in the action that Wilkes brought against Wood, the Under-Secretary, Pratt ruled that precedent could not make legal what was illegal. General warrants, under which the authorities could 'force persons' houses', break open their desks and seize their papers, were 'totally subversive of the liberty of the subject' and 'contrary to the fundamental principles of the constitution'. The damages awarded by London juries helped the finances of Wilkes and the other forty-eight, some of whom had had nothing whatever to do with N° 45, as well as maintaining public excitement and bringing more humiliation to the government. In a similar case in 1765, *Entick v Carrington*, Pratt, who had become Lord Camden, confirmed the illegality of general warrants and made the famous pronouncement that 'with respect to the argument of state necessity, or a distinction which has been aimed at between state offences and others, the common law does not understand that kind of reasoning . . .'[25]

Wilkes had the ministry on the run; his successes made him over-confident. Against the advice of Temple, who had subsidised the cases against the Government, he made two serious mistakes. Having set up a printing press in his own house, he reprinted N° 45, which made it impossible for him to deny authorship, and he printed a dozen copies of part of an obscene poem called 'An Essay on Woman' together with another paper which included a parody of the *Veni Creator*. These laid him open to charges of blasphemy and obscenity. Probably 'An Essay on Woman' was not by Wilkes but by Potter. The notes, which were by Wilkes, were a burlesque of Bishop Warburton's notes to Pope's 'Essay on Man' and were ascribed to that divine who was a member of the House of Lords. Wilkes soon paid the penalty for disregarding the advice of his friends.[26]

On Parliament's return on November 15 Wilkes was attacked in the Commons for the *North Briton*, and in the Lords for 'An Essay on Woman' and the *Veni Creator*. In both Houses the government bent the rules. In the Commons Wilkes's complaint of a breach of privilege should have been heard before Grenville's message from the King, but the Speaker had been primed and the Government's majority was obedient. The royal message was heard first and, despite the efforts of Pitt who intervened some forty times in defence of Wilkes and the freedom of the press, the House decided that N° 45 was a libel and ordered it to be burned by the common hangman.[27]

The Lords voted an address to the King to order the Attorney General to prosecute Wilkes for publishing 'An Essay on Woman'. Here the ministry was on much weaker ground. Of all people Sandwich, Egremont's successor as Secretary of State, had taken the lead in the plan to use the 'Essay' against Wilkes. Evidence was obtained by bribing Wilkes's foreman; blackmail and forgery were also employed, in which the Reverend John Kidgell, allegedly overfond of choirboys, the author of a pornographic novel, *The Card*, and the chaplain to Lord March, played a prominent part. Later he in his turn tried to blackmail March, a Lord of the Bedchamber and a rake as notorious as Sandwich, over the forgery. If the government was vulnerable over the methods used by these guardians of public morals to obtain their evidence on the 'Essay', a more immediate difficulty was that Wilkes had never published it. Indeed he had taken great care not to.[28]

The government repaired that omission by publishing it themselves. It was read to the Lords by Sandwich, to whom it had originally been dedicated. Dashwood, now Lord Despencer and a courtier, who had cooperated with Sandwich in collecting evidence against their former friend, commented that it was the first time he had heard Satan preaching against sin. Lord Lyttleton asked that the poetry reading should cease, but the peers, postponing their sense of shock till they had enjoyed more of it, shouted 'go on'. Bishop Warburton then 'called his God to witness' that he had not written any of the notes. Nobody on earth had ever thought he had. Pitt asked why the Government did not search Warburton's study for heresy and the general hypocrisy was not lost on the London public. *The Beggar's Opera* was playing at the time, and after Macheath's line 'But that Jemmy Twitcher should peach I own surprises me', the audience cheered, and Sandwich was from then on known as Jemmy Twitcher.[29]

Nevertheless Wilkes was in deep trouble; and he was immediately faced with a more pressing danger. A recent Secretary to the Treasury and a toady of Bute, Samuel Martin, who had been not inaccurately described in the *North Briton* as 'a mean, abject, low-lived and dirty fellow', had in the Commons denounced the unnamed author as a 'cowardly rascal, a villain and a scoundrel',[30] words which were clearly designed to lead to a duel. Wilkes, who had already enhanced his reputation by his coolness and courage in a duel with Talbot, the Lord Steward, was the last man to evade a challenge, and he sent a note in which he 'whispered' in Martin's ear that he was the author. At their consequent meeting in Hyde Park, Martin shot Wilkes in the groin. Seriously wounded, Wilkes told Martin to escape and at first thought the incident was just an ordinary 'matter of honour'. He later changed his mind. The grounds for suspicion were: Martin had waited for eight months after the insult before seeking satisfaction; he had been practising his shooting during those months; the choice of weapons according to the so-called laws of honour lay with Wilkes, yet in his letter of challenge Martin had specified pistols; in 1762-63 Martin received £41,000 from the civil list for 'secret' and 'special services'. All in all, Horace Walpole was probably right to talk of 'a plot against the life of Wilkes'.[31]

Londoners were still firmly on Wilkes's side. When, at the order of both Houses of Parliament, the common hangman half-heartedly attempted to burn N° 45 at the Royal Exchange, he was able to burn only part of it. A crowd of some 500 rescued the rest and pelted the Sheriffs and the City Marshall with mud. The glass of the coach of one Sheriff, Thomas Harley MP, was smashed. The rioters, some of whom cried that the Duke of Cumberland and Lord Temple supported them, were encouraged, the Sheriffs told the House of Lords, 'by gentlemen in coffee-houses and balconies'. Nearly 200 constables were present, but nobody tried to help them: 'the mob were all of the same side' and their cry was 'Wilkes and Liberty'. The City grandees were likewise inactive: the Lord Mayor was in the Mansion House less than 100 yards away 'doing his own business'. No magistrate appeared on the scene, and the Riot Act was not read. The King was exasperated by the outrage, the Speaker complained of the 'very high insult lately offered to the authority of Parliament', and the Commons thanked the Sheriffs for their efforts. The Common Council of the City did not.[32]

The clamour of the people, Grenville told Charles Yorke, could not be appeased by a change of ministers: 'It was no longer a cry for the Duke of Newcastle, Lord Hardwicke or even Mr Pitt, but for Pratt and Wilkes.' By his courageous and irreverent stand against the government, Wilkes articulated the hostility of the middling and inferior sorts to the elite's monopoly of power and place and their resentment against an unfair tax system, all the greater in a time of economic trouble. In addition Wilkes had chosen an issue which was not merely libertarian. Because of their frequent use of excise and customs officers against merchants and shopkeepers, general warrants were widely hated. These ingredients produced Wilkes's extraordinary popularity.[33]

Having evaded the attentions of a Scottish lunatic who attempted to break into his house in order to murder him, and of government spies who watched him, Wilkes slipped over to Paris to see his daughter and to recuperate. Whatever his original intention, he did not return to face the Commons or his trial. Despite sending a medical certificate by two doctors, he was expelled from the House without being heard and before the prosecution against him had come to court. Scarcely more judicial was his trial before Lord Mansfield, whom Wilkes justifiably called his 'personal enemy'. Two months earlier Mansfield had told the King that no man had ever behaved so shamefully as his fellow Chief Justice, Pratt, in denying His Majesty justice; not even Judge Jeffries, the feline courtier added, had acted with 'greater violence' than Pratt. Determined to make restitution, Mansfield allowed a material alteration in the charges against Wilkes the day before the trial. Wilkes's solicitor, who was probably in the pay of the Treasury, acquiesced. Not content with having obtained evidence by bribery, the prosecution embellished it with forged additions. The jury was evidently packed, Mansfield himself objecting to one man who had displeased him in an earlier libel case. The judge's interpretation of the law of libel did not, in any case, leave much for a jury to do, and Wilkes was duly convicted. When he did not appear for sentence, he was outlawed. The foreman who betrayed him had a worse fate. No printer would employ him or 'associate with him', and he killed himself.[34]

In the Commons, on a motion declaring general warrants illegal, Pitt declared that if the House did not pass it they would be the disgrace of the present age and the reproach of posterity. The House did not flinch from being both. Not until 1766, after Rockingham had succeeded Grenville, did the Commons finally condemn general warrants as illegal and, if executed upon a member, a breach of privilege. It was a belated double victory for Wilkes.[35]

Return

In 1765 it was Bute's turn to be accused of organising a mob. The Duke of Bedford, already unpopular in London for his part in negotiating the peace, defeated a bill which, by preventing the import of foreign silks, would have given some protection to the Spitalfields weavers. Two days running some 8000 picketed Westminster, and MPs were jostled. Bedford was hit by a stone, and his coach was wrecked. Bedford House in Bloomsbury Square was then assaulted by a large and well-disciplined mob. More than 300 soldiers defended the house; acting with great restraint they did not fire even with 'the people bursting into the gates' and pelting them with stones. The Riot Act was ignored, but with darkness coming on a cavalry charge aided by infantry eventually dispersed the mob, trampling down hundreds, said Grenville who was present, yet killing none. Bedford told the King that Bute was 'the exciter of this mob, that he was at the bottom of it'. Once again a nobleman was unable to believe that he was the author of his own unpopularity, or that people like weavers could act on their own initiative.[36]

Though Wilkes was well away from the scene, some accused him of organising the riots. The ministry was already weak and divided, and the King wanted a new one, which Mansfield thought would be a victory for the mob. Two of George III's sons lamented to Grenville 'the horrid situation' of the kingdom; Grenville was more concerned that 'with a mob at our doors' there was 'no government within to repress it'. He was, however, able for the moment to impose his demands upon the King and his ministry limped on till July.[37]

Wilkes was not alone in conjuring ineptitude from ministers and Parliament. Indeed Pitt thought every important measure of the Grenville ministry was wrong. Grenville treated the American colonists with all the finesse he had displayed over the *North Briton*, combining a neglect of colonial grievances with a pedantic enforcement of British rights. Not for him the wisdom of Walpole, who after his defeat over the English excise, refused to try to tax America! The culmination of Grenville's policy, the Stamp Act, slipped through Parliament almost as easily as the average capital statute, but produced serious riots in America and a boycott of British goods. Pitt 'rejoiced' at American resistance. The Rockingham ministry described the riots not as inexcusable violence or rebellion but as 'matters of importance', which indeed they were; they had largely nullified the Stamp Act and they caused Rockingham to repeal it. Unfortunately the ministry twinned its repeal with a Declaratory Act which made a bombastic proclamation of British legislative supremacy over the Americans 'in all cases whatsoever'. All the same, Pitt and Camden were nearly alone in opposing it.[38]

The advent of the Rockinghams to office did Wilkes as little good as the succeeding administration of Pitt, now Lord Chatham, and Grafton. Chatham's illness in December 1766 and his virtual withdrawal from business three months later left Grafton as the head of an administration which included, apart from Chatham himself, several members who favoured conciliation of America. Yet because American policy was devised by Charles Townshend, its American record was even more disastrous than its two predecessors'. Townshend's solution of the American problem was the reassertion of British authority by the imposition of customs duties and a remodelling of colonial governments. Like their predecessors the Townshend measures passed easily enough through Parliament but intensified opposition in America, leading later to the Boston 'massacre' of 1770 in which five people were killed in an attack on a customs post. The Wilkes and American issues reacted on each other. The British colonies enjoyed more liberty than any colonies elsewhere. Yet, not surprisingly, many Americans began to see themselves, like Wilkes, as victims of British tyranny, while many Englishmen thought their own liberties were also threatened. Others feared that the English *canaille* might follow the American example and embrace republican ideas.[39]

Discontent had indeed been growing at home. 1766 had seen serious food riots lasting from July to December. Sixty-eight places in twenty counties were affected, and mills, hayricks and warehouses were burned. 1767-68 was one of the coldest winters of the century, and food prices remained high, producing economic distress and industrial unrest in London and elsewhere. The Government, now effectively without Chatham, had little prestige and less popularity. More important, Wilkes's creditors on the continent were losing patience. MPs could not be imprisoned for debt, and Wilkes decided to end his exile. On his return he summed up his position. 'What the devil have I to do with prudence?' he asked his timorous advisors. 'I owe money in France, am an outlaw in England, hated by the King, the Parliament and the bench of bishops. I must raise a dust or starve in a gaol.' He would stand for the City, he told them, with 'general warrants and the good nature of my fellow citizens' as his qualification.[40]

Defeated in the City by 'ministerial influence assisted by private malice', Wilkes announced he would stand for Middlesex in five days time. Temple provided him with the necessary qualification of landed property, and nothing was left to chance.

For all his surface flippancy, Wilkes was a meticulous political organiser. Forty thousand handbills were issued urging Wilkes's supporters to keep the peace and 'to convince the world that liberty is not joined with licentiousness'. Only one of Wilkes's two opponents, Sir William Proctor, appeared on the hustings at Brentford, where he was jeered and hissed. But the peace was kept both there and on the Acton Road. At Hyde Park Corner, however, the mob behaved, according to the *Annual Register*, 'in a very outrageous manner'. They were provoked by Proctor's procession carrying a flag with the inscription 'No Blasphemer'. The City Marshal's son was knocked off his horse, several carriages were badly damaged, and only those sporting *N° 45* were allowed through.[41]

Wilkes's easy victory, in the words of a supporter, caused 'great public rejoicings throughout the metropolis and in other places'. The *Annual Register* was less enthusiastic: 'the mob paraded the whole town from east to west, obliging everybody to illuminate and breaking the windows of such as did not do it immediately.' Lord Bute, the Duke of Newcastle and many others had their windows broken. The Duke of Northumberland saved most of his by providing the mob with ale. A tea broker and a West Indian merchant were among the leaders of the mob.[42]

The King stayed up all night 'full of indignation at the insult', and an alarmed government ordered troops to be held in readiness. Yet disorder mounted. On the second night illumination was again demanded and all doors had 'No 45' written on them, as did all the carriages. There were cries of 'Wilkes and no King', but nobody was hurt and the damage almost entirely consisted of broken glass. Benjamin Franklin thought that the illuminations exceeded 'the greatest occasions of rejoicing' ever seen in London, and during the next five weeks seven additional regiments were brought into the London area.[43]

The Lord Chancelor, Camden, complained that 'a criminal' had in open daylight thrown himself upon the country as a candidate, 'his crime unexpiated . . .' Yet for the government Wilkes's chief crime was to have won, something which the opposition naturally welcomed. 'Whatever men may think of Mr Wilkes's private character,' the Duke of Richmond wrote to Newcastle, 'he has carried his election by being supposed a friend to Liberty, and I think it will show the Administration, that though they may buy Lords and Commons and carry on their measures smoothly in Parliament, yet they are not so much approved of by the Nation.' The exertions of the mob had powerfully reinforced that message.[44]

Shortly after his return to England, Wilkes had written to the King begging clemency. The King took no notice, which was presumably what Wilkes expected; otherwise he would not have sent his letter by a footman. He announced that he would surrender to the Court of King's Bench and on April 20 he did so.[45]

The Massacre of St George's Fields

On Wilkes's first appearance Mansfield, farcically, refused to recognise him because he had surrendered voluntarily. On his second, though he had had to arrange his own arrest, Mansfield refused him bail. A great crowd at Westminster, deeming that denial unduly vindictive, decided to grant it themselves. They removed the horses from Wilkes's coach and drew it to the City instead of to the King's Bench prison, Wilkes protesting that this was all very irregular and that he was the King's prisoner and must obey the law, which amused the crowd and drew their cheers. He eventually escaped from his supporters and took himself off to prison in disguise, receiving congratulations from Temple on 'your wise and humane discouragement of all tumult and disorder'.[46]

The government was less pleased. It had yet again been made to look ridiculous and had only Wilkes himself to thank for his being safely in gaol. Moreover no rioter had been arrested on a day which the Secretary of State called 'a disgrace to civil government'. From then on there was a crowd outside the prison and rioting was endemic. On May 7 Wilkes's outlawry was again argued in court, but in his absence, despite Glynn's protests. Once again Mansfield postponed decision. His delaying tactics may have seemed clever to the government, but they did nothing to assuage the exasperation of the populace. On the next day, by speaking to them from his window, Wilkes managed to disperse the crowd which was demonstrating against his continued imprisonment, but on the ninth the prison lobby was demolished.[47]

Parliament was opened the following day. A large crowd assembled at Westminster shouting 'Wilkes and Liberty', and 'a great body of people' gathered in St George's Fields outside the prison, also thinking that Wilkes would be allowed to attend Parliament. The Southwark magistrates had three weeks earlier received a letter from the Secretary of State, Lord Weymouth, an idle, gambling and, according to Walpole, 'inconsiderable, debauched young man'. The letter urged the JPs not to delay calling for troops, told them they would be blamed for any riots and asserted that 'a military force' could never be 'employed to a more constitutional purpose than in the support of the authority and dignity of the magistracy'.[48]

According to Almon, who was with Wilkes at the time, the soldiers were 'rude and brutal' with the people, who until then had been quiet. William Hickey also thought the soldiers were the aggressors. According to others the crowd had brushed aside a detachment of the Scots Guards. In any case, when summoned by the prison Marshal, two Southwark magistrates found that a verse beginning

> *Venal judges and Minister combine*
> *Wilkes and English liberty to confine . . .*

had been stuck on the prison wall. Instead of ignoring it, the magistrates ordered the verses to be torn down. This provoked disturbances and turned a demonstration into a riot. Justice Gillan, who Hickey thought 'a blockhead', read the Riot Act and was struck on the head by a stone; he was more angry than hurt. The culprit, 'a young man in a red waistcoat', was chased by an officer and three guardsmen, but they bayonetted and shot a man, William Allen, who had not even been in the crowd, let alone involved in the incident. Inevitably the killing made the crowd 'more riotous and violent' during the next two hours.[49]

The Riot Act was read a second time and the soldiers ordered to shoot. Evidently firing at random, they killed between six and eleven people and wounded others. A number of these were returning home from work and had not been rioting. Probably a reluctance to fire on their fellow countrymen, which one soldier was heard to express, led to some of the troops firing over the heads of the rioters and killing passers by. Approving 'the vigour' of the justices, the King wrote to Weymouth that evening: 'bloodshed . . . seems to me the only way of restoring due obedience to the laws.' He was wrong. The 'Massacre' of St George's Fields led not to due obedience but to weeks of almost constant rioting, beginning that evening with attacks on the houses of two of the Southwark magistrates. At one riot outside the House of Lords, to the shout of 'Wilkes and Liberty' was added the cry that 'it was as well to be hanged as starved'.[50]

George III conveyed through a letter from the Secretary at War, Lord Barrington, his high approval of the conduct of the army, though it was, at best, incompetent. Barrington's letter to the Foot Guards had promised that in the event of 'any disagreeable circumstance' they would have 'every defence and protection' from the law and 'this office'. The government kept its word. A coroner's inquest could not be avoided and that found the three soldiers guilty of murder; but a grand jury, consisting *inter alia* of three placemen MPs, P.C. Webb (Wilkes's old enemy), two other placemen, two JPs who had been at the 'Massacre' and an army contractor, threw out the charges against two of the soldiers, including Mclauchlan, who had probably killed Allen. The remaining soldier, Maclane, was tried and acquitted while Mclauchlan was allowed to escape. Before that Lord Mansfield had found no difficulty in giving bail to the accused on the same day that he once more refused it to Wilkes.[51]

Wilkes's supporters indicted Justice Gillan for murder. Despite being defended by the Attorney General, the Solicitor General, the Secretary to the Treasury and a future Speaker of the Commons, and despite being treated with marked favour by the bench, Gillan was not confident of the outcome. The reversal of roles was too much for him, and he fainted twice before being acquitted. The ordinary criminal classes were made of sterner stuff.[52]

Wilkes's popularity was now prodigious. The middling sort were impressed by his having evaded the mob and delivered himself to gaol; the inferior sort were delighted by his defiance of the ministry and enraged by the 'Massacre'. He was the champion of the discontented. The symbol of resistance to arbitrary government, he embodied the virtues of liberty and independence. 'Since the fall of Lord Chatham,' Burke wrote, there had been no hero of the Mob but Wilkes.[53]

In November 1767 the King's speech had stressed the difficulties of the 'poorer sort of my people'. In the new year the price of bread rose sharply, and industrial troubles broke out all over the country. In London there were strikes, riots and demonstrations by watermen, tailors, coopers, glass grinders, hatters, sawyers, sailors, weavers and coalheavers. These disturbances were at first not connected with Wilkes; indeed, caused by inflation, low wages and unemployment, they had begun in January while he was still abroad. But the political and industrial troubles inevitably fertilised each other – the weavers and the coalheavers were prominent supporters of Wilkes – and, combined, they for some weeks reduced London to a state of confusion bordering upon anarchy. At the time Mansfield believed that unless vigorous action was taken there would be a revolution in ten days. And, later, Grafton believed that the Wilkite agitation encouraged 'a resistance to all legal authority'. The ministry, like the mob, personified the issue: Barrington thought Wilkes had scattered a firebrand throughout the kingdom, and the King thought the expulsion of Wilkes from Parliament 'very essential'. Food riots at Hastings and elsewhere did nothing to raise confidence.[54]

Meanwhile the legal farce had one more scene. On June 8 Wilkes appeared again at Westminster Hall before Mansfield who, jostled on his way to court, had been left in no doubt of the crowd's view of the case. In a masterly disquisition on the law of outlawry, the Lord Chief Justice dismissed one by one all the allegations of Wilkes's counsel. Having complained of the shameful tumults and the 'various terrors' that had been 'hung out', he reassured the court that threats of 'personal violence' would have no influence. He then stunned his audience by announcing, despite all he had previously said, that Wilkes's outlawry must be reversed. The most probable explanation of this astonishing performance is that Mansfield wrote the first part of his judgment while he intended to uphold Wilkes's outlawry and, when he changed his mind, he did not want to disturb his superb legal exposition.[55]

Subsequent events showed that Mansfield had not altered course because he or the ministry favoured leniency. Probably the cause was fear of the crowd and the anonymous threats he had received; hence his otherwise redundant assertions that he would do his duty 'unawed' and that the judges had nothing to do with the prosecution of Wilkes. Mansfield was cold but not courageous; even the King he courted found him timid and 'but half a man'.[56]

The verdict saved Wilkes from a future without legal rights and a long period of imprisonment. There were the usual celebrations all over England. But the next scene was not farce. Ten days later, the court did not dare to sentence Wilkes to the pillory, which would have brought triumph for him and humiliation for the government, but imposed a fine of £1000 and imprisonment for twenty-two months for the republication of N° 45 and the alleged publication of 'An Essay on Woman'. This decision was scarcely defensible. After all, Wilkes had already suffered, and his outlawry had been judged illegal. More important, general warrants, too, had been declared illegal, and he had gained damages for the government's illegal seizure of his papers; the general contention of N° 45 was correct, even if violently stated, and he had not in fact published 'An Essay on Woman'. It is not the job of courts to apologise for other people's errors or their own, but a nominal sentence would have been appropriate. Wilkes's immediate reply was to announce that he was recommencing his action against 'the first and great criminal', Lord Halifax, over his behaviour in 1763.[57]

Expulsion and re-election

His supporters immediately paid the fine, and prison was from Wilkes's own point of view probably the best place for him. He was sent money and a mass of gifts by, among others, Americans who identified his cause with theirs, as indeed did many Englishmen. While Wilkes was able to see anybody he wanted and was free to write what he liked, incarceration placed a useful constraint on his activities and protected him from accusations of fomenting riot. And had it not been for George III and Wilkes himself, imprisonment would have been the end of the Wilkes affair. The King was still anxious to expel Wilkes from the Commons; his premier, Grafton, the Lord Chancellor, Camden, and one Secretary of State, Shelburne, were not. Camden warned that they should consider what would happen if Wilkes were re-elected; hence he preferred pardon to punishment. Grafton promised Wilkes that if he kept quiet he could keep his seat. Wilkes, for whom silence held small advantage, responded with a petition to the Commons and an address to the freeholders of Middlesex. The ministry felt impelled to act.[58]

Wilkes also published the unfortunate letter Weymouth had sent the Surrey magistrates before the riot in St George's Fields, adding the preface that since the letter had been written three weeks before 'the fatal 10th of May', 'the horrid massacre' had been planned well in advance and the 'hellish project had been brooked over by some infernal spirits without one moment's remorse'. As usual Wilkes was extreme in his language, yet, by abandoning the caution in the use of force that eighteenth-century governments customarily enjoined on JPs and, instead, encouraging them to use it, Weymouth had given him cause. Wilkes included some additional insults to Lord Barrington for his letter thanking the troops. The Lords resolved that Wilkes's communication was 'an insolent, scandalous, and seditious libel'.[59]

In the same week, the death of Wilkes's fellow member caused another election in Middlesex. Serjeant Glynn, who had been Wilkes's counsel in all his cases, was the Wilkite candidate, and Sir William Beauchamp Proctor, who had been beaten by Wilkes earlier in the year, was the candidate of both the court and the aristocratic opposition. As a riposte to the slogan 'Wilkes and Liberty', the ingenious Sir William devised the cry of 'Liberty and Proctor'.*[60]

Proctor tried also to compete with the Wilkites in patronising Brentford public houses and in mustering a crowd. He spent over

---

* In *Sybil*, the hero's response to the placards saying 'vote for McDruggy and our young Queen' was 'vote for our Young Queen and Egremont' which, added Disraeli, 'was at least more modest and turned out more popular'.[61] In Proctor's case it did not.

£1000 on providing drink and for two guineas a day he hired an Irish bodyguard which was to act, he claimed, as 'assistants to the civil magistrates'. That may have been his intention, but according to Walpole his 'mob . . . by folly or mismanagement proved the sole aggressors'. After Proctor's men had cleared the hustings because Glynn was well ahead, Glynn asked Sir William to control his mob. Proctor, said Glynn, 'made me no answer and left me'. In the ensuing violence, Clarke, a Wilkite lawyer, and Hopkins, a constable, were killed; many others were hurt. Two of Proctor's 'assistants to the civil magistrates' were found guilty of murder, but the civil magistrates then came to their assistance, and they were eventually freed.[62]

At the turn of the year Wilkes was overwhelmingly elected Alderman of Farringdon Without, polling 1300 out of 1500 votes; even the constables in the City were devoted to him. Wilkes's petition was heard at the end of January, and he was accompanied from prison to Parliament by a large concourse. Westminster was so crowded that the lobby had to be cleared, but there was no disorder. Horace Walpole thought the contest between Wilkes and the government was 'between faction and corruption' and that 'of two such common whores the richest will carry it'. Certainly the outcome was never in doubt, yet the ministry took no chances. As usual it rigged the rules. Contrary to the opinion of Dunning, the Solicitor General, and the Lord Chancellor, Wilkes was prevented from putting his case except on two points. And in order to maximise its vote the government included four counts in the resolution of expulsion: the publication of *N° 45,* the publication of 'An Essay on Woman', his imprisonment and the preface to Lord Weymouth's letter. Burke wondered how these four alleged offences merited expulsion. Like Burke, Wilkes's old antagonist, George Grenville, attacked the obvious injustice of accumulating the four articles in one resolution and, warning that Wilkes's popular favour 'extended to the distant parts of the kingdom', he advised the House to look forward: Wilkes would certainly be elected, and what then? Undeterred, the Commons voted for expulsion by 219 to 137. The Guards had to be summoned to quell riots in Drury Lane.[63]

Announcing his decision to stand again, Wilkes told his constituents that his courage was not 'appalled', and he carried Grenville's warning one stage further. 'If ministers,' he wrote, 'can once usurp the power of declaring who *shall not* be your representative, the next step is very easy, and will follow speedily. It is that of telling you whom you *shall* send to Parliament, and then the boasted constitution of England will be entirely torn up by the roots.' Nobody was silly enough to stand against Wilkes and he was returned unopposed. That night he was serenaded 'by gentlemen on horseback' and the gaol was illuminated. The House of Commons promptly expelled him again and declared him 'incapable' of being elected to Parliament.[64]

Wilkes's adherents formed the Society of Supporters of the Bill of Rights, the first reforming body set up outside Parliament to inform and influence the electorate and to seek electoral control of Parliament. The Society evolved radical programmes for legal and parliamentary reform, though despite its name its primary purpose, at least in Wilkes's eyes, was to pay Wilkes's debts and to get him into Parliament. Those who believed that the priority should be reversed soon left the Society.

Wilkes was being selfish of course, yet his instinct was sound: the popularity of the Middlesex election dispute and of reform stemmed from his personification of the issues, not from their own intrinsic attractions. On March 16 Wilkes was elected for the third time, his opponent being unable in the face of a large and hostile crowd at Brentford to find anybody brave enough to nominate him, though there was 'not the least riot'.[65]

So far the government and the Commons had merely made themselves ridiculous and the mob had treated them with some tolerance, enjoying Wilkes's easy victories. The announcement that the government had found a serious candidate raised the temperature. When some merchants decided to deliver a fawning address against sedition to the King, the Wilkites organised a counterdemonstration. The result, not surprisingly, was an outright victory for the popular side. The gates of Temple Bar were shut against the merchants, and the bearer of the address lost it when he was forced to leave his coach. By the time it was recovered, he was in no condition to present it. Nearly all the merchants turned back; the others arrived at St James's covered in dirt. Some noblemen were dragged from their coaches, two of which were broken. A Wilkite hearse representing the deaths of Allen and Clarke was drawn down Pall Mall past the Palace. When the Horse Guards appeared, 'the rabble, whose spirit of mischief is only equalled by their timidity immediately retired and left a large vacancy before the Palace'. Retirement before a cavalry charge when unarmed is an enlarged definition of timidity; others thought the mob 'most audacious' and 'determined'. Indeed the crowd, having ignored the reading of the Riot Act, had stood its ground when faced by the Foot Guards and dared them to fire. As well as crying 'Wilkes and Liberty', 'many of the mob', reported the same observer, 'cried Wilkes and no King, which is shocking to think on'. Seventeen rioters were arrested, but only five were sent for trial, and all were discharged by what the King termed 'the factious and partial conduct of the grand jury' which, if not checked, would lead to anarchy.[66]

The government's new champion was no more suitable for Middlesex than Sandwich had been for the 'Essay'. The one qualification possessed by Colonel Luttrell, who had been induced to give up the borough (Bossiney in Cornwall) that had been bought for him, was his hostility to Wilkes. The magistrates made careful preparations to keep order; so did the Wilkites. On polling day Wilkes's forces paraded in strength with bands, cavalcades and processions of coaches. Publicans between Knightsbridge and Brentford sold their beer cheaply in honour of Mr Wilkes. Most of Luttrell's cavalcade failed to attend and most of those who did appear failed to get beyond Hyde Park Corner, where they were pelted. Luttrell himself owed his safety at Brentford to Wilkes's supporters. From then on the proceedings were peaceful, and Wilkes gained almost four times as many votes as Luttrell. Church bells were rung, and there were illuminations all over the city, but no rioting.[67]

George III, seldom one to learn from experience, thought that in resolving by 197 to 143 that Henry Luttrell 'ought to have been returned a Member for Middlesex and not John Wilkes Esq' the Commons 'would greatly tend to destroy that outrageous licentiousness that has been so successfully raised by wicked and disappointed men'. In fact it inflamed the 'licentiousness'. Protest meetings were immediately held. With the help of the Society for the Protection of the Bill of Rights and of the Rockingham Whigs, eighteen counties petitioned the King. Five days after the Commons vote, Wilkes had to leave prison to see a judge in chambers and on his way back the crowd once again removed his horses to pull his coach themselves and once again he had to escape from them in order to return to gaol. On the next day the King got a very different reception. On his way back to St James's from the House of Lords crowds shouted 'Wilkes for ever, not Luttrell'.[68]

By emphasising the gulf between constitution rhetoric and reality, the Commons' decision caused an upsurge of radicalism that had not been seen that century. The veil that draped the anomalies of the electoral system was torn down by the government itself. Its self-exposure was in fact unnecessary. As Dowdeswell suggested, there was an alternative to declaring the loser the winner: to leave Middlesex represented by only one MP. Such a solution would have been unpopular but still greatly preferable to what the Commons did; it would also have been legal.[69]

Summing up the position in January 1770, the Lord Chancellor, Camden, denounced the ministry's 'violent and tyrannical conduct' which had spread 'a spirit of discontent . . . into every corner of the kingdom'. If nothing was done, he wondered whether despair would not drive the people to becoming their own 'averagers' and to redressing their grievances themselves. Camden was not alone in his worries. Such a sober and respected MP as Sir George Savile talked of Hampden and ship money. Wesley thought the state was in

danger. The King himself thought his crown almost depended upon
the expulsion of Wilkes. Grafton later described the internal state of
the country at the time as 'really alarming': the struggle over the
Middlesex election had kept alive the spirit of riot which threatened
to bring all government and lawful authority into disrespect. Even
David Hume, of all people, became agitated about English 'licentiousness or . . . frenzy of liberty' and thought the crisis should be
resolved by a showdown 'between the Mob and the Constitution'.
The King's aunt, Princess Amelia, was resigned to going to Holland
rather than live in a country ruled by Wilkes.

Yet all the fears were groundless. The state was strong. Wilkes had
no desire to rule, and neither he nor his followers sought a violent
overthrow of lawful authority. Still less revolutionary was the
aristocratic opposition who supported him on the rights of electors.
Wilkes's release from prison was celebrated throughout England –
church bells rang all day in Somerset – and in America, and his first
visit to the City drew the biggest crowd since the coronation. Yet he
did nothing when he was free. Without leadership the agitation
subsided, and the aristocratic opposition fell apart. Even the Wilkites
split.[70]

George III at last achieved a stable administration by sending Lord
North to the Treasury. Junius defied the gravest of the King's
chaplains to recite without laughing the catalogue of the ministry –
North, Barrington, Weymouth, Gower, Ellis, Onslow, Rigby,
Dyson and Sandwich – and told George III that their very names
were 'a satire upon all government'. Instead of repealing all the
Townshend duties, that satire retained the Tea Duty as a continuing
assertion of British authority in America, and the country continued
its slow drift to disaster.[71]

The printers' cases

Wilkes had begun the first number of the *North Briton* with an
eloquent if unhistorical hymn to the liberty of the press: 'the firmest
bulwark of the liberties of this country . . . this most sacred weapon,
left for the defence of truth and liberty.' The English press was indeed
uniquely free from censorship in advance, yet the bulwark was, as
usual, anything but firm. So far from defending truth and liberty,
most of the journalists were in the pay of the government or the
opposition. And the government had a number of profane weapons
against the press, most notably the law of sedition. By using *ex officio*
informations the Attorney General could initiate prosecutions
without the assent of a grand jury, and Lord Mansfield had
reaffirmed the traditional but controversial practice that it was for the

judge, not the jury, to decide whether or not a publication was a libel. As a result the conviction of hostile journalists was common-place. In answer to a question from Mme de Pompadour as to how far the liberty of the press extended in England, Wilkes was much more realistic than he had been in print. 'That is what I am trying to find out,' he answered. As we have seen, he soon did.[72]

The Commons had often declared the reporting of its debates to be a breach of privilege. In 1760 and 1761 printers had been summoned to the bar of the House, effectively silencing the newspapers till 1768. Yet the press had been growing fast in numbers, circulation and importance, and in the wake of the Middlesex election its reporting of Parliament became more daring. Irritated by the growing number of generally critical reports, and probably resenting the advent of competition from a popular press and public opinion, the Commons decided to teach the press a lesson. In February 1771, on the complaint of Colonel Onslow who had been called a 'paltry, insignificant insect' for raising the matter, the Commons ordered the arrest of two and, later, six more printers; when that proved unproductive, it asked the King to issue a royal proclamation 'for apprehending' them. Publication of parliamentary reports was an essential preliminary to making a connection between MPs and the public, as Wyndham the Tory leader had understood during the years of the Tories' exclusion. So here was another crucial issue between oligarchy anxious to keep government to itself and the popular party anxious to make Parliament accessible to the voters and thereby achieve representative government.[73]

Alderman Wilkes and John Almon, printer of the *London Evening Post*, had ready an audacious and well-contrived plan of action. They sought to defend the press and defeat the pretensions of the Commons by using the City of London's claim to an exclusive jurisdiction within its boundaries. The Commons, by persuading the King to issue a proclamation whose legality was doubtful, had given Wilkes his opportunity. One of the wanted printers, Wheble, got himself arrested by his chief compositor, Carpenter, and appeared before Wilkes at the Guildhall. Wilkes wrote to Halifax, who was again Secretary of State, that as he had found no legal cause of complaint against Wheble, he had thought it his duty to adjudge that Wheble 'had been apprehended in the city illegally in direct violation of the rights of an Englishman and . . . to discharge him'. Instead of Wheble being arrested, Carpenter was charged with assault. The same day a Commons messenger tried to arrest Miller, Almon's printer, whereupon Miller charged the messenger with assault and had him arrested by a constable who had been primed. Brass Crosby, the Lord Mayor, Wilkes and Alderman Richard Oliver, sitting in the Lord Mayor's bedchamber because of his gout, discharged Miller and granted the messenger bail on the charge of assault. The Society of Supporters of the Bill of Rights voted each of the defiant printers £100 for defending the rights of Englishmen.[74]

The Commons were incensed and George III, who had cautioned North against acting against the printers while thinking 'this strange and lawless method' of reporting debates should be ended, now told him that the authority of the House would be annihilated if the Lord Mayor and Alderman Oliver were not instantly committed to the Tower, adding rather lamely that Wilkes was 'below the notice of the House'. Nevertheless the Commons, even less wise than the King, ordered the attendance of Wilkes as well as the others. Wilkes made it clear that he would only attend 'in his place', that is to say as member for Middlesex. The House, making a fool of itself as it nearly always does when dealing with the press, tore out from the minute book of the Lord Mayor's court the page relating to the case of the Commons messengers, 'the act,' said Chatham, 'of a mob, not a Parliament'. Most of the opposition, the *Annual Register* recorded, had left the House, 'declaring that they would not be witnesses to such an unprecedented act of violence . . .' The House had embarked, said an MP, on 'another contest with the people . . . more dangerous than the former one'.[75]

On their successive visits to the Commons, Crosby and Oliver were escorted by 'amazingly great' crowds. On March 25 the House voted by 170 to 38 to send Oliver to the Tower, Crosby having earlier been allowed home because of his gout. On the twenty-seventh the Lord Mayor was drawn to Westminster by his supporters not his horses; the crowd was 'prodigious' and most of it 'appeared to be respectable tradesmen'. A number of MPs were 'insulted in the grossest manner, and some in very high office narrowly escaped with their lives'. Charles Fox, who in the earlier debate had disparaged 'the voice of the people', and his brother, 'the two cubs', were pelted and bruised and their carriage damaged. North's coach was smashed, and he himself who had been mistaken for Fox was hurt as well as frightened, having to be rescued by Meredith, an opponent. It took five hours and the efforts of the most popular MPs to disperse the crowd outside the House.[76]

Things were little better inside. 'Don't let us be like a mob here,' Burke urged, but his words had no effect. The Commons 'mob' refused to allow Crosby to be represented by counsel and most of the opposition accordingly quitted the House. Crosby said that his case had been prejudiced and would add nothing more. He was sent to join Oliver in the Tower. The ministry, mindful of the King's rumoured instruction to have 'nothing more to do with that devil Wilkes', did not dare touch him. They were repeatedly asked whether they considered him above or below the law. Eventually

Wilkes was ordered to attend on April 8. Knowing that he would not come and knowing that it could not punish him, the House avoided the difficulty by adjourning until the ninth. The printers were not prosecuted, and debates went on being reported though the government was still able to prevent reports by 'spying strangers' and clearing the gallery, which North frequently did. The Commons had been humiliated; and Wilkes, the City, the crowd and the printers had won.[77]

Sheriff and Lord Mayor

Wilkes was elected Sheriff of the City in July of that year, despite the court's strenuous efforts to defeat him, efforts which came to light when a letter from North's secretary, Robinson, was sent to the wrong Mr Smith, a Wilkite, who published it. Wilkes proved a good Sheriff. He and his colleague, Bull, ordered the production of an accurate list of electors, refused to execute warrants of impressment, issued regulations for the better treatment of debtors by bailiffs, visited the gaols regularly, continued their predecessors' practice of keeping the army away from the hanging processions to Tyburn, and forbade the practice of bringing prisoners into court in irons. On leaving office Wilkes and Bull suggested the ending of capital punishment for many 'inferior crimes where mercy too seldom heals the rigour of justice' and claimed that 'it was our care, while we paid a due obedience to the laws now in force, to alleviate their harshness by lenity and tenderness to every unhappy object'. They received a unanimous vote of thanks from the Livery.[78]

In October 1772 Wilkes stood as candidate for Lord Mayor of London. Although he won the most votes, the Court of Aldermen broke its usual custom and returned the second candidate, James Townsend. On Lord Mayor's day the crowd tried to turn back Townsend's carriage 'crying that Wilkes must go first', which would have been difficult as he had decided to keep away. In the evening a crowd of about 3000 appeared at the Guildhall. Ladies arriving for the party were asked for money 'to drink Mr Wilkes's health'. One gentleman had a part of his hair cut off and others were molested, but nobody seems to have been badly hurt. The crowd attacked the iron gates, and the Honourable Artillery Company had to be called in. Townsend accused Wilkes of hiring the mobs. Wilkes cited his absence in defence and maintained that the riot could have easily been suppressed but for the incompetence of the Sheriff.[79]

The next year saw the only mob led by Wilkes in person. When the Speaker sent a notice to all sheriffs to summon their members to attend, the City's sheriffs summoned Wilkes, not Luttrell, and

Wilkes led his supporters to Westminster. The House refused to hear him but Wilkes kept control and confined the crowd's activities to marching up and down. There was no violence.[80]

At the third attempt Wilkes duly became Lord Mayor. The cheating of the previous two years made the popular enthusiasm all the greater. Church bells were rung, and once again the crowd drew Wilkes's coach from the Guildhall to the Mansion House. The competition for the honour of drawing him was so intense that one of his admirers was killed and another was badly hurt. That night, in the last Wilkite riot, Alderman Harley had his windows broken. At the Lord Mayor's Show the crowds were bigger and more enthusiastic than ever before, but the Lord Mayor enjoined 'decorum', and there was no trouble. At the height of his popularity, Wilkes was a successful and diligent Lord Mayor.[81]

Wilkes in Parliament

Parliament had been dissolved at the end of September, and though the court tried hard even advertising for 'Two gentlemen of Fortune and Honour', nobody could be found to oppose Wilkes and Glynn on the hustings. The new Parliament contained about a dozen Wilkites whom Wilkes called his twelve apostles. Yet he made little more mark on the Parliament of 1774 than he had on the last Parliament of George II, when he had had no apostles and had himself been an obscure follower of Pitt.[82]

Wilkes's opinions ruled out his being popular or effective in Parliament. He was years ahead of his time, which is something the House of Commons never is. It always the guardian of the conventional wisdom or folly of the age; and while George III was the embodiment of that 'wisdom', Wilkes was not in sight of it. Yet even if his political views had been more in tune with his duller and more ambitious fellow politicians', he probably would have had little influence. Because of his geniality and wit, it was very difficult to dislike Wilkes, as Dr Johnson eventually discovered. The trouble was that he did not much like his colleagues, and not surprisingly, he was not prepared to offer the House the flattery it required, calling it 'the most corrupt assembly in Europe'. Once, in a powerful speech urging peace with America, he referred to its inmates as 'a set of idle, listless, loitering, lounging, ill-informed gentlemen at Westminster'.[83]

In his first interventions in the House, Wilkes made clear that ingratiation with either the King or the ministerial majority was far from his mind. The anniversary of the execution of Charles I should be celebrated as a festival, he suggested, not kept as a fast; and fearing that the present Parliament would be as 'profligate' as the last, he talked of parliamentary prostitution. His Majesty remained a favourite target throughout the parliament.[84]

Wilkes continued his opposition to the government's American policy and, after Burke and Chatham, he was the most eloquent advocate of reconciliation with the colonists, while judging the course of events better than them. In February 1775, speaking against an address to the King declaring Massachusetts in rebellion, he said that a successful resistance was a revolution not a rebellion, and wondered 'whether in a few years the independent Americans may not celebrate the glorious era of the revolution of 1775 as we do that of 1688'. The war, when it came, he dubbed 'an unjust felonious war' which would be 'fatal and ruinous to the country', and he was the first to recognise that the colonies were now 'the free independent states of America'. After Saratoga he told the Commons that the troops should be recalled and that we should 'enter into a federal union' with the colonists and sign a commercial treaty. Like Burke, he found the government's use of Red Indians repugnant, and in an allusion to Lord Barrington's letter after St George's Fields wondered whether that gentleman had yet thanked the Indian tribes in the King's name for 'scalping and tomahawking his American subjects'.[85]

In all this, naturally, Wilkes was not on the popular side. Violence against other countries makes the blood, at least of non-combatants, run faster. In addition, harvests were good and the American war had brought increased prosperity. At that time, said Gibbon, the Archangel Gabriel would not have been heard on America, and Wilkes was no archangel. Patriotism and economics made the war generally popular until it was seen to be going irretrievably wrong.[86]

Wilkes, of course, favoured parliamentary reform. In February 1776 he proposed 'a more equal representation of the People in Parliament'. Cornwall had as many members as Scotland, and as few as 5723 people could elect an effective majority of MPs. The House should strive so far as possible 'to make the theory and practice of the Constitution coincide' and therefore restore to the people 'their original share in the legislature'. The rotten boroughs should be amputated, laying 'the axe to the root of corruption and treasure influence, as well as aristocratical tyranny'. Since 'the meanest mechanic, the poorest peasant and day-labourer' had important rights respecting his liberty, his property and the price of his labour, some share in the power of making the laws which they were expected to obey should be reserved for them.[87]

Wilkes's remarkable speech was too brilliant and witty for its subject and for its audience, if Wilkes hoped it to have any effect. But probably he did not, or he would not have included a favourable reference to Oliver Cromwell. In reply Lord North was 'very jocular', supposing that Wilkes was not serious. Owners of the rotten boroughs would not be disposed to sacrifice 'so beneficial a species of property' and amputation was always dangerous. North's jocularity and his views on seats as property rather than as means of representation were vastly more in accordance with the sentiments of the House than what a newspaper called Wilkes's 'very ingenious and public-spirited speech'. His motion was rejected without a division.[88]

Wilkes also favoured 'unlimited' religious toleration, supporting measures for the relief of dissenting ministers and teachers, and welcoming the 'just relief' granted to Roman Catholics in 1778. He would not even persecute an atheist.*[89] Told by Dundas, the Lord Advocate, that he had abandoned his promise to extend the Catholic Relief Act to Scotland because of the virulent opposition to it there, Wilkes warned the government a year before the Gordon Riots that 'an example of a fatal nature' had been given to the London mob. Wilkes's political views precluded conventional political success in Parliament, and he was not prepared to change them either to gain favour with the court or win support from the crowd.[91]

The demagogue and the constitution

The court, the opposition aristocrats and the Wilkites all had different ideas of the constitution, and all thought they had legitimacy on their side. George III never doubted the rightness of the government's actions and lamented the unique 'licentiousness' of the times; the Rockingham Whigs thought the crown with its vast patronage and secret cabals threatened the constitution and stirred up disaffection; the Wilkites believed that the government should govern with the consent of the people, not by force, and lamented the unique 'corruption' of the times.[92]

Wilkes was disliked by George III and the political elite because, by extending opposition from the cosy arena of Westminster to the world outside, he threatened their monopoly of the political system. What a time we live in, lamented the King, 'when a parcel of low shopkeepers pretend to direct the whole legislature'. For the opposition Whigs, as much as for George III and the Court politicians, differ as they might over the influence of the Crown, that monopoly was part of the order of things and was not to be disturbed: the British constitution had been settled by the Revolution of 1688

---

* Wilkes was irreverent, saying of Dr Johnson that 'liberty is as ridiculous in his mouth as religion in mine'. He also told Boswell that he would 'no more value being raised in the same body than being raised in the same coat, waistcoat and breeches'. On the other hand he attended church regularly. He seems to have been a deist.[90]

and had attained perfection. As Wilkes put it in 1767, 'the Whigs in power turn Tories, tho' alas the Tories do not turn Whigs!' Three years later Burke partly agreed: 'historical patriotism' and being 'a Whig on the business of a hundred years ago,' he maintained, was 'consistent with every advantage of present servility.' Some action was needed, he thought, because George III was breaking the constitution; yet there was nothing wrong with the constitution or the country that would not be mended by the return of the Rockinghams to office.[93]

The court's and the High Whig view of the constitution was best expressed by the young Charles Fox, long before he became a 'man of the people'. Asking who were the best judges of the public welfare, the people at large or the Commons, Fox pronounced unhesitatingly in favour of 'this House'. He paid 'no regard whatever to the voice of the people'. It was 'their business . . . to choose us . . .' If MPs were 'drawn from the direct line of justice, by the threats of a mob, the minority within doors need only assault [MPs] by their myrmidons without, to gain their ends upon every occasion. Blows will then carry what their arguments can not effect, and the people will be their own agents, though they elect us to represent them in parliament'. The inevitable result would be 'universal anarchy'. Fox therefore stood up 'for the constitution, not the people', and for 'the independency of parliament' despite the 'loudest huzza of an inconsiderate multitude'.[94]

For much of the country the constitution worked well; Fox rightly pointed to the size of the Empire, the magnificence of the metropolis, 'the immensity of our commerce and the opulence of our people'. The British constitution was the envy of other countries, and Britain was the most powerful state in Europe. Yet to take pride in British prosperity and liberty and to contrast them with absolute monarchy, Popery and wooden shoes was one thing; to claim that the system as it was in the 1760s and 1770s was the perfect and glorious embodiment of the principles of 1688 was quite another.[95]

Parliament had replaced the people and the people had become the mob. The Commons prided itself upon taking an independent view. MPs saw themselves as 'virtually the nation'. The real nation was subordinate and its opinions had little effect, even at elections. The wider public – the 'middling' and 'the inferior' sets – did not know what MPs did or said because Parliament proscribed reports of parliamentary debates. If they sought to influence MPs by petitioning, their adherence to a petition was largely discounted on the grounds that only the signatures of the well-to-do carried weight. To the parliamentary placemen, the majority of the Middlesex freeholders were 'no better than an ignorant multitude' whose opinions were worthless. At one point North even threatened that petitions to the King to dissolve Parliament were a breach of privilege. Newspapers and pamphlets attacking the ministry were prosecuted for libel, and the judges, not the jury, decided the issue. 'A pretty system,' Chatham summed up, 'jurors who may not judge, electors who may not elect, and suffering subjects who ought not to petition.'[96]

The elite and the court concurred that the primary duty of the governed was to obey with a good grace. Typically the King's speech of 1763 referred to 'that spirit of concord and that obedience to law which is essential to good order'. The Wilkite radicals saw both the 'multitude' and its duties in a very different light. A nation as sensible as the English, Wilkes replied in *N° 45*, would 'see that a spirit of concord, when they are oppressed, means a tame submission to injury . . . Every legal attempt of a contrary tendency to the spirit of concord,' Wilkes went on, would be 'deemed a justifiable resistance, warranted by the spirit of the English constitution.'[97] Was Wilkes's own resistance so warranted? The answer depends on a judgement of his methods, the amount of violence he used, the conduct of his opponents and the nature of the issues.

Wilkes has received the censure of both schools of historians, being disliked by Whigs for his morals and by Tories for his politics. As both schools have pointed out, he was unquestionably a demagogue – indeed in claiming *Provoco ad populum* as his motto he virtually called himself one. Yet his demagoguery was distinctly abnormal: he was no orator, mob or otherwise, and only once did he himself lead a mob. His first battle was won in the law courts, not the usual arena of demagogues, and his triumphs were over issues that had little to do with bread-and-butter politics or with religion. They were largely libertarian.[98]

Wilkes was certainly 'a pumper-up of popular fears and rages' – H.L. Mencken's definition of a demagogue – in his exploitation of the contemporary dislike of the Scots, though he did not thereby forfeit the friendship of such Scotsmen as Boswell and Hume.*[99] And on general warrants, the right of election and the freedom of the press he certainly took the popular side. But so did Chatham and Burke. On many other issues Wilkes followed a markedly unpopular line. Improvement of prison conditions, religious toleration and opposition to a war were matters which no ordinary demagogue would have touched, still less espoused.

---

* Wilkes's attitude may have been decisively affected by an incident with a Scottish barrister whom he had engaged to conduct his election petition in 1754. The barrister failed to do the work and refused to return his fee, suggesting that Wilkes could go to law about it. Instead of taking that advice, Wilkes drew his sword and was immediately given the money and an obsequious farewell.[100]

'Wilkes and Liberty' was not the first popular cry, nor was there anything new in politicians playing the popular card against the court. Chatham, as we have seen, had recently alarmed both George II and the Duke of Newcastle; and David Hume called him a 'formidable demagogue' as well as a 'wicked madman' – Wilkes was in good company. A less reputable precursor was Alexander Murray. For defying the Commons Murray had been acclaimed by the London populace with cries of 'Murray and Liberty'; later he plotted to assassinate George II. Though Wilkes was as far from being a Jacobite as it was possible to be, Wilkite radicalism and Jacobitism had some things in common: the 'liberty' slogan, the number 'forty-five' and the same colour, blue; more important, a number of Wilkites had been Jacobites, and there was some correlation between Wilkite and Jacobite electoral support. In any case the crowd had not been a passive bystander in the first half of the century, and use of the mob was in certain circumstances a recognised political tactic. Though Newcastle had deplored Chatham's recent 'violence', he was true to his more distant political past when in 1768 he initially took a far from apocalyptic view of the Wilkite riots. 'Wilkes's merit is being a friend of liberty,' he told the Duke of Richmond, 'and he has suffered for it, and, therefore, it is not an ill symptom that it should appear that that is a merit with the Nation.' The crowd's activities were welcomed by members of the oligarchy when they shared its objectives. Only when they felt threatened by them did they become enthusiasts for law and order. Six weeks later, when with the spread of 'economic riots' the disturbances had grown, Newcastle no longer considered the rioters to be 'the Nation' but 'a mad lawless mob'.[101]

'Many in the House,' wrote Burke shortly after St George's Fields, 'find a use in mobs.' Indeed the distinction was less between those politicians who on occasion approved of mobs and those who did not than between those whose popularity could bring a crowd onto the streets without expense and those who had to pay. The political riots or demonstrations that were mounted free of charge were not, of course, all entirely spontaneous; such things are rare, if not impossible. Almost invariably there must have been some encouragement and organisation. Thus a plentiful distribution of handbills produced 'a prodigious crowd' at the Mansion House to escort the Lord Mayor, Brass Crosby, to the Commons on March 19, 1771. The encouragement was sometimes purely political; occasionally, the politics was strengthened by a dash of drink. As one contemporary satire put it:

> See the mad populace in swarms appear
> Inspired at once by liberty and beer.[102]

Though the hiring of mobs by politicians or their agents at elections was commonplace, Lord Bute's 'butchers and bruisers' and Sir William Proctor's 'assistants to the civil magistrates' are the only mobs known to have been hired in London in the Wilkite period. Probably, however, there were others. Certainly, allegations of hiring or organising a mob were freely bandied: Beckford was accused in 1761, Newcastle a year later, Temple in 1763, Bute in 1765, the ministry in 1769, and both the Lord Mayor and Lord North in 1771. Junius even accused the King of having mobs 'notoriously hired to surround your coach or stationed at the theatre'. During the riots outside Parliament over the printers' affair in 1771, James Townsend remarked that he always knew where a mob came from and that 'the sailors' mob' was hired by the government. North plaintively replied that nobody could suppose he 'hired this mob. I never had a hand in any.' That rang true: even North could scarcely have organised a mob which nearly killed its hirer.[103]

However much other politicians employed the mob, the Wilkite use of it was different, both in objectives and scale. Wilkes was not playing the game of 'place'. On the few occasions when he tried to get a place, he did not use the crowd; he tried private solicitation. When he did bring in 'the publick' – the phrase 'public opinion' came into general use at the same time as 'Wilkes and Liberty' – he brought them in not merely to help himself but on an issue.[104]

The Wilkites used the crowd to show the oligarchy how the public felt. In thus extending the public's role, Wilkes was thought by Grafton to have overstepped what was permissible, whereas Chatham had not. Coming from an aristocratic colleague of Chatham's who had been tormented by Wilkes, that opinion was to be expected. And though it was widely shared it partly rested on two misconceptions. Firstly, Wilkes was blamed for industrial disturbances which were caused by the economic dislocation of the 1760s; only later were they at all connected with him. Secondly the greater strength of extra-parliamentary opinion in 1769-70 was only partially due to the organisational efforts of the Society of Supporters of the Bill of Rights or to the political skills of Wilkes himself. No less important were the issue – there would never, Burke told Rockingham, be 'a matter so well calculated to engage' the people as the Middlesex election – and the public's increasing awareness of politics. London was almost a city state, and it did not concede unquestioning precedence to Westminster. The 'corrupt' system could not be left for ever undisturbed.[105]

All the same the alarm of the parliamentary classes was understandable. Public agitation could easily get out of hand. The ruling elite were too small a minority to feel secure, and their means of quelling riots were primitive. In his 1751 Enquiry, written in the hope of rousing the civil power from its lethargy, Henry Fielding claimed that growing wealth had brought an accretion of power to 'the commonalty' and asserted from experience that the civil power by itself had difficulty in suppressing 'a mob of chairmen or servants, or a gang of thieves and sharpers'. How then, he wondered, could it deal with 'a general riot of the people'? Grafton was not much roused from lethargy in 1768. 'Our ministers, like their Saxon ancestors,' wrote Horace Walpole, 'are gone to hold a Witenagemot at Newmarket.' Grafton preferred Newmarket with his courtesan, Nancy Parsons, to London with its mobs, and his ministry's attempts to deal with what appeared to be 'a general riot of the people' by constant use of the army did not allay the fears of the respectable. Brought up on the classics, they abhorred mob rule and they knew that violence had heavily contributed to the fall of the Roman Republic – which, like eighteenth-century Britain, had lacked a proper police force.[106]

A good classical scholar, Wilkes had reasons other than the Roman precedent for seeking to control the violence. Not fighting a brief isolated skirmish but engaged in a long-running quarrel with the ministry, Wilkes had to make consistent display both of his popularity with the middling and inferior sets and of the vindictive hostility and violence of the court. Unrestrained popular violence would have defeated both objectives and made a mockery of the Wilkite claims to be defending the constitution and the principles of 1688. The middling set would have been shocked and changed sides, and what Wilkes regarded as the arbitrary and tyrannical conduct of the court would have been justified or obliterated by the Wilkite violence. Equally no violence at all – possible only by abandoning all use of the crowd – would have left the Wilkites disarmed and defeated. A careful balance had to be struck and, in general, it was. Violence was kept to the minimum, the middling set was not scared away and some of it took part in the demonstrations.

In general the authorities, too, struck a balance. Henry Fielding's brother and successor as Bow Street magistrate, Sir John Fielding, was reluctant to use troops, though he had only 80 constables at his disposal; it was only after three days of rioting following Wilkes's first election for Middlesex that he called for the aid of the military. Only once during the Wilkite disturbances did the authorities throw off restraint. The unwise stationing of Scottish troops at the prison, their undisciplined killing of Allen, the presence of weak magistrates and, above all, Lord Weymouth's letter urging the benefits of military force, led to the unnecessary 'massacre' of St George's Fields. There had been disasters before – Hexham in 1761 and Bridewell two years later – but with far greater excuse. As a rule, the mildness of the authorities mirrored the mildness of the rioters.[107]

Except when they organised a demonstration with almost military precision or a ritual execution of 'imaginary criminals of rank', the Wilkites had a more difficult task than the authorities in striking the right balance of violence and restraint – which for them was a large crowd and minimum violence. They could not control the crowd in the way that the government controlled the army and the constables. Unlike Bedford's bruisers or Proctor's mob, Wilkite rioters were not, in the present-day phrase, a 'rent-a-crowd'. The Wilkite mobs were not hired; nor did they engage in looting. Money was not the motive. The Wilkite movement was genuinely popular, something which the King and the oligarchy did not accept. It suited them to believe that the mob was 'mad' and 'lawless', that it had no real grievances but was being manipulated by evil men; or, as George III told North during the printers' riots, 'the violence . . . has been encouraged by men of some property who dare not avow it'.[108]

The rioting London crowd, as Dr Rudé's pioneering researches showed, was not composed of vagrants, criminals and the unemployed: 'a mob that can read,' wrote an observer in 1769, 'and a Ministry that can not think are sadly matched.' Nor was it usually made up of the 'middling set' or even of the aristocracy and the well-to-do. In 1779, however, Charles James Fox, Lord Derby and the Duke of Ancaster joined and led the rioters celebrating a court martial's triumphant vindication of Admiral Keppel. They helped to break, first, Lord George Germaine's windows and then Lord Sandwich's gates at the Admiralty, forcing 'Jemmy Twitcher' to flee with his mistress, Miss Ray, through the garden to the Horseguards where he 'betrayed most manifest panic'. The windows of Lord North in Downing Street also suffered and the Guards were needed to prevent the house being entered. Sandwich was Wilkes's enemy, but Wilkes had nothing to do with the riots. A few days later when Keppel dined in the city, the windows of Fox and other opposition leaders were broken 'at the instigation,' Walpole thought, of the Court.[109]

Usually, however, the public violence of the aristocracy was confined to duels. Observers occasionally noted that the Wilkite crowd was 'a crowd of the better sort', or that many of the mob were of 'a better class', or that it was 'a mob that can read'. Yet the ordinary 'political' rioters or demonstrators, that is to say the Wilkites, were largely drawn from the 'inferior set': labourers, servants, journeymen and small traders. They were mainly wage earners rather than the self-employed with a sprinkling of tradesmen and others of the better sort including the occasional gentleman. They were not riff-raff and they were not 'mad' or 'lawless'.[110]

In general, indeed, the Wilkite crowd was not much less orderly than Charles Fox and the gentlemen of Brooks's, though Wilkites themselves sometimes complained of its disorder and bullying. Often it was scarcely violent at all. Perhaps the best known act of a Wilkite mob was the pulling out of his carriage of the august Austrian ambassador and the chalking of 'No 45' on the soles of his boots – not treatment that any diplomat would welcome, but more of an indignity than a dangerous piece of violence. Again, when the Wilkite John Percival appeared in court, the Surrey recorder, Sir Fletcher Norton, a former Attorney General and future Speaker, denounced riots and radicals and extolled the virtues of obedience and loyalty for an hour and a half. He then sentenced the rioter, presumably by now stupefied with boredom, to two years imprisonment. What had Percival done? He had committed the outrage of chalking '45' on the coat of Justice Capel.[111]

'Violence,' wrote George III's biographer, 'was the pleasure of the mob.'[112] If so, the Wilkite mob was unusually restrained in its pleasure. But the phrase is, perhaps, a good one in that it conveys the idea that the Wilkite mob was not vicious; it tended to be good humoured in its violence. There was no lynching. Indeed the Wilkite crowd never killed anybody. One Wilkite died in the scramble to have the honour of drawing Wilkes's coach to the Mansion House when he became Lord Mayor. The other deaths were all inflicted by Proctor's mob or the army. There was almost no violence against persons, though the unpopular Harley was pelted and pulled from his coach in 1770. Even the violence against property was nearly always restricted to the breaking of windows and the destruction of coaches. The riots after Wilkes's first election for Middlesex were thought by Burke to have been 'exceedingly exaggerated' and by Walpole to have been like other election riots but with less damage than usual.[113]

The 'printers'' mob in 1771 when North, the 'Fox cubs' and other MPs were badly roughed up was exceptional, but then so was the provocation: Oliver had already been sent to the Tower, guilty of no greater offence, in the City's eyes, than administering the law, and Crosby was sure to follow him. Government and opposition differed on the crowd outside the chamber. Wedderburn, who had again changed sides to become Solicitor General, implied that it was a mob hired by the city magistrates. The two City sheriffs who were MPs, Baker and Martin, did not think the crowd deserved to be called a mob: they were 'respectable citizens, men of property [who] thought it their duty to accompany' the Lord Mayor to Westminster. Whatever it was, citizenry, mob or an 'assembly of people', it undoubtedly got out of hand, and its excesses throw into relief the normal control or self-restraint of the Wilkite crowd.[114]

That restraint was all the more remarkable in that the togetherness and equality of crowds, their belief in their cause, and the reversal of

roles implicit in the riot or demonstration must have exhilarated the
Wilkites. For a time as they marched or rioted, the Wilkite crowd
had cast off their subordination in an aristocratic society and were
ruling – or at least baiting their habitual superiors. 'The pleasure,'
wrote Wedderburn, 'which the rich and powerful feel in governing . . . their inferiors is not half as strong as that which the
indigent and worthless feel in subverting property, defying law, and
lording it over those whom they were used to respect.' That was
largely true, but if the Wilkites had been 'worthless' they would
presumably have subverted property by destroying it. In fact they
destroyed little. Walpole wrote of the crowd that attended Wilkes to
Parliament in January 1769, that it was well behaved and had been
'soon dispersed by his order'. And, he continued, Wilkes's committees 'who had regimented the mobs of London and Westminster
conducted them with composure and regularity'.[115]

'All opposition,' Burke told an unresponsive Rockingham in 1775,
'is absolutely crippled if it has no sort of support without doors.'
Government was so strong in the eighteenth century that an
established ministry was only overthrown in a war: Walpole's,
Newcastle's and, later, North's. Hence to gain influence or office an
opposition needed the support of either the King or the populace, a
point which the Rockingham Whigs never grasped. Fox soon
changed his mind about the independence of Parliament and the
subordination of the people when the hidden premise of his argument
– that George III and the majority of the Commons agreed with Fox
or *vice versa* – ceased to apply. When, after Fox fell out with North,
it no longer held, and he and his friends were a minority, the
Commons soon ceased to be the repository of all political and
constitutional wisdom and became the corrupt and subservient tool
of the executive. By 1780 Fox was proclaiming the duty of
Parliament 'to conform to the sentiments of the people'. Yet the
Rockinghams for some time continued to be Whigs 'on the business
of a hundred years ago'.[116]

Unlike the Rockinghams, Wilkes did use the crowd without
compunction and with success. He was one of the few opposition
Whigs on the business of the present day. Quoting Montesquieu in
his support, he maintained that civil dissensions were 'favourable to
freedom', and that corruption was more dangerous than civil discord.
True or not, the view that public agitation could not be uniquely
improper when bribery, corruption and the manipulation of elections
were taken for granted was not implausible. After all, as the Tories
had sporadically recognised during their days of exclusion, there was
no chance of the 'corrupt' system miraculously reforming itself.
Public agitation was the only way of achieving change; the alternative
was to wait for defeat in war. Indeed the belief that any use of the

crowd was illegitimate implied that politics should be entirely a one class matter or a mere dispute between the King and the Whig oligarchy, and that the sole political function of the middling and lower sets was to do what they were told.[117]

That may have been the ideal, but it was not the practice and, only intermittently, the theory of Georgian England. Popular support or hostility could determine the survival of both ministers and measures. Politicians out of office frequently championed the cause of the people against Parliament. In the 1730s Bolingbroke maintained that the people could give instructions to their MPs who were, therefore, delegates. Twenty years later the Tory MP, Sir Roger Newdigate, thought the people were 'as good judges of their own interest and honour' as either House of Parliament. Wilkes was following a long opposition tradition in calling the people 'a higher tribunal than parliament'. Chatham was more explicit: ' . . . when the liberty of the subject is invaded, and all redress denied him,' he told the Lords, 'resistance is justified.' A few years later Fox was still more outspoken: when the laws afforded no relief 'the people would inevitably take up arms, and the first characters in the kingdom would be seen in their ranks'.[118]

Clearly any such right of rebellion, however circumscribed and however theoretical, included a right to demonstrate or riot; riots, after all, involved a much lower level of violence than rebellion. Indeed a riot was widely recognised to be a defensible method of conveying to Parliament that a measure – such as the Cider Tax – was unpopular and should be repealed. It acted as a public opinion poll. Though the public were frequently reviled in Parliament as 'the rabble', 'the despicable mechanics', 'the refuse of the people', 'the scum of the earth' – Sir Francis Burdett said thirty years later that the people of England were only insulted in the House of Commons – much attention, at least in theory, was paid to the popular part of the constitution. Only the King or the mob, Lord North said in 1771, could remove him.[119]

A few of the parliamentary opposition were able to see that there was more to the activities of the Wilkite mob than madness, manipulation and class hatred. Chatham thought a prudent concession on the part of the government would return the people to 'a state of tranquillity'. Sir George Savile considered that the people were not ignorant dupes and that their grievances should be redressed. Edmund Burke, not always reliable on popular politics, accused 'the violent instruments of government' of treating the people as an obnoxious enemy and thought there was 'nothing inglorious in yielding to the people of England'. Popular violence was caused, he added, by popular grievances. There were 'two ways of raising mobs: one by hiring; another by provoking.' Burke thought the ministry had both hired and provoked mobs.[120]

Yet the government ruled out concessions. Lord Mansfield characteristically maintained that they would only encourage further violence. Instead of giving prudent attention to public grievances, the typical governmental reaction was to talk of 'outrageous and detestable mobs' or of 'this spirit of outrage and violence', and, like Rigby, to claim that heeding popular clamour would be to substitute 'the caprice of the multitude' for government by law.[121]

The flaw in that argument was that the caprice of the multitude turned out to be a better guide to the constitution than the decisions of the ministry and Parliament. The declaration of Wilkes's ineligibility and the substitution of Luttrell as MP for Middlesex were the weakest parts of the Commons's case.* Yet the expulsion of Wilkes in the first place was also inexcusable and without precedent. He had already been expelled in the last Parliament for *N° 45* and 'An Essay on Woman'. They provided no excuse for expelling him again. The only new accusation against him, an alleged libel on Lord Weymouth, was a matter that should have been pursued in the courts, as even Blackstone recognised. As Chatham said, there had been 'a dangerous violation of the English constitution' and the people were 'justly incensed'. Both legally and constitutionally the mob was right and the guardians of the constitution wrong.[123]

In most of the ministry's own actions, indeed, caprice was more conspicuous than law. Over Wilkes, as over America, George III and his ministers brought most of their troubles on themselves. Oppositions were generally ham-strung. The political system and the social structure normally prevented the emergence of political issues except those of war and peace and taxation. The political class was by and large satisfied – with good reason – and nobody else could make other than local demands. Wilkes was the great provider of issues, yet even they would have fizzled out but for the government's aggressiveness. Much of Wilkes's popularity stemmed from his role as defender of traditional liberties against governmental attack.

---

* The nearest parallel to the Wilkes case occurred in 1961, when Mr Benn having become Lord Stansgate had to resign his seat at Bristol and then won the resulting by-election with an increased majority. The Conservative candidate, Mr St Clair, petitioned an electoral court which found that Mr Benn was disqualified from being both a member of the House of Commons and a candidate and that Mr St Clair had been duly elected. The House voted to agree with the electoral court. Whatever the wisdom of that decision, it differed from the Wilkes case in that as the law then stood Mr Benn was not eligible to sit in the House of Commons. Mr St Clair then made a declaration which further differentiated Bristol from Middlesex. He undertook to resign his seat if and when Mr Benn became eligible to stand, and he honoured his undertaking. Nevertheless Mr Benn forced a change in the law just as Daniel O'Connell did in 1828 by winning the by-election in County Clare. To avoid a succession of Wilkes cases, Wellington was forced to bring in Catholic Emancipation.[122]

'I hold it to be the great reproach of our age and nature,' Wilkes told his (former) constituents on his release from prison, 'that our fellow-subjects have been basely murdered by an inhuman soldiery in St George's Fields and other hired ruffians at Brentford, without a single victim to the public justice of our country . . . or to the violated laws of God and man.' Wilkes's rhetoric was overblown, but his facts were correct. The ministry organised the escape of the killers of Allen, and there was no inquiry and no regret for what Burke called 'an act of atrocious violence'. Much the same happened after the killing of the Wilkite Clarke by Proctor's mob.[124]

If the killers of Allen and Clarke were entitled to mercy or better, then surely so were the two Spitalfields weavers who had merely damaged silk in a loom, and three of the seven Stepney coalheavers who were condemned under a stretched interpretation of the Waltham Black Act, endorsed by Mansfield and his brethren. Yet the weavers and coalheavers were hanged while the killers of the Wilkites and some other murderers were pardoned or allowed to escape. Murder, said the Middlesex petitioners, was 'abetted, encouraged and rewarded' by the government.[125]

Once again the rhetoric was excessive, but when its interests were involved the government was clearly not the impartial upholder of the law; nor were the judges. In political cases, they were highly political. Mansfield, great lawyer in other spheres though he was, consistently behaved in the Wilkes affair more as a member of the government than as an independent judge. And not only against Wilkes and his followers. P.C. Webb, the Solicitor to the Treasury who had coordinated the prosecution of Wilkes in 1763-64, was clearly guilty of perjury; Mansfield engineered his acquittal. Wilkites like Glynn, Townsend and Oliver were not alone in thinking that the laws, the judges and the administration of justice had fallen into disrepute; more conventional opposition politicians and lawyers like Camden, Chatham, Dunning and Burke thought the same. Much of the discontent was due to Mansfield's treatment of libel cases and to the feeling that the courts in Westminster Hall and the Court of St James's were too closely connected.[126]

The King was not conspiring to subvert the law any more than he was conspiring to subvert the constitution. Yet the Wilkites had more justification for thinking that they were the victims of a legal conspiracy than Burke and the Rockinghams had for thinking that they were the victims of a political one. The fear of arbitrary government in the 1760s and 70s was not irrational. Successive ministries consistently behaved worse and more violently than Wilkes. In 1768 a Wilkite journalist could plausibly allege no fewer than twelve illegalities by the authorities against him. The Wilkites had grounds for regarding themselves as the upholders of the law and the government as the breakers of it. Without Wilkes and the crowd, government would have become more arbitrary.[127]

George III's biographer thought it doubtful that the Crown could ever behave unconstitutionally: if the Crown could get away with unconstitutional behaviour, it became constitutional.[128] If the same realistic standards are applied to Wilkes and the crowd, then their behaviour, too, was thoroughly constitutional. General warrants were declared illegal, the Middlesex election was never repeated, the 1769 resolution of the House of Commons declaring Wilkes ineligible was at last expunged, printers were never again prosecuted for publishing reports of Parliamentary debates, and the freedom of the press was strengthened. In addition, the causes with which Wilkes himself, though not the crowd, was associated, such as parliamentary reform and religious toleration, also triumphed in the end.[129]

If stricter standards are sought, there can be no sure answer. When the rules are uncertain, nobody can know when they are broken. The English constitution has no independent existence of its own. It merely remains as it is, until somebody changes it. It is always in transition and, in part, indeterminate – particularly so in the reign of George III when conspiracy theories were rife. Some thought the King intended decisive constitutional change – Parliament was to look on while a cabal of the closet and the backstairs was substituted in place of a national administration; some believed that the aim of the great Whig families was an aristocratic republic with a doge as a figurehead; others feared that Wilkes and the radicals were out to establish rule by the mob. The King and his supporters, the opposition Whigs and the Wilkites all sought to shift the constitution in their direction. None of them wholly succeeded and all of them hovered on its borders.[130]

During the row over the printers, Burke disagreed with those who were 'against disturbing the public repose; I like a clamour whenever there is an abuse. The fire-bell at midnight disturbs your sleep, but it keeps you from being burned in your bed.'[131] Moderate violence could perform a useful service in highlighting grievances, checking abuses, deterring arbitrary government and preventing revolution. Yet 'a clamour' is only of value if it is indeed the firebell and not the fire. George III and most of the political world could not distinguish the two. For them, clamour or violence merely demonstrated the licentiousness of the mob, to which the only proper reaction was suppression; equally, on the other hand, the absence of clamour demonstrated the people's contentment and vindicated the conduct of the government. Hence the crowd was always either cowed or licentious.[132]

Notwithstanding the King's belief that Wilkes's expulsion was 'a measure whereon my Crown almost depends', the Wilkite crowds were indeed the firebell. They had no thought of overthrowing the King or the constitution. The Wilkites wanted to alter the ways of the government not bring it down. They were trying to preserve or recover their rights and liberty, to counter what Wilkes called 'all the oppressions which ministerial rage and revenge can invent' and to root out 'the remains of arbitrary power and star-chamber inquisition'.[133]

The disturbances were a useful reminder to the parliamentary classes that there was another political world outside Westminster and St James's, and that there were limits to the abuses that this outside world would tolerate. Arguably, of course, they were damaging later, in that during the next serious disturbances they scared the authorities from taking action against the rioters. Yet the government and the magistrates treated the Gordon Riots differently from the Wilkite disturbances not because of frightened memories of Wilkes but because, initially at least, Gordon's mobs did not greatly worry them. The elite regarded the Wilkites, despite or because of their relative lack of violence, as a serious threat; anti-Popery rioters they did not. In consequence they were mistaken both times. The Wilkite riots were the firebell which they mistook for the fire; the Gordon Riots were the fire which they mistook for the firebell.

Wilkes's career illustrates the impossibility of drawing a clear distinction between governmental 'force' which is legal and legitimate and nongovernmental 'violence' which is illegal and illegitimate. There is no such clear distinction. In bringing people onto the streets or encouraging them when they were there, the Wilkites were acting violently against governmental force (or violence) whose legality was often at best doubtful. The judges were usually political; the legislators were seldom judicious. Political agitation outside Parliament affected the behaviour of both and, on the whole, improved it.

In the eighteenth century two strands of protest can be differentiated although they occasionally intermingled: one, which ran from the Sacheverell Riots to the Jewish Naturalisation Bill to the Gordon Riots, was the producer and product of prejudice and fanaticism; it served no useful purpose. The other, which ran through many food riots, the turnpike riots, some of the election riots and the Wilkite disturbances, had a strong feeling for law or custom and was seeking either to make the authorities do their job or to reform them; often its violence was almost non-violent, and it was usually salutary. Hans Stanley, an opponent of Wilkes, must have had the Wilkite crowds in mind when he told Parliament in 1772 that compared with the fury of religious ones, political mobs were as 'harmless as doves'. The truth of that was seen eight years later.[134]

SIXTEEN

The Gordon Riots

When tumult lately burst his prison door,
And set plebeian thousands in a roar
When he usurp'd authority's just place,
And dared to look his master in the face;
When the rude rabble's watchword was – destroy,
And blazing London seem'd a second Troy . . .

William Cowper, 'Table Talk'

Our danger is at an end, but our disgrace will be lasting, and the month of June 1780 will ever be marked by a dark and diabolical fanaticism which I had supposed to be extinct.

Edward Gibbon

Une émeute qui dégénéreroit en sédition est devenue moralement impossible [en Paris] . . . Paris est à l'abri de l'alarme et de la terreau quie George Gordon jeta dans Londres dernièrement . . . La sédition excitée à Londres par Lord Gordon a donc parue comme un rêve aux Parisiens . . .

L.S. Mercier, 1783[1]

With the exception of the 'Fifteen' and the 'Forty-five', the Gordon Riots were by far the most violent episode in eighteenth-century England, producing what the *Annual Register* called 'one of the most dreadful spectacles this country ever beheld'. 'Let those who were not spectators of it,' its account continued, 'judge what the inhabitants felt when they beheld at the same instant flames ascending and rolling in clouds from the King's Bench and Fleet prisons, from New Bridewell, from the tollgates on Blackfriars Bridge, from houses in every quarter of the town, and particularly from the bottom and middle of Holborn, where the conflagration was horrible beyond description.'[2]

The years 1779-84 saw invasion scares, ignominious defeat in the American war, industrial riots, religious disturbances, near revolt in Ireland, denunciation of the Crown in Parliament, a reform movement in the country, a government so feeble that it seemed bound to collapse, fluctuating ministries and almost every symptom of discontent and decay. To Sir Herbert Butterfield the years 1779-80 were 'quasi-revolutionary'; in his view the catastrophe of revolution was only narrowly escaped, while to Professor Cannon 1783-4 were, perhaps, still more dangerous years, with contemporaries talking of the possibility of civil war.[3]

The North ministry contained, said an observer, 'the most jarring councils and the most divided opinions'. In 1779 Lord North was so paralysed that when one Secretary of State died it took him eight months to appoint another. The government was losing the war. That summer a French attack on Plymouth, where there were guns but no gunpowder, or elsewhere on the South coast where there were neither, was narrowly avoided because the ineptitude of the French fleet exceeded that of the British. Hardy, the elderly English admiral in command only because better officers distrusted the ministry, successfully evaded battle and took refuge in Spithead; North later said that had Hardy known the state of the French fleet he would have 'earnestly sought an engagement'. As Cowper put it:

> . . . admirals, extoll'd for standing still,
> or doing nothing with a deal of skill . . .[4]

The cotton industry was depressed by the calamitous war. In the autumn large mobs attacked buildings and machinery in five Lancashire towns. Some 2000 people who assaulted a mill at Chorley were repulsed, losing two killed and eight wounded. Strongly reinforced by the Duke of Bridgewater's colliers, a mob estimated by Josiah Wedgwood to number 8000 returned the next day and destroyed the machinery. The same happened at Altham before the arrival of Sir George Savile's Yorkshire Militia prevented further violence.[5]

North's paralysis extended across the Irish Channel. The American colonists had set Ireland an example – 'We are all Americans here . . .' wrote an Irish peer in 1775 – while the combined effects of British commercial restrictions and the American War had reduced the Irish economy to more than usually desperate straits. If the Irish were not given relief they might, thought Rockingham, be forced into resistance; Shelburne wondered if North wanted a new war to misconduct; and Fox, as usual going further, maintained that when good faith was exhausted, 'violence or resistance' were regrettably justified. As well as the support of the English opposition, the Irish had the means of resistance: fears of a French invasion had given colourable cause for the formation of independent companies. The chances of the French being the first opponents of these Irish volunteers were remote. Yet North could not be induced to read the papers on Ireland, even when they were specially summarised. In November a Dublin mob of some thousands attacked the Attorney General's house and surrounded and intimidated the Irish House of Commons. Violence worked. Now North not only read the papers, he acted. Just in time the ministry made concessions generous enough to still the agitation and only the English opposition was disappointed.[6]

Defeat in war is ever the most potent agent of discontent, reform and revolution – had the Wilkes crisis coincided with military failure, the outcome might have been very different. Although the entry of France and Spain into the American war initially increased its popularity in England, its economic hardships and military disasters brought reform to renewed life and the aristocratic opposition to temporary unity.

The aims of the County Associations or petitioning movement, which Butterfield saw as the nub of the crisis, were far from revolutionary: the restoration of national morals and the preservation of the constitution by economical and parliamentary reform. The movement's progenitor, Rev Christopher Wyvill, a rich absentee clergyman with suspected Unitarian leanings, accurately described his weapons of political warfare as 'argumentation and legal assemblies of people, petitions, remonstrances, associations, engage-ments to vote against corruption and corrupt men'. Not much danger of violence there, certainly. Wyvill who had secured forty-one petitions by April 1780 was aiming at the upper strata, from the magnates to the prosperous freeholder, and was determined to prevent popular agitation being used as an excuse for opposing reform. In that he succeeded, until the Protestant Association and the Gordon Riots infected not only the word 'association' but any form of popular political participation with the taint of violence. Yet there was in any case little in his programme to excite popular enthusiasm.[7]

The ministry's policies and George III's system which maintained them were under attack in Parliament as well. Even that epitome of rectitude, Sir George Savile, implied a threat when he presented the Yorkshire petition: the petitioners expected it to be granted, but 'should it be refused,' he said, 'here I leave a blank . . . .' Fox and Burke were more explicit. Fox, whose views had veered almost 180 degrees since the days when he had attacked Wilkes, with whom he now shared a platform, told the Commons that if economical reform by Parliament was thwarted by the administration, 'the people would have recourse to other means of redress.'[8]

Nothing, Wilkes had said eighteen months earlier, seemed stable and secure except the ministerial majority in the Commons. In 1780, not even that was secure. Dunning's famous resolution on the need

to diminish the increasing influence of the Crown was passed on
April 6. An adjournment of Parliament caused by the illness of the
Speaker probably saved the ministry. During it, the government's
managers regained control of their flock, demonstrating that the
resolution was well founded and that its passing was an aberration.
On the eve of the Gordon Riots, therefore, the ministry seemed again
secure, even if nothing else did.[9]

Ironically it was not the folly of that 'bunch of imbecility', as Dr
Johnson called the North ministry, that caused the Gordon Riots, but
one of its sensible measures. An act had been passed in 1778 to relieve
'His Majesty's subjects professing the Papist Religion from certain
penalties and disabilities' imposed upon them by a statute of 1699. It
removed the threat of life imprisonment from 'Papist bishops, priests
or Jesuits' and other Roman Catholics who kept or taught in schools;
and it removed the restrictions on a Catholic buying, holding or
inheriting land. These concessions were granted only to those
Catholics who took a special oath of allegiance prescribed in the act.[10]

In 1774 North's government had passed the Quebec Act which
gave official recognition and full toleration to the Catholic Church
in Canada. The English Relief Act, however, did far less. It was, as
Lord Mansfield said later, not even 'a toleration', it only took away
'the penalties of one Act out of many'. That one act had nevertheless
been onerous. Its virtual repeal, strongly favoured by politicians like
Burke and by judges like Mansfield and Camden, for once in
agreement, had come less from the ministry's espousal of religious
toleration than from the course of the American war. With setback
following setback in America, and France and Spain about to enter
the war on the American side, the ministry needed to conciliate
Roman Catholics and encourage their enlistment in the army. The
Scottish Highlands were looked on as a promising recruiting ground,
and secret negotiations were entered into with first Scottish and then
English Catholics. An additional reason was the fears of Irish
landlords that large numbers of their Catholic tenants would be
seduced by American promises of free land and toleration into
following the 55,000 Irish Protestants who had recently emigrated to
a freer and more prosperous life across the Atlantic. One Irish
landlord, Sir George Savile, was asked by the ministry to introduce
the bill in the Commons. Another, Lord Rockingham, supported it
in the Lords. Nobody opposed it in either House, not even Lord
George Gordon.[11]

Not untypically of the North administration, a bill whose origins
lay in the desire to get army recruits from Scotland applied in the end
only to England and Ireland. The government's promise to extend
the same relief to Scottish Catholics produced what the *Annual
Register* called 'a furious spirit of bigotry and persecution' and fierce

riots erupted in Edinburgh, Glasgow and elsewhere. In Edinburgh a new Roman Catholic chapel was burned, and the house of the bishop, who had once been the Chevalier's surgeon, was pulled down. Houses and shops of people thought to be Catholic were attacked and Catholic leaders had to take refuge in Edinburgh Castle. This was violence of a quite different order from that of the Wilkite disturbances.[12]

The Scottish campaign of violence, like the Irish, worked. When called upon by Wilkes to make good its promise over Catholic relief in Scotland, the government announced that the bill would not be extended to that country. The price of the government's ignominious surrender to the Scottish mob, replied Wilkes – who knew what he was talking about – would be similar outrages in London.[13]

Lord George Gordon was invited to Scotland and became president of a number of religious associations. And having seen what 'bigotry' had achieved in Scotland, the English zealots who had formed the London Protestant Association issued a similar invitation. A younger son of the Duke of Gordon – he had £600 a year and his brother £20,000 – Lord George had entered the navy straight from Eton. Almost his first action as a midshipman was to complain of the corrupt system which supplied the seamen with biscuits riddled with weevils, and he became 'the sailors' friend'. On the West Indian station, Gordon was horrified by slavery and the 'bloody treatment of the negroes'; he was correspondingly impressed by the freedom and equality of American society. Deciding when on leave in England to enter politics, in 1774 he became MP for the pocket borough of Luggershall at the age of 23, and as he voted regularly with the opposition, his political attitudes soon became as objectionable to the government as his naval behaviour had long been to the Admiralty – which considered him a 'damned nuisance wholly unsuitable for promotion'. After ten years as a lieutenant and a final unsuccessful request for a command, Lord George resigned his commission in 1777, telling Sandwich, the First Lord, that he declined to 'imbue his hands in the blood of men struggling for freedom'.[14]

After a holiday with him the year before, William Hickey remembered Gordon as 'a gay, volatile and elegant young gentleman of engaging manners' who, like his companions, drank a good deal; and it was later said of him that if he had called the Archbishop of Canterbury the Whore of Babylon, it was the only whore his Lordship disliked. In the Commons, however, though he was capable of good satirical invective, Gordon was often a relentless bore. Once he emptied the chamber by reading an entire Irish pamphlet on a subject which had nothing to do with the motion before the House. The next day he read to the House an account of two debates in the Irish House of Lords, a number of letters from the Secretary of State to the Lord Mayor of Dublin, and various extracts from the Irish papers, and then announced that 'for the instruction of the House' he would read the same pamphlet he had read the day before. It was so good he thought it ought to be read every day of the week.[15]

Gordon was contemptuous not only of the ministry but of all the parliamentary factions. Since 'justice for the people [was] not to be expected from either party', he belonged to the 'party of the people'. As such he was unique and he took himself with appropriate seriousness, once assuring the House that nobody was more competent to speak on the conduct of the Church than he was. He put much store on his consistency, ignoring the fact that his 'purpose' of repealing the Catholic Relief Act was itself inconsistent with his failure to oppose its passage through Parliament.[16]

Lord George was not, however, the only man to take his 'purpose' (and his abilities) seriously, otherwise the Roman Catholic leader Lord Petrie would not have sought to persuade him to abandon it, nor would Lord North have attempted to bribe him. The issue that had most enraged Gordon since his entry into the Commons was 'the mad cruel and accursed American war'. He regarded it as an attempt by arbitrary power to procure unconditional submission, and demanded that North call off from the colonies 'his butchers and ravagers'. The war was intimately connected with the religious issue. Five years earlier the Quebec Act had been vehemently opposed by Chatham, Shelburne, Richmond, Wilkes, Savile and the City not only as a popish measure but chiefly as an unforgivable provocation of the Protestant American colonists. The Catholic Relief Act was even worse: its object was to arm papists against those same Protestant colonies.[17]

Opposition to the Relief Act therefore combined two sets of people. Much the larger set were those who were opposed to it on traditional religious and political grounds. Such men were not merely 'a mean set of people' – Lord Petrie's description of the Protestant Association – or crude sectarian bigots: 'Revolution principles' could be invoked. Horace Walpole, who called himself an 'honest . . . heathen', was against Catholic relief. So was the City of London's Common Council. John Wesley inveighed against the 'purple power of Rome', praised the Protestant Association and insisted that no government should tolerate Roman Catholics. Popery was still generally associated with tyranny and 'wooden shoes', and Britain was at war with the Catholic powers, France and Spain.[18]

For the second group anti-Catholicism was part of more radical attitudes. The heirs of 'the good old cause' – Gibbon wrote of 40,000 Puritans as from the time of Cromwell starting out of their graves –

these radicals were more concerned with traditional worries about liberty, believing that both American and British freedom could be secured only by an American victory. Gordon, who thought Popery 'synonymous with arbitrary power', belonged to this second set. He used to drink success to America's arms, he deplored the eagerness with which the papists supported the 'unhappy civil war against the Protestants in America', and he thought the Relief Act demonstrated the 'hypocritical, underhand dealings of a despicable' ministry. All the second group and many of the first shared Lord George's opinion of the North government.[19]

From 1779 onwards Gordon's language in Parliament was almost uniformly violent. In May 1779 he maintained that Scotland was ripe for insurrection and rebellion. In November the Scots, like the Irish, were ready to break with the ministry, and the government would find 120,000 men at his back. In March 1780 he claimed to have 160,000 men at his command in Scotland who, if the King did not keep his coronation oath, were determined to cut off his head. A month later he called both the King and the ministry popish, and in the same week he confided to the House that though the Protestants had not yet determined to murder the King they considered themselves absolved from allegiance to him. At the time he was attacking George III in public, Gordon was using his privilege as a duke's brother to have four private audiences with him. At one of them he read the King that same Irish pamphlet for an hour.[20]

Possibly these were the ravings of a madman; many reckoned him deranged. Horace Walpole thought most Gordons were mad and Lord George especially so – though he later considered him to have 'more knavery than mission'. Gordon was certainly ambitious and singleminded to the point of fanaticism. He had, Charles Turner told the Commons well before the Gordon Riots, 'a twist in his head, a certain whirligig which ran away with him' whenever religion was mentioned. In Scotland Gordon not only took a leading part in the activities of the Kirk, he dressed and looked like a Presbyterian with his hair lank and unpowdered. Similarly, when he became a Jew he preserved, said a contemporary, 'the sanguinary proofs' of his circumcision and would receive only those of his new faith who had beards of the requisite length. But fanaticism is not the same as madness. In the eighteenth-century people who did or said unusual things were often assumed to be insane: Major Cartwright's advocacy of parliamentary reform rendered his normality suspect, and a man who left all his money to the poor was adjudged mad and his will upset. At least before the riots, Lord George seems not to have been insane, and if they had succeeded nobody would have thought him mad after them. In any case, crazy or not he had given Parliament and ministry ample forewarning of mischief and violence.[21]

At the end of May Gordon told the Protestant Association that he was not 'a lukewarm man himself', and that if they intended just to talk and not to act they should get another leader. Notwithstanding strong dissent within the Association from those who foresaw trouble, it was decided to hold a mass meeting at St George's Fields on Friday June 2 before presenting a 'Protestant petition' to Parliament. Gordon added that if less than 20,000 people attended him he would not present his petition. In the event about 60,000 assembled in St George's Fields, and they were each handed a blue – the colour of Wilkes and also the early Hanoverian Tories – cockade or rosette, which had been made at a cost of £2500. Despite the intense heat Lord George marched his force round the field three or four times, and then one division crossed Westminster Bridge, another Blackfriars Bridge, and a third London Bridge. The last on its march through the City was evidently joined by a non-religious, poorer and partly criminal element. The rest, according to an observer, had 'a vulgar furious zeal upon their countenances'.[22]

By mid-afternoon all the divisions had arrived at Westminster, a vast concourse jamming every approach to the Houses of Parliament, Palace Yard and Westminster Bridge. The young Frederic Reynolds, the son of Wilkes's solicitor, observed that the mob had received the addition of 'many thousands of disorderly persons' but that it was largely composed of decently dressed people who displayed 'all the outward and visible signs of hypocrisy and starvation'. Westminster Hall was invaded and the Court of King's Bench was forced to adjourn. A similar invasion of the House of Lords was prevented by the doorkeepers, but peers were attacked on their way to the House. Lord Bathurst, the Lord President of the Council, lost his wig and had his legs kicked. The Bishop of Lincoln was seized by the throat and the wheels removed from his carriage. The Duke of Northumberland was assaulted and relieved of his watch, while Lord Mansfield 'narrowly escaped with life'. Later, deputising for the absent Lord Chancellor who was lucky enough to be indisposed in Tunbridge Wells, Mansfield, so the Duke of Gloucester told Walpole, 'quivered on the Woolsack like an aspen'.[23]

The Duke of Richmond, introducing his motion in favour of annual parliaments and manhood suffrage, regretted the situation in which their lordships presently found themselves and deplored the riotous proceedings then going on in New Palace Yard. Otherwise ignoring the hubbub outside and the dishevelled appearance of many of his listeners, he proceeded with his prepared speech on the growing corruption of government until he was eventually interrupted by a peer telling the House that one of their number was in serious danger from the mob. 'At this instant,' said a report it was 'hardly possible to conceive a more grotesque appearance than the

House exhibited. Some of their lordships with their hair about their shoulders; others smutted with dirt; most of them as pale as the ghost in Hamlet, and all of them standing up, in their several places, and speaking at the same instant. One lord proposing to send for the guards; another for the justices or civil magistrates; many crying out, Adjourn, adjourn! while the skies resounded with the huzzas, shoutings, or hootings and hissings in the Palace-yard. This scene of unprecedented alarm continued for about half an hour.'[24]

Very few of the Lower House suffered severely from the mob and Lord North fared much better than in 1771, this time only losing his hat. Yet the din from the crowd outside was no less than in the Lords. Lord George Gordon – who had arrived 'so faint with heat and dust' that he needed 'an orange and some wine and water to recover me which I took upon the table of the House' – moved to have his petition taken into immediate consideration. A heated debate began and several times Gordon came out of the House to give the crowd bulletins on its progress. His appearances and 'inflammatory' speeches were greeted with loud cheers and kept the demonstrators excited and angry. In one speech he told them, 'Lord North calls you a mob'; on another occasion 'the Member for Bristol [Burke] . . . is no friend to your petition'; later he told them that they had 'got a very good prince, who as soon as he shall hear the alarm has seized such a number of men, will no doubt send down private orders to his ministers to enforce' the prayer of their petition. John Anstruther, who later became Chief Justice at Calcutta, heard Gordon say that the Scots had carried their point by 'their steadfastness and firmness'; and the Chaplain of the House of Commons heard him say that the Scotch had had no redress 'until they pulled down the mass-houses'. Then, evidently realising how far he had gone, the demagogue warned the mob against 'evil minded persons, who would rise amongst them to incite them to mischief, the blame of which would be imputed to them'. Despite appeals to do so, in none of his speeches did he tell the crowd to go home; he could not, he explained, take that on himself. Indeed, he hinted that so long as they filled the lobby, it was impossible for the House to divide and defeat his motion.[25]

Observing Gordon's incitement of the crowd, his fellow members had no doubts as to who was to blame. One told Gordon that he would kill him if any of the mob entered the Chamber; another followed him around with the same intention. When soldiers had at last cleared the crowd out of the lobby and a division was possible, only seven members supported Gordon's motion and 192 opposed it. Lord George's attempted intimidation had failed; his incitement had not. The belated summons of some Foot and Horse Guards enabled MPs to go home; but though an intelligent justice,

Addington, contrived their departure from Westminster in good humour, not all the crowd did the same. Instead many went to two 'mass-houses'. The Sardinian ambassador's chapel near Lincoln's Inn Fields was ransacked and burned down; the Bavarian ambassador's chapel and house near Golden Square were plundered but not burned. Both chapels were used by English Catholic gentry.[26]

The conduct of the soldiers and the authorities on the first day was typical of their behaviour throughout, until on the sixth day the King intervened. The troops invariably behaved well but were ham-strung by lack of orders from the civil authorities and by uncertainty about their legal position; the authorities remained feckless and inadequate. They had had full warning of the great crowd Lord George Gordon intended to bring to Westminster, but they had taken virtually no precautions. On April 6 the ministry had called on the Guard to be in readiness to deal with a far smaller mob which was expected to accompany Fox to a meeting of the Westminster Association in Westminster Hall. Those precautions had turned out to be unnecessary, and that may have helped to produce the government's complacency in June. With a few exceptions the justices were similarly incompetent and remained so throughout the riots. Gordon believed many of them had signed the petition.[27]

Until the Commons found that the milling crowd in the lobby prevented a vote being taken, it did nothing to quieten or disperse the mob. The House did not even attempt to control Gordon himself, let alone arrest him; and after postponing consideration of bills about duties on post-horses and hair powder, it adjourned until June 6. On the third the Lords debated what the Lord President called 'the great fall from dignity which their Lordships had suffered' and tried to find out whether the government or the magistrates were to blame. The answer seemed to be the former. Richmond was gratified that ministers had recovered from their 'panic' but lamented their failure to control the mob or to anticipate the disturbances; he ascribed the trouble not to the Relief measure but solely to the Quebec Act. Then, after Shelburne had similarly condemned both the ministry and the Quebec Act and advocated a police force on the French model, and Rockingham had maintained that Gordon should have been prosecuted and the military not called out, Richmond spoke for some two hours in favour of his bill to effect more equal representation and annual parliaments. Lord Stormont, a Secretary of State, replied that since the British constitution was generally acknowledged to be the wisest that had ever been created it would be folly to change it. Whether the events of the previous day and night constituted a weaker argument for the introduction of manhood suffrage or for the perfection of the British constitution was not discussed.[28]

On Saturday June 3 London was generally quiet, though a 'vast

concourse' assembled in Covent Garden to see the thirteen people
who had been arrested the previous night at the Sardinian Chapel
taken to Bow Street by soldiers. Unfortunately, many of those
arrested had been innocent bystanders, and within three days eleven
of them had been released. On Sunday 4 the 'blue cockade mob'
returned to work, destroying a Catholic chapel in Moorfields and
damaging neighbouring houses, including that of the priest. On
Monday, the King's official birthday, Irish Catholic chapels in
Wapping and Aldgate were destroyed and Irish Catholic houses and
a school in Moorfields were badly damaged. The houses of two
justices who had taken action against rioters were pulled down, and
that of Sir George Savile was only saved from destruction by the
arrival of the Guards.[29]

For Parliament's meeting on Tuesday, the Guards cleared and
guarded lanes to enable MPs to reach the House. George Crabbe
found that this only made the mob 'more insolent: they boldly
paraded the streets with colours and music', mostly armed with sticks
or bludgeons, and all wearing the blue cockade. Two crude anti-
Catholic handbills entitled 'England in Blood' and 'True Protestants,
no Turncoats' were widely distributed. 'England in Blood', which
urged the necessity of 'persevering against the infernal designs of the
Ministry', was reputedly written by Gordon's secretary, Robert
Watson.[30]

If the military did not intimidate the mob, the mob for once did
not intimidate a justice, Hyde, who showed himself conspicuously
ready to act against it. In consequence no peer received more than
verbal violence except for the First Lord of the Admiralty.
Sandwich's head was cut, his coach was damaged and, though his
coachman turned it round, the crowd stopped it before it reached the
Admiralty. The First Lord was forced to take refuge in a coffee
house.[31]

Many MPs found reasons for not attending, but some 200 passed
unanimously a number of resolutions on the tumults. Burke, who
had been threatened on his way in, condemned those who had misled
the people to such violent outrages and censured the government for
that relaxed state of the police which could not even protect the
legislature from violence. The consequence was 'a bludgeoned mob
and an armed soldiery'. Reports of Fox's speech differ, but he seems
to have been still more evenhanded, condemning the violence but
unable to support the government since they had dissolved the bands
of society and disgraced everyone associated with them.[32]

One member hinted at the expulsion of Lord George Gordon. The
idea excited much opposition and was dropped. Gordon did not
oppose the resolution condemning the riots, but he was again
wearing a blue ribbon, which after a threat from the other side of the

House his friends removed by force. In what he himself called 'rather a long speech', he told the House that if it would appoint a day to discuss the petition and 'promise to do it to the satisfaction of the people' he was sure they would disperse. Evidently not sobered by what had happened since the House had last adjourned, Lord George wished to harangue the crowd as he had on Friday, but was prevented by his friends 'not without a degree of violence'. Fearing an attack, the House then adjourned. Understandably, the King told North, who had met Gordon the day before, that what the Commons had done fell far short of what was required: allowing Gordon, 'the avowed head of the tumult', to remain at large encouraged the continuation of it. The House met again two days later, then hurriedly adjourned until June 19. That concluded Parliament's inglorious part in the Gordon Riots.[33]

Maybe on Tuesday members thought that to take action against Lord George would jeopardise their own safety. Escape from the House was difficult enough as it was. Having read the Riot Act, Justice Hyde ordered the Horse Guards to disperse the mob. MPs were able to leave, but the crowd had their revenge by moving to St Martin's Street where they attacked Hyde's house and destroyed it. With no magistrate present an ensign who arrived with about thirty Foot Guards was himself reduced to making a speech. Its only effect was to produce jeers. So, the resources of oratory exhausted, the ensign marched his troops away and the mob clapped them on the back. The mob had fire engines and used them to prevent neighbouring houses being burned.[34]

The crowd had been led to Hyde's house by one James Jackson, a huge man on a carthorse waving a flag. Now shouting 'A-hoy for Newgate', he made George Dance's brand new prison, where four rioters were held, the next target. The assault had evidently been planned and was efficiently executed. Marvellously recreated by Dickens in *Barnaby Rudge*, the fall of Newgate was witnessed by George Crabbe. 'They broke the roof, tore away the rafters, and having got ladders they descended. Not Orpheus himself had more courage or better luck; flames all around them, and a body of soldiers expected, they defied and laughed at all opposition.' Returning a few hours later Crabbe found Newgate 'open to all; anyone might get in, and what was never the case before, anyone might get out. I did both . . .' All the 117 prisoners had in fact got out, including three who were due to be executed later that week.*[35]

---

* 'They turned all the thieves and robbers out of Newgate,' Benjamin Franklin commented at the time, 'and instead of replacing them with an equal number of other plunderers of the public, which they might easily have found among the Members of Parliament, they burnt the building.'[36]

Other buildings destroyed were the Police Office of Sir John
Fielding in Bow Street, Justice Cox's house in Great Queen Street,
and Lord Mansfield's house in Bloomsbury Square. Lord North's
official residence in Downing Street was also attacked, but some
Light Horse charged and expelled the mob. Two Catholic schools in
Bloomsbury and Soho were destroyed, as were the houses of a justice
and a constable who had been active against the rioters. Lord
Mansfield's furniture was thrown into the street and burned and his
books destroyed. The mob 'afterwards forced their way into his
Lordship's wine cellars and plentifully bestowed it upon the
populace'. Forty guardsmen were present, but in the absence of a
magistrate their commander refused to act. Eventually a justice did
arrive accompanied by more troops. Having read the Riot Act, which
was ignored by the crowd, Justice Durden asked the officer to order
his troops to fire. Colonel Woodford, who had spent most of
Saturday and much of Sunday with Gordon, his brother-in-law,
complied with the request, but only about fourteen soldiers seem
to have obeyed the order, and some of those deliberately fired over
the heads of the crowd. Nevertheless half a dozen people were
killed in the first shooting since the beginning of the riots, and the
crowd dispersed. So, unfortunately, did the soldiers, thinking the
affair was at an end. The mob thought differently and returned to
burn down Mansfield's house. The Archbishop of York, who lived
in the same square, narrowly escaped, and Lambeth Palace was saved
from attack by the presence of 150 soldiers who remained there till
August.[37]

Clerkenwell, Bridewell and New Prison were also stormed and
emptied of their contents. By the next day more than 1500 convicts
had been freed. 'The Protestant cause has received,' Burke commented, 'a powerful reinforcement from Newgate since last night',
but he thought the worst was over. Here he was wrong by twenty-
four hours: the day on which he wrote, 'Black Wednesday', was the
worst of the lot.[38]

By that time blue flags were hung from most houses, 'No Popery'
signs were everywhere, and the wearing of blue cockades had
become almost universal. According to Grafton even the Secretary
of State's servants were wearing them as a passport. Justice Hyde's
country house in Islington was destroyed, though Mansfield's,
Kenwood at Hampstead, was saved. Another active justice, Wilmot,
lost the furniture of his private house and had his office destroyed.
Catholic houses, shops, public houses and offices were attacked in
Westminster, the City and further afield. The worst scene was the
assault on Langdale's distillery in Holborn. Although Langdale, a rich
Roman Catholic, had long been expecting an attack, he was given
no protection. By giving money and drink to potential attackers he

tried to protect himself. This worked for a time but on Wednesday evening his premises were attacked and fired and his stocks of liquor – much larger than usual because he had anticipated an increase in duty – began to flow. Drinking large quantities of unrectified spirit would by itself have inflamed the rioters, but much of the spirit was itself on fire, as were all Langdale's large premises and surrounding houses. The crowd allowed two fire engines to work. Unfortunately they were pumping out spirit not water and spread rather than confined the inferno. Men, women and children in varying degrees of intoxication were burned in the street; others were killed by falling buildings.[39]

All the remaining prisons save one were attacked and their prisoners released: most were burned down – the one great penal reform of the century. The Bank of England was attacked three times. Earlier it had been vulnerable, but by now it was well defended by, amongst others, the Guards, the Northumberland Militia, the voluntary London Military Association, and the former colonel of the Buckinghamshire militia, Alderman Wilkes.[40]

Some were suspicious of Wilkes during the troubles and, characteristically, he fuelled their suspicions with a joke. When the messenger carrying the Royal Proclamation of June 7 arrived at the City's Common Council, Wilkes, remembering past encounters, moved that he be committed. Wilkes feared that the government's military incursions threatened the City's traditional liberties. But, the advocate of religious toleration, he played an energetic part in putting down the riots he had foreseen. If others could not distinguish between the Wilkes and Gordon mobs and causes, he had no difficulty. In his diary, normally a notably uninformative document confined to recording where and with whom he dined without even disclosing the menu, Wilkes wrote: 'fired six or seven times . . . killed two rioters directly opposite to the great gate of the Bank.' Prominent in defence of Catholics as well as the Bank, he afterwards received the special thanks of the Privy Council.[41]

Burke was premature about the weakening of the riots because it was only on that Wednesday morning that the government at last took action. If it had not, much of London, as Walpole feared, would probably have burned that 'Black Wednesday' night, accompanied by fighting in the streets between the rioters and the new citizens' defence associations that had been formed; anarchy, revolution of one sort or another, or even the arrival of a Scottish army might have followed. But George III, finally exasperated by 'the great supineness of the civil magistrates' and determined there would be 'one magistrate in the kingdom' who would do his duty, summoned a Privy Council, which finally empowered the military to use force without the permission of a magistrate. As a result, heavy casualties were inflicted on the assailants of the new Blackfriars Bridge, and the Bank was successfully defended. The new order was not issued until the evening, and it took time for the government's new-found firmness to take full effect. Soldiers had been gathered in London during the last few days: Hyde Park was said to resemble 'the field of Malplaquet before the battle', and by Wednesday evening nearly 10,000 men were under arms. Yet Lord Amherst claimed still to be short of troops, and though warning had been given of the attacks on the prisons they were not properly defended. In addition it was not until the seventh that Amherst, who evidently found the London mob a more difficult opponent than the French army in America, accepted expert advice and secured London, Westminster and Blackfriars Bridges. That was the crucial strategic move, which separated the mobs and enabled the army to gain ascendancy.[42]

By Thursday June 8 it had become unsafe to wear a blue cockade. Battles were fought in St George's Fields and in Fleet Street where the rioters attacked the Horse Guards and were repelled by the bayonet, leaving about twenty dead and many wounded; riots continued in Southwark and Bermondsey, and a Catholic shop was destroyed in the City. More soldiers had arrived, however, and the military were at last in control. The following day Lord George Gordon was arrested by three King's messengers who got into his house by pretending to be clergymen, and he was sent to the Tower.[43]

Bath, Bristol, Birmingham and Hull also saw disturbances. But only in Bath, where a Roman Catholic chapel and a priest's house were burned and the priest assaulted, and where one, possibly innocent, rioter was executed, were they serious.[44]

The City and the government

Both the ministry and the City were abysmally feeble in their efforts to put down the Gordon Riots. In 1780 the City was even more opposed to the government than it had been for most of the eighteenth century. The ministry was weak, contained no popular figure, was clearly losing the American war and was widely thought to be on its last legs. A few riots, it was plausible to think, might finish it off or induce it to give way on the Catholic Relief Act, as it had in Scotland. Moreover the cause of the riots was one with which a great many people sympathised. Cowper wrote in February of the general suspicion 'of a fixed design of government to favour the growth of popery', and Gordon thought that 'many of the magistrates and almost all the creditable constables had signed the petition'. Hostility to the Pope and all he stood for – in normal times almost part of the national identity – had been intensified by the entry of the main Catholic powers into the American war. Patriotism and bigotry marched – or ran – hand in hand.[45]

There were, too, particular personal reasons for the abject behaviour of the City leadership. The Lord Mayor, Brackley Kennett, had been a waiter in a brothel before graduating to a brothel of his own. Though both posts should have accustomed him to dealing with disorder, they evidently had not. Whenever he was asked to take action during the riots he gave an evasive answer and shuffled away. On Sunday June 4 he went to Moorfields with a detachment of Guards and spoke to a crowd which was burning a chapel. When it paid no attention, he simply retired into a house, leaving the Guards outside with no orders and with nothing to do save protect the house in which the Lord Mayor was skulking. Similarly, Kennett's two later jobs, tavern keeper and wine merchant, might have instilled notions about safeguarding property. But when told that it was his duty to prevent a fire, he merely replied that 'the mob had got hold of some people and furniture they did not like and were burning them, and where was the harm in that?' Admittedly the City marshals and constables were highly reluctant to deal with the mobs, in some cases openly sympathising with them; and the Mayor's requests for troops were belatedly and inadequately met. Yet Kennett, like many others in the City, was clearly determined that the mob should not take a dislike to him. At one point he said that he had orders to employ the military if necessary, 'but I must be cautious what I do lest I bring the mob to my house. I can assure you,' he added, 'that there are very great people at the bottom of the riot.'[46]

Most of the City magistrates had a similar outlook. They made themselves scarce from the beginning, or having called for troops they lost their nerve and disappeared, or they remained on the spot and when the troops arrived they refused to act. Conceivably the justices were influenced by memories of the Wilkite prosecution of Gillan after St George's Fields, but much more probably their cowardice was caused by sympathy with the rioters and by knowledge of what had happened to the homes of such active magistrates as Hyde and Wilmott. On June 7 the Deputy Clerk of the City told Stormont that only very few JPs had attended because they were frightened of having their houses destroyed. Readers of Smollett and Fielding would not have been surprised; Justices Frolic, Thrasher and Buzzard were still in office. Well might Mansfield talk of the magistrates' 'neglect' and 'native imbecility'.[47]

After seeing 'the Protestants' looting at 'leisure in full security' the ruins of the Old Bailey as though they were 'lawfully employed', Dr Johnson remarked: 'such is the cowardice of a commercial place'; but that was only part of it. The City was not merely cowardly; it favoured and encouraged the rioters. As late as June 7 the City's Common Council took the highly provocative step of agreeing to petition the House of Commons against the Relief Act. It had passed a similar resolution two days before Gordon's march. Only when the riots were 'no longer merely a question of religion' and the violence seemed to have stopped serving their purposes did the City authorities change sides. It was only then that their duty coincided with their prejudices, and only then that they stopped neglecting it.[48]

The government suffered from no such conflict between their prejudices and their duty, yet apart from George III they still neglected it. Probably the Houses of Parliament should not be blamed for what Johnson called their 'great tameness'.[49] They were there to do what they were told, not to take independent action. There is no such excuse even for a cabinet of nonentities. Not to arrest Gordon until after the riots were over was as cowardly as anything done – or not done – by the City authorities. To leave him at large and allow him to take part in the proceedings of Parliament on the Tuesday, while refusing to discuss his petition, was the worst possible mixture: the first did nothing to discourage the rioters; the second did nothing to satisfy them.

The government's attitude to the use of the army was similarly negligent. It summoned many additional units to London and encouraged the use of troops, but it did nothing to see that their deployment served any useful purpose. Until the Wednesday, Londoners were accustomed to see soldiers arrive at the scene of a riot, watch what was going on, occasionally appeal for order, and then march away again. The experience of the Coldstream Guards was typical. On June 4 a detachment formed a ring round a bonfire in Moorfields; the Lord Mayor would not allow them to do anything, so the mob hurled furniture over their heads onto the fire. On the next day another detachment, incapacitated by a magistrate's refusal to give it orders, could only stand and watch a chapel on the Ratcliff Highway being pulled down. The ineffectiveness of the troops was not their fault; unlike the City or the government, the army came very well out of the whole episode. Put in an intolerable situation by the authorities, the soldiers retained their discipline and did everything required of them, provided it was lawful.[50]

The sole cause of the army's impotence was the view of the law that was passed on to it by the government. This was clearly set out in a letter from the Secretary at War, Jenkinson, to Stormont, the Secretary of State. 'It is the duty of the troops, My Lord, to act only under the authority and by direction of the civil magistrate. For this reason they are under greater restraints than any other of His Majesty's subjects, and when insulted are obliged to be more cautious

even in defending themselves.' If therefore there were no civil
magistrates present at a riot, or if when present they refused to give
any direction to the army, there was, on this view, nothing that the
troops who had been summoned to the scene could do, for to open
fire would lay them open to civil penalties. So they could either stay
and witness the violence, or they could turn about and march away
again. Either course was ignominious and excited the derision of the
rioters; it even tended, as Jenkinson claimed, to encourage them.[51]

The traditional misapprehension of the law voiced by Jenkinson
did not lead to difficulty so long as the magistrates did their duty.
Yet, as Mansfield told the Lords immediately after the riots, the Riot
Act had been misunderstood: every private individual, and soldiers
above all, had not only the right but the duty to put down
disturbances and to use force if necessary; they did not need the
sanction of a magistrate. Clearly Mansfield was correct. The
government's belated action was in full accordance with the law.[52]

Yet, even though they knew that the magistrates were failing in
their duty and were stultifying the use of troops, ministers did
nothing. In 1768-69 the government had been alarmed by the minor
violence of the Wilkite crowds, and though the provocation had been
slight the army had received the King's congratulations after killing
seven people at St George's Fields. Yet in 1780 faced with near
rebellion and with no bending of the law required, ministers were
content to wring their hands. Even at Wednesday's meeting of the
Privy Council only the Lord President and one or two others
supported the King in favouring decisive action. Luckily, when
Wedderburn was called in, the normally evasive Attorney General
gave unequivocal advice that officers could themselves decide to fire
on the mob without the intervention of a magistrate. And that was
enough for the King. 'So let it be done,' he said.[53]

Who was responsible?

At the end of the riots Gillray published a picture of a villainous rioter
wielding a club:

> Tho' he says he's a Protestant, look at the print.
> The face and the bludgeon will give you a hint.
> Religion he cried in hopes to deceive
> While his practice is only to burn and to thieve.

Was the destruction merely the outcome of senseless mob violence
or did the rioters have a serious religious or political objective? Or –
a third possibility – should the riots be divided into two parts: the

first stage being the work of genuine religious fanatics and the second that of criminals out for plunder?[54]

So far as it is now possible to do so, Professor Rudé discovered who the rioters were. Of the 110 accused whose occupations are known, nearly three-quarters were wage earners; the rest included twenty-two small employers, shopkeepers and independent crafts-men, four soldiers, six sailors, one apothecary (who was acquitted) and one public executioner, Edward Dennis (who was convicted and released). There seem to have been few who were unemployed. A small criminal element was there from the beginning – otherwise the Duke of Northumberland and other peers would not have had their pockets picked on their way to the Lords on June 2 – and later some criminals took advantage of the riots: two women were raped and killed. But despite the emptying of the gaols the criminal element seems not greatly to have grown. The overwhelming majority of the released prisoners were from debtors' prisons; only 134 were released from Newgate, 119 from Bridewell and almost 100 from other prisons for criminals, while some 1500 were released from the debtors' prisons, the King's Bench and the Fleet. Probably the debtors were no more inclined to take part in the disturbances than was militiaman Gibbon, who remained the whole week in Islington because he was 'not apt, without duty or of necessity, to thrust' himself into a mob. Maybe the 'convicts and all kinds of desperadoes' that Horace Walpole and others noted as being involved were better at evading arrest than their fellow rioters. But only three or four of the 160 who were tried had criminal records. Indeed a high percentage received from their neighbours or employers testimonials of their good characters which seem to have been superior to those of many of the prosecution witnesses.[55]

The spectacle of blazing prisons was particularly disturbing to the law abiding, yet their destruction and the small number of private houses that were substantially damaged show the mob's careful selection of targets. The only scene of drunken frenzy and indiscriminate destruction was at Langdale's Brewery in Holborn, and even there the rioters believed the brewery contained a Catholic chapel. Only in Holborn, because of the fire at the brewery, were an appreciable number of Protestant houses damaged. As a rule the only Protestant houses in danger were those belonging to active justices and to prominent supporters of Catholic relief. Similarly no indiscriminate attack was made on Roman Catholics. Only sixty Catholic houses were destroyed or damaged, and virtually none of these were in places where the Catholic population was heavily concentrated. It was not the Catholic population as a whole that was singled out, but Catholics of substance. That differentiation, added to the assaults on those engines of oppression of the poor – the prisons – and on the Bank of England make plain a substantial 'class' element in the riots. Religious feeling directed the violence at Roman Catholics; social feeling excluded poor Roman Catholics from that violence.[56]

Walpole, whose printer had been on the streets observing the rioters, reported on Thursday June 8 that most of them were apprentices and that plunder and drink were what they chiefly sought. Inevitably much was drunk but, except at Langdale's brewery, that was clearly not the main objective of the rioters. Inevitably, too, there was some looting but not much. Usually what was taken from buildings was burned, not stolen, and only eight of the accused were found guilty of theft. Dickens was probably much nearer the mark than Walpole when in *Barnaby Rudge* he described most of the rioters as being like 'mere workmen who had a certain task to do'. Yet the most striking fact about them is the one which Erskine brought out at Gordon's trial: none of the 44,000 who had signed Gordon's petition were among those 'convicted, tried, or even apprehended on suspicion'. If they were involved, they were even better at evading arrest than the criminals.[57]

The third possibility, mentioned above, that the riots should be divided into two unconnected stages, largely accommodates Erskine's telling point. Gordon's friend, Sir Philip Jennings Clarke MP, claimed at his trial that those who thronged the lobby of the House of Commons on Friday evening were already different from those who had marched from St George's fields. That was partly true, and if the riots are to be separated into two parts a dividing line as early as that is the only remotely plausible one – after all, the mob at the Commons went off to sack the ambassadors' chapels. The trouble is that at the time Gordon drew no such line. His speeches to the crowd on June 2 leave no doubt that he regarded them as his followers. And his attitude did not change later.[58]

From his own account Gordon seems all along to have been much less concerned with London's safety than with his own – he feared he would be murdered by Irish papists and even considered asking the government for a guard. When he went to see Lord North in Downing Street on Monday June 6, North told him that if he 'would leave town, matters would subside'. Gordon refused this appeal. His sole contribution to helping matters subside was to advise 'the immediate repeal of the Popish Bill'. On the Tuesday the demagogue issued a handbill criticising the riots and urging 'a legal and peaceable deportment', yet he still wore his blue cockade to the House of Commons and did not disown the mob that swarmed round Westminster. He did, however, when he came out, exhort the people 'to go home'. They went instead to Justice Hyde's house and Newgate.[59]

On Wednesday when Lord George went to Buckingham House to ask for a private audience with the King, George III very correctly refused to see him until he had shown 'proof of his loyalty and allegiance' by doing all in his power to quell the disturbances. Gordon could not provide that proof, but he was able to tell Stormont that he could be of great service in putting a stop to the riots. He would not have thought, presumably, that he had great influence over drunken criminals. And in an advertisement, which he sent to the newspapers on that day and which appeared in some of them on Thursday June 8, he told how he had in three places exhorted the mob to be peaceable but had had no effect 'because Lord George Gordon [was] not able to give them any assurances that the Act would be repealed'. That advertisement encapsulated Gordon's attitude and conduct throughout: ostensibly favouring law and order while indicating to the rioters that they should continue with their depredations until the government gave in. And they interpreted him, Walpole wrote, in spirit not in letter. Lord George never came near complying either with North's request to quieten the tumults by leaving London or with the King's to do everything he could to stop them. Gordon's own behaviour refutes the idea that it was 'an unconnected riot' which did the destruction. While some very young men and prostitutes who can scarcely have paraded with the Protestant Association in St George's Fields joined in, the riots did not change their character halfway through or at any other time. On the Tuesday the Protestant Association criticised the violence and urged 'a legal and peaceable deportment', but not until Gordon had been sent to the Tower did it unequivocally disavow any connection with the riots and declare its 'utmost abhorrence of such atrocious conduct. Responsibility for the riots therefore lies squarely on Lord George and the Protestant Association.[60]

Ambitions limited to repeal?

Both Gordon and the Protestant Association must have known that to march many thousands of people to Westminster was liable to produce violence. That was why many of the Association's leaders opposed his plan. They had seen the effects of religious propaganda in Scotland: Catholic mass houses and other premises had been destroyed. And they had seen the effect of that violence on the ministry: the extension of the Catholic Relief Act to Scotland had been abandoned. In America, too, as Gordon was presumably aware, mobs had not long before successfully intimidated representatives assembling. Almost certainly, therefore, Lord George and the Protestant Association expected London and England to copy

Edinburgh and Scotland; hence Gordon's reminder to his audience outside the Commons that the Scots had got nowhere until 'they pulled down the mass-houses'.[61]

The riots can be regarded as a straightforward anti-Catholic agitation, albeit with a growing component of social protest, whose limited and feasible objective was in the tradition of the Sacheverell Riots and the campaign against Walpole's Excise Bill; Lord George and the Protestant Association were campaigning for the repeal of the Catholic Relief Act and nothing more.[62] On this minimalist view of Gordon's ambitions he apparently had much to gain and little to lose. He probably expected the government to agree straightaway to his demands. He would then have struck a blow against a war he deplored, a government he despised and a religion he detested. He would also have shown himself a politician of considerable account. Or, if the ministry did not immediately surrender to the intimidation of 60,000 people, a riot or two, a Roman Catholic chapel pulled down here and there, would surely do the trick. Once again Lord George Gordon would be the hero of the hour. Or, at worst, there would be no concession, and the government would step in to put an end to the violence. Even in the worst predictable case, therefore, little damage would have been done. The risks were not high.

The failure to unearth a masterplan for the riots either at the time or later is not surprising; for one thing the secretary of the Protestant Association destroyed all the relevant papers as soon as he learned that Gordon had been arrested. For another, in all probability, no such plan existed because it was not necessary. All that was needed was the stoking up of fanatical anti-Catholic feeling, which had been going on for months, and the initial show of force. If, for one reason or another, that did not prove to be enough, the activities of a very few people on the spot would be sufficient to point the crowds in the right direction. And that is what happened. Many, including the Archbishop of York, spoke at the time of well-dressed people leading the attacks, and clearly there were some. One such, Henry Maskall, a pro-American radical, was tried and acquitted. Probably, though, most of the well-dressed men were spectators or temporary drunken participants, like Fox in the Keppel Riots the year before.[63]

The Protestant Association having set the match to the flame did not need to pile much fuel on the fire, though almost certainly it piled some. Prosecution witnesses referred at the trials to having seen people with lists of houses 'that had to come down'. No such lists have ever been discovered, but there was undoubtedly much direction: the fire spread only to selected targets, and fire engines were used to confine the damage to the intended victims. The rioters presumably (and correctly) thought that many people supported what they were doing, a belief which would tend to make them careful of Protestant property. Had there been no direction, the damage would have been much greater, and no warning of intended attacks would have been given; nor would the mobs have been suitably equipped.[64]

Anti-Catholic though the riots blatantly were, not all those taking part in the destruction had the same ideas or objectives. Some were anti–Catholic enthusiasts; some had it in for the authorities and were taking the first chance since the Monmouth Rebellion to revolt under aristocratic leadership and the banner of religion; some were against both the Pope and the government; probably some were just bored, and others only wanted to destroy. But the riots did not change character or direction; they merely became larger and more violent. Nobody planned their development; it was a graduated response to the government's inaction – the rioters naturally gaining confidence from their successes and from the absence of effective opposition.[65]

The government, unfortunately, had no conception of a graduated response. Gordon's – on this view – limited expectations were foiled by the wholly unpredictable inadvertence of the ministry, which combined the maximum provocation with the minimum of effective force. That folly, added to the criminal negligence of what a City observer called 'the scoundrel magistrates', let the violence of the rioters and, in the end, the army exceed all foreseeable bounds.[66]

A revolutionary uprising?

On another interpretation, Lord George expected his show of force against a notoriously 'weak' government to produce something much more far-reaching than the repeal of the Relief Act: at the very least the ending of the American war. Before the riots he had, after all, used violent and revolutionary language; not only had he conjured up the threat of revolt and civil war, he had obliquely likened 'the Elector of Hanover' to both Charles I and James II. And when a man's subsequent actions are consistent with his earlier threats, as was Gordon's behaviour from his insistence on the Protestant Association's march on Westminster to the end of the riots, there must be some presumption that his language accurately translated his intentions.[67]

Lord George was an embittered and ambitious young man, an extreme radical and a religious enthusiast – a combustible amalgam. That the crusade he was leading was apparently reactionary does not preclude him having had revolutionary designs. Much as the new conservatism of the 1980s can be viewed as either radical or reactionary, the 'No Popery' agitation of 1780 can be seen as both reactionary and revolutionary. The conduct of the Gordon mobs was similarly ambivalent. In any case revolutions do not have to be left wing or progressive; nor do they have to aim to transform society.* If, as in Professor Zagorin's definition, a revolution 'is any attempt by a subordinate group through the use of violence to bring about a change of government or its policy . . .' then Gordon was evidently making a revolutionary attempt.[69]

Furthermore revolution in 1780 was far from unthinkable. Gordon was not the only politician to use the language of threat and violence. The orthodox opposition leaders were also doing so, and Sir James Lowther, one of the seven MPs to support Gordon on the day of the march, had recently told the government that should it not grant his petition he would recommend the people of Cumberland not to pay their taxes, and if the government tried to dragoon them there would be 'the most horrid consequence'. Political language was violent because the times were so bad and the government so weak. The calamitously incompetent government and the opposition Whigs, Butterfield pointed out, had brought the country's institutions into contempt and had loosened 'the fabric of the state'. Above all the country faced military disaster – something the British had not known for many a long year. Pitt's victories in the Seven Years War had consolidated the Hanoverian regime; now George III and Lord North's defeats in the American war were undermining it.[70]

Writing fifteen years later Gordon's secretary and biographer, Dr Robert Watson, maintained that in 1780 Gordon could certainly have 'overturned the government, and founded a constitution agreeable to the wishes and true interest of the people – a hundred thousand men were ready to execute his orders, and ministers trembled for their safety'. The government was only saved from destruction, Watson contended, by 'the unprincipled lawless banditti' who began the riots. 'It is supposed,' Watson continued, 'that whoever is master of the bank and the tower will soon become master of the city, and whoever is master of the city will soon be master of Great Britain; with this belief, a plan was laid to seize them both, and to bring the matter at once to a crisis.' But before what Watson rightly called 'this daring project' could be put into execution, the military fired upon the people who suffered dreadful carnage and were obliged to yield to superior force.[71]

Watson, who himself was undoubtedly a revolutionary in the 1790s, may have merely fathered his own ideas onto Gordon. Yet save in one respect his account is not intrinsically implausible. The

---

* Nor do counter-revolutions have to be socially conservative. The objective of the peasants of Calabria who, rising under Cardinal Ruffo in 1799 overthrew the French-installed Neapolitan Republic and restored the Bourbon monarchy, was to seize the wealth and properties of the rich.[68]

exception is his attempt to blame the mobs for the failure of the
revolution. Their excesses, he claimed, led 'the timorous and those
unaccustomed to revolutionary movement' to withdraw from the
scene. But if such men were frightened away by the burning of a few
Catholic chapels, they were unpromising material for revolutionary
attacks on the Bank of England and the Tower. The revolutionary
crisis – if it was one – was created by the 'lawless banditti' and
nobody else could have done it. Watson may have been complaining
about the order in which the selected targets were attacked – Dr
Johnson and the *Annual Register* concurred in the view that if the
rioters had at the beginning struck at the Bank of England they would
probably have secured it – but on the first day Gordon incited them
to attack mass-houses not the Bank; the lower priority given to it
was thus not their fault. Probably, therefore, Watson was just being
sensibly cautious. To have added to his talk of revolution an
endorsement of the Gordon Riots when they were still very much in
people's minds, and fears of renewed public disorder were high,
would have been a close flirtation with sedition. In that dangerous
year, 1795, condemnation of both riots and rioters was almost
obligatory.[72]

That apart, Watson's version chimes with what Gordon said before
the riots and with what the mob did during them. Anti-Catholicism
was the main fuel of the agitation, and the tumults duly began with
disciplined and discriminating assaults on Roman Catholic chapels
and property. After those essential preliminaries, attacks were
launched or planned on the houses of the Prime Minister, the Lord
Chancellor, the opposition leaders, the Archbishop of Canterbury,
the Archbishop of York, the Lord Chief Justice, the Bow Street
magistrate and other justices, on the prisons and on the Bank of
England – a hit-list which comprised the whole spectrum of authority
except the King. No wonder Lord Mansfield spoke of 'a systematic
plan to destroy the constitution and overturn the government'!
Whatever the war cries that were used, the targets were more
appropriate to insurgents bent on revolution and peace with America
than to drunken mobs intent on loot and mindless destruction and
allegedly defending Protestant England from the danger of Popery.[73]

Whether or not revolution was carefully planned, how nearly was
it achieved? Lord North, like the City magistrates, was supine but,
unlike them, showed no signs of cowardice. Nodding at one of his
heavily-armed dinner guests some hours after the attack on Downing
Street, North said he was not 'half so much afraid of the mob as of
Jack St John's pistol'. That same Wednesday night Horace Walpole
assured Lady Ossory that there was no panic; the Duke of Gloucester
had taken his four nieces to Ranelagh for the evening. The theatres,
too, remained open, but then so they did in Paris on almost all the

major *journées* of the French Revolution. And if there was not quite
panic, there was general consternation and the largest exodus from
London 'since the Plague'. As in the 'Forty-five', some fled as far as
Holland. The Royal Exchange Insurance Company refused to
cooperate with the government for fear of reprisals from the mob.
Many 'well affected' people did the same. Dr Johnson called it 'a time
of Terror' and thought there had been 'an universal panic'. Fear and
rumour reigned; it was even thought that rioters were about to
release lions from the Tower and lunatics from Bedlam.[74]

The ministry, too, was bewildered and apprehensive. On the
Wednesday morning the Speaker, Sir Fletcher Norton, told Gordon
that the government was almost dissolved by the rioters. Lord
Hillsborough, a Secretary of State, wrote that they threatened not
only 'the total destruction' of London but 'the subversion of the
government'. And the King later told Parliament that the outrages
had 'overborne all civil authority' and threatened the 'subversion of
all legal power'. The government was nearly swept away together
with law and order.[75]

Of course, even a dissolved government would not necessarily
have served Gordon's purpose. But serious talk of revolution was
symptomatic of the weakness and decay of civilian administration.
Asking himself what was the civil power, a clergyman answered 'a
power that will be civil to the mob'. Without the army, he believed,
they would have been lost. The outcome did indeed depend upon the
soldiers: on the orders they were given and on their obedience to
them. Because of its defeats in America the army lacked both prestige
and popularity. Two months before the riots, Sir Charles Bunbury
had criticised the nation's small return for the immense sums that had
been spent on it, and had catalogued its 'memorable transactions' in
America. In 1778 it had evacuated Philadelphia; in 1779 it evacuated
Rhode Island; in 1780 nobody knew where it was. The ministry was
attempting, Bunbury scoffed, 'to keep a large army incognito'. For
the first five days of the riots the soldiers must have wished they had
remained incognito instead of being made conspicuously ridiculous
by the magistrates and the government.[76]

According to Watson, Lord George told the mob in the Commons
lobby that 'the military were generally disaffected'. That view or
hope was not a madman's fantasy. Some onlookers thought early on
that the soldiers were not unsympathetic to the presumed aims of the
rioters. They were heard to say at the burning of the Sardinian
Chapel: 'Great fools! Why did they not pull down the buildings? The
fire might have hurt their neighbours.' Stormont was told that
somebody had put into their heads that to assist Catholics would be
a breach of their oaths and therefore they would not fire on anybody
'destroying Romanish chapels'. Many people thought they would

not fire on the rioters and might even join them. Some Coldstream Guardsmen were said to support Gordon, and not all the troops ordered to fire in Bloomsbury Square obeyed the order.[77]

In general, however, the troops did what they were told, even though their orders ensured their ineffectiveness and brought them into ridicule. How long they would have endured such humiliation is unknowable. On Wednesday June 7 the King's decision 'to provide for the public safety of the state' by changing their orders brought it to an end and enabled the army to suppress the 'rebellious insurrections' and save the capital. Had matters been left to the King's ministers, they would probably have gone on doing nothing until London had been burned down and the 'rebellious insurrections' had sprouted into revolution.[78]

Conclusion

Dickens portrayed the riots as the outcome of a deep and carefully planned conspiracy. That was a common view at the time. Mansfield held it. So did Stormont. Burke wrote of the 'principal movers in this wicked business who have hitherto eluded . . . scrutiny'. And Colonel John Stuart, who was the first to suggest that the three bridges should be held and who wrote intelligent accounts of the riots to his father, Lord Bute, said that having seen the prisoners they all appeared too wretched to have been able to plan 'so deep and well conducted a project'.[79]

The opposition, the French and the Americans were all suspected of being behind the 'wicked business'. Few seem to have suspected Gordon of more than encouraging the riots, though Walpole wondered what 'seditious plans' were incorporated with 'his Calvinistic reformation'. Presumably most people thought him too mad to have formed a more extensive design. Yet even if he was mad, that would not rule him out; and if anybody planned the 'project', it was Lord George. He was indeed questioned by the Privy Council who found no evidence of his having planned a revolution. (What evidence it expected to find other than what he had said or done is not clear; it can hardly have hoped for a confession.) Unlike Wilkes, Gordon surely was a revolutionary. But whatever his dreams or hopes of a revolution – and almost certainly he aimed, at least, to force an end to the war – he is unlikely to have formulated such a clear-cut plan as the one outlined by Dr Watson. Apart from anything else, any such plan would presumably have had to be abruptly aborted, if the ministry had quickly agreed to repeal the 'Popish Act'. The element of intention in events is seldom high. Gordon's assurance to the mob on the first day that the military were disaffected suggests that in planning violence he may have calculated the attitude of the army – a vital consideration for any revolutionary leader – but the near-revolutionary opportunity that had arisen by the Wednesday was probably created by Gordon's revolutionary hopes, a disastrous war, the activities of the rioters, religious prejudice and the paralysis of the government rather than by a carefully premeditated programme of revolution.[80]

'Few events in the annals of Britain,' Watson wrote, 'have excited more attention than the riots of 1780, and perhaps none are in greater darkness.' The darkness is still there, but the attention soon wandered. The riots of 1780 were much the biggest civil tumult since the Monmouth Rebellion. Yet until recently they have received strikingly little notice. The best modern survey of the period dismisses them in half a sentence. Much as the crowd's part in the Glorious Revolution was soon obliterated, the mob's near toppling of the state in 1780 was quietly buried.[81]

In the eighteenth century, as in others, few people disapproved of violence as such; the cause or the objective of the riot determined for the majority the view they took of it. Hence the City's initial support for the tumults of 1780. A similarly pragmatic approach today involves judging violence by the degree of provocation, by its objectives, by the casualties and damage it caused, and by its success or failure. By all these criteria the Gordon Riots stand condemned, even though the government bears much of the blame.

The ministry's capitulation to the Scottish Protestants came near to encouragement, but there was no provocation. The 'ruffian apostle' and his 'pious insurgents'[82] were not alone in seeking the repeal of a mild measure of relief for Roman Catholics, yet only the ultrabigoted could think such an objective justified violence. The government was palsied and the war was disastrous, yet only the ultradiscontented could think that the situation justified a revolutionary uprising.

The damage done in the Gordon tumults was incomparably greater than that wreaked by the Wilkite mobs whose destructiveness scarcely went beyond the breaking of windows. Like the Wilkites, the Gordon rioters killed nobody, though since many of them were armed that was partly fortuitous. Their own casualties were, however, heavy. The art of dispersing rioters without mowing them down by gunfire, so brilliantly displayed in the Sacheverell riots, had been largely forgotten; in 1780, because of the rioters' arms, quelling the tumults without using guns would, except in the early days, have been more difficult. Some officers disliked shooting the rioters and tried other methods with success, but the army – or rather the rioters – paid heavily for the authorities' indifference to the subject of riot control. According to the *Annual Register*, the troops killed 285 rioters and another 173 were taken to hospital: 'The number of those who perished from inebriation and in the ruins of the demolished houses is not known, but is conceived to have been very considerable.' The total who died was probably between 800 and 1000. A Grenadier Guards sergeant recorded that on two nights of the riots his walk brought blood through his stockings.[83]

The riots were a total failure. So far from bringing revolution, they revived the ministry. The Relief Act was not repealed. Indeed only eleven years later a larger measure of relief to Roman Catholics than that of 1778 was passed without trouble at a time when relief to Protestant Dissenters was being refused. Admittedly, Catholic emancipation did not come until 1829, but it was the man who suppressed the riots, George III, not the rioters, who was responsible for that. Finally, the Gordon Riots produced no incidental benefits. They did not draw the attention of the authorities to grievances that needed to be redressed. Rather they sought to undo the alleviation of injustice. In no way defensive, they were purely coercive.

The flames of London's prisons did not alarm the possessing classes into setting up a more effective police force. 'Liberty' was still as important as 'property', and a 'French' police, it was felt, would endanger the first even if it safeguarded the second. Hence Newgate's destruction which released 139 prisoners was far less influential than the fall of the Bastille which freed a mere seven: four forgers, one sexual offender, one English and one French lunatic were released. All the same after June 1780 the propertied nation was suspicious of all extra-parliamentary agitation, and radicals, in particular, became much more wary of popular demonstrations and the mob. In that sense the English reaction to the French Revolution began well before its outbreak.[84]

SEVENTEEN

Aftermath and Recovery

The flames of London which were kindled by a mischievous madman admonished all thinking people of the danger of an appeal to the people.

Edward Gibbon

. . . it was a doubt whether the nation should be ruled by the sceptre of George the third, or the tongue of Fox.

Dr Johnson

At Carlton House Wilkes *proposed the toast:* The King – long life to him – The Prince of Wales: Since when have you become so loyal? – Wilkes, *with a bow*: Ever since I have had the honour of knowing your Royal Highness.[1]

More than 450 people were arrested during and after the Gordon Riots: 160 eventually stood trial, of whom 62 were sentenced to death and 85 were acquitted. As early as June 15, Burke, along with the King and Wilkes one of the few to come well out of the riots, wrote to Wedderburn advocating mercy for the convicted rioters. After a lengthy intrigue Wedderburn had just been made Baron Lough-borough and Chief Justice of the Court of Common Pleas, but he did not manage his legal transition with the smooth dexterity of his political transformations. His response to Burke was to deliver a charge to the grand jury of Surrey designed to inflame opinion against the rioters. It was more a speech of an Attorney General than a Chief Justice; Loughborough had not yet taken over from Wedderburn.[2]

Burke followed up his letter to Loughborough with appeals to other members of the 'Nominal Cabinet', who with the King decided which of the condemned should be executed. He proposed that there should be no executions until all the trials had been finished; then six, at most, of the worst offenders should be hanged at six different places on the same day. Burke favoured mercy because there had already been great slaughter of the rioters on the streets, because the convicted had been deluded by the complete 'impunity' of those who had committed the same offences in Edinburgh, and because many 'of the lower and some of the middling' people of London were 'in a very critical disposition' and in general approved the principles of the rioters. Such people should be humbled and not irritated, Burke suggested, and the government should therefore proceed with firmness and delicacy, especially since 'none of the list-makers' or the managers had been caught. Finally, he contended, the execution of one man fixed the attention and excited awe; the execution of multitudes dissipated and weakened the effect. Burke hoped, too, that in selecting the criminals for exemplary punishment the government would not, as the champions of the Protestant Association recommended, punish the 'offenders for plunder' and spare 'the offenders from principle'. Common plunderers were executed in considerable numbers anyway; the offenders from principle would be the only ones who would furnish an example.[3]

Nobody, of course, paid the smallest attention to Burke's arguments. If he was right in thinking that mercy would show 'the wisdom and steadiness of government', North's ministry was unlikely to be merciful. Revenge came more easily than clemency; and irresolution during the riots was followed by violence after them. Considering that 'the chief delinquents' had not been discovered and many of those convicted were 'a poor thoughtless set of creatures, very little aware of their offence', the nominal cabinet ordered an inordinate number of executions. Probably no eighteenth-century popular rising in Western Europe had been so severely punished. Twenty-five men, women and children were hanged. According to Horace Walpole, seventeen of those hanged were under eighteen; certainly at least one was a boy of fifteen and another a girl of sixteen.[4]

Lord George Gordon was charged with high treason but not tried till the following February – when he was brilliantly defended by Erskine, his junior counsel, and by Kenyon. Lord Mansfield★ told the jury that they had to consider two points: whether the multitude had committed acts of violence with the intention of forcing a repeal of the Catholic Relief Act and, if so, whether Gordon had incited or promoted the insurrection with the same intention. If he had, then he was guilty of treason – the doctrine of constructive treason under which the London apprentices and Dammaree and Purchase had been

★ The court consisted of Mansfield and three other judges. The presence of Mansfield illustrates the gulf between eighteenth and twentieth century ideas of judicial impartiality. Mansfield's own house had been burned down, and in a powerful speech in the House of Lords he had denounced the riots. In addition, he had thought it 'more decent' because of the injury he had suffered not to attend the nominal cabinet when it decided upon the punishment of the convicted rioters. Yet he did not think it 'more decent' not to preside at Gordon's trial.[5]

sentenced to death. The answers seem fairly clear yet, after a trial which lasted without a break from 8 am until nearly 5 am the following day the jury found Lord George not guilty. Erskine, who had expected a conviction, fainted.[6]

The defence stressed that nobody connected with Lord George or belonging to the Protestant Association had been convicted. And Erskine asked why Gordon should be condemned for not foreseeing trouble, when the government had not foreseen it either. The ministry had not provided 'a single soldier, no nor even a constable to protect the state'. These two points may have been sufficient to defeat the Solicitor General's telling final speech and Mansfield's damning summing up. More probably the jury just did not accept Mansfield's definition of the law and thought that Gordon's behaviour, however culpable, did not amount to treason. Or maybe they were mostly Dissenters and were determined to acquit anyway. Whatever the reasons Gordon went free.[7]

Cabinet ministers were probably relieved. In any case they, the other guilty men, did even better than Gordon: they escaped blame and the opposition did not. A number of people at the time, including the Archbishop of York and Lord Bute, suspected the opposition of being behind the riots. For politicians to believe that a mob had been organised by their opponents was common form. Bute had always been prone to such suspicions and Markham, the Archbishop of York, was a courtier prelate.* Yet even though the rioters had been particularly hostile to such opposition leaders as Rockingham, Burke and Savile, and the opposition factions were no more behind them than were the Americans or the French, who were likewise implausibly accused, the rumour of opposition involvement was propagated outside the parliamentary circle and widely believed.[9]

Richmond immediately recognised both the damage the riots would do to future popular causes and the help they would give to the ministry. And indeed, far from finishing it off they strengthened it. 'The strange convulsions,' crowed the Secretary at War, had restored 'tranquillity'; there was a natural rallying to the forces of order, however shaky those had proved. Even more helpful to the ministry was Clinton's capture of Charleston, which gave hope that the American war was not yet lost; and after attempting a coalition with Rockingham, North dissolved Parliament in September catching the opposition unready. Even so, he did far worse than he expected. Where opinion mattered, the opposition was successful, winning eleven out of the twelve metropolitan seats, four-fifths of

---

* He was one of only four peers to protest against Chatham's funeral and monument being at public expense, a piece of sycophantic churlishness which pleased the King. And he warned his clergy that membership of associations for parliamentary reform was 'foreign' to their clerical functions and 'not the road to preferment'.[8]

the English counties, and two-thirds of the English boroughs with over 1000 voters. Where opinion did not count, in most of the smaller boroughs and in Scotland, the ministry prevailed. So the opposition gained a moral victory, and North a majority.[10]

The Gordon Riots had deepened the split in the opposition: the Rockinghams were firm for religious toleration and law and order; and the leading Chathamite, Shelburne, was equivocal over the riots and hostile to the ministry, condemning the use of the military and urging the formation of a police force on the French model. The Chathamite remnant, far weaker in parliament and less crammed with pocket boroughs than the Rockinghams, strongly favoured parliamentary reform, holding before the riots decorous public meetings in its support. After them Shelburne complained that Rockingham was 'obstinately stopping the free course of popular spirit' which offered the only possibility of successful opposition to the court.[11]

The Rockinghams were divided. The Duke of Richmond favoured manhood suffrage and Fox, drawn to the Rockinghams less by political attitudes than by his social life and his hereditary hatred of Shelburne, was a convert to reform. Overnight he had become the 'man of the people' and seemed to countenance popular agitation. To Rockingham and most of his followers, however, neither the end nor the means was acceptable even before the riots. They supported economical reform because it would, they thought, appreciably diminish the power of the crown, thereby increasing their own; they had no enthusiasm for parliamentary reform because it would diminish their influence as well as the Crown's. It would also have reduced their ability to keep their own taxation unwarrantably low. Hence the loss of their boroughs was too high a price for removing North and ending the war. Bringing down the ministry was left to the Americans.[12]

Wyvill and the Associated Counties[13]

Wyvill's scheme of a collection of County Associations to bring pressure to bear on Parliament was open to denunciation as 'an anti-parliament'. Yet the objects to be achieved by such pressure were limited: no further granting of public money until public extravagance was curbed and sinecures and unmerited pensions were abolished; plus an additional hundred county MPs and triennial parliaments. 'Moving the people of England to carry out so small a reform,' John Jebb, one of the founders of the radical Society for Constitutional Information, told Wyvill, 'would be tempesting the ocean to drown a fly.' Wyvill had no desire to move the people of

England and if MPs, magnates and the relatively prosperous voters
– a small minority of the English people – were amenable to quiet
persuasion, then Wyvill had chosen the right approach.[14]

In contrast the London radicals, many of whom were Dissenters,
believed the Commons should represent persons not property and
favoured far-reaching reform of Church and state. Wyvill's subtleties
on the need to win over those with an interest in the current system
were not for them; if they steadily pursued the right way, John Jebb
believed, all would be well. The programme of the Westminster
Subcommittee drawn up by Jebb advocated universal manhood
suffrage, equal electoral districts – rights which had been enjoyed 'in
the times of the immortal Alfred' – secret ballots and indeed
everything that was later included in the Chartists' six points.[15]

Yet the radicals were little more likely than Wyvill to tempest the
ocean. Parliamentary reform held limited popular appeal. In
unrepresented Birmingham Joseph Priestley found 'indifference' to
the question, and on the other side Lord North could point to the
absence of petitions for reform from the large unrepresented towns
and to the tranquillity of the 'satisfied multitude'. The radicals'
proposals alarmed many of those who had originally supported
reform; they did not stir the populace.[16]

Reform had no popular hero. Wilkes's day was over, Wyvill had
no urban appeal, and Fox's emergence as 'the idol of the people' was
too sudden and ephemeral. Furthermore British opinion is seldom
excited by abstract arguments. All the Wilkite struggles had been on
concrete issues: not general warrants as such but the arrest of Wilkes
under a general warrant; not merely the right of election but the
expulsion and disqualification of Wilkes and the substitution of
Luttrell; not the freedom of the press but the attempted arrest of
printers and the sending of the Lord Mayor to the Tower.
Parliamentary reform, too, could possibly have been made concrete
and popular if it had been adopted by a united opposition. That at
least was what the Duke of Richmond believed: when Lord
Rockingham told him that reform was not popular out of doors he
replied: 'you and we can soon make it so.' Whether or not he was
right, the attempt was not made, Parliamentary reform was even less
popular with the Marquess than it was out of doors.[17]

In 'the portentous crisis from 1780 to 1782', Burke claimed
fourteen years later, there was 'much intestine heat [and] a dreadful
fermentation. Wild and savage insurrection quitted the woods, and
prowled about our streets in the name of Reform.' The Gordon
rioters prowled about the streets and were near wild insurrection, but
not in the name of reform. The reformers did advocate reform, but
they kept off the streets and neither preached nor practised savage
insurrection. The Rockinghams did not prowl about the streets or

preach parliamentary reform, yet it was they rather than the reformers who hinted at insurrection and generated the intestine heat. Burke, himself, maintained that if Parliament was not allowed to control the civil list, debate would be at an end and 'the people must do what parliament had refused'. Fox told a mass meeting in Westminster Hall that the people 'must be ministers of their own deliverance' and reminded his audience that their brethren in America and Ireland 'had taught them how to act'.[18]

Despite the posturing, the Rockinghams had no intention of calling out the people, who anyway would not have answered their call. Nor had Wyvill, who thought that his means of persuasion on virtuous men, 'united by reason alone', would overcome all opposition. And reason, combined with the impact of war taxation and military defeat, did initially influence some of the gentry's attitude to reform, much as food prices and unemployment influenced the lower set's propensity to riot. But only in those very exceptional circumstances could his County Associations' persuasions prevail against immediate self-interest and the rights of property. So, at least after the Gordon Riots, Wyvill was as far away from securing parliamentary reform as he was from seeking savage insurrection.[19]

Economic reform was taken over by the parliamentary opposition. Parliamentary reform was not. Wyvill's Association movement, by its very nature, implied the wish and the need to exert pressure on Parliament; yet outside Yorkshire he had little pressure to exert. The number of enlightened gentry was insufficient for his purposes, and there was no chance of Parliament voluntarily espousing its own reform. In eschewing popular support and unseemly popular activities, Wyvill removed from the propertied classes an excuse for opposing parliamentary reform; but in so doing he also removed almost their only reason for supporting it. Parliament would adopt reform only under duress in order to avoid something worse; the populace was the only available engine of duress, and revolution or social unrest were the only things worse than reform. However moderate his aims, therefore, and however reasonable his methods, the cautious and high-minded Wyvill was not much more realistic than the visionary London radicals and rather less so than the rash and ambitious Lord George Gordon.[20]

Moderation and sweet reason left the parliamentary classes cold towards parliamentary reform; radical demands made them hot and frightened and even less addicted to reform, while popular violence, as the Gordon Riots showed, made them even more conservative. Possibly the only winning combination would have been a proposal for moderate parliamentary reform backed by mass nonviolent demonstrations. Yet such a combination was doubly unattainable: the reformers could not keep all their ranks moderate, and the populace could not be aroused to enthusiasm for proposals which apparently did not affect them. And after the Gordon Riots probably even that impossible combination would not have overcome the deep conservatism of the propertied nation.

1779–80 were certainly crisis years; Catherine the Great thought every European power was in a state of crisis in 1780. Yet those years in England demonstrate the truth of Churchill's remark that a number of simultaneous crises do not necessarily add to the difficulty of coping with them. Reverses are not always cumulative; they may cancel each other out.[21]

The Gordon Riots threatened the ministry yet they weakened both Wyvill's movement and the aristocratic opposition, and in the end they strengthened the government. Wyvill and the reformers forswore violence, the French did not invade, the Gordon tumults were in the end suppressed, Ireland was appeased for the time being, and the industrial riots in Lancashire were quelled. Violence was contained, and save during the Gordon Riots the country never came close to degenerating into that near-anarchy that might have provoked insurrection or revolution. Though two elements of a revolutionary situation were present – a feeble government and failure in war – final defeat did not come till later, and the regime only faced a serious challenge from Lord George and the London mobs. Had North fallen after the passage of Dunning's resolution, he would merely have been replaced, as he was two years later, by the leaders of the parliamentary opposition. Revolutions are unexpected; the government was wholly unprepared for the Gordon conflagration. George III and Lord North's lack of nervousness over revolution is not therefore conclusive, especially as neither of them was notably prescient; yet except in the first fortnight of June 1780 they evidently had small cause for alarm.[22]

The King v Fox

North's eventual fall – the result of defeat in the American war, not of revolution – brought an interlude of instability worse than the 1760s. None of the four ministries that came into office in less than two years enjoyed the full confidence of both King and Commons. In the struggle between the Rockinghams and the King for the control of the executive, few holds were barred on either side. The Rockinghams did not let issues or public concerns deflect them from their main purpose of gathering patronage and giving 'a good stout blow to the influence of the Crown'; George III called the Rockinghams 'the leaders of sedition' and came near to treating them as such, narrowly preferring their installation in office to his own abdication.[23]

The King had to invite Rockingham to succeed North, yet the new ministry was a coalition in which the Shelburne group was almost as powerful in the cabinet as the Rockinghams. The administration, said Fox, was 'to consist of two parts, one belonging to the King, the other to the public'. In fact neither belonged to either, though the Shelburnes were closer to the King than the Rockinghams to the public. The ministry temporarily quietened Ireland by allowing her to initiate her own laws and by repealing the Declaratory Act. Like North's earlier concessions these stemmed not from British generosity but from the pressures of the American war and the threat of Irish violence. 'The American revolution, the fleets of Bourbon showing on your coasts, and the volunteer army being themselves dissatisfied,' an MP told the Irish Parliament, 'are the circumstances alone . . . which gave this country a constitution.'[24]

In England political violence was a possibility only in 1783-84, when many Frenchmen thought this country was on the verge of a revolution, and some Englishmen feared civil war. George III had resolved not 'to be dictated to by Mr Fox' and, after Fox had resigned on the indefensible grounds that Rockingham's successor, Shelburne, had been named by the King and not chosen by the cabinet – in which there was anyway a clear majority for Shelburne – he was determined never again to employ him. Fox had supplanted Wilkes as the King's least favourite politician. Nevertheless, when Fox joined with North to defeat Shelburne on the peace terms, George III failed to save himself from a 'desperate faction' and was forced to accept on their own humiliating terms the 'unnatural' coalition of Fox and North. Just two years earlier Fox had said that the North ministry should expiate their disgraceful measures 'on the public scaffold'; now instead of beheading he was embracing them.[25]

Fox's opposition to Shelburne and his alliance with North crippled the reformers – Pitt's motion for reform was massively defeated by 293 to 149. It was no good, Wyvill pointed out in the *York Chronicle*, Fox making an able speech in favour of reform when the people of England knew he had formed an administration decisively against it. The coalition – the original basis, presumably, of Disraeli's remark that 'England does not love coalitions' – was deplored on every side. North's old associate, John Robinson, referred to its 'violence'. The most respected Rockingham of all, Sir George Savile, was shocked by it. The independents were outraged. Wilkes called it a 'monstrous, unnatural union . . . for the division of the public spoils'. And George III was determined to get rid of it as soon as he could.[26]

The coalition's India Bill gave the King his opportunity. Although it was in many respects a brave attempt which reflected Burke's sympathy for subject peoples, it was massively unpopular because it offended eighteenth-century instincts about the sanctity of charters and property rights and transferred, said the Younger Pitt, 'the immense patronage and influence of the East to Charles Fox in or out of office'. The general reaction was the same as Fox's would have been, had anyone else made a bid for the India patronage.[27]

Yet the bill passed easily through the Commons, while outside the clamour rose and India stock fell. Only the Lords remained, and they virtually never defeated the government. Yet the House of Lords was the King's poodle not the ministry's. Pitt conveyed to George III his willingness to form a ministry, provided the King secured the bill's defeat by making his views known. The King duly authorised Lord Temple, Pitt's cousin, to inform peers that anybody who supported the bill would be considered his enemy, and enough of their lordships obediently complied. North and Fox were dismissed, and Pitt became First Lord of the Treasury.[28]

The Commons denounced Temple's action as a high crime and misdemeanour, stigmatising anyone who advised the King to dissolve Parliament as an enemy of the country. Yet George III's dispatch of Fox and North turned out to be the most popular thing he had ever done. Pitt denied all knowledge of the intrigue that had preceded it and was believed. The City of London thanked the King for his constitutional use of his prerogative and rejoiced in the dismissal of the coalition. Petitions followed from all over the country. There were more of them in support of George III than the combined total of petitions over the Jewish Naturalisation Act, the Cider Tax, the Middlesex election, the Catholic Relief Act and economic and parliamentary reform. Buoyed up by this public support, Pitt refused to resign even though he suffered more than twenty defeats in the Commons, including votes of censure.[29]

At the end of February Pitt received the freedom of the City of London after a graceful speech from Mr Chamberlain Wilkes extolling his 'superior ability and purity of public virtue'. On his return he was attended, his brother who was with him recorded many years later, by 'a vast concourse' which removed his horses and drew his coach. Outside Carlton House the mob stopped and hissed. Eventually it was persuaded to move on, and in St James's Street opposite Brooks's, chairmen, waiters and members of that club, armed with bludgeons, 'launched a desperate attack on Pitt's coach. They succeeded in making their way to the carriage and forced open the door. Several desperate blows were aimed at Mr Pitt . . .' He was rescued by the chairmen and members of White's, where he took refuge. Pitt's servants were badly bruised and his carriage nearly wrecked. His brother recognised two of Fox's friends among the attackers. As Bernard Shaw once remarked, 'the quality and the mob' are not two classes but the same people.[30]

Not for the only time, Brooks's was out of tune with popular feeling. At a meeting in Westminster Hall Fox was hissed and hooted and greeted with cries of 'No coalition!', 'No Grand Mogul!', 'No usurper!', 'No Turncoat!', 'No Traitor!', 'No Dictator!' – a fairly comprehensive condemnation. He was easily defeated and forced to leave the hall.[31]

With Pitt and the King ignoring their successive defeats in the Commons, the coalition's obvious weapons were refusal to vote supply and refusal to pass the Mutiny Act. It delayed them both, but went no further. To refuse supplies, Fox was warned, would lead to 'your being execrated and probably torn to pieces by the people'. Also the independent members would have been alienated. So on March 8 Fox unconvincingly explained that while it was the ancient practice of the House to withold supplies until grievances were redressed, they would not do so now because of the country's difficulties. Instead he moved a remonstrance, which was passed by only one vote, and shortly afterwards Parliament was dissolved.* [32]

The influence of the Crown and the force of public opinion routed Fox and North in the election. Anglicans and Dissenters, the traditional supporters of the King and radical opponents united against the coalition. Wilkes, who received £1000 from the King's election fund in narrowly winning Middlesex, Wyvill, Jebb, Richmond and nearly all the prominent reformers sided with Pitt, who won both a moral victory and a large majority.[33]

Election violence, coming usually from above and being for a safe purpose, was not much affected by the post-Gordon fear of using the mob. Serious rioting occurred in the elections for Buckinghamshire – the only contested poll there between 1734 and 1830 – Liverpool, Coventry and Leicester. But much the worst violence was at Westminster where the government spent almost a third of its entire election fund trying to beat Fox. The naval hero, Hood, was the clear leader, and the main contest was for the second seat between Fox and a much more consistent reformer, Sir Cecil Wray. No ingredient of a popular election was lacking – bribery, intimidation, drink, regular riots, even murder – and some unusual ones were added. The Foxite mob was led by Irish chairmen hired from Spitalfields, while the government side had Hood's sailors, described by their opponents as 'a gang of fellows, headed by naval officers and carrying His Majesty's colours'. Battle was regularly given round the hustings in Covent Garden and further afield. In one skirmish a constable was killed and the Guards took fifteen rioters to Newgate. In another incident, the King had a detachment of Guards marched to Covent

---

* Almost certainly the Mutiny Act was a far less powerful weapon than was generally assumed: no Mutiny Act was in force from 1698 to 1702 without anybody noticing much difference.

Garden not to quell a riot but to vote. Fox gained the help of Lord George Gordon and those whom Pitt called 'the Duchess of Devonshire and other Women of the People'. The Prince of Wales, escorted by a band of prize-fighters, also lent his support, as did his former mistress, Perdita Robinson. And at the end of 'forty days' riot and forty days' confusion', Fox just got home. The mob demolished the hustings, Fox was chaired by his supporters and, preceded by a banner proclaiming 'The Man of the People' and, followed by the state carriages of the Duchess of Portland and the Duchess of Devonshire, he was carried in triumph to Devonshire House.[34]

Why the King won

Each side thought the other had breached the conventions of the constitution. Since those conventions were evolving, the exact state of the constitution was as uncertain in 1784 as it was in the sixties and seventies. For that reason Tom Paine thought there was no such thing as the English constitution, a view nowadays not confined to radicals.[35] In any case, despite what George III called its 'beauty, excellence and perfection', the constitution provided little guidance either to him or his opponents and probably both of them breached it. The problem is germane here only in that unconstitutional behaviour by the King might have provoked a violent reaction. In the event, constitutionally improper or not, the King's actions evoked not violent opposition but strong popular support.[36]

In the earlier crises of the King's reign it was George III and his ministers who made the mistakes; in 1783-84 it was his opponents who blundered. In the previous troubles George III was identified with the actions of his ministries. So in 1762-3

> *When Scots, or Slaves to Scotsmen, steer'd the helm,*
> *When peace, inglorious peace, disgrac'd the realm . . .*[37]

and again in the later Wilkite controversies, the King shared in the obloquy showered on ministers by the City and the public. Then it was he and his allies who were thought guilty of 'violence', arbitrary designs and unconstitutional behaviour; in 1783-84 it was his enemies who were regarded as dangers to the constitution. When Fox's India Bill was attacked in the City as an invasion of commercial rights and interest, George III was seen as the City's ally not its enemy, a change in his position which went far deeper than his laboriously acquired political skills or his momentary enjoyment of unconstitutional monarchy. At the beginning of his reign George III, though more popular than his predecessors, was not much loved, and his turbulent

first decade brought him no increase in affection. That came later
when longevity came to his aid. Custom stales politicians; it matures
kings. The longer monarchs are on the throne, the greater their
prestige and the more they become a valued part of people's lives.
With George III that process had begun by the early eighties, though
his popularity only became near-idolatry after his seeming madness
in 1788. The King's reputation was enhanced by his steadfastness in
the Gordon Riots and, so far from being held against him, the failure
of the American war made him into a focus of patriotism and an
island of stability in a sinking world; Rodney's victory in the Battle
of the Saints and the relief of Gibraltar also enhanced his prestige.
Whether the country won or lost, the King always gained.[38]

In internal politics, too, he gained even when seeming to lose. The
Rockinghams' economical reforms diminished the Crown influence
but enhanced its reputation; they freed George III from the charge of
corrupting Parliament. Similarly, the Fox-North coalition, initially a
defeat, soon brought the King great popularity. Finally the King was
helped by the Prince of Wales, whose excesses served to emphasise
the solid bourgeois virtues of his father. The influence of Wesley and
others had brought the beginnings of a new moralism into English
society. Wilkes was not affected by that development, but he disliked
the Prince of Wales and his toast at Carlton House to the King's long
life was not merely witty; it represented a change in public
attitudes.[39]

Before Pitt, Chatham, who had been more applauded at George
III's coronation than the King himself, had been the century's only
great and popular statesman. So, like the King, Pitt enjoyed the
benefits of dynasty, and the House of Hanover could not have
triumphed without the House of Pitt; even with Pitt, it was a close
run thing, only in retrospect seeming inevitable. Young, uncorrupt
and unstained by the factional squabbles of the reign, Pitt made all
the other politicians seem tawdry and shopsoiled. In carrying out
economic reform, the Rockinghams had been careful, as Gordon
pointed out, to preserve their own pickings and sinecures; the
relatively poor Pitt emphasised his singularity by practising economical reform at his own expense. When in January 1784 the Clerkship
of the Pells worth over £3000 a year fell vacant, Pitt suppressed the
post instead of taking it for himself.[40]

No less important than the popular transformation of George III
and the freshness, probity and abilities of Pitt was the unpopularity
of Fox and of what Dundas called 'that insolent aristocratical band'.
Thwarted at court, the Foxite Whigs' only possible route to power
was popular favour. But unlike the Tories during their period of
proscription, the Whigs did not espouse radical policies to gain public
support; the oligarchy remained impotently Venetian at a time when

George III was resolved above all else not to be its Doge and when the plebeians were stirring. Some twenty years later Fox realised that opposition could gain strength only from 'movements' out of doors, not in Parliament, but in 1782–84 the Whigs remained obsessed with the world of Westminster.[41]

Whig reiteration of their conspiracy theory that only 'secret influence' kept them out of office in the end made it a reality. It helped to make them so obnoxious to George III that eventually he did conspire to remove them from office. Yet their theory long preceded his conspiracy, and the practice, though not the theory, was vastly popular. Out-of-date oligarchical politics made even less impression on the public than on the King. Where Wilkes had been seen as the victim of tyranny and the defender of traditional liberties, the Rockinghams were seen as nobody's victims but as defenders of their own traditional privileges. Under the first two Georges the Tories were proscribed; under George III and Rockingham Whigs proscribed themselves.[42]

And so, despite the constitutional battle, the years of crisis ended peacefully. They were, as the King told John Robinson, 'bad times, bad times indeed'. But, with the supreme exception of the Gordon Riots, they were not violent.[43]

The Gordon tumults tainted all popular meetings and movements, yet they had only a little to do with Wyvill's failure and still less with Fox's. Wyvill was already in trouble before then and would have failed even if Fox had not split the reformers. Only briefly during the war was there much disposition to change a system which usually seemed to work and which certainly suited the only people who had the power to change it. Junius once warned Wilkes against 'perpetual union' with the mob:[44] Wyvill needed no such advice; he never contemplated the briefest liaison. Not that the crowd would have responded to his wooing. His cause was neither immediate enough nor personified. And without the crowd the reformers were too few and largely toothless.

The same was true of the Whig cause. Blocked by what they believed to be the unconstitutional behaviour of Pitt and the King, the Foxites could theoretically have recalled 1688 and appealed to arms. Yet just as for a situation to be revolutionary there must be at least some revolutionaries, so for a civil war to break out there must be men on both sides ready to fight. The King would have lacked neither champions nor followers. Early in 1783 there had been mutinies in both the army and the navy as well as unrest in the militia. The disaffection arose, however, not from military enthusiasm for Fox and North but from the government's breach of the men's terms of enlistment and from its failure to pay them. Though entitled to release from the army because of the end of the war, the

77th Highlanders were ordered to the West Indies. Refusing to go, they nearly killed their colonel, defeated a detachment sent to subdue them and occupied Portsmouth citadel for a week. Lord George Gordon's support was solicited. He did not help them, but the government gave in and nobody was punished. From December 1783 to April 1784, the most serious period of the political struggle, the troops were quiet and would unquestionably have supported the King. Fox would at best have had only what Wyvill called 'his gamesters from Brooks's' and their chairmen. There was nobody, probably not even Fox himself, who wanted to kill George to make Charles Fox king. An appeal to arms would have been a much worse gamble for Fox than any even he had ever taken at Brooks's or Newmarket, and nobody seems to have contemplated it.[45]

Had Fox enjoyed the popularity of the elder Pitt, of the Wilkes of a dozen years before or even of Sacheverell, he would have probably won without any call to arms. The King believed that 'violence if met by firmness is commonly repelled',[46] yet firmness in 1783-84 would have been difficult if he had faced a clear majority of the Commons supported by the London mob, whether violent or not. An alliance between the third and fourth estates would surely have given the King pause. In such circumstances he could scarcely have risked dismissal of the coalition and, if he had, the crowd would probably have secured its return within days. In reality, neither Fox nor the issue commanded popular backing, and there was no reason why either should. Fox was a hero only to his followers: his conduct had alienated the public. Monarchy has often enjoyed great popular favour; aristocracy has enjoyed it seldom. And anyway in 1783-84 most of the aristocracy sided with the King. So, in those years the chances of civil war or serious violence were remote.

Recovery

With the Younger Pitt securely in office, Britain, for the first time in a quarter of a century, enjoyed good stable government and national resurgence began. Pitt was not free of trouble, however. Ungenerously, he supported the decision of the High Bailiff of Westminster not to return Fox to Parliament and instead to grant Wray a scrutiny of the votes. As that expensive and unworkable procedure dragged on, the ministry's majority dwindled. Eventually the majority disappeared and Pitt's parliamentary defeat was celebrated with two nights of rioting. Those who refused to illuminate their windows in honour of Fox had them broken. The new bacchanalian generation, Walpole observed, was not averse to being 'rioters under the Princeps Juventutis'.[47]

Despite the fast growth of trade and the economy, the restoration of the nation's finances, groggy from the war, impelled the raising of higher revenue. Pitt's multifarious new taxes excited much opposition, and he had to withdraw some of them. Only one, however, provoked violence: a tax on retail shops imposed in 1785. Lord George Gordon was prominent in the campaign against it. Pitt conceded that the levy was 'severe', but claimed that as it would lead to higher prices it would in the end be paid not by the shopkeeper but by the consumer. The shopkeepers agreed about the tax's severity but not about its victims. They rioted, and Pitt was burned in effigy. Downing Street was attacked in June and Pitt did not dare to return there. Eden, still in opposition, was gladdened that it was now dangerous to be a neighbour of 'the popular Minister'. When Pitt went to the City in November, he received some 'rough compliments from ye mob', and the windows of his carriage were broken. Other means of persuasion were also used. Fox, Wilkes and the other metropolitan MPs attended a large meeting of shopkeepers in the Guildhall which demanded repeal, and Fox continued to press the matter in Parliament. There was no further violence, and in 1789 the Shops Tax, like the Cider Tax twenty years earlier, was withdrawn. By then, the Exchequer had recovered from the American War. Britain was the only state in Europe whose finances were sound.[48]

Paradoxically the accession to office of Pitt the reformer made most reform if anything more difficult. The spectacle of an honest, immensely capable young man at the head of affairs made reform seem less relevant, particularly as the disasters of the American War were soon blocked from memory by economic growth and industrialisation, the 1780s seeing one of the fastest expansions in the country's history. Certainly Pitt was no more successful in achieving parliamentary reform as First Lord of the Treasury than he had been when he was not in office. Probably the Commons would in any case have turned it down in 1785, but just possibly demonstrations or even petitions might have persuaded MPs to look kindly on reform at a time of peace and prosperity. Pitt's proposals were far too cautious to excite public enthusiasm. They were not, however, too cautious to excite royal and aristocratic antagonism and Pitt lost by 74 votes.[49]

Chatham had not espoused parliamentary reform until excluded from office; Pitt's zeal for reform cooled as he became more securely ensconced in power. The system of 'Old Corruption' inevitably seemed less tarnished when consistently surveyed from 10 Downing Street than from further afield, though it never tarnished Pitt himself, who remained wholly uncorrupted. And Pitt was bound to be affected by the political climate and the attitude of his colleagues. The natural supporters of the government were opposed to reform, as of course was the King. So Pitt increasingly contented himself with far-reaching but relatively unobtrusive financial, trade and administrative reforms.[50]

In 1785 Pitt's Solicitor General attempted to create a unified police force with stipendiary magistrates on the Bow Street model for the whole of the metropolis. The gallows groaned, said Sir Archibald Macdonald, with crowds of young men – nine out of ten of those hanged in London were under twenty-one – but still crime increased; severe punishments were ineffectual. He proposed, therefore, 'a total reformation' of the police to abolish 'thief-taking', which led to the lives of innocent men being sworn away, and to improve detection. Most people, however, preferred groaning gallows to a 'French' police force. 'Many foreigners,' said the paper which later became The Times, 'have declared that they would rather lose their money to an English thief, than their liberty to a Lieutenant de Police.'*[51]

Pitt was in general agreement with his friend, Sir Archibald Macdonald's proposals. Another friend, Wilberforce, later said that Pitt was convinced of 'the improper severity of our laws' and contemplated a plan to make the whole code less sanguinary. Yet by 1787 Pitt thought it would be dangerous to take any step which might remotely discredit the existing system.[53]

The American War had ended the use of American colonies as a receptacle for convicts, and for them slave labour was cheaper anyway. In consequence, by the mid 1780s Britain's prisons and the hulks, which had been pressed into service as additional prisons, were bursting at the seams. Burke, who from time to time tried unavailingly to make Parliament shoulder its responsibility for the criminal law, claimed that there were 100,000 convicts liable to transportation, and Wilberforce equally unsuccessfully tried to persuade Pitt to build penitentiaries. Burke was successful, however, in preventing the choice of West Africa as a penal colony, pointing out that the gallows would be merciful in comparison. Indeed when Africa had been tried 10 years earlier, 334 out of 746 sent there had died and the remainder had disappeared. Eventually the government chose Botany Bay not as an imperial settlement but as the cheapest

---

* Although the metropolis had to wait until 1829 for a proper police force, the London magistracy was reformed in 1792. A number of prominent men including the poet Laureate, Henry James Pye, became magistrates. Luckily Pye was a better magistrate than poet.[52]

† In 1787 the government was able to get Lord George Gordon safely out of the way and to take revenge for his earlier acquittal. Gordon wrote a pamphlet trying to prevent the first shipment of convicts to Botany Bay and was prosecuted for an alleged libel on the 'Judges and Administration of the Laws of England'. He was also prosecuted for libelling Marie Antoinette. After escaping for a time, he was sentenced to five years imprisonment and to provide exorbitant sureties for his good behaviour thereafter before he could gain his release. He never did.[55]

way of dealing with felons, most of whom were guilty of minor theft.[54]

Something of the same happened over religion. The Dissenters had grounds for thinking that Pitt would support repeal of the Test and Corporation Acts. His father had sympathised with the Dissenters, comparing them favourably with the bishops. They had strongly supported Pitt in the 1784 election and the continued imposition of civil disabilities by religious tests was surely alien to his reforming mind. Yet Pitt consulted the Bishops with a result as predictable as consulting the judges on reform of the criminal law – all but two wished to retain the Anglican monopoly – and he came down decisively against repeal. This was perhaps Pitt's biggest mistake in home politics. Had he supported equal rights for the Dissenters, or had he merely kept quiet (as Burke, who did not forgive them for supporting Pitt in 1784, did until the French Revolution), the King and the bishops would probably have defeated repeal in the Lords, but the Dissenters would have still regarded Pitt as an ally and would have remained more moderate in their advocacy of reform. Above all they would have felt more kinship with the unreformed British constitution and been less impressed by later events across the Channel.[56]

Nevertheless, until much later, Pitt strongly supported the abolition of the slave trade. Wilberforce, who undertook the task on Pitt's recommendation, was optimistic of success. In warning the abolitionists to expect opposition from men 'not encumbered by either Honour, Conscience or Humanity' who would do everything to preserve 'their great goddess interest', John Wesley, a long-time opponent of slavery, proved a more accurate prophet. As each year more than 40,000 African negroes were taken across the Atlantic in British ships, Liverpool, London and Bristol did indeed have a considerable interest in the matter. The slave trade, said a naval captain, was carried on by oppression and cruelty which frequently ended in murder. Its defenders claimed on the contrary that the notorious 'middle passage' was the happiest period of a slave's life; one apologist picturing it as a pleasure cruise, much as Chief Justice Ellenborough later described transportation to Botany Bay as 'a summer's excursion' to a milder climate. The two cruises provided living conditions which initially were comparable: over 40 per cent of the second consignment of convicts to Australia died on ship or on arrival, a mere 9 per cent of the third consignment: not less than 12.5 per cent of the slaves, according to Wilberforce, died on the middle passage and not less than 4.5 per cent on arrival; on one crossing one third of the slaves expired.[57]

African negroes were even less 'of the same species' as members of Parliament than British convicts, yet the violence done to them attracted more opposition. Still, the goddess interest was easily able to block abolition, and the agitation's only result was Sir William Dolben's act limiting the number of negroes a ship could carry in proportion to its tonnage. Dolben, who had taken the trouble to go on board a slave ship in the Thames, was horrified by its arrangements; so were at least some sailors. Slaves were packed, said Lord Stanhope, 'like books on shelves'. Dolben's bill, strongly backed by Pitt, passed easily through the Commons but only scraped through the Lords, where Thurlow, the Lord Chancellor, helpfully described it as the result of a 'five days fit of philanthropy'. Over the slave trade all the giants – Pitt, Fox and Burke as well as Wilberforce – were for abolition, but, so the member for Amersham contentedly put it, 'the dwarfs, the pygmies' beat them. It was all right to be generous with one's own property, he thought, but not with the property of others. The great Whig landowners had similar fears, and Boswell thought that abolition would not only be robbery but also 'extreme cruelty to the African savages'. Disagreeing strongly with Johnson, he believed in company with many clergymen that slavery was a state sanctioned by God.[58]

Assassination attempts and the Regency Crisis

George III, who was opposed to all reform and thought Wilberforce a Methodist hypocrite, had troubles of his own. In 1786 as His Majesty was getting out of his carriage at St James's Palace a woman tried to stab him twice. The King immediately reassured his entourage that he was not hurt and ordered them to 'take care of the poor woman – do not hurt her'. George III had judged the situation correctly. Margaret Nicholson was not an enraged shopkeeper, a disappointed reformer, or some other disaffected subject. She merely thought the Crown was rightly hers, a belief that kept her in Bethlehem Hospital for the rest of her life. Four years later a smartly dressed man threw a stone at the King as he was travelling in state to open Parliament. John Frith was acquitted of high treason, the jury being satisfied of his lunacy, and the following year he, too, was sent to an asylum.[59]

Yet George III had rather less to fear from mad would-be assassins than fom his own doctors. In 1788 his illness precipitated a crisis over the arrangements for a regency. He had difficulty in walking, he could not sleep, his hearing and eyesight deteriorated, and he was frequently delirious. Once he talked for nineteen hours on end. Almost certainly he was suffering from porphyria, a physical illness which often produces mental disability in the form of delirium. Porphyria, however, was a disease unknown until many years afterwards, and the King's doctors thought the trouble was mental. They used the word 'disorder' not insanity, but they thought his delirium was effectively madness – Catherine the Great expressed surprise that the King had any wits to lose. Lurid stories were spread about the King's odd behaviour, though the most famous – that he shook hands with an oak tree in Windsor Park under the impression that it was Frederick the Great – has, sadly, been disproved. The doctors made no headway and insisted on the King's removal from Windsor to Kew, which would be more convenient for them. George III agreed to go only when he was told that he would otherwise be taken by force.[60]

Probably the King's recovery had begun well before Francis Willis, a clergyman who with his son kept a private madhouse in Lincolnshire, was called in. Willis's treatment has been described by modern medical experts as 'intimidation, coercion and restraint'. Whenever the King, who anyway had a well-grounded dislike of the medical profession, objected to this regime, as when he tore off irritants which had been placed on his legs to blister them, he was placed in a strait-waistcoat for hours, often with his legs tied to the bed and a band tied across his chest. Not surprisingly, the King expressed his hatred of all physicians, but chiefly of the Willises, as they treated him 'like a madman'. When Willis sanctimoniously informed him that like Christ he went about healing the sick, George III rejoined that Christ had not got £700 a year for doing so. The Willises, as John Wilkes told his daughter, ruled by fear, and the King was naturally afraid, imagining that they were going to murder him.*[61]

There was scant possibility of any other violence during the Regency Crisis. The last four years, fruitful for the country and the ministry, had been barren for the opposition. Factious and demoralised, divided and ineffective, the Foxites seemed destined to remain out of office for as long as George III lived. These gloomy prospects were transformed by his apparent insanity. That for them was the next best thing to his dying; Fox indeed talked of his 'civil death'. If the Prince of Wales became Regent without restrictions on his powers of patronage, the ministry would become and remain Whig. In their excitement the Foxites began squabbling over the spoils,

---

* In 1801 when he was stricken again, the King was subjected to even worse violence. At first he merely suffered similar indignities to those of 1788: blistering of the legs and emetics to make him more amenable. When, fed up with this treatment, the King abused the Willises (this time the two sons) and told them to leave Windsor, they took his abuse as a sign of his insanity not of his good sense, and with the consent of the Queen and the government they kidnapped him. With the Willises as his gaolers, the King was imprisoned at Kew for over a month until he gave the Lord Chancellor an ultimatum that unless he was freed and allowed to join his family he would sign no more papers. Only this royal threat to down pens and strike ended the kidnapping.[62]

while their leader's impatience for power was making the acquisition of the spoils increasingly chimerical. Replying to Pitt's motion to appoint a parliamentary committee to search for precedents, Fox asserted that the Prince had a clear right 'to assume the reins of office' and that Parliament had no discretion in the matter. The irony of 'the man of the people' expounding High Tory doctrines of the royal prerogative and hereditary right was stark; and Pitt who remarkably had, as a child, written a verse tragedy with a similar plot, was able to 'un-Whig' Fox, if not for life as he vowed, at least for the duration of the King's illness.[63]

Burke made matters worse by accusing Pitt of 'unpardonable violence' in charging others with near treason for upholding the rights of the Royal Family. Yet, unlike Fox, Burke based his position on constitutional principle, though barely a Whig one even 'in the business of one hundred years ago'. Burke overcame his usual dislike of extra-parliamentary action to propose a strong public remonstrance, not realising that his principle and Fox's lack of it were equally unappealing: they were supporting an unpopular Prince against a popular King and a popular minister. As usual the Whig leaders were out of touch with opinion out of doors. Showing himself a better judge, a Yorkshire supporter warned the party against wakening 'that spirit among the mob which was so injurious to us' at the last election. It would have been still more injurious in 1788-89, and once again the battle of the public addresses was decisively won by the government.[64]

Even so, victory in the country and in Parliament would not have been enough to save Pitt, had the King remained incapacitated. Miraculously, George III survived the Willises' attentions and in February was pronounced free from complaint. Loyal demonstrations took place all over the country.

> Bright shone the roofs, the domes, the spires,
> And rockets flew, self-driven.

In London the illuminations, said the *Annual Register*, were 'literally general'. The crowds were immense and London traffic jams were inaugurated. When the Archbishop of Canterbury wondered if a thanksgiving service in St Pauls might tax the King's health, George III told him that he had twice read how his physicians had treated him and if he could stand that he could stand anything. On the way back from the service Pitt's carriage was drawn to Downing Street by the populace. The celebrations everywhere were peaceful. Only the opposition was discomforted, and the only violence in the crisis came from the royal doctors.[65]

EIGHTEEN

The Revolutionary Decade

We have enjoyed . . . the benefit of those original principles of our constitution . . . It is this union of liberty with law, which, by raising a barrier equally firm against the encroachments of power, and the violence of popular commotion, affords to property its just security, produces the exertion of genius and labour, the extent and solidarity of credit, the circulation and increase of capital; which forms and upholds the national character, and sets in motion all the springs which actuate the great mass of the community through all its various disciplines.

William Pitt, February 17, 1792

Meet the evil; reform those who are adverse to your constitution by reforming its abuses; reform . . . the representation of the people in this House: keep your word with the public . . . proceed immediately to the abolition of that infernal traffic, the slave trade; show them the constitution of this country in its perfection . . .

Charles Fox, December 3, 1795

In England . . . everything has a constitution, except the nation . . . no such thing as a constitution exists in England.

Thomas Paine, Rights of Man, *1791-2[1]*

'Very great Rebellion in France' was all that Parson Woodforde recorded of the fall of the Bastille between entries in his diary about Somerset's bad weather and the purchase of a fine crab for one shilling. The parson was not exceptional. For most Englishmen 1789 was less remarkable for the outbreak of the French Revolution than for George III's recovery from apparent madness. 'Annus Mirabilis', Cowper's fortunately forgotten epic, commemorated that happy event, not the French revolution:

> *The spring of eighty nine shall be*
> *An era cherished long by me . . .*
> *The symbol of a righteous reign*
> *Sat fast on George's brows again.* *[2]

---

* In hardly less painful verses Cowper felicitated the sea not only on being the foundation of the country's empire but also on providing waves for His Majesty's bathing at Weymouth.[3]

Though few shared Fox's extravagant enthusiasm for the fall of the Bastille, the British ambassador in Paris thought that France should henceforth be considered 'a free country', and the belief that France was belatedly following England's freedom-loving ways was one mistaken cause for English satisfaction. Another was expressed by a future prime minister, the young Robert Jenkinson, who had been present at the attack on the Bastille.

In a widely praised maiden speech he said there was now nothing to be feared from 'that once formidable rival'. (In fact, of course, much as British dissension à la Montesquieu invigorated Britain, French revolutionary discord strengthened France.) With its heady proclamation of equal rights the Revolution had most appeal for those Englishmen who did not possess them: it provided ammunition for the Dissenters' campaign for repeal of the Test and Corporation Acts. Indeed for many people the Revolution made its initial impact second hand as a weapon in the Dissenters' claim for religious and political equality. In consequence for churchmen, opposition to the Dissenters and to the French Revolution tended to go together.[4]

In November 1789 Dr Richard Price, the Unitarian minister at Hackney, preached to the London Revolution Society (named after 1688 not 1789) a sermon 'On the love of our Country'. Price, both a distinguished economist who had influenced Pitt and a philosopher who had been urged by George Washington to become an American, and who had once proposed a European 'confederacy' to stamp out war, cited 'the right to choose our own governors' and 'to cashier them for misconduct' as principles of the English Revolution, and made a strong plea for equal representation and for an end to the 'Test Laws'. He concluded with a paean of praise and thanksgiving for the 'glorious' revolution in France. The Revolution Society then sent an address to the French National Assembly congratulating it on the Revolution. Both on his own account and because he was an adherent of Burke's arch-enemy Lord Shelburne, Price had long enjoyed Burke's hostility. Now his coarsely phrased and aggressive sermon, together with the congratulations the Society conveyed to Paris, provoked Burke into writing his *Reflections on the Revolution in France*, a book which was originally intended to be at least as much an attack on Price and the English Dissenters as on the French Revolutionaries.[5]

The *Reflections* came out a year later, and George III thought every gentleman should be grateful to Burke. In the end probably many of them read it; it had a large sale and vast influence both at home and abroad. Yet until its predictions were verified by the course of French events, Burke's magnificent tract seemed an exaggerated response to the Revolution – it made him unpopular in his own party, and he found Pitt 'dead and cold' on the subject. Initially, indeed, Burke's pamphlet was a tonic to radicalism, provoking some thirty-eight replies, many of them from Dissenting clergymen. One of these was by Joseph Priestley, another prominent Unitarian campaigner and one-time friend of Burke, who was denounced as an extremist in the *Reflections*. Like Price, Priestley had been in Shelburne's think tank and was a distinguished scientist and political theorist who may have provided Bentham with his formula of 'the greatest happiness of the greatest number'. In 1785 he had talked of Rational Dissent being gunpowder 'laid grain by grain, under the old building of error and superstition, which a single spark may hereafter inflame, so as to produce an instantaneous explosion'. This foolishly incendiary metaphor allowed him to be depicted as an ecclesiastical Guy Fawkes, intent on blowing up churches. Priestley's qualification, that it would be absurd to expect and 'in vain to attempt' a revolution until things were ripe, gave churchmen only limited reassurance.[6]

The 'Church and King' Riots

Priestley was minister in Birmingham where the Dissenters' campaign over the Test and Corporation Acts had produced particular bitterness, partly because the locally weak Anglicans feared the Dissenters would gain political control if their disabilities were removed, partly because the Unitarians were so influential, and partly because of Priestley himself. Priestley fired the first shot with a sermon the day after Price's. In the local pulpit war that followed, Dissenters were charged with holding 'republican principles and with almost demolishing' Christianity; Anglicans were merely stigmatised as 'viciously prejudiced . . . persecuting and abusive'.[7]

By 1791 Priestley was expecting trouble; he told Price that he had long since drawn his sword against the Church and was prepared to take the consequences. The economic situation of Birmingham did nothing to calm rising religious tempers. In addition to the habitual poverty of many, a change of fashion from buckles (a Birmingham speciality) to laced shoes had brought serious unemployment to the town. Furthermore, most of the town's employers and its intellectual and social elite were Dissenters. In any display of hostility to them, therefore, political and religious prejudice could be happily joined to social and economic resentment.[8]

To commemorate 1688 Priestley had helped to form a revolutionary society, which organised a reform dinner for 'any Friend of Freedom' on Bastille Day in 1791. The *Birmingham Gazette* contained a threatening announcement that the names of those attending would be published in a halfpenny pamphlet. A widely circulated handbill attacking Parliament, Pitt and the clergy and maintaining that the

Crown was growing 'too weighty' for the King helped to inflame loyalists, as did an equally inflammatory answer urging support of the King against republicans and regicidal supporters of the revolution. Slogans vowing 'Destruction to the Presbyterians' and 'Church and king for ever' began appearing on walls. Tumult was in the air, and Priestley decided to miss the dinner, much as Fox and Sheridan stayed away from a similar function in London. Despite Priestley's absence from the Royal Hotel and the presence of an Anglican chairman, some ninety diners were greeted on arrival with inapposite shouts of 'No Popery' and with mud and stones on departure. When all the hotel windows were broken, the magistrates who, well aware of likely trouble, had 'dined in town that day', joined in the cry of 'Church and King' and merely directed the mob away from the hotel to the Unitarian meeting-houses; one of them, Brooke, had a motive other than sectarian for doing so: his own house adjoined the hotel.[9]

The rioters duly moved off to attack two meeting houses to the glory of 'Church and King'. One was burned; the other, which was surrounded by buildings, was pulled down, and only its furniture was burned. Priestley's home, a mile and a half away at Fairhill, Sparkbrook, was next destroyed, together with his valuable scientific equipment and his fine collection of manuscripts. Dr Spencer, a JP, was present, shouting 'Church and King' and urging the rioters not to hurt each other. Priestley himself who had been playing backgammon with his wife escaped just in time. Most of the country gentry were away, watching an archery contest in Staffordshire. But on the next day Lord Aylesford persuaded the rioters, who were armed with bludgeons, to leave the ruins and return to Birmingham. Though well meant, this turned out to be inept. With nobody to stop them, the mob attacked Dissenters' homes in the city and broke into the two gaols, releasing the prisoners.[10]

Up till then the authorities had been indulgent. But if to attack meeting-houses was fair game, to attack prisons was poaching, and belatedly the magistrates swore in several hundred special constables. Unfortunately, this was done with such little discrimination that rioters as well as the respectable citizens were enrolled, the result, apparently, of confusion not intention. This new constabulary was not surprisingly worsted – losing one killed and several wounded – in a fight at the sacking of the home of another prominent Dissenter whose well-stocked cellar caused more casualties than did the fighting. That battle was decisive: the special constables and the magistrates allowed the mob a free hand until the military arrived two days later on the seventeenth. Cries of 'No Popery' were still occasionally heard, but the religious orientation of most of the rioters was less erratic. Throughout the four days the targets were carefully selected and the destruction meticulously controlled. Initially all Anglicans, whether diners or not, were spared. An elderly church-woman who occupied a large house owned by a Dissenter was escorted to safety together with her furniture before the house was burned down. Only in the last attack of the riots, an assault on the Edgbaston house of the Anglican botanist Dr Withering, like Priestley and James Watt a member of the Lunar Society, a notable scientific and philosophical club, were the rioters repelled by a strong force of knife grinders and 'some famous fighters from Birmingham', recruited by Withering.[11]

At this point the Dragoons arrived from Nottingham – the government was prompt in sending troops; the delay was due to the slowness of eighteenth-century communications. The rioters went back to work, if they had any, though for the next few days 'depredations' continued further afield. In all, during the four days of riots four dissenting meeting-houses were damaged and twenty-seven houses attacked or threatened. They belonged to reformers who had attended the dinner, to Dissenters, or to members of the Lunar Society.[12]

This blow to Birmingham's intellectual life had been dealt in the name of 'Church and King'. The name of the Church, at least locally, had not been taken in vain; and understandably perhaps, the King expressed satisfaction that Priestley had suffered from doctrines that he and his party had instilled, and that 'the people' saw them 'in their true light'; nevertheless he could not 'approve of their having employed such atrocious means of showing their discontent'. Others were less fastidious. Since it strengthened the hands of government, the Lord Lieutenant of Ireland was not 'sorry even for this excess, excessive as it has been'.[13]

Despite the violence being avowedly in support of the govern-ment, Dundas, the new Home Secretary, quickly saw its dangers, believing the chief cause of the riots to be the 'levelling principle' which would not necessarily operate in support of the government for long. His later claim to regard all riots with equal abhorrence was therefore genuine. The Foreign Secretary likewise did not 'admire riots in favour of government much more than riots against it'.[14]

Anxious to bring the rioters to trial, Dundas naively pressed the Birmingham magistrates to make a more energetic search for the instigators. Such a search would have come uncomfortably close to home, and the magistrates remained dilatory over prosecutions and condoned public hostility to prosecution witnesses. These were in any case reluctant to come forward, and juries were no less reluctant to convict. In the end only seventeen people were prosecuted and only four were convicted, of whom two were hanged and two were pardoned. Samuel Whitbread MP claimed that at least one of the pardons bore a distressing similarity to the 'famous case of McQuirk'.[15]

That apart, the government was only at fault in making no public criticism of the riots and in largely ignoring the conduct of the Birmingham JPs. After the Gordon Riots, Kennett, the Lord Mayor, was tried and convicted; after the Priestley Riots the Birmingham magistrates were left untouched. Yet they were at least as culpable. Coleridge wrote of the 'sable-vested instigators', and the JPs, like the Anglican clergy and landowners, were almost certainly behind the riots. Not that those in front were a hired mob; they were willing workers. The army commander was surprised that the rioters had not done battle under 'the standard of sedition'; and whether their enthusiasm stemmed mainly from religious bigotry, political ardour or a 'levelling principle' is hard to say. No doubt, as in the Gordon Riots, motives varied; probably, for some, a cry against Parliament would have done nearly as well as 'Church and King' – some of the Birmingham rioters were believed to be involved in anti-enclosure riots in Sheffield immediately afterwards, and a year later people in Birmingham shouted 'No Presbyterians and Tom Paine for ever'. Certainly an apparently reactionary slogan could coexist with quasi-revolutionary sentiments, but probably most of the rioters were genuine supporters of 'Church and King'. Priestley thought so, as presumably did the magistrates since they did nothing to prevent and little to stop the destruction. In any case the first serious violence of the revolutionary era was instigated not by radicals or Dissenters but by the upholders of property, the constitution and the Church.[16]

The Reform Societies and the Loyalist reaction

By 1789 conditions in the Bastille were far better than in any English prison. Yet not only Fox and the Dissenters welcomed its fall. Lord George Gordon's natural fellow-feeling for the exploit was tinged with envy – he was still in the English Bastille, the rebuilt Newgate – and he requested the French National Assembly to solicit his release. In only marginally improved verse Cowper told the Bastille

> There's not an English heart that would not leap
> To hear that ye were fall'n at last.

More unexpectedly, Horace Walpole exchanged congratulations on the fall of the Bastille with Hannah More, who later doubted the benefits of Sunday Schools because of the danger of children learning to read Tom Paine as well as the Bible; and the caricaturist Gillray, later a fierce loyalist, contrasted the new French liberty with Pittite

oppression. Less surprisingly, England's drowsy radicalism, tran-
quillised by five years of peaceful prosperity, was slowly awakened
by the revolution.

The inert
Were rous'd, and lively natures rapt away!

Yet the prosperity continued beyond 1789, and only Tom Paine's
Rights of Man brought radical ideas before a wide public. The Society
for Constitutional Information gradually revived and new societies,
marking the entry of working men into politics, were founded to
procure not revolution but reform. The most important of them, the
London Corresponding Society, founded in January 1792 and largely
composed of artisans and tradesmen, expressed 'their abhorrence of
tumult and violence'; universal male suffrage was to be achieved by
'reason, firmness and unanimity alone'.[17]

At least until they were driven underground by repression, the
radical societies remained loyal, pacific reformers not revolutionaries.
But just how reform could be obtained without violent revolution
was a mystery to everybody outside the societies and probably to
some within them. Even Wyvill's more influential and less ambitious
Yorkshire Association had found Parliament impervious to peaceful
persuasion. Ten years on, it was still more so. Parliament, said the
Whig MP Charles Grey in 1794, would never reform itself.
Nevertheless the radicals – the 'English Jacobins' to their opponents,
though they were more 'Girondin' than 'Jacobin' – believed they
could obtain universal suffrage by argument, propaganda, petitions
and pressure. In their eyes a system, under which seats were openly
advertised for sale and some 11,000 people elected a majority of the
Commons, was so obviously unrepresentative that reform was
inevitable. Yet in the eyes of the great majority that system had made
the country not only much freer but also much richer and much more
successful than its rivals. Divine right had effectively been transferred
from the King alone to the whole parliamentary constitution. In
consequence conservatives feared that even moderate reform would
maim that sacred instrument, while such outlandish contrivances as
annual parliaments and manhood suffrage would, they were sure,
produce anarchy and social revolution. To prevent such a reversion
to 1641–42, all innovation became taboo; and the unreformed
constitution that the radicals considered indefensible turned out
instead to be impregnable.[18]

The gulf between radicals and conservatives both rendered
compromise impossible and obscured the distinction between legal
peaceful reform and illegal violent revolution. When the mere
advocacy of a wider suffrage was deemed seditious – the Attorney

General adjudged a plan for representative government treasonable – the line between peaceful and violent change was necessarily blurred. The resulting repression occasionally drove some reformers to contemplate violence and revolution. At the same time, to conservatives, the means the radicals used or intended were scarcely relevant. They considered working men's intrusion into politics an infringement of the political nation's rightful monopoly, a point on which initially the London Corresponding Society itself had qualms. 'If Mr Paine' manages to move 'the lower classes', even Christopher Wyvill could write in 1792, everything 'we now possess will be at the mercy of a lawless and furious rabble.' In any case conservatives deemed even peaceful persuasion of Parliament illegitimate. More important, it was not the radicals' means but their ends which troubled them. To the propertied, universal suffrage was little preferable to revolution, since it was merely its prelude. What the Duke of Portland called the 'the inundation of levelling doctrines' would see to that. Political reform would inevitably produce social upheaval, and to be deprived of wealth and privilege by Act of Parliament was a scarcely more inviting prospect than to be stripped of them by violent revolution.[19]

'The aristocracy,' wrote Thomas Hardy, the founder of the L.C.S. and an acquaintance of Lord George Gordon, 'is trembling in every joint for their exclusive privileges.' Trembling or not, the aristocracy was determined to hold on to what it regarded as its rights and, in a time of what Fox called 'violence and extremes', to defend both them and the constitution without being over-fastidious in its methods. While the radicals maintained that the violence came from the government – the reformers had not yet, said one of them in 1795, been reduced to opposing force to force – the government and conservatives saw the radicals as allies of any enemy country, intent on imposing the French mode of government by violence. The reformers' peaceful professions were discounted, and reform was taken to be the same as revolution. Hence Wyvill, whose alliance with Pitt was ruptured by the war and by Pitt's abandonment of reform, was surely right in believing that universal suffrage could not be achieved without civil war.[20]

Yet, to begin with, even the chief conservative bugbear, Tom Paine, seems to have envisaged a peaceful transition to a democratic paradise. The most influential and hostile of all the replies to Burke's conservative manifesto, Paine's *Rights of Man*, came out in March 1791; its second part appeared a year later. Though lacking Burke's profundity and marvellous rhetoric, Paine too was a pamphleteer of genius. A masterpiece of rationalist common sense, *Rights of Man* is full of memorable phrases and written in a plain, lucid style easily understood by people not normally reached by political argument; hence its phenomenal sale. By 1793 in its two parts it had sold some 200,000 copies; Wolfe Tone reported that it was the Bible of Belfast and, translated into Gaelic, it penetrated as far as Stornoway. After attacking Burke's weakest point, his flattering picture of the French *Ancien Régime*, Paine derided George III as 'Mr Guelph', the Church as a 'mule animal', the constitution as non-existent, and the social system as 'the whole puppet show of state and aristocracy'. Basing himself on natural rights he preached an uncompromisingly demo-cratic message: the nation could not be governed as before, and the people had the right to abolish any form of government. Part II, which was still more radical, even contained a carefully worked out social programme. Both parts showed how nebulous was the dichotomy between revolution and reform. Paine did not advocate violence or illegality; indeed he opposed rebellion and explained why even a bad law should be obeyed, something that Lord George Gordon would never have done. Yet Paine clearly expected an English Revolution – without explaining how it would happen – and his objectives could not be gained without one.[21]

Like most other European leaders, Pitt at first viewed the French Revolution with notable calm. Wholly lacking counter-revolutionary fervour, he had no intention of crusading against the Revolution – as late as February 1792 he was prophesying fifteen years of peace – or against its English admirers. Though, just possibly, he may himself have privately sympathised with Paine, Pitt initially had little fear of the English seeking to imitate what was happening in France; the French 'infection' could be caught only if it was 'imported'. His issuance in May 1792 of a Royal Proclamation against seditious meetings and writings seems to have been as much caused by high politics as by plebeian stirrings. To promote parliamentary reform Charles Grey, Thomas Erskine and a few other opposition Whigs had just formed the Association of the Friends of the People. Even though it was a very moderate body which thought the radical societies' aims could not be accomplished without violence and which refused all intercourse with them, Pitt saw a chance to split the opposition Whigs by winning over their conservative majority with a strong line against sedition. Tom Paine was the government's other target. Proceedings were begun against him for seditious libel, a form of government advertising which sharply augmented his sales. Warned by the poet Blake that his life was in danger, Paine escaped to France.[22]

The May proclamation produced a gratifyingly loyal response and the government felt no serious alarm until the autumn when a bad harvest and the end of a boom brought fast-rising food prices and riots and industrial disputes in Scotland and Ireland as well as in

England. Dundas, in Scotland, feared that the military would not be able to cope 'with open sedition'. Then, as later in the decade, the cause of reform needed the help of economic distress to prosper. Yet apart from Paine virtually all the reformers confined themselves to the country's political ills and ignored its stomach. Nevertheless, the abolition of the French monarchy and the French military victories brought further vigour to the radical cause. The London Corresponding Society doubled its membership in a month and told the new French Convention that Britons were preparing to become free like the French.[23]

The government and the conservative Whigs were not alone in worrying about Tom Paine and revolutionary subversion. Conservative England's francophobia was inflamed by the very events which inspired the radicals. The September massacres and the English radicals' trafficking with the French Convention further fuelled patriotic zeal and governmental anxiety. In December the government called out the militia and John Reeves, a former chief justice in Newfoundland and a talented placeman, founded with government encouragement 'The Association for Preserving Liberty and Property against Republicans and Levellers'. Reeves had struck oil. Much as George III received twice as many loyal addresses on his recovery from illness as the combined total of those submitted in all the agitations of the last forty years, so Reeves's association easily dwarfed all the Reform Societies in popularity. Money flooded in and loyal associations – perhaps 1500 of them – sprang up all over the country, vigilantes against reform and sedition. Reeves, said Coleridge, was 'Captain Commandant of the Spy-gang'. Radicals were harried and heresy hunted. Intimidation did not stop short of violence. 'Church and King' mobs attacked reformers' houses. Paine was extensively burned in effigy, and his printers and booksellers were imprisoned or driven to America. Nor was propaganda neglected. Hannah More's tracts, enjoining on 'the lower classes of the people' satisfaction and gratitude for the existence and charity of the rich, easily outsold Paine. In Birmingham loyalists were thought to outnumber their opponents by six to one.[24]

The execution of Louis XVI and France's declaration of war inevitably generated further anti-French ardour. In refusing to back down over the French threat to Holland, Pitt enjoyed overwhelming national and parliamentary support. Cowper expressed a common view: the French had made him 'sick of the very name of liberty'. Wilkes similarly wrote of 'the bloody savages of Paris'. With loyalism rampant, radicalism recoiled. It was only revived by the harsh sentences passed on Scottish reformers, partly for promoting the circulation of Paine's works – on that count the government should have been prosecuted for sedition. Burns wrote 'Scots wha hae'. More practically the L.C.S. decided to be represented at a British Convention in Edinburgh.[25]

To a century in which in wartime everything associated with the national enemy becomes anathema, the radicals' continued use, despite the war with France, of French terms like convention and citizen seems gratuitous provocation.* And it was highly provocative in 1792-4 both to the government and to the patriotic feelings of the overwhelming majority; yet the reformers were merely being old fashioned. A very different attitude had been taken in earlier contests. To Addison's disgust, the fashion dolls advertising the latest French fashions came to England throughout the War of the Spanish Succession – and every later war until Napoleon put a stop to it. In the War of the Austrian Succession French ships continued until 1748 to be insured at Lloyds. In the Seven Years War the Duke of Newcastle travelled down to Sussex with ten French servants. More recently Admiral Rodney, detained in France during the American war as a debtor, had had his debts paid by a French admiral and was allowed to return to England to command the English fleet, defeating the French at the Battle of the Saints; and in the same war Boulton and Watt sent their first engine to France together with much new technology. The English radicals admired the French Revolution because it had transformed politics and society; they failed to realise that it had also transformed international relations and war.[27]

In Scotland, where economic depression and opposition to the war had brought a radical boom, the Edinburgh convention was easily broken up by the government – only thirty constables were needed – and the English delegates were prosecuted for sedition. These Scottish trials, presided over by Lord Braxfield whom even the Lord Advocate considered 'violent and intemperate', were, like their predecessors, scandalous. The Scottish criminal law was in some ways more civilised than the English, but at that time Scottish judges emphatically were not. Though it had certainly not sought violent revolution, the convention may well have crossed the ill-defined frontier dividing legal reforming activity from sedition. Braxfield made that irrelevant, however, by effectively abolishing the frontier, inventing a doctrine whereby sedition could be committed unintentionally. In his view the constitution was virtually perfect and a campaign to extend the franchise merely created discontent among the rabble who had no rights to representation; therefore to champion parliamentary reform was 'to all intents and purposes' sedition. After hectoring the defendants and the hand-picked juries, he handed out

---

* In England in the 1914-18 war, the First Sea Lord, Prince Louis of Battenberg, was forced to resign because of his German name; in the United States, sauerkraut was renamed 'liberty cabbage'.[26]

sentences of fourteen years' transportation. Despite the judges' behaviour and Whig appeals, the ministry refused to intervene either in favour of the earlier victims or against Braxfield. Pitt thought the judges would have been 'highly culpable' not to suppress such dangerous doctrines by punishing the delinquents. Public opinion agreed. No democrat could move, wrote Coleridge, 'without receiving some unpleasant proof of the hatred' of his opinions felt by the great majority of the people.[28]

The savage sentences worked in Scotland, but failed to intimidate the English radicals. The London Corresponding Society, having held a large public meeting, planned a convention. The Society for Constitutional Information fell in with the idea. The best radical orator, John Thelwall, deprived of a regular meeting place by loyalist pressure on tavern keepers and threatened by 'bludgeon-men' allegedly hired by Robert Jenkinson MP and other protectors of the constitution, still managed to draw audiences of over 600. The government decided to squash the growing radical movement by following the Edinburgh example. Probably it was influenced still more by its wish to deepen the Whig split from Fox. Thomas Hardy, Horne Tooke – Wilkes's one-time ally who had been influential in the L.C.S., the Constitutional and other societies – John Thelwall and nine others were arrested. One act was passed suspending *habeas corpus*; another maintained that 'a treacherous and detestable conspiracy had been formed for subverting the existing laws and constitution and for introducing the system of anarchy and confusion which had lately prevailed in France'.[29]

While the radicals were imprisoned under harsh conditions in the Tower, arms were found in a bankrupt's house in Edinburgh and a treasonable conspiracy uncovered. The plot lacked substance though not ambition: after the troops had been subverted, the authorities were to be seized and a provisional government proclaimed. Hardly anybody, however, would have anything to do with the scheme, and the conspirators' arsenal consisted of just four battle axes and eighteen pikeheads. The leader, Robert Watt, had been a government informer who had either, as he claimed, been converted to radicalism or, as Coleridge believed, was acting as an *agent provocateur* in order to regain his former employment. He and another were convicted, and Watt was executed (though spared disembowelling and quartering). For the English prisoners the only reassuring feature was that the trial was fair; Braxfield had been kept off the bench.[30]

Like the Scots, the English radicals were alleged to have procured arms, but most of the indictment against them concerned their proposed convention. To many, extra-parliamentary associations of any kind were constitutionally suspect: even Wyvill's assiduously moderate association had been widely regarded as 'anti-parliamentary'; and 'conventions' were especially dubious. After all, the precedents were hardly reassuring. Leaving America aside, Irish conventions had recently wrested concessions from the British government. Worse still, of course, was the current French regicidal 'Convention'. Not surprisingly, wrote Thelwall, the name convention became the '*war-whoop* of the tribe in power'. More substantially, noboby was sure what an English convention was supposed to do. Was its object, as the radicals claimed, merely to persuade Parliament of the need for reform? Or was its aim, as loyalists asserted and Paine had seemingly advocated in late 1792, to supplant Parliament and thus pave the way to revolution?[31]

Even if it was the latter, the government's decision to prosecute the radicals for high treason, of which they were almost certainly innocent, rather than for the non capital crime of sedition, of which they were probably guilty, was rash and violent. The Attorney General Sir John Scott (later Lord Eldon) ignored some sound legal advice to content with sedition. High treason was defined in the statute of 1351 as compassing the death of the King or levying war against him. Even in 1794 planning a convention to press for parliamentary reform did not closely resemble either of those activities; clearly therefore the rusty old blunderbuss, 'constructive treason', would have to be primed once more. That unpopular doctrine – which entailed judges distending the statute's words well beyond their natural meaning and which was subjected to a withering attack by William Godwin in a pamphlet, '*Cursory Strictures*', published a week before the first trial – had not hit its target in 1781: a jury had acquitted Lord George Gordon of levying war against the King, even though he had been implicated in serious riots. Now juries had to be persuaded that, although the radicals had used no violence whatever, they had been compassing the King's death by demanding parliamentary reform and preparing for a convention.[32]

The Attorney General opened Hardy's trial with a nine-hour speech of endless intricate detail – 'nine hours', exclaimed Thurlow, 'then there is no treason by God.' Scott's long-windedness was all the more glaring in that all previous treason trials had been completed in one day; this one took eight days and was uniquely 'labyrinthian'. Hardy's counsel, Erskine, though in poor health, frequently worsted the ponderous Scott, brilliantly refuting the Crown's view of 'constructive treason' and establishing that Hardy's proposals for reform were closely based on those of the Duke of Richmond. In cross-examination he brought prosecution witnesses to Hardy's aid and the government's allegations about the procurement of arms dwindled into a few pikes for self-defence against illegal loyalist attacks. Erskine was also able to show that Burke, now the high priest of the constitution's infallibility, had in the past denounced its defects in language stronger than any used by the reformers. The same was true of Richmond, who, having said in 1785 that Parliament would not reform itself, had added, 'it is from the people at large that I expect any good'.[33]

Eyre, the Lord Chief Justice, had recommended prosecutions for high treason; in his direction to the grand jury he had enlarged the scope of treason (for which he was excoriated by Godwin) going like Parliament far to prejudge the case; and at the trial itself he did not conceal his political views, telling the jury that men of rank should ensure that their reforming opinions did not find their way 'into the minds of the lower orders of the people'. Yet he conducted the trial with courteous fairness, and his summing up was only marginally in favour of conviction. As Scott later complained, Eyre had more doubt at the trial whether high treason had been committed than when he had given his original advice. He may even have been influenced by the evidence. The jury certainly was. After retiring for three hours it acquitted Hardy.[34]

While he was in the Tower, Hardy's house had been attacked by a 'Church and King' mob, causing the death of his wife in childbirth. Now popular sentiment had changed. Eyre complained during the trial of improper behaviour within and without doors. At the end of Erskine's seven-hour speech, 'an irresistible acclamation pervaded the court, and to an immense distance round'; Erskine had to ask the populace to disperse before the judges could enter their carriages. Every evening Erskine was cheered when he left the court, while Scott and the judges were hooted and hissed. Hardy's acquittal exicted tumultuous acclaim. A large crowd drew him in a coach to Piccadilly; the celebrations brought the arrest of twenty-six people, only one of whom was 'of a low cast'. In the provinces mail coaches bringing the news were cheered. Yet, despite the verdict and its popularity, the government obstinately embarked on a second trial, that of the old and ill Horne Tooke. Presumably it thought a packed jury would do its duty.[35]

Unlike Hardy, Horne Tooke was as active in his own defence as his counsel, Erskine. His strictures on the Attorney General's behaviour reduced that luminary to tears; nor did he spare the Lord Chief Justice. When Eyre accepted evidence of the Revolution Society's approval of some of the French Assembly's actions as tending to show republican sympathies, Tooke said it was fortunate that they had not said there were good things in the Koran, or they might have been charged with Mohammedanism. He called Pitt, Richmond, Fox, Sheridan and Wyvill as defence witnesses to show that his allegedly treasonable conduct was little out of line with theirs in the early 1780s. After pleading some uncharacteristic lapses of memory, Pitt eventually admitted that in 1783 he had attended a meeting with Horne Tooke which had included some 'delegates'; it was therefore something of a convention. This time Eyre's summing up was favourable to the accused and the packed jury took only eight minutes to acquit. In his speech thanking them, Horne Tooke expressed the hope that the Attorney General would be more cautious in future. He was not: Thelwall was brought to trial. 'Constructive treason won't do, my Lord,' the King told the Lord Chancellor, 'constructive treason won't do.' Yet only after its third humiliation – Thelwall's acquittal – did the ministry abandon what Godwin justifiably called its 'sanguinary plot' to eliminate the radical leaders by extending the doctrine of constructive treason.[36]

However salutary for the government, which was driven to less violent courses, the London acquittals, products of three separate juries' good sense and Eyre's humane integrity, were less therapeutic for radicalism than the Edinburgh convictions and Braxfield's licenced brutality. The membership of the London Corresponding Society shrank; the Society for Constitutional Information effectively died. Wilting radicalism was confronted by a blooming conservatism begotten by the French Revolution. The Terror in France had convinced most people that the so-called universal rights of man were both fraudulent and a mortal threat to the historic constitutional rights of Englishmen. The protection of those traditional rights and the need to head off the sort of struggle of the poor against the rich that had happened in France made continued dissension among the upper orders seem now a dangerous self-indulgence. Hence what Coleridge called a 'panic of property', and what Wyvill thought was more a fear of anarchy, solidified the propertied nation into a patriotic party of order and converted the rich to regular churchgoing. The formal junction of the Portland Whigs and the ministry in July 1794 made the parliamentary elite more united than it had been since the Restoration. Only a small Foxite remnant stayed in opposition. The rest formed a garrison to defend the citadel of the British constitution against the French, the poor and all innovation. Even slavery and the slave trade, both of which had been swept away by France, were, like the Game Laws, preserved by England.[37]

At a lower level the garrison was later reinforced by the recruitment of a corps of Volunteers, based on the loyalist associations. Its ostensible object was local defence against French invasion, but like the Irish Volunteers in the American war, the English Volunteers had a more immediate task than repelling foreigners; unlike the Irish, however, their target was not the government but the disaffected. Obviously any arming of 'the people' had to be undertaken with considerable caution – Pitt's first appeal was addressed to 'gentlemen of wealth and property' – and initially only the ultra reliable were entrusted with weapons.

Nevertheless by 1804 there were some 400,000 of them, a vast popular movement usually exuding and enforcing loyal contentment. The Volunteers, said the Chiswick Armed Association, 'restored a due principle of subordination among the different classes of the people . . . rendered disloyalty unfashionable and insurrection almost impossible'. No wonder men were transported for laughing at them drilling! All the same, not all the Volunteers – they elected their officers – were safely docile. Like militiamen in 1795, many led food riots in 1800-1 and, in Wolverhampton, Volunteers told a magistrate that they had never intended 'to give security to the human oppressor, whilst the poor are starving in the midst of plenty'.[38]

The nature of the violence

The severe fright that the propertied nation had conceived regarding the poor and the Revolution was not a reflection of the violence that had actually occurred since 1789. A particularly blatant act, enclosing large tracts of common land to the benefit of the absentee landowner and a local fox-hunting clergyman, set off serious riots at Sheffield in 1791. But enclosure riots had occurred when France was safely absolutist. The same applied, of course, to the frequent food and industrial riots of the early nineties. As Fox said of tumults at South Shields, Yarmouth and elsewhere, the sailors sought an increase in wages, not the overthrow of the constitution. Apart from such traditional outbreaks, virtually all the violence came from the supporters of the government, not its opponents.[39]

The Priestley Riots were nearly the most serious of the 'Church and King' disturbances. In Manchester on the same day similar destruction had only been averted by the leading reformer of the town Thomas Walker, a churchman, being also the chief magistrate and taking preventive measures; in Norwich the house of the Whig reformer and clergyman, Dr Parr, was besieged for three days; in Sheffield a reforming JP was attacked. In December 1792, when Walker was no longer in office, 'some hundreds of people' attacked his house and those of three other reformers. 'Persons of respectable appearance' cheered them on with cries of 'Church and King forever, lads, down with the Rump'! The magistrates did not intervene against the mob, but Walker was prosecuted for high treason for having defended his house with gunfire aimed safely high. A clerical magistrate concocted evidence from a drunken weaver, which the Crown lawyers must have known was perjured, yet they still brought the case. Though Walker was acquitted, his business was ruined.[40]

A declaration of twenty-six leading citizens of Nottingham against the war – their opposition was on economic not ideological grounds – led loyalists to start military exercises and hire gangs to intimidate those who favoured peace. In June 1794 the local Tories went further. They raised a mob which in five days of rioting attacked the property and the persons of the war's supposed opponents. Many people were 'baptized' (ducked) and one man died. A mill belonging to a Unitarian was set on fire. Possibly the same would have happened to much of the town but for the army's arrival – the water pipes had been cut in preparation. Once again the JPs did virtually nothing. Indeed the mayor helped rioters enter victims' homes and provided general encouragement. Like the Birmingham magistrates in 1791 he escaped punishment and so, effectively, did the rioters.[41]

In North West England alone, twenty-five recorded instances of loyalist violence occurred in the first half of the 1790s, and almost as many in Northumberland and Durham. In April 1794 a mob of 3000 or 4000, armed with clubs and stones and urged on by the local parson who shouted 'that's a Jacobin, that's another', attacked South Lancashire reformers meeting in a pub at Royton. The local constables let events take their course, and the grand jury refused to find true bills against any of the rioters. Instead, six of the reformers were arrested, treated roughly in prison, and charged with assault.[42]

In some of the incidents rich reformers were the targets, but in many others poor men were victims – in loyalist riots people as well as property were often attacked. So the 'Church and King' disturbances in England were not part of a war of the poor against the rich, any more than were similar tumults in Brussels, Naples and Madrid. They were attempts, promoted or tolerated by the authorities, to cow 'Jacobins' and Dissenters. As some food rioters complained in Birmingham in 1795: 'You did not shoot us when we were rioting for Church and King . . . but gave us good ale and spirits to urge us on. Now we are rioting for a big loaf we must be shot at and cut up like bacon pigs.'[43]

The most deadly disturbance of the 1790s, the Bristol Bridge Riot, was similarly no embryonic radical uprising. Tolls on the new Bristol Bridge were to be paid only until accumulated retained profits had topped £2000, and in 1792 the townspeople were informed that tolls would cease at Michaelmas the next year. Yet in 1793 the bridge commissioners, who were closely intertwined with Bristol Corporation, an unpopular self-elected oligarchy, announced that tolls would continue as before. Believing they were being cheated, a crowd twice burned down the toll gates. When on the second occasion the mob paid no attention to the Riot Act, the Herefordshire Militia opened fire, killing a non rioting passer-by and wounding a few others. Tension naturally rose, but the trustees did nothing to lower it or to explain their actions.[44]

The next day, Sunday September 29, the Riot Act was read three times, and three times again the following morning, without leading to any action either by the crowd or the authorities. In the evening a few boys broke into the toll house and burned its furniture, while a small force of militia which tried to stop the bonfire was beaten off with stones and oyster shells. Drums beat to arms and a crowd of over 500 gathered to see what the trouble was. The mayor and alderman arrived at the head of the militia. As soon as some stones were thrown the militia opened fire in both directions. The crowd, most of whom would not, of course, have been aware that the Riot Act had been read in the morning, fled in panic, but ten were killed and more than fifty wounded. Most of them were 'respectable tradesmen'. Some claimed that bodies were carried away or thrown into the river and that about forty people were killed. Even on the official figures the casualties exceeded those of every other disturbance except London in 1780 and Hexham in 1761.[45]

Despite recent economic difficulties, no radical slogans were chanted by any of the mobs. Radicalism scarcely existed in Bristol – the town did not even boast a reform society. The causes of the trouble were the unpopularity of the Corporation and the general belief that tolls were being wrongly perpetuated. Whatever was claimed later, the authorities did not at the time think they were suppressing a dangerous radical agitation. Only their own manifest incompetence and lack of authority led them to overreact.[46]

Far less lethal but much more dangerous to the government were the 'Crimp' Riots a year later: they were in London, they concerned recruitment to the army, and they did involve radical agitation. The country's recruiting methods had long been detested by all its potential victims. Because the army itself was unpopular, volunteers were always insufficient – particularly so in 1794 when the government was aiming to bring one in ten men of military age under arms; hence compulsion was inevitable. The army's equivalent of the press gang was the 'crimp' and 'crimp houses'. Crimps were like pimps, except that they dealt in recruits not prostitutes and operated an 'atrocious and inhuman traffic'. Men were inveigled into crimp houses by violence, fraud or prostitutes, and then effectively kidnapped before being marched in handcuffs to be sworn into the army by a JP.[47]

In August 1794 resentment against this remarkable system was all the greater because balloting for the City of London militia was in progress. Anybody balloted had to join or buy a substitute, which rendered the militia system little more popular than crimping and increased the general feeling of insecurity. The discovery outside a crimp house of the bound body of a man who had been crimped and had presumably died trying to escape, set off a week of rioting. 'A mixed multitude of men, women, boys and children' attacked many of the crimp houses, moving quickly from place to place to evade arrest, though in the end four death sentences were passed. The mobs were methodical and moderate. They did not loot and they attacked crimp houses not the crimps. The military response was efficient and restrained.[48]

The rioters shouted 'No war, no soldiers', and 'Liberty and no crimps'; the cry 'Liberty, Fraternity and peace with France' was also heard. Inflammatory handbills protesting against the government's 'tyranny' were distributed, and an able magistrate believed that premeditated riots had been excited by 'the leaders of the seditious societies'. Almost certainly he was right. The radicals opposed the war and, like many others, they abhorred the government's sleazy recruiting arrangements. But a little encouragement was all that was required. The system produced its own opposition.[49]

Up to 1795, therefore, the poor had shown no disposition to 'class' violence or to insurrection. Violence was used against, not by, reformers. Just as it had been in the first half of the century, the mob was a conservative force. As commonly happens, the rich exaggerated the threat to themselves from the poor because they mistakenly projected onto the poor their own greater solidarity. The poor did, however, resent not having enough to eat.

The crisis of 1795

The 1794 harvest was deficient, and the 1794-95 winter was the third worst of the century; the milk froze in the milkmaids' pails in London, and Parson Woodforde's chamber pots froze 'above stairs' in Norfolk. In March 1795 food riots began in Cornwall, Sussex and the Midlands. So far from suppressing them, the militia – notably in Portsmouth, Chichester and Plymouth – sometimes joined or even led them. A few regular soldiers did the same. The government had begun building barracks in order to segregate the army from disaffected civilians, but its expensively inefficient programme was far from complete. Many soldiers lived in leaking buildings, and those still living in billets had to pay the inflated food prices out of their pay. On April 15 more than 300 men of the Oxfordshire militia put Newhaven under drunken military control; the next morning the town had to be retaken by regular infantry with artillery and cavalry support.[50]

Between April and July the price of wheat more than doubled and disturbances spread all over the country – in Paris near-famine conditions produced two popular uprisings. Even Pitt's friend

Wilberforce favoured peace with France. Once again radicalism
revived. 'Sedition,' said the active Gloucestershire magistrate, prison
reformer and one-time Whig radical, Sir George Onesipherous Paul,
'will take the advantage of acting on an empty stomach.' In London
at the end of June the London Corresponding Society held a public
meeting – an attendance of 100,000 was implausibly claimed – which
passed resolutions denouncing the war and the high cost of food and
demanding manhood suffrage, the dismissal of 'guilty ministers' and
recognition of 'the brave French Republic'. Though only the words
were violent, order did not last for long. Seditious handbills appeared
in their hundreds; large crowds roamed the streets shouting, 'Damn
the King, Damn Pitt, we will have bread at 6d a loaf'; and more
crimp houses were destroyed. This time the crimp house disturbances were shorter and less serious, yet Pitt's windows were broken
in Downing Street and the Foot Guards, the Horse Guards and the
militia were needed to quell them.[51]

Food riots intensified. In many places mobs prevented food being
moved out of their district. The popular 'cry of want of bread,'
lamented Onesipherous Paul, 'has gained almost the whole people to
the side of plunder, they think it justifiable to seize [barges] and sell
the corn.' Indeed, he added, they would have to live by plunder
unless the authorities could 'restore protection' to the canals and
roads. Many authorities, however, did not even try to do so. The
distress was so palpably genuine that they frequently sided with the
crowd against the food merchants and against the movement of corn.
Taxation populaire enjoyed wide official toleration. When a mob
seized a wagonload of corn in Leicester it was allowed to keep it; only
when stones were thrown did the troops open fire, killing three and
wounding eight. Inevitably these inward-turned blockades hit the
larger towns, dependent on the movement of food. In Birmingham,
Sheffield and the cotton towns in Lancashire, mills and warehouses
were attacked. The authorities responded with volleys and bayonet
charges. Two rioters were killed in Birmingham and another two in
both Sheffield and Rochdale. The army was stretched.[52]

The disastrous wheat harvest of 1795 deepened the crisis, and the
course of the conflict with France brought neither relief nor
diversion. Military disasters fed public hostility to the war and food
riots continued in the autumn. In London the L.C.S. held another
large public meeting at which 'the system' was denounced, Thelwall
ascribing all the sufferings of the poor to 'corrupt and vicious
parliaments'. Despite the extravagant oratory and some threatening
resolutions the meeting was orderly but, like its predecessor in June,
it built up tension. At the opening of Parliament three days later Pitt
was 'surrounded' and cursed by a mob. George III, recorded Parson
Woodforde who was present, 'was very grossly insulted by some of

the mob'. He was hissed, hooted and groaned at by vast crowds shouting 'No Pitt, No War, Bread, Bread, Peace, Peace'; a man in the crowd selling 'The Rights of Man for a penny' was arrested and rescued. Shortly before the King arrived at the House of Lords one of the windows of his coach was broken by a pebble or, as he and Woodforde much less probably thought, by a bullet fired from an air gun; on his way back another stone hit the coach. Woodforde thought the mob was composed of 'the most violent and lowest democrats'. Five of 'the rascals' were arrested, but no one was tried.[53]

High food prices – not sedition or reforming opinions – were the root of the trouble. That was not understood, however, and memories of the Gordon Riots and more recent Parisian disorders made some riposte from the government inevitable. *Habeas corpus*, which had only been restored in June, was immediately suspended, and troops were rushed to London. To judge from his conversion of the pebble-throwing incident into a dastardly attempt at assassination, as well as from his remark to Wilberforce that his head would be off in six months were he to resign, Pitt was in a state of near panic. Yet the ensuing legislation was rather less alarmist. The first bill, as Erskine complained, enshrined the judicial doctrine of constructive treason in statute law. Pressure on the King to change either his ministers or his measures became statutorily treasonable. The second bill effectively banned public meetings of more than fifty people and the sort of lectures that Thelwall had been giving.[54]

The Foxites and the radicals combined, for once, against these 'Gagging Acts'. Coleridge privately grieved his own inactivity – his feelings were 'all too delicate for use' – but publicly maintained that the bills were 'conceived and laid in the dunghill of despotism'. Petitions flooded in and enormous public meetings were held. In the Commons Fox said that if the bills were opposed by the great majority of the nation, then 'obedience . . . was no longer a question of moral obligation and duty, but of prudence,' a statement reminiscent of his pronouncements in 1780 and one that he was soon forced to explain away. Despite the agitation the new measures were popular in the country and even more so in Parliament. Remarking that the legislation was chiefly directed against 'the lower orders', the Duke of Bedford reminded their Lordships that while 'they can do without us, we can not do without them'. Nevertheless the acts passed both Houses by a majority of more than five to one. 'Patriotism', the L.C.S. noted, ebbed and flowed with the 'price of provisions', and radicalism was dealt a heavier blow by the next year's fall in food prices than by the Gagging Acts. The most serious riots in 1796 had little to do with either radicalism or food prices. They were caused by a bill augmenting the militia, and as in 1757 they were exacerbated by rumours that militiamen would be forced to serve overseas.[55]

A Reign of Terror?

Of the possible views of the repressive legislation of the 1790s – it was a reasonable response to a revolutionary danger; there was such a danger, but the response was exaggerated; the various acts were a hysterical reaction to a nonexistent danger; or there was little such danger, but the legislation was warranted – the last seems nearest the mark. The radicals were not numerous or powerful, yet the war was unpopular, and unrest was considerable when food prices were high. The government had little means of knowing the exact cause of that unrest, but it knew what had happened in 1780 and was determined to avoid a repetition. In addition, further large public meetings would have had no practical effect except to lead to more violence – from loyalists, more probably, than from the reformers. Even before 1795, loyalists had been taking the law into their own hands. Even worse, they had formed, said Erskine, 'a sort of partnership of authority with the executive power' to bend the law by intimidation. By 1795 preventive legislation was virtually unavoidable and was preferable to the unbridled intolerance of individuals. Above all the government could not afford to take risks with the French: invasion was as great a danger as rebellion.[56]

Throughout the decade Fox, Sheridan and a few others made a gallant defence of civil liberties. Having denounced the 1795 legislation's 'flimsy pretext', Fox correctly averred that repression drove men 'to force and violence'. Yet Britain could not have behaved at home as she had in previous wars. The American struggle had been widely regarded as a civil war; the dissent was permitted, though unpopular. Chatham had called the war unjust in its principle and ruinous in its consequences; Savile thought it a 'justifiable rebellion'; Lord Effingham refused to take his regiment to America. Yet whether or not Britain was now really at war, as Pitt claimed, 'with armed opinions', the war with France was certainly not a civil one; and though Fox, who never understood the French Revolution or grasped the difference between the French and American wars, sometimes seemed to want the French to win, his defeatism was not a privilege the government could extend to others. The resistance and violence offered by the English Jacobins were, as Horne Tooke put it, only that of 'the anvil to the hammer', but the government's measures, by the standards of later wars, were not excessive.[57]

Fox likened 'the Crown party here' to the French Jacobins and talked, like others, of Pitt's 'Reign of Terror'. Sheridan, too, was far from alone in bracketing Pitt with Robespierre. Had the treason trials gone the other way, such language might have been appropriate in 1794, when Godwin thought 'terror was the order of the day'. At all other times its use indicated a life sheltered from awareness of the real terror, red and white, practised in France and Ireland. Not that the English repression was unreal. Reformers were harassed and silenced, juries were sometimes packed, magistrates sometimes acted illegally, some prisoners were framed, most were convicted, some radicals after being beaten up by loyalists found themselves not their tormentors in the dock, many people were harshly treated in prison and about one hundred were incarcerated for months without trial, others had their careers and businesses ruined. Thelwall, who circumvented the law by ostensibly discoursing on ancient history, suffered, as he said, from 'mad violence' and four times narrowly escaped assassination. He was attacked by a mob at Derby, defending himself with a pistol; at Yarmouth his lectures were broken up by ninety armed sailors organised by the mayor, the clergy and officers of the militia. Overt radicalism was stifled and driven to violent conspiracy.[58]

Yet such repression and intimidation were far short of a reign of terror. The law was tarnished but not overthrown. Though 'McCarthyism' was rife, the government did not run amuck. Save in 1798-99, some opposition survived in the press as well as in Parliament. (Fox's Libel Act of 1792, supported by Pitt, had cut the government's power over the press.) The radicals who appeared before the Privy Council were seldom browbeaten. Thelwall told Pitt and his fellow members of the Council that it was 'no part of the law or constitution of this country' to answer their questions. Spence, who thought the landlords should be 'scalped' of their lands, told the Privy Council that if the people's 'burden and grievances were not attended to they must look at the consequences'. When summoned as a witness at Horne Tooke's trial, Pitt was roughly handled by the defence; Robespierre would not have submitted to similar treatment. Again, both the Attorney General and the judges were sometimes criticized for being too favourable to the accused – not an accusation ever levelled against Herman or Fouquier-Tinville in the Revolutionary Tribunal. The contrast in the violence of the two countries was demonstrated by the experience of Paine himself. In England Paine was considered an extremist, convicted of seditious libel in his absence and outlawed. In France he was nearly lynched when mistaken for an aristocrat and, after courageously opposing the execution of Louis XVI, he was clapped into gaol for being too moderate. He only escaped the guillotine by chance and illness.[59]

About 200 prosecutions for sedition were launched in the entire decade – Pitt's government was more restrained against the 'Jacobins' than the Whigs had been against the Jacobites in 1715-16 and 1745-46. Apart from the treason trials in 1794, only twelve men were prosecuted for that crime, only one successfully. The Seditious Meetings measure, though potent as a deterrent, was only once pressed into service in the courts. Similarly the 1797 act making the encouragement of naval or military disaffection a capital offence produced only one prosecution, which did however lead to the execution of Robert Fuller even though he was illiterate and feebleminded and the jury had recommended mercy. Most of the prosecutions for sedition occurred before the panic of 1795, and many would have been launched even in normal times. The man, who verbally, damned and buggered the King and would as soon have shot him 'as a mad dog', cannot have been greatly surprised to face legal reprisals. And when a printer claimed that all the royal children were bastards since the Queen was 'a whore' – an unlikely supposition – he should have been aware that he was testing the limits of government tolerance.[60]

Fox claimed that Pitt's system was more cruel and oppressive than 'any devised by the See of Rome or the Spanish Inquisition' and during the 1796 general election he contended that there had never been a more detestable government. It had attempted, he said, 'the lives of more innocent men at home than Henry VIII'. At that time the government had in reality attempted the lives of only slightly more people than the total of Henry VIII's wives. Later in the decade, leaving out the naval mutineers whom even Fox put in a different category, only two men were executed for offences against the state. Henry VIII sent the same number of his wives to the scaffold.[61]

Ireland and the mutinies

The level of violence that was common in France in the revolutionary decade was confined in the British Isles to Ireland. And it was there that the chief danger to Britain lay. In Ireland the penal laws had made the Irish Catholic, in Burke's phrase, 'a foreigner in his own land', and by 1778 only 5 per cent of that land remained in Catholic hands. The Catholic Relief Acts of that year and 1782 had permitted Catholics to hold property in the same way as Protestants. Yet the political and economic concessions, prised out of London by the Irish Volunteers during the American war, had left the Protestant Ascendancy inviolate and the Irish government – 'worm-eaten furniture,' Burke called it – even more corrupt than before. Ireland was still much more a misgoverned and neglected colony than one half of a dual monarchy. Britain appointed the Viceroy and controlled patronage; otherwise an oligarchy of Protestant landowners had a virtual monopoly of power. Nothing was done for the great majority of the country; about seven-eighths of the fast-growing population was disaffected, and with no English-style Poor Law to cushion their poverty the Irish peasants lived in conditions worse than any in Western Europe.[62]

In Ireland, as in Britain, the French Revolution fertilised radical ideas and produced reform societies. The Society of the United Irishmen, founded in Belfast and Dublin to unite Protestants and Catholics, sought to make 'all Irishmen citizens – all citizens Irishmen'. The instrument was to be parliamentary reform; like the English radicals, the United Irishmen had virtually no social programme. To lessen the military threat posed by a disaffected Ireland during the war with France, Pitt pressed Dublin into passing two more Catholic Relief Acts. But although these removed most Catholic disabilities and at last gave Catholics the franchise, they stopped short of allowing Catholics to sit in Parliament and of other parliamentary reform. In consequence, they were almost as far from satisfying the ambitions of the United Irishmen as were the United Irishmen from addressing the needs of the landless poor.[63]

Irish violence in the 1790s came initially from the Defenders, a Catholic secret society originally formed to defend Catholics against attack from its Protestant equivalent – the Peep O'Day Boys, later the Orange Society – and from the Irish government. In a mere two months in 1793, sixty-eight Defenders were sentenced to death, and a few months later, in a battle between 2000 Defenders and the militia, eighty Defenders were killed. If it was not yet civil war, civil battles were common. Until 1795, however, the aspirations of the United Irishmen were peaceful as well as solely political. The Society was not republican and did not seek to end the British connection. Yet the aim of peaceful reform by consent was even more unrealistic in Ireland, rent by racial and religious divisions, than in England. Government repression (the Society was officially suppressed in 1793), the implausibility of peaceful reform, the recall of a liberal viceroy, economic slump, continued support of the French Revolution and the massacre of Catholics in Armagh – all these drove the United Irishmen into alliance with the Defenders and converted them to seeking by force of arms an independent Irish republic with French assistance. Few conversions have proved more disastrous.[64]

The British government made much of French Revolutionary interference in other countries' affairs; Pitt complained of the French propagating their system 'from the mouth of their cannon' and calling the result 'the will of the people'. The French Convention's decree of November 19, 1792 had indeed offered fraternity and assistance to all peoples wishing to recover their liberty. Pitt called it an attack not only on every government in Europe but on 'the human race'. Yet it was hardly implemented. And in fact British interference in French internal affairs long preceded French interference in the United Kingdom. It was Britain's attempted exacerbation of civil war at Toulon and in the Vendée, where the peasants had risen against conscription, that prompted the Directory to seek revenge in Ireland.[65]

In December 1796 a French expeditionary force eluded the British navy and arrived in the teeth of a great gale in Bantry Bay in South West Ireland. Had the appointed landing place been in the North, the invaders would have been greeted with enthusiasm; in the South there was no glimmering of a Catholic rising. More serious, the invaders were leaderless. The French Commander in Chief, General Hoche, who had not revealed his orders to anybody, was no nearer his own force than was the British fleet. And without him, the French naval commander, like Forbin in 1708, refused to land despite the pleas of the army commander. After a few days of waiting for Hoche, 'the Protestant wind' dispersed the French fleet, and for the moment the danger was over. Ireland was defended by very few regular soldiers and, had the French landed, a revolutionary government on the continental pattern would surely have been established in Dublin. That would have been only the beginning. Interested in land not parliamentary reform, the Irish people would have fought a war against landlords and presumably won it. England, the exiled U.I. leader Wolfe Tone observed, who was with the French fleet, had not had such an escape since the Armada.[66]

A few months later the Royal Navy seemed in no condition to repel a squadron of merchantmen, let alone an armada. The nation faced, a subordinate told the First Lord of the Admiralty, 'the most awful crisis these kingdoms ever saw'. At a time when Britain confronted France almost alone and her navy was outnumbered by the combined navies of Spain, France and Holland, the Channel fleet had mutinied. In view of the navy's crucial importance to the country's safety and the government's perpetual anxiety over 'seditious men . . . with treason in their mouths and rebellion in their hearts' creating trouble, rudimentary prudence might have dictated providing the navy's seamen with decent conditions of service. But to the Admiralty and the Government that sort of prudence was extravagance. Economy came first. 'The fleet,' Pitt told the Commons in 1796, was 'more respectable and more formidable than ever before.' For ordinary seamen life in the navy was certainly formidable. Unfortunately nothing was done to make it respectable. Indeed so far from sailors' conditions having improved, they had deteriorated.[67]

Despite the sharp inflation, the seamen's pay was still anchored where it had been set in 1653; merchant seamen could earn four times as much. In addition the old abuses still flourished. Pay was not only inadequate; it was often months or even years late. The press gang still dogged the sea ports. The food was usually abominable, and pursers cheated the men out of their proper rations. The sick and wounded received no pay at all. The seamen's allocation of prize money was derisory. Discipline was harsh. Although good captains like Collingwood virtually did without it, flogging had if anything grown more pervasive, men being beaten for trifling offences that required at worst a reprimand. The regulations had long laid down that no sailor was to receive more than twelve lashes with the cat-o'-nine-tails without a court martial, but 'of late years,' wrote Admiral Duncan, 'every captain has taken upon him to establish rules for himself'.[68]

While conditions had grown worse, many of the new men in the navy were less ready to endure them. To make the fleet more formidable than before and to offset the huge desertion rate forced by the atrocious conditions on board ship, more sailors were needed than the scouring of the prisons and the press gang could provide – the navy grew from 16,000 men before the war to 114,000 in 1797. Quotas were therefore imposed on counties and sea ports to furnish recruits roughly in proportion to their population. To meet their quotas, local authorities had to offer bounties to volunteers, which attracted men in debtors' prisons, 'disqualified attorneys and cashiered excisemen, clerks dismissed from employment and other individuals in similar cases'. Such men were more literate, of a higher social standing, less inured to brutality, and likely to be more politically conscious and more radical than previous naval recruits.* Even more ominously, Henry Luttrell, formerly the government's champion against Wilkes in 1769, now Lord Carhampton and Commander in Chief in Ireland, had been illegally sending suspected Irish Defenders to the British navy. Many magistrates had done the same. In total, Irishmen probably made up more than 10 per cent of the fleet, and on some ships more than half the seamen were Irish. Most of them had been dispatched to the navy to reduce the danger of an explosion in Ireland. Their likely effect on the British fleet was ignored.[70]

Lavish warning had been given of impending trouble. Wilberforce expected a mutiny. Since the beginning of the war seamen had sent many letters complaining of violent officers on various ships and asking their Lordships of the Admiralty to intervene. In 1794 one ship had mutinied at home and another in the Mediterranean. Two years later, the complaints extended to pay and food, and Captain Packenham told Lord Spencer, the First Lord, that the captains who were asking for their own pay to be increased thought that the men were also entitled to a rise and that unless something was done for

---

* Admiral Sir Thomas Trowbridge, a brave sailor who had commanded the *Culloden* and had a distinguished career under Nelson, thought trouble was always caused by 'lawyers', by which he meant 'fellows that can read and write'. Asked to define mutiny, he replied: 'Whenever I see a fellow look as if he was thinking, I say that's mutiny.'[69]

them they would certainly take steps to get it themselves. Then in March 1797 the men of the Spithead fleet sent eleven petitions to their retiring admiral, the popular Lord Howe, pointing out that although the cost of living had doubled they had had no rise and could not support their families. Howe sent the petitions on to the Admiralty, who did nothing. In the previous month a run on the banks and a serious financial crisis had given economy an even higher priority, and the Admiralty did not even mention the petitions to Lord Bridport, Howe's successor.[71]

The seamen were less inert. Since the Admiralty did not deign to reply to the complaints, a strike or mutiny was the only route to improvement. At last aware that mutiny was planned, the Admiralty decided to squash the discontent by ordering the fleet to sea. Bridport, who sympathised with the men's grievances and knew the order to be folly, had to comply. The men felt no such compulsion. On April 16 when the order was given, they merely gave three cheers – the pre-arranged signal. The mutiny had begun. Its immensely capable leaders – no overall leader was ever identified, though the key man was probably Valentine Joyce, a quartermaster's mate and a United Irishman who had been imprisoned for sedition – retained unanimity among their followers, used minimal violence, kept their demands moderate and maintained strict discipline. Even flogging survived. Continually stressing that if enemy ships appeared they would immediately go to sea to fight them, they conciliated traders and commercial men by continuing the defence of merchant ships. In short, nothing was changed except that the fleet was ultimately under the control of the men's 'Delegates' or 'General Assembly', not its officers.[72]

Bridport warned the Admiralty that to act as it suggested and employ 'vigorous and effective measures for getting the better of the crews' would be futile. In consequence the government eventually acted with more sense than outrage. But its acclimatisation to the new situation took time: having dashed down to Portsmouth, Spencer pompously refused to meet the men; ignoring their requests over food, leave and better treatment of the sick, he offered an inadequate pay increase which Delegates rejected. Spencer capitulated on pay, while still ignoring food and leave. The men, he ordained, were to return to duty at once and be forgiven. That word immediately created misgivings. The Delegates decided that an Act of Parliament embodying the government's decision must be passed and that a pardon from the King must be issued to the whole fleet. The latter was a sensible precaution. The mutineers of 1794 had been promised pardon and then hanged.[73]

The King's pardon arrived quickly, but more pomposity over procedure held up the Act of Parliament and kept suspicions alive.

Meanwhile the Admiralty decided to show its muscle. It ordered its captains to see that the marines' arms were kept ready even in harbour and 'in the first appearance of mutiny to use the most vigorous means to suppress it'. The fleet had been returning to normal; 'tranquillity and order' had been restored, Lord Spencer contentedly noted. Only the Admiralty's folly and the government's dilatoriness reactivated the mutiny. Admiral Colpoys, deciding that enough was enough, tried to prevent the Delegates coming on board his ship. The men refused to obey their officers, and the first lieutenant, Peter Bover, killed one of them. Shouting 'Blood for Blood' the men fired back. Some three men on each side were killed and several wounded before Colpoys admitted defeat. Bover was nearly lynched but was saved by Valentine Joyce. Luckily popular, he was merely placed under arrest, together with Colpoys and the ship's captain.[74]

The Delegates determined it was time to get rid of unpopular officers. More than 100 were put ashore. The new mutiny required a new pardon if the men were not to be at risk. By a happy stroke the government decided to entrust the final negotiations to Lord Howe. Unlike Spencer, Howe dealt directly with the delegates; old and immobile though he was, he visited every ship. The government gave in on food, leave and redress of grievances as well as on pay. Howe even conceded the dismissal of unpopular officers: one admiral, four captains and over fifty other officers and warrant officers were removed. On May 15 the affair ended without recrimination and with a wealth of loyalty, wine and Rule Britannias. Two days later Bridport at last put to sea. The seamen's grievances were generally agreed to be justified, and the granting of their petitions 'occasioned universal satisfaction'. The seamen had achieved their victory without excesses and with minimum violence. 'I am entirely with the seamen in their first complaint,' wrote Nelson, 'we are a neglected set.'[75]

A few days before the triumphant ending at Spithead, the crews of the ships anchored at the Nore, off Sheerness, had mutinied in support of the Channel fleet. On the Sandwich, the largest ship there, conditions were even worse than any at Portsmouth. Built for 750 men, the Sandwich now contained over 1500. A reduction was 'absolutely necessary' the ship's doctor had told the captain in March, adding that the air was 'so impregnated with human effluvia that contagious fevers must inevitably be the consequences'. The captain concurred, but could do nothing. On May 12 the crews of the Sandwich and other ships sent their most unpopular officers ashore.[76]

On hearing on the nineteenth that peace had been made at Spithead, the seamen at the Nore's obvious course was to pocket the gains and accept a pardon, as did the squadrons at Torbay and at the

Cape. Instead, they held out for more concessions, while pretending that those already made were flawed. Nearly all the men's new demands were not unreasonable, and had the Nore been the first mutiny most of them would probably have been granted. But Spithead had given the government and the country a severe fright. Antiwar addresses were still being received. Major, if overdue, concessions had been made to the Portsmouth seamen, and the government was in no mood to make any more. For the Nore men to expect the government and the country to give a repeat performance was a crass miscalculation.[77]

Because they were relighting a fire which everybody else thought had been satisfactorily extinguished, and because their objectives were not clear, the Nore leaders had a far more difficult task than their predecessors. Not only were they opposed by a now much more hostile and militant ministry, their followers were inevitably less unanimous than the men of the Channel Fleet. Many seamen thought it pointless to continue a struggle that had already been won. Even if, therefore, the leadership at the Nore had been of the calibre of that at Spithead, it probably could not have brought the dispute to a happy ending. But it was not. No attempt was made to preserve a blur of anonymity over an ostensibly collective leadership. Probably the real leaders were Irish and did remain collectively anonymous; but, if so, they lost full control by allowing or encouraging other men to put themselves forward as apparent directors. In any case, though he had not planned or begun the mutiny, Richard Parker soon became its all too conspicuous and pretentious leader.[78]

A former schoolmaster and a quota man released from a debtor's prison, Parker had recently joined the *Sandwich*. In the navy twice before, he had on the first occasion challenged his captain to a duel; on the second, again a midshipman, he had been disrated for a minor act of disobedience before ill health led to his return to civilian life. Possessing naval experience as well as intelligence and education, Parker was a natural choice for leader. Whatever his past attitudes, however, Parker now thought rank entitled him to respect and, unlike Joyce at Portsmouth, he styled himself 'President' and adopted the trappings of power. As a result he became a focus for the resentment not only of the government but of many of his nominal followers.[79]

From the outset the Nore mutiny was more violent and aggressive than its predecessor. An expedition was mounted to seize eight gunboats lying in Sheerness harbour and shots were fired at the fort. Some officers were 'ducked', a curious ceremony which led to near drowning, and then sent ashore. Others were tarred and feathered or flogged. Howe thought a deal could and should be done with the men. 'The extravagances of the seamen are not attended to in the manner they ought to be,' he told Portland, ascribing 'neglect' of the seamen's complaints 'to the incompetency of the persons who have the immediate superintendence in the department.' The head of that department, Spencer, had no intention of attending to the complaints. He journeyed to Sheerness, but once again refused to meet the delegates and was determined to make no concessions. He was in fact barely asked for any. By that stage all the men wanted was a ratification of the Spithead terms for them and a promise that their additional points would be considered. Howe would have leapt at that offer but Spencer, fortified by the knowledge that the men were not united, was intent on their capitulation and subsequent pardon.[80]

Like their forerunners in the Channel fleet, the Nore seamen continually reaffirmed their loyalty, maintaining their action to be not mutiny or rebellion but merely a strike for improved conditions. At least after the mutineers' rejection of Spencer's terms, that was not a contention that the authorities could accept. Declining to deal with people they regarded as rebels, the Admiralty resolved to starve them into submission by denying them food and water, and the government took action in Parliament. Bills, passed almost unanimously, made incitement to mutiny punishable by death, and gave the Admiralty power to declare a ship in a state of rebellion, whereupon anybody remaining on the ship became a felon or a pirate; anybody having intercourse with the ship also committed a capital offence. Sheridan pointed out that the government's ill treatment of the sailors was responsible for the mutiny. Pitt could see no ill treatment: the mutiny was the consequences of foreign malevolence; it was not a national product.[81]

The arrival at the Nore of most of Duncan's North Sea squadron which was supposed to be blockading the Dutch Fleet – expected shortly to take an invading army to Ireland or England – was a doubtful blessing for the mutineers. It provided valuable reinforcements, but it hardened opinion against them. Desertion in the face of the enemy was mutiny, if not treachery, of the most dangerous and disgraceful brand. And the enlarged band of insurgent sailors had at hand no counterstroke to the government's siege which would not reinforce the general conviction that their defiance was more a rebellion than a strike. Lacking the bargaining power of the Channel fleet – they had no public support, they were not united and their escape would be difficult – they could only force the authorities to treat with them by threatening damage to the country; and such action would be largely self-defeating, since it would fan both the hostility of the public and the misgivings of their own followers. Yet, as in the case of many industrial workers who used no violence on strike, inactivity would be merely an overture to surrender. Hungry and depressed, the seamen would soon return to duty.[82]

Accordingly the Delegates decided to blockade London. All ships except those carrying perishable goods were to be stopped. The seamen were themselves being besieged; all their supplies had been cut off. Their own counter-blockade was more an attempt to break out of the government's stranglehold and to obtain fresh food and water than anything else. Yet, inevitably, it incensed the commercial men who thought it was all the work of 'lurking traitors'. The seamen went on protesting their loyalty to the King – who, however, was happy in the thought that lack of fresh water would soon oblige them to submit – and blamed 'His Majesty's perverse ministers' for concealing from their countrymen 'the slavery' under which seamen had laboured for many years. They also relaxed their blockade to let through all trading ships. The authorities did not reciprocate. When the mutineers sent fifty of their sick to a hospital ship, the admiral refused to admit them, and the sick men were returned to their own ships. The only treatment they received was the stuffing of their pockets with government proclamations demanding their surrender.[83]

The mutineer's blockade had failed to move the government. They themselves were running short of supplies. Their leaders decided that the fleet should escape to the open sea. Their ultimate destination is uncertain. But evidently some ships were to sail to the Texel, and others to Ireland and France. The order to sail was given, but not one ship obeyed it. The men were now mutinying against their leaders. Yet when two ships left Sheerness not for the Texel but to return to duty, they were fired on by the rest of the fleet. All the same the mutiny was in its final throes, and its leaders were soon under arrest.[84]

'Remember,' Richard Parker wrote in his dying declaration, 'never to make yourself the busy body of the lower classes, for they are cowardly, selfish and ungrateful.' What the rank and file should have been grateful for, Parker did not say, but he maintained that the mutiny had been beaten only because the delegates had checked 'the violence and turpitude of their masters'. Had the Delegates been as violent as their followers, 'necessity would have obliged a compliance to our demands'. Parker, who died bravely, hoped his would be the only execution. That wish was vain. Fifty-nine others were sentenced to death, of whom twenty-nine were hanged from the yardarm.[85]

The mutineers at both Spithead and the Nore always stressed the industrial nature of the disputes and their fundamental loyalty to the King; the government harped on their political and seditious origins. Both had good reason: a 'political' mutiny was an even more perilous undertaking for those taking part than one caused by industrial grievances; conversely, if the mutinies had been sparked purely by bad pay and conditions, the fault was entirely the government's, whereas if they had been fomented by 'Jacobin agitation', ministers would be largely absolved from blame. And both were right. The mutinies would never have erupted had the seamen's conditions of service not been abominable; the *Annual Register* thought it surprising that the men had not risen before. Yet the only respect in which those conditions had deteriorated since the beginning of the war – the fall in the value of their pay because of inflation – would probably not by itself have been enough to precipitate rebellion. Even if recruitment to the navy had been normal, the fleet might not have been immune to the radical ideas of the time. But the influx of quota-men and Irish malcontents produced a significant number of sailors affected, or disaffected, by French Revolutionary and United Irish ideas. The new men and the new ideas together made the seamen's chronic grievances seem acute and intolerable. Resigned resentment was turned into rebellious determination.[86]

Burke and many others feared that Howe's concessions had put an end to all naval discipline. In fact they prevented far worse troubles: had governmental obduracy driven the mass of loyal seamen to embrace the ideas of their Irish or 'Jacobin' leaders, the consequences would have been explosive. Yet neither the concessions nor the stringing up of thirty of the mutineers prevented further unrest. Three marines were shot at Plymouth in July for plotting to destroy the barracks, blow up the arsenal and overturn the government. Mutinous conspiracies were also discovered in the Channel fleet after it had to put to sea. And in the following year there were mutinies in the Channel fleet and in St Vincent's squadron off Cadiz. Nevertheless, within months of the end of the Nore mutiny, the British navy was inflicting heavy defeats on all its enemies. At the celebrations after the victory at Camperdown Admiral Duncan was fêted by the London crowd, but Pitt's coach was stoned, and he needed an armed guard for his return from St Paul's.[87]

Rebellion

In Ireland, Burke lamented, virtual war had been 'declared between property and no property, between . . . the rich and the poor'. It was caused, he added, partly by circumstances but more by the fault of the government: the mass of the people were subjected 'to the capricious and interested domination' of a 'small monopolising junto'. Early in 1797 some Irish peers petitioned for complete Catholic emancipation and in March, shortly before seceding from Parliament, Fox urged the British government to adopt lenient and healing measures. Even at that late hour, political conciliation would probably, as Burke believed, have warded off revolt, though it would not have eliminated the violence that had been endemic for some fifty years. In any case, believing rebellion inevitable, the Irish Whigs, too, seceded from their Parliament, and both the Viceroy in Dublin and Pitt in London preferred coercion to concession.[88]

Ulster was terrorised by the Defenders and the United Irishmen. The populace were so powerful and desperate, a clergyman averred, that no individual could risk resistance. Alarmed by the prospect of another Bantry Bay, the government decided that the least risk lay in terrorism of its own. It placed most of the province under martial law, defending itself by citing the British government's proclamations during the Gordon Riots. The two situations were not in fact similar; martial law had been avoided in 1780. But to the Irish government genuine precedents were as dispensable as legality. General Lake, MP for Aylesbury and later also an Irish MP, was the ideal counter-terrorist: a brave soldier devoid of imagination, humanity and political sense. 'Nothing but terror,' he maintained, would 'keep [the Irish] in order.' Lake's troops, mainly Irish Catholics, also warmed to their task, not complicating their search for arms by distinguishing the guilty from the innocent. Both the armed and the unarmed were killed and their houses burned as a warning to others. Flogging and torture were additional tools of disarmament. A soldier more distinguished than Lake, General Sir John Moore, acknowledged that 'enormities . . . entirely disgraceful to the military' were committed. The Orangemen used by the Government were even more brutal. Yet Lake's barbarity was effective. Ulster was extensively disarmed, and the Republican movement was quelled. The fragile union of Protestant and Catholic disaffection was shattered, and sectarianism resumed its sanguinary sway.[89]

Both the French and the United Irishmen missed their best chance in 1797. The United Irishmen would have done better to rise than suffer subsequent emasculation; and the French should have sent another expeditionary force. But the end of the *Ancien Régime* had not much altered Paris's attitude to émigré claims of massive disaffection at home. After the Irish failure to stir at Bantry Bay the French felt, as in the 1740s, that the indigenous rising should occur before they invaded. And, like the English Jacobites, the United Irishmen elected to wait for a French invasion, which their own inactivity discouraged and postponed.[90]

Lord Moira, an Irish landlord and a good soldier, told the English House of Lords that he had seen in Ireland 'the most absurd as well as the most disgusting tyranny that any nation ever groaned under'. The Irish government's successful tyranny in the North brought it troubles in the South. The judicial murder of William Orr, a Presbyterian farmer in Antrim, gave the United Irishmen a

Protestant martyr. Convicted on perjured evidence he was executed, despite the jury's recommendation to mercy and despite a flood of petitions to the Viceroy, Lord Camden; General Lake insisted that clemency would impair his own violent achievements. Catholics, driven out of the North, confirmed and spread the news of barbarities in Ulster. In the South the United Irishmen improved in numbers and in organisation. By February they had on paper 280,000 men of whom 170,000 were outside Ulster. To oppose them, the government had available some 77,000 troops of all kinds of which all but 11,000 were Irish.[91]

The government set about disarming the South with even greater savagery than it had employed in Ulster. Once again both the innocent and the guilty were shot and had their houses burned. Indeed to be innocent was a handicap. Men were flogged until they confessed where their arms were hidden. Those who had no arms to confess had no means of ending their ordeal. To relieve the monotony of flogging, torture was also employed. 'Half-hanging', loosening the rope round a man's neck every time he lost consciousness, and 'pitch-capping', placing a cap of molten pitch on the victim's head and then setting fire to it, were especially popular. Once again these methods discovered a large quantity of arms, but this time they produced not quiescence but revolt.[92]

At the end of 1797 Carhampton, who like General Lake favoured ferocity, was succeeded as Commander in Chief by Sir Ralph Abercromby, who like General Moore did not. Abercromby noted on arrival that the lower classes hated the gentlemen because they oppressed them and the gentlemen hated the peasants because 'they know they deserve to be hated'. Appalled by what he had seen on a tour of the South, Abercromby issued his celebrated censure of the Irish army for being 'in a state of licentiousness which must render it formidable to everyone but the enemy'. The abuses, he later added, could 'scarcely be believed'. As the Irish oligarchy only found it difficult to believe that anybody should publicly object to abuses, Abercromby's candour led not to their correction but to his own removal. Regretting 'the general alienation of the minds of the people from government' and 'the relaxed discipline' of the Irish army, Abercromby was forced to resign. To his successor, General Lake, the brutality of his troops was congenial and proper.[93]

The government had penetrated the United Irish organisation, but it lacked enough evidence to bring the leaders to trial, and legal scruples which were notably absent from its treatment of the peasantry prevented it from arresting them. A new informer at the heart of the organisation, however, enabled it to arrest fifteen of the leaders on March 12; the most important, Lord Edward Fitzgerald – the Irish Lord George Gordon – evaded arrest but was captured on

May 19, four days before the rebellion was planned to start. Little else in the way of planning was discernible, and nothing had been coordinated with the French who, in the end, arrived in the wrong place at the wrong time with too small a force. The United Irishmen had no strategy and no clear idea of appropriate tactics. Their organisation had been paralysed by the arrests and by the government's campaign of terror. Not even the planned date of the rising was widely met.[94]

Instead of being a planned uprising led by the United Irishmen, the rebellion was more a succession of defensive sectarian revolts by men made desperate by government oppression and fears of Orange persecution. There was a sporadic progression from provoked and scattered insurrection to inchoate but bloody civil war; and, in so far as anybody was in charge, it was the Defenders not the United Irishmen. Only in the belated and ineffective risings in Ulster were the ideals or the delusions of the United Irishmen still just alive. In the South, the Catholic peasants did not fight for a non-sectarian Ireland, parliamentary reform or an independent Irish republic, but for their own safety, the restoration of their land and the supremacy of their religion. The rebellion, Lord Moira told the Prince of Wales, was caused by 'immediate and local outrage to the feelings of the lower classes'; General Moore thought the same. Elsewhere, in much of occupied Europe such feelings led to popular risings against the French oppressors and the revolution. Only in Ireland did they produce a popular rising on the other side.[95]

With the professional classes supporting the authorities, the Irish peasant rising was, amongst other things, a class war. Like its prelude, the rebellion was also counter-terror against terror. In Ulster when the United Irishmen were in control, prisoners were taken and the rules of war were observed by the rebels, though not by their opponents. Elsewhere those rules did not apply. Atrocities abounded. Quarter was seldom given. Prisoners and non-combattants were massacred on both sides. In class wars, it has been said, 'it is the side that wins that kills most'. And as the brave but ill-armed rebels were usually defeated by the well-armed and only slightly more disciplined government troops, the slaughter came overwhelmingly from the government side. 'Strange indiscipline in the troops, perfect incapacity in the officers,' a Whig peer reported from Ireland. 'The government itself,' he continued, proceeded 'from a union of English imbecility and Irish ferocity.' Pitt, who with a very uncharacteristic blend of imbecility and ferocity had just fought a duel with Tierney, sent no British reinforcements for the first fortnight of the rebellion. He did urge the Viceroy to curb the atrocities, but only after his appointment of Lord Cornwallis – who arrived five weeks into the revolt – to succeed both Camden as

Viceroy and Lake as Commander in Chief, did the government achieve a union of sense and moderation.[96]

Even then, that union was not immediately achieved in the field. The reprisals and the retribution after the rebellion were as lethal as the civil war itself. 'The violence of our friends,' wrote the new Viceroy in early July, 'and their folly in endeavouring to make it a religious war, added to the ferocity of our troops who delight in murder, most powerfully counteract all pleas of conciliation.' During and after the rebellion some British officers, like Moore, tried conciliatory clemency with fruitful results, but most of them, like Lake, practised maximum severity, if not the extermination favoured by many loyalists. Lake's predilection for making 'severe examples' extended both the duration and the area of the war. Anybody found in civilian clothes within miles of a military action, Cornwallis complained, was 'butchered without discrimination'. 'Murder,' he remarked of his troops, 'appears to be their favourite pastime.' And in savagery there was little to choose between his Protestant yeomanry and his Catholic militia.[97]

In 1798 anything between 20,000 and 70,000 people lost their lives in Ireland. About 30,000 is perhaps the best guess, probably almost as many as died in the French Terror of 1793-94, not counting the far greater carnage in the Vendée. Most of the killing was done by Irish soldiers and Irish rebels. Yet the Irish government's policy was determined by British politicians, and the slaughter perpetrated by the Irish troops was encouraged and accepted by British officers and gentlemen; Cornwallis had under his command no fewer than forty-three British generals – 'the worst in Europe,' thought Lord Buckingham, a former Viceroy. Furthermore, British officers presided over the courts martial which until Cornwallis brought them under control were little more discriminating in their vengeance than the gangs of marauding Irish Yeomanry. The Viceroy thought his leading officials were 'a violent set of men'. Indeed the attitude of the Protestant Ascendancy to the Catholic population resembled that of Lord Chesterfield to the Scots during the 'Forty-five'. 'All good Protestants,' wrote Buckingham, believed extermination of the Catholics to be 'the only cure for the present and the only sure preventive for the future.' Another nobleman hoped that a new rising would provide the opportunity to annihilate a million or two of the Catholic inhabitants. A new rebellion was ruled out, however, by Cornwallis having at his disposal 140,000 British troops, of whom about half were regular soldiers. There were only 26,000 British soldiers in Wellington's army at Waterloo.[98]

Like the French in Ireland, the British botched their interventions in France. Both governments acted on the promptings of overoptimistic émigrés out of touch with their own countries, and in both cases the native inhabitants paid the penalty, suffering and perpetrating dreadful atrocities. Coleridge's poem 'Fire, Famine and Slaughter', caught the horrors of civil war in both countries:

'Twill make a holiday in Hell![99]

Hunger and peace

Fox, who had been given a general idea of the United Irishmen's aims by Lord Edward Fitzgerald, was horrified by the violence in Ireland. Pitt, too, was shaken, and some opposition peers protested at the 'atrocious cruelties'. But most of England viewed the carnage with indulgent detachment. The English, as Burke had complained, were not interested in Irish affairs. This general indifference was not shared, of course, either by the Irish living in England, many of whom had been driven to Lancashire by the Orange terror, or by the English Jacobins, many of whom had been by this time driven underground to revolutionary republicanism, if not altogether out of politics. When in 1797 the French demanded a rising in England to accompany an invasion, Dr Robert Watson claimed that 200,000 men were ready to rise in England and 50,000 in Scotland. All such estimates were highly imaginative. The 'United Englishmen' and 'United Britons', both created in 1797-98, were dedicated to physical force but were too weak to employ it. Revolution was merely an aspiration, but as usual the government was aware of the conspiracy. Its preventive arrests disposed of any revolutionary threat and destroyed any chance of the Irish rebels being helped by an English diversion. Fox's toast at a Whig Club dinner to 'the sovereignty of the people of Great Britain' nearly landed him in the Tower, but General Bonaparte invaded Egypt instead of the British Isles, and England remained quiescent during the Irish rebellion.[100]

In the following year the government suppressed the radical societies by name and at the same time prohibited all combinations of workmen – the French Revolutionaries had done the same in 1791, and nobody in later years had tried to undo it. Much more dangerous, however, than largely Irish plotting, workmen's associations or the manufacture of a few pikeheads was the near famine of 1799-1801. The 1799 harvest was deficient and that of 1800 worse. The wholesale price of wheat doubled between September 1799 and July 1800. 'Very great grumbling amongst the Poor,' Woodforde recorded in Norfolk. Because of inflation the real wages of building workers in 1800 were lower than they had been for 200 years. The people were nearly 'starving for want of food', Lord Liverpool told the cabinet, and in the coming winter were 'likely to starve also for want of raiment'. The death rate duly rose, though not so sharply as in 1795–96.[101]

Beginning at the end of 1799, food riots continued for the next eighteen months. The most intensive disturbances were in the Midlands in September 1800. In Nottingham the military fired a volley to little effect and in Birmingham a millowner defended his premises with blunderbusses, killing one attacker and wounding another. Unusually, food rioting then spread to London, which saw its worst violence since the Gordon Riots. One handbill asked:

> Fellow countrymen, how long will ye quietly and cowardly suffer yourselves to be thus imposed upon and half-starved by a set of mercenary slaves and government hirelings? . . . Let them not exist a day longer. Ye are the sovereignty. Rouse then from your lethargy . . .

A week of rioting followed, in which the crowds took care to smash all street lights to hinder identification. They were after the middlemen – which from the government's point of view was preferable to ministers or magistrates. The Lord Mayor was accused by the Lord Chancellor, Loughborough, of behaving like his predecessor in 1780, but London was saturated with troops, and his moderation, mirroring that of the mob, was effective.[102]

Four months earlier, George III had survived two assassination attempts in one day. In the morning when he was watching a military review in Hyde Park a spectator standing near him was wounded. Almost certainly the bullet was intended for the King. The official story – that a guardsman had fired accidentally – involved two improbabilities: that a guardsman had mistakenly been issued with ball ammunition instead of powder and that he had aimed horizontally instead of vertically without anybody noticing. The soldiers themselves believed it was an assassin's bullet. That evening James Hadfield fired a shot at the King as he entered his box at Drury Lane for the first English performance of *The Marriage of Figaro* and only missed by a yard. Despite its being his second escape of the day, the King displayed his customary coolness and stayed till the end of the performance. The audience insisted on the newly popular national anthem being sung twice before the opera could begin, and Sheridan provided an additional verse of higher quality than the usual ones before examining Hadfield with a magistrate. The crowd outside was less loyal than the audience in the theatre. The King was hissed, and one of his escort was unhorsed.[103]

Hadfield had been wounded in the head in Flanders and discharged from the army on the grounds of insanity: 'When mad he would call himself Jesus Christ and God.' Brilliantly defended at his trial by

Erskine, he was found insane and sent to join George III's previous assailants in Bedlam. The man who had put him up to the crime, Bannister Truelock, soon followed him there. Truelock was intimate with both God and Hadfield, claiming to have been pregnant with the Messiah for twenty-five years. Though never a member of any radical society, he was a democrat who had talked of George III's death ushering in a republican era. Whether or not, therefore, Truelock's millenarian fantasies had been evident before Hadfield's crime or were only a subsequent precautionary indication of insanity, both assassination attempts were probably political.[104]

Scarcity and high prices brought agitation all over the country. Lord Liverpool's prediction to the cabinet proved all too accurate. 'The poor are absolutely starving for want of both food and clothing,' Lord Lilford's agent told him from Lancashire, 'an industrious family in full work cannot earn more than half meat.' In the North West and elsewhere the riots were more political and better organised than they had been in 1795. In November troops had to be recalled from Portugal. A Wigan magistrate complained of some very seditious members of 'the lowest classes . . . preaching up resistance to government'. Handbills were circulated in Birmingham entitled 'Vive La Republic'. The Midlands were reported to be very much disaffected towards government. In Yorkshire the Lord Lieutenant, Fitzwilliam, conceded that 'the lower orders of the people of the West Riding talk'd of revolution as a remedy for famine', though he did not think any of the 'supposed conspirators important'.[105]

By March 1801 government had virtually broken down in the South West. Numerous companies of Volunteers mutinied, leading many disturbances and refusing to suppress others. No less an authority than the local army commander, General Simcoe, confessed that 'the law of the country was totally overthrown'. Yet there and everywhere else the rioters were concerned with food, not democracy or revolution. Although the radicals could stimulate food riots, they were too few to do much more. The government's relief measures – in some areas perhaps half the population was receiving assistance – and private charitable giving, together with swarms of soldiers, prevented mass starvation or anarchy. Fortunately, the fine harvest of 1801 and the revival of trade that followed the peace ended the crisis. In those circumstances, Lord Fitzwilliam was told, 'pernicious doctrines [would] not be disseminated with much effect'. Having always thought that food prices and the stagnation of trade were the only subjects that 'collected' large crowds, he did not need much convincing. In this dearth only two rioters were executed as opposed to ten in 1795-96 – an indication that the government kept its nerve.[106]

Before peace was made, Pitt had been succeeded by Addington. The Irish rebellion and its violent aftermath had convinced him of the need to change the governance of Ireland. Only union with Britain could break the political monopoly of the Irish Protestants. In such a union, Catholic Emancipation would produce only a small Catholic minority in the Westminster legislature, whereas in a nominally independent Irish House of Commons it would entail an overwhelming Catholic majority. Without Catholic Emancipation, Cornwallis pointed out, England would be making a union 'with a party in Ireland' instead of with 'the Irish nation'. Yet, owing to Protestant intransigence, Loughborough's betrayal of Pitt – Junius had said thirty years before that even treachery could not trust him – and George III's obstinate misunderstanding of his coronation oath, that was the only union permitted.[107]

Events had moved a long way since 1780. To many of the elite, Roman Catholicism now seemed to be a bulwark against revolution. The Prince of Wales came to the conclusion that Catholicism was the 'only religion for a gentleman' and, unlike the Protestant Dissenters, the English Roman Catholics had been granted substantial further relief. Yet George III was still as adamantly anti-popish as any Gordon rioter.[108]

The King's treatment of Pitt was a throwback to his eviction of the Fox-North coalition. At a levée he loudly instructed Dundas that he would consider any man who supported Catholic Emancipation his 'personal enemy – the most Jacobinical thing I ever heard of'. After protesting at such an improper attempt 'to make use of Your Majesty's name', Pitt resigned, thus leaving office in much the same circumstances in which he had entered it seventeen years before. The difference between the two clashes was that George III's intervention was this time disastrous, wrecking any chance of Britain uniting with 'the Irish nation'. As had already become habitual, England made concessions to Ireland only when threatened with violence; and Catholic Emancipation was fatally postponed for twenty-eight years.[109]

NINETEEN

Indebted to Providence?

Through all the stages of the Revolution military force has governed; public opinion has scarcely been heard. But . . . I still believe that in every civilized country (not enslaved by a Jacobin faction) public opinion is the only sure support of any government.

William Pitt, February 3, 1800

Chief Justice Eyre stated that it was an ostentatious and boasting conspiracy, and . . . it was much in favour of the accused, that they had neither men, money nor zeal to effect the purposes with which they were charged . . . There was a camp in a back shop, an arsenal provided with nine muskets, and an exchequer containing nine pounds and one bad shilling; all to be directed against the whole armed force and established government of Great Britain.

R.B. Sheridan, 1795

I told him the English were not a people who would soon be moved to violent acts, they had too general a sense of the advantages they derive to put everything to risk.

Joseph Farrington, November 26, 1795[1]

Writing in January 1790 to Edmund Burke, with whom he had stayed and got on well two years earlier, Tom Paine predicted that the French Revolution would certainly be 'a forerunner to other revolutions in Europe'. Not only did Paine prove memorably unfortunate in his choice of correspondents, he also turned out to be a poor prophet. The Revolution in France was not the first of many similar ones elsewhere. The Belgian Revolution was largely a reaction against the Emperor's liberal reforms. Kosciuszko's Polish rising was more a war of independence against a Russian army of occupation than a revolution. Only in the miniature state of Geneva did the inhabitants manage a (very moderate) French-type revolution of their own making. All the other European revolutions were achieved by the bayonets of the French army. One short answer, therefore, to the question why there was no revolution in Britain is that French bayonets could not cross the English Channel.[2]

With hindsight England's avoidance of revolution is not a matter for surprise. France was more the odd man out in undergoing a revolution than was Britain in escaping one. Yet, in 1790, Paine's confidence that the French example would be widely followed was not far fetched. On the Continent the *Ancien Régime* did not look rock solid and, only a few years after the Gordon Riots and the loss of America, even British stability seemed in question. A few weeks before the fall of the Bastille a British aristocrat made an inventory of current evils: noblemen and gentlemens' abandonment of the country, justices' fear of felons, the poor's need to plunder because not provided for, ladies not daring to live in the country, evasion of taxes, enclosures of common land, venal corporations, trade and manufacturing overstrained, bankruptcies in every town, laws 'unenforceable being multiplied beyond comprehension'. As a result, he predicted, there would 'come a distress, a famine and an insurrection, which the praetorian guards, or the whole army can not quell; or even the Parliament pacify . . .' As Sir Lewis Namier long ago remarked, those words would have been remarkably prescient, if they had been written of France not England.[3]

Subsequent events in France might have been expected to lend reality to the forebodings of the future Lord Torrington. In fact they did the opposite. Had the relative moderation of 1789-91 been preserved, as Paine expected, the English governing elite might have had greater cause for worry. 'A spark,' Peter Pindar wrote in 1791,

> *will now set kingdoms in a blaze,*
> *That would not fire a barn in former days.*

But the Revolution's doctrines were not widely disseminated in Britain until Paine's book was published in February 1791; and by the time they had sunk in the French model admired by Paine was no longer in existence. Revolution had been seen not to produce tolerant moderation. Even if Jacobinism became the ideal, that too had failed to last. More important, before Jacobinism was overthrown it had produced the September massacres, the Terror and the execution of Louis XVI, as well as the French declaration of war – all of them providing for most Englishmen an effective inoculation against revolutionary ideas. Even Wordsworth, the democrat, recoiled 'from the bare idea of a revolution'. The Jacobins' successor, the Directory, was not a regime that many could wish to reproduce elsewhere; and its treatment of Switzerland, by which it tainted 'the bloodless freedom of the mountaineer' and mixed 'with Kings in the low lust of sway', completed the disillusionment of Coleridge, Wordsworth and other former sympathizers. Unlike the corrupt and

arrogant Directory, the culmination of the revolution predicted by
Edmund Burke – the military dictatorship of Napoleon Bonaparte –
did have its English admirers, but it was a far cry from the principles
of 1789. The course of the French revolution was thus the English
conservatives' highest card. And France, Britain's traditional adversary when the home of Popery and absolute monarchy, was no less
her enemy when transformed into the headquarters of secular
republicanism and Bonapartist military despotism. Hence another
explanation of why there was no revolution in Britain runs: because
there was a revolution in France.[4]

Long British experience, as well as the recent French turmoil,
backed the conservative case. Despite its glaring anomalies the British
constitution enjoyed enormous esteem. Its achievement in keeping
the institutions of King, Lords and Commons in balance, preserving
liberty by preventing both absolute monarchy and mob rule, was
considered one of the wonders of the world. The now very popular
George III was far from alone in thinking the constitution a thing of
'beauty'. It was generally venerated as the prime source of prosperity
at home and of triumph abroad. Hence the conclusion that it would
be madness to forsake such a trusty, efficacious and English
instrument for newfangled, Godless and foreign contraption, apt to
import the violence and upheavals of Paris, was a compelling one
even when put by controversialists far less eloquent than Burke.
Patriotism gave the home team a powerful advantage.[5]

That team never lacked either players or supporters. Many
clergymen, journalists, schoolteachers and others felt it their duty to
wage 'literary warfare . . . to wield the pen and shed the ink' against
'the most dangerous enemy which ever disturbed the peace of the
world'. These voluntary propagandists denounced Jacobinism as the
enemy of religion, the monarchy, morality and all social order; they
pointed to the dangers that Jacobinism held for even the poorest in
the land; and they stressed the need to preserve the British way of
life in its traditional and unblemished entirety. Even the waltz, since
it required the partners to embrace, was a threat to morals and
propriety and thus an aid to Jacobin subversion.[6]

The conservative counter-attack which had great popular appeal
was assisted by the incoherence of the radical case. As was seen
earlier, the radicals – save for Paine, Thelwall, Coleridge and a few
others – proposed only political reform and had no social programme
to benefit the deprived. They thus alienated the rich without winning
the poor. The elite feared that widening the franchise would soon
engender social revolution, while to 'our poorer brethren', Coleridge
pointed out, political reform meant little except a change of rulers.
The London Corresponding Society claimed that a truly representative Parliament would bring 'the necessaries of life more within the

reach of the poor'. To most people that was not obviously so. Although Paine did outline an imaginative programme for a welfare state and favoured progressive taxation and the end of primogeniture, he eschewed any further interference with the sacred rights of property. Even Paine was no egalitarian, and most radicals were far more cautious. The only issue that really mattered to the poor – their poverty – was largely ignored. Not only, therefore, were the means by which the radicals hoped to achieve their widely differing aims obscure and seemingly inadequate, those objectives themselves inspired scant enthusiasm. Hence the conservatives scarcely had to win the argument because the radicals decisively lost it.[7]

Much more important, of course, than intellectual controversy was what John Wesley had called the 'great goddess interest'. Writing from London in May 1792, Talleyrand warned the French government that to believe England was 'on the eve of revolution' was mere self-deception. The truth was, he explained, that the mass of the nation was generally indifferent to all those political discussions which caused so much stir in France; 'attached to the constitution by ancient prejudices, by habit, by continued comparison of its lot with that of the people of other states, and finally by prosperity', it saw no advantage in a revolution, the dangers of which it knew from its own history. The English, Talleyrand added, were a people 'occupied without intermission by its commercial interests'. In the same dispatch Talleyrand informed his superiors that the English constitution was equally dear to the peers whose privileges it consecrated, to the rich whom it protected, and to the entire body of the nation to whom it assured all the liberty they wanted.[8]

In England there was no question of that 'aristocratic revolt' which in France had led up to 1789 – 'the patricians began the revolution,' said Chateaubriand, 'and the plebeians completed it.' The English patricians committed no such imprudence. Unlike its French counterpart the English peerage had almost no legal privileges. It was not a caste, as Tocqueville pointed out, and its pre-eminent position was never threatened. Yet the English nobility was little – if at all – more open than the French and, according to Burke, it treated its inferiors with less 'familiarity'. Further, although the taxation system in England looked and, in many ways, was fairer than the French, it was on the whole rather more biased in favour of the rich. Not surprisingly, therefore, the great English magnates were both absolutely and relatively richer at the end of the century than they had been in 1700. Many peers profited from 'Old Corruption' – the government's wholesale distribution of sinecures, pensions and other payments to those it wanted to reward. And as in the Pennsylvanian political boss's definition of an honest politician – one who, when bought, stays bought – they remained securely attached to their spoils. All in all, except possibly for Poland, the English aristocracy was more firmly in control of the state than any other in Europe. No wonder Wordsworth railed against 'the insolence and presumption of the aristocracy', and no wonder the main aristocratic reaction in Britain was in favour of the established order![9]

Much the same was true of the commercial and manufacturing rich. Before 1789 British industrialists sometimes found they were treated with greater respect in France than in England, where the gentry were liable to regard them as 'poor mechanics no better than the slaves who cultivate their vineyards'. All the same, there was more of an identity than a conflict of interest between the great landowners and the commercial rich. The landed and monied interests were far less separated in England than in France. Many landowners were heavily involved in finance and trade, and men of commerce were allowed to pursue their business without interference from the British government. *Laissez faire* at home had been British policy *de facto* long before Adam Smith's *The Wealth of Nations* made it *de jure*. Furthermore in a matter of primary concern to the commercial rich Britain was pre-eminent: Pitt had restored the national finances by 1789; those of almost every other country were in disarray. However much, therefore, commercial men might resent many politicians' ignorance of economic matters or feel frustrated by their own inferior status, the English system offered them solid blessings; and any desire some of them had to emulate France was quickly crushed by the September massacres and the Terror. The English economy continued to grow and, with the interests of manufacturers and merchants lying emphatically on the side of the ruling aristocracy and against 'the English Jacobins', their support of the regime was not in doubt.[10]

Those lower down the social scale had a similar outlook. Montesquieu had warned his French contemporaries that if any foreign power threatened the English state 'the lesser interests would give way to the greater and all would unite to support the government'. And indeed patriotism, reinforced both by governmental and aristocratic pressures and by class fears aroused by Tom Paine, predisposed the middle classes to ally themselves with those above them against the national enemy. Economic interest pointed the same way. The fast expansion of the economy in the second half of the century had brought a consumer boom and an increase in both the prosperity and the extent of the middle class (a phrase that was used in 1790). Property was more widely held, and the professions continued to grow. Between 1760 and 1800 the number of families living in modestly comfortable circumstances increased, perhaps, by 10 per cent to about a quarter of the population. In any internal struggle, too, the propertied nation knew which side it was on. It even accepted Pitt's Income Tax with relative equanimity.[11]

The Prussian, Archenholz, thought in 1786 that never had a nation enjoyed so much prosperity for so long. As in underdeveloped countries today, however, growing prosperity had barely trickled down to the other three-quarters of the population. From mid-century the working class (an expression first used in 1789) was affected less by the growth of the economy than by the growth of the population and the slow growth in agricultural productivity – a combination which for many kept wages either hardly in line with prices or lagging well behind them. The total of a family's earnings not the wages of the father was what mattered, there were large variations between trades and areas, and some of the poor fared quite well. But far more of them were getting poorer, and acute poverty was widespread, peaking in the crisis years of 1795–96 and 1799–1801. The living conditions of the English lower classes, which appalled the Russian novelist Karamazin, were compared by defenders of the slave trade, the Foxite Samuel Whitbread pointed out, to those of negro slaves in the West Indies – to the advantage of the latter! The Sheffield poet Joseph Mather, who could not read or write, made the same comparison and came to much the same conclusion:

> Like them I must continue
> To be both bought and sold,
> While negro-ships are filling
> I ne'er can save one shilling,
> And must, which is more killing,
> A pauper die when old.[12]

Nevertheless patriotism was far from being confined to the middle classes. The English, thought the painter Joseph Farrington, were 'the most national people in Europe', and Pitt skilfully played on national feelings. All the same the multitudes of the poor had no clear economic interest in repudiating the levelling doctrines of the French Revolution and defending, instead of seizing, the possessions of their social superiors. Precautions, additional to repressive legislation, were therefore necessary. Once again the morals of the lower classes were subjected to searching scrutiny and censure; campaigns were launched both to improve their morals and to preserve the sabbath from any taint of pleasure. The elite had long followed the Bishop of Wells's advice, given at the time of the Sacheverell Riots, to keep the right of resistance from the knowledge of the people, since they were too apt to exercise it. Now their theoretical right was removed altogether. Just when it looked as if they might exercise it, Dundas decided that it could not be safely granted to 'the generality of mankind'.* More practically Burke took the trouble to point out that even if the throats of all the rich were cut, the suppers of labourers would not even for one night be turned into banquets – an assertion perhaps more likely to give the poor dangerous ideas than to foster their grateful acceptance of poverty.[14]

Religion provided better protection for the rich than doubtful calculations about the self-interest of the labouring classes. This 'divine cement' of the social order was considered the most effective producer of 'contentment in the lowest situations'; and the Church of England, strengthened by the Anglican Evangelical Revival led by Wilberforce and others, was vastly influential in promoting social stability. Like the Methodists who showed a greater concern for the poor, it proclaimed rebellion to be a sin, emphasising to its often declining congregations the lower classes' religious duty to remain socially and politically subordinate to King and government:

> Our constitution's orthodox
> And closes with our creed . . .

Cruder indoctrination of the poor came from pious laymen. Hannah More's conservative blacksmith told her readers that instead of being jealous because of others being richer in this world, 'I read my Bible, go to Church and look forward to a treasure in heaven'. In her charity schools she allowed 'no writing for the poor', her object being 'to train up the lower classes in habits of industry and piety'. Miss More consoled the poor man with the information that his wife ranked below him, and she solaced his wife with the intelligence that she was superior to her children. In her view an all-wise providence had permitted famine in 1801 to demonstrate the benefit the poor gained from the existence of the rich; the latter, she stressed, provided charity as a matter 'of favour not of right'.†[15]

Whether or not such propaganda was effective in diverting the ambitions of the poor from seeking treasure on earth – it did not after all prevent massive food rioting – the charity was a reality. Sheer benevolence was one factor; Pitt thought the recent display of beneficence had never been surpassed. In addition, not only did the

---

* In the same debate an MP quoted probably the best remark ever made on 'this perilous doctrine' from Andrew Fletcher of Saltoun: 'That it were to be wished, that all government should think resistance lawful, and all subjects should think it unlawful.'[13]

† More was not the only publicist keen to protest too much on behalf of the established order. In 1792 Archdeacon Paley produced his disarmingly entitled Reasons for Contentment. This may have been an attempted atonement for his earlier likening of the rich to a few pigeons who gorged themselves while the rest of the starving flock fought to protect them. This famous analogy was not popular with Paley's wealthy patrons, and he never got a bishopric. Yet in the 1790s the plebeian pigeons never rose to challenge his contention that this order of things was of benefit to all.[16]

rich not want their throats cut, they needed the poor to fight for them in the army and navy. Who is to defend the country, Erskine asked the government in 1795, but the 'insulted people whom you calumniate?' Charitable subscriptions were therefore substantial. In Nottingham in 1795-96 successive town meetings raised money to provide food tickets and bread for those in need. Much the same happened elsewhere both in that crisis and in 1800-01. Parson Woodforde thought the sum collected in his parish was 'very great indeed'. In 1795-96 the poor gained more money from charitable gifts than they did from the poor rates.[17]

The Poor Law

Canning believed that the Poor Law saved England from revolution. In *Ancien Régime* France most of the poor – between 5 and 10 per cent of the population – were destitute or nearly so, and in Paris in 1789 the figure was well over 60 per cent who depended on private subsidy; the government played little part. In England, by contrast, relief had long been achieved mainly by public provision (called by Halevy 'a kind of state socialism'), a system which attracted the admiration of many foreign visitors. Even so, in the southern half of the country in the 1790s a large surplus of agricultural labourers lived in extreme poverty for much of the year. Observers demonstrated that it was not possible to live on the wages of an agricultural worker. Despite believing that the poor's 'situation in life' was better than they 'deserved at the hand of God', Wilberforce himself was active in the years of dearth, yet the philanthropic efforts of the Evangelicals were concentrated on helping the black slaves shipped across the Atlantic; those on their doorstep were fed with Hannah More's religious tracts.[18]

Whatever the beneficial economic effects of the increased pace of enclosure after 1760, which on occasion was violently resisted, the social costs were dire. Nineteen out of twenty enclosure bills, wrote Arthur Young, injured the poor. The number of totally landless labourers (who could no longer keep their own livestock and were thus wholly dependent on wages) multiplied, seasonal unemployment grew, expenditure on poor relief was greatly increased, and real wages still fell. In the crisis year of dearth and inflation, 1795, the Berkshire magistrates – seven squires and eleven clergymen meeting near Newbury at the Pelican Inn in Speenhamland – decided that a labourer's wages should be supplemented out of the rate on a scale varying with the price of bread, and that he should be paid an allowance for his wife and each child. Although justices elsewhere had earlier done much the same, Speenhamland gave its name to the system which was soon espoused by eighteen counties.[19]

Early in 1796, maintaining that the poor were in 'a state scarcely consistent with the character of a civilized country', Whitbread introduced a bill empowering magistrates to fix a minimum wage, an option fully in accordance with English precedent and one which Devon JPs had already taken. He was backed by Fox but the bill was rejected, Pitt arguing that the hardships of the poor were not as great as Whitbread claimed and that 'the unassisted operation of principles' was a more effective remedy than interference by authority. Like the rest of the government, Pitt seems initially to have had little idea of the extent of the poor's distress, but his apparent dogmatism was mitigated by a promise to bring forward proposals of his own. The next year, however, his imaginative ideas received even shorter shrift than Whitbread's. Parliament did nevertheless recognise the principle of 'Speenhamland' and that system had much the same effect as a minimum wage.[20]

In denouncing 'Speenhamland' for being the cause of the country's economic woes, *laissez-faire* doctrinaires muddled cause and effect. Subsidising wages and providing family allowances out of the rates did not pauperise or demoralise the working classes, nor overpopulate the southern counties. The system was a humane and necessary remedy for evils that were already present.[21]

Speenhamland's eleven clergymen and seven squires were thus wiser than their critics. Deploring interference with the laws of commerce which were 'the laws of God', Burke thought magistrates and the state should not interfere with the free market and should leave the poor to the mercies of private charity and to the consolations of the next world. In this case 'the wisdom of our ancestors' embodied by the Speenhamland magistrates was a much better guide than 'God'. Had Burke's view been adopted, England might have seen roaming packs of vagrants terrorising the countryside as in prerevolutionary France or even invading towns and cities, as they did Paris in 1788-89; certainly many people would have starved to death. In the event, nothing of that sort happened. 'Speenhamland' ensured a very minimal subsistence for all – something the French Revolutionaries never achieved in France, despite their rhetoric. The Poor Law could not itself prevent food riots, but it was a powerful tranquilliser. Canning was at least half right.[22]

Jacobins and Jacobites

Pitt told Parliament that, faced with two such horrible alternatives as the re-establishment of a popish pretender or that 'desolating system of anarchy' produced by the French Revolution, he would unhesitatingly chose the Pretender.* He was sure, however, that everybody was equally prepared to risk their lives in opposing 'either Jacobitical or Jacobinical principles'. His predecessors between 1715 and 1759 had felt no such certainty. That crucial difference between the fight against the Jacobins and the one against the Jacobites was demonstrated by Pitt's foundation of the Volunteers. For George I or George II to have similarly armed the people would have ended the dynasty. As Hume pointed out, because the succession was disputed, they did not dare to arm their subjects. Even in 1756-58, George II and the Newcastle Whigs were deeply alarmed by the prospect of the new militia putting arms into the hands of their Jacobite enemies. Yet in the 1790s the Volunteers could be formed without endangering the crown of George III.[24]

In the 1790s the government took that risk in the well-founded belief that it had more to fear from armed Frenchmen than from armed Englishmen. In 1803 over half of the almost 400,000 Volunteers had firearms. Often as hungry as anybody else, they were unreliable enforcers of order, frequently leading food riots instead of stopping them. But, though they were misled, said General Simcoe, they were not Jacobins; and he, not the radical Major Cartwright who optimistically believed the general arming to be the most likely cause of parliamentary reform, turned out to be right. Much to the surprise of conservatives and the disappointment of radicals, the Volunteers never tried to use their armed strength to enforce political demands. Even so, the government did not press its luck. As soon as the invasion scare was past, it began winding down its Volunteers.[25]

Together with the Yeomanry and the Cardigan Militia the Volunteers helped to nullify the only French landing in Britain. Shortly after Bantry Bay, the French 'vomited', in Lord Liverpool's phrase, 'a set of ragamuffins . . . on our coast'. The ragamuffins – a charitable description of some 1000 half-starved criminals and military dregs called by the French 'the Black Legion' and commanded by a piratical American – were intended to burn down Bristol and spread general panic, but after some futile depredations at Ilfracombe the main force disembarked at Fishguard and surrendered within hours.[26]

A serious French invasion would have been accorded a very different reception from that given to the Pretender and his Highlanders. As in 1745 the City would have panicked – even Fishguard set off a run on the Bank of England. But although the

---

* In 1796 the French considered the possibility of sending Charles Edward's brother, Cardinal York, to Ireland to lead a rising.[22]

French would have received a little more help from some of the populace than the Jacobites had done, they would have encountered far more hostility. In 1794 even radicals and pro-French opposition Whigs were convinced that virtually everybody would 'turn out' to oppose an invasion. After 1795 the days of 'Church and King' enthusiasm and violence were over, but loyalism remained sufficiently strong to produce a flood of Volunteers in 1798. Soon afterwards the government discouraged 'the arming' of the urban poor, yet in 1801 Godwin gloomily noted that 'even the starving labourer in the alehouse [had] become a champion of aristocracy'.[26]

A revolutionary situation?

Short of a successful French invasion, a revolutionary situation in England could have arisen only from a breakdown of government, military defeat, a mass insurrection, the defection of the armed services, a *coup d'état* by the 'English Jacobins', or by a combination of some of them. The French Revolution was caused by a breakdown of the old order; the government lost control, and the National Assembly gained it – more or less. Whatever the dangers in 1779-80, there was no possibility of such a breakdown in England during the next twenty years. Parliament, steeped in the pride of legitimacy and history, never for one moment considered stepping aside to allow some chaotic new body to take control. The governing elite never lost its self confidence, and men of property were solidly behind it. The English state was the strongest in Europe.[28]

Such a state would not obligingly collapse. To be replaced it had to be overthrown. Yet the chances of a mass insurrection were almost as remote as an English 1789. No aristocratic leadership was obtainable. However disaffected were Fox and his followers the last thing they wanted was rebellion or revolution: although he toasted the sovereignty of the people, Fox was opposed to universal suffrage – even in 1797 he favoured going no further than giving the vote to householders – and boasted that he had not read the second part of Paine's *Rights of Man*. Middle-class leadership was only a little more available. Describing Jacobinism as 'the revolt of the enterprising talents of a country against its property', Burke attributed the French Revolution to a conspiracy between the moneyed interest and a sinister bunch of literary atheists. In England, as was seen above, the country's enterprising talents were safely harnessed to their own interest and that of property; the moneyed men, too, were allied to the regime by sentiment and profit and no Continental-type intelligentsia existed, atheist or otherwise. Inevitably there were a few radical barristers like Felix Vaughan, who joined the L.C.S., but a legal system that trained its practitioners to be wary of such innovations as putting an end to the burning alive of female forgers effectively precluded the nurturing of swarms of dangerously revolutionary lawyers of the sort that Burke saw as largely composing the French *Tiers Etat*.[29]

Besides, many middle-class reformers were disillusioned by the violence of the mob's hostility to them in the 'Church and King' riots. The current government of England, one of them wrote, was as good as the people deserved. Thomas Walker thought that the people had been kept too uneducated to appreciate the need for reform. In any case most middle-class radicals favoured reform, not insurrection or revolution. Furthermore in the second half of the decade urban radicalism was crushed by the government's repressive legislation. Without gentry or adequate middle-class leadership, lower-class agitation was insufficiently focussed to lead to organised rebellion.[30]

Revolutionaries in the labouring classes were also thin on the ground. The country, a Foxite peer conceded in 1792, was overflowing with loyalty. Though the loyalist tide receded a little after 1794 and rioting women were heard to say that they would soon see the 'downfall of all ye clergy and of every rich person', radical doctrines made limited impact except when harnessed to popular grievances. The social crisis created by the riots over high food prices in 1800-01 was certainly serious – General Simcoe concluded that in March 1801 Devon and Somerset were 'in a complete state of anarchy'. Yet the government and the rich made strenuous efforts to contain it, and it was in any case a long way from mass political insurrection. Similarly there was nothing approaching a political breakdown at the top. Hence no revolutionary situation or opportunity arose.[31]

Pitt was well aware of the armed forces' crucial role not only in repelling invasion but also in preserving the political system from internal revolt. Yet the government's handling of the army and navy was much more negligent than its treatment of the lower classes. By turning a blind eye to all the warning signals of impending trouble in the fleet, it precipitated mutinies which laid Britain open to invasion and which were politically – as well as militarily – the most perilous moment of the revolutionary decade. The mutinies were not instigated by the United Irishmen or by the radical societies, but the United Irishmen had planned a naval revolt in the previous year and might well have taken advantage of Spithead and the Nore in 1797. When he learned what had happened Wolfe Tone lamented the loss of a marvellous opportunity. Even as it was, members of the U.I. were prominent in the mutinies. Similarly a number of the leaders had been members of the 'Jacobin' societies, and Painite ideas are

discernible in their petitions. Lord George Gordon's former secretary, Dr Robert Watson, a prominent member of the London
Corresponding Society, was active in Portsmouth at the time.
Because Joyce and the other leaders, mindful of the need to maintain
unanimity, stuck to the industrial grievances which were all that
concerned the great majority of loyal seamen, the Spithead mutiny
appeared much less political than its successor at Sheerness. Yet
though divisive political notions were kept beneath the surface,
sedition was not absent from the Channel fleet, some of which talked
of sailing to Brest.[32]

Most of the sailors in the British fleet were patriotic and only
interested in their own practical grievances. On the face of it,
therefore, they were not promising revolutionary material. Yet the
crew of the battleship *Potemkin*, largely reruited from peasants, had
long been the despair of radical agitators, until in 1905 an inedible
dinner of maggotty soup touched off an explosion. Had the British
government's sensible handling of the 1797 mutinies not been in
sharp contrast to its feckless fumbling before them, had it not
immediately granted the army a pay rise to stop the mutinies
spreading ashore, or had the Nore ships been able to maintain their
blockade of London, then almost anything might have happened on
land or sea. In particular parts or all of the Spithead fleet or the Nore
squadron might have sailed to France or Holland. For either to have
done so would have been a more drastic and damaging step than that
taken by the *Potemkin* mutineers who merely surrendered their ship
to the Romanian authorities – in 1905 Romania, unlike France or
Holland in 1797, was a neutral not an enemy country.[33]

If the navy was the nation's chief line of defence against the foreign
enemy, the army was the government's main protection against
internal revolt. In social disorders there was always the danger that
the private soldiers might side with their rioting social equals rather
than obey their officers' orders. Hence Pitt sought to isolate the
troops from the populace by housing them in barracks instead of
alehouses. (The French army, which had proved an unreliable
buttress of the monarchy, lived among the people, not in barracks.)
Otherwise the government took no better care of its soldiers than of
its sailors. Troops were sent to Flanders without proper clothes. In
the terrible winter of 1794–95, the government relied on charitable
gifts to provide them with greatcoats. Even shoes were scarce. The
government did nothing to cut down army flogging, and only the
dangers laid bare by the naval mutinies concentrated its mind on the
inadequacy of soldiers' pay.[34]

When the Spithead mutiny broke out 'disaffection and discontent'
were evident in the Guards and, despite the pay increase that these
events evoked, the artillery mutinied at Woolwich while the Nore

mutiny was at its height – one of the few events, according to Wilberforce, which 'waked' the Prime Minister. The Woolwich artillery riot was suppressed the next day by cavalry and the Guards. Earlier a newly raised Irish regiment had mutinied at Exeter when ordered to amalgamate with another regiment of the line. The mutineers fired at some of their officers and attacked Exeter castle. Only a fierce attack by some Dragoons in which 'some had their noses cut off, others their arms [and] a great many [were] disabled' restored good military discipline. In 1800 the royal Duke of Kent provoked a mutiny in the garrison at Gibraltar by his attempted imposition of Prussian-type discipline. Several men were killed, and the Duke was recalled in disgrace.[35]

But military mutinies were rare, and despite the government's reckless disregard of its soldiers' welfare and its failure to take precautions against sedition – only one-third of the London garrison were stationed in barracks, off-duty soldiers could wander about London in civilian clothes, and many Irishmen were enlisted in the Guards – the regular army remained loyal and, unlike the militia and the Volunteers, it had no record of disobedience in dealing with ordinary disturbances. Since a similar military willingness to suppress more dangerous risings was virtually certain, a revolutionary *coup d'état* had no chance of success unless the army, or at least the bulk of it in London, had been previously won over.[36]

The Despard conspiracy, which was unearthed and probably magnified by the government in 1802-03, revealed that there was some disaffection in the third battalion of the First Guards, but not enough to do much damage even if the conspiracy itself had been better conceived. At Colonel Despard's trial the Attorney General admitted that the story he was putting forward was improbable, and Sergeant Best, Despard's defence counsel, made much of that theme:

> Fourteen or fifteen persons assemble together at a common tap-house with no other fire-arms than tobacco pipes, form a conspiracy to overturn a government [which is] supported by the unshaken loyalty of many millions . . . by what arms? Not a pike, gun, sword, pistol . . . Yet with these forty or fifty men of buckram, the Tower was to be taken, the Bank was to be seized, the India-house was to be overturned, the King was to be seized in the midst of his Guards as he was going to the House of Lords, and the two Houses of Parliament taken most complete possession of.

It was indeed, concluded Sergeant Best, a 'ridiculous scheme'.

Even if the conspirators had managed to capture the Tower and a few other public buildings, what then? Disraeli's Sidonia pointed out that it was not hard to reach Jerusalem – the difficulty was to know what to do when you got there. Despard would have had the same problem. As he himself conceded, a few desperados could capture the Tower and the Bank, but far more men would be needed to hold them. The country was at peace and, far from being defeated, it had gained some spectacular naval victories. No revolutionary situation existed, and no mass insurrection would have come to the aid of the conspirators. Only a French invasion could have lent the *coup* credibility, and there was no near prospect of one. Even if, therefore, the government had not aborted the plot by arresting its leaders, the Despard conspiracy would have been as doomed and as futile as Robert Emmet's Irish rising the following year.[37]

Despard made no substantive defence, only calling character witnesses. Nelson testified that 'no man could have shown more zealous attachment to his sovereign and his country than Colonel Despard did'. But that had been twenty years ago, and he had not seen Despard since. Even so, Nelson impressed the jury as much as he did at Captain McNamara's trial later that year for killing a man for insulting his dog and won Despard a recommendation to mercy. Fox concluded, however, that he himself was almost the only man in London who would have reprieved the colonel, and Despard and six other conspirators, all of them soldiers, were hanged for high treason. There was also some plotting in the North of England, but it had little support, and the Despard affair demonstrated that a *coup d'état* was no likelier a route to successful revolution than was mass rebellion.[38]

Eighteenth-century England had much in common with the twentieth-century United States. Both were intensely nationalistic, nearly always successful in war, and the richest countries in the world. Money is as important in contemporary American politics as property was in eighteenth-century Britain. In both political systems influence and patronage, not to say 'corruption', were prominent. The American President's powers are similar to those of George III. (With his impeccable private life, that monarch would have made a safely dull presidential candidate.) In Britain a large part of the population was deprived of the franchise; in America a large percentage declines to exercise it. There are the same vast disparities of wealth in the United States today as there were in eighteenth-century Britain, and now America too has a vast underclass. The chief difference between contemporary America and eighteenth-century England is that the former is more violent. But in the United States, as in England 200 years ago, habit, the governing myths and the magic of authority procure the consent of the great majority. Nobody except a few cranks and fanatics expects or fears an American revolution.[39]

An English revolution in the eighteenth century was not much more likely. History showed, Swift argued early in the century, that the common people would revolt only against 'a very bad government indeed'. And shortly before the American war Priestley maintained that the English had always borne extreme oppression for long periods before rising. Whatever may be thought of the oppression, both men proved better judges of the English people than Tom Paine. In 1688–89, Paine complained, the nation had been 'left out of the question'. He expected them 100 years later to remedy their exclusion by imitating their enemy across the Channel. Yet very few Englishmen showed any inclination to do so. Much as they had disappointed Milton after the Civil War – from being in 1644 the people to whom God revealed himself 'as his manner is, first to his Englishmen', they became in *Paradise Regained*

> . . . *but a herd confus'd,*
> *A miscellaneous rabble . . .*
> *They praise and they admire they know not what –*

and were later to distress Dickens by their lethargic lack of radical fervour, the English people in the 1790s demonstrated themselves to be obstinately conservative.[40] But so, of course, did the British government and the propertied elite.

Any assessment of the violence of the eighteenth century should try to avoid both anachronistic hypercriticism and nostalgic applause. The first approach would over-emphasise the relative indifference to injustice, suffering and death which pervaded all classes, while ignoring some strong mitigating factors. The most important of these was probably the backwardness of medical knowledge at that time. Average life-expectancy was only about 35 years, and if some among the higher orders lingered beyond three-score and ten, that was no thanks to their doctors, as the case of George III showed. Almost nobody was a stranger to acute pain. Gnawing hunger was for many people another powerful foe of good temper. The nerves of eighteenth-century Englishmen – and women – must have been very frequently stretched beyond endurance. Hence disagreements more easily became quarrels, and antagonisms rapidly progressed from words to blows. The Hanoverian in the Clapham Hackney carriage would have tolerated violence more readily than his modern counterpart and he would have had more pressing reasons for translating his feelings into actions. Aspirin, indigestion tablets and other placebos must have considerably reduced the urge to violence. Perhaps the cause for surprise is that they have not had more effect.

Complacency and nostalgia are equally misplaced. To some it may be tempting to bemoan the absence of a 'moral crowd' today, to think that instead of Hume's predicted 'euthanasia' of absolute monarchy, the English constitution now languishes under the anaesthetic of democracy, and to regret that near-universal access to peaceful means of protest such as the ballot box and letters to the press has brought more direct action into lamentable disrepute. Some grievances are sore enough, it may be felt, to justify a quick riot. Just as many people in the eighteenth century thought the riot was a healthy national tradition expressing rugged English libertarianism,[41] so a return now to the good old days of 'Wilkes and Liberty' would restore the vigour of the Body Politic.

That is clearly fantasy. The existence of collective moral outrage presupposes great injustice; it is surely better to avoid such provocations than to hanker after violent reactions against them. There is the further point that innocent victims are an almost inevitable accompaniment of 'spontaneous' rioting. Even collective virtue in a crowd is likely to provoke a collective reaction from a government. Finally, the crowd is plainly not always virtuous. Overall one might possibly regret the passing of the 'moral economy', but that is not the same as endorsing its violent expression.

Eighteenth-century England was neither a lawless killing ground nor a Quaker utopia. Should that be attributed to skilful government, to sheer good luck or, as William Warburton believed, to the special providence of God? According to Bishop Bossuet in his funeral oration on the Queen of England, Mary of Modena, revolutions are always 'caused by the weakness or the violence of princes. When rulers neglect to acquaint themselves with the business of government or with the state of their armies . . . to watch over the laws and to observe moderation,' Bossuet continued, then the people's 'patience will be exhausted and the extremes of violence' will menace the regime. Only in their neglect of the army did Pitt and the cabinet fail to meet Bossuet's requirements for stability. So, if the Bishop was right, England's avoidance in the 1790s of the extremes of revolutionary violence owed as much to the competence and moderation of the government as to the traditional patience of the English people.[42]

Abbreviations

Add. Mss.	Additional Manuscripts
A.H.R.	Agriculture History Review
A.R.	The Annual Register
B.I.H.R.	Bulletin of the Institute of Historical Research
B.L.	British Library
B.S.S.L.H.	Bulletin of Society for Study of Labour History
Burke	The Works of the Right Honourable Edmund Burke, 6 vols, Henry G. Bohn, London, 1855-6.
Burke's Corr.	The Correspondence of Edmund Burke, 9 vols, eds. T. W. Copeland and others, Cambridge and Chicago, 1958-70.
Cav.	Cavendish Debates, 2 vols, ed. J. Wright 1841-2
C.J.	Commons Journals
E.B.	Encyclopaedia Britannica, 11th ed., 1911
Ec. H.R.	Economic History Review
E.H.R.	English Historical Review
G.M.	The Gentleman's Magazine
HC 1715-1754	The House of Commons 1715-1754, 2 vols, ed. R. Sedgewick, London, 1970
HC 1754-1790	The House of Commons 1754-1790, 3 vols, eds. Sir Lewis Namier and J. Brooke, London, 1964
HC 1790-1820	The House of Commons 1790-1820, 5 vols, ed. R. G. Thorne, London, 1986
H.M.C.	Historical Manuscripts Commission
H.W.	The Yale Edition of Horace Walpole's Correspondence, 41 vols, gen. ed. W. S. Lewis, Newhaven 1937-1984
J.B.S.	Journal of British Studies
J.H.A.	Journal of Historical Association
J.M.H.	Journal of Modern History
J.S.H.	Journal of Social History
L.J.	Lords Journals
P.H.	Cobbett's Parliamentary History of England from the Earliest Period to the year 1803, ed. William Cobbett

P.M.	Political Magazine
P. & P.	Past and Present
P.R.	The Parliamentary Register or History of the Proceedings and Debates of the House of Commons [House of Lords], ed. J. Debrett
P.S.	Political Studies
S.H.	Social History
S.P.	State Papers
S.T.	A Complete Collection of State Trials compiled by T. B. Howell, 33 vols, 1816–1826
T.R.H.S.	Transactions of the Royal Historical Society
W.O.	War Office Papers

All books were published in London unless otherwise stated.
Full details of a book are usually given only the first time it is cited.

Notes

Introduction: A Violent Society?

[1] R. Coupland (ed.): *The War Speeches of William Pitt* (1940), 20; *Brickdale's Parliamentary Diary* (in Bristol University Library), Vol V, 27 March 1771: H. Arendt: *On Violence* (1970), 79

[2] Milton: *Paradise Lost,* Bk VI, ll 220, 593-8.

[3] J. Danielou: *Prayer as a Political Problem* (1967), 106; A. Manhattan: *The Catholic Church Against the Twentieth Century* (1950), 77, 117, 121: J. Mack Smith: *Mussolini* (1981), 24, 114; Arendt, 35n.

[4] P. Zagorin: *Rebels and Rulers 1500-1660,* (Cambridge, 1982), 2 vols.; I, 18-9.

[5] G. Sorel: *Reflections on Violence* (1915), 195, 200-1; cf. P. Wilkinson: *Terrorism and the Liberal State* (1986), 19.

[6] M. Harrison: *Crowds and History* (Cambridge, 1988), 182-91.

[7] R. Segwick (ed.): *The Letters of King George III to Lord Bute* (1939), 156; J. Locke: *Two Treatises of Government* (P. Laslett, ed., Cambridge 1960), eg II. s16-20, 176, 179, 222; J. Dunn: *The Political Thought of John Locke* (Cambridge, 1982), 165; Cav. I, 592.

[8] Murray in Holderness S.P. 36/123 ff. 51; T. Hayter: *The Army and the Crowd in the Mid Eighteenth Century* (1978), 188; Cav. I, 146; E. Mossner: *The Life of David Hume* (1954), 181; PH XVII, 221; *Grenville Papers* (4 vols., J. Smith ed. 1852), II, 139.

[9] C. Friedrich: *The Pathology of Politics* (New York 1972), 1-5, 10-2, 14, 57-8, 68, 227-8; C. Tilly: Collective Violence in European Perspective in H. Graham and T. Gurr (eds.), *Violence in America* (Beverley Hills, 1979), 109; J. Dunn: *Western Political Theory in the Face of the Future* (Cambridge, 1979), 6.

[10] J. Cockburn (ed.): *Crime in England 1550-1800* (1979), 50; F. Dunne: *Mr Dooley Remembers* quoted in F. J. Harrison: *The Common People* (1984), 19; Michael Jones in the *Sunday Times,* 4th December 1988; R. Wells: Counting Riots in Eighteenth Century England (*B.S.S.L.H.*, 1978), 68-70.

[11] H. Perkin: *The Origins of Modern English Society, 1780-1880* (1969), 280; R. Porter: *English Society in the Eighteenth Century* (Harmondsworth, 1982), 114; J. Plumb: *The First Four Georges* (1956), 14-5, 20; G. Kitson Clark: *The Making of Victorian England* (1965), 59-60; A. Briggs: *The Age of Improvement* (1960), 426-7; D. Marshall: *Eighteenth Century England* (1974), 2.

[12] A. Macfarlane: *The Justice and the Mare's Ale* (Oxford, 1981), 1-26, 173-99; J. Beattie: *Crime and the Courts in England 1660-1800* (Oxford, 1986), 112, 624; J. Sharpe: *Crime in Early Modern England 1550-1750* (1984), 175: J. Sharpe: The History of Violence in England: Some Observations, *P & P* no. 108 (1985), 215.

[13] B. Pascal: *Pensees* (Harmondsworth, 1966), III, 60, 46; PD 3S, IX, 389; D. Defoe: *A Hymn to the Pillory,* in J. G. Boulton (ed.), *Selected Writings of Daniel Defoe* (Cambridge, 1975), 101; Sorel, 105.

[14] E. Fromm: *The Anatomy of Human Destructiveness* (Harmondsworth, 1977), 58.

[15] Macfarlane, 173-86; R. Cobb: *The Police and the People* (Oxford, 1970), 88-9, 325-7; F. Ford: *Political Murder* (Cambridge, Mass., 1985), 5-6, 31, 55-7, 105-10, 178-81, 194-9, 239, 382-3.

[16] Ford, 193-4.; M. Gibb: *Buckingham 1592-1628* (1935), 316-7.

[17] *Lord Eldon's Anecdote Book* (eds. A. Lincoln and R. McEwen, 1960), 124-6.

[18] *The Northamptonshire Mercury* 29 April, 6 May, 2 September 1751, in C. Morsley: *News from the English Countryside* (1979), 15-20; AR 1771, 96; J. Wesley: *Journal* (8 vols., N. Curnock ed. 1909-16) V. 265-6; D. Nokes: *Jonathan Swift* (Oxford, 1985), 228.

[19] J. Jones: *The First Whigs* (Oxford, 1961), 144; R. Hutton: *Charles II* (Oxford, 1989), 406-8; F. Maitland: *The Constitutional History of England* (Cambridge, 1948), 318-9, 386.

[20] W. Lecky: *A History of England in the Eighteenth Century* (9 vols., 1878-90), III, 504-8.

[21] W. McNeill: *The Pursuit of Power* (Oxford, 1982), 117, 124-34, 142; J. Boswell: *Life of Johnson* (Oxford, 1957), 21 March 1783, 1195.

[22] J. Wain: *Samuel Johnson* (1974), 280; R. Malcolmson: *Life and Labour in England 1680-1780* (1981), 18-9, 163-4; Perkin, 18-22; PH XXXI, 1072.

[23] J. Plumb: Political Man, in J. Clifford (ed.), *Man Versus Society in Eighteenth Century*

Britain (Cambridge, 1968), 15-6; J. Harrison: *The Second Coming* (1970), 7-9, 221.

24 G. Lampedusa: *The Leopard* (1988), 99.

25 L. Colley: *In Defiance of Oligarchy* (Cambridge, 1985), 276.

26 H. Dickinson: *Liberty and Property* (1979), 152, 240, 281; PH X, 557; Hayter, 102; G. Shelton: *Dean Tucker* (1981), 177.

27 C. Cruise O'Brien (ed.), (Harmondsworth, 1986), 173.

28 Cav. I, 312; PH XVI, 567.

29 J. L. & B. Hammond: *The Bleak Age* (Harmondsworth, 1947), 19.

30 Le Blanc, quoted in E. Smith: *Foreign Visitors in England* (1889), 104; Disraeli: *Sybil* (1845), Bk. I. Ch. I.

31 cf. D. Cooper: *The Lesson of the Scaffold* (1974), 20-1.

32 W. Holdsworth: *A History of English Law* (17 vols. 1903-72), XI, 557; M. Misson: *Memoirs and Observations in his Travels over England* (1719), 218.

33 Misson, 218; Defoe: *A Hymn to the Pillory*, in Boulton ed., 101; H. Walpole: *Memoirs of King George II*, (3 Vols. J. Brooke ed., New Haven, 1985), III, 39-40; C. Chenevix Trench: *Portrait of a Patriot* (Edinburgh, 1962), 186; T. Smollett: *The Expedition of Humphrey Clinker* (1771), (Oxford, 1989), 3, 102-3; C. Lloyd: *Lord Cochrane* (1947), 129; Holdsworth, XIII, 268.

34 J. Archenholz: *A Picture of England* (1791), 309; G. Howson: *It Takes a Thief* (1987), 140; L. Radzinowicz: *A History of English Criminal Law and its Administration* (5 Vols., 1948-86), II, 329-32; H. Fielding: *Amelia* (1752), Bk. I, Ch. IV.

35 Boulton (ed.), 57; T. Smollett: *Roderick Random* (1748), (Oxford, 1981), 310; L. Crompton: *Byron and Greek Love* (1985), 14-6, 54-62, 159; R. Trumbach: London's Sodomites, *J.S.H.* (1971), vol. II, 10-1.

36 Howson, 288; AR 1763, 67; PH XXI, 388-91; *Burke Corr.* IV, 350-1.

37 Crompton, 159-67, 300.

38 Crompton, 168-9, 254-5.

39 C. de Saussure: *A Foreign View of England in the Reigns of George I and George II* (1902), 111-2, 177, 200; C. L. Baron de Pollnitz: *Memoirs* (2 vols., 1739), II, 456-7; B. de Muralt: *Lettres sur les Anglais* (Cologne, 1727), 2-3; F. de la Rochefoucauld: *A Frenchman's Year in Suffolk 1784* (Woodbridge, Suffolk, 1988), 17; Smith, 38-9, 126-7.

40 H. Meister: *Letters Written during a Residence in England* (1799), 20-1; HW, IV, 312; H. Bleackley: *The Hangmen of England* (1929), 79-80; C. Morris (ed.): *The Illustrated Journeys of Celia Fiennes, 1682-1712* (Exeter, 1982), 185, who had only once 'had reason to suspect' that she had seen some highwaymen; D. Defoe: *A Tour Thro' the whole island of Great Britain* (2 vols., 1972); M. Cranston: *John Locke* (Oxford, 1985), 165-6.

41 Cranston, 166; M. Grosley: *A Tour to London* (1772), I, 16, 48-9, 60-2; J. Langbein: Shaping the Eighteenth Century Criminal Trial, *University of Chicago Review*, vol. 50, no. 1 (1983), 44-5.

42 T. Smollett: *The History of England from the Revolution to the Death of George II*, (5 vols., 1823), II, 494, III, 356, 360; T. Smollett: *Travels through France and Italy* (1949), 36, 218.

43 Saussure, 190; Pollnitz, II, 470; Grosley, I, 62; C. Hibbert: *King Mob* (1958); C. Moritz: *Travels, Chiefly on Foot, Through Several Parts of England in 1782* in Pinkerton, *A General Collection of Voyages*, (1808), vol. 2, 517; Misson, 33; Archenholz, 113, 322-3; H. Meister: *Letters Written During a Residence in England* (1799), 170, 289-90; *Boswell's Column*, (M. Bailey, ed. 1951), 344.

44 D. Hume: *A Treatise of Human Nature* (L. Selby-Bigge, ed., 1975), 56; D. Hume: *Essays, Moral, Political and Literary* (Oxford, 1963), 475.

45 E. Halevy: *England in 1815* (1949), 148-9, 170, 588; R. Hole: *Pulpits, Politics and Public Order in England 1760-1832* (Cambridge, 1989), 19-21, 79, 97; PH XVIII, 1007.

45 J. Viner: Man's Economic Status, in Clifford (ed.), 30.

47 J. Ehrman: *The Younger Pitt* (2 vols., 1969-83), I, 315.

48 PH XXXIII, 131; *Burke Corr.* IV, 335.

49 D. Forbes: *Hume's Philosophical Politics* (Cambridge, 1985), 275, 320; Fromm, 268-70; 253; J. Stevenson: *Popular Disturbances in England 1700-1870* (1979), 3-4.

50 Arendt, 79; G. Le Bon: *The Crowd* (1896), V, X, 1-2, 8-13, 35, 55.

[51] H. Fielding: *Amelia* (1752), Bk. I, Ch. II; Shoemaker: The London Mob in the Early Eighteenth Century *J.B.S.* vol. 26 (1987), 298, 303-4.

[52] J. Swift: *A Discourse of the Contests and Dissentions Between the Nobles and the Commons in Athens and Rome* (F. Ellis, ed., Oxford, 1967) 97, 88-91, 105-8, 120, 115, 150; *Jude*, 13-6.

[54] Nokes, 219, 270-1.

[54] C-L Baron de Montesquieu: *Considerations on the Causes of the Greatness of the Romans and their Decline* (J. Lowenthal ed. New York, 1965), 93-4, 87-8; C. Courtney: *Montesquieu and Burke* (Oxford, 1963), IX; Burke V, 249 (*Letters on a Regicide Peace*).

[55] *The Papers of Thomas Jefferson* (J. Boyd ed. Vols. 11 & 12, Princeton, 1955), XII, 356-7, 442; S. Padover: *Jefferson* (1942), 155-60.

[56] A. Lintott: *Violence in Republican Rome* (Oxford, 1968) 1-5, 208.

[57] G. Rudé: *Wilkes and Liberty* (Oxford, 1965), 181-4; J. Shy: *Towards Lexington* (Princeton, 1965), 43, 377; Macfarlane, 178, 190-3; see Chapter XII below.

[58] W. Hazlitt: *The Spirit of the Age 1825* (1910), 316.

[59] Burke, V, 93: *Thoughts and Details on Scarcity*; Cav. II, 480; Smollett, II, 521; T. Cleary: *Henry Fielding* (Waterloo, Ontario, 1984), 294; H. Battestin: *Henry Fielding* (1989), 514, 546, 677, 680.

[60] Cav. I, 318; C., L., and R. Tilly: *The Rebellious Century 1830-1930* (1975), 2, 85; J. L. and B. Hammond: *The Skilled Labourer* (1979), 16.

[61] J. Dunn: *Modern Revolutions* (Cambridge, 1972), 15; Cobb, 85-91; J. Mackintosh: *Vindiciae Gallicae* (1791), 174; B. Moore Jr.: *Social Origins of Dictatorship and Democracy* (Harmondsworth, 1977), 505-6.

PART I Legitimacy in Dispute

[1] Sermon XVI, Preached on Thanksgiving-day, for the suppression of the late Unnatural Rebellion, in 1746. *The Works of William Warburton, 1811*, IX, 336-7.

I Prelude: The Glorious Revolution

[1] PH IV, 206; *S.T.* XI, 881, J. Kenyon: *Revolution Principles* (Cambridge, 1977), 80.

[2] T. Paine: *Rights of Man* (Harmondsworth, 1985), 144, 154; B. Manning: *The English People and the English Revolution* (1976), 11-18, 76-87, 108-11, 124-38; P. Zagorin: *The Court and the Country* (1969), 323; Zagorin: *Rebels and Rulers 1500-1660*, II, 147-50, 184-5; C. Hill: *The World Turned Upside Down* (Harmondsworth, 1984), 19, 24.

[3] PH IV, 206; R. Latham (ed.): *The Shorter Pepys* (1984), 109-10, R. Hutton: *The Restoration* (Oxford, 1985), 90-6, 185; T. Harris: *London Crowds in the Reign of Charles II* (Cambridge, 1987), 36-9, 60-3.

[4] Latham (ed.) 893-5; Harris: The Bawdy House Riots of 1668, *H.J.* 29, 3, (1986), 537-56.

[5] Holdsworth, VIII, 318-21; G. Keeton: *Lord Chancellor Jeffreys and the Stuart Cause* (1965), 105; D. Ogg: *England in the Reign of Charles II* (Oxford, 1967), 513-4, 522.

[6] R. Dunn: The London Weavers' Riot of 1675, *Guildhall Studies in London History* Vl. I (1973-5), 21-3; J. Miller: *James II* (1989), 27.

[7] Harris: *London Crowds*, 76-7, 107-8, 131-9, 155-88.

[8] Ogg, 647-50; J. Carswell: *The Porcupine* (1989), 198-222; M. Cranston: *John Locke* (Oxford, 1985), 220-7; D. Milne: The Results of the Rye House Plot (*T.R.H.S.* 5th ser. vol. I (1951), 91-3; M. Ashley: *John Wildman* (1947), 232-48. For the view that there was one 'whole conspiracy' and the Whig leaders were guilty, see R. Ashcraft: *Revolutionary Politics and Locke's Two Treaties of Government* (Princeton, 1986), 338-405; and J. Salmon: Algernon Sidney and the Rye House Plot, *History Today* 4 (1954), 698-705.

[9] J. Beckett: *The Aristocracy in England 1660-1914* (Oxford, 1986), 403; PH IV, 206; Dryden: *Absalom and Achitophel,* LL. 686-7, 727-8, 733-4.

[10] P. Earle: *Monmouth's Rebels* (1977), 78-80, 54; R. Clifton: *The Last Popular Rebellion* (1984), 142-3, 154-6.

[11] Clifton, 202, 92-100, 288-9, 185-9, 161-2, 190; Earle, 28, 31-3, 98, 100, 111, 132, 195; I. Roots in Roots (ed.), *The Monmouth Rising* (Devon, 1986), 12-3; Dunning, 11, 13.

[12] W. Wigfield: *The Monmouth Rebels* (Gloucester, 1986), IX-X; Earle, 17-21, 24, 6-12, 14-5, 4-5, 31-3, 191-5, 204; R. Dunning: *The Monmouth Rebellion* (Wimborne, 1984), 61-4, 69, 79; Clifton 67-71, 252-61, 272-6, 283.

[13] Earle, 60-6, 77-8, 103, 111; Wigfield in Roots ed., 31, 43; Clifton (who puts the rebel numbers at 3,000) 245-8, 163-5, 192-5, 154-5, 180; P. Backscheider: *Daniel Defoe* (Baltimore, 1989), 35-40; Ashley, 252-60.

[14] Clifton, 184, 199-224; Dunning, 28-30, 37-44, 52; Wigfield, VIII; Earle, 89-90, 98-102, 114-34, 136-8, 195; Roots (ed.), 12-3, 35.

[15] *S.T.* XI, 371-3, 379; Earle, 161-2, 167-75, 178-81; Keeton, 318-331.

[16] Roots, 191; R. Hutton: *Charles II* (Oxford, 1989), 210-1; Clifton in Roots (ed.), 52-6; Clifton, 239, 292-2; Keeton, 330-1, 463, 496; Earle, 38, 167-8; G. Elton: *Policy and Police* (Cambridge, 1972), 387-8; Zagorin: *Rebels and Rulers,* II, 19, 21.

[17] Dunning, 52-5; Earle, 172 175-7; Clifton, 239-40; K. Thomas: *Man and the Natural World* (1983), 174; D. Rumbelow: *The Triple Tree* (1982), 174-5.

[18] M. Ashley: *The Glorious Revolution of 1688* (1968), 166-8, 271-3, 183-4; J. Childs: *The Army, James II and the Glorious Revolution* (Manchester, 1980), 174-5, 164, 177-8, 205-6, 96.

[19] K. Feiling: *A History of the Tory Party 1640-1714* (Oxford, 1924), 233-4; W. Speck: *Reluctant Revolutionaries* (Oxford, 1989), 86-7, 7; J. Jones: *The Revolution of 1688 in England* (1984), 291, 294-7; R. Beddard: *A Kingdom without a King* (Oxford, 1988), 19, 24; Childs: *The Army,* 139, 184-94.

[20] Speck, 191-5. 226-30, 239-40, 243-4; Jones, 297-8; Lord Macaulay: *History of England* (6 vols. C. Firth ed., 1913), III, 1157-8; Miller: Proto-Jacobitism? The Tories and the Revolution of 1688-9, in Cruickshanks and Black (eds.): *The Jacobite Challenge* (Edinburgh, 1988), 12-3.

[21] Beddard, 6-7, 34-5.

[22] B.L. Add Mss 32095, Fol. 306; J. Pocock: The Fourth English Civil War, *Government and Opposition* vol. 23, no. 2 (1988), 153-5, 159.

[23] Harris, 183-6, 223-6; W. Sachse: The Mob and the Revolution of 1688, *J.B.S.* vol. IV, no. 1 (1964), 24; B.L. Add. Mss 41805, fols, 156-7, 178; J. Miller: *Seeds of Liberty* (1988), 29, 57-8, B.L. Add Mss. 36707, fols. 47-8; Beddard, 23.

[24] Beddard, 29-34; Add Mss 36707, fol. 50; K. Lindley: Riot Prevention and Control in Early Stuart London *T.R.H.S.* 5th ser. vol. 33 (1983), 124-6; *The Diary of John Evelyn* (E. S. de Beer ed., Oxford, 1955) vol. IV, 609; Keeton, 451.

[25] O.E.D.; Sachse, 23.

[26] Macaulay, III, 1206-8; Sachse, 28-9; Beddard, 34, 39, 41-3, 173.

[27] Beddard, 38, 42-5, 75-82; Sachse, 30; Beddard: The Guildhall Declaration of 11 December, *H.J.* XI, 3, (1968), 406, 411.

[28] H.M.C. Portland II, 420-1; Macaulay, III, 1206-10, 1214-5; Keeton, 450-4; M. Beloff: *Public Order and Popular Disturbances 1660-1714* (Oxford, 1938), 41-3; Sachse, 32-3.

[29] G. H. Jones: The Irish Fright of 1688, *B.I.H.R.* vol, LV (1982), 148-53; R. Clifton: The Popular Fear of Catholics during the English Revolution in P. Slack (ed.): *Rebellion, Popular Protest and the Social Order in Early Modern England* (Cambridge, 1984), 129-31, 145-7, 158-61; Childs: *The Army,* 195; Sachse, 30-1, 35-6.

[30] Sachse, 30-5, 40; Beddard: *A Kingdom without a King,* 50, 107-8.

[31] Beddard, 49-53, 58-60, 180; Miller: *James II,* 206-8.

[32] Beddard, 52-3, 179, 63-4, 6, Beddard: The Guildhall Declaration, 410-0; Add Mss 3209, fol. 306.

[33] Beddard, 11, 64-5; Childs, 418; G. De Krey: *A Fractured Society* (Oxford, 1985), 56-7; H.M.C., Portland III, 420.

[34] J. Western: *Monarchy and Revolution* (1985), 303-4; D. Ogg: *England in the Reigns of James II and William II* (Oxford, 1955), 226-7; B. Hill: *The Growth of Parliamentary Parties 1689-1742* (1976), 32-5.

[35] A. McInnes: When was the English Revolution? *History* vol. 67 (1982), 385-92; Western, 346-7, 356, 397-402; L. Schwoerer: *No Standing Armies!* (Baltimore, 1974), 151-4, 189; J. Carter in G. Holmes (ed.): *Britain After the Glorious Revolution 1689-1714* (1967), 40-2, 55-6; A. Lossky: The General Crisis of the 1680's, *European Studies Review* vol. 10, no. 2 (1979), 178-96; J. Childs: 1688, *J.H.A.* vol. 73, no. 239 (1988), 421.

[36] A, McInnes: The Revolution and the People, in Holmes (ed.), 80-93; Carter in *idem*, 47; J. Brewer: *The Sinews of Power* (1989), 22-4: Jones: *The Revolution of 1688*, 326-31; J. Plumb: *The Growth of Political Stability in England 1675-1725* (1967), 13; Beckett, 404; (Hampden); D. Brogan: *The Price of Revolution* (1951), 13; G. Holmes: *British Politics in the Age of Anne* (1987), 185-7, 194, 208-10.

[37] N. Sykes: *Church and State in England in the Eighteenth Century* (Cambridge, 1934), 30-3, 315; G. Cragg: *The Church and the Age of Reason 1648-1789* (Harmondsworth, 1978), 59-60; Kenyon: *Revolution Principles,* 86, 116; G. Bennett in Holmes (ed.), 157-63; G. Holmes: *Politics, Religion and Society in England 1679-1742* (1986), 191-4, 201-2; De Frey, 6, 19-22, 75; Western, 371-6; PH VI, 859 (Bishop Burnet).

[38] 14 Charles II c IV; Cragg, 52, 56, 60-1, 98-9; J. Dunn: *Political Obligation in its Historical Context* (Cambridge, 1980), 55; Erskine-Hill: Literature and the Jacobite Cause in Cruickshanks (ed.), 49; Harris, 80; Kenyon, 4, 20, 34, 64-5, 85.

[39] Kenyon, 140 (Defoe); Bennett in Holmes (ed.), 155, 159.

[40] PH VI, 857, (Burnett); Erskine-Hill in Cruickshanks (ed.), 50; M. Thompson: The Idea of Conquest in Controversies over the 1688 Revolution, *Journal of Historic Ideas,* vol. 38 (1977), 40-3; Bennett in Holmes (ed.), 169.

[41] Kenyon, 88-9; D. Szechi: *Jacobitism and Tory Politics 1710-1714* (Edinburgh, 1984), 41, 53-4, 196-7; E. Gregg: Was Queen Anne a Jacobite? *History,* LVII (1972), 358-75.

[42] Locke Laslett (ed.), 10-2, ch. XIX paras 222-42; Dunn: *The Political Thought of John Locke,* 47-8; Ashcraft, 390-405, 545-51, 575-7; Cranston, 207, 211-3; R. Ashcraft and M. Goldsmith: Locke, Revolution Principles and the Formation of Whig Ideology, *H.J.* 26, 4 (1983), 773-5, 786, 184-91; Pocock, 162. The extent of Locke's early influence is a matter of scholarly controversy. For the minimalist view see Dunn: *Political Obligation in its Historical Context,* 62-76; and Kenyon, 1-2, 17-20, 51; for the modified traditional view see Ashcraft and Goldsmith, 723-800; and Holmes: *British Politics* XXXIII-IV.

[43] Ashcraft, 572-89; Dunn: Locke, 10, 33; J. Pocock: *Virtue, Commerce and History* (Cambridge, 1985), 64-7, 223-30.

[44] Kenyon, 110, 125; Dickinson: *Liberty and Property,* 88-9; Ashcraft, 565-6.

[45] Dryden: *The Medal,* 86-7, 80; Plumb: *The Growth of Political Stability in England 1675-1725,* 133-5; J. Jones: *Country and Court in England 1658-1714* (1983), 2, 7, 22; De Frey, 5-6, 17-8, 70-2, 177-9, 191-2, 202; D. Hayton: The Country Interest and the Party System 1689-c. 1720, in C. Jones (ed.), *Party and Management in Parliament 1660-1784* (Leicester, 1984), 45-6, 65.

[45] Holmes: *British Politics,* 97, 114-5, 218, 231; Ford: *Political Murder,* 188-94; W. Speck: 'The Most Corrupt council in Christendom' in C. Jones ed., 45-62; Hume: Of the Original Contract, *Essays,* 457-8.

II The Sacheverell Riots

[1] *The Tryal of Dr Henry Sacheverell before the House of Peers . . .* (Jacob Tonson, London, 1710), 35, 61; G. Aitken (ed.): *Later Stuart Tracts* (New York, 1969), 278.

[2] F. Ellis (ed.) Introduction to Swift's *Discourse,* 2, (Prussian Minister); J. Sharpe: *Early Modern England* (1987), 199 (Swift).

[3] Western, 140; P. Earle: *The Making of the English Middle Class* (1988), 6-9, 86-9.

[4] Western, 93-4; H.M.C. Portland III, 430; W. Doyle: *The Old European Order 1660-*

1800 (Oxford, 1978), 43; D. Coleman: *The Economy of England 1450-1750* (Oxford, 1977), 6, 15-6, 100-2, 120; E. Kerridge: *The Agricultural Revolution* (1967), 328-32; De Frey, 192-3; D. Szechi and D. Hayton: John Bull's Other Kingdoms in C. Jones (ed.), *Britain in the First Age of Party 1680-1750* (1987), 247.

[5] Locke in C. Macpherson: *The Political Theory of Possessive Individualism* (Oxford, 1964), 223; Holmes: *Politics, Religion and Society* 249-79, 304, 316.

[6] Holmes: *British Politics,* 377-8; P. Dickson: *The Financial Revolution in England* (1967), 17-35, 54-6; H. Dickinson: *Bolingbroke* (1970), 69: Feiling: *A History of the Tory Party 1640-1714,* 407-8; W. Hoskins: Harvest Fluctuations and English Economic History 1620-1759, *A.H.R.* XVI (1968), 28-31.

[7] G. Bennett: Conflict in the Church, in Holmes (ed.), 162-9; E. Evans: The Anglican Clergy of Northern England, in C. Jones (ed.), 223-4; De Frey, 75, 112-20.

[8] G. Holmes: *The Trial of Dr Sacheverell* (1973), 12-4, 142, 52-3, 17, 43-7; Kenyon, 91-6, 112, 115; Holmes: *British Politics,* 107n.

[9] *The Tryal,* 31-46; Holmes, *Trial,* 62-9, 141n; J. Plumb: *Sir Robert Walpole* (2 vols. 1956-60), I, 146-7.

[10] *The Tryal,* 44; Holmes: *Trial,* 78-9, 84-5; 88-9, 110-1.

[11] Holmes: *Trial,* 80-9; Lecky I, 51-3; Kenyon, 131.

[12] Holmes: *Trial,* 279-82; Kenyon, 128, 10-1, 200-1; Kenyon in N. McKendrick (ed.): *Historical Perspectives* (1974), 44-5; H.M.C. Portland III, 435.

[13] Holmes: *The Sacheverell Riots,* 60-1; H. Mansfield Jr.: *Statesmanship and Party government* (Chicago, 1965), 171-3; Stanhope and Parker in *The Tryal,* 74, 71, 103.

[14] Holmes: *Trial,* 111-3. G. Holmes: The Sacheverell Riots, *P. & P.,* 72 (1976), 68-70.

[15] R. Sharpe: *London and the Kingdom* (3 vols. 1894), II, 634, 644; Lecky I, 53; Holmes: *Trial,* 156.

[16] *The Tryal,* 22-3; Holmes: *Trial,* 131-3; Ashcraft and Goldsmith, 789.

[17] Holmes: *Trial,* 156-7, 135-42.

[18] Sharpe, II, 644; Holmes: *Trial,* 157, 160.

[19] Holmes: *Trial,* 146-55, 161; H.M.C. Portland IV, 533; *The Tryal,* 96, 102-3.

[20] H.M.C. Portland IV, 532; Holmes: *Trial,* 161.

[21] Holmes: *Trial,* 161-6; H.M.C. Portland IV, 532.

[22] Holmes: *Trial,* 169-72; E. Gregg: *Queen Anne* (1984), 305-6.

[23] Holmes: Riots, 56-7, 74; Holmes: *Trial,* 171-2.

[24] Holmes: Riots, 61-2, 64, 74; Holmes: *Trial,* 169, 173-4.

[25] H.M.C. Portland IV, 533-4; PH VI, 846.

[26] H.M.C. Portland IV, 532-3; Holmes, 68-70.

[27] Beloff, 51; Kenyon, 144; Harris, 153-7, 164-72, 188.

[28] Holmes: Riots, 56-83; *Trial,* 156-78.

[29] Holmes: Riots, 73-85, cf. E. Canetti: *Crowds and Power* (Harmondsworth, 1984), 16-7, 20-1, 32.

[30] Holmes: Riots, 70n; *Trial,* 175-6.

[31] PH VI, 885; Holmes: *Trial,* 209, 220, 227-9; Gregg, 306; Plumb, II, 150.

[32] Holmes: *Trial,* 234-5; Stevenson: *Popular Disturbances,* 20; L. Eardley-Simpson: *Derby and the Forty Five* (1933), 13; H.M.C. Portland IV, 539.

[33] H.M.C. Portland IV, 537; B. Hill: *Robert Harley* (New Haven and London, 1988), 124-30; Holmes: *Trial,* 249-54; Holmes: Riots, 55n; J. Swift: *Journal to Stella* (2 vols. H. Williams ed., Oxford, 1986), I, 42.

[34] PH VI, 916-7; Holmes: *Trial,* 251-5, 259; Holmes: *British Politics,* 107n, 353; Swift: *Journal to Stella* I, 342; II, 469.

[35] Sir C. Petrie: *Bolingbroke* (1937), 185.

[36] Swift: *Journal to Stella* II, 415-7.

[37] D. Nokes: *Jonathan Swift* (Oxford, 1985), 219; PH VI, 846.

[38] J. Morley: *Walpole* (1980), 186-8; R. Hatton: *George I* (1978), 199, 202, 289-90.

III The Protestant Succession and the 'Fifteen'

1 Smollett, II, 299-301; Kenyon: *Revolution Principles*, 175; J. Baynes: *The Jacobite Rising of 1715* (1970), 105.

2 B. Lenman: *The Jacobite Risings in Britain 1689-1746* (1980), 30-5, 49-54, 75-8, 284.

3 W. Ferguson: *Scotland, 1689 to the Present* (Edinburgh, 1978), 55-6; G. Trevelyan: *England Under Queen Anne* (3 vols. 1941-2), II, 341-5; Lenman, 88-9, 286; F. McLynn: *The Jacobites* (1985), 84.

4 E. Gregg: Marlborough in Exile 1712-1713, *H.J.* XV, 4 (1972), 594-617; Szechi: *Jacobitism and Tory Politics 1710-14*, 16, 38-9, 165.

5 L. Colley: *In Defiance of Oligarchy* (Cambridge, 1975), 177-8; Szechi, 12-3, 17-20, 27-8, 39, 173, 183, 187-91, 197, 200-2; Hill: *Robert Harley*, 174-5, 206-9.

6 Szechi, 199, 182-91; Bolingbroke: *A Letter to Sir William Wyndham* quoted in Petrie: The Jacobite Activities in South and West England in the Summer of 1715, *T.R.H.S.* (4 ser. XVIII, 1935), 86.

7 Hill, 95-6, 167-8, 206; Colley, 17, 26.

8 Dickinson: *Bolingbroke* 120-3, 129-31; E. Cruickshanks: *Political Untouchables: The Tories and the '45* (1979), 2-5; N. Landau: *The Justices of the Peace 1679-1760* (Berkeley, 1984), 78-95, 303-9; HC 1715-54, I, 19, 62.

9 A. Foord: *His Majesty's Opposition 1714-1830* (Oxford, 1964), 19, 52-3; C. Emden: *The People and the Constitution* (Oxford, 1956), 175; PH VII, 50-3; W. Speck: The General Election of 1715, *E.H.R.* XC (1975), 509, 512-3, 518; HC 1715-54, I, 20-1; Colley, 18, 120-2, 177, 186, 146.

10 The writer was probably, not certainly, Robethon. HC 1715-54, I, 23-4.

11 Lecky, I, 209-10; N. Rogers: Riot and Popular Jacobitism in Early Hanoverian England in Cruickshanks (ed.), *Ideology and Conspiracy* (Edinburgh, 1982), 72, 74-5.

12 HC 1715-54, I, 284; J. Fitts: Newcastle's Mob *Albion* 5/1 (spring 1973), 41-5; N. Rogers in Cruickshanks (ed.), 74-5.

13 Hatton: *George I,* 134-6.

14 Hatton: 35-6, 52-4, 59-68; J. Owen: *The Eighteenth Century 1714-1815* (New York and London, 1976), 5, 95; W. Speck: *Stability and Strife, England 1714-1760* (1977), 169.

15 Boswell: *Johnson,* 17th September 1777, 840-1, 1195; Smollett, II, 312; M. Mack: *Alexander Pope* (New Haven and London, 1985), 775-7, 926; P. Monod: *Jacobitism and the English People, 1688-1788* (Cambridge, 1989), 40, 121-2, 347-8.

16 Lecky, I, 211n; N. Rogers: Popular Jacobitism in Provincial Context, in Cruickshanks and Black (eds.), 129.

17 Hoskins: Harvest Fluctuations, 22-3, 30; PH VII, 73, 104-8; Hill, 65-7, 70; N. Rogers: Popular Protest in Early Hanoverian London, *P. & P.* 79 (1978), 73.

18 A. Luce and T. Jessop (eds.): *The Works of George Berkeley, Bishop of Cloyne* (1956), VIII, 87-8.

19 Stevenson: *Popular Disturbances in England 1700-1870,* 20-1; Monod, 185-92; Lenman, 123-4.

20 T. Horne: *The Social Thought of Bernard Mandeville* (1978), 3-7.

21 Fitts: Newcastle's Mob, 41-2; Smollett, II, 311-2; Rogers: Popular Protest, 93-4, 72-3; Rogers in Cruickshanks (ed.), 76; G. Rude: *Hanoverian London 1714-1808* (1971), 207.

22 W. Ward: *Georgian Oxford* (1958), 55; Monod, 182.

23 Rogers in Cruickshanks (ed.), 70-85; Monod, 185-94; HC 1715-54, I, 62; PH VII, 111.

24 Smollett, II, 318-9; I George I c.5; see CH. VI below.

25 Petrie: Jacobite Activities, 92; Gregg: Marlborough in Exile 1712-1714, 617.

26 Dickinson, 134-5; Petrie, 87, 85; Colley, 29-31; McLynn: *The Jacobites,* 82.

27 Baynes, 22-4, Petrie, 94-105; Colley, 29-30.

28 Cruickshanks (ed.): *Ideology and Conspiracy,* 3; A Compleat History of the late Rebellion, quoted in Sir C. Petrie: *The Four Georges* (1946), 38.

29 Ferguson, 56-7; Lenman, 89-90, 93-4, 97-101, 107-8; Holmes: *P.R.S.* 93-4, 105-6, 110, 115-27.

30 Lenman, 133-4, 137-8, 149-52, 205; B. Lenman: *The Jacobite Cause* (Glasgow, 1986),

50-1; E. Gregg: The Jacobite Career of John, Earl of Mar, in Cruickshanks (ed.), 180-2; F. McLynn: Issues and Motives in the Jacobite Rising of 1745, *The Eighteenth Century* vol. 23, no. 2 (1983), 99.

[31] Lenman: *The Jacobite Risings,* 153-4; Luce and Jessop (eds.), VIII, 93; Rockingham to Newcastle, 17th May 1768, B.L. Add. MSS 32990, ff. 83-6.

[32] Ferguson, 65-8; Baynes, 37-8, 80-1, 129, 133-8, 146-53.

[33] Lenman, 118-21; Baynes, 82, 86-90, 97-104; McLynn, 99-100.

[34] Baynes, 106, 110-27; Monod, 318-27.

[35] Baynes, 162-70, 178-9.

[36] Lenman, 124, 156-61; Baynes, 183, 189, 193, 196-7.

[37] Baynes, 190-1, 195; Plumb, I, 218-21.

[38] Baynes, 188-95; Luce and Jessop, eds., VIII, 90-8; Hatton, 176-7.

[39] Rogers: Popular Protest, 75-6; Lenman, 156; Fitts, 41-9.

[40] Rogers: Popular Protest, 78-83; Fitts, 44-9; B.L. Add. MSS. 5832.

[41] Rogers: Popular Protest, 78, 87, 90-4, 100.

[42] Smollett, II, 340-2; Lecky, I, 216-7; H. Erskine-Hill: The Political Career of Dr Johnson, in Cruickshanks and Black (eds.), 168, PH VII, 303, 336, 300-1.

[43] B. Williams: *Stanhope* (Oxford, 1932), 410-4, 459-62; Plumb, I, 277, 363, 369: Speck: *The Electorate in the First Age of Party,* in C. Jones (ed.) (1987), 60-2.

[44] Fitts, 49.

IV The Rise and Fall of Walpole

[1] PH VIII, 1185, 1203-4; Undated Memoranda B.L. Add. MS. 47096 (unfol.).

[2] Howson: *It Takes A Thief,* 3-4; Beattie: *Crime and the Courts in England 1660-1800,* 516-8; J. Carswell: *The South Sea Bubble* (1960), 114-8, 120-1, 125-6, 129-30, 133, 217.

[3] PH VII, 682 (Shippen), 686 (Walpole); Plumb: *Sir Robert Walpole,* I, 306-9, 316, 327-8, 352-4; Carswell, 133-4, 163, 229-33, 236-40, 267; Dickson: *The Financial Revolution,* 95, 111-2, 172-4, 187-90.

[4] W. Coxe: *Memoirs of the Life and Administration of Sir Robert Walpole, Earl of Orford* (3 vols. 1798), II, 191-6, 209, 216; Dickson, 147-8, 159-62; W. Laprade: *Public Opinion and Politics in 18th Century England* (Westport, 1971), 237-8.

[5] Plumb, I. 342-4; Carswell, 115-6, 17-8, 241-2; Coxe, II, 212, 216; J. Beckett: Cumbrians and the South Sea Bubble, *Transactions of the Cumberland and Westmoreland Antiquarian and Archaeological Society,* new ser., 82 (1982), 144, 148.

[6] HC 1715-54, II, 205; PH VII, 903-10; Carswell, 263-4.

[7] Coxe, II, 553-4, 557; G. Bennett: Jacobitism and the Rise of Walpole, in McKendrick (ed.), *Historical Perspectives,* 76, 82; Cruickshanks: *Political Untouchables,* 9.

[8] Bennett, 70-92; Cruickshanks: Lord North, Christopher Layer and the Atterbury Plot 1720-23, in Cruickshanks and Black (eds.), 92-106, where she argues that the plot was a serious affair; Laprade, (Defoe) 265; Plumb, II, 40-9.

[9] Coxe, II, (Onslow) 557; H. Walpole: *Memoirs of King George II,* III, 131; Plumb, II, 46; B. Hill: *Sir Robert Walpole* (1989), 117-8.

[10] J. Black in J. Black (ed.): *Britain in the Age of Walpole* (1984), 15-6; E. Thompson: *Whigs and Hunters* (Harmondsworth, 1985), 21-4; E. Cruickshanks and H. Erskine-Hill: The Waltham Black Act and Jacobitism, *J.B.S.* 24, nr. 3 (1985), 358-65; Monod, 115-8.

[11] Radzinowicz, I, 4, 77, 308, 480, 641, 621, 10, 18, 549, 309, 627, 675-6; P. Yorke: *The Life and Correspondence of Philip Yorke, Earle of Hardwicke* (3 vols., Cambridge, 1913), I, 135-6, 151-2; Landau, 163-4; GM 1741, 161; Thompson, 174-5, 182-9.

[12] Coxe, II, 203-4; Earl of Egmont: *Diary of Thomas Perceval, afterwards first Earl of Egmont* (3 vols. 1920-3), I, 265-6, 368: Pope: *Satire IV of Dr John Donne Versified,* II, 140-3; HC 1715-54, I, 470-1; Mack: *Alexander Pope,* 577; Colley, 205; A. Scull: Law, Order and Power, in S. Cohen and A. Scull (eds.): *Social Control and the State* (Oxford, 1983), 211.

[13] Lord Hervey: *Memoirs of the Reign of King George II* (R. Sedgewick, ed., 1931), 186-7, 458-9; J. Plumb: The Walpoles, Father and Son in J. Plumb (ed.): *Studies in Social History* (1955), 195-6.

[14] J. Gay: *Fable XIV* II, 63-6, in J. Gay: *Poetry and Prose* (2 vols., V. Dearing ed. Oxford, 1974), II, 429; J. Bergin: *Cardinal Richelieu, Power and the Pursuit of Wealth* (New Haven and London, 1985), 251; I. Christie: *Myth and Reality in Late Eighteenth Century British Politics* (Berkeley, 1970), 36-1; HC 1715-54, 508-11, 568-71; Yorke: *Hardwicke*, II, 334, 429.

[15] Smollett, II, 463; Dickinson: *Bolingbroke*, 13, 46, 126-8, 311-2, 345; HC 1715-54, II, 294, 376; Walpole: *George II*, I, 156.

[16] Act I, Scene I: Act III, Scene XVI, *The Beggar's Opera* 1728; S. Armens: *John Gay Social Critic* (New York, 1966), 51, 61; P. Rogers: *Eighteenth Century Encounters* (Brighton, 1985), 100.

[17] Swift: *On Poetry, A Rhapsody*, II, 161-4; P. Rogers: *Grub Street* (London, 1972), 249; Pope: *Epilogue to the Satires, Dialogue* II, ll. 27-9, 44-5; Cleary, 38; PH X, 319-41.

[18] Montesquieu: *Considerations*, 87-8, 93-4; J. McClelland: *The Crowd and the Mob* (1989), 92-5; N. Hampson: *Will and Circumstance* (1983), 17-9.

[19] J. Downie: Walpole, "The Poet's Foe" in Black (ed.), 171-88; M. Harris: Print and Politics in the Age of Walpole in *idem*, 192, 196-8, 201; Egmont: *Diary*, I, 7, 9; P. Rogers: *Grub Street*, 338; M. Mack: *The Garden and the City* (Toronto and London, 1969), 160n.

[20] Nokes: *Jonathan Swift*, 288-90; Mack: *Alexander Pope*, 683-5, 714-9; Pope: *Epilogue to the Satires, Dialogue* II, 140-5; Thompson, 306. For the possible silencing in the twenties see Thompson, 278-94; Rogers in *Eighteenth Century Encounters*, 75-92 strongly disagrees; Mack, 402-6 leans slightly toward Rogers.

[21] Swift: *"To Mr Gay"*, LL 154-6.

[22] Gay, *Fable IX*, Dearing II, 411; Hume: Of the Independency of Parliament, *Essays*, 44-5; Bolingbroke: *The Spirit of Patriotism*, in I. Kramnick: *Bolingbroke and his Circle* (Cambridge Mass., and London, 1968), 75; H. Fielding: *Amelia*, Bk. II, Ch. 2.

[23] HC 1715-54, II, 159; Coxe, III, 569 (Dodington).

[24] Pope: *Epilogue to the Satires*, I, LL 159-68.

[25] Gay: *Fable XIII*, LL 99-100, Dearing, II, 425; Coxe, I, 377; B. Kemp: *Sir Francis Dashwood* (1967), 21-4.

[26] J. Leopold: The Levellers Revolt in Galloway in 1724, *Scottish Labour History Society Journal*, 14 (1980), 20; G. Eyre-Todd: *History of Glasgow* (Glasgow, 1934), III, 132-41; Coxe, II, 440-1; HC 1715-54; I, 520, 522-3.

[27] Nokes, 280-96; Coxe, II, 468.

[28] Hervey, 207-9, 86-7, 646, 750-1; Mack: *The Garden and the City*, 133.

[29] Price: The Excise Affair Revisited in S. Baxter (ed.) *Britain's Rise to Greatness* (Berkeley and London, 1983), 266; PH VIII, 1278; Adam Smith: *The Wealth of Nations*, Bk. V, Ch. II.

[30] E. Hughes: *Studies in Administration and Finance 1558-1825* (Manchester, 1934), 117-27, 171; Brewer: *The Sinews of Power*, 145-9, 161, 214; Egmont: *Diary*, I, 363.

[31] Boswell: *Johnson*, 212n; PH VIII 1058-9, 1325-6.

[32] PH VIII, 965, 946; Smollett, II, 509-11; Hughes, 294-304; Plumb, II, 240.

[33] PH VIII, 968-70, 1061; P. Mathias and P. O'Brien: Taxation in Britain and France 1715-1810, *Journal of European Economic History*, V (1976), 611-21.

[34] Hervey, 123-4, 128-9; Coxe, I, 370-1, 378-9; P. Langford: *The Excise Crisis* (Oxford, 1975), 37-40.

[35] PH VIII, 947, 952-6, 972, 1051; *The Correspondence of Jonathan Swift*, IV, (H. Williams ed., Oxford, 1965), 107.

[36] PH VIII, 972, 951, 961; Egmont: *Diary*, I, 306; Coxe, I, 371.

[37] Dickinson: *Bolingbroke*, 233-4; Plumb, II, 250-2; R. Turner: The Excise Scheme of 1733, *E.H.R.* vol. 32, 2nd ser. (1979), 38-9, 42.

[38] L. Sutherland: The City of London in Eighteenth Century Politics in R. Pares and A. Taylor (eds.), *Essays Presented to Sir Lewis Namier* (1956), 51-4; Hervey, 130, 138; N. Rogers: *Whigs and Cities* (Oxford, 1989), 5-6, 15-9, 35-42, 128-9, 165-7, 402-4.

[39] N. Rogers: Resistance to Oligarchy in J. Stevenson (ed.): *London in the Age of Reform* (Oxford, 1977), 3-6; PH VIII, 1305-6; Hervey, 146.

[40] PH VIII, 1269, 1279-80, 1297-9; Egmont: *Diary*, I, 353.

[41] Hervey, 147-8; PH VIII, 1305-7.

[42] PH VIII, 947 (Pulteney); Sharpe, III, 37; Langford, 46, 54-5; Turner, 44; PH IX, 477 (Walpole).

[43] Egmont: *Diary*, I, 348, 355, 357, 365, 359-60; GM 1733, 44, 98, 155; Hervey, 154-162, 168-9.

[44] Hervey, 164-5; Egmont, I, 361-2; Turner, 45.

[45] Hervey, 165-7; GM 1733, 153, 212-3, 266-7; Coxe, I, 404; PH IX, 7-8.

[46] Hervey, 169-70; P. Langford: *A Polite and Commercial People, England 1727-1783* (Oxford, 1989), 28; PH VII, 945-7, 987, 1020, 1040, 1089-90.

[47] PH XIII, 959; Langford: *The Excise Crisis*, 25.

[48] Langford, 99; see Ch. II above.

[49] Langford, 124-50.

[50] Langford, 110-23; Yorke, I, 135-6; Plumb, II, 316-8; HC 1715-54, I, 310; II, 567; PH IX, 452.

[51] Colley, 162, 334; R. Malcolmson: A Set of Ungovernable People in J. Brewer and J. Styles (eds.): *An Ungovernable People* (1983), 93-102.

[52] Malcolmson, 103-6; Yorke, I, 155-6; PH IX, 1298 (*Hardwicke*); Thompson, 256-7; G. Rudé: *Paris and London in the Eighteenth Century* (New York, 1971), 201.

[53] GM 1736, 421-2; Hervey, 567-9; Langford: *England 1727-1783*, 44-6; PH IX 1290, 1295.

[54] PH IX, 1039; Earle, 51: Lord Mahon: *History of England* (3 vols., 1837), II, 282-4; M. D. George: *London Life in the Eighteenth Century* (Harmondsworth, 1985), 46-8; A. Scott: *The Early Hanoverian Age* (1980), 37-8.

[55] GM 1736, 422, 484; Rudé: *Paris and London*, 204-12.

[56] Coxe III, 352, 358-60; Mahon, III, 245-6; Egmont, II, 302, 305; Hervey, 569-70; Rudé, 213-21; George, 48, 322.

[57] W. Scott: *The Heart of Midlothian* (1818), Chs. II & III; Dickinson & K. Logue: The Porteous Riot 1736, *History Today* vol. 22 (1972), 272-5.

[58] GM 1736, 42, 548; Coxe, III, 361; Dickinson and Logue, 274-80.

[59] Coxe, III, 360-8; Dickinson and Logue, 277-8.

[60] Coxe, III, 365-7; Hervey, 659-61, 705-8, 734-8; Dickinson and Logue, 279-81.

[66] Langford: *Excise*, 132, 150; HC 1715-54, I, 46; Coxe, III, 577; K. Wilson: Empire, Trade and Popular Politics in Mid-Hanoverian Britain: The Case of Admiral Vernon, *P. & P.* 121 (1988), 77, 89-90, 94.

[62] B.L. Add. Mss. 47096 (unfol.); Wilson, 81, 89-91, 104-6.

[63] Egmont: *Diary*, III, 243-4; J. Owen: *The Rise of the Pelhams* (1957), 20, 28, 87; N. Rogers: The Urban Opposition to Whig Oligarchy, in M. and J. Jacob (eds.): *The Origins of Anglo-American Radicalism* (1984), 133-4; Feiling, 39; B.L. Add. Mss. 47096.

[64] PH XII, 415-27, 434-5; Smollett, III, 77-84; Langford: *England 1727-1783*, 185-6; Owen, 106-10; Hill, 79-82; G. Keeton: *Trial by Tribunal* (1960), 30-4.

[65] PH X, 404-5 (Walpole), 341; PH IX, 1295; P. Rogers: *Grub Street*, 99.

[66] see Ch. XII below; PH VIII, 1185; IX, 458-9 (Wyndham); IX, 1288-91 (Carteret); X, 437-8 (Pulteney); IX, 1295 (*Hardwicke*).

[67] PH IX, 1295-6, 1299; Hervey, 567, 573-4.

[68] PH VIII, 1185; IX, 477; X, 400-5, 442-3.

[69] A. Charlesworth (ed.): *An Atlas of Rural Protest in Britain 1548-1900* (1983), 44, 47, 82-5.

[70] Colley, 146.

[71] Cruickshanks and Erskine-Hill, 359-65; J. Broad: Whigs, Deer-Stealers and the Origins of the Black Act, *P. & P.* 119 (1988), 71; HC 1715-54, I, 57; Monod, 95-125; Dickinson: *Liberty and Property*, 45; Rogers: The Urban Opposition to Whig Oligarchy, 135-9; Rogers: Popular Jacobitism in Provincial Context, in Cruickshanks and Black (eds.), 130-7; Rogers: *Whigs and Cities*, 84-5, 172.

[72] F. Hill: *Georgian Lincoln* (Cambridge, 1966), 38-41; N. Pevsner and Harris: *Lincolnshire*, 112.

[73] PH X, 451; HC 1715-54, II, 160; PH IX, 1311-2 (Walpole); PH VIII, 1185-6 (Wyndham); Smollett, II, 521; PH IX, 1289-94 (Carteret).

[74] Thompson: *Whigs and Hunters,* 210-2; I George I, C.5; Coxe, III, 376; Coxe, II, 455; Yorke, I, 154-5, 134.

[75] Landau: *The Justices of the Peace,* 164, 310-3; Hervey, 566; Brewer and Styles (eds.), 124.

[76] Holmes: *P.R.S.,* 177-8; PH X, 431-2; A. Babington: *A House in Bow Street* (1969), 48-9; Lecky, I, 452-3.

[77] *Essay on Riots,* GM 1738, 7; PH X, 438, 444 (Pulteney), 408-10 (Lyttleton).

V   Jacobitism and the 'Forty-five'

[1] W. Coxe: *Memoirs of the Administration of Henry Pelham* (2 vols., 1829), I, 303; W. Scott: *Waverley* (1818), Vol. I, Ch. XXVII; Lenman: *The Jacobite Risings in Britain, 1689-1746,* 256-7.

[2] Black in Black (ed.): *Britain in the Age of Walpole,* 2-3, 156-7; J. Nef: *War and Human Progress* (1950), 156.

[3] J. Black: *British Foreign Policy in the Age of Walpole* (Edinburgh, 1985), 138-9.

[4] Cruickshanks: *Political Untouchables,* 38-49, 115-47.

[5] H. Richmond: *The Navy in the War of 1739-48* (1920), II, 75, 77, 82-5, 93; Cruickshanks, 53, 57-8, 63-4.

[6] F. McLynn: *Charles Edward Stuart* (1988), 87-8, 111-3, 117-22, 127-30.

[7] Hume: Of the Parties of Great Britain, *Essays,* 73n; McLynn: Issues and Motives, 111-3, 116; Szechi and Hayton in C. Jones ed., 225-9, 277-8.

[8] Lenman, 146-9, 245-9, 254-5; McLynn: *The Jacobites,* 61-2; GM 1745, 442, 496; A. Youngson: *The Prince and the Pretender* (1985), 167-70.

[9] Fielding's 'A Serious Address to the People of Great Britain', quoted in R. Jarvis: *Collected Papers on the Jacobite Risings* (2 vols., Manchester, 1971-2), II 177-80; Scott: *Waverley,* II, Ch. X.

[10] Jarvis I, 7-20; Lenman, 249-55; McLynn: *Charles,* 151-5.

[11] W. Coxe: *Memoirs of Horatio, Lord Walpole* (1802), 284; Lenman, 254-8; Fergusson, 150-1; R. Mitchison: *A History of Scotland* (1970), 339; GM 1745, 442; Youngson, 103-6, 210-2.

[12] F. McLynn: *The Jacobite Army in England 1745* (Edinburgh, 1983), 8-11, 24-5; McLynn: *Charles,* 168-73; Youngson, 107, 212-3.

[13] Scott: *Waverley* (preface); Jarvis, II, 26-34, 202.

[14] Jarvis, I, 105-16, 120-8, 232-4; GM 1745, 599-60, 611.

[15] Cruickshanks, 89.

[16] Coxe: *Pelham,* 258, 274-5; GM 1745, 539-40; W. Speck: *The Butcher* (Oxford, 1981), 212; Yorke: *Hardwicke,* I, 469, 473; Wesley: *Journal III,* 211-2; Eardley-Simpson: *Derby and the Forty Five,* 139-42, 271.

[17] PH XIV, 451; Eardley-Simpson, 109.

[18] GM 1745, 613-4; K. Tomasson: *The Jacobite General* (Edinburgh and London, 1958), 98-103.

[19] McLynn: *Jacobite Army,* 80.

[20] Cruickshanks, 86-7; Jarvis, II, 85-7.

[21] GM 1745, 621; Jarvis, II, 10, 209; Yorke, I, 477.

[22] e.g. Cruickshanks, 100, and McLynn: *Jacobite Army,* 130-2, 141, 197-8, and Eardley-Simpson, 205-10, 227, 229.

[23] McLynn: *Charles,* 188-90.

[24] e.g. Macdonald of Sleat, and F. J. McLynn. See McLynn: *Jacobite Army,* 130, 197-8.

[25] Vol. II, Ch. XI.

[36] W. Scott: *Redgauntlet* (1824), Introduction.

[27] McLynn: *Jacobite Army,* 124.

[28] F. McLynn: *France and the Jacobite Rising of 1745* (Edinburgh, 1981), 9, 78-82, 86-7, 90, 133, 161, 234.

[29] McNeill: *The Pursuit of Power,* 180; Jarvis, II, 224.

[30] GM 1746, 41, 80-2; McLynn: *France,* 146-60, 164-5.

[31] GM 1746, 179; McLynn: *France,* 3-4.

[32] Smollett, III, 170.

[33] Colley, 34, 41; GM 1745, 554; R. Robson: *The Oxfordshire Election of 1754* (Oxford, 1949), II; McLynn: *Jacobite Army,* 30,38.

[34] PH XI, 711; McLynn: *Jacobite Army,* 9; Black, 138.

[35] McLynn: *France,* 17; A. Ayer: *Thomas Paine* (1988), 45.

[36] Boswell: *Johnson,* 840-1, 1195, 380-4; Erskine-Hill: The Political Character of Samuel Johnson, in Cruickshanks and Black (eds.), 161-2, 165-6; HC 1715-54, II, 394; Monod, 273.

[37] Hume: Of the Protestant Succession, *Essays,* 492-8; Forbes, 93-6; F. Mossner: *The Life of David Hume,* 180.

[38] McLynn: Issues and Motives, 99, 110.

[39] Western: *Monarchy and Revolution,* 144; For the French attitude, see McLynn: *France,* 17, 61, 81, 90, 104, 120, 134, 162, 177.

[40] Scott: *Waverley,* I, Ch. XXVII; J. Clark (ed.): *The Memoirs & Speeches of James, 2nd Earl Waldegrave, 1742-1763* (Cambridge, 1988), 11-2; McLynn: *France,* 25.

[41] HC 1715-54, II, 545; McLynn: *Charles,* 187.

[42] Fielding in Jarvis II, 220, 226-9; HW III, 178, 177n, 180; N. Rogers: Popular Disaffection in London during the Forty-Five, *London Journal,* Vol. I, no. 1 (1975), 6, 10; Smollett III, 170; N. Rogers: Resistance to Oligarchy in Stevenson (ed.): *London in the Age of Reform,* 17-7; Rudé: *Hanoverian London,* 155-6.

[43] Youngson, 116; Cleary: *Fielding,* 209-10; Battestin: *Henry Fielding,* 398-402; GM 1745, 522-6, 579-80, 666; HW III, 180-1; GM 1746, 105; Smollett III, 169; A. Carlyle: *Autobiography,* quoted in Scott: *The Early Hanoverian Age,* 160.

[44] Rudé: *Hanoverian London,* 157.

[45] Tomasson, 109; GM 1745, 665; Hamilton: *The Origin and History of the First or Grenadier Guards* (3 vols.,1874), II, 134-5; C. Chenevix-Trench: *George II* (1973), 233-4.

[46] McLynn: *Jacobite Army,* 129.

[47] Youngson, 66, 128-9.

[48] Smollett III, 171-2, GM 1745, 622, 624-5; Yorke I, 467, 483-4.

[49] Tomasson, 142-59; GM 1746, 61.

[50] Youngson, 140-1, 249-50.

[51] Smollett III, 179; Tomasson, 201-2.

[52] Tomasson, 203-18.

[53] Tomasson, 219-25.

[54] Youngson, 143-6; McLynn: *Charles,* 251-63; J. Prebble: *Culloden* (1961), 66.

[55] Tomasson, 254-62.

[56] Hamilton, II, 120-1; Nef, 156-9, 305; Gibbon: *The Decline and Fall of the Roman Empire* (6 vols., 1954), Ch. XXXVIII, IV, 109; Youngson, 111.

[57] A. Sorel: *Europe and the French Revolution* (A. Cobban and J. Hunt eds., 1969), 108-13; Defoe in Boulton (ed.), 104, 270; PH XIX, 364n-70n, 424-5, 430-1.

[58] C. Barnett: *Britain and Her Army,* (1970), 140, 241-2; J. Fortescue in A. Turberville (ed.): *Johnson's England* I, 72; E. Longford: *Wellington, Pillar of State* (1972), 441-2, HW III, 174, 204.

[59] Lenman: *The Jacobite Risings,* 273, 282; Mitchison, 340-1.

[60] G. Harris: *The Life of Lord Chancellor Hardwicke* (3 vols., 1847), II, 166-7; GM 1745, 518-20, 577-9, 625-6, 667; Yorke I, 457-63; GM 1746, 366-7; Youngson, 225-6.

[61] Youngson, 209-10; Scott: *Waverley* I, Introduction, II, Chs. XVIII, XLIII.

[62] Jarvis I, 256; Speck, 95, 113-4; Youngson, 248.

[63] HW III, 188; Walpole, I, 70; Speck, 128; Prebble, 140; GM 1746, 272.

[64] Speck, 186, 113; Yorke I, 475, 483; Lenman, 262; Youngson, 259; Prebble, 172.

[65] GM 1746, 241-2; Speck, 145-7.

[66] Prebble, 120-3, 130; Youngson, 258-9; Speck (who denies any killing in cold blood), 145-7, 161.

[67] Prebble, 132-7; Speck, 141, 147-8; Yorke, I, 531.

[68] By Professor Speck in his authoritative and fair biography *The Butcher,* 161.

[69] Speck, 161, 148-9; Prebble, 133-8.

[70] GM 1746, 219-20; Youngson, 261; Yorke I, 531; Speck, 148-56. The conjecture is Dr Speck's.

[71] Speck, 148-56, 159-61.

[72] Lenman, 264; Smollett III, 166; Speck, 164-8; Yorke I, 421, 524-5.

[73] Speck, 168-70; GM 1746, 324.

[74] Samuel Butler: *Hudibras* ll. 101-2; GM 1746, 366-7; Lenman, 256, 259, 260; Ferguson, 153; G. Donaldson: *Scotland, the Shaping of a Nation* (1980), 114, 166-7; Speck, 183-5, 187.

[75] Carlyle, quoted in Ferguson, 153; Prebble, 304, 237.

[76] B. Disraeli: *Coningsby* (1844), Bk. I, Ch. III.

[77] Clark (ed.), 155; Chenevix-Trench, 236.

[78] Prebble, 141-6, 239, 315-6; GM 1746, 270; Speck, 156-62.

[79] Prebble, 244-6, 256-63; Jarvis, II, 255, 258-9, 283; Smollett, III, 183.

[80] Tomasson, 196; Coxe: *Lord Walpole,* 301-3; Mossner, 181; GM 1746, 391-4; Chenevix-Trench, 237-8.

[81] McLynn: *Jacobites,* 105.

[82] D. Ogg: *Europe of the Ancien Regime 1715-1783* (1965), 43; Mossner, 177.

[83] Jarvis II, 195-7; Cleary, 215.

[84] W. Raleigh (ed.): *The Works of George Savile, Marquess of Halifax* (Oxford, 1912), 219.

PART II   Powers and Grievances

[1] H. Garth and C. Wright-Mills (eds.): *From Max Weber* (1970), 78.

VI.   The Army and the Riot Act

[1] Sir L. Namier: *England in the Age of the American Revolution* (1930), 7; PH IX, 470; Boswell: *Johnson,* 749-50.

[2] J. Houlding: *Fit for Service* (Oxford, 1981), 55-89; R. Whitworth: *The Grenadier Guards* (1974), 25.

[3] Maitland, 278-80; Schwoerer: *No Standing Armies!,* 11-2, 19-32, 51-72, 103, 121-32, 139-46, 4; N. Phillipson: *Hume* (1989), 82-3.

[4] Schwoerer, 155-89; M. Thomson: *A Constitutional History of England 1642-1801* (1938), 292-4; Lecky I, 509-13.

[5] C. Clode: *The Military Forces of the Crown* (2 vols., 1869), I, 398; A. Guy: *Oeconomy and Discipline* (Manchester, 1985), 6-11; Brewer: *The Sinews of Power,* 29-32.

[6] PH IX, 1311-2, 1323-4, 1334; Langford: *England, 1727-1783,* 35.

[7] PH X, 400-5; Lindley: Riot Prevention and Control in Early Stuart London, 109-26; Harris: The Bawdy House Riots of 1668, 539-41; Allen: The Role of the London Trained Bands in the Exclusion Crisis, 1678-1681, *E.H.R.* LXXXVII (1972). 287-303.

[8] J. Western: *The English Militia in the Eighteenth Century* (1965), 57-8, 63; PH IX, 205.

[9] J. Swift: *Gulliver's Travels, A Voyage to Brobdingnag* (1726), Ch. 6; J. Pocock: *Politics, Language and Time* (1972), 104-41; W. Blackstone: *Commentaries on the Laws of England* (4 vols., Oxford, 1765-9), I, 402-4.

[10] Forbes, 172; Doyle: *The Old European Order 1660-1800,* 241-2; A. Skinner, in McKendrick (ed.), 96-7, 118-9, 123; Kramnick, 166; Dickinson: *Liberty and Property,* 184-6; PH IX, 1340; L. Colley: *Namier* (1989), 85.

[11] Hervey, 525; E. Steiner: Separating the Soldier from the Citizen, *S.H.* 8 (1983), 21, 33; D. Defoe: *The Complete English Tradesman* (Gloucester, 1987), 220-1; J. Brereton: *The British Soldier* (1986), 7-11, 25, 28-31; Holdsworth XI, 401-5; Brewer, 49-51.

[12] Brereton, 5; PH XI, 1442, 1448, 1459: Clode, I, 223-5, 229-35; Blackstone, I, 401-2.

[13] P. Clark: *The English Alehouse* (1983), 181, 289; PH IX, 281; Guy, 7; J. Bohstedt: *Riots and Community Politics in England and Wales 1790-1810* (Cambridge, Mass., 1983), 172-3, 284.

[14] Kiernan: Foreign Mercenaries and Absolute Monarchy, *P. and P.* 11 (1957), 74-7, 80-3; Brewer, 41-3.

[15] Holdsworth, VIII, 324-5, 330-1; X, 705-8; A. Dicey: *Law of the Constitution* (1885), Ch. VIII.

[16] I George I, Stat. 2, cap 5; Holdsworth, VIII, 328-9; Rogers: Popular Protest in Early Hanoverian London, 70-5.

[17] J. L. and B. Hammond: *The Village Labourer 1760-1832* (Gloucester, 1987), 121.

[18] Holdsworth, VIII, 331; Radzinowicz, III, 125, 136-7; Hayter: *The Army and the Crowd*, 10-2.

[19] GM 1757, 430; AR 1768, 227-34; *Memoirs of William Hickey* (3 vols., ed. A. Spencer, 1918-9), I, 92-4.

[20] Hervey, 566; Napier, quoted in C. Townshend: *Political Violence in Ireland* (Oxford, 1984), 97.

[21] Hayter, 31-2; Hervey, 566; Brewer and Styles (eds.): *An Ungovernable People*, 124.

[22] Blackstone, I, 401; E. Thompson: The Moral Economy of the English Crowd, *P. & P.* no. 50 (1971), 121; Clode, II, 628; Hayter, 170; Brewer, 52-3.

[23] Radzinowicz, III, 118-9; J. Shy: *Towards Lexington* (Princeton, 1965), 43, 380; D. Baugh: *British Naval Administration in the Age of Walpole* (Princeton, 1965), 7-8; Hayter, 28.

[24] PH IX, 442; J. Cannon (ed.): *The Whig Ascendancy* (1981), 46; Bohstedt, 57.

[25] Hayter, 42; Cav. I, 10, 315; see Ch. XV below.

[26] Nef: *War and Human Progress*, 19-22, 86-8.

[27] Houlding, 66, 166-172, 395; Hayter, 3, 16, 34.

[28] Hayter, 182; R. Wells: *Wretched Faces* (Gloucester, 1988), 266-7; McNeill: *The Pursuit of Power*, 187-8.

[29] S.P. 35/10, ff. 61-2; W.O. 34/103, ff. 5-7; Clode, II, 620-1.

[30] Holdsworth, X, 705-7; Radzinowicz, III, 124-5.

[31] W.O. 35/10, 55, 8-10; Clode, II, 623-5.

[32] W.O. 35/10, ff. 11-12; Clode, II, 625-7; Hayter, 13; S.P. 36/123, ff. 51-2.

[33] S.P. 36/123, ff. 51-2; Radzinowicz, III, 129-30.

[34] Harrison: *Crowds and History*, 298; CH. XVI below.

VII   Crime and the Criminal Law

[1] Yorke, I, 135; Burke, VI, 106; Cleary, 38.

[2] Radzinowicz: *A History of English Criminal Law*, I, 3-5, 76-7.

[3] C. Emsley: *Crime and Society in England 1750-1800* (1987), 203-4; Blackstone: *Commentaries*, IV, 4; J. Innes and J. Styles: The Crime Wave: Recent Writing on Crime and Criminal Justice in Eighteenth Century England, *J.B.S.* XXV (1986), 21-9.

[4] Sir William Meredith MP in 1772, PH XVII, 238; T. More: *The Works of Lord Byron* (17 vols., 1847), VI, 320; CJ 20, (1723) 208, 211-4, 217; S. Lambert (ed.): *House of Commons Sessional Papers of the Eighteenth Century* (Wilmington, 1975), I, 37-8; Thompson: *Whigs and Hunters*, 245-7.

[5] D. Hay: War, Dearth and Theft in the Eighteenth Century, *P. & P.* 95 (1982), 146-7; Radzinowicz, I, 10-1, 548-9, 22-3, 6-56.

[6] P. Marsden: *In Peril before Parliament* (1965), 151-2; Sir J Stephen: *A History of the Criminal Law in England* (3 vols., 1883), I, 396; Lord Birkenhead: *Famous Trials* (New York, n.d.), 446-8.

[7] Lord Justice Mackinnon: The Law and the Lawyers, in Turberville (ed.): *Johnson's England*, II, 301-2; J. Langbein: The Criminal Trial before the Lawyers, *University of Chicago Law Review*, vol. 45 no. 2 (1978), 282-4; M. Cottu: *De l'Administration de la Justice Criminelle en Angleterre* (Paris, 1822), 92; Jeffreys quoted in the *Second Report on Criminal Law 1836*, 6n.

[8] Beattie: *Crime and the Courts in England 1660-1800*, 345-8; G. Bullett: *Sydney Smith, A Biography and a Selection* (1951), 173-5; *Second Report on Criminal Law*, 1836, 8.

[9] Langbein: *Shaping the Eighteenth Century Criminal Trial*, 123, 118-9; J. Cockburn: *A History of English Assizes 1558-1714* (Cambridge, 1972), 114-5; P. King: Decision-Makers and Decision-Making in the English Criminal Law 1750-1800, *H.J.* 27, 1 (1984), 52n-53.

[10] Holdsworth, XI, 567-8; VI, 518-9; Lecky I, 501-2; M. Ignatieff: *A Just Measure of Pain* (New York, 1978), 31-4; Beattie, 299-308, 312-3, 339, 339n, 350-1; Rumbelow: *The Triple Tree*, 30; Howson: *It Takes a Thief*, 96, 127; W. Treloar: *Wilkes and the City* (1917), 124-5.

[11] Anon: *Old Bailey Experience* (1833), 59-60; Rumbelow, 106-7; Sharpe: *Crime in Early Modern England 1550-1750*, 37; Cottu, 73, 91, 96-100, 102; Beattie, 313, 340, 376-8, 410, 376, 415, 396-9, 425-6; T. Humphreys: *A Book of Trials* (1953), 25.

[12] Mackinnon, 298; W. Rubinstein: The End of Old Corruption in Britain 1780-1860, *P & P*. 101 (1983), 56, 60.

[13] Pope: *The Rape of the Lock*, III, ll.19-22; M. Madan: *Thoughts on Executive Justice* (1785) Appendix 142-3; H. Cockburn: *Circuit Journeys* (Edinburgh, 1888), 327-8; K. Miller: *Cockburn's Millenium* (1975), 266-7.

[14] AR 1790, 207-8, 223-7, 264-7; Beattie, 410-3, 419-30; Langbein, 22, 52-5.

[15] Hay: Property, Authority and the Criminal Law in Hay et al. (eds.) *Albion's Fatal Tree* (Harmondsworth, 1977), 43; H. Fielding: *Tom Jones* (1749), bk. 18, ch. II; Walpole: *Memoirs of King George II*, I, 116, II, 211n; Langbein, 19-21.

[16] Radzinowicz, I, 121, 116, (Eldon); J. Brooke: *King George III* (1972), 310-1; R. Postgate: *That Devil Wilkes* (1956), 219-20; AR 1770, 109; AR 1771, 96.

[17] Hay, in Hay (ed.) 52; GM 1758, 42-3, 91; F. Dostoyevsky: *The Idiot* (1868), Pt I, ch. V; G. Kjetsaa: *Fyodor Dostoyevsky* (1988), 85-90; GM 1783, 711; GM 1766, 436.

[18] Macfarlane: *The Justice and the Mare's Ale*, 195n; Sharpe, 68; B. Mandeville: *An Inquiry into the causes of the Frequent Executions at Tyburn 1725*, (University of California, 1964), 16; PH XXVIII, 141.

[19] Howson: *It Takes a Thief*, 95-7, 184, 233-67; Stephen, I, 402-3, 415; Cockburn is more optimistic than Stephen, pointing out that only about ten per cent of those convicted of felony were actually executed, but he concedes that in 1616 nine 'witches' were hanged on the sole 'perjured and uncorroborated evidence of a small boy': Cockburn, 120-32, 228; *Second Report on the Criminal Law*, 4-5, 74, 79; A. Koestler: *Reflections on Hanging* (1956), 111.

[20] H. Fielding: Introduction to *A Voyage to Lisbon* (1755), 195-6; Radzinowicz, II, 326-46; Battestin, 577-8, 683; FM 1733, 99-100, 493.

[21] Radzinowicz, I, 50-8, 425n-426n; Thompson, 21, 256-8; Plumb: *Walpole*, II, 237-8.

[22] PH XIX, 237-8, and quoted by Dickens in his preface to *Barnaby Rudge* (1841).

[23] Beattie, 430-1, 438, 453; F. McLynn: *Crime and Punishment in Eighteenth Century England* (1989), 129.

[24] GM 1724, 510; GM 1733, 661; R. Wearmouth: *Methodism and the Common People of the Eighteenth Century* (1945), 95; P. Linebaugh: *The London Hanged* (1991), 142-3; McLynn, 122-4.

[25] J. Rule: Wrecking and Coastal Plunder in Hay (ed.), 187; AR 1763, 77, 71; AR 1791, 25; Radzinowicz, I, 468, 14n; PH XIX, 236-7; Crompton: *Byron and Greek Love*, 170-1.

[26] Gurr: Historical Trends in Violent Crime, *Crime and Justice* vol. 3 Chicago, 1981, 299, 312-5; Sharpe: The History of Violence in England, *P. & P*. 108 (1985), 207, 214-5; K. Wrightson: *English Society 1580-1680* (1982), 160-1; Radzinowicz, I, 30, 30n; R. Palmer: *The Age of the Democratic Revolution* (Princeton, 1964), II, 372.

[27] Radzinowicz, I, 151, 148; Beattie, 144-6, 178-9; Mandeville, 1.

[28] N. Douglas: *Old Calabria* (1955), 64, 312-3; W. Paley: *Principles of Moral and Political Philosophy* (1817), II, 268-9, 272, 277, 302.

[29] Radzinowicz, I, 481-3, 12-3.

[30] PH XIX, 235-41; J. Carswell: *The Old Cause* (1954), 222, 374; F. Fletcher: *Montesquieu and English Politics 1750-1800* (Philadelphia, 1939), 195; N. Hampson: *The Enlightenment* (Harmondsworth, 1982), 155-6; Hibbert: *King Mob*, 162-3.

[31] H. Fielding: *An Enquiry into the Causes of the Late Increase of Robbers etc.* 1751 (1784),

345, 432, 423, 455; Cleary, 10-1, 257-8, 263-4; Battestin, 459-60, 513-22, 547-52, 564-71.

[32] Walpole: *George II*, I, 175; Radzinowicz, I, 348, 336-7; Moore VI, 318-22; Holdsworth III, 302; O. Goldsmith: *The Vicar of Wakefield* (1766), ch. XXVII; Fletcher, 189-92.

[33] PH XXVIII, 14607; Brewer. The Wilkites and the Law in Brewer and Styles (ed.), 167-9; R. Coupland: *Wilberforce* (1945), 49; Radzinowicz, I, 641, 341-2, 340-9.

[34] M. Oakeshott: *Rationalism in Politics* (1962), 114; Radzinowicz, I, 498-9, 256.

[35] See e.g. Emsley, 240; Innes and Styles, 384-5, 421-30; Langbein: Shaping the Eighteenth Century Criminal Trial, 36-41; J. Langbein: Albion's Fatal Flaws, 99-100, *P. & P.* 98 (1983), 117-8; Sharpe: *Crime in Early Modern England 1550-1750*, 149; King, 25, 39.

[36] Innes and Styles (for the defence) 425-9; Madan, 43; Blackstone, IV, 4; Thompson, 23, 197; Lambert, I, 37-8.

[37] Innes and Styles, 421-5 (for the defence); Sharpe, 70; Cockburn, 100-2; Emsley, 27.

[38] A. Ekirch: *Bound for America* (Oxford, 1987), 1, 17, 21-2, 26-7, 62, 140, 156, 227; Beattie, 500-13; 450-1; Ignatieff, 20.

[39] Langbein: Shaping the Eighteenth Century Criminal Trial, 37-41; Innes and Styles, 423-5 (both for the defence); Radzinowicz, I, 632-40; Beattie, 144-5, 507.

[40] King, 25; Baker in Cockburn (ed.), 43; McLynn, 257-9.

[41] E. Wakefield: *Facts Relating to Punishment and Death in the Metropolis* (1831), 65, 95, 131-2, 149-50, 172, 79-80; Beattie, 421-3, 430-6; Babington: *A House in Bow Street*, 112.

[42] Beattie, 233, 494, 549-50, 584-5, 630-1; Babington, 112-3, 149-50; GM 1786, 102.

[43] D. Hume, B,: *Commentaries on the Law of Scotland* (2 vols., Edinburgh, 1844), 10-1; AR 1784-5, 193-4; GM 1786, 363; GM 1783, 891.

[44] G. Pearson: *Hooligan* (1983), *passim*; PH XXVIII, 146-7; G. Trevelyan: *English History in the Nineteenth Century and After 1782-1919* (1937) IXV, 5, 72; B,. Schilling: *Conservative England and the Case against Voltaire* (New York, 1976), 57-60.

[45] W. Cole: Trends in Eighteenth Century Smuggling, *Ec.H.R.* 2nd ser. X, no. 3, (1957-8), 395-7, 405-9; P. Deane: *The First Industrial Revolution* (Cambridge, 1984), 223-4; M. Weisser: *Crime and Punishment in Early Modern Europe* (New Jersey, 1979), 119-21.

[46] McLynn, 185-9, 193-4; Winslow: Sussex Smugglers, in Hay (ed.), 119-24, 133-46, 160-6; Battestin, 465-6; GM 1765, 195; B. Bushaway: *By Rite* (1982), 208; D. Hawkins: *Cranborne Chase* (1983), 19-20.

[47] S. Ayling: *John Wesley* (1979), 240; McLynn, 172-3, 183, 192, 196-7; M. Rediker: *Between the Devil and the Deep Blue Sea* (Cambridge, 1987), 72-3; HW, X, 288; Plumb: *Walpole* I, 121-2, II 237; *The Diary of Thomas Turner* (D. Vaisey ed., Oxford, 1985), 122; J. Woodforde: *The Diary of a Country Parson 1758-1802* (J. Beresford ed.,, Oxford, 1963), 130-1, 292, 421-2, 475-6, 535.

[48] McLynn, 63-4; P. Haining: *The English Highwayman* (1991), 100.

[49] Howson, 3-5, 111, 115, 171-2, 180-4; D. Defoe: *Street Robberies Considered* (1728), 49; Fielding: *An Enquiry*, 335; Fielding: *A Voyage to Lisbon*, introduction; J. Styles: Sir John Fielding and the Problem of Criminal Investigation in 18th Century England, *T.R. H.S.* 5th ser. 33 (1983), 132-3; G. Rudé: *Criminal and Victim* (Oxford, 1985), 123-6.

[50] Fielding: *Tom Jones*, Bk. XII, ch. XIV; Misson, 67-8; Fielding: *An Enquiry*, 455.

[51] Hay in Hay (ed.), 52.

[52] Grosley, I, 62, 84-8; Saussure, 111-2; Pollnitz, II, 471; Fielding, quoted in J. Brewer: *The Common People and Politics, 1750-1790s* (Cambridge, 1986), 26.

[53] R. McGowen: 'He Beareth not the Sword in Vain', *Eighteenth Century Studies* (1987-8), 200, 205-7.

[54] Wesley: *Journal*, IV, 427-8; Sheehan in Cockburn (ed.) 229-45; Linebaugh in idem, 246-69; Linebaugh: *The London Hanged*, 33; Backscheider, 489-90; Clifton: *The Last Popular Rebellion*, 228.

[55] Rumbelow, 153-4, 196-7; Sheehan in Cockburn (ed.), 235-6; Linebaugh in idem, 251-2; Wakefield, 145, 151-71; C. Hibbert: *The Road to Tyburn* (1955), 135.

[56] Radzinowicz, I, 166; Sheehan in Cockburn (ed.) 243; Rumbelow, 164-5; Howson, 271-3; Bleackley, 50-2.

[57] Linebaugh in Hay (ed.), 67; Walpole: *George II*, III, 106; GM 1733, 154; Mandeville, 23, 34; Defoe, 52; Muralt, 49; Misson, 124; Saussure, 124.

[58] Mandeville, 20-2; *Boswell's Column* (M. Bailey ed., 1951), 345-7; Fielding: *An Enquiry*, 449-50; Swift: *Clever Tom Clinch Going to be Hanged*, ll.19-20; cf Wakefield, 175-6.

[59] Szechi in Cruickshanks & Black (eds.): *The Jacobite Challenge*, 60-3; C. Vulliamy: *John Wesley* (1954), 158.

[60] F. Gill (ed.): *Selected Letters of John Wesley* (1956), 50; Knox: *Enthusiasm*, 540; Ayling, 139.

[61] Pollnitz, II, 458; Misson, 124; Saussure, 124-5; Hibbert, 143; Cav.. II, 12.

[62] Fielding, 450; Holdsworth, XI, 565; Mandeville, 25; Howson, 276; Cooper: *The Lesson of the Scaffold*, 6.

[63] M. Foucault: *Discipline and Punishment* (Harmondsworth, 1979), 59-65; McLynn, 269-70, 276; Bleackley: *The Hangmen of England*, 29-31, 130, 143; Fielding, 450-4; Mandeville, 37-46; AR 1798, 47; Cooper, 6-7; 14-5.

[64] Linebaugh in Hay (ed.), 65-117; Hibbert, 147-9; McLynn, 271-2; AR 1763, 96; AR 1769, 160; Ignatieff, 22.

[65] Mandeville, 36-7; Fielding, 450; Wakefield, 178-82; Radzinowicz, I, 464; III, 345.

[66] Babington, 48-9; Mayer in Cohen and Scull (eds.): *Social Control and the State*, 24; Landau, 124; Speck, 169; cf. Clark, 123-36.

[67] J. Carswell: *From Revolution to Revolution England 1688-1776* (1973), 87; HC 1715-54, I, 9-13; P. Rogers: *Henry Fielding* (1978), 208; M. Raeff: *The Well Ordered Police State* (New Haven and London, 1983), 137-41; Schilling, 78-9; Lambert (ed.), 34-5; OH XVI, 756.

[68] J. Cannon: *Aristocratic Century* (Cambridge, 1984), 151-3; Schilling, 83-99; C. Hill: *The Century of Revolution 1603-1714* (Edinburgh, 1961), 77; for the continuing strength of the Anglican Church and religion see J. Clark: *English Society 1688-1832* (Cambridge, 1985), 87-93, 136-41, and passim.

[69] R. Hole: *Pulpits, Politics and Public Order in England* (Cambridge, 1989), 86-7, 127-30; Radzinowicz III, 142-3 (Wilberforce).

[70] Goldsmith: *The Traveller*, II 351-2; Ayling, 157; Fielding: *Enquiry* 356; C. Emsley: An Aspect of Pitt's Terror, *S.H.*, 6, 2, (1981), 175; T. Smollett: *The Adventures of Peregrine Pickle* (1751), ch. 49; C. Searle: Custom, Class Conflict and Agrarian Capitalism, *P. & P.* 110 (1986), 121, 129-32.

[71] Hay in Hay (ed.) 38-9, 44-6; Langbein: Albion's Fatal Flaws, 107; King, 37, 52.

[72] See, for example, *Joseph Andrews* (1742) bk. 2, ch. 11, bd. 4, ch. 3; *Amelia* (1751), bk. 1, ch. 2; *Voyage to Lisbon* (1755), 258-9; *Roderick Random* (1748), chs. 17 and 41; *Humphrey Clinker* (1771), June 12-4; *The Life and Adventures of Sir Lancelot Greaves* (1760-1), chs. 10-2; Battestin, 497-8.

[73] *Grenville Papers* (4 vols., W. Smith ed., 1852), I, 359.

[74] King, 28, 31-4; McLynn, 88-90; Yorke: *Hardwicke*, I, 144-6; Wesley: *Journal*, VII, 32; AR 1774, 155; AR 1784-5, 202, 247; AR 1788, 208, 215.

[75] Thompson, 263-9; Dickinson, 161-2; Goldsmith: *The Traveller*, l. 418.

[76] G. Hay in Hay (ed.) 52; and Ignatieff in Cohen and Scull (eds.), 77, 94-5.

[77] Rediker, 245.

[78] Cleary, 102; Battestin, 220-1; Gay: *Polly* 1729 (1923) Act I, Scene I; PH XXVII, 821-2; Armens: *John Gay*, 59-61.

[79] Walpole: *George II*, I, 30; McLynn, 133; cf Goldsmith: *The Vicar of Wakefield*, ch. XXVII; G. Gatrell: Crime, Authority and the Policeman State in F.M.L. Thompson (ed.), *The Cambridge Social History of Britain 1750-1950* (3 vols. Cambridge, 1990), 251.

[80] Wrightson, 160; L. Stone: *The Crisis of the Aristocracy 1558-1641* (Oxford, 1965), 118-20; V. de Sola Pinto: *Enthusiast in Wit* (1962) 162-3; Downie: The Attack on Robert Harley MP, *The National Library of Wales Journal* XX (1972), 42-3; Walpole: *George II*, 76; Sharpe, 95-9; Nokes: *Jonathan Swift*, 148.

[81] Gay: *Fables XXI*, 45-6; Fielding: *An Enquiry*, 355-63; Clark (ed.): *The Memoirs and Speeches of James, 2nd Earl of Waldegrave*, 43, 46; Clark: *English Society 1688-1832*, 360, 108.

[82] Sharpe, 103, 118, 176, 183; Fielding: *An Enquiry*, 363; Defoe: *The Complete Tradesman*, 221; *Joseph Andrews*, Bk. II, ch XIII; Bk IV, ch. VI; cf *Amelia*, Bk. IV, ch. V; Langford: *England 1727-1783*, 118-9.

[83] Goldsmith: *The Vicar of Wakefield*, ch. XXVII; Swift: *A Modest Proposal* (1729).

[84] J. Kenyon: *The Popish Plot* (Harmondsworth, 1974), 205-6; G. Williams: *Artisans and Sans-Culottes* (1968), 87-8.

[85] Rogers: *Henry Fielding*, 50; P. Wagner: The Pornographer in the Courtroom, in P-G. Boucé (ed.): *Sexuality in Eighteenth Century Britain* (Manchester, 1982), 126-7; Mack: *Alexander Pope*, 568.

[86] Cleary, 39; Radzinowicz, I, 422-7; McLynn, 137-9.

[87] Boswell: *Johnson*, 19th September 1777, 849; Bleackley, 120-2; Howson, 221-2.

[88] Radzinowicz, I, 452-3; P. Langford: *Public Life and the Propertied Englishman 1689-1798* (Oxford, 1991), 20; *Tom Jones*, Bk. 7, ch. 9; HW XXI, 184.

[89] Radzinowicz, I, 450-472; Vulliamy, 332; Rumbelow, 166; AR 1777, 87-8.

[90] Goldsmith: *The Deserted Village* II 316-7; Beattie, 526, 463, 88.

[91] Beattie, 453n-5n; Bullett, 178-9; E. Robinson: An English Jacobin, *Cambridge Historical Journal* XI (1955), 350.

[92] Radzinowicz, I, 4-5, 213, 477-8; Lecky, I, 407; A. Aspinall: *Politics of the Press 1780-1850* (1949), 37; Lord Campbell: *Lives of the Lord Chancellors* (10 vols., 1868), VIII, 108; Ehrman: *The Younger Pitt*, II, 81, 391.

[93] PH XIX, 235-41 (Meredith); Radzinowicz, I, 151-64, for the view that Parliament expected the law to be enforced; Hay in Hay (ed.), 48-9, 56-7, for the view that it did not, because a harsh penal code tempered by mercy enhanced the effectiveness of terror and enabled 'the rulers of England to make the courts a selective instrument of class justice'.

[94] PH XXVI, 195-9.

[95] Blackstone, IV, 4; Holdsworth, XI, 560-1; Radzinowicz, I, 448-9.

[96] Holdsworth, XI, 560.

[97] PH XXVI, 1056-9; Radzinowicz, I, 287-93, 245, 147, 447, 509; IV, 331; Lecky, VI, 249; J. Edwards: *The Law Officers of the Crown* (1964), 141.

[98] N. Gash: *Mr Secretary Peel* (1961), 335, 329-33, 336-42; Radzinowicz, I, 577-95; IV, 303-11, 317-23.

[99] McLynn, 17-8.

[100] Hume: Of the First Principles of Government, *Essays*, 29; Paley, vol. 2, bk. 2, ch. 2, 120-9; Arendt: *On Violence*, 47-8.

[101] GM 1783, 891; Hay in Hay (ed.) 48-53; Clark, 412.

[102] B. Disraeli: *Sybil* (1845) Bk. I, ch. 1; E. Thompson: Patrician Society, Plebian Culture, *J.S.H.* 7,4, (1974), 397; Gay: *Fables*, 1738, III in Dearing II, 387; *Memoirs of the Life of Mr James MacLean* (1754), 103; H. Amory: Henry Fielding and the Criminal Legislation of 1751-2, *Philological Quarterly*, L, 2 (1972) 191-2.

[103] Canetti: *Crowds and Power*, 491; Hampson: *The Enlightenment*, 271 (de Maistre); Radzinowicz, III, 104; Bleackley, 18-9, 29-40, 85-7, 94.

[104] AR 1780, 275-6; Bleackley, 114-5, 119, 124-31; Radzinowicz, I, 187n.

VIII   The Press Gang

[1] Hume: Of Some Remarkable Customs, *Essays*, 379; PH XIX, 82.

[2] Hume: Of Some Remarkable Customs, 376, 379; J. Morley: *Voltaire* (1906), 78-9; J. Ashton: *The Industrial Revolution* (1948), 110.

[3] Edward Barlow in Rediker: *Between the Devil and the Deep Blue Sea*, 32; J. Bromley: *The British Navy and its Seamen after 1688* (1984), 149; D. Baugh: *British Naval Administration in the Age of Walpole* (Princeton, 1965), 231; D. Baugh (ed.): *Naval Administration 1715-50* (1977), 89-91.

[4] J. Bromley (ed.): *The Manning of the Royal Navy* (1974), 164, 174; G. Best: *War and Society in Revolutionary Europe 1770-1870* (1982), 40; Admiral Sir Herbert Richmond in

Turberville (ed.): *Johnson's England*, I, 48-9; PH, XIV, 402.

5 PH, XI, 428; N. Rodger. *The Wooden World* (1986), 164, 174; S. Gradish: *The Manning of the British Navy during the Seven Years' War* (1980), 29, 203-5; Mackesy: Strategic Problems of the British War Effort, in Dickinson (ed.), *Britain and the French Revolution 1789-1815* (1989), 153; *Lord Eldon's Anecdote Book*, 52; C. Lloyd: The Press Gang and the Law, *History Today* (1967), 686; R. Middleton: *The Bells of Victory* (Cambridge, 1985), 34-5.

6 HC 1715-54, II, 497, 503; Baugh (ed.) 123-4, 145-6; Rodger, 109-10.

7 Rodger, 40-1, 60, 85-7, 116-8, 134, 14, 218-20; Best, 32-3, 41; Baugh (ed.), 90; Smollett: *The Adventures of Roderick Random* ch. XXV; Ogg: *Europe and the Ancien Régime 1715-1785*, 160-1; In his scholarly defence of the Admiralty and the Navy in the Seven Years' War, *The Wooden World*, Dr Rodger (14) concedes that Smollett was not 'wholly unacquainted with the Navy', but points out that 'in picaresque novels, a man is not upon oath'. While Smollett doubtless often exaggerated, that seems insufficient reason for ignoring him, especially as there are no contemporary factual accounts of life at sea. Admiralty documents are not an adequate substitute.

8 Gradish, 87-97; Rediker, 33, 259; PH XIV, 402; Best, 41, 147; Rodger, 41, 98, 132-5.

9 Nef: *War and Economic Progress*, 234.

10 AR 1770, 161; *Roderick Random*, ch. XXIV; ST XVIII, 1323; PH, XIX, 83-4; Lecky, III, 537, 539; G. Williams: *History of the Liverpool Privateers* (London & Liverpool, 1897), 292, 269.

11 Williams, 194.

12 Wesley: *Journal*, IV 328-9; R. Brooke: *Liverpool 1775-1800* (Liverpool & London, 1853), 457-8; Williams, 194, 237-8, 319, 423; Stevenson, 39-40; Best, 146-7; Ehrmann, II 496-8; Stevenson: The London Crimp Riots of 1794, *International Review of Social History* 16 (1971), 41; N. McCord and D. Brewster, Some Labour Troubles of the 1790s in North East England, *International Review of Social History*, 13, 3 (1968), 377-81.

13 Lloyd, 688.

14 Baugh (ed.), 127-9; Baugh, 178; Stevenson, 39-40; Lloyd, 688-9.

15 Rodger, 176; Williams, 102; AR 1770, 147; McCord and Brewster, 380.

16 Baugh, 153; Lecky, III, 537-8.

17 Hume, 379; PH XI, 428; ST XVIII, 1323-60; Holdsworth IV, 329; X 381-2; Colley, 140.

18 Rodger, 168-70, 172; Gradish, 59-61; Lloyd, 689; Baugh, 159-62.

19 PH XVIII, 1402-3; AR 1770, 157, 160, 163; AR 1776, 192; Sharpe: *London and the Kingdom*, III, 106-7; H. Bleackley: *Life of John Wilkes* (1917), 256.

20 Baugh (ed.), 101; Bromley (ed.), XXIV, XXIII, XXXVII; *Wesley's Journal, A Selection* (E. Jay (ed.), Oxford, 1987), 45; PH XI, 419; Lloyd, 686.

21 Baugh, 34-9; Bromley 149-50, 159; Baugh (ed.) 91-2; Gradish, 107-10; Bromley (ed.), XXIX-XXXIII; PH XI, 428, 431; Holdsworth XI, 401.

22 PH XIX, 82-103; HC 1754-90, III, 71; Gradish, 55.

23 Baugh, 112-3, 138; Gradish, 74-5.

24 Baugh, 230, 377-83; J. Lind in D. Horne and M. Ranson: *English Historical Documents 1714-1783* (1957), 589-91; PH XI, 414-35; XII, 52-9, 86; XIV, 538-63; Gradish, 1, 14, 50, 108-10, 209; Bromley, 150; Bromley (ed.), XL-XLI.

25 Gradish, 55, 203-4; PH XI, 417; Rodger, 164; D. Medley: *English Constitutional History* (Oxford, 1925), 517; Bromley: In the Shadow of Impressment, in M. Foot (ed.): *War and Society* (1973), 184-5; Hume: *Essays*, 380.

IX   The Game Laws and Cruelty to Animals

1 Blackstone: *Commentaries*, II, 411-2; M. Carter: *Peasants and Poachers* (Woodbridge, Suffolk, 1980), 9-10; Woodforde, 361.

2 P. Munsche: *Gentlemen and Poachers* (Cambridge, 1981) 117; C. and E. Kirby: The Stuart Game Prerogative, *E.H.R.* XLVI (1931), 238-54; Blackstone, II, 417.

[3] Stephen: *History of the Criminal Law*, III, 281; C. Kirby: The English Game Law System, *The American Historical Review*, 38 (1932-3), 240-1, 250; Blackstone: *Commentaries*, IV, 175; Munsche, 170-1.

[4] Munsche, 28, 12, 81-2; Blackstone, II, 412; Thompson: *Whigs and Hunters*, 99-101; PR XLIV, 237, 243; Woodforde, 136-7; Fielding: *Joseph Andrews*, bk III, ch. IV.

[5] Munsche, 19-21, 3-6, 195; PR XLIV, 234, 241-2.

[6] Munsche, 22, 50-1, 28-32, 38-42; McLynn: *Crime*, 211.

[7] Munsche, 23, 44-7, 113-5, 167; McLynn, 207-8.

[8] Munsche, 23, 44-7, 113-5, 167; McLynn, 211; D. Brogan: *An Introduction to American Politics* (1954), 186.

[9] Crabbe: *Tales from the Hall*, XXI, 11 263-6.

[10] Munsche, 25-26; D. Jones: The Poacher, a Study in Victorian Crime and Protest, *H.J.* 22, 4, (1979), 825, 859; Carter, 76.

[11] Munsche, 106-7, 118-21, 219; S. Smith: Spring Guns and Man Traps, in G. Bullett: *Sydney Smith, a Biography and a Selection*, 147; Malcolmson, 114.

[12] Hay, 207, 236-44, 252; Munsche, 24-7, 193, 76-8, 87, 91-101, 104-7, 161-3, 231; P.D.N.S., VIII, 1292-8; PR XLIV, 243; PD XXXV, 345; Jones, 855.

[13] Munsche, 69; Hawkins: *Cranborne Chase*, 73; McLynn, 213.

[14] Kirby, 248-9; Munsche, 25-71, 70; Woodforde, 260.

[15] J. Innes: Politics and Morals, in Hellmuth (ed.): *The Transformation of Political Culture* (London and Oxford, 1990), 68-9; Munsche, 125, 72; H. Hopkins: *The Long Affray* (1985), 166-8.

[16] P.D.N.S., XIII, 1267, 1268; XVII, 19-20, 23, 26, 28; Hopkins, 166; Carter, 17.

[17] Munsche, 71-5, 210; Carter, 16.

[18] P.D.N.S. XIII, 1266-7; Bullett, 138-9.

[19] P.D.N.S., XIII, 1256; XII, 939 (Eldon); AR 1827, 116-7.

[20] P.D.N.S., XVII, 267 (Eldon); XIII, 1259-62; E. Turner. *Roads to Ruin* (1950), 23-4; Hopkins, 172.

[21] Bullett, 136-7; L. and J. Stone: *An Open Elite?* (Abridged edition, Oxford, 1986), 161-2, 203-4, 226-9; N. Rogers: Money, Land and Lineage, *S.H.* 3 (1979), 445-6; A. Young: *Travels in France and Italy 1792* (1976), 55-6, 64-5.

[22] P.D.N.S., XIII, 1262; XII, 642 (Suffield); XVII, 21, 34, 23-5, 296; XV, 719 (Peel); XII, 937-40 (Eldon and Wellington); Third Series, VII, 134, 255-6; Turner, 26-31.

[23] R. Malcolmson: *Popular Recreations in English Society 1700-1850* (Cambridge, 1979), 45-50, 56-7, 67-71, 118-22; Brooke: *Liverpool*, 266-7; M. Linklater and C. Hesketh: *For King and Conscience* (1989), 89, 92-3; K. Thomas: *Man and the Natural World* (1983), 144-5, 183-4.

[24] *The Leeds Intelligencer*, in Morsley, 49.

[25] Thomas, 144-5, 159-60; Ayling: *John Wesley*, 262; J. Boswell: *London Journal 1762-3* (1951), 160-1.

[26] Thomas, 143-4, 180-1, 185, 190-1, 290-1; L. Stone: *The Family, Sex and Marriage in England 1500-1800* (Harmondsworth, 1982), 162-3; Porter: *English Society in the Eighteenth Century*, 312-3; *Turner's Diary*, 250, 292; J. Golby and A. Purdue: *The Civilisation of the Crowd* (1984), 55.

[27] Thomas, 185-6; Le Bon: *The Crowd*, 43-4; Friedrich, 72; Fromm, 184-5; Henry Brand, quoted in Golby and Purdue, 55.

[28] PH XXXV, 207; Smith: The Suppression of Vice, in Bullett, 165.

[29] PH XXXVI, 833-4, 839; R. Sales: *English Literature in History* (1983), 21; Archenholz: *A Picture of England*, 262-3.

[30] D.N.B.; P.D.N.S., XVII, 738.

[31] PR VI, 282-3; McLynn, 211; Trevelyan: *England in the Nineteenth Century and After*, 151; Hopkins, 79.

[32] PR XLIV, 568, 560, 243, 563, 245; P.D.N.S., IX, 645 (Shelley); J. Pollock: *Wilberforce* (Tring, Herts., 1977), 143; Young, 207-8; T. Paine: *Rights of Man*, 74-5; Hopkins, I (Cobbett), 78, 184.

[33] PR XLIV, 237 (Curwen); GM 1788, 817-8; GM 1756, 384-5; Langford: *England 1727-*

1783, 301; Thornhill in Turner, 19; Blackstone, II, 412; P.D.N.S., XIII, 451.

[34] Hawkins, 57-8; P.D.N.S., XII, 939-40 (Eldon); *White's Natural History of Selborne* (W. Williams ed., 1965), Letter VII, 30; Munsche, 148-50.

[35] P.D.N.S., VIII, 542 (Shelley).

[36] GM 1788, 819; Porter, 70, 81; Lord Templewood: *Ambassador on Special Mission* (1946), 46; P.D.N.S., XVII, 21; PR, LXIV, 236, 569; P.D.N.S. XXXV, 339; Munsche, 188.

[37] PR XLIV, 565 (Pitt), 242 (Fox); P.D.N.S., XVII, 22-3; Smith: The Game Laws, in Bullett, 107.

X   Election Skulduggery

[1] PH XV, 499; Walpole: *Memoirs of George II*, II, 7; *Humphry Clinker*, May 19.

[2] E. Jacob: *The Fifteenth Century 1399-1485* (Oxford, 1961), 415; G. Haskins: *The Growth of English Representative Government* (Philadelphia, 1948), 117; Beloff: *Public Order and Popular Disturbances 1666-1714*, 49.

[3] Holdsworth: *A History of English Law*, X, 573; Beloff, 49-50, 54-5; HC 1745-90, I, 402; HC 1790-1820, II, 402-3; N. Gash: *Politics in the Age of Peel* (1953), 148; De Frey, 247.

[4] Gay: *An Epistle to the Earl of Burlington*, II 51-2; Robson: *The Oxfordshire Election of 1754*, 16 (Francis); HC 1715-54, I, 116-21; HC 1790-1820, I, 232; Namier: *The Structure of Politics at the Accession of George III*, 65, 159; F. O'Gorman: *Voters, Patrons, and Parties* (Oxford, 1989), 17, 59, 107-9, 146-8, 334-5.

[5] D. McAdams: Electioneering Techniques in Populous Constituencies 1784-96, *Studies in Burke and his Time* 14 (1982), 43; Clode: *The Military Forces of the Crown*, I, 195-203.

[6] J. Cannon: *Parliamentary Reform 1640-1832* (Cambridge, 1973), 24-5, 29-31; *The Freeholder's Plea against Stock-jobbing Elections of Parliament Men* (1701), probably by Defoe, in Dickinson, *Liberty and Property*, 118; Colley, 137; C. O'Leary: *The Elimination of Corrupt Practices in British Elections 1868-1911* (1962), 173-8, 229-33.

[7] HC 1715-54, I, 329; HC 1745-1790, I, 385; J. Sack: The House of Lords and Parliamentary Patronage in Great Britain, 1802-1832, *H.J.* 23, 4 (1980), 914; Namier, 166, 148-50; HC 1790-1820, I, 44; II, 380; J. Phillips: *Electoral Behaviour in Unreformed England* (Princeton, 1982), 46-7, 52-6; Ogg: *Europe of the Ancien Régime 1715-1783*, 46 (Paley).

[8] CJ 25, 210; Smollett, III, 431; HC 1715-54, I, 349, 198, 375; HC 1754-90, I, 402; O'Gorman, 127-8.

[9] P. Lawson: Grenville's Election Act 1770, *B.I.H.R.* LIII (1980), 218; HC 1715-54, I, 206.

[10] Carswell: *From Revolution to Revolution*, 86n; HC 1715-54, I, 116-23, 245, 318.

[11] Egmont: *Diary*, I, 85-6; HC 1715-54, I, 245; II, 413-4; Dickson: *The Financial Revolution*, 220.

[12] HC 1715-54, I, 359; Colley, 124; Robson, 136-7; Namier, 167, 167n; R. Edwards: *The Nabobs at Home* (1991), 14, 48, 53-4; Lawson, 218-28.

[13] O'Gorman, 178-9; Cannon, 42; Holmes: *PRS*, 14-24; G. Veitch: *The Genesis of Parliamentary Reform* (1964), 84; PH IX, 474; Colley, 169; Langford: *The Excise Crisis*, 164.

[14] see Head of Chapter; Rousseau: *Du Contrat Social*, Bk. III, ch. XV.

[15] O'Gorman, 33-8, 43-53, 66-7, 225-7, 232; HC 1754-1790, I, 47, 51-2, 214; Rogers: *Whigs and Cities*, 203, 211.

[16] Phillips, 65-72, 80-1, 86, 136-8; HC 1754-90, I, 86-9, 286-8; S. Ayling: *Edmund Burke* (1988), 98-100; O'Gorman: Electoral Deference in 'Unreformed' England 1760-1832, *J.M.H.* 56 (1984), 402-4, 408-9, 412.

[17] I. Christie: *Stress and Stability in Late Eighteenth Century Britain* (Oxford, 1984), 54; Moritz: *Travels through several parts of England in 1782*, 17; E. Eyck: *Pitt versus Fox* (1950), 225; HC 1754-90, 364, 394-5; R. Browning: *The Duke of Newcastle* (New Haven and London, 1975), 332.

[18] Backscheider, 446-7; Phillips, 16-9, 24-35; Hempton, 43; HC 1715-54, I, 290; *Jackson's Oxford Journal* in Robson, 62.

[19] PH IX, 476; Namier, 195.

[20] O'Gorman: *Voters*, 28-9, 142-3, 158-62, 170-1; Phillips, 77-81; Ayling: *John Wesley*, 265; Warburton, X, 130-1.

[21] HC 1715-54, I, 349, 215, 204; HC 1790-1820-, II, 16, 200, 445; HC 1754-90, I, 366, 417-9; Robson, 51-3.

[22] PH XVII, 148; E. Lascelles: *Life of Charles James Fox* (Oxford, 1939), 26; HC 1754-90, I, 395-6; HC 1790-1820, II, 397; PH XXI, 687.

[23] HC 1715-54, I, 211, 310, 200; II, 110; HC 1790-1820, II, 58.

[24] Holdsworth, X, 575n; PH XXII, 1391; Colley, 162.

[25] S. Johnson: Life of Savage in *Lives of the Poets* (2 vols., Everyman edition, 1953), 82-3, 87; Pope: *The First Satire of the Second Book of Horace Imitated*, 1. 82; Fielding: *Tom Jones*, Bk. 8, ch. 11; Thompson: *Whigs and Hunters*, 211-2.

[26] HC 1715-54, I, 197, 205, 303; PH VII, 961-5; PH XIV, 221-5; HC 1754-90, I, 277, 357; Langford: *Public Life and the Propertied Enlgishman*, 128.

[27] Colley, 18; HC 1715-54, I. 286.

[28] Colley, 162; Browning, 8-9; HC 1715-54, I, 292, 287; N. Rogers: Aristocratic Clientage, Trade and Independency: Popular Politics in Pre-Radical Westminister, *P. & P.*, 61 (1973), 88-9; CJ, 21 (1727) 46.

[29] HC 1715-54, I, 279; HC 1790-1820, II, 257, 349; Gash, 137; Beckett, 443.

[30] Boswell: *Johnson*, 5th April 1775, 609-10; O'Gorman: Electoral Deference, 396, 402-6, 412.

[31] HC 1715-54, I, 302; HC 1754-90, 213; Landau: *The Justices of the Peace*, 37-8, 45; PH XV, 496-7; Clark: *The English Alehouse*, 324.

[32] HC 1754-90, I, 455; HC 1715-54, I, 337, 306.

[33] Rogers, 85; HC 1715-54, I, 339; Namier, 78, 78n.

[34] Holdsworth, X, 569, 596n; Harrison: *Crowds and History*, 183.

[35] CJ 21, 46; Brooke: *Liverpool*, 303.

[36] HC 1715-54, I, 203-4; Stevenson, 24.

[37] Plumb: *Sir Robert Walpole*, I, 316-8; HC 1715-54, I, 279.

[38] J. Owen: *The Rise of the Pelhams* (1957), 315-6; HC 1715-54, I, 318-21.

[39] HC 1715-54, I, 284; Battestin, 485-7; Robson, 62, 97-8, 128; Rogers, 81; Landau, 281-3; M. Thomis: *Politics and Society in Nottingham 1785-1835* (New York & Oxford, 1969), 144-5.

[40] Rogers, 74; HC 1715-54, I, 286; GM 1741, 275; Owen, 9.

[41] Egmont: *Diary*, III, 219-20; Rogers, 73-5, 97, 75; R. Roberts: Eighteenth Century Boxing, *Journal of Sport History* 4 (1977), 250-3.

[42] CJ 24, 37; GM 1741, 665.

[43] HC 1715-54, I, 286-8; Rogers, 92-4, 98-102; Walpole, I, 9; McLynn: *Crime*, 223-4; Battestin, 472-6, 483, 485, 490-1.

[44] J. Brewer. *The Common People and Politics 1750-1790s* (Cambridge, 1986), 32; McAdams, 43-7; HC 1754-90, I, 402; see Ch. XVII below.

[45] Thomis, 144-5, 155-65; HC 1790-1820, II, 317-9.

[46] HC 1754-90, I, 344; O'Gorman: *Voters*, 136, 147-8, 151-5; Rogers, 105; HC 1715-54, I, 370.

[47] HC 1715-54, 331-2; Rogers, 91-2; N. McKendrick, J. Brewer, J. Plumb: *The Birth of a Consumer Society* (1983), 241-2; HC 1754-90, I, 246, 437-8, 443; McAdams, 37-8; Stevenson, 27-8.

[48] HC 1790-1820, II, 242, 228; McAdams, 52-3.

[49] HC 1754-90, I, 372; Stevenson, 27; T. Perry: *Public Opinion, Propaganda and Politics in Eighteenth Century England* (Cambridge, Mass., 1962), 75; Plumb, II, 321.

[50] PH XIV, 208, 211.

[51] PH XVI, 400; HC 1790-1820, II, 451.

XI Food Riots

[1] GM 1739, 7; Colley: *In Defiance of Oligarchy*, 159; GM 1766, 525; Booth: Food Riots in the North West of England 1790-1801, *P. & P.* 77 (1977), 91.

[2] As not all riots were reported, their exact number is not known, and there are difficulties of definition; R Wells: *Wretched Faces* (Gloucester, 1988), 90-6; G. Rudé (*The Crowd in History 1730-1848*, 35-6) found two-thirds of 275 disturbances to be food riots; J. Bohstedt (*Riots and Community Politics in England and Wales 1790-1810*, 14-5, 235) found the percentage to be 39.

[3] J. Walter and K. Wrightson: Dearth and the Social Order in Early Modern England, *P. & P.* 71 (1976), 26, 36-7; R. Rose: Eighteenth Century Price Riots and Public Policy in England, *International Review of Social History*, VI (1961), 280-1, 283; J. Walter: Grain Riots and Popular Attitudes to the Law in Brewer and Styles (eds.), *An Ungovernable People*, 53, 56, 59, 64, 71, 76, 79-80.

[4] Kerridge: *The Agricultural Revolution*, 345; Hoskins: Harvest Fluctuations and English Economic History 1620-1759, 21, 29-30; Thompson: The Moral Economy of the English Crowd in the Eighteenth Century, *P. & P.* 50 (1971), 110.

[5] Hoskins, 22-4 (Defoe); Kerridge; 328, 334-5; 347; Deane: *The First Industrial Revolution*, 65, 31-2, 145; Coleman: *The Economy of England 1450-1750*, 102-3, 114-21; E. Wrigley: The Growth of Population in Eighteenth Century England: A Conundrum Resolved, *P. & P.* 98 (1983), 127, 143-4; N. Crafts: English Economic Growth in the Eighteenth Century, *Ec.H.R.* 2nd ser. XXIX (1983), 232-4; R. Jackson: Growth and Deceleration in English Agriculture, 1660-1790, *Ec.H.R.* 2nd ser. XXXVIII, no. 3 (1985), 333, 339, 342, 349-50.

[6] L. Schwarz: The Standard of Living in the Long Run: London 1700-1860, *Ec.H.R.* 2nd ser. XXXVIII (1985), 25, 28-9, 31, 35; Jackson, 340-1, 346-7, 351; M. Flinn: Trends in Real Wages, 1750-1850, *Ec.H.R.* 2nd ser. XXVII no. 3 (1974), 408; G. von Tunzelmann: Trends in Real Wages, 1750-1850, Revisited, *Ec.H.R.* 2nd ser. XXXII (1979), 38-40, 45-6; K. Snell: *Annals of the Labouring Poor* (Cambridge, 1987), 28-40, 223-4, 312; La Rochefoucauld: *A Frenchman's Year in Suffolk, 1784*, 4, 18, 78; J. Ellis: Urban Conflict and Popular Violence, The Guildhall Riots of 1740 in Newcastle upon Tyne, *International Review of Social History* XXV (1980), 334-6.

[7] Wells, 1-2, 35, 52-5, 69-71; D. Williams: Were Hunger Rioters Really Hungry? *P. & P.* 71 (1976), 72-4.

[8] Snell, 28-36, 72-3, 104-11, 356-7; *The Diary of Thomas Turner 1754-1765* (Vaisey ed.) 42, 56-7, 67-8, 80-2, 85-92, 117-9, 122-5, 139-40, 246, 268, 316; Malcolmson: *Life and Labour in England 1700-1780*, 76-80; Woodforde: *The Diary of a Country Parson 1758-1802*, 168, 424; Clifford (ed.): *Man versus Society in Eighteenth Century Britain*, 44; George: *London Life in the Eighteenth Century*, 173; Battestin, 513.

[9] J. Post: *The Last Great Subsistence Crisis in the Western World* (London and Baltimore, 1977), 75; Wearmouth, 62; Williams, 72-4; W. Stern: The Bread Crisis in Britain 1795-96, *Economica* new ser. XXI (1964), 172-3; Booth, 102-4; Charlesworth (ed.): *An Atlas of Rural Protest in Britain 1548-1980*, 83.

[10] Wearmouth, 22, 29, 34; Bohstedt, 84-7; Thompson, 111; A. Randall: The Gloucestershire Food Riots of 1766, *Midland History* X (1985), 84-5.

[11] Wearmouth, 32; AR 1766, 124-5; Charlesworth & Randall: Morals, Markets and the English Crowd in 1766: A Comment, *P. & P.* 114 (1987), 211.

[12] Bohstedt, 34, 27-31; Malcolmson: A Set of Ungovernable People in Brewer and Styles (eds.), 118; Booth 95.

[13] Thompson, 78-9.

[14] Locke: *First Treatise on Civil Government*, 42; Dunn: *Locke*, 43; St. Thomas Aquinas: *Summa Theologica* in A. D'Entrères (ed.), *Selected Political Writings* (Oxford, 1948), 171; Wells, 10-1; C. Dobson: *Masters and Journeymen* (1980), 144-5; *The Northampton Mercury*, 6 April 1772, in Morsely, 77.

[15] Holdsworth, IV, 375-9; VI, 346; XI, 466; Thompson, 96.

[16] Beloff, 66-7, 69; Rose, 289-90; Thompson, 84, 88, 96n; Holdsworth, XI, 466;

Bleackley: *Life of John Wilkes*, 288-9; P. Corfield: *The Impact of English Towns 1700-1800* (Oxford, 1982), 89.

[17] J. Stevenson in A. Fletcher and J. Stevenson (eds.): *Order and Disorder in Modern England* (Cambridge, 1985), 235-8; Charlesworth (ed.), 3-5, 63, 118, 86; Williams: Morals, Markets and the English Crowd in 1766, 56-7, 69-73; E. Fox Genovese: The Many Faces of Moral Economy, *P. & P.* 58 (1973), 164-5; Snell, 99-103; Of course as Charlesworth and Randall point out in their Comment (202-5) on William's article, by no means all riots were reported, and the peaceful areas were affected by the turbulence elsewhere.

[18] Rudé: *Paris and London in the Eighteenth-Century*, 296.

[19] Malcolmson: *Life and Labour*, 109; Wells, 177-8; Wearmouth, 19, 78; Langford: *Public Life*, 474; Bohstedt: Women in English Riots 1790-1810, *P. & P.* 120 (1988), 103.

[20] Wearmouth, 44-5; GM 1766, 549, 598; Rudé: *The Crowd in History*, 255.

[21] GM 1766, 436; AR 1766, 137, 139.

[22] Hammond: *The Village Labourer*, 120-1; Bohstedt: Women, 119-20; B.L. Add. Mss 35607, fol. 312.

[23] Wearmouth, 54; Add. Mss 35607, fol. 309-10.

[24] Rudé, 22-3, 30, 37-8; J. Stevenson and R. Quinault, (eds.) *Popular Protest and Public Order* (New York, 1975), 48-9; J. Rule: *The Experience of Labour in Eighteenth Century Industry* (1981), 14-6, 31; Bohstedt: *Riots*, 13, 44-5, 166, 168-75, 195-201; Booth, 87-90.

[25] Malcolmson in Brewer and Styles (eds.), 93 116-21; Rogers: *Whigs and Cities*, 292-3; Wearmouth, 20-1.

[26] Booth, 97; W. Shelton: *English Hunger and Industrial Disorders* (1973), 107.

[27] See Chs. III and X above; *The Journal of John Wesley* (ed. Curnock) III, 98-104, 129, 188-91; Wearmouth, 144-5; J. Walsh; Methodism and the Mob in G. Cuming and D. Baker *Popular Belief and Practice* (Cambridge, 1972), 218.

[28] Landau, 53, 93-5; Colley, 152-3, 162, 287; Thompson: Patrician Society, Plebian Culture, *J.S.H.* 7 no. 4 (1974), 403-4; Stevenson & Quinault (eds.) 41-2; Stern, 171.

[29] GM 1756, 409; Shelton, 99, 111-2; Randall, 80-86.

[30] Hayter, 65-6; D. Hempton: *Methodism and Politics in British Society 1750-1850* (1987); 232; Thompson: Moral Economy, 95; *Turner's Diary*, 82; Wells, 32-4, 196-7, 217, 328, 348; Stern, 174.

[31] GM 1756, 577; B. Williams: *The Life of William Pitt* (2 vols., 1913), I, 287-8; B. Dobree (ed.): *The Letters of George III* (1935), 42.

[32] Hayter, 84-7, 170; Bohstedt, 37; Thompson: Patrician Society, 403-4.

[33] Wearmouth, 59, 65, 85; Bohstedt, 48, 66, 95-8; Wells, 82; Thompson: The Moral Economy, 12; GM 1756, 545.

[34] P.R. 1768 vol. II, 259-64; A. Cobban: *Edmund Burke* (1929), 191; *Thoughts and Details on Scarcity*, Burke V, 83-4, 92, 100; Boswell: *Johnson*, 446.

[35] Bohstedt, 58-62, Thompson, 129-31.

[36] Booth, 100-1, 105; Ellis, 338.

[37] Bohstedt, 41-2, 47, 55-8, 232; Booth, 105.

[38] Add. Mss 35607, fol. 312; Wells, 156; Thompson, 121.

[39] Hayter, 85, 79, 18; Randall, 92.

[40] GM 1756, 491; Hayter, 28, 47, 52-3; Houlding, 61-2.

[41] Wearmouth, 22, 35-6; *Adams Weekly Courant*, 14 October 1766 in Morsely, 57; Rose, 288.

[42] GM 1740, 355-6; Ellis, 341-5; Feiling, 97; Wearmouth, 20-1, 70; cf AR 1766, 139.

[43] *The Wealth of Nations*, Bk IV, ch. V, in Ehrman: *The Younger Pitt*, II, 445.

[44] G. Shelton: *Dean Tucker and Eighteenth Century Economic and Political Thought*, (1981), 78-9.

[45] Walter and Wrightson, 35-6; Wearmouth, 54-5.

[46] GM 1765, 44, 195, 394, 567; W. Shelton: *English Hunger*, 25; Williams; *Morals, Markets and the English Crowd in 1766*, 62.

[47] M. D. George: *England in Transition* (Harmondsworth, 1953), 98-9, 137; W. Shelton, 26-7; Williams, 62-4.

[48] Walpole: *Memoirs of the Reign of King George III*, II, 366; AR 1766, 137; W. Shelton, 34-5, 42.

[49] AR 1766, 224-6; W. Shelton, 46-8; J. Money: *Experience and Identity* (Manchester, 1977), 248-9.

[50] GM 1766, 398, 548, 490; AR 1766, 149, 226-7.

[51] W. Shelton, 95-101, 107, 114, 119-21.

[52] PH XVI, 648, 251, 281-3; Walpole, II, 372-3, 378-9, 388.

[53] *Essay on Riots*, GM 1739, 7; Langford, 446-7.

[54] GM 1766, 399; P.R. 1766, vol. 2, 100-4, 259-64; PH XVI, 235-6, 242-3; Kerridge, 335, 380-1, 386-90.

[55] AR 1768, 90.

[56] GM 1766, 598; Wearmouth, 60, 84, 74.

[57] BL Add. Mss 32867, fols. 6-10, 94-7; GM 1756, 408-9; Wearmouth, 81-2; Charlesworth (ed.), 112-3; Hay (ed.), 49-50.

[58] Thompson: Patrician Society, 404; Bohstedt, 64-6; Wells, 276-9.

[59] GM 1766, 549, 598-9; AR 1766, 151; Randall, 88-9; Hayter, 120-1; PH XVI, 391.

[60] GM 1740, 465; Ellis, 346-8; Boothe, 105-6; Wells, 279-80.

[61] A. Coles: The Moral Economy of the Crowd: Some Twentieth Century Food Riots, *J.B.S.* XVIII (1978), 157-76.

[62] Fromm: *The Anatomy of Human Destructiveness*, 18, 24, 145, 251-4; Booth, 105; Tilly: *The Rebellious Century 1830-1930*, 50-1, 128-9, 135, 145-52, 192, 233; W. Thayer: *The Life and Times of Cav.our* (2 vols., 1911), I, 314; D. Mack Smith: *Cav.our*, (1985), 72-3.

[63] PH XVI 236, 378; Hay in Hay (ed.), 49-50; Wells, 331; Christie: *Stress and Stability*, 153-5.

[64] GM 1739, 7; Rose 290; Ehrman, II, 154, 44-5; 464-8; Stern, 178-80.

[65] Malcolmson in Brewer and Styles (eds.), 118-23.

[66] Wells, 178-81; K. Polanyi: *The Great Transformation* (Boston, 1957), 186-7, 295-6; Bohstedt: *Riots and Community Politics*, 238, 54-5, 66-7, 222-3; Bohstedt: Women in English Riots, 1790-1810, 112.

XII Industrial Disputes

[1] Dobson: *Masters and Journeymen*, 112, 185; Shelton: *Dean Tucker*, 40; Pocock, quoted in Corfield: *The Impact of English Towns 1700-1800*, 84.

[2] Grosley: *A Tour to London*, I, 66; George: *England in Transition*, 53-5.

[3] A. Coats: Changing Attitudes to Labour in the Mid Eighteenth Century in M. Flinn and T. Smout (eds.), *Essays in Social History* (Oxford, 1974), 78-9, 87; D. Baugh: Poverty, Protestantism and Political Economy in Baxter (ed.), *England's Rise to Greatness 1600-1763*, 76-81, 101-2; Horne: *The Social Thought of Bernard Mandeville*, 67-71.

[4] Coats, 80-3, 90-1; G. Shelton, 126-32, 165, 173-4; Hume: Of Commerce, *Essays*, 266; Horne, 92-4; Baugh, 84-6; Adam Smith: *The Wealth of Nations* (ed. A Skinner, Harmondsworth, 1974), Book I, ch. 8, 184, 176, 181.

[5] Jackson, 333, 339, 345-51; Crafts: English Economic Growth in the Eighteenth Century. A Re-Examination of Dean and Cole's Estimates, 232-4; P. Lindert and H. Williamson: English Workers' Living Standards during the Industrial Revolution: A New Look, *Ec.H.R.* 2nd ser., XXXVI, no. 1 (1983), 13; Schwarz, 25, 28-31, 35.

[6] Holdsworth, XI, 466-8; Malcolmson: Workers' Combinations in Jacob (eds.), *The Origins of Anglo-American Radicalism*, 150-2.

[7] Holdsworth, XI, 476-7, 483-96; Dobson, 15, 25, 38-9; Pelling: *A History of British Trade Unionism*, (Harmondsworth, 1963), 21.

[8] Rudé: *The Crowd in History*, 67, 72.

[9] Perkin, 32; G. Rude: *Europe in the Eighteenth Century* (1985), 65.

[10] Adam Smith, 169-70; P. Mantoux: *The Industrial Revolution in the Eighteenth-Century* (1935), 456; Rule: *The Experience of Labour in the Eighteenth Century*, 155, 178-81.

[11] Dobson, 39-40, 60-2, 65-6; Mantoux, 81; Rule, 111-2; Battestin, 524; E. Thompson: Time, Work-Discipline and Industrial Capitalism, in Flinn and Smout (eds.), 60.

[12] Dobson, 17; Rudé, 66-8; Hammond: *The Skilled Labourer*, 153.

[13] Dobson, 45.

[14] Mantoux, 79-81; Dobson, 32; Rule, 183, 186; Malcolmson, 159.

[15] Dobson, 20, 32; Rule, 160-1; Houlding, 65-8; Hammond, 126-7.

[16] Dobson, 31-32.

[17] GM 1738, 658; Rule, 163, 187.

[18] G. Shelton, 112-3; 40; Langford: *Public Life and the Propertied Englishman*, 461; Colley: *In Defiance of Oligarchy*, 151.

[19] G. Shelton, 112; George, 44-50.

[20] Beloff, 82-7; De Krey, 57-8; McLynn: *Crime*, 220, 226-7, 322; 5 George I cap. 23; see also Ch. XV below.

[21] AR 1768, 57-60, 99, 101-2, 105-6, 108-9, 111, 114, 120-1, 124, 129-30, 139; Schwarz, 31; W. Shelton: *Enlgish Hunger and Industrial Disorders*, 141-6, 158, 165-78, 184-202.

[22] Hammond, 15; J. Fewster: The Keelmen of Tyneside in the Eighteenth Century, *Durham University Journal* NS XIX-XX, (1957-9), 24-5, 67-74.

[23] *The [London] Gazetteer and the New Daily Advertiser* Sept 4th 1775, quoted in Brooke: *Liverpool 1775-1800*, 327-34; A. Wardle: Some Glimpses of Liverpool During the First Half of the Eighteenth Century, *Tr. of the Historical Society of Lancashire and Cheshire*, 97 (1945), 151.

[24] R. Rose: A Liverpool Sailors' Strike in the Eighteenth Century, *Journal of the Lancashire and Cheshire Antiquarian Society*, LXVIII (1958), 88-9; *London Gaz. and N.D.A.*, Sept 4th, in Brooke, 328-30, 334, 339; Williams: *History of the Liverpool Privateers*, 555-6.

[25] *London Gaz. and N.D.A.* Sept 4th in Brooke, 328, 340-3; Rose, 89-90; Williams, 556-9.

[26] Brooke, 329, 333, 335; Rose, 90-1; Williams, 557-9; AR 1776, 44 (History).

[27] Brooke, 325-6, 343; Corfield, 162.

[28] AR 1776, 44 (History); Christie: *Stress and Stability*, 147; Brooke, 343-4; Williams, 559-60.

[29] E. Hobsbawm: The Machine Breakers, in *Labouring Men* (1986), 7-10; Mantoux, 410-1.

[30] Mantoux, 409-11; Hammond, 402-3.

[31] AR 1779, 228-9, 233; Hammond, 43-5.

[32] Rule, 163; M. Thomis: *The Luddites* (New York, 1972), 15-6; Mantoux, 413-5.

[33] Hammond, 11; McLynn: *Crime*, 303.

[34] G. Shelton: *Dean Tucker*, 109-11; A. Smith, 114-5, 383-4; D. Ricardo: *The Principles of Political Economy and Taxation* (1817), ch. XXXI.

[35] A. Mathias: *The Transformation of England* (1979), 8-9; C. Driver: *Tory Radical* (New York, 1946), 17-8; C. Hill: *Reformation to Industrial Revolution* (1967), 219.

[36] Hammond, 126-8; Rule, 163.

[37] Sir J. Clapham: *A Concise Economic History of Britain* (Cambridge, 1949), 239; George: *London Life in the Eighteenth Century*, 182; Davis: The Rise of Protection in England, 1689-1786, *Ec.H.R.* 2nd ser., XIX, 306, 309-10.

[38] Davis, 316; AR 1769, 81, 124, 136, 138; Hammond, XIX-XX, 168-77; George, 193-5.

[39] L. Colley: Eighteenth Century English Radicalism before Wilkes, *T.R.H.S.* 5th ser., 31 (1980), 17; GM 1739, 8-10; Hayter, 170.

[40] GM 1737, 378; George: *Transition*, 142-3.

[41] Hammond, 149-50; Rule, 131-2.

[42] Smith: *The Wealth of Nations* Bk I, ch. X, 246; Perkin, 182 (Carlyle), 184-9; Malcolmson, 157.

[43] Crouzet: The Impact of the French Wars on the British Economy in Dickinson (ed.), 194-6, 205-6; C. Emsley: *British Society and the French Wars 1793-1815* (1979), 28-30, 82-5; Wells, 18-9, 56-7, 75, 169-71; A. Goodwin: *The Friends of Liberty* (1979), 454-5.

[44] E. Thompson: *The Making of the English Working Class* (Harmondsworth, 1982), 550-5; Christie, 138-9; Wells, 171-3.

[45] McCord and Brewster, 367-76, 383; Wells, 171-2.

XIII Duelling

[1] Holdsworth: *A History of English Law*, V, 200; R. Baldick: *The Duel* (1965), 120; *Waverley*, II, ch. XXIII.

[2] J. Clark: *English Society 1688-1832* (Cambridge, 1985), 93-106; H. Perkin: *The Origins of Modern English Society 1780-1880* (1969), 237-52, 273-5; Burke: *Reflections of the Revolution in France* (O'Brien, ed.), 170; O. Christie: *The Transition from Aristocracy 1832-1867* (1927), 22-3; Defoe: *The Complete English Tradesman*, 213.

[3] G. Kelly: Duelling in Eighteenth Century France, *The Eighteenth Century*, 21, no. 3 (1980), 239, 239n; P. Ziegler: *Addington* (1965); 356-7; Stone: *The Crisis of the Aristocracy*, 248-9; Smollett: *Humphry Clinker*, September 28, 283.

[4] J. Gilchrist: *A Brief Display of the Origin and History of Ordeals* (1821), XXI; E.B., 640; Hampson: *The Enlightenment*, 68; V. Kiernan: *The Duel in European History* (Oxford, 1988), 25-6, 82, 97-8, 109-10, 167; F. Billacois: *The Duel* (New Haven and London, 1980), 21, 33-40, 70-5, 144-62, 175-88.

[5] A. Wise: *The History and Art of Personal Combat* (1971), 65, 86, 119; Billacois, 28, 32, 99n, 237-8; Kiernan, 80-3; Holdsworth, IV, 304; V, 200; Baldick, 65.

[6] Baldick, 70.

[7] Holdsworth, I, 579; V, 201; VI, 309; Baldick, 68-71; Latham (ed.): *The Shorter Pepys*, 866, 871; Western: *Monarchy and Revolution*, 85; Miller: *James II*, 121.

[8] Holdsworth, V, 199; Kiernan, 75.

[9] Holdsworth V, 199-201; Stephen, III, 99-102; Billacois, 83; P.D., 3rd ser., LXXIII, 764, 1019 (Lord Howick).

[10] Macaulay, V, 2266-70; Trevelyan: *England under Queen Anne*, III, 103, 245; H. Dickinson: The Mohun-Hamilton Duel, Personal Feud or Whig Plot?, *Durham University Journal* (1965), 159-65.

[11] Dickinson, 159-65; Swift: *Journal to Stella*, Letter LV, II, 570-2; D.N.B.; J. Aylward: Duelling in the Eighteenth Century, *Notes and Queries* CLXXXIX (1945), 32-4; Baldick; 71-2; Wise, 146-52.

[12] ST XIX, 1185-6, 1213, 1196, 1227-8; AR 1765, 208-12; Chilchrist, 83-6.

[13] HW XXII, 284, 293; ST XIX, 1178; AR 1765, 211-2; A. Rowse: *The Byrons and Trevanions* (1978), 125-9; L. Marchand: *Byron* (1971), 18.

[14] Carswell: *The Old Cause*, 46, 66-7, 96.

[15] Baldick, 72-3, 98-100; Gilchrist, 147-8, 222-34; P.D. 3rd ser., LXXIII, 808.

[16] Plumb, I, 247-8; Egmont, I, 221; Coxe: *Memoirs of the Pelham Administration*, I, 9; *Lord Hervey's Memoirs*, XXVII-XXX.

[17] Coxe: *Memoirs of Horatio, Lord Walpole*, 258; HC 1715-54, II, 510, 548.

[18] PH XX, 1101-4, 1116-20; E. Lascelles: *The Life of Charles James Fox* (Oxford, 1939), 84-5; C. Hobhouse: *Fox* (1947), 89.

[19] PH XXI, 293-6; Lord E. Fitzmaurice: *Life of William, Earl of Shelburne* (2 vols., 1875), II, 75-7; Gilchrist, 118-22.

[20] PH XXI, 295, 319-27; Gilchrist, 136.

[21] Gilchrist, 186-7; AR 1798, 43-4; R. Reilly: *William Pitt the Younger* (New York, 1979), 358-9.

[22] Lord Rosebery: *Pitt* (1902), 138-40; Reilly, 359-61; W. Roberts: *Memoirs of the Life and Correspondence of Hannah More* (4 vols., 1834), III, 31-2, 60.

[23] W. Hinde: *Castlereagh* (1981), 164-8; P. Dixon: *Canning* (1976), 137-8.

[24] N. Gash: *Mr Secretary Peel* (1961), 162-7; C. Chenevix Trench, *The Great Dan* (1986), 89-94.

[25] E. Longford: *Wellington, Pillar of State* (1972), 185-8.

[26] Sir C. Petrie: *George Canning* (1946), 107.

[27] EB, (Duelling) 641; Kiernan, 191.

[28] Baldick, 42-4; Wise, 174.

[29] EB, 640.

[30] Holdsworth, V, 200; Paley, I, 275-6; Kelly, 249-51; EB, 642; Gilchrist, XXXI-XXXII, 282-3.

[31] Baldick, 120; B. Mitchell: *Alexander Hamilton* (New York, 1976), 370-1.

[32] Fielding: *Tom Jones*, Bk. VII, ch. XIII; R. Gilmour: *The Idea of the Gentleman in the Victorian Novel* (1981), 27-8; Gilchrist, 234.

[33] Aylward, 46; *The Manchester Mercury* in Morsely, 103; Gilchrist, 83.

[34] R. McGowen: 'He Beareth not the Sword in Vain', *Eighteenth Century Studies* (1987-8), 194, 202, 207; Sykes, 326-7; EB, 639; Wesley: *Journal*, IV, 271; Kiernan, 172; Paley, I, 272-6.

[35] Yorke: *Hardwicke*, II, 589; Aylward, 72; Gilchrist, 323-33.

[36] Kiernan, 111-2; PD 3rd ser., 1020.

[37] Gilbert: Law and Honour among 18th Century British Army Officers, 79-86; Hobbes: *Leviathan* (Oxford, 1909), 72; Gilchrist, XIV-XIX; Kiernan, 111-2, 59, 101.

[38] Dixon, 138; AR 1789, 208-10; Gilchrist, 149-52, 56-60; *Lord Eldon's Anecdote Book*, 151; Halevy, 453n; PD, 3rd ser., LXXIII, 762-71, 802-14.

[39] Trevelyan, III, 24; Baldick, 180-3.

[40] E. Royle and J. Walvin: *English Radicals and Reformers 1760-1848* (Brighton, 1982), 95; Boswell: *Johnson*, 1228; Coupland: *Wilberforce*, 177, 239; *Grafton's Autobiography* (W. Anson ed.) (1898), 392-3n; L.J. XXVI, 188-91; R. Ketton-Cremer: *Norfolk Assembly* (1957) 162-4.

[41] Baldick, 175-6, 157.

[42] Gilchrist, 96-9, 158, 156-7, 161-4, 146, 253-4, 165-6, 122-4, 212, 335, 256-9, 321; GM 1746, 439; *Medwin's Conversations of Lord Byron* (E. Lovell Jr. ed., Princeton, 1966), 56; Fielding: *Tom Jones*, Bk. XVI, ch. II.

[43] Gilchrist, 195-9; Baldick, 97-101.

[44] Smollett: *Travels Through France and Italy*, Letter XV; L. Marchand (ed): *Byron's Letters and Journals* (12 vols., 1973-82), III, 93-5; Gilchrist, 250-1.

[45] Latham (ed.), 866.

[46] PD, 3rd ser., LXXIII, 811, 1023; Gilchrist, passim; Kiernan, 7-8, 191.

[47] Kiernan (who thinks duelling was declining before the Revolution), 185, 187, 204-5; D. Andrew: The Code of Honour and its Critics, *S.H.* 3, (1980), 409, 410n, 423; GM 1783, 485, 443; Clark, 110, 114.

[48] A. John: War and the British Economy 1700-1763, *Ec.H.R.* VII, no. 3, 329; Dickinson: *Bolingbroke*, 69; Cannon: *Aristocratic Century*, 120; Beckett: *The Aristocracy in England 1660-1914*, 409; Disraeli: *Sybil*, Bk. I, ch. II; Gilchrist, 60-1; Andrew, 423.

[49] PD, 3rd ser. LXXIII, 330, 762-71, 802-14; Baldick, 113-4.

[50] Kiernan, 269-70, 198, 263, 277-9; Mack Smith: *Cavour*, 47; Baldick, 135-6.

[51] Macaulay, V, 2446.

[52] AR 1798, 69; Andrew, 433.

[53] Hopkins: *The Long Affray*, 168.

[54] Burke: *Reflections*, 150-1; cf. N. Elias: *The Court Society* (Oxford, 1985), 239-40.

[55] Kelly, 236-7, 251-4; Clark, 113; N. Hampson: The French Revolution and the Nationalism of Honour, in Foot (ed.), *War and Society*, 207.

[56] Bacon: Of Revenge, *Essays*, 1625.

[57] Baldick, 65; Nietzsche, in Nef, 409; Montaigne: Cowardice, The Mother of Cruelty, in *Essays*, 1580 (1898), Bk II, vol.II, ch. 27, 228-31; Billacois, 61-7, 83, 239; Marchand (ed.), VI, 188-9; VII, 184, 95-6; IX, 102.

[58] Marchand (ed.), 162, 182; III, 251; Marchand: *Byron*, 279; Roberts: Eighteenth Century Boxing, 246-53; Lord Knebworth: *Boxing* (1931), 22-7; Malcolmson: *Popular Recreations*, 42-3.

[59] Malcolmson, 145-6; Cranston: *John Locke*, 243; Archenholz, 323.

[60] A. Nevins: *Ordeal of the Union* (2 vols., New York & London, 1947), I, 56; Kiernan, 117.

[61] Le Bon: *The Crowd*, 2, 5, 7-9, 12-4, 35, 45; Friedrich, 71-2; Billacois, 7, 81-2, 152; McClelland, 10-4, 210-5; Hamilton, II, 262-3.

PART III Avoidance of Revolution

[1] W.S. Churchill: *Lord Randolph Churchill* (1907), 481.

XIV The 'Jew Bill', Pitt and the Militia

[1] T. Perry: *Public Opinion, Propaganda and Politics in Eighteenth Century England* (Cambridge, Mass., 1962), 143; J. Western: *The English Militia in the Eighteenth Century* (1965), 178, 151.

[2] Smollett, III, 391, 360; HW, IV, 411; Sir C. Petrie: The Elibank Plot, *T.R.H.S.* 4th ser., XIV (1931), 175-92; Monod: *Jacobitism and the English People 1688-1788*, 84, 88, 205-9, 217-9, 242, 345.

[3] Walpole: *Memoirs of the Reign of King George II*, I, 12, 17-9, 141, 152-3, 32; 49, 6; Clark (ed): *The Memoirs and Speeches of James, 2nd Earl Waldegrave 1742-1763*, 158, 206; GM 1753, 292-3; J. Clark: *The Dynamics of Change* (Cambridge, 1982), 36, 43; Monod, 33-4, 230; L. Sutherland: The City of London and the Devonshire-Pitt Administration 1756-7, *Proceedings of the British Academy*, 46 (1960), 148-9; Rogers: *Whigs and Cities*, 173-4.

[4] C. Roth: *A History of the Jews in England* (Oxford, 1949), 205-6, 214-5; L. Sutherland: Samson Gideon and the Reduction of Interest 1749-50, *E.H.R.* XVI (1946), 16-8, 21-2.

[5] L. Sutherland: Edmund Burke and the Relations Between Members of Parliament and their Constituents, *Studies in Burke and his Time* (1968), 1008; Perry, 75-6; Boswell: *London Journal*, 146; Roth, 216-9; G. Shelton: *Dean Tucker*, 80-4.

[6] Robson: *The Oxfordshire Election of 1754*, 89; PH XIV, 1394; Perry, 85-7, 118-20; Lecky I, 264-5; Smollett, III, 348.

[7] Robson, 94; PH XV, 91-4, 101-2, 119-28, 132-3, 154-5; Smollett, III, 384n on the bishops; Walpole, I, 240-1; Egmont: *Diary*, I, 360; W. McNeill: *Plagues and Peoples* (Harmondsworth, 1979), 161.

[8] HW XXXV, 150; Robson, 106, 97-8; HC 1754-1790, I, 59-61; A. Babington: *A House in Bow Street* (1969), 102-3; J. Treherne: *The Canning Enigma* (1989), 48.

[9] Perry, 121-2, 179, 41-2.

[10] Clark (ed.), 153, 173, 64-72; HW, IV, 411; Walpole II, 142; Clark, 237-9; Browning: *The Duke of Newcastle*, 232, 241, 248-52, 261; Yorke, II, 309-10.

[11] Yorke, II, 311, 279, 337; Clark, 280; HW, IV, 585; V, 12-3; Walpole, II, 184-5; Clark (ed.), 185; AR 1758, 11; M. Peters: *Pitt and Popularity* (Oxford, 1980), 61-3; P. Langford: Pitt and Public Opinion 1757, *E.H.R.* LXXXVIII (1973), 54; Sutherland: The City of London and the Devonshire-Pitt Administration 1756-7, 153-8; *Turner's Diary*, 55, 62; Grenville, I, 172-3.

[12] Hoskins, 31: Charlesworth (ed.), 86-7; GM 1756, 408-9, 447-8; Wearmouth, 26-7; HW, IV, 585; V, 12-3; Yorke, II, 337; in his massive study, Dr Clark strongly contends that Pitt won office not through his support out of doors but through behind-the-scenes intrigue, 8-9, 231-82.

[13] HW, V, 17; Sir C. Grant Robertson: *Chatham and the British Empire* (1966), 71; Clark (ed.) 152.

[14] Walpole II, 223-5; Add. Mss 32867, fol. 97; Colley, 274; Williams: *The Life of William Pitt, Earl of Chatham*, I, 280-1, 288, 293, 302-10.

[15] Kemp: *Sir Francis Dashwood*, 12, 26-7, 162, 166; Feiling, 49, 43; Schwoerer, 190-5; Pocock: *Politics, Language and Time*, 120-7, 146; GM 1756, 408; see Ch. VI above.

[16] I. Roots: *The Great Rebellion 1642-1660* (1966), 57; PH X, 405; Hervey, 154.

[17] Western, 104-7, 116, 127-34; Nef, 202; Middleton: *The Bells of Victory*, 9; Williams, I, 278-9; Yorke, II, 262-5; PH, XV, 743-4.

[18] Walpole, II, 181, 208, 216, 246-8, 254, 259; HW, V, 10, 23-4, 100; GM 1756, 432-3; Williams, I, 294-317.

[19] Langford, 57, 65-6, 70-2; Williams, I, 311-3; Clark (ed.) 205-6; HW, V, 87; Yorke, II, 372, 410-1.

[20] HW, V, 87; Clark, 295, 366, 385-6; D. Jarrett: *The Begetters of Revolution* (1973), 36;

Williams, I, 375-7; PH IX, 1291; Namier: *England in the Age of the American Revolution*, 73-4; for a blow-by-blow account of the high political manoeuvrings, see Clark, 354-447.

[21] Western 138-40.

[22] G. Lefebvre: *The French Revolution from 1793-1799* (2 vols., 1962-4), 45-7; J. Godechot: *The Counter-Revolution* (Princeton, 1981), 212-3, 322-5; R Brooks: Domestic Violence and America's Wars, in Graham and Gurr (eds.): *Violence in America*, 311-20; L. Glassey: Local Government in Jones (ed.), *Britain in the First Age of Party*, 166; Beloff, 115, 121, 127; Wesley: *Journal*, III, 135-41, 151, 182-6; IV, 223-4; R. Knox: *Enthusiasm* (Oxford, 1950), 50n.

[23] Western, 128-9, 251, 254, 245, 140-1; Langford: *Public Life*, 266-7.

[24] GM 1757, 430, 384; Western, 122, 130-1, 140-1, 298-300; Shelton: *English Hunger and Industrial Disorders*, 111, 129.

[25] Hayter, 98-9; Western, 295; Walpole, II, 271.

[26] Walpole, II, 271; GM 1757; 431; Hayter, 100-3; Western, 291-2; Landau, 291.

[27] GM 1757, 430; Western, 292-4, 298; Sir F. Hill: *Georgian Lincoln* (Cambridge, 1986), 106-7; Hayter, 99-105.

[28] Yorke, III, 35-6; Hill, 107; Sir L. Namier and J. Brooke: *Charles Townshend* (1964), 55; GM 1757, 529; Shelton, 111, 129.

[29] E. Wigham: *Strikes and the Government 1893-1974* (1976), 91-2.

[30] GM 1757, 591; Yorke, III, 33; Western, 295-6, 141-2; Peters, 106-7; Walpole, II, 272; Hayter, 107.

[31] PH XV, 871-926; BL Add. Mss 32880 fols. 172, 180-2; Yorke, III, 44-52; Peters, 106-12, 29, 149-50; Browning, 264-5. In his *Bells of Victory*, (esp. 19-22, 49, 139, 211-32) Mr Middleton argues that Pitt's part in the war has been exaggerated by later historians, dazzled by the victories, that his role was largely parliamentary not administrative and that he neither directed nearly every branch of government nor had a long-term strategy. Not only historians, however, but many contemporaries thought Pitt had made a decisive contribution. Waldegrave was a contemporary, and his other remark that Pitt had 'hitherto conducted the war with spirit, vigour and tolerable success' was evidently written, Dr Clark points out, before the great victories of 1759. Clark (ed.) 153, also 220-1.

[32] GM 1761, 137-8; Wearmouth, 30, 82; Western, 141-2, 298; *The Leeds Advertiser* in Morsely, 35; Cav., 1, 334.

[33] J. McCague: *The Second Rebellion* (New York, 1968), 178-9, 74-5, 93, 103, 121, 135-7, 149, 112, 137, 148; Friedrich; 67-8; J. Richardson: *The New York Police* (New York, 1970), 138, 143, 144-5. Mr Richardson thinks the casualties were lower than the contemporary figures, but gives no evidence.

[34] Western, 129, 253-4, 296-300, 141; McCague, 17-9, 95, 8-9, 118-9, 192, 128, 174, 187; Richardson, 132-3, 140, 146.

[35] McCague, 184-6, 165-6, 174-5; Richardson, 145-6; GM 1758, 191, 239.

[36] HW, V, 491; Walpole, III, 58-9, 108-9; Western, 154-61, 171, 176-83; Z. Rashed: *The Peace of Paris* (Liverpool, 1951), 176; Ketton-Cremer, 155-6; *Turner's Diary*, 175; G. Nordman: Choiseul and the Last Jacobite Attempt of 1759, in Cruickshanks (ed.) 201-17; McLynn: *Charles*, 449-54

XV   Wilkes and Liberty

[1] R. Sedgwick (ed): *The Letters from George III to Lord Bute*, 232; B. Dobrée (ed): *The Letters of King George III*, 52; C. Chenevix Trench: *Portrait of a Patriot*, 90, 291.

[2] HC 1754-90, I, 348-9; The Political Register 1768 (2), 255.

[3] K. Feiling: *The Secret Tory Party 1714-1832* (1938), 8; But the story is doubtful. See HC 1754-90, I, 348-9.

[4] Bleackley: *The Life of John Wilkes*, 17; Kemp: *Sir Francis Dashwood*, 130-6; G Martelli: *Jemmy Twitcher* (1962), 43-9; *Grenville Papers*, I, 176-7, 222-4; Chenevix Trench, 11, 13, 21-4.

[5] Lecky, III, 134; J. Boswell: *On the Grand Tour, Italy, Corsica and France 1765-6* (1955), 58; J. Brewer: *Party Ideology and Popular Politics at the Accession of George III* (Cambridge, 1981), 163, 171, 196-9.

[6] Boswell, 53; Sir L. Namier: *Personalities and Powers* (1955), 39-58; Brooke: *King George III,* 258-9; Dobre (ed.), 113, 122.

[7] Cav., I, 232; for Halifax, see D.N.B.; A. Hamilton: *The Infamous Essay on Woman* (1978), 105, 117; Martelli, 39-41; Gray: The Candidate of The Cambridge Courtship, 11. 15-7; H. Walpole: *Memoirs of the Reign of King George III* (4 vols., 1851), I, 272; R. Porter: Mixed Feelings, the Enlightenment and Sexuality in Boucé (ed.), *Sexuality in Eighteenth Century Britain,* 12-3.

[8] William Dowdeswell in *Burke Corr.* II, 70; Lecky, I, 183.

[9] J. Almon: *The Correspondence of the Late John Wilkes* (5 vols., 1805), I, 33-45, 91-2; HC 1754-90, III, 311; P. Quennell: *Four Portraits* (1945), 195; R. Rea: *The British Press in Politics 1760-1774* (Lincoln, Nebraska, 1963), 23-32.

[10] H. Butterfield: *George III, Lord North and the People 1779-1780* (1949), 3; Clark: *The Dynamics of Change,* 22-3, 26, 454-6; Brewer, 10-2; AR 1762, 47.

[11] O. Hufton: *Europe, Privilege and Protest 1730-1789* (1980), 124, 128: Shelton: *English Hunger and Industrial Disorders,* 141-7; Brewer, 17-8; G Rudé: *Wilkes and Liberty* (Oxford, 1962), 103-4.

[12] W. Fryer: King George III, His Political Character and Conduct, *Renaissance and Modern Studies,* VI (1962), 82-4; R. Pares: *King George III and the Politicians* (Oxford, 1953), 99-102; H. Butterfield: *George III and the Historians* (1957), 253-60.

[13] AR 1763, 40-2; Sharpe: *London and the Kingdom,* III, 69; AR 1761, 237; Williams: *Pitt,* I, 158-9, II, 121; J. Brewer: The Misfortunes of Lord Bute, *H.J.* XVI, I (1973), 5; Cav., I 10.

[14] Brewer, 5-6; Sedgwick (ed.), 167-71; Brooke, 100-1.

[15] Churchill: The Candidate, II, 281-2; Shelburne's Memorandum on the events of 1762, in Fitzmaurice: *Shelburne,* I, 186; Almon, I, 75; cf. J. Schumpeter: *Capitalism, Socialism and Democracy* (1950), 149.

[16] AR 1763, 34-8; Kemp, 65; P. Wordland: Extra-Parliamentary organisation in the Making, *Parliamentary History* 4 (1985), 115-6, 132; AR 1766, 46-7; PH XVI, 206-7.

[17] Boswell: *London Journal,* 256, 295; PR 1768 (2), 273-80; The *North Briton No. 45* in Hamilton: *The Infamous Essay on Woman,* 79-86; PH XV, 1270; Rashed, 209.

[18] Hamilton, 48, 71, 80; PH XV, 350; Rea, 33-43; Lecky: III, 71, 75; Thomson: *A Constitutional History of England 1642-1801,* 196-7.

[19] Almon, III, 198; I, 100-1; Namier and Brooke: *Charles Townshend,* 101.

[20] Almon, III, 199, 203-7; PH XV, 1360.

[21] AR 1763, 135-9; Almon, I, 103-8; Bleackley, 104; Prebble: *Culloden,* 292-3.

[22] Christie: *Myth and Reality in Late Eighteenth Century British Politics,* 57, 61; S.T. XIX, 984; Yorke: *Hardwicke,* III, 488; Almon, III, 109.

[23] Almon, I, 117; AR 1763, 139, which has "class" not "set"; S.T. XIX, 985, 987-990.

[24] Brewer: *Party Ideology,* 168; Almon, V, 285; R. Postgate: *That Devil Wilkes* (1956), 123; Boswell: *London Journal,* 320; *Grenville Papers,* II, 78.

[25] AR 1763, 87; Rudé, 29; PH XV, 1402; Rea, 48-9, 59-69; S.T., XIX, 1167, 1073.

[26] Almon, I, 139-41; Hamilton, 138-40; Rea, 70-1.

[27] Almon, II, 1-4; PH XV, 1354-61; Rea, 72-4.

[28] *Grenville Papers,* II, 153-5; PR 1768 (3), 221-4; Hamilton, 93-5, 100, 106, 111-6, 120, 145-52, 157-8, 172-3, 176-80; PH XIX, 115.

[29] Postgate, 77, 88; HW, X, 110-1; Walpole, I, 312-4.

[30] Bleackley, 132; Namier: *England in the Age of the American Revolution,* 366-70.

[31] Almon, II, 16-7, 989; Walpole, I, 314, 317-8; Eyck: *Pitt versus Fox,* 133-4; PH XIX, 114.

[32] PH XV, 1380-84; Walpole, I, 331; AR 1763, 144-5; Rea, 77.

[33] *Grenville Papers,* II, 234-5, 239; J. Brewer. English Radicalism in the Age of George III, in Pocock (ed.), *Three British Revolutions* (Princeton, 1980), 334-42.

[34] Postgate, 81n, 88; Almon, II, 36, 41-6; III, 109-15; S.T. XIX, 1075-9; P.R., 1768 (2), 221-4; Hamilton, 157-8, 177-81, 190, 248; *Grenville Papers,* II, 239, 277-8.

[35] PH XV, 1400-3, XVI, 207; Sir C. Grant Robertson (ed.): *Select Statutes, Cases and Documents* (1947), 454.

[36] *Grenville Papers*, III, 163-4, 167-72; Cav., I, 146; Hayter: *The Army and the Crowd*, 130-2, 167, 174-5.

[37] Sedgwick (ed.), 240-1; *Grenville Papers*, III, 169, 175.

[38] PH XVI, 97, 83, 91, 104, 164-5; J. Miller: Origins of the American Revolution (1945), 104-17; L. Gipson: *The Coming of the Revolution 1763-1775* (1954), 90-5, 101-15; Murrin: The Great Inversion, in Pocock (ed.), 387-92; J. Hoffman: *The Marquis* (New York, 1973) 64, 105, 108-14.

[39] Namier and Brooke, 159-60, 167-79; E. Robson: *The American Revolution 1763-1783* (1955), 45, 64-7; Shy: *Towards Lexington*, 312-8, 394-7; Doyle: *The Old European Order 1660-1800*, 49; Murrin in Pocock (ed.), 399.

[40] See Ch. XI above; Brewer, 17-8; AR 1768, 76; Bleackley, 185.

[41] Almon, III, 265-8; AR 1768, 82-3, 36; HC 1754-90, I, 331-2; Chenevix Trench, 215; J. Brewer: The Number 45, in Baxter (ed.), *England's Rise to Greatness*, 367.

[42] Almon, III, 269, AR 1768 86; Rude, 42.

[43] Lecky, III, 132; Hayter, 138-40; Chenevix Trench, 218.

[44] AR 1768, 92; Grafton: *Autobiography*, 199; Rude, 45-6.

[45] Almon, III, 263-5; AR 1768, 84.

[46] S.T. XIX, 1084-92; AR 1768, 100; Bleackley, 197-8; *Grenville Papers*, IV, 279-80.

[47] Rudé, 48-9, S.T. XIX, 1093-4; *Grenville Papers*, IV, 293.

[48] AR 1768, 108; Walpole, II, 176-7; III, 136, 205; Almon, III, 274-6.

[49] Almon, III, 277-9; Hickey, I, 92-4; AR 1771, 196-9; Cav., I, 336; Rudé, 50-1.

[50] Rudé, 51-2; AR, 1768, 108, 110-12, 9; Hickey: *Memoirs*, I, 94; Dobrée, 57; J. Brooke: *The Chatham Administration* (1956), 357-8.

[51] AR 1768, 111, 151; PR, 1768, (3) 179-86; (2) 421; Cav., I, 67-73, 317; O Sherrard: *The Life of John Wilkes* (1930), 187.

[52] AR 1768, 137-8; PR, 1768, (3) 171-9; Almon, III, 280; J. Brewer: The Wilkites and the Law in Brewer and Styles (ed.), *An Ungovernable People*, 132.

[53] *Burke Corr.* I, 349.

[54] PH XVI, 381; AR 1768, 96-124; Grafton, 188-90, 202; Walpole, III, 206n; Cav., I, 7-8, 66; Dobrée (ed.) 51-2.

[55] S.T. XIX, 1085, 1098-1116; Bleackley, 201-2.

[56] S.T. XIX; Walpole, III, 223-5; 1754-90, III, 189; Sedgwick (ed.), 157.

[57] AR 1768, 127; P.R. 1768, III, 110-1; Sherrard, 189.

[58] Grafton, 196-201; Fitzmaurice, II, 162; Feiling, 107-8.

[59] Almon, III, 273-6; Cav., I, 139-51, 307-15.

[60] Rudé, 59; AR 1768, 193.

[61] Disraeli: *Sybil*, II, Ch. I.

[62] AR 1768, 193-5; Rudé, 59-61; Cav., I, 95-9

[63] Walpole, III, 297; Postgate, 138; Grafton, 227-8; PH XVI, 538-40, 546-75; Bleackley, 211-7; Hamilton: *First of Grenadier Guards*, II, 201.

[64] AR 1769, 72, 75; PH XVI, 577-80; Bleackley, 217-218.

[65] Rudé, 61-2; Cav., I, 354-5; AR 1769, 75, 79, 82.

[66] AR 1769, 84, 87, 195-6; Cav., I, 380; Rudé, 63-5; *Grenville Papers*, IV, 415-7; Dobrée (ed.), 57.

[67] AR 1769, 90; Fitzmaurice, II, 188; Bleackley, 221-23; PH XVI, 585-8.

[68] Dobrée (ed.), 57; Cannon: *Parliamentary Reform 1640-1832*, 63-4; Rudé, 135, 138, 70-1.

[69] Feiling, 109-10; Hoffman, 217-251.

[70] PH XVI, 845; Walpole, IV, 38-43; *Burke Corr.* II, 96-7; Grafton, 229, 195; Forbes: *Hume's Philosophical Politics*, 134, 187-92; Woodforde, 66.

[71] J. Cannon (ed.): *The Letters of Junius* (Oxford, 1978), 191.

[72] A. Turberville: *Men and Manners in the Eighteenth Century* (Oxford, 1929), 47; Rea, 201; Watson, 98; Cav., II, 89-116, 121-48.

[73] P. Thomas: The Beginning of Parliamentary Reporting in Newspapers 1768-1774, *E.H.R.* LXXIV (1959), 623-5; Cav., II, 257, 324; Rea, 7, 141-3, 150-1, 204-5; Lecky,

III, 257; AR 1771, 81, 183-4; PH, X, 802-3.

74 Cav., II, 383, 405-6; AR 1771, 131, 186, 188; Almon, V, 57-61; P. Thomas: John Wilkes and the Freedom of the Press (1771, *B.I.H.R.* XXXIII (1960), 87-91; Rea, 206-8.

75 Dobrée (ed.), 76-7; Almon, V, 61; Rude, 159-60; Postgate, 177; AR 1771, 64-6, 187-8; Thomas, 92-3; Cav., II, 407, 421-2, 436-8; 448.

76 AR 1771, 68; Cav., II, 442-67; PH XVII, 145-55; Thomas, 94.

77 AR 1771, 67-70, 85, 105; Rudé, 162-3; *Brickdale Diary*, (in Bristol University Library) V, 43-67; Cav., II, 467-80; Thomas, 93-97.

78 AR 1771, 117, 121, 142-3, 146; Sharpe, III, 120-3; Postgate, 181-2.

79 Bleackley, 277; Rudé, 169, Sharpe, III, 134.

80 AR 1773, 90-5; Sharpe, 137; Sherrard, 258-9.

81 H. Walpole: *Last Journals* (2 vols Doran ed. 1859), I, 163-5, 262, 420-1; Bleackley, 282-5; Rudé, 170-1.

82 HC 1754-90, I, 334; Bleackley, 287.

83 Walpole: *Last Journals*, I, 525-6; II, 173; PH XXI, 897; PH XIX, 811, 1339-40.

84 PH XVIII, 183-4, 217-9, 358-77, 736; XIX, 115-6, 1061-2, 1007-8.

85 PH XVIII, 238-40, 734-5, 1009-10, XIX, 418-27, 563-76, 708, 791, 813, 815, 1006-7, 1343.

86 Rudé: *Hanoverian London 1714-1808*, 174-5; Eyck, 210.

87 PH XVIII, 1286-98.

88 PH XVIII, 1297-8; *Public Advertiser* in Bleackley, 305, 68.

89 PH XX, 242-6, 309-20.

90 Boswell: *Johnson,* 895-6; Postgate, 200.

91 PH XX, 309-20, 242-6, 280-2.

92 AR 1763, 40-2; Brewer: *Party Ideology,* 252-6.

93 Sedgwick (ed.), 208; Christie: *Myth and Reality,* 198; E. Burke: *Thoughts of the Causes of the Present Discontents,* in *Edmund Burke on Government, Politics and Society* (B. Hill ed., 1975), 80-1.

94 PH XVII, 145-50.

95 PH XVII, 147.

96 PH XVI, 670, 698, 892; Cav., I, 229, 234-5; Rea, 142-3, 176-88, 252; Feiling, 111, (Chatham).

97 AR 1763, 40-2; PH XV, 1331; *North Briton No. 45,* in Hamilton, 83.

98 Lecky, III, 74; Brooke: *Chatham Administration,* 230; PH XIX, 575.

99 R. Rovere: *Senator Joe McCarthy* (1960), 204; F. Brady: *Boswell's Political Career* (New Haven and London, 1965), 36, 46-7.

100 Sherrard, 37.

101 Forbes, 130; Colley, 173; Brewer, 21; Monod, 33-4, 85-6, 92, 230-1, 345-6; See Introduction and Ch. III above; Rudé: *Wilkes and Liberty,* 46; Brooke, 358.

102 Rudé, 196; R. Cobb: *A Second Identity* (1969), 275, 278; AR 1771, 83; Lascelles: *The Life of Charles James Fox,* 33.

103 Cav.. II, 468-75; AR 1769, 198; Cannon (ed.), 25; *The Brickdale Diary,* V, 27th March 1771.

104 Quennell, 195; P. Kelly: Radicalism and Public Opinion in the General Election of 1784, *B.I.H.R.* XLV (1972), 83-4.

105 J. Steven Watson: *The Reign of George III* (Oxford, 1960), 138-9; *Burke Corr.* II, 155.

106 Fielding: *An Enquiry,* 330-4; HW, X, 274; Lintott: *Violence in Republican Rome,* 1-5; 89, 200-8; R. Porter: *Gibbon* (1988), 28-30, 80, 109-10.

107 Hayter, 136-9; AR 1763, 99.

108 cf. Tilly in Graham and Gurr (eds.), 110; AR 1771, 89, 91; Dobrée (ed.), 78; and eg. Cav.. I, 323.

109 Rudé, 181-3; *Grenville Papers,* IV, 425n (Mrs Montague); Shoemaker: *The London Mob in the Early Eighteenth Century,* 284-5; AR 1779, 198-201, 285; Walpole, II, 342-3, 350; Lascelles, 80.

110 AR 1771, 83; Cav.. II, 454n; Rudé, 15, 181-3.

[111] See Ch. XVII below; 1768, 3, 118; Brewer in Brewer and Styles (eds.), 133-4.

[112] Brooke: *King George II*, 149.

[113] AR 1770, 111; Cav.. I, 309; Sherrard, 177.

[114] Cav.. II, 468-74.

[115] Canetti: *Crowds and Power*, 17-21, 66-7, 379-82; *Grenville Papers*, IV, 264; Walpole: *Memoirs of George III*, 111, 314.

[116] *Burke Corr*. II, 51-2; PH XVIII, 155; XX, 1379; Butterfield: *George III, Lord North and the People 1779-1780*, 225-6; Burke (Hill ed.), 80-1.

[117] PH XIX, 121; Colley: Eighteenth Century English Radicalism before Wilkes, 14.

[118] Kramnick, 172-7; PH XV, 133; XIX, 136, 570; PH XVI, 748.

[119] PH XVI, 696, 804, 805; Cav.. II, 480.

[120] PH XVI, 748, 699; Cav.. I, 29, 126, 308, 525; II, 475; *Brickdale's Parliamentary Diary*, V, 27th March 1771; AR 1768, 27.

[121] PH XVI, 961, 698; Cav.. I, 6, 18; AR 1768, 271.

[122] M.A.J. Wheeler-Booth: The Stansgate Case, *The Table*, 1961, 23-56.

[123] Cav.. I, 144; *Burke*, VI, 126-31; PH XVI, 819-20.

[124] Almon, IV, 14-9; Burke (Hill ed.), 98; Cav.. I, 306-18, 6-30; PR 1768 (2), 421; AR 1769, 69, 75-77, 80-1; Brewer in Brewer and Styles (eds.), 148-9.

[125] AR 1769, 198; Radzinowicz, I, 55-6; Rudé, 203-4; the Kennedy brothers were reprieved in 1770, see Ch. VII above.

[126] S.T. XIX, 1172-6; Cav.. II, 99, 105, 121-3, 127, 133, 139-42; PH XVI, 819, 1306-7; Rea, 116-9, 158.

[127] P.R. 1768, (3), 119-20; Brewer, in Brewer and Styles (eds.), 143, 148.

[128] Brooke: *King George III*, 254-5, 176-7, 152.

[129] Rea, 224.

[130] Colley: *Namier*, 63-4.

[131] Burke, I, 92 (March 7th, 1771).

[132] eg. North in Cav.., I, 351.

[133] Pares, 49n; Sherrard, 298; PR 1768 (2), 407.

[134] PH XVIII, 261.

XVI   The Gordon Riots

[1] Cowper: *Table Talk*, II 318-23 in *The Poetical Works of William Cowper* (H. Milford, ed., 1950), 23; Lecky, III, 523; L. Mercier: *Tableau de Paris* (Amsterdam, 1783), VI, 26-8.

[2] AR 1780, 261.

[3] Butterfield: *King George III, Lord North and the People 1779-80*, v-vi, 27, 35; J. Cannon: *The Fox-North Coalition* (Cambridge, 1969), xi.

[4] PH XX, 1111; Butterfield, 55-6, 61-4, 129-30; Cowper's *Table Talk* (written January 1781) 11 192-201.

[5] AR 1779, 228-9, 233; Mantoux, 411-3; Hammond: *The Skilled Labourer*, 43-5.

[6] PH XX, 639, 665, 1226-8; Butterfield, 89-94, 100-4, 155-7, 169-88; Doyle, 303; AR 1779, 223-4; M. Elliot: *Partners in Revolution* (New Haven and London, 1982), 11-2.

[7] C. Johnson: *Revolution and the Social System* (Stanford, 1964), 13-4, 21; E. Black: *The Association* (Cambridge, Mass., 1963), 33; Butterfield, 184, 187, 225-6, 285-7; J. Gascoigne: Anglican Latitudinarianism and Political Radicalism in the late Eighteenth Century, *History* 71 (1986), 32-3; N. Phillips: Edmund Burke and the County Movement, *E.H.R.* 76 (1961), 257, 260, 275.

[8] Fryer: King George III, 98; PR XVI, 184; Butterfield, 251-2; PH XXI, 184-5, 190-1; and see Ch. XVII below.

[9] PH XIX, 1344; Walpole: *Last Journals*, II, 395; PH XXI, 617-8.

[10] Boswell: *Johnson*, 1174; J. de Castro: *The Gordon Riots* (1926), 8-10; C. Hibbert: *King Mob* (1958), 18-9.

[11] J. Steven Watson, 197-9, 235; S.T. XXI, 645; de Castro, 4-9; Butterfield, 75; B. Bailyn:

Voyagers to the West (1987), 26, 31, 43-4, 49; B. Bailyn: *The Peopling of British North America* (1987), 9, 39.

[12] The Irish Parliament passed a similar bill; AR 1780, 256; Lecky, III, 508-9; de Castro, 5n, 13-4; Black, 135-6, 142-4.

[13] PH XX, 280-2; see CH. XV above.

[14] R. Watson: *The Life of Lord George Gordon* (1795), 6, 12-7; HC 1754-90, II, 513; P.M. June 1780, 407.

[15] Hickey: *Memoirs*, II, 81-8; PR XVI, 172-8.

[16] Hibbert, 7; PR XVI, 337, 347; PH XXI, 149.

[17] de Castro, 20-3; Walpole: *George III*, II, 378-80; PH XVIII, 1011; PH XIX 1094, 1122, 1198-9; Lecky, III, 502-3.

[18] Hibbert, 20-5; Walpole: *George II*, III, 124; Ayling: *John Wesley*, 264-5.

[19] Rogers: Crown and People in the Gordon Riots, in Hellmuth (ed.), 42; Rudé: *Hanoverian London*, 174-5, 220-1; R. Watson, 15; Hickey, II, 72; PH XIX, 1198-9, 1331-2.

[20] PH XX, 622, 1107-8; PR XVI, 346; PM April 1780, 282, 321; PR XVII, 128-9, 352-8; Walpole: *Last Journals*, II, 362-3, 410.

[21] Walpole: *Last Journals*, II, 362; HW XXV, 55; HC 1715-90, II, 514; PR XVII, 128-9; Hibbert, 165-9; Schilling: *Conservative England and the Case against Voltaire*, 102.

[22] *Lord George Gordon's Narrative*, B.L. Add. Ms 42129, 1, 8-13; AR 1780, 257; S.T. XXI, 568-70; de Castro, 24-31.

[23] AR 1780, 257; PH XX, 665; Lecky, III, 511; Hibbert, 36-8; Walpole, II 403-4; HW XXXIII, 175.

[24] PH XXI, 664-9; de Castro, 38; Hibbert, 40-3.

[25] S.T. XXI, 508-9, 514; 523-6, 529; *Gordon's Narrative*, 14-22; AR 1780, 258; HW XXXIII, 177; Hibbert, 38, 43-5.

[26] PM June 1780, 420-1; HW XXXIII, 172-8; HW XXV, 54; Hibbert, 45-51; J. Nicholson: *The Great Liberty Riot of 1780* (1985), 36-8.

[27] Walpole, II, 391, 401; PH XIX, 591-3, 670; HW XXV, 53; *Gordon's Narrative*, 21; Hibbert, 42, 65.

[28] CJ, 37, 2nd June 1780; PH XI, 672-88; I. Christie: The Marquis of Rockingham and Lord North's Offer of a Coalition, *E.H.R.* LXIX (1954), 391; Hibbert, 53-5.

[29] de Castro, 56, 48-9, 52, 58-61, 63-4; Rudé, 222.

[30] AR 1780, 260; de Castro, 192, 76-8; Hibbert, 66; PM, June 1780, 434; D.N.B. for Watson.

[31] S.T. XXI, 537; de Castro, 79.

[32] PR XVII, 360; PM, June 1780, 432; de Castro, 80-2.

[33] *Gordon's Narrative*, 45-6, 39-40; Dobrée (ed.), 143; PH XXI, 660-4; PR XVII, 360; Hibbert, 67-9.

[34] de Castro, 82-3, 85; Hibbert, 68-71.

[35] Lecky, III, 514-5; de Castro, 91-2; Hibbert, 73-7; Linebaugh: *The London Hanged*, 335-6.

[36] de Castro, 224-5.

[37] AR 1780, 261; *Gordon's Narrative*, 26-32; S.T. XXI, 664; Walpole, II, 407; de Castro, 85-6, 97-9, 103-5, 74-5.

[38] *Burke's Corr.*, IV, 247; Hibbert, 79-81.

[39] PM, June 1780, 437; Grafton: *Autobiography*, 313; PH XXI, 709; AR 1780, 261; de Castro, 87, 122-3, 131-4.

[40] S.T. XXI, 504; de Castro, 105, 141-3; AR 1780, 262.

[41] Add. Mss. 30866, f.241; *Gordon's Narrative*, 42; Rudé: *Hanoverian London*, 180-1; Bleackley, 362-6.

[42] *Burke Corr.*, IV, 242-3; Add. Mss. 27828, f.127; AR 1780, 261; Rogers, 47-9; Hibbert, 91-2, 103, 111-2; Hayter, 153-7.

[43] HW XXXIII, 192; PM, June 1780, 442; de Castro, 167, 172, 180-1; *Gordon's Narrative*, 57-8.

[44] AR 1780, 264; Money: *Experience and Identity*, 210; Pollock: *Wilberforce*, 11.

[45] Lecky, III, 503n, 520-1; *Gordon's Narrative*, 21.

[46] W.O. 34/103, f.13; de Castro, 56, 51; Sharpe, III, 181-2; Hibbert, 64-5.

[47] de Castro, 72, 119-22; PH XXI, 698.

[48] Boswell: *Johnson*, 1054; Add. Mss. 27828, f.127; Sharpe, III, 185; PR XVII, 362; Rudé, 277, 327, 334-5.

[49] Boswell, 1053.

[50] W.O. 34/103, f.14; S.T. XXI, 664; Hibbert, 55, 63-4, 74, 81-3.

[51] Clode: *The Military Forces of the Crown*, II, 636-7.

[52] PH XXI, 691-8; Holdsworth, X, 364-6, 705-9; see Ch. VII above.

[53] Hibbert, 91-2; AR 1780, 226.

[54] J. Miller: *Religion in the Popular Prints 1600-1832* (Cambridge, 1986), no. 85.

[55] HW XXV, 54; Rudé: *Paris and London in the Eighteenth Century*, 283, 280n, 280, 281; Hibbert, 130-1; Quennell, 118; AR 1780, 275-7.

[56] Rudé, 284, 286; Stevenson, 84.

[57] HW XXXIII, 190, 189; Rudé, 281-3; *Barnaby Rudge*, Ch. 52; S.T. XXI, 620.

[58] S.T. XXI, 578, 514, 529; Rudé: *Hanoverian London*, 221.

[59] *Gordon's Narrative*, 28-31, 38-40, 47-8; de Castro, 66, 87.

[60] *Gordon's Narrative*, 42, 47-53; HW XXXIII, 185, 175; S.T. XXI, 571, 578, 510, 638, 629-30; PM June 1780, 430, 444; de Castro, 113-4, 142-3, 156, 181-2, 235, 66, 194; Hibbert, 88-9.

[61] *Gordon's Narrative*, 1, 8-10; S.T. XXI, 526; Lecky, III, 510; Miller: *Origins of the American Revolution*, 346, 354.

[62] Stevenson, 77-8, 86.

[63] Hibbert, 84, 103-4, 123-6; Nicholson, 67; Rogers, 49-50; S.T. XXI, 653-88; Ch. XIV above.

[64] HW XXV, 63; de Castro, 133, 219, 234; Rudé: *Paris and London*, 279-80.

[65] Shoemaker, 303-4; Rogers, 52; Rudé, 289-92.

[66] de Castro, 108, 161; Hayter, 166.

[67] de Castro, 18, 24, 57; Hibbert, 25-6.

[68] Godechot: *The Counter-Revolution 1789-1804*, 329-36.

[69] F. Furet: *Interpreting the French Revolution* (Cambridge, 1981), 123, Zagorin: *Rebels and Rulers 1500-1660*; I, 7-10, 17-24; Johnson, 10, 28-9.

[70] de Castro, 187; Butterfield, 379-80; K. Chorley: *Armies and the Art of Revolution* (1943), 38-9, 108, 244-5.

[71] R. Watson, 22-3.

[72] R. Watson, 22; AR 1780, 262; Boswell: *Johnson*, 1055; de Castro, 105, 229.

[73] Ph XXI, 694; *Burke Corr.* IV, 241; HW XXV, 63; McNeill: *The Pursuit of Power*, 186; Nicholson, 48, 59, 64.

[74] HW XXXII, 189-92, 197; Boswell, 1055; Hibbert, 107-9, 124; P. Rogers: Grub Street, 119.

[75] *Gordon's Personal Narrative*, 48; Walpole: *Last Journals*, II, 312; de Castro, 192, 202-4; PH XXI, 689.

[76] Butterfield, 27, 35, 379; de Castro, 110, 202; PH XXI, 393.

[77] R. Watson, 21; Walpole, II, 469; Hayter, 183-4; Hibbert, 55, 63-4, 79, 82-3, 93-4.

[78] PH XXI, 689; HW XXXIII, 194; Hayter, 184; de Castro, 203-4; Lecky, III, 521-2.

[79] PH XXI, 694, 730; *Burke Corr.* IV, 256; de Castro, 182-3.

[80] HW XXV, 61-2; de Castro, 217-31; *Gordon's Personal Narrative*, 61-3; McLynn: *Crime*, 238-9; Chorley, 24.

[81] Watson, 31; Stevenson, 76; Nicholson, i-ii; I. Christie: *Wars and Revolutions* (1982), 138.

[82] Walpole's descriptions in de Castro, 55, and HW XXXIII, 186.

[83] AR 1780, 262-3; HW XXXIII, 193; Hayter, 3, 16, 166, 175, 182-6; Whitworth: *The Grenadier Guards*, 32-3.

[84] Stevenson, 90; J. Thompson (ed.): *English Witnesses of the French Revolution* (Oxford, 1938), 52-3; D. Bindman: *The Shadow of the Guillotine, Britain and the French Revolution* (1989), 36, 14-5; McLynn: *Crime*, 237-8.

XVII Aftermath and Recovery

[1] *Autobiography*, 192 (World's Classics, Oxford, 1907); Boswell, 11th June 1784, 1292; Bleackley: *Life of John Wilkes*, 376; *Lord Eldon's Anecdote Book*, 16.

[2] Rudé: *Paris and London*, 275; *Burke's Corr.* IV, 247–50, 254–6; AR, 1780, 277–86; Campbell: *Lives of the Lord Chancellors*, VIII, 37–48.

[3] Some Thoughts on the Approaching Executions and Some Additional Reflections on the Executions, *Burke* V, 513–21; *Corr.* IV, 247–50, 254–8.

[4] Burke V, 514, 519; Hufton, 281–2; Walpole: *Last Journals*, II, 424; HW XXV, 67; Rudé: *The Crowd in History*, 209.

[5] PH XXI, 694–8; *Burke's Corr.* IV, 255.

[6] ST XXI, 644–7; Walpole, II, 443.

[7] ST XXI, 557, 612n, 647; Walpole, II, 443.

[8] PH XIX, 1254; G. Veitch: *The Genesis of Parliamentary Reform* (1964), 77.

[9] AR 1780, 137–40; de Castro, 229–30; Christie: *Myth and Reality*, 110–3.

[10] Fitzmaurice: *Shelburne* III, 83–4; HC 1754–1790, I, 86–7; O'Gorman, 295–7; Christie, 109–32.

[11] PH XXI, 680–1; Christie, 111–3; J. Norris: *Shelburne and Reform* (1963), 125–8; Fitzmaurice III, 107.

[12] J. Derry: *Charles James Fox* (1972), 94–5, 99, 105; Cannon: *Aristocratic Century*, 145–6.

[13] Ch. XVI above.

[14] E. Black: *The Association*, (Cambridge, Mass. 1963), 51, 51n; Langford: England 1727–1783, 553; Debrett IX, 713–4; Veitch; 76.

[15] M. Fitzpatrick: Heretical Religion and Radical Politics in Hellmuth (ed.), *The Transformation of Political Culture*, 359; Christie; *Wilkes, Wyvil and Reform* (1962), 78–9; Gascoigne, 29–30.

[16] Money: *Experience and Identity*, 159; Debrett IX, 711, 713; Christie, 114–7, 120, 168; N. Phillips: Edmund Burke and the County Movement, *E.H.R.* 76(1961) 271.

[17] Christie, 123; Walpole II, 364.

[18] *A Letter to a Noble Lord, Burke* V, 118, 116, PH XXI, 190–1, 184–5; Butterfield, 225–60.

[19] Black, 33.

[20] Butterfield, 193–6, 220–2, 375–80; Veitch, 66–7; Jarrett: *The Begetters of Revolution*, 167–8.

[21] Sorel: *Europe and the French Revolution*, 119; W. S. Churchill: *The Hinge of Fate* (1951), 456–7.

[22] R. Chorley: *Armies and the Art of Revolution* (1943), 34, 38–9, 108; Pares: *King George III and the Politicians*, 199, and *E.H.R.*, LVX, 526–9.

[21] Christie: *Wars and Revolutions*, 140; Fitzmaurice III, 225.

[24] Fitzmaurice III, 137; Walpole II, 526; Elliott: *Partners in Revolution*, 12; P. Kelly: British and Irish Politics in 1785, *E.H.R.* XL (1975), 536, 556.

[25] J Cannon: *The Fox-North Coalition* (Cambridge, 1969), 163; Dobrée (ed.), 160–1, 164–5; PH XXII, 692–3.

[26] Debrett IX, 709, 736; Black, 107; Christie: *Wilkes, Wyvill and Reform*, 191–2; HC 1754–1790, III, 408–9; PH XXIV, 22–3; Dobrée (ed.), 173–4; Walpole II, 591–2.

[27] Cannon, 108–12; Sir L. Namier: *Crossroads of Power* (1962), 171; Feiling, 157.

[28] Cannon, 128–31; P. Kelly: British Politics 1783–4, *B.I.H.R.*, LIV (1981), 62–4.

[29] Debrett XII, 421, 447–9, 516–7; Ehrman, I, 129–34; GM 1784, 70; Cannon, 185–7.

[30] GM 1784, 204; Ehrman I, 140–1; G. B. Shaw: *Everybody's Political What's What* (1944), 30.

[31] Debrett XIII, 205–7; Lascelles: *Fox*, 144.

[32] Debrett XIII, 268–77; Derry: *Fox*, 201; Kelly: British Politics 1783–4, 73, 77.

[33] HC 1754–1790, I, 89–96; O'Gorman, 295–7; Kelly: Radicalism and Public Opinion in the General Election of 1784, *B.I.H.R.* XLV (1972), 88.

[34] AR 1784–5, 191–2; GM 1784, 314, 381–2; McAdams: *Electioneering Techniques in Populous Constituencies 1784–96*, 33–4, 43, 47; HC 1754–1790, I, 337; Derry, 207–8; Pitt's phrase, Ehrman I, 217–8.

[35] Paine: *Rights of Man*, 71–3, 131, 191–2; J. Clark: *Revolution and Rebellion* (Cambridge, 1986), 90; Brooke, 254–5.

[36] Dobrée (ed.), 128.

[37] C. Churchill: *The Candidate* in *Poetical Works* (2vols. 1804),11. 277–8.

[38] L. Colley: The Apotheosis of George III: Loyalty, Royalty and the British Nation 1760–1820, *P.&P.* 102 (1984), 95, 102–4; Brooke, 230–1, 316–7; cf. Paine: *Rights of Man*, 128.

[39] Colley, 104; Langford, 581–2; See head of chapter.

[40] Colley, 94; Ayling: *Edmund Burke*, 120–1; Butterfield, 298; Ehrman I, 152.

[41] Feiling, 145; Cannon, 237.

[42] J. Brewer: Rockingham, Burke and Whig Political Argument, *H.J.* XVII, (1975), 196.

[43] Cannon, 113–4; AR 1781, 137–40.

[44] Cannon (ed.): *The Letters of Junius*, 426.

[45] Cannon, 233, 86; GM 1783, 89–90, 171, 263, 266–7, 345–6, 357, 626, 711; J. Prebble: *Mutiny* (Harmondsworth, 1972), 211–59; Walpole II, 579–80, 601, 619, Christie: *Wilkes, Wyvill and Reform*, 221.

[46] Brooke, 218.

[47] Ehrman, I, 161, 217–23; C. Bayley: *Imperial Meridian 1780–1830* (1989), 2–3; Lascelles: *Fox*, 174; McAdams, 50–1.

[48] Ehrman I, 161, 253–4, 254n; Crouzet in Dickinson (ed.), *Britain and the French Revolution 1789–1815* 189–91; Hibbert: *King Mob*, Woodforde, 286–7, 361; GM 1787, 144–7; AR 1789, 208; Sorel, 120–2.

[49] Ehrman I, 164, 223–8, 234, 608–9; Young, 212, 251; Cannon: *Parliamentary Reform 1640–1832*, 91–4.

[50] W. Rubinstein: The End of Old Corruption in Britain 1780–1860, *P.&P.* 101 (1983) 55–7, 71–3, 77; R. Harris: *Political Ideas 1760–1792* (1963), 157–8; Dobrée (ed.), 192–3; Brewer: *The Sinews of Power*, 86–7.

[51] PH XXV, 888–94; D. Philips: 'A New Engine of Power and Authority', The Institutionalisation of Law Enforcement in England 1780–1830 in V. Gattrell, R. Lenman and G. Parker, (eds.): *Crime and the Law* (1980), 168.

[52] Radzinowicz: *A History of the Criminal Law* III, 121–7, 133–7.

[53] Ehrman II, 124–9; PD XIX (1811) LXXVI–VII; PH XXVI, 1058; see Ch. VII above.

[54] PH XXV, 391–2, 431–2; PH XXI 388–90; R. Hughes: *The Fatal Shore* (1987), 39–40, 615, 66, 72; PH XXVIII, 1223–5; J. Holland Rose: *William Pitt and National Revival* (1911), 434–43.

[55] Hibbert, 158–67; Nicholson, 84–90.

[56] Ehrman II, 57–73, 85–6; G. Ditchfield: The Parliamentary Struggle over the Repeal of the Test and Corporation Acts, 1787–1790, *E.H.R.* LXXXIX (1974), 553, 562; Sykes: *Church and State in England in the Eighteenth Century*, 341; F. Lock: *Burke's Reflections on the Revolution in France* (1985), 42–3; J. Cookson: *The Friends of Peace* (Cambridge, 1982), 11–6.

[57] Pollock: *Wilberforce*, 58, 75, 102, 89, 96; Coupland: *Wilberforce*, 94, 101, 103; Wesley's *Journal*, V, 445–6; Vi, 143; Wesley's *Letters* (Gill ed.), 164, 215–6; A. Turberville: *The House of Lords in the Age of Reform, 1784–1837* (1958), 213; see Ch. VII above; Hughes, 145–8.

[58] cf. Fielding in *Joseph Andrews*, quoted in Ch. VI above; Pollock, 82–3, 105–8; Coupland, 93–6, 116; H. Butterfield: Charles James Fox and the Whig Opposition in 1792, *Cambridge Historical Journal* IX (1947–9), 297, 313; Boswell: *Johnson*, 876–8; Fletcher: *Montesquieu and English Politics 1750–1800*, 233–4.

[59] Pollock, 129, 179; AR 1786, 233–4; AR 1790, 194, 197, 204–5.

[60] Brooke, 322–30, 392; PH XXVII, 692–704; J. Derry: *The Regency Crisis and the Whigs in 1788–9* (Cambridge, 1963), 5; I. Christie: George III and the Historians – Thirty Years on, *History* 71 (1986), 206–8; T. Blanning: *The Origins of the French Revolutionary Wars* (1986), 59.

[61] Brooke: 329–41; C. Hibbert: *George IV* (1972), 86–7; Chenevix Trench: *Portrait of a Patriot*, 355.

[62] Brooke, 369–73.

[63] PH XXVII, 704–13; Derry, 67–74, 79; C. Whibley: *William Pitt*, (Edinburgh and London, 1906), 4–6.

[64] PH XXVII, 713–5; Derry, 53–4, 156–65, 169, 116–7, 127–30; Ayling: *Edmund Burke*, 186–91.

[65] Cowper: *On the Queen's Visit to London*, in *The Political Works of William Cowper* (H Milford ed. 1934), 11. 13–4; Ehrman I, 662–6; AR 1789, 200, 202; Brooke, 341–3.

XVIII The Revolutionary Decade

[1] Coupland (ed.): *The War Speeches of William Pitt*, 21; PH XXXII, 465; Paine: *Rights of Man*, 191-2.

[2] Woodforde, 355, 344-9; Cowper: '*Annus Mirabilis 1789*', ll, 32-3, 44-5.

[3] Cowper: 'On the Benefit Received by His Majesty from Sea-bathing.'

[4] J M Thompson (ed.): *English Witnesses of the French Revolution* (Oxford, 1938), 53; C. Yonge: *The Life and Administration of Lord Liverpool* (3 vols, 1868), 13, 16; N. Gash: *Lord Liverpool* (1984), 16, 21; G. Williams: *Artisans and Sans-Culottes* (1968), 6-8; see Introduction above.

[5] C. Robbins: *The Eighteenth Century Commonwealthman* (Cambridge, Mass.1959), 335-45; A. Cobban (ed.): *The Debate on the French Revolution 1789-1800* (1950), 4-6, 14, 59-64; Goodwin: *The Friends of Liberty*, 106-12, 130; W. Hall: *British Radicalism 1791-1797* (New York, 1976), 160-2; Lock: *Burke's Reflections on the Revolution in France*, 42-3, 51-2, 65-9, 77-8; F. Dreyer: The Genesis of Burke's Reflections *J.M.H.* 50 (1978), 464-6, 474-8.

[6] Burke: *Reflections on the Revolution in France* (O'Brien ed.), 18, 22; Lock, 107, 31, 47-9, 132-4, 144, 85-6, 158; Godechot: *The Counter-Revolution*, 65-6; Butterfield: Charles James Fox and the Whig Opposition in 1792, 294-5; J. Boulton: *The Language of Politics in the Age of Wilkes and Burke* (1963), 80-2; Robbins, 347-8; Cobban (ed.), 4-5, 9-10, 436-40;; E. Halevy: *The Growth of Philosophic Radicalism* (1949), 122; Money: *Experience and Identity*, 219-21.

[7] R. Schofield: *The Lunar Society of Birmingham* (Oxford, 1963), 193-201, 357-8; Hole: *Pulpits, Politics and Public Order in England 1760-1832*, 120n; R. Rose: The Priestley Riots of 1791, *P.&P.*18 (1960), 70-2; PH XXIX, 1434; Money, 210, 222-3.

[8] Cookson: *The Friends of Peace*, 12; Rose, 72; Berg, 288-9, 304-8; Schofield, 358.

[9] AR 1791, 25-6; A. Holt: *A Life of Joseph Priestley* (1931), 154-8; Schofield, 359; Rose, 72-3, 81; PH XXIX, 1438-41; Goodwin, 179.

[10] AR 1791, 26; PH XXIX, 1440-1; Rose, 73; Holt, 159-63; Goodwin, 181-2; J. Money: Freemasonry and Loyalism in England, in Hellmuth (ed.), 253-4; Veitch, 185-6.

[11] AR 1791, 26-8; PH XXIX, 1435; Rose, 73-6; P. Brown: *The French Revolution in English History* (1965), 79; Priestley in Cobban (ed.), 424-5; Schofield, 121-7.

[12] AR 1791, 28-9; Ehrman II, 132-3; Rose, 75-6.

[13] Dobrée (ed.), 212; H.M.C. Dropmore II, 133, 140; Rose, 77.

[14] Ehrman II, 133-4; PH XXIX, 1445-6; H.M.C. Dropmore II, 136.

[15] Rose, 82; Holt, 172-5; PH XXIX, 1444; see Ch. XVI above.

[16] Derry: *Charles James Fox*, 313-5; Radzinowicz IV, 135-6; PH XXIX, 435; Goodwin, 181; Brown, 80-2; Cobban (ed.), 424-5.

[17] Hibbert: *King Mob*, 168n; Cowper: *The Task*, V, ll.389-90; HW XXXI, 323, 321; Bindman: *The Shadow of the Guillotine*, 13-5, 33-37, 89; Wordsworth: *The Prelude*, X, 123-4; Thompson: *The Making of the English Working Class*, 80, 163-72; M. Thale (ed.): *Selections from the Papers of the London Corresponding Society 1792-1799* (Cambridge, 1983), 10.

[18] Cobban, (ed.), 336.

[19] Veitch, 202 (Wyvill); Goodwin, 193, 209; ST XXIV, 277; T Schofield: Conservative Political Thought in Britain in Response to the French Revolution, *H.J.* 29,3, (1986),604; Butterfield (Portland), 325.

[20] Veitch, 216, 323; M. Thomis and P. Holt: *Threats of Revolution in Britain 1789-1848*

(1977), 2, 6-7, 11, 13.

[21] Boulton, 88, 134-50, 250, 256-7; W. Doyle: *The Oxford History of the French Revolution* (Oxford, 1989), 169; J. Ann Hone: *For the Cause of Truth* (Oxford, 1982), 12; Paine, 51, 82, 71-2, 59, 143, 156, 160-2, 265-6, 269.

[22] Blanning: *The Origins of the French Revolutionary Wars*, 62, 71-3, 80-2, 87-9, 120-3; Godechot, 154-5; Ehrman II, 42-3, 47-52, 79-80, 87-8, 91-2, 108-10, 120-1, 172-9, 185-93; R. White: *The Age of George III* (1968), 201; Black, 218-21, 228; D. Powell: *Tom Paine* (1985), 213-4.

[23] Ehrman II, 92-4, 106, 149-50, 215-25; Goodwin, 24, 241-8, 252-3, 263.

[24] R. Dozier: *For King, Constitution and Country* (Lexington, Kentucky, 1983), 32-4, 48-67, 90-2; Brown, 83-6; Colley: The Apotheosis of George III, 122; Money: Freemasonry and Loyalism in England, in Hellmuth (ed.), 243-5, 254-5; Woodforde, 427-9; H. Dickinson: Popular Loyalism in Britain in the 1790s, in Hellmuth (ed.); 527-8; Cobban (ed.), 276-7, 415; S. T. Coleridge: *Lectures 1795 on Politics and Religion* (London and Princeton, 1974), 303; N. Roe: *Wordsworth and Coleridge, the Radical Years* (Oxford, 1988), 98-9; E. de Montluzin: *The Anti-Jacobins 1798-1800* (1988), 21; S. Pedersen: Hannah More Meets Simple Simon, *J.B.S.* 25 (1986), 112; Money: *Experience and Identity*, (1986),112; Money: *Experience and Identity*, 231.

[25] Brown, 89, 95-9; Blanning, 148-9, 155-9; Bleackley, 392.

[26] A.J.P. Taylor: *English History, 1914-45* (Oxford, 1965), 14; D.W. Brogan: *Politics and Law in the United States* (Cambridge, 1961), 91.

[27] Nef, 161-3; McKendrick, Brewer, Plumb, 43-6; C. Wright and C. Fayle: *A History of Lloyd's* (1928), 80; *Turner's Diary*, 160.

[28] Goodwin, 286-306, 313; Palmer: *The Age of the Democratic Revolution* II, 477-8; Hall 182-96; ST XXIII, 766; PXXXX, 1575-6; Campbell VIII, 144-6.

[29] Ehrman II 393-6; T. Parsinnen: Association, convention, and anti-parliament in British radical politics, 1771-1848, *E.H.R.* 88 (1973), 514; C. Emsley: Repression, 'terror' and the rule of law in England during the decade of the French Revolution, *E.H.R.* 100 (1985), 809-10; Mrs Thelwall: *The Life of Thelwall* (2 vols. 1837), I, 130-61; Goodwin, 195, 218-20, 320-5, 334-8; Williams, 77-80; Campbell VIII, 306.

[30] Thelwall I, 186-9; ST XXV, 10-1; Roe, 181-2; Goodwin, 334-6; Thomis and Holt, 17-8; ST XXIV, 198-200.

[31] ST XXIV, 201-10; 1293-5; Thelwall, I, 116; Parsinnen, 509-12; J. Dinwiddy: Conceptions of Revolution in the English Radicalism of the 1790s in Hellmuth (ed.), 543-5; Brown, 134-6.

[32] Holdsworth VIII, 397-21; XIII, 161-3; *Lord Eldon's Anecdote Book*, 55-7; Maitland:*The Constitutional History of England*, 478; ST XXIV, 210-32 (where the pamphlet is ascribed to the radical, Felix Vaughan, Hardy's junior counsel), 908-9; W. St Clair: *The Godwins and the Shelleys* (1989), 130-1; Campbell VIII, 305-6.

[33] ST XXIV, 419, 861, 589-602, 653-62, 687-9, 681-2, 708-9, 879, 918-22, 913-6, 1047-65; Campbell VIII, 307, 310; Holdsworth XIII, 162-3; Brown, 127.

[34] ST XXIV, 200-32, 1308, 1362, 1371, 659-60, 681-2, 688-9, 861-5, 1293-1384; PH XXXI, 1088-9; *Lord Eldon's Anecdote Book*, 57.

[35] ST XXIV, 970n, 1383; Campbell VIII, 312, 317-8; Eldon, 101; Williams, 95; Royle and Walvin, 73.

[36] ST XXV, 97, 370-396, 400-2, 713-8, 739-46; PH XXXI, 1095-6; Cambell VIII, 147, 318-26; Ehrman II, 397-8; Thelwall I, 351-61; Holdsworth VIII 317-8; XIII, 163; W. Godwin: *Caleb Williams*, 1794 (Oxford, 1982), preface.

[37] Thompson, 149-53; J. Western: The Volunteer Movement as Anti-Revolutionary Force 1793-1801, *E.H.R.* 71 (1956), 603, 605, 610; Coleridge, 30-1; Cobban (ed.), 17, 130; Bayly: *Imperial Meridian*, 100.

[38] Western, 607-8, 613 and *passim*: Ehrman II, 328-9, 401-2, 486-9; Dozier, 131-55; Dickinson in Hellmuth (ed.) 523-6; R. Wells: *Insurrection, The British Experience 1795-1803* (Gloucester, 1983), 21-2; L. Colley: Whose Nation? Class and National Consciousness in Britain 1750-1830, *P.&P.* 113 (1986), 109, 114; Bohstedt, 49-51, 82, 115.

[39] Goodwin, 164-6; Derry, 336-7; Schilling, 178-80.

[40] A. Booth: Popular Loyalism and Public Violence in the North-West of England 1790-1800, *S.H.* 8 (1983), 299-302; Thompson, 82, 122-3, 130, 141; Brown, 124-5, 183; Goodwin, 265; PH XXXII, 374-5.

[41] M Thomis: *Politics and Society in Nottingham 1785-1835* (New York and Oxford, 1969), 170-9; Booth, 299; Dozier, 160.

[42] Booth, 297-302; Dickinson in Hellmuth (ed.), 529-32; Dozier, 159-61.

[43] Booth, 305-9, 312; Rudé: *The Crowd in History*, 137-9.

[44] P Jones: The Bristol Bridge Riot and its Antecedents, *J.B.S.* XIX, 2 (1980), 83-5; M Harrison: To Raise and Dare Resentment, *H.J.* 26, 3 (1983), 562-7; AR 1793, 45.

[45] AR 1793, 45-6; GM 1793, 951; Jones, 85-6; Harrison, 568-71, 576, 584.

[46] Harrison, 561-2, 572-6, 580

[47] C. Emsley: *British Society and the French Wars, 1793-1815* (1979), 12, 33; J. Stevenson: The London 'Crimp' Riots of 1794, *International Review of Social History* 16 (1971), 40-2.

[48] AR 1794, 24-5; GM 1794, 63; Stevenson, 43-9, 55-7; Erhman II, 451.

[49] Stevenson, 46-55, 58; Rudé: *Hanoverian London*, 253.

[50] R. Wells: *Wretched Faces, Famine in Wartime England 1793-1801* (Gloucester, 1988), 37, 99-105, 420-9; Woodforde, 481; Thompson: Moral Economy, 112-3, 124.

[51] Wells, 135-8; Rudé: *The Crowd in the French Revolution* (Oxford, 1959), 144-57; Pollock; *Wilberforce*, 130-1; Ignatieff: *A Just Measure of Pain*, 98-9; Thale (ed.), 252-5; Goodwin, 372-4; AR 1795, 29.

[52] Wells, 107-17, 430-8; Hall, 202-3; Williams, 99.

[53] Wells, 37, 139-140; Hone, 17-8; Thale (ed.), 314-20; Roe, 146-7, 173-4; Woodforde, 506-7; AR 1795, 37-9.

[54] Ehrman II 455-8; PHXXXII, 272 (Pitt), 470-6 (Erskine); Coupland: *Wilberforce*, 164.

[55] J. Farington: *Diary* (R. Garlik and A. Macintyre (ed.s) New Haven and London, 1978), II, 404, 455; PH XXXII, 367, 377, 383-5; 454-9; Thale (ed.) 322-30; Roe, 145, 153-4; Cookson, 153; Coleridge: Reflections on Having Left a Place of Retirement, l., 48 in *Poetical Works* (Oxford, 1962); Coleridge: *Lectures*, 288; PR XLIII, 186; Wells, 141-3; Western: *The Enlgish Militia in the Eighteenth Century*, 223, 298, 301.

[56] Goodwin, 273-4; Emsley: *British Society*, 48-9; Brown, 131-3; 154; R. Reilly: *William Pitt the Younger* (New York, 1979), 316.

[57] PH XXXII, 277-82, 364-7, 459; PH XIX, 367; Langford: *England 1727-1783*, 583; Hobouse: *Fox*, 203-5, 212; Jarrett: *The Begetters of Revolution* 148-9; Coupland (ed.), 244; Blanning, 158-9; Rosebery: *Pitt*, 28-9; PH XXXI, 450; Goodwin, 395.

[58] PR XLIII, 325; PH XXXI, 1077-85; PH XXXII, 353; Godwin, 2; R. Cobb: *The Police and The People* (Oxford, 1970), 131-50, 205-9, 335-56; C. Emsley: An Aspect of Pitt's 'Terror', *S.H.* 6,2 (1981), 155-74; Emsley: Repression, 802-3, 815, 816, 821, 824; AR 1797, 15-6; Thompson: *The Making of the English Working Class*, 174, 179-80, 192-3; Cookson, 2, 13, 83, 116-7, 259; Williams, 74, 104-6; Goodwin, 29-30, 367-8, 380-3, 404-6, 411-6.

[59] Thelwall I, 165-71; Hall, 152-3; Campbell, VIII, 324; Lefebvre: *The French Revolution* II, 70; Ayer: *Thomas Paine*, 114, 118-9, 128-31; Powell, 194, 218-44.

[60] Emsley: Aspect 156-9, 174; Emsley: Repression, 813-5; 822; Brown, 154.

[61] Hobhouse, 220: Thompson, 181; Emsley: Repression, 814-7.

[62] Ayling: *Edmund Burke*, 99, 116-7, 261; Elliott: *Partners in Revolution*, 3, 7-8, 11-2; R. Kee: *The Green Flag* (1972), 35-7, 41-3; T. Pakenham: *The Year of Liberty* (1972), 29-32; AR 1798, 152; I. Christie: *Stress and Stability in Late Eighteenth Century Britain* (Oxford, 1984), 118-20., 118-20.

[63] Elliott, 21-8, 36-9, 51-2; AR 1798, 154-5; Ehrman II, 221-2, 424; Kee, 42, 44, 52-3, 126, 155.

[64] Kee, 43-4, 58-61, 66-74; AR 1798, 155-6; Elliott: *Partners XIII*, 28-35, 39-50, 71-2, 95-7, 107-8; M. Elliott: *Wolfe Tone* (New Haven and London, 1989), 213-25, 244-50; *Burke Corr.* IX, 117, 26.

[65] Coupland (ed.), 37, 40, 46-7, 56, 69, 94, 249-51; Blanning, 136-7; M. Duffy: British Diplomacy and the French Wars 1789-1815, in Dickinson (ed.), 134-6; Doyle, 255-7;

Ehrman II, 298-9, 303-4, 321-5, 568-78; Godechot, 227-8, 242-5, 256-60.

[66] Elliott: *Partners*, 111-5, 119-21; Elliott: *Wolfe Tone*, 323-32; Kee, 81-4; *Burke Corr*. IX, 222-8; Wells: *Insurrection*, 62-3; Palmer II, 498.

[67] C. Gill: *The Naval Mutinies of 1797* (Manchester, 1913), 262-7; G. Mainwaring and B. Dobrée: *Mutiny, The Floating Republic* (1989), 7, 23; McCord and Brewster: Some Labour Troubles of the 1790s in North East England, 379-83; AR 1797, 207; Coupland (ed.), 144, 163.

[68] AR 1797, 207-8, 219, (History); Mainwaring and Dobrée, 8-11, 14-5, 18-9, 23, 59-65, 245-7, 255-6; Gill, 268-88; D. Walder: *Nelson* (New York, 1978), 220-1; A. Bryant: *The Years of Endurance* (1942), 185-6, 190.

[69] *Lord Eldon's Anecdote Book*, 20.

[70] Mainwaring and Dobrée, 15-6, 101, 125; Elliott: *Partners*, 137-40; AR 1797, 208; Emsley: *British Society*, 52-3.

[71] Mainwaring and Dobrée, 8-11, 23-4; Gill, 6-8, 14-5; Pollock, 157; Deane: *The First Industrial Revolution*, 190-3; Emsley, 59.

[72] AR 1797, 208-9, 293-41; Mainwaring and Dobrée, 36, 39; Gill, 18-21, 25-7, 38, 43, 255n; Bryant, 186-7; Elliot, 143.

[73] Gill, 31-40; Mainwaring and Dobrée, 42-51; AR 1797, 241-4; Bryant, 188-9; AR 1797, 210.

[74] AR 1797, 26, 211-3; *Burke Corr*. IX, 333, 338-9; Mainwaring and Dobrée, 83-5, 92-4; Gill, 47-66, 86-92.

[75] Gill, 68-81; Mainwaring and Dobrée, 89, 94, 97, 108, 113-8; AR 1797, 214, 219; Walder, 222-3.

[76] Mainwaring and Dobrée, 126-7; Gill, 102-6.

[77] Mainwaring and Dobrée, 137-9; Gill, 134-40, 256-7; Cookson, 162; AR 1797, 28, 50, 245-7.

[78] Mainwaring and Dobrée, 188-9; Gill, 110-1, 129-30, 157-61, 249-50, 255-7; Elliot, 143-4.

[79] Mainwaring and Dobrée, 121-2; Gill, 124-8, 381; AR 1797, 31, 33; Bryant, 194-5.

[80] Mainwaring and Dobrée, 148-55, 218; AR 1797, 31-4; Gill, 145, 151-61, 186-8, 382; Bryant, 195.

[81] Gill, 191, 213, 155-6, 192-4, 203-7, 211, 382-3; Mainwaring and Dobrée, 182, 191-4.

[82] Gill, 155-6, 162-81, 213, 257-8; Mainwaring and Dobrée, 175-82; AR 1797, 32, 314; Wells: *Insurrection*, 88.

[83] Mainwaring and Dobrée, 194, 200-1, 250, 254; Gill 181-6; AR, 1797, 216; Bryant, 196-7.

[84] Gill, 214-40; Mainwaring and Dobrée, 216-31, 236; AR 1797, 35; Elliott, 135.

[85] Mainwaring and Dobrée, 274-5, 237-43; AR 1797, 217; Gill, 248-9.

[86] AR 1797, 207-8, 219; Gill, 299-314, 358; Wells, 90-1, 95.

[87] *Burke Corr*. IX, 317, 347-8; AR 1797, 37, 50; Wells, 100-1, 105-7, 111, 149; Gill, 318; Best: *War and Society in Revolutionary Europe 1770-1870*, 136; C. Oman: *Nelson* (1947), 227.

[88] *Burke Corr*. IX, 188-9, 254-8, 331-4; AR 1797, 151-2; AR 1798, 159; PH XXXIII, 152-5, 170; Hone, 34-5; Bayly, 87-9; Wells, 6, 67, 154; Elliott: *Partners*, 165, 211-2.

[89] Kee, 84-90, 97; *Burke Corr*. IX, 117, 121, 295, 305-6; AR 1797, 258-64; Palmer II, 501; Elliott, 125-8; Wells 63, 112-4.

[90] Elliott: *Partners*, 119, 124, 150, 153; 161-2; Elliott: *Wolfe Tone*, 359, 365; Wells, 63.

[91] Bryant, 235-6, AR 1797, 51-2; Kee, 92, 94, 99; Wells, 120.

[92] Pakenham, 67-101; Kee, 97-100.

[93] *Burke Corr*. IX, 116-7, 339; Pakenham, 59-68, 82, 100-1; Elliott: *Partners*, 191-3; Kee, 87.

[94] Kee, 95-6, 101-3, 114-5, 132-4; Elliott, 77-9, 168, 199-200, 212-5; AR 1798, 162; Wells, 154, 131-7.

[95] Elliott, 165-8, 195-9, 235-7; Kee, 109, 118, 128-31; Pakenham, 274 (Moira), 334 (Moore); Doyle, 365-8.

[96] Pakenham, 132-5, 145-6, 153-6, 165-70, 175, 183-90, 225-7, 234-7, 251-6, 261, 276,

290-4, 301; G. Brenan: *South From Granada* (1957) 168; G. Brenan: *The Spanish Labyrinth* (Cambridge, 1960), 318-23; Kee, 103-21, 129-31.

[97] Kee, 105-7, 122-4, 140-1; Pakenham, 183-5, 256, 297, 304-11; 325, 333-4; AR 1798, 89-96; Palmer II, 502-3.

[98] Pakenham, 305, 310-1, 321-5, 334, 371-4, 382-4, 387-93; _M. Elliott: Ireland and the French Revolution, in Dickinson (ed.), 99; S. Schama: *Citizens* (1989), 791-2; Lefebvre II, 119-20; Kee, 123, 151-60; Palmer II, 491, 503; See Chapter V above.

[99] Elliott: *Partners in Revolution*, 56-7, 83-6, 91; Cobb, 111-2; Coleridge: *Fire, Famine and Slaughter*, l.16.

[100] Elliott, 210-2, 144-50, 174-89, 252; *Burke Corr.* IX, 114; AR 1798, 210-7, 41; Dinwiddy in Hellmuth (ed.) 551, 559-60; Wells, 71-8, 121-8, 141-6, 151-3, 175; Hobhouse: *Fox*, 230-1.

[101] Goodwin, 453-5; Doyle, 149; Emsley: Repression, 817, 320; Woodforde, 591; Wells: *Wretched Faces*, 1, 18-9, 36-9, 51-2, 59-62, 65 (Lord Liverpool) 69-71; Crouzet in Dickinson (ed.), 205; Elliot, 256-8.

[102] Wells: *Wretched Faces*, 120-32, 421-3; Goodwin, 463; Hone, 93; Stevenson: Food Riots in England, in Stevenson and Quinault (ed.s), 56-7; J. Stevenson: Social control and the Prevention of Riots in England, 1789-1829, in A. Donajgrodzki (ed.), *Social Control in Nineteenth Century Britain* (1977), 42-3.

[103] AR 1800, 13-6; Wells: *Wretched Faces*, 156-9, 370-1; Brooke: *King George III*, 315.

[104] J. Harrison: *The Second Coming* (1970), 210-1; Campbell VIII, 246-52; Wells, 148-9.

[105] Booth: Food Riots in North West England 1790-1801, 100-4; Wells: *Wretched Faces*, 149-54, 160, 285, 301; Wells: *Insurrection*, 182-4, 209.

[106] Wells: *Wretched Faces*, 153-60, 267-73, 285, 302; Bohstedt, 49-51; Brown, 160; Charlesworth (ed.), 103; Wells: *Insurrection*, 224-5.

[107] Pakenham, 387-90, 403; Reilly, 346-50, 384-5; Rosebery, 222-3; Cannon (ed.): *The Letters of Junius*, 247; Thomson: *A Constitutional History of England 1642-1801*, 267-8; Macaulay III, 1411-3.

[108] Schilling, 249; Ehrman II, 81-4; Hibbert: *George IV*, 172.

[109] Cannon: *The Fox-North Coalition*, 133, 143; Dobrée (ed.), 240-4; Kee, 182-6; see Ch XVI above.

XIX 'Indebted to Providence'?

[1] Coupland (ed.), 277; PH XXXI, 1065-6; *Diary*, II, 414.

[2] *Burke Corr.* V, 412, 415; VI, 67-76; Powell, 157, 160-3, 168-9, 176; Palmer II, 50-1, 146-56, 179-87, 280-4, 292-3, 300-10, 317-22, 332-3, 368, 374-91, 399-413, 436-7, 444; Rudé: *Revolutionary Europe 1783-1815* (1964), 42-3, 215-22.

[3] Namier: *Crossroads of Power*, 193; Jarrett, 1-2, 7.

[4] Paine, 57; Peter Pindar: *The Rights of Kings* (1791) in Schilling, 141-2; Blanning, 131-2, 143; AR 1798, 88; Roe, 2-3, 13, 181, 237-9; S. Gill: *William Wordsworth* (1989), 107-8, 128-9; R. Holmes: *Coleridge, Early Visions* (Harmondsworth, 1990), 202-3; Coleridge: *France An Ode*, ll.77, 81; Burke: *Reflections*, 342, 204-5.

[5] Dobrée (ed.), 128; Sorel, 394; Dickinson, 272-5; Dinwiddy in Hellmuth (ed.) 541; F. O'Gorman: Pitt and the Tory Reaction to the French Revolution 1789-1815, in Dickinson (ed.), 35-7; PH XXXII, 394; Coupland (ed.) 29, 99, 277-8; Christie: *Stress and Stability*, 181-2.

[6] Dickinson in Dickinson (ed.), 104-12, 119-25; Montluzin, 1-4, 10-5; Hempton, 225.

[7] Dickinson: *Liberty and Property*, 246, 254-318; Dickinson in Hellmuth (ed.), 522-3; Coleridge: *Lectures*, 10, 48; Thale (ed.), 18; Sales: *English Literature in History*, 136-7; Thompson, 174-6; J. Schofield, 620-2.

[8] Pollock, 75; Veitch, 209-10; Christie, 93.

[9] C. Lucas: Nobles, Bourgeois and the Origins of the French Revolution, *P. & P.* 60 (1973), 98-9, 116-7; Rudé, 82; Schama, 40, 47, 116-8; Paine, 224-8; Burke: *Reflections*, 243-5; A. Tocqueville: *L'Ancien Régime* (Fr. M. Patterson, Oxford, 1947), 88-9;

Cannon: *Aristocratic Century*, 7-8, 90-2, 125, 141-3, 147; Stone: *An Open Elite?* 131-42, 164-6, 283-90, 298-9, 305-6; Mathias, 127-8, 287-8; Mathias & O'Brien: Taxation in Britain and France 1715-1810, 616, 629-35; Young: *Travels in France and Italy 1792*, 172; Porter, 70-81; Rubinstein: The End of 'Old Corruption' in Britain, 1780-1800, 55, 57, 71-3; Roe, 187; Phelps Brown: *Egalitarianism and the Generation of Inequality*, 310-20, 373-9.

[10] Jarrett, 257; Burke: *Reflections*, 209-11; Pocock: *Virtue, Commerce and History*, 195, 200; Barrington Moore Jr.: *Social Origins of Dictatorship and Democracy*, XIV, 30-1; Ehrman II, 147-50; Crouzet: The Impact of the French wars on the British Economy, in Dickinson (ed.), 191, 200-2.

[11] Montesquieu: *De L'Esprit des Lois*, Bk. XIX, Ch. XXVII, in Sorel, 384; Colley: Apotheosis, 97; Cookson, 77, 80; McKendrick, Brewer, Plumb, 1-6, 9-10, 24-9, 51, 77, 102-3; Christie, 91-2; Langford *Public Life*, 353.

[12] Archenholz, 346; *Human Development Report 1990*, 32-3, 42-4, 59; P. Corfield: Class by Name and Number in Eighteenth Century Britain, *History* 72 (1987) 56-7, 48; Baugh: Poverty, Protestantism and Political Economy, in Baxter (ed.) 90; PR XLIV, 31; see Chs. XI and XII above; Joseph Mather: The File-Hawker's Lamentation, in R. Lonsdale (ed.), *The New Oxford Book of Eighteenth Century Verse*, (Oxford, 1984) 789, 855.

[13] PH XXXII, 450.

[14] Colley: Whose Nation? 97, 116; Colley: Apotheosis, 97; PH VI, 846; Ch II above; PH XXXII, 467-9; Burke: *Thoughts and Details on Scarcity*, Burke V, 84.

[15] Hole, 90, 111-2; Schilling, 79, 83, 97; Sykes, 267, 397-9, 405-6; Wearmouth, 262-5; Cobban (ed.), 415; Hall, 52.

[15a] Paley: *Moral and Political Philosophy* (7th ed. 1790), I. 105.

[16] Baugh, 91, 106-7; PH XXXII, 105 (Pitt); PH XXXI, 1097 (Erskine); Thomis, 5-6; Woodforde, 482-4, 600; Stevenson: in Donasgrodzki (ed.), 41-3.

[17] J. Hamburger: *James Hill and the Art of Revolution* (Greenwood, Connecticut, 1977), 19n; K. Polanyi: *The Great Transformation* (Boston, 1957), 93; O. Hufton: Towards an Understanding of the Poor in Eighteenth Century France, in J. Bosher (ed.), *French Government and Society 1500-1850* (1973), 145-9, 160-4; R. Cobb: *A Second Identity* (Oxford, 1969), 155; Halevy: *The Growth of Philosophic Radicalism*, 205; La Rochefoucauld, 206-8; Snell, 28-36, 104; Langford: *Public Life*, 456; D. Marshall: *Industrial England 1776-1851*, 79-80; M. Blaug: The Myth of the Old Poor Law and the Making of the New, in Flinn and Smart (eds.), 143; Pollock: *Wilberforce*, 140, 170-3.

[18] Snell (who convincingly reinstates the case put forward by the Hammonds), 106, 109, 138-227, 312; AR 1769, 116; J. Neeson: The Opponents of Enclosure in Eighteenth Century Northamptonshire, *P. & P.* 105 (1984, 120, 129; J. Steven Watson: Parliamentary Procedure as a Key to the Understanding of Eighteenth Century Politics, *The Burke Newsletter* 3 (1962), 123-4; Hammond: *The Village Labourer*, 41, 19, 78-84, IX-XI, 97-111, 163-5; HC 1754-1790, I, 181.

[19] PR XLIV, 19-34; PH XXXII, 700-15; Polanyi, 289-90; Hammond, 86-7, 135-42, 149-52; Perkin, 185-8; Rosebery, 168-71; Ehrmann, II, 471-5.

[20] Blaug, 123-44; J. Marshall: *The Old Poor Law 1795-1834* (1984), 23, 35-7, 42-6; Snell, 56, 109.

[21] *Thoughts and Details on Scarcity, Burke*, V, 100, 92, 83-5; Burke: Speech on Conciliation with America, 22 March 1775; Lock, 18-9, 164; Schama 306-7, 324-5; Polanyi, 86, 93; Christie: *Stress and Stability*, 104-5, 114-5, 216-7; Doyle, 399-401.

[22] Monod, 107.

[23] PH XXXII, 355; Hume: Of the Protestant Succession, *Essays*, 494; Western: The Volunteer Movement, *passim*; Chs. II, IV and XV above.

[24] Colley: Whose Nation? 114-5; Bohstedt: *Riots and Community Politics*, 51-6, 63; Best, 148.

[25] Elliott, 116-8; Roe, 251-7; Lefebvre II, 189.

[26] Deane, 193; Williams, 79; Emsley: *British Society*, 68-9; Dinwiddy in Hellmuth (ed.), 552-5; Booth: Popular Loyalism, 310-2; Cannon: *Aristocratic Century*, 165.

[27] Cobb: *A Second Identity*, 267-81, 158; Doyle, 20-1, 210-3; Sorel, 565; Brewer: *The Sinews of Power*, XVII-XVIII, 24.

[28] PH XXXII, 353, and PH XXX, 725 (Fox); J. Dinwiddy: Charles James Fox and the People, *History* LV (1970), 343-6; Burke: *Reflections*, 211-4, 128-32; Pocock, 208, 202-3; Roe, 243-4.

[29] Booth: Popular Loyalism, 309-12; Goodwin, 139, 492; Thompson, 200.

[30] PH XXX, 10 (Wycombe); Bohstedt: Women in English Riots 1790-1810, *P. & P.* 120 (1988), 103; R. Wells: The Revolt of the South-West 1800-1801, *S.H.* 6 (1977), 722 (Simcoe); Chorley: *Armies and the Art of Revolution*, 24-5, 34.

[31] C. Gill: *Naval Mutinies*, 53-4, 306-9, 313, 323-47; Wells: *Insurrection*, 93, 96-103; Thompson, 183-4; Elliot, 137-44; Chorley, 132-4.

[32] H. Seton-Watson: *The Russian Empire 1801-1917* (Oxford, 1967), 599; A. Ulam: *Lenin and the Bolsheviks* (1969), 292-4; Chorley, 119, 131-6.

[33] Chorley, 129, 138-43, 175, 242; Schama, 373-6, 421; Hampson: The French Revolution in Foot (ed.) *War and Society*, 205; Young, 145; Emsley: *British Society*, 37-8; Steiner, 24-5.

[34] Wells: *Insurrection*, 105; Whibley: *William Pitt*, 177; Stevenson: *Popular Disturbances*, 147-150; Hibbert: *George IV*, 178.

[35] Chorley, 243; Emsley: *British Society*, 43; Stevenson in Donajgrodzki (ed.), 34-6.

[36] ST XXVIII, 392-423, 378-80, 447-51; M. Elliott: The Despard Conspiracy Reconsidered, *P. & P.* 75 (1977), 46-61; Disraeli: *Tancred*, 1847 Bk. II, Ch. XI; Wells: *Insurrection*, 221-5, 237-48; Hone, 104-16; Chorley, 11-3, 23, 34, 38-9, 155-8; C. Johnson: *Revolution and the Social System*, 14-6, 49-50, 56.

[37] ST XXVIII, 459, 524, 528; Chapter XIII above; J. Dinwiddy: The Black Lamp in Yorkshire 1801-1802 *P. & P.* 64 (1974), 116-23; F. Donnelly and J. Baxter: The Revolutionary Underground in the West Riding: Myth or Reality, *P. & P.* 64 (1972), 127-32.

[38] J. Pocock: 1776, The Revolution Against Parliament, in J. Pocock (ed.), *Three British Revolutions* (Princeton, 1980), 286; and Murrin in *idem*, 369-70; Langford: *England 1727-1783*, 618.

[39] Swift: A Sermon upon the Martyrdom of King Charles I, *Irish Tracts and Sermons 1720-1723* (H. Davis, ed. Oxford, 1948), 229; J. Priestley: An Essay on the First Principles of Government, in H. Dickinson (ed.), *Politics and Literature in the Eighteenth Century* (1947), 134-7; see Ch. 1 above; Paine, 154, 264-6; D. Wolfe: *Milton in the Puritan Revolution* (New York and London, 1941), 249-66; J. Milton: *Areopagitica* in *Milton's Prose* (ed. M. Wallace, World's Classics, Oxford, 1947), 313; C. Hill: *Milton and the English Revolution* (1977), 91, 160-2, 167, 206, 209, 418, 426: Milton: *Paradise Regained*, Bk III, ll 49-52; N. & J. MacKenzie: *Dickens* (Oxford, 1979), 273-4.

[40] Langford: *Public Life and the Propertied Englishman 1689-1798*, 469; Halevy: *England in 1815*, 148-9, 170, 588; and see Introduction above.

[41] For Warburton see Part I, note I; Sorel, 81 (Bossuet).

INDEX